The Quality and Economic Significance
of Anticipations Data

The Quality
and Economic Significance
of Anticipations Data

A CONFERENCE OF THE
UNIVERSITIES–NATIONAL BUREAU COMMITTEE
FOR ECONOMIC RESEARCH

A REPORT OF THE
NATIONAL BUREAU OF ECONOMIC RESEARCH, NEW YORK

PUBLISHED BY
PRINCETON UNIVERSITY PRESS, PRINCETON
1960

C

RELATION OF NATIONAL BUREAU DIRECTORS TO
PUBLICATIONS REPORTING CONFERENCE PROCEEDINGS

Since the present volume is a record of conference proceedings, it has been exempted from the rules governing submission of manuscripts to, and critical review by, the Board of Directors of the National Bureau. It has, however, been reviewed and accepted for publication by the Director of Research.

(*Resolution adopted July 6, 1948
and revised November 21, 1949*)

Contents

ix

CONTENTS

CONTENTS

The Quality and Economic Significance
of Anticipations Data

Introduction

ALBERT G. HART

COLUMBIA UNIVERSITY

FRANCO MODIGLIANI

CARNEGIE INSTITUTE OF TECHNOLOGY

GUY H. ORCUTT

UNIVERSITY OF WISCONSIN

The economics of expectations, which was the subject of the conference reported in this volume, has rather suddenly taken shape as a professional discipline. Theoretical speculation about the nature and role of economic anticipations has been intense ever since the Swedish school opened up the field nearly thirty years ago. But until fairly recently, the study of expectations was limited almost entirely to mere surmise. Now there is content, thanks to the rapid creation of an impressive body of statistics, many sets of which are reviewed in this volume.

This conference, held at Princeton on November 8 and 9, 1957, should be seen in the context of other efforts here and abroad. In the United States, the primary sources of data have been the investment-intentions survey conducted jointly by the Department of Commerce and the Securities and Exchange Commission, and the consumer-intentions survey conducted under the auspices of the Board of Governors of the Federal Reserve System by the Survey Research Center at the University of Michigan. Perhaps equally important in laying the foundation for development was a project on business expectations and planning launched in 1949 at the University of Illinois, sponsored by the Merrill Foundation, under the leadership of Howard Bowen and Franco Modigliani. The project led not only to interesting field work, but also to a systematic search for data, and to the recruiting for this line of inquiry of a group of talented research workers.

A conference held at Ann Arbor in 1951 brought together a good deal of evidence on and analysis of short-term forecasting.[1] When in 1954 the Federal Reserve Board set up five "task groups" to consider the development of economic statistics, no less than three were assigned to work on the statistics of expectations—a field which a few years earlier had not existed. One group, under the chairmanship of George Terborgh, worked on business investment intentions; a second, under the chairmanship of Arthur Smithies, on consumer expectations and intentions. The third, under the chairmanship of Martin Gainsbrugh, worked on "general

---

[1] *Short-term Economic Forecasting*, Studies in Income and Wealth, Princeton University Press for the National Bureau of Economic Research, 1955.

business expectations," the complex of factors—orders, sales expectations, inventory control, pricing, and scheduling of production and employ-ment—which affect operating decisions.[2]

A meeting devoted to the impact of uncertainty on business decisions was held in 1955 at the Carnegie Institute of Technology under the auspices of the Committee on Business Enterprise Research of the Social Science Research Council.[3] Uncertainty was also the focus of a British meeting in 1953, which, however, did not deal with empirical materials.[4] A meeting of European students working along the lines of the IFO–Institut in Munich was held in 1957.[5]

Nature and Uses of Expectational Data[6]

What seems to mark off the papers here from earlier work in this expanding international enterprise is the maturing of a consensus about the place of anticipations in the economic process. The predictive value of expectations is systematically studied to aid us in forecasting, to tell us what kind of information the stated expectations contain, and to give clues to how the economic process (jointly with other social processes) generates expectations.

No student of anticipations can afford to be scornful of their use in forecasting. Concern with forecasting originated the Commerce–SEC, the Michigan surveys, and such private surveys as McGraw–Hill's, and makes possible their continuance on an adequate scale. Furthermore, the sur-veys proved reliable in predicting major changes in the sectors they cover, and are widely viewed as one of the most useful services offered by economic research to government and to business. The process of develop-ing new and retrospective measures of anticipations and of testing antici-pations as direct forecasts of the variables predicted continues to be a fruitful one, as several papers in this volume demonstrate.

However, direct forecasting is not the only use of anticipations data—nor, indeed, their most promising use. Most such data are at their best when used as *ingredients* in forecasting models which combine them with other variables in ways that allow for their biases and for the interaction

[2] The reports of the five task groups are published together in a hearings volume of the Joint Committee on the Economic Report, *Reports of Federal Reserve Consultant Committees on Economic Statistics*, 1955.

[3] The proceedings, under the editorship of Mary Jean Bowman, were published as *Expectations, Uncertainty, and Business Behavior*, Social Science Research Council, May 1958.

[4] Issued as a symposium edited by C. F. Carter, G. P. Meredith, and G. L. S. Shackle, *Uncertainty and Business Decisions*, Liverpool, University of Liverpool Press, 1954; second enlarged edition, 1957.

[5] The IFO–Institut is also the publisher of the first journal in the field (*IFO–Studien*, issued semiannually).

[6] For a fuller discussion, see the monograph in the Illinois series by Modigliani and Cohen. (For full citation, see p. 15, n. 10.)

of economic forces. More fundamentally, anticipations data are one of our basic sources of evidence on how firms and households make the decisions which in our decentralized society guide the whole course of economic development. To account satisfactorily for economic change, we need to develop and test hypotheses about the way experience shapes people's view of the future, the way this view of the future shapes their decisions, and the way further experience reshapes forecasts and plans. The resulting insights in turn can enhance our ability to forecast. Every forecasting technique must rest at crucial points on an assumption that some observed uniformities will continue into the future. As we gain more background knowledge, we become able to shift the assumptions from ones about surface phenomena to ones based on more reliable, deep-seated relationships. Specifically, we can get more reliable uniformities for expectations by considering intentions (to install plant and equipment, for example) as *conditional* and analyzing them through models which make room for divergence from expectations in the conditioning variables (in the example, manufacturing sales).

Anticipations data can be placed in two broad classes, though the line of demarcation cannot always be sharply drawn.[7] First, there are anticipations relating to the future behavior of the *environment*, that is, to the course of variables which the person answering does not control, such as the demand for his products by customers, the availability and cost of his inputs, and the state of the market for financing. Second, there are anticipations about *future actions of the economic unit* for which he speaks, such as the scheduling of the use of materials and equipment in its possession. The first class of anticipations are perhaps best termed *market anticipations* or *forecasts*; the second, *intentions* or plans. Close to the border of the two classes are anticipations which hinge on the interaction of the economic unit and its environment—for example, forecasts of the inventory of finished products, which reflect both output and price decisions and customers' demand.

In static economic models we often picture decisions as depending solely on the situation at the moment of decision—a firm's plant, staff, and inventory as they have developed cumulatively through past transactions, and its current rate of sales. To use the models for the analysis of change we divide time into "periods," and treat each period's events as setting the stage for the next. But in a world where many decisions will have results that run through many future periods, and where people making such forward-looking decisions are well aware of the processes of change, it is often more appropriate to view decisions as depending on the expected future behavior of the environment. Then the interesting question about a reported anticipation will be not so much whether it correctly

---

[7] For a classification of expectations see the *Reports of the Federal Reserve Consultant Committees.*

pictures what is going to happen as whether it correctly pictures what the decision makers involved think will happen.

When we think of what decisions can be registered by finding out about intentions, we realize that intentions may be more or less conditional. At the extreme of unconditional decisions, we have *commitments*, such as signed construction contracts on which orders to execute a decision have been issued and which can be altered only by a rare kind of emergency action that reverses an action already going on. Orders to execute are also issued on matters which an economic unit cannot settle unilaterally. For example, a firm often sets a selling price and instructs its agents to sell all they can at that price; the price can be regarded as an intention, but sales under it can only be forecast.

On beyond the commitments for the near future which must be made at once to carry on business, an economic unit commonly has long-range *plans*. To frame plans is also a form of decision. But next year's intended actions need not be embodied in immediate orders to execute, and the eventual action may in the end diverge sharply from that now contemplated. A plan of this sort is like a body of guesses about what future course will be adopted *if* anticipations do not change significantly before the intentions involved must solidify into commitments. The fact that such a plan will in all probability never be executed without major amendments does not make it useless for understanding the actual decisions, however. Long-range plans give orientation to current actions—for instance, a railroad would be foolish to commit itself to new rolling stock unless it could look forward to maintaining its line in usable condition. Any action which is more than a reflex can be made sense of only as a link in a chain of intended actions, even though the later links are still to be forged.

Thus decisions are related to the expectations held by the economic unit through a *planning function*. Actions conditionally decided upon are related by a *realization function* to initial plans and to the later development of the conditioning factors (for example, sales in relation to plant and equipment installations in the second half of a budget year). Both functions can be studied in data on expectations.

Behind the two relations lies the problem how expectations are generated by experience through a relation we may call the *forecast function*. It is reasonable to suppose, as most dynamic theoretical models imply, that the forecasts which people report are based chiefly on extrapolations of relevant experience. But what experience they deem relevant, how they ordinarily combine the elements, and how far special occasions bring in special data or lead them to switch forecasting formulas are questions of fact, on which we can seek data through a study of anticipations data. The problem is not yet under control, but we seem to have reached the stage where it is standard procedure to scrutinize data for clues to the forecast function as well as to the planning and realization functions.

On one major area we so far have little concrete information. In principle, every expectation is held with some degree of uncertainty. It should be possible to ask people to state confidence limits for at least some estimates, or to tell us whether they ever adopt different "strategic assumptions" about a single variable for different planning problems in hand simultaneously, so as to play safe over a range of possibilities. This is an area which is wide open for future research.

Content of the Volume

Part I contains two papers whose authors look normatively at the planning process—working back from the problems to be decided into the forecasts needed for rational decision. Charles C. Holt opens his paper (itself an exercise in forecasting!) with a brief survey of past and present uses of forecasts and then discusses the impact of new decision methods on needs for forecasts (which prove to be stiffened in some ways, but relaxed in others). He concludes with a presentation of a concrete decision analysis and its specific forecast requirements. Henri Theil considers forecasting in its relation to government policy-making. He presents an analysis of the accuracy of the Dutch model predictions (both conditional and unconditional), which is followed by a section, mainly theoretical, on the problem of governmental decisions based on econometric models.

In Part II are the papers which focus most sharply on the formation of expectations. George Katona brings to bear cross-lights from psychology plus the insights of a research team who have firsthand experience with several types of expectation surveys. Robert Ferber illustrates the strengths and difficulties of comparing bodies of evidence, and Albert G. Hart, those of a check from internal evidence. Broadly speaking, the papers confirm our advance impression that relatively simple extrapolation patterns "explain" a large part of the variance of expectations. Katona makes it plain that "general economic conditions" as well as personal experience with the variable to be forecast have a marked influence on respondents, and Hart suggests that extrapolation of recent levels and rates of change leaves an "unexplained" residue which contains an appreciable part of the predictive value of expectations.

Part III is devoted primarily to reports on series not previously available for systematic professional scrutiny. F. Thomas Juster and Morris Cohen, in particular, report on the first stages of research enterprises which seem likely to yield valuable time series. James J. O'Leary, on the other hand, offers a rather tantalizing glimpse into a body of data which seems fairly well established as a continuing series but so derived that it is hard to publish results.

Part IV brings together reviews of series already scrutinized at earlier conferences but so important that review should be fairly continuous. Arthur Okun's paper comes last because its central emphasis on combining expectational indications with each other and with related data makes it an effective review of almost the entire field of the conference.

Acknowledgments

On behalf of the participants in the conference, thanks are due to the Universities–National Bureau Committee for Economic Research for initiating and sponsoring the meeting, and to the Woodrow Wilson School of Public and International Affairs at Princeton University for lending its admirable conference facilities. The planning committee was composed of Albert G. Hart, *Chairman*, George Katona, Stanley Lebergott, Robert E. Lipsey, *Secretary*, Franco Modigliani, Geoffrey H. Moore, and Guy H. Orcutt. The manuscript has gained much in clarity from the charts of H. Irving Forman.

PART I

Forecasting Requirements from the Business Standpoint

CHARLES C. HOLT

GRADUATE SCHOOL OF INDUSTRIAL ADMINISTRATION,
CARNEGIE INSTITUTE OF TECHNOLOGY

At present, forecasting requirements as defined by current business practice consist largely of a few common-sense generalizations distilled from experience. However, the situation promises to change. Recent years have seen a significant innovation in the form of quantitative decision models. As applied to particular problems, these methods call for specific forecast information. Consequently as their use expands, forecast requirements will become more clearly defined.

In the present paper I shall try to foresee the nature of such future forecast requirements. The analysis will focus on the kinds of information the forecaster is asked to supply and will not deal directly with the methods used to obtain the information.

The Accelerating Use of Forecasts

Before World War I, forecasting by business firms was largely confined to a few firms which forecast their aggregate sales. Later efforts to improve the quality of the forecasts gradually led to the development of market research groups that concentrated on relevant industry considerations. However, the impact of general business conditions was generally ignored, a fact which led to serious errors in 1920-21. These costly experiences revealed the need for improved procedures, and some progressive companies began to establish specialized statistical and economic research groups to engage in general economic forecasting. By the end of the twenties forecasting was well established in the largest financial centers

NOTE: The research was undertaken for the project, Planning and Control of Industrial Operations, under contract with the Office of Naval Research. Reproduction of this paper in whole or in part is permitted for any purpose of the United States Government. The author gratefully acknowledges comments and criticisms of this paper by G. L. Bach, K. J. Cohen, Jacques Dreze, I. T. Ellis, Franco Modigliani, and Martin Shubik.

where interest centered largely on future security and commodity prices. The fact that the severe depression of the early thirties, and the recession of 1937-38, were "missed" by most forecasters provided a further impetus to the formation of full-time, professional forecasting departments.

A survey conducted in 1940 under the auspices of the Graduate School of Business of Stanford University[1] showed that out of a sample of thirty-one large corporations, eight had organized economics or statistical research departments engaged in forecasting external business conditions, while about fifteen prepared detailed sales forecasts for periods up to a year in advance. Even at this late date, however, roughly half of the companies surveyed did not engage in organized forecasting.

The extreme uncertainty which characterized the economic outlook after World War II greatly stimulated the forecasting efforts of corporations. In 1950 the Controllership Foundation surveyed a typical cross section of thirty-seven progressive corporations with activities in the forecasting area.[2] Of these, twenty-nine forecast general business conditions, twenty-six through organized staffs of their own, and three through outside research and advisory organizations. The growth in forecasting activity by business firms has continued to the present. Although many concerns still are extremely casual about their forecasting, it is unusual to encounter a fair-sized firm which makes no provision for it.

Now that forecasts are widely viewed as almost indispensable for business decisions, it is pertinent to ask why the widespread use of forecasting was so long delayed. Perhaps the primary reason was the lack of adequate data on the industry and national levels. It was not until the thirties that the data collection programs of the government began to assume their present form. Also in the early days business managers thought that the forecasts were unreliable and that they could guess as well as anyone—a contention often supported by the facts. The lack of agreement on forecasting methods and the wide diversity in results made agreement on forecasts difficult and hence they were of little use in coordinating departmental activities. Even good forecasts would have been of little use since few corporations engaged in organized planning. Actions tended to be taken in terms of current events rather than future developments. Where forecasts were employed, difficulties were encountered in determining their implications for action. The profusion of variables and the presence of uncertainty posed almost insoluble decision problems when only judgment could solve them.

As time passed some of these limitations diminished. When the more progressive business firms had demonstrated the usefulness of forecasts, competitive pressures stimulated the remaining companies to follow suit.

[1] P. E. Holden, L. S. Fish, and H. L. Smith, *Top Management and Control*, Stanford University Press, 1941.
[2] *Business Forecasting—A Survey of Business Practices and Methods*, Controllership Foundation, 1950.

Current Uses of Forecasts and Their Requirements

The uses of forecasts are now so varied that in many firms hardly a department is untouched by their influence. For example, forecasts are used in allocating sales effort and establishing sales quotas, in budgeting advertising expenditures, in planning that involves sources and applications of funds, in establishing prices that take into account both forecasted cost and forecasted sales volume, in establishing the need for the expansion of plant and equipment, in making purchase commitments for raw materials and components, in guiding product development and research into areas of potentially high profits, and in planning production, inventory, employment, and personnel training.

In addition, the adoption of an official company forecast is sometimes used as a planning procedure. A requirement that all plans be based on the same forecast gives some assurance that the plans will be consistent. Indeed it may be more important that all departments use the same forecast than that the forecast be accurate. Strictly speaking, coordination is required on a planning rather than on a forecast level, but the present form in which forecasts are prepared makes difficult the separation of the two. The "adoption" of a forecast may also serve a control function, but my paper will have little to say on this point.[3]

Despite the many contributions of forecasting to business planning, Solomon Ethe of the National Industrial Conference Board, as recently as 1956, pointed out that while many companies in industries faced with cyclical demands or with long lead-times of production face problems in the control of production, only a few have discovered how sales forecasts can help to solve them.[4]

Frank D. Newbury summarized the present-day thinking of many business managers when he said that they cannot escape forecasting while remaining responsible for a business enterprise—the question every executive faces is not *whether* he will forecast but rather *how* he will forecast. Any organized plan, he concludes, is better than no plan.[5]

Clearly the essential role of forecasts in decision-making is understood, but it is significant that this has not been followed up by a fundamental analysis of the functions of forecasts.

Ethe proposes the following criteria for choosing a forecasting system:[6]

1. Operating executives must understand how the forecasts are obtained

[3] Although the relations between forecasts, plans, and action decisions are becoming increasingly clear, the further problem of controlling an organization so that the actions are carried out has yet to be adequately treated. However, important fundamental research is under way.

[4] Solomon Ethe, "Forecasting in Industry," *Studies in Business Policy*, No. 77, National Industrial Conference Board, 1956, p. 70.

[5] Frank D. Newbury, *Business Forecasting*, McGraw–Hill, 1952, pp. 2–3.

[6] Ethe, p. 74.

and have confidence in the results. One of the chief objections to the more complicated mathematical methods is that an executive untrained in mathematics and statistics cannot understand how the forecasts are arrived at, and therefore tends to doubt, discredit, or ignore them.

2. Obviously the method chosen must result in fairly accurate forecasts—accurate both in the size of the average error and in the number of times "complete misses" take place.

3. The forecasts should be produced with a minimum of elapsed time and with adequate lead.

4. Sales forecasts should be provided in units and product groupings most readily useful to the company.

5. When selecting a forecasting method, a company should weigh the cost and the workload impact on its staff against possible benefits.

Newbury also recognizes the problem of obtaining the confidence of business managers but attributes the difficulty to the lack of forecast accuracy. He points out that engineering methods are often not understood but their results are accepted because their methods are known to "work."[7]

Herbert V. Prochnow presents the following specifications for successful forecasting:[8]

1. *Precisely correct* forecasts are "freakish accidents" and cannot be established as a measure or goal of satisfactory forecasting performance. Mistakes of the past should not lead to even greater future errors because of undue concern about "consistency" and "reputation." In a drive for "pinpoint" results there is serious danger that the basic direction of general business may be lost.

2. Although a forecaster with an above-average record typically is a skilled economic analyst who has a ready command of basic statistics and is aware of the numerous limitations of the data, he must not be afraid to make "estimates" and draw tentative conclusions from fragmentary information.

3. A forecaster needs a wide circle of personal contacts in business, government, universities, and private research organizations, as sources both of up-to-date information and of valuable interpretations.

4. Successful forecasting is a continuous process, involving the constant sifting of new information and statistics to find further support for the current forecast or sufficient reason to modify it. All too frequently business forecasting is done only once or twice a year and largely forgotten in the interim, with understandably poor results.

5. Successful forecasters make a special point not only to use outside

7 Newbury, p. 21.

8 Herbert V. Prochnow (ed.), *Determining the Business Outlook*, Harper, 1954, pp. 16-17.

contacts for information but also to check their forecasts with other informed individuals.

6. Successful business forecasting requires the ability to exercise an extraordinary amount of independent judgment, to project reasoned opinions—backed by experience—rather than hopes and desires, to maintain a broad point of view rather than merely that of an industry, company, union, occupation, or political party, and to weigh the different forces at work helping to shape the future course of business.

These specifications and injunctions, based on current forecasting practice, are not without value, but in many respects they are vague. Obviously our present knowledge of requirements for forecasts and forecast methods leaves much to be desired.

New Decision Methods and Their Impact

Since the second World War two developments have occurred which will have a tremendous impact on business decision-making in the future: (1) fundamental research on rational decision-making, and (2) the development of electronic computers. Both developments owe much to government-supported research. Thus far their application has been largely confined to the more progressive companies, but the results have been sufficiently encouraging to stimulate both further research and computer purchases. The time may not be too far distant when competitive pressures will speed the introduction of the new techniques on a broad scale.

OPERATIONS RESEARCH AND MANAGEMENT SCIENCE

Operations research dates back to the Battle of Britain when some scientists were called in as consultants to work on problems of military decisions. The successes of the scientific approach were so dramatic that similar teams were formed in the United States to consult with military organizations. After the war, the interests of the operations researchers shifted to business decisions. While they have not been conspicuous for doing fundamental research on decision methods, they have linked the theoretically oriented people and the practical managers in the business world. Other persons whose basic interests were similar but somewhat broader began to work on "management science." They endeavored to bring to bear on the problems of decision-making the knowledge available from the social and physical sciences and mathematics.

Most of this work could be called work on statistical decision theory, broadly interpreted.[9] The essence of the approach is to quantify a decision

---

[9] No effort will be made here to acknowledge the large number of contributors to the field.

problem by using the precise language of mathematics to describe the objectives to be sought, the relationships between the objectives, and the controlled and uncontrolled variables—the controlled variables being those influenced by the decision-maker. In its new form the decision problem becomes a mathematical problem amenable to solution by powerful mathematics and computers. This type of analysis has important implications for forecasting when it is extended to deal with (1) dynamic decision problems extending through time, and (2) uncertainty.

ELECTRONIC COMPUTERS

Much of the optimism associated with statistical decision analysis would not exist were it not for the availability of large-scale electronic digital computers. It is easy to transform a difficult problem involving many interacting variables and having repercussions that extend far into the future into a mathematical problem that has no known analytic solution. But even though general solutions may not be available, the powerful methods of numerical analysis may make solutions for particular cases quite feasible by means of electronic computers. And if numerical methods do not solve the problem, a quantitative simulation on an electronic computer may supply information on the key elements involved.

To date business firms have shown their greatest interest in the ability of electronic computers to solve routine data-handling chores. But as time goes by they increasingly will appreciate the computers' power to contribute to the solution of the really important decision problems involved in "running the business."

The beginning impact of these developments can currently be observed at some professional society meetings where a new kind of businessman can be heard discussing production problems in terms of marginal cost, machine capacity in terms of queuing theory, warehousing problems in terms of linear programming models, and decision optimality in terms of computer capacity. The next few decades will see a rapid acceleration in the application of the new methods to decision making.

IMPLICATIONS FOR FORECASTING

In any quantitative decision analysis with a time dimension, the future values of variables are explicitly stated—future values obtainable only by forecasts. *Without forecasts, the decision problem cannot be solved.*

When a quantitative analysis is made of a decision problem, it provides a basis for determining what information about the future is relevant. If the desired outcome (i.e. the decision criterion) is affected by the interrelationship between the current decision action and a future value of a variable, or if the current action influences any future actions which have such a relationship, then the future value of the variable is relevant.

Otherwise the future value of the variable is irrelevant and need not be forecast.[10]

The question of which variables are relevant and should be forecast depends entirely upon the particular decision problem being faced. It must be faced anew in each new decision analysis. The forecast requirements on the time span to be covered, information on forecast errors, and the costs of forecasting also are highly specific to a particular problem.

However, as a result of research on decision models appropriate to particular kinds of decision problems, we know something about the *kinds* of forecast requirements to be expected. Insofar as these analyses anticipate the decision-making of tomorrow, we can infer future forecast requirements.

More Exacting Forecast Requirements

Often the forecast requirements imposed by decision models are more exacting than those governing present practice. A general classification is presented below.

TIME PATTERNS

When the implications for action of a forecast are unclear, there is little point in trying to predict exact fluctuations. However, when they *are* clear, and when the action depends critically upon the time patterns of fluctuations, forecasts must be more refined.[11] For example, purchase and sales decisions by speculating warehouses may depend upon the exact time patterns of buying and selling prices forecasted.[12] The time pattern of price fluctuations is also important in analyses of security transactions subject to the capital gains tax.[13]

Current forecasting practice tends to cumulate variables over relatively long periods. For example, sales are often forecast on an annual or quarterly basis rather than monthly, weekly, or daily. The need for greater precision in forecasting the time pattern is found in several kinds of decision problems:

[10] For a rigorous development of the concept of irrelevance, see Franco Modigliani and Kalman J. Cohen, "The Role of Anticipations and Plans in the Economy of the Firm and Their Use in Economic Analysis and Forecasting," *Studies in Business Expectations and Planning*, Bureau of Economic and Business Research, University of Illinois, 1957, which they summarized in "The Significance and Uses of *Ex Ante* Data— A Summary View," *Proceedings of the Conference on Expectations, Uncertainty, and Business Behavior*, Mary Jean Bowman (ed.), Social Science Research Council, May 1958; see p. 3, Introduction to the volume.

[11] One implication of such a requirement is that we need to refine our analysis of seasonal patterns particularly in the direction of developing the theory of estimation.

[12] A. Charnes, W. W. Cooper, Jacques Dreze, and M. H. Miller, "Optimal Horizon and Decision Rules for the Warehousing Problem," forthcoming.

[13] R. F. Gemmill, "The Effect of the Capital Gains Tax on Asset Prices," *National Tax Journal*, June 1957, pp. 289-301.

1. Sometimes the future of certain variables will be found to be of conditional relevance depending upon the forecast future of other variables. For example, if a product can be sold in two markets, one of which is distinctly more profitable than the other, a forecast of sales in the profitable market will indicate whether or not the total output can be disposed of there. If the answer is positive, the sales potential of the second market is irrelevant. If it is negative, the variable is important and should be forecast. Such a situation would tend to require an accurate primary forecast.

2. How far ahead a forecast must reach may depend on the time pattern forecast. For example, if a short-term sales forecast indicates that plant capacity will be exceeded, a long-term sales forecast will be required to determine whether capacity should be expanded. Unless the short-term forecast indicates such a need, the long-term forecast is irrelevant to the current decision. Consequently, the short-term forecast must be relatively accurate. The same situation occurs when the forecast must be extended until a given action must be made. For example, a warehouser with an inventory on hand, in deciding whether to sell at existing prices or wait for higher prices, will need to forecast prices up to some alternate selling date. Frequently the length of time will depend on the values that the variables may assume in the future. Thus, it may be necessary to forecast only so far as to make sure that certain levels will not be exceeded. If such assurance is not forthcoming, the period must be extended and more detailed forecasting of the time pattern of fluctuations during the added period provided.

3. Some decision analyses indicate that the future values of some variables are relevant only up to definite fixed points in time. As time passes, the forecast period gradually contracts until a point is reached when it suddenly lengthens again. In such a situation a forecasting horizon of fixed length might not produce the needed information. Some business firms forecast their sales to the time when inventory will be at its minimum level and the danger of run-outs the greatest. That forecasting to such an inventory "crisis point" is best was clearly demonstrated in a number of production and inventory control decision analyses.[14]

NUMBER OF FORECASTS

Currently many decisions are made by clerks by common-sense methods, with no clear distinction between where the clerk's forecasting leaves off and his decisions begin. For example, in deciding how many of a particular product or part to order in any particular month, a clerk may check

[14] Franco Modigliani and Franz E. Hohn, "Production Planning Over Time and the Nature of the Expectation and Planning Horizon," *Econometrica*, January 1955, pp. 46-66. Also A. Charnes, W. W. Cooper, and B. Mellon, "A Model for Optimizing Production by Reference to Cost Surrogates," *Econometrica*, July 1955, pp. 307-323.

the storage bin to gauge how many units are on hand and then look at the sales record to see how many units were sold in recent months; on this basis he "forecasts" and also orders. The making of any one such decision would be of little consequence to a large firm, but the sum of all these judgmental decisions by clerks may virtually run the factory. Thus improvement in the quality of minor decisions and their coordination with more vital ones is a matter of great importance for business organizations. Quantitative decision analyses on this level will greatly increase the number of forecasts that are required. They will probably be supplied by relatively simple formulas, but they should also be consistent with the aggregate forecasts which are being used for decisions higher in the organization.

THE FORECAST OF RELATIONSHIPS

Not only will forecasts be required for particular variables, but the relationships between variables must also be forecasted. This is readily apparent in situations in which there is an interaction between the company's actions and the values that relevant variables will take in the future. For example, to price a product, a company must take into account the effect of price on sales volume. Here the forecaster is essentially asked to produce a demand curve.

The separation of the uncontrolled variables from the controlled considerably clarifies the job of the forecaster. Currently, when a sales department is asked for a forecast of dollar sales, it is being asked in part to anticipate the price and sales promotion decisions that higher management will make—presumably on the basis of the sales forecast. This lack of separation of the controllable from the uncontrollable partly explains the phenomenon of sales forecasts being officially "adopted" by a top level management committee of the operating departments. Such a "forecast" is part forecast, part plan and decision, and part a control commitment to put the decision into effect. To the extent that the forecaster can meet the exacting requirements of supplying forecasts of relations, it will be possible to separate forecasting of the uncontrolled variables from these other functions.

PROBABILITY DISTRIBUTIONS OF FORECAST ERRORS

Although forecasters are well aware that they do not and cannot make perfect forecasts, and although statisticians have emphasized errors of estimate, it is still a rare forecast that carries with it an estimate of its probable error. With the advent of decision models that include analyses of risk, some information on probable forecast errors is usually essential to weigh the risks and obtain an optimal decision. The exact information required will vary from problem to problem. For example, a decision model for scheduling heating oil production requires that the probability distributions of sales forecast errors be estimated.[15] If a buffer stock is carried as a hedge against forecast errors, an estimate is required of the upper tail of the sales forecast error distribution. Where the forecast horizon depends upon the delivery time, the relationship between the size of the forecast error and the forecast horizon may have to be estimated.

FORECAST PERFORMANCE AND COST

Some decision analyses become sufficiently refined to require estimation of the relationship between forecast errors and the resulting cost of worsened decisions. Also the costs of producing the forecasts by alternative methods are needed. By considering the costs of both the forecast errors and the forecasts themselves, a firm can select the best method of making forecasts for a particular decision. Only in the context of a complete decision analysis can this problem be treated adequately. Unfortunately the determination of the cost of forecast errors is an extremely subtle problem because there are usually several alternative ways of coping with the uncertainty associated with forecast errors.

Less Exacting Forecast Requirements

Most problems involving the time dimension call for a planned sequence of actions. However, only the first step can be translated into action. And plans for the future can be revised if new information develops in the interim. This fact has several important implications in relaxing forecast requirements.

IRRELEVANCE OF MOST OF THE FUTURE

Rigorous decision analyses show that much of the future is absolutely irrelevant to the decision at hand.[16] A decision analysis of great generality goes further to prove that most of the future is irrelevant in deciding a first move for any given level of optimality.[17] Decision analyses may show that the distant future is not irrelevant in that it *does* influence the present decision, but the size of the influence is relatively small. If the cost advantage of the forecast is less than the cost of producing the forecast, the forecast is termed practically irrelevant.[18] This further reduces the variables to be forecast.

15 A. Charnes, W. W. Cooper, and G. H. Symonds, "Cost Horizons and Certainty Equivalents: An Approach to Stochastic Programming of Heating Oil," *Management Science*, April 1958, pp. 235-263.
16 Modigliani and Cohen.
17 A. Dvoretzky, J. Kiefer, and J. Wolfowitz, "The Inventory Problem," *Econometrica*, April 1952, July 1952, pp. 187-222 and pp. 450-466 and a simplified version of the results is presented by J. Laderman, S. B. Littauer, and Lionel Weiss under the same title in the *Journal of the American Statistical Association*, December 1953, pp. 717-732.
18 Modigliani and Cohen.

In time we will learn the determinants of the forecast horizon, but at present little is known. Some variables may be conditionally irrelevant (either absolutely or practically) unless particular developments are foreseen in forecasting other variables.

REVISIONS

Another implication of the fact that decision analysis need indicate only the best first move is the probability that new information will become available by the time the second move is to be made, which will allow the future to be forecast more easily and cheaply. The question of how often to make forecast revisions can be studied by quantitative decision analysis, but provision also must be made for the cost of replanning on the basis of the revised forecast. There is no gain in getting new estimates unless they will be used.

MINIMIZING THE COST OF ERRORS

A decision analysis includes consideration of the penalties attached to forecast errors, presumably solving how best to prepare for a probable error and to recover from its effects once it has occurred. Precautionary devices, such as holding inventory as a buffer, may be so cheap that there is little need to strive for accuracy.

Furthermore, when a short-term forecast is in error, the decision-maker learns about it quickly and can take corrective steps. Statistical decision analyses and computers facilitate the replanning process. A fast response decreases the penalty associated with forecast errors and further relaxes the forecast requirements.[19] Note that replanning, in some cases, will be profitably done more frequently than reforecasting.

When the cost of forecast errors is weighed against the cost of improved accuracy, the decision may well favor a crude but cheap forecasting method. Several decision analyses that were applied to actual industrial operations tended to bear out this contention, which suggests that business firms should perhaps *first* concentrate on decision analyses rather than on improved forecasting.

STATISTICAL CONTROLS

The application of control procedures similar to those used in quality control may relax forecast requirements. Already, under some systems,

[19] The fast response to forecast errors finds its limiting case where the feedback of information is instantaneous (as is often found in servo mechanisms). Feedback and feed forward (i.e. forecasting) are alternatives in the sense that decision making can be improved by either. This point is developed by W. W. Cooper and H. A. Simon in *Short-Term Economic Forecasting*, Studies in Income and Wealth, Vol. 17, Princeton University Press for the National Bureau of Economic Research, 1955, pp. 352-359.

forecasts are allowed to stand without revision until errors of a certain magnitude occur. Further developments in this direction offer promise of decreasing the cost both of forecasting and of replanning.

Implications of a Production and Employment Decision Analysis

Some of the foregoing points may be clarified by describing a particular decision analysis. Take the problem of planning the aggregate levels of production and employment for a factory to minimize the total of payroll costs, overtime costs, hiring and layoff costs, costs of holding inventory, and the penalty of inventory run outs.[20] When the cost relationships can be approximated by a quadratic cost function, the costs can be minimized by using linear decision rules in setting production and employment. Decision rules calculated for a particular factory were:

$$(1) \quad P_t = \left\{ \begin{array}{l} +0.4630_t \\ + .2340_{t+1} \\ + .1110_{t+2} \\ + .0460_{t+3} \\ + .0130_{t+4} \\ - .0020_{t+5} \\ - .0080_{t+6} \\ - .0100_{t+7} \\ - .0090_{t+8} \\ - .0080_{t+9} \\ - .0070_{t+10} \\ - .0050_{t+11} \end{array} \right\} +0.993 W_{t-1} + 153 = 0.464 I_{t-1}$$

$$(2) \quad W_t = 0.743 W_{t-1} + 2.09 - 0.010 I_{t-1} + \left\{ \begin{array}{l} +0.01010_t \\ + .00880_{t+1} \\ + .00710_{t+2} \\ + .00540_{t+3} \\ + .00420_{t+4} \\ + .00310_{t+5} \\ + .00230_{t+6} \\ + .00160_{t+7} \\ + .00120_{t+8} \\ + .00090_{t+9} \\ + .00060_{t+10} \\ + .00050_{t+11} \end{array} \right.$$

[20] For a complete analysis see Charles C. Holt, Franco Modigliani, and Herbert A. Simon, "A Linear Decision Rule for Production and Employment Scheduling," *Management Science*, October 1955, pp. 1-30; and Charles C. Holt, Franco Modigliani, and John F. Muth, "Derivation of a Linear Decision Rule for Production and Employment," *Management Science*, January 1956, pp. 159-177.

where P_t = units of product that should be produced during the forth-coming month, t

W_{t-1} = employees in the work force at the beginning of the month (end of previous month)

I_{t-1} = units of inventory minus units on back order at the beginning of the month

W_t = employees required for the current month, t (employees that should be hired is therefore $W_t - W_{t-1}$)

O_t = a forecast of units of product that will be ordered for shipment during the current month, t

O_{t+1} = the same for the next month, $t+1$, and so on.

The calculation of these rules from the cost estimates is roughly a five-minute job on an (intermediate) electronic computer. Decisions on production and employment can be calculated in a few minutes simply by inserting the initial conditions and forecasts into the rules. While the rules yield the first period decisions explicitly, there is an implicit tentative plan for future production and employment decisions obtainable if such information is needed for other decisions. I now turn to the forecast implications.

1. The implications for action of the forecasts of future sales (or orders) are clear. If the forecasts change, desirable production and employment will change correspondingly. The rules demonstrate that a decision cannot be made without a forecast of some kind.

2. In an absolute sense the *infinite* future is relevant for the decisions. However, the weights applied to the forecasts decline to very small values beyond the first twelve months, and for practical purposes are irrelevant. The length of the forecast horizon depends upon the particular cost relationships found in a factory to which this decision analysis is applied. The forecast weights decline much more rapidly for production than for employment. By the fourth month the weight for the former is down to 10 per cent of the weight for the first month. For employment this does not happen until the ninth month. Thus production will tend to respond to relatively short swings in forecast sales (the forecast time pattern is important here), while employment will reflect the weighted average of future sales over a fairly long time.

3. When a forecast error occurs the decision rules make compensatory adjustments in production and employment with a minimum of cost. The net effect of previous forecast errors is reflected in the initial conditions (i.e. the inventory and the number of employees on hand at the beginning of the current month, I_{t-1} and W_{t-1}. For example, if sales in the previous month were higher than anticipated, this would appear as a reduction in inventory, which will explicitly influence the production and employment decisions.

21

4. If uncertain sales are viewed as being drawn from a joint probability distribution, the forecasts that should be used are the expected values of the sales in the future periods. No other information about the probability distribution is relevant to the decisions.[21]

5. An explicit cost function allows the cost of forecast errors to be estimated.[22] The function used in this analysis related total cost for many time periods to linear, square, and cross-product cost components in the following variables: work force, production rate, inventory level, errors in forecasting orders, and actual orders. Eliminating from the cost expression the three controlled variables (work force, production rate, and inventory level) gives a function for minimum cost expressed as the sum of linear, square, and cross-product cost components in actual orders and forecast errors. By using an identity illustrated with the variables x and y,

$$(3) \qquad\qquad E(xy) = (Ex)(Ey) + \rho_{xy}\sigma_x\sigma_y$$

where E = the mean or expected value operator

ρ_{xy} = their correlation coefficient

σ_x = the standard deviation of x

we can obtain a complicated expression for average cost per period of time in terms of means, standard deviations, and correlation coefficients of orders and forecast errors.

To understand the cost components, we might assume that there were no forecast errors and ask how much costs would be increased by fluctuations of orders about their mean. Then costs would rise by

$$(4) \qquad\qquad \sum_{M=0}^{\infty} \alpha_M \rho(O_t, O_{t+M})\sigma_O^2$$

where $\rho(O_t, O_{t+M})$ = the autocorrelation function of orders

σ_O = the standard deviation of orders

α_M = a constant indicating the importance of the cost component.

The α_M's are dependent upon the cost structure of the factory. For the particular factory studied, the values shown in the accompanying diagram were obtained, indicating that a high correlation between sales of one- and two-period separations would increase costs; for three- through thirteen-period separations it would decrease costs.

---

[21] Herbert A. Simon, "Dynamic Programming under Uncertainty with a Quadratic Criterion Function," *Econometrica*, January 1956, pp. 74-81.

[22] For a more complete discussion of the cost of forecast errors see C. C. Holt, Franco Modigliani, J. F. Muth, H. A. Simon, *Planning Production, Inventories and Work Force*, Prentice–Hall, forthcoming, Chap. 9.

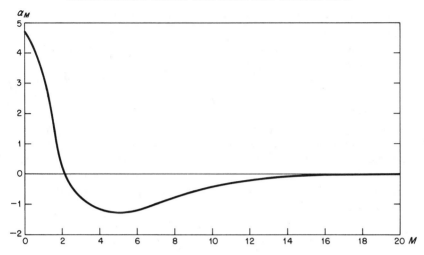

With the costs of these order fluctuations as a basis for comparison, we can determine how much costs would increase if sales did not fluctuate but random forecast errors were introduced. Costs would rise by

$$(5) \qquad \sum_{L=0}^{\infty} \beta_L \sigma_\epsilon^2(L)$$

where $\sigma_\epsilon(L)$ = the standard deviation of forecast errors for a lead time L

β_L = a constant, indicating the importance of this cost component.

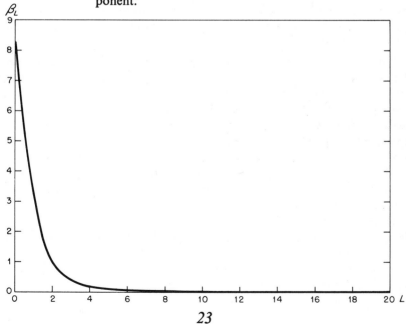

For the factory under consideration, the values shown in the second diagram were obtained. Note that the costs resulting from forecast errors decline rapidly as the lead-time is extended, emphasizing the relative importance of short-term forecasts. Although there are many other cost components associated with accurately forecast variations of sales and random forecast errors, here they are so small that they can be neglected.

Admittedly the above expressions for the costs of forecast errors are somewhat unwieldy. However, an explicit cost function and the optimal decision rules make possible an easy calculation on a computer to determine the costs that result from decisions based on different forecast methods. By weighing the different costs against the costs of obtaining the forecasts a choice can be made of the best forecasting method for the particular factory.

Conclusion

The approach to forecast requirements advocated here is subject to two different criticisms:

1. Many of the forecast requirements derived from quantitative decision analyses have long been known and even put to use. Thus it is unnecessary and unfortunate to use formalisms such as "statistical decision theory" that are foreign to the practical world of business.

2. While current forecasting and decision-making are largely an art, formal quantitative decision analyses are strictly scientific and the gap between the two is too great to be bridged, especially at the top management levels where unknowns and intangibles dominate the decision problems and judgment provides the solutions.

While there is merit to both points, it does not follow that formalized decision analyses should not or will not be used. Indeed, the fact that many of the conclusions arrived at through formal decision analyses are consistent with the conclusions reached by practicing managers on the basis of common-sense and experience is reassuring. Were this not so the applicability of the new methods would be in question. Formal decision analyses have a potential for carrying further than judgment.

Although the decision problems faced by top level management are the most difficult ones to subject to formal quantitative analysis, the fundamental *qualitative* knowledge obtained from the formal study of lower level decisions is of significant value in making the judgmental top level decisions, and some of the concepts may clarify the issues involved in top level decisions. For example, the notion of relevance may show what variables need to be forecast. Formal decision analyses will contribute to top level decision-making and the related forecast requirements long before they are suitable for direct application at that level.

It is likely that in the future a business executive will not insist on understanding the detailed methods of the forecaster any more than those of the engineer. He will have confidence in forecasts that work, and statistical decision analysis will be his best basis for judging a forecaster's performance.

For economists, the widespread use of explicit forecasts in formal quantified planning and decision analyses will greatly improve the reliability, consistency, and significance of their anticipation data. Finally, by the intensive study of the decision problems faced by businessmen, including the constraints arising from organizational structures and the costs of decision-making, economists should be better able to suggest and verify hypotheses on the relationships between anticipations data and business behavior.

C O M M E N T

Ira T. Ellis, E. I. du Pont de Nemours and Company

Charles Holt reviews the scarcity of forecasting before 1940 and notes that even now there is a lack of adequate data at the industry and national levels. He outlines the current uses of forecasts by business firms and also describes what characteristics they should have. For example, the forecasting system should be able to produce timely results given in units and product groupings most readily usable by the company. And he provides a sample decision problem for planning an aggregate level of production and employment for a factory in order to minimize the total cost of production, including payroll costs, overtime costs, hiring and layoff costs, costs of holding inventory, and the cost of inventory depletion.

The paper is largely theoretical. It seems to be more concerned with the detailed planning or control of production than with the preparation of sales forecasts, for example. Yet economic advisers are more concerned with the general business outlook or "climate" within which businessmen must carry out their operations at some time in the future.

His discussion breaks new ground in the general field of decision-making and rationally planned production by top management in a particular company. The author properly notes that there are many other problems at this level besides the preparation or use of forecasts. Upper echelon decisions are not generally made on the basis of mathematical computations alone; much judgment is involved.

Martin Shubik, General Electric Company

In his paper, Charles Holt attempts to draw the implications which decision analyses hold for forecasting. He presents a highly readable historical discussion as background for his central theme, which is the interrelationship between forecasting, planning, and making action decisions. The incremental cost of information is investigated and its incremental worth in terms of improved decision-making is taken into account.

While Holt does an excellent job of stressing the modern decision theory point of view, there are several points to which more emphasis should have been given. One is sensitivity analysis. Holt discusses the concept of the relevant forecast horizon, the horizon obtained by introducing a concept of reasonable error. He also stresses the need to state the probable error when making a forecast. Both points are special instances of the general problem of sensitivity analysis encountered often in linear programming applications. When we find out whether our results will change much if there is a slight change in a parameter, we can judge the need for accuracy.

Another topic that is not adequately treated is the possibility of using machine methods for contingent forecasting. Holt stresses the importance of separating the controlled from the uncontrolled variables in a decision analysis. However, the latter variables may themselves be sorted according to whether they are, or are not, amenable to statistical treatment. One of the most promising features of the utilization of machines in anticipations work is that it will enable firms to evaluate the implications of a variety of contingencies. After examining the different outcomes, a plan can be selected which seems best under a broad range of eventualities. In this manner more effort on planning may be substituted for more effort on forecasting.

The modern approach to forecasting deals with the interactions between the information inputs and the business as a decision-making entity. As Holt points out, it is vital to compare continuously the costs of control of decision and information procedures with the costs of changing physical processes (such as the production cycle) and with the costs of improving forecasting. Forecasting and the decision processes are regarded as part of the variable costs of production rather than as elements of overhead.

In the section, "Implications of a Production and Employment Decision Analysis," the change in the nature of the content of the paper may be too great. Holt refers to an article in *Management Science* for the complete analysis of the example quoted. Nevertheless, the change of pace from a more or less nontechnical discussion to the specification of a twelve-time-period decision rule is so large that anyone who has not read the paper referred to is likely to feel somewhat disoriented.

Holt's paper, which bridges the gap between present work in the theory of decision-making and its applications to the problems of businessmen, helps to clarify one of the problems in present economic theory. Traditionally the theory of the firm has been based on the concept of a rational man operating in an environment about which he is fully informed. More recent models, however, have introduced an environment replete with uncertainties. One of the basic problems of economic man in the latter circumstances is to decide how much he is willing to pay for information whose worth he cannot evaluate in advance. Even if he knows what he wants, he still has this problem, and, as Simon and others point out, his goals may not be well defined.

Simon has suggested that the economists' concept of rational man should be replaced by his concept of "satisficing man."[1] I have not yet found a precise statement of the axioms of behavior for Simon's "satisficing" man, but the reading of Holt's paper has suggested one possible operational interpretation which reconciles these concepts and appears to correspond generally to current business practice. The businessman operates in an environment which can best be described as a multivariate system over which he has partial control and about which he has incomplete knowledge. His time is divided between (1) conforming to the system, and (2) improving that part of it which is under his control. The first behavior pattern corresponds to the operations of a "satisficing" man: he does not know precisely what he wants or precisely what his environment is or how he can manipulate it, but he has learned to stay alive in a "satisfactory" manner. As an economic man, however, he may perceive that a change in one or more of the parameters describing his environment would be advantageous. He then instigates a study aimed at changing his methods of production scheduling, forecasting, inventory control, or other procedures. This is a process of adaptive maximization and differs from the straightforward maximization process implicit in most of the theory of the firm, in that uncertainty about environment and goals, as well as the cost of information and decision-making, are explicitly regarded as part of the system.

[1] Herbert A. Simon, *Models of Man*, Wiley, 1957, pp. 204-205.

27

Forecasting in its Relation to Government Policy-Making

HENRI THEIL

NETHERLANDS SCHOOL OF ECONOMICS · ECONOMETRIC INSTITUTE

Private firms, especially large ones, usually have sizable central planning departments. Western governments, although their economic problems are more weighty and complex, do not generally employ such assistance. One finds when traveling through the administrative centers of Western countries only small staffs, at scattered locations. One reason may be the idea that looking into the future in a comprehensive, consistent, and centralized fashion is close to socialist planning. Another may be that our knowledge of the mechanism of economic systems is still so primitive that the economist's advice is not always of value.

The situation is slightly different in the Netherlands. After World War II the Central Planning Bureau was established. It now has some ninety employees, half of them graduate economists.[1] One of its tasks is to supply a system of coherent forecasts of the development of certain macro-economic variables in the next year (the annual "Central Economic Plan"), including predictions based on alternative government policies.

The tool employed is an econometric equation system. The Plan 1955, for example, was based on a system of 27 linear (or linearized) relations of which 11 were behavior relations; 4, institutional relations; and 12, definitions. There were two consumption functions, one for wage income and one for nonwage income. The endogenous variables included price indexes as well as volumes and values. The price indexes (of consumption goods, investment goods, etc.) were described as functions of the wage level and the import price level, the latter two variables being considered as exogenous.[2]

In the following section I shall evaluate briefly the accuracy of recent Dutch predictions.[3] I shall then proceed to the problem of decision-making by means of econometric models.

[1] For a description of the activities of the Bureau in comparison with similar operations carried out in the United Kingdom, see R. L. Marris, "The Position of Economics and Economists in the Government Machine: A Comparative Critique of the United Kingdom and the Netherlands," *Economic Journal*, December 1954, pp. 759-783.

[2] The equation system in its complete form has been published in the *Centraal Economisch Plan 1955*, The Hague, 1955, pp. 110-119.

[3] See also my "A Statistical Appraisal of Postwar Macroeconomic Forecasts in the Netherlands and Scandinavia," a paper read at the Rio de Janeiro Meeting of the International Statistical Institute (1955). This paper will be published in the Proceedings of the Meeting.

Measuring the Accuracy of the Dutch Model Predictions

INTRODUCTION

The analysis of the accuracy of forecasts must be distinguished carefully from a verification of the forecasting procedure. In point predictions (in contrast with interval predictions), a forecasting procedure is a *method* of deriving predictions with the following properties: the forecasting errors have a zero mean, or a zero median, or a zero upper quartile, and so forth. Verification amounts then to a statistical test of the null hypothesis that the observed prediction errors are drawings from a parent characterized by such properties, against some specified alternative hypothesis. Clearly, verification is possible only if the forecaster states explicitly what kind of probability properties his errors are supposed to have. For the Dutch macroeconomic forecasts this is not the case. Nor are probability properties of the disturbances of the equation system, like variances and covariances, specified explicitly. Accuracy analysis, on the other hand, does not require probability assumptions since it is concerned with the empirical variation of the forecasts around the "actual" quantities which they serve to predict.

This section is devoted to an accuracy analysis of the Dutch forecasts. Such an analysis can be carried out at three distinct levels:

1. The forecast values are taken as given and are compared with the corresponding actual values. This is a straightforward approach, which, unlike 2 and 3 below, can be applied irrespective of the existence of an equation system.

2. The exogenous variables are separated from the endogenous ones, and the observed values of the former are inserted in the equation system. The corresponding values of the endogenous variables are then derived and compared with the observed endogenous values. (The forecast here is conditional upon the exogenous variables being as observed.)

3. For each (structural) equation of the model, the variable explained is separated from the explanatory variables, and the observed values taken by the latter are inserted in the equation. The corresponding computed value of the variable explained is then compared with the observed value. For example, if the equation system contains a function describing consumption as dependent on income, prices, and other exogenous and endogenous variables, then the values taken by the latter variables determine a certain consumption figure, which can be compared with the observed amount in order to judge the accuracy of the consumption function.

My analysis here will be confined to approaches 1 and 2.

ON THE ACCURACY OF THE UNCONDITIONAL FORECASTS

The analysis is based on the development of twenty-three variables from 1949 through 1955, 1952 being excluded.[4] A summarizing picture of all pairs of forecasts and corresponding observed changes is given in Chart 1. Predicted (percentage) changes are defined as

$$(1) \qquad P = \frac{p_t - a'_{t-1}}{a'_{t-1}} \, 100$$

CHART I

Comparison of Actual and Predicted Percentage Changes,
23 Variables, 1949–1955, Excluding 1952
(predicted values taken as given)

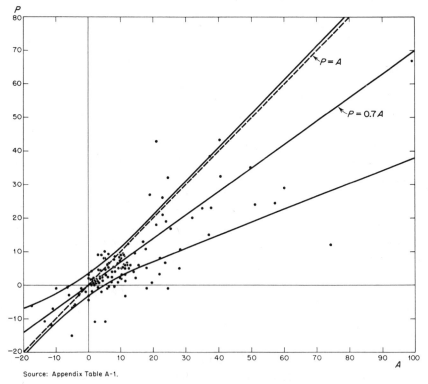

Source: Appendix Table A-1.

where p_t is the predicted level of some variable in year t and a'_{t-1}, the actual level of the preceding year as it was known when the forecast was made. The latter value is to be distinguished from a_{t-1}, which is the actual

[4] For 1952, alternative forecasts were prepared, a fact which hampers a satisfactory appraisal. For a survey of the relevant figures, see Table 1, p. 43.

level in $t-1$ according to later statistical data. This level is used in the definition of the actual change:

$$(2) \qquad\qquad A = \frac{a_t - a_{t-1}}{a_{t-1}} \, 100$$

The distinction between a'_{t-1} and a_{t-1} removes the disturbing effect of imperfect statistical knowledge of the preceding year, which is desirable because this imperfection has nothing to do with the quality of predictions for the next year.

Chart 1 shows that the majority of the points are situated in the "correct" first and third quadrants, implying that there are relatively few turning-point errors. But it shows also that most of the points in the first quadrant are below the line of perfect forecast (the broken line through the origin), which implies a bias toward underestimation of changes. More precisely, the percentage distribution of the 134 forecasts over the categories is as follows: turning-point errors[5]—12; correct-sign predictions —88, of which 65 were underestimation of changes[6] and 24 were overestimation of changes.

To compare these results with those obtained by two well-known "naïve" forecasting methods—the no-change extrapolation ($P \equiv 0$) and the extrapolation of last year's change ($P \equiv A_{-1}$)—the inferiority of the $P \equiv 0$ method is well illustrated if all points of Chart 1 are shifted vertically until they reach the horizontal axis. While this reduces the number of turning-point errors to zero, the picture as a whole is considerably worse. The implications of the method $P \equiv A_{-1}$ are illustrated in Chart 2. The distribution over turning-point errors and underestimation and overestimation of changes is as follows:[7] turning-point errors—20; correct-sign predictions—80, of which 39 were underestimation of changes and 41 were overestimation of changes. Although the bias toward underestimation appears to be absent, again the picture as a whole is evidently worse.

The comparisons are favorable to the Dutch forecasts but the forecasts are far from perfect.

1. There is the bias toward underestimation of changes, which can be formalized by the regression:

$$(3) \qquad\qquad P = 0.7A$$

implying that the predictions are on the average equal to 70 per cent of the corresponding observed changes. This regression is indicated by the solid upward sloping line through the origin of Chart 1.

---

[5] Including nonzero predictions of zero changes and zero predictions of nonzero changes. The frequency of these cases is 4 per cent.

[6] The (rare) cases of perfect forecasts have been equally divided between underestimation and overestimation.

[7] See footnotes 5 and 6.

CHART 2

Comparison of Actual and Predicted Percentage Changes,
23 Variables, 1949–1955, Excluding 1952
(predicted values derived from extrapolation of previous year's change)

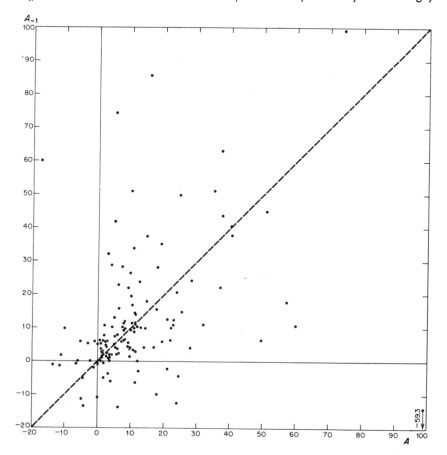

2. The residuals around the regression line do not have constant variance. A closer inspection of Chart 1 suggests that the variance is least near the origin and that it increases when we proceed in a north-eastern or southwestern direction. This can be formalized by the "scedastic" regression:

(4) $(P-0.7A)^2 = 10+0.1A^2$

The two curvilinear solid lines of Chart 1 are the functions

(5) $P = 0.7A \pm \sqrt{10+0.1A^2}$

33

FORECASTING AND GOVERNMENT POLICY-MAKING

which describes the forecasts according to the regression $(0.7A) \pm$ the standard deviation.[8]

ON THE ACCURACY OF CONDITIONAL FORECASTS

For 1949-54 an analysis of the conditional forecasts, based on approach 2, was carried out by Lips and Schouten.[9] It was based upon the development of 14 variables, of which 5 are price indexes; 5, volumes; and 4, values; so, as a whole, there are 84 conditional forecasts (P_C) and corresponding observed changes (A). Chart 3 shows that the forecasts are substantially better than the unconditional forecasts (Chart 1). The percentage distribution over turning-point errors and underestimation and overestimation of changes is as follows;[10] turning-point errors—19; correct-sign predictions—81, of which 44 were underestimation of changes, and 37 were overestimation of changes.

The bias toward change underestimation is much less important than it was for the unconditional forecasts and may not exist at all. The rather large number of turning-point errors is partly due to the inclusion of 1952, which was quite stable and showed minor changes relative to 1951. It also reflects the inclusion of five price indexes (instead of the three in the analysis of the unconditional forecasts), which were relatively stable in four of the six years. Obviously, when small changes are involved, the danger of turning-point errors is greater than in the case of substantial changes.

COMMENT

The unconditional forecasts, though imperfect, are not bad when compared with naïve methods, and the conditional forecasts are even better. Hence most of the errors in the unconditional predictions must be due to erroneous predictions of future exogenous values. Furthermore, while the unconditional forecasts show a clear tendency toward underestimation of changes, the conditional forecasts do not. Hence there must be a similar bias in the predictions of future exogenous values.

[8] The coefficients 0.7, 10, 0.1 of the two regressions are derived from the values for 1949-51 and 1953 in the following iterative manner. First, the median (m') of the individual ratios P/A are used as a preliminary estimate of the coefficient m in the regression $P = mA$; next, the squares of the deviations $P - m'A$ are grouped according to increasing order of $|A|$ and plotted in a scatter against the square of A. This yields the values 10 and 0.1 mentioned above. The final estimate of m is obtained by taking a weighted average of the ratio P/A, the weights being equal to $A^2/(10 + 0.1A^2)$. This is in accordance with weighted regression theory. For an alternative approach based on the "second regression line," see my *Economic Forecasts and Policy*, North–Holland, 1950.

[9] J. Lips and D. B. J. Schouten, "The Reliability of the Policy Model of the Central Planning Bureau," a paper read at the Hindsgavl Meeting of the International Association for Research in Income and Wealth, 1955 (*Income and Wealth Series VI*, London, Bowes and Bowes, 1957, pp. 24-51).

[10] See footnotes 5 and 6.

CHART 3

Comparison of Actual and Predicted Percentage Changes
14 Variables, 1949–1954
(predicted values derived by use of observed exogenous values)

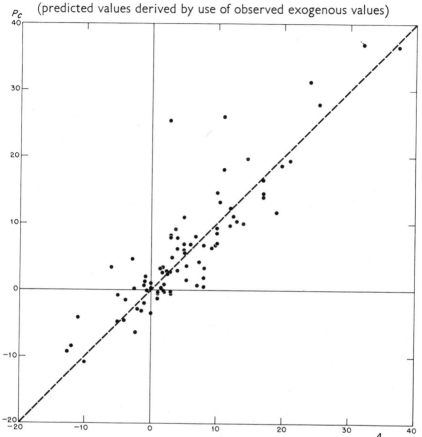

But other factors contributed to the relatively good showing made by the Dutch forecasts:

1. The scarcity of turning-point errors owed much to the scarcity of turning points, thanks to strong upward trends for most of the variables in most of the years studied.

2. The Central Economic Plans were sometimes published rather late in the year to which they refer.[11]

3. The model contains many important exogenous variables. The change

[11] This "advantage" should not be overestimated. If we take the preliminary forecasts for 1949-51 and 1953 that were prepared around January (the final predictions for 1954 and 1955 were published rather early), we arrive at forty-four predictions. About 80 per cent of them are closer to the corresponding observed changes than no-change extrapolations, half the remainder consist of ties. Similarly, the extrapolations $P \equiv OA_{-1}$ are worse than about 70 per cent of these forecasts.

in the volume of exports, for instance, is largely exogenous from the Dutch point of view and the total amount of exports is considerable in relation to the national product. Another such variable is the wage level. Although the central government cannot change wages arbitrarily, it must consent to wage increases; and this makes the wage level effectively exogenous. Clearly, the insertion of the observed values of these variables in the model must contribute to the quality of the conditional forecasts of the endogenous changes.

4. The equation system underlying the conditional forecasts (that of Plan 1955) is one of a series of successive systems which are the result of theoretical and empirical experimentation. Although the systematic analysis of Lips and Schouten was the first of its kind, such experimentation, too, must contribute to the quality of the conditional forecasts for the earlier years of 1949-54.

These special features may partly explain the difference between the findings reported here and those of Christ's analyses of the predictive power of Klein's models of the United States economy.[12]

The Use of Forecasts in Decision-Making

The exposition in this section is mainly theoretical; it is presented in general, rather than in numerical terms. A more detailed treatment is presented in my monograph, *Economic Forecasts and Policy* (North-Holland Publishing Company, 1958). I shall confine myself to the static variant of the theory.

Consider a policy-maker (who may or may not be government employed), who has certain *instruments* $(x_1, \ldots, x_m)$ at his disposal and who is interested in certain *noncontrolled variables* $(y_1, \ldots, y_n)$. The relationship between these variables is supposed to be linear, and may be written briefly:

$$(6) \qquad y = Rx + s$$

where x and y are column vectors of instruments and noncontrolled variables respectively, R a $n \times m$ matrix of multiplicative coefficients, and s a column vector of additive coefficients. The elements of the multiplicative structure (i.e. the elements of R) describe the effectiveness of the various instruments for the various noncontrolled variables.

Assuming that (6) describes the relationship between instruments and noncontrolled variables during a certain period, and that the policy-maker must choose among alternative actions (i.e. alternative x-vectors),

[12] C. F. Christ, "A Test of an Econometric Model for the United States, 1921-1947," in *Conference on Business Cycles*, Special Conference 2, National Bureau of Economic Research, 1951, pp. 35-107; also his "Aggregate Econometric Models," *American Economic Review*, June 1956, pp. 385-408.

the criterion will be derived by the introduction of a preference function which is supposed to be quadratic:

(7) $\quad w(x, y) = a'x + b'y + \frac{1}{2}(x'Ax + y'By + x'Cy + y'C'x)$

Hence, in mathematical terms, the policy-maker's problem consists of maximization of (7) subject to (6). This is largely comparable to the consumer's problem of maximizing a utility function subject to a linear budget constraint. However, classical demand theory ignores problems of uncertainty, which are vitally important here, because of the role played by predictions. Most economic models, from which reduced forms of the type (6) are derived, contain exogenous variables *not* controlled by the policy-maker. An example is the import price level in the Dutch equation system. Such variables do not fall under x. Instead their values have to be predicted before they are included in the vector s. Thus s is a rather heterogeneous mixture: it includes values assumed by certain exogenous variables and also disturbances.

The policy-maker will have in general an imperfect knowledge about the parameter matrixes of his constraints, and especially about s. To handle the problem in a probabilistic manner, we must assume that the policy-maker's preferences satisfy the Von Neumann–Morgenstern axioms, and that his preference function (7) is such that, if he is in an uncertain situation, he maximizes expected utility.

THE LOSS OF WELFARE DUE TO SUBOPTIMAL DECISIONS

First I shall disregard all problems of uncertainty and derive the policy-maker's "best" x (to be denoted by x^0), given preferences and constraints. Then w_x is the utility level attained when the vector x is applied:

(8) $\quad w_x = w(x, Rx+s) = k_0 + k'x + \frac{1}{2}x'Kx$

where $k_0 = b's + \frac{1}{2}s'Bs$

(9) $\quad k = a + R'b + (C+R'B)s = \begin{bmatrix} I & R' \end{bmatrix} \begin{bmatrix} a & C \\ b & B \end{bmatrix} \begin{bmatrix} 1 \\ s \end{bmatrix}$

$\quad K = A + R'BR + CR + R'C' = \begin{bmatrix} I & R' \end{bmatrix} \begin{bmatrix} A & C \\ C' & B \end{bmatrix} \begin{bmatrix} I \\ R \end{bmatrix}$

K being a square and symmetric matrix independent of s. Maximization of (8) with respect to x gives

(10) $\quad x^0 = -K^{-1}k$

Comparing the parameter matrixes R and s with the parameters of the consumer's budget constraint (i.e. with prices and income), and supposing that the elements of these matrixes take alternative values, we see that (10) can be regarded as the policy-maker's analogue of the consumer's demand functions. I shall call them the *optimal reaction functions*. The corresponding functions of the noncontrolled variables (y) are found by substituting (10) into (6). It is immediately apparent that the functions are all linear in s. This, too, is comparable with consumer's demand theory. For, if the utility function is quadratic, the Engel curves are all straight lines; and these curves describe the consumer's optimal purchases as dependent on the additive coefficient of his constraint (i.e. on his income).

If the policy-maker applies the instrument vector x^0, then he arrives at the maximal welfare level attainable:

$$\text{(11)} \qquad \begin{aligned} \hat{w} &= k_0 - \tfrac{1}{2}k'K^{-1}k \\ &= k_0 - \tfrac{1}{2}x^{0'}Kx^0 \end{aligned}$$

If he applies any other instrument vector x, then the level attained is given by (8). Subtracting (8) from (11), we find the *loss of welfare* due to the suboptimal decision x:

$$\text{(12)} \qquad \begin{aligned} \hat{w} - w_x &= \tfrac{1}{2}[x^{0'}Kx^{0'} - 2x^{01}Kx + x'Kx] \\ &= -\tfrac{1}{2}(x - x^0)'K(x - x^0) \end{aligned}$$

which is a quadratic form in the decision error $x - x^0$, the matrix of this form being $-\tfrac{1}{2}K$.

This result suggests that K should be a negative-definite matrix. I shall not go into detail here, but confine myself to the following remarks. If the generalization of consumer's demand theory is carried out consistently, substitution and complementarity relationships can be defined in a natural manner. In particular, there is a substitution matrix of order $m + n$ and rank m, containing substitution terms for all pairs of variables, instruments as well as noncontrolled variables. Consider then that submatrix of order $m \times m$ of the substitution matrix that corresponds to pairs of instruments only. It can be shown that this submatrix is equal to the inverse of K. Hence the matrix of the loss of welfare is determined by substitution and complementarity relationships among instruments.

THE LOSS OF WELFARE DUE TO IMPERFECT PREDICTIONS

The loss defined above is associated with a certain x, and is entirely independent of how the decision is arrived at. Consider now the loss of welfare due to imperfect forecasts. Suppose that the policy-maker's actual constraint is given by (6), but that he thinks that his constraints are

$$\text{(13)} \qquad y = Rx + s_e$$

If $s_e \neq s$, the additive structure of the constraints in the relevant period is predicted imperfectly. It is also possible to proceed under the more general assumption that the multiplicative structure is known imperfectly, so that the matrix R of (13) must be replaced by $R_e \neq R$. This is, however, beyond the scope of the present paper. The special attention given to the case $R_e = R$ can be justified by reference to the empirical finding that the large difference between the quality of the conditional and the unconditional forecasts is due to deficiencies in the prediction of future exogenous values. The values, as far as they belong to noncontrolled exogenous variables, are components of s, not of R.

If the policy-maker assumes that his constraints are given by (13), he chooses that x which will maximize utility under these conditions. This x is different from x^0. Actually, it is not difficult to see that the resulting decision error $x - x^0$ is only the change in x according to the optimal reaction functions that would take place if the constraints changed from (6) to (13). Given the linearity of these functions in s, we find that the decision error resulting from the prediction error $s_e - s$ equals

$$(14) \qquad\qquad x - x^0 = H(s_e - s)$$

where (cf. equations (9) and (10))

$$(15) \qquad\qquad H = -K^{-1}(C + R'B)$$

Combining (14) with (12), we find for the loss of welfare due to the forecasting error $s_e - s$:

$$(16) \qquad\qquad -\tfrac{1}{2}(s_e - s)' F(s_e - s)$$

where

$$(17) \qquad\qquad F = H'KH$$

It will prove convenient in the following discussion to use a utility scale (or loss-of-welfare scale) which is fully numerical. Given the assumption that the Von Neumann–Morgenstern axioms are satisfied, this means that we should define a zero and a unit. A zero has already been defined as the loss of welfare which corresponds to a perfect forecast ($s_e = s$). I shall define the unit as the loss of welfare that results from no-change extrapolation; that is, as the loss which occurs if the policy-maker acts under the assumption that s equals the additive structure of the constraints in the preceding period, s_{-1}. Writing the components of the additive structure as deviations from the corresponding components of the preceding period (so that s_{-1} becomes a zero vector), gives what will be called the *failure* of the forecast s_e:

$$(18) \qquad\qquad \text{fail } s_e = \frac{(s_e - s)' F(s_e - s)}{s' F s}$$

The failure is obviously zero for a perfect forecast,[13] one for a no-change

---

[13] The failure can also be zero for particular imperfect forecasts since F may be semi-definite, e.g. if $m < n$ (fewer instruments than noncontrolled variables). In that case a class of vectors $s_e \neq s$ exist of which the errors $s_e - s$ "compensate" each other in such a way that they do not affect the choice for x.

extrapolation, and it has no finite upper limit. Similarly, the *success* of a forecast is defined as the excess of the welfare level attained over the level corresponding to the no-change extrapolation, measured in the same unit:

$$(19) \qquad \text{suc } s_e = 1 - \text{fail } s_e$$

The success is one if the forecast is perfect, zero if it is a no-change extrapolation, and it can take negative values.

The justification of the definitions is threefold.

1. The policy-maker is always able to keep failure and success between zero and one, provided his information is of sufficient quality and provided that the multiplicative structure of the preceding period is known (for then he can derive s_{-1} as $y_{-1} - R_{-1}x_{-1}$, the -1 indexes being interpreted as referring to the previous period).

2. They are related to the comparison with naïve forecasting methods.

3. They can be easily brought in connection with the bias toward underestimation of changes.

To grasp the last assertion, consider the simple case in which the changes in all components of the additive structure are proportionally underestimated. Since I wrote $s_{-1}=0$, this assumption implies

$$(20) \qquad s_e = (1-\theta)s$$

θ being a scalar in the interval $(0, 1)$. If for θ the average mentioned for the Dutch forecasts (30 per cent) is taken and combined with (20) and (18), the result is a failure of 0.09 and hence a success of 0.91; a result independent of the numerical characteristics of the policy-maker's constraints as well as of those of his preferences.

THE POSSIBILITY OF A NEGATIVE PARENT SUCCESS

The picture of the Dutch forecasts presented here is too favorable. When the underestimation of changes is not proportionate, the success is reduced. I shall discuss in particular the pattern of errors which was observed in the unconditional forecasts and also the success of the forecasts in a statistical population rather than in some specified case.

Suppose that the change in the additive structure $(s - s_{-1} = s - 0 = s)$ consists of a systematic part $(\bar{s})$ and a stochastic part (u):

$$(21) \qquad s = \bar{s} + u$$

The stochastic part is supposed to have a zero mean and a finite covariance matrix which is independent of the instruments:

$$(22) \qquad Eu = 0 \qquad E(uu') \text{ independent of } x$$

Perfect forecasting of the additive structure of the constraints implies perfection with respect to both $\bar{s}$ and u, but I shall not make this assumption. Instead, I shall write for the predicted additive structure s_e:

$$(23) \qquad s_e = \beta_s \bar{s} + \beta_u u + v$$

where β_s and β_u are scalars defined according to

$$(24) \qquad \beta_s = \frac{E(\bar{s}' F s_e)}{\bar{s}' F \bar{s}} \quad \text{and} \quad \beta_u = \frac{E(u' F s_e)}{E(u' F u)}$$

Given these β-definitions, the relation (23) is merely a definition of the vector v. I shall call the elements of this vector "forecast disturbances" since (23) can be regarded as a parent regression of s_e on $\bar{s}$ and u, provided that the elements of these three vectors are interpreted as "observations" on three "variables." Another proviso is that we interpret this regression in the sense of Aitken's method of generalized least-squares, the inverse of the residual covariance matrix of this method being replaced by the positive-definite (or semi-definite) matrix $-F$.

The relevance of (23) can be shown as follows. If $0 < \beta_s < 1$, then the change in the additive structure, as far as its systematic component ($\bar{s}$) is concerned, can be said to be underestimated. If $\beta_u \neq 1$, the forecast is imperfect for the stochastic component. If $\beta_u = 0$, nothing is achieved in this respect—which will be frequently true. As to the forecast disturbances v, they make it possible to take account of the hyperbolic standard deviations of the residuals around the empirical regression developed in the analysis of unconditional forecasts. Assume:

$$(25) \qquad E(v' F v) = h_s \bar{s}' F \bar{s} + h_u E(u' F u)$$

h_s and h_u being fixed positive scalars. The second term on the right can be regarded as a constant, given the assumption that the covariance matrix of the stochastic component u is independent of the instruments; compare (22). Hence (25) describes the expectation of a quadratic form in the forecast disturbances as a general linear function of the same quadratic form in the elements of the systematic part of the additive structure of the constraints. If we compare the forecast disturbances v with the residuals $P - 0.7A$ and recall that their squares can be approximately described as linearly dependent on A^2, we see that assumption (25) is closely related to this empirical result.

Next I shall introduce the concepts of failure and success in a parent population. They are obtained by replacing sample moments by corresponding parent moments, and will be indicated by "Fail" and "Suc," respectively:

$$(26) \qquad \text{Fail } s_e = \frac{E[(s_e - s)' F(s_e - s)]}{E(s' F s)}; \quad \text{Suc } s_e = 1 - \text{Fail } s_e$$

41

Then, using (21)–(25), we find after some algebraic rearrangements:

(27) $\qquad$ Suc $s_e = p(2\beta_s - \beta_s^2 - h_s) + q(2\beta_u - \beta_u^2 - h_u)$

where

(28) $\qquad$ $p = \dfrac{\tilde{s}'F\tilde{s}}{\tilde{s}'F\tilde{s} + E(u'Fu)}$ $\quad$ and $\quad q = 1 - p$

The interpretation of this result is as follows. If the systematic part $\tilde{s}$ of the change in the additive structure of the constraints is sufficiently large compared with the stochastic variation of u, then p is close to one and q close to zero. In that case (27) becomes effectively

(29) $\qquad$ Suc $s_e = 2\beta_s - \beta_s^2 - h_s$

which means that the prediction achievements for u are then irrelevant. The maximum of (29), given h_s, is reached for $\beta_s = 1$; and this maximal value equals $1 - h_s$, which will generally be positive. If, on the other hand, $\tilde{s}$ is a vector of sufficiently small elements, (27) becomes approximately

(30) $\qquad$ Suc $s_e = 2\beta_u - \beta_u^2 - h_u$

Here everything depends on the forecaster's achievements for the random component u. If he is unable to achieve anything in this direction (i.e. if $\beta_u = 0$), then the success takes a *negative* value $(-h_u)$. This means that the policy-maker should not use his forecast s_e at all. He should act under the assumption of a zero change in the additive structure, in which case his success is zero. This does not mean that he should take no measures. Since the adaptation of his instruments at the beginning of the preceding period will in general have been suboptimal owing to prediction errors for that period he should adapt the instruments to the correct additive structure of the previous period. He should, however, disregard his ideas about the additive structure of the new period, for this would lead to a larger loss—not necessarily in a particular sample case, but in the parent population of such cases.

ISOLATED REDUCTIONS OF PREDICTION ERRORS

Quite frequently a forecaster is advised to revise his prediction in a particular direction. For example, he may be advised to change the first element of the predicted additive structure s_e. It might seem that this advice should be adopted if it brings the element closer to the corresponding component of the additive structure s, but this is not necessarily true. To see this, consider the numerator of the failure of s_e: $(s_e - s)'F(s_e - s)$. If the failure matrix F is diagonal, the numerator is a weighted sum of squares of the forecasting error of the additive structure, the weights all having the same sign. Then a numerical reduction of any component of $s_e - s$ is desirable, irrespective of whether the error component obtains a different

TABLE 1

Predicted and Actual Percentage Changes in Dutch Macroeconomic Variables, 1948-1955

Variables	1948 A	1949 P	1949 A	1950 P	1950 A	1951 P	1951 A	1952 •P	1952 A	1953 P	1953 A	1954 P	1954 A	1955 P	1955 A
Price indexes:															
Commodity exports	0	−3.0	−6.0	+9.0	+4.0	+13.0	+17.0	—	+1.7	−7.0	−11.0	−4.5	0	0	+1.0
Commodity imports	+5.3	−3.0	−3.0	+12.4	+12.4	+21.0	+22.9	—	−1.5	−12.0	−11.5	−6.7	−5.0	0	+1.8
Consumption	+4.0	+3.0	+5.4	+5.0	+9.2	+9.0	+10.0	—	−0.8	−3.1	0	+2.0	+3.6	+1.7	+1.0
Quantities and volumes:															
Commodity exports	+44.9	+24.0	+51.0	+23.0	+19.0	+27.0	+35.0	—	+4.0	+4.0	+14.0	+6.0	+11.4	+5.0	+10.3
Commodity imports	+8.7	+9.0	+11.0	+20.0	+32.0	+9.0	+3.0	—	−12.6	+19.0	+24.0	+10.6	+28.2	+0.8	+7.2
Consumption	+5.8	−2.0	−0.9	+2.0	0	−1.0	−2.3	—	+1.9	+4.5	+3.7	+6.2	+5.9	+2.3	+7.3
Industrial production	+19.4	+8.0	+10.0	+6.0	+13.0	+10.0	+5.0	—	0	+6.0	+12.0	—	—	—	—
Construction activity	+41.7	+8.0	+5.0	+8.0	+5.0	+3.0	0	—	−2.4	+18.0	+21.0	—	—	—	—
Available labor force	+4.6	+1.1	+2.5	+0.6	+1.5	+1.0	+1.3	—	+1.1	+1.1	+1.4	+1.7	+2.6	+1.4	+1.3
Labor productivity	+10.1	+4.0	+7.4	+4.7	+5.2	+4.2	+1.0	—	+2.2	+5.2	+6.2	+1.6	+0.7	+0.6	+3.4
Employment in private sector	+5.8	+0.6	+2.4	+1.2	+2.9	+1.5	+1.5	—	−0.6	+1.4	+1.8	+2.3	+4.2	+1.3	+2.7
Employment in public sector	−2.0	−1.8	−1.1	−10.9	−13.5	−5.8	−4.3	—	+6.2	+5.3	+7.9	+2.4	+6.0	+2.1	+1.6
Money values:															
Commodity exports	+43.5	+23.0	+37.6	+32.5	+40.5	+43.4	+40.2	—	+5.9	−0.6	+2.8	+1.2	+11.4	+5.0	+11.4
Commodity imports	+15.7	+6.4	+6.3	+35.1	+49.6	+32.1	+24.6	—	−13.9	+9.3	+6.2	+3.2	+21.9	+0.8	+9.1
Consumption	+10.1	+1.3	+4.4	+6.5	+9.1	+7.7	+7.9	—	+1.1	+2.3	+3.6	+8.3	+9.7	+4.0	+8.3
Net investment (incl. inventories)	+33.8	+9.3	+10.7	+29.0	+60.0	−6.1	−17.5	—	−59.3	+66.9	+99.1	+12.1	+74.3	−10.9	+5.2
Value added in private sector	+16.8	+3.1	+10.4	+6.7	+11.9	+8.5	+8.1	—	+4.0	+2.1	+9.8	+6.1	+11.0	+3.1	+11.4
Government wage bill	−0.8	−0.7	−6.5	−3.2	+11.4	+5.4	+7.9	—	+1.3	+7.3	+9.8	+9.5	+14.4	+8.9	+11.1
Government commodity purchases	+20.5	+6.7	+23.7	+5.0	+12.5	+42.9	+21.0	—	+10.8	+26.1	+22.8	−0.5	+6.3	−0.4	+8.0
Indirect taxes minus subsidies	+62.9	+38.5	+37.3	+14.9	+14.6	+16.9	+25.4	—	−3.8	+4.6	+3.2	+5.3	+10.7	+1.1	+2.1
Exports of services	+50.9	+2.0	+10.0	+8.0	+22.0	+15.0	+37.0	—	+7.6	−11.0	+2.0	−1.0	+5.8	+0.7	+19.5
Imports of services	+28.7	−2.0	+4.0	+5.0	+28.0	−1.0	+18.0	—	+9.7	−1.0	−10.0	+5.1	+17.9	+2.2	+14.7
Surplus on the balance of services	+85.5	+5.9	+15.5	+10.8	+17.7	+24.5	+57.2	—	+5.9	−15.1	−5.1	−6.3	−4.5	−1.0	+24.5

43

sign. For the alternative case, in which the failure matrix is not diagonal, it is sufficient to consider an example; say, $n=2$ and

$$-F = \begin{bmatrix} 1 & -0.9 \\ -0.9 & 1 \end{bmatrix}$$

Take further the forecasting error $s_e - s = \{1 \quad 1\}$. The numerator of the failure of s_e is then equal to 0.2, apart from sign. Suppose also that it is suggested that the forecast of the second component of s be changed from 1 to a. The numerator of the failure becomes then (apart from sign): $1 - 1.8a + a^2$, the minimum of which is 0.19, which is reached at $a=0.9$; and it exceeds the level 0.2 mentioned above whenever a is outside the interval (0.8, 1). Clearly, the non-diagonality of F implies that the elimination of the second component of the prediction error is far from desirable. Replacing $s_e - s = \{1 \quad 1\}$ by $\{1 \quad 0\}$ increases the failure fivefold! This holds more generally. If the failure matrix is not of the diagonal type (and there is no reason why it should be), a reduction of one particular component of the prediction error $s_e - s$, the other components remaining the same, does not necessarily lead to a failure reduction. It may be that it is better to raise the component than to reduce it. In the above example, if the original error $s_e - s$ equals $\{1 \quad \frac{1}{2}\}$, the failure is reduced by raising the second component to the 0.9 level, given the value 1 of the first component. The reason is that if F is not diagonal, the components of the error $s_e - s$ may compensate each other *via* their influence on the decision error.

C O M M E N T

JOHN W. LEHMAN AND JAMES W. KNOWLES, Joint Economic Committee

The opportunity to review Henri Theil's paper is particularly welcome in view of the constant concern of the staff of the Joint Economic Committee with the problems with which he deals. Judging from his paper, work on the day-to-day difficulties of forecasting in relation to government policy-making results in professional thinking along similar lines, regardless of country. Our own experience provides the basis for our comment on Theil's analysis.

ON THE THEIL PAPER

Theil prefaces his discussion of the Dutch forecasts with the observation that most Western governments rely on small, scattered staffs to make forecasts. In the sense that many of the analytical personnel are dispersed among numerous operating agencies, this is true of our own government —though our Committee staff numbers from eleven to thirteen and the

NOTE: The views expressed are those of the authors and do not necessarily represent the views of the Joint Economic Committee or individual members of that Committee.

staff of the Council of Economic Advisers from thirty to fifty, which is not small considering the methods of operation. However, the reasons Theil adduces for decentralization do not apply here. The collection and processing of the basic data, as well as the formulation of detailed operating programs, take place in the various departments and agencies. By being on the spot, individual technicians working on different aspects of the policy problems acquire a more intimate knowledge of the basic procedures.

One method Theil uses to determine the accuracy of the Dutch projections is to compare the forecast values with the corresponding observed values. He defines the former in terms of predicted percentage changes from the actual level of the preceding year as it was known when the forecast was made. The actual values employed are percentage changes computed in the light of later data, both for the preceding year and for the forecast year. He states that this "removes the disturbing effect of imperfect statistical knowledge of the preceding year, which is desirable because this imperfection has nothing to do with the quality of predictions for the next year."

Theil is correct that the forecaster's imperfect knowledge of the base year needs to be taken into account, but his assumption that it has nothing to do with the quality of the forecast is open to serious challenge. For example, there may be several "actual" values as successive revisions are made in the data, so that the result obtained by his method will depend in part on how much time has elapsed between the making of the forecast and the evaluation of its accuracy. More important is the fact that Theil's method of adjustment will yield valid results only under the following rather restricted conditions:

1. The definition of the predicted and actual values as percentage changes must be logically consistent with the structure of the model and with its variables; that is, the predictions must actually have been expressed in this manner. Some complex variables are not readily definable as predicted percentage changes. The predicted figure of government expenditures, for example, is a budgeted sum resting on assumptions that would not necessarily have been altered even if a different estimate of the actual figure for the preceding year had been available. For the net change in investment—especially in inventories—the predicted value is the arithmetical difference between the beginning and ending values of the net stock of investment goods, but it is actually projected in terms of changes in gross values and changes in prices and depreciation or capital consumption.

2. The statistical data system must remain substantially unchanged in all of its detail between the time that the actual value for the preceding year is estimated as a basis for the forecast and the time at which the

evaluation is carried out. Otherwise, a different percentage change may occur simply because of a change in the data system.

3. Possible changes in the data system must not have been allowed for in the preparation of the forecast.

4. The predictions must not be affected by any difference that arises between the estimate of each variable for the preceding year available when the forecast was made and the estimate available when the forecast is appraised. Frequently this will not be true. For example, when stock and flow variables such as gross inventories, change in inventories, sales, and output are explicitly or implicitly incorporated into the system, a difference in the estimate of the initial values might result in a significantly different forecast.

5. The forecast is adjusted for the estimated effects of predicted changes in policies resulting from the forecast.

It is not clear to us that these conditions are met by the forecasts Theil evaluates.

We also question whether the forecasting qualities of an equation system can be tested by comparing its predictions with the predictions yielded by some "naïve" forecasting method. A naïve model is one selected in a specific instance without regard to its adaptability to the task at hand. No method is inherently naïve.[1] Hence, a comparison of the type made by Theil may be quite inconclusive unless the method selected is naïve from the standpoint of the forecasting problems involved.

Perhaps a more important consideration is whether Theil actually confronts his model with a test of its crucial requirements in comparison with the performance of such a naïve model. If the Dutch model is supposed to produce only estimates of the magnitude of change when all the variables are continuing in the same direction, one should ask whether any simple alternative gives equal or better results. This is similar to part of the test Theil made. In approximately 20 per cent of the cases his model is about equal in effectiveness to the method which projects the percentage change of the previous year. The other 80 per cent of the cases are fairly evenly distributed between those in which the complex set of equations gives poorer results and those in which it gives better results. If we eliminate the exogenous variables from consideration, the equation system seems to turn in a slightly better performance.

If, on the other hand, interest is in the turning points, there appears to be no significant difference between the results given by the more and less sophisticated procedures. The naïve model missed all true turning points but never forecast a false one.. The multi-equation model predicted about

[1] James W. Knowles, "Relation of Structure and Assumptions to Purpose in Making Economic Projections," *Proceedings of the Business and Economic Statistics Section of the American Statistical Association*, September 1956, pp. 7-23.

two-thirds of the turning points, but called eight which did not occur. About 12 per cent of all errors were at turning points, but if the exogenous variables had been perfectly known, 19 per cent of the errors would be at turning points, compared to 20 per cent for the naïve method. Since the only improvement which the model provides at the turning points is due to errors in forecasting the exogenous variables, we would invert Theil's conclusion and say that the successes in the unconditional predictions must be due to the degree of failure achieved in predicting these values.

These findings lead us to conclude that our own reluctance to invest scarce funds in complex mathematical systems has been justified, just as it has been in previous tests. Our conclusion is reinforced by Theil's observation that the model seems to produce a tendency toward consistent underestimation such that the predicted values, on the average, are about 70 per cent of the actual values. The errors in predicting the exogenous values may be due to a tendency to avoid predicting large changes, or changes in direction, on the theory that this is a more conservative or less "risky" practice. We offer the suggestion because we have observed this psychology in business and government forecasting in this country. If this is true, better results might be achieved by concentrating on improving the prediction of the exogenous variables rather than on formulating an elaborate mathematical procedure for predicting the endogenous variables.

Our reluctance to accept Theil's appraisal of the accuracy of these forecasts can be traced mainly to the belief that each projection should be evaluated in the light of how well it served the purpose for which it was designed rather than by testing the degree to which actual events correspond to the prediction. General economic projections used in government policy-making are not forecasts, strictly speaking, since they are intended to lead to decisions during the forecast period. The decisions may call for program changes which alter the assumptions on which the projections are based. For example, a projection indicating a deflationary tendency in the coming year might result in policies which would check the implied decline. Under these conditions, an evaluation of the forecast in terms of its correspondence to observed events would be irrelevant and misleading. The vital question is whether or not any alternative projection would have provided a better basis for policy-making.

There are three tests of the quality of a prediction:

1. Were the projected quantities the best estimates which could be derived from the assumptions used?

2. Would other assumptions have been more efficient or appropriate for the particular prediction?

3. Since the prediction was stated in terms of and derived from assumptions through the use of an economic model, was the model's

structure the best one for the particular conditions surrounding the prediction?[2]

Only the first of these tests has been applied by Theil. It would be interesting to see what results he would get by applying the other two.

ON THE JOINT ECONOMIC COMMITTEE PROJECTIONS

Perhaps it would be useful to describe some of our experience at the Joint Economic Committee. The first purpose of the staff projections is to set forth for the Committee's evaluation the nature and magnitude of any adjustments necessary to achieve the objectives of the Employment Act, along with the implications for the economy if the adjustments are not forthcoming. A second purpose is to provide a basis for an internally consistent program aimed at achievement of the nation's major economic goals. These purposes have led to the development of a highly aggregative model, one containing none of the detailed industry-by-industry or product-by-product "goals" which might be appropriate where there exists detailed government direction of the day-to-day operations of the economy. The statistical testing of our projections involves three readily identifiable areas.

Evaluation of the Underlying Data. Through its Subcommittee on Economic Statistics, the Joint Economic Committee has brought technical comment and public expression to bear on the accuracy and adequacy of the underlying statistical data. The Subcommittee has held hearings and published reports itself and has also presented material before Congressional committees concerned with appropriations for statistics and assisted in the development of new statistical programs and techniques. Most of these activities have been directed toward those statistics which underlie all national economic projections.

Testing the Hypotheses. The particular purposes and structure of our projections dictate a number of the procedures used and explain our concern with the underlying statistics. The staff prepares a national economic budget, showing projected incomes and expenditures for government, business, and consumers. On the expenditure side, we rely heavily upon budget plans for the government sector. In the business sector, we use such series as the Department of Commerce—Securities and Exchange Commission and McGraw-Hill surveys of business plans for plant and equipment expenditures, the Dun and Bradstreet surveys of businessmen's expectations (first made at the request of the Joint Economic Committee in 1947), and the recently inaugurated *Newsweek*–National Industrial Conference Board survey of capital appropriations. In the

---

[2] See footnote 1. A projection should be appraised *ex post* in the light of the information, framework of measurement, and analytical tools available *ex ante*. However, innovations can be incorporated to determine whether their use would have produced a better forecast.

consumer sector, we use such materials as the field surveys of consumer intentions and expectations, conducted by the University of Michigan Survey Research Center for the Federal Reserve Board and other groups.

On the supply side, however, the staff has developed production functions as a basis for computing a "potential" output of the economy believed to be consistent with "maximum employment, production, and purchasing power."[3] The published estimates are derived from trends in labor force, employment, hours of work, and output per man-hour—in government, agriculture, and total private nonagricultural activity. Up to now data problems have precluded use of more complex models. We look forward to development of usable production models that take into consideration both capital and labor inputs, with allowance for such influences as the ratio of output to capacity, and changes in product mix, in hours of work, in the age distribution of the capital stock, and in technology.

Usefulness of the Projections. The regular examination of the value of the projections for policy-making is another important feature of our testing procedure. In the Committee's report on the 1956 *Economic Report of the President*, the staff presented an estimate of the potential output (supply) for 1956, made at the beginning of the year, of $327.4 billion in 1947 prices. In February 1957, actual GNP for 1956 in 1947 prices was estimated at $330.4 billion. Actual demand, therefore, was $3.0 billion or about 0.9 per cent above the advance estimate of potential output.

How could this difference be accounted for in terms of employment, hours of work, and productivity? First, employment exceeded the assumed long-term trend. The labor force increased 1.5 million compared to an average increase of 800,000 to 900,000 per year, while unemployment was 3.8 per cent rather than the assumed 4 per cent. This could account for an excess of output over potential of about $4.3 billion. Hours of work, slightly longer than previous trends indicated, accounted for an excess of output of $2.7 billion. Finally, output per man-hour in the private non-farm sector apparently failed to increase in 1956. This resulted in output falling $4.0 billion below the level possible if output per man-hour had reached the trend value as then estimated, demonstrating the difficulty in using year-to-year movements of this ratio—especially when such preliminary data are used as a basis for forecasting.

The staff also estimated that the January 1956 *Economic Report* and the budget implied a demand for gross national product in 1956 of $400 billion, in fourth quarter of 1955 prices. Before being compared with the actual figure for 1956, this figure must be raised by about 1 per cent ($3.7 billion) to allow for revisions in July 1956 of the 1955 basic statistical data from

[3] See *Potential Economic Growth of the United States during the Next Decade*, Materials prepared for the Joint Economic Committee by the Committee Staff, Joint Committee Print, 83d Cong., 2d sess., 1954.

which the projections were made. It must also be raised by about 2.3 per cent ($9.3 billion) to allow for price increases in 1956. Combined, the adjustments increase the assumed GNP for 1956 to $413.0 billion. The figure reported in the fall of 1957 was $412.4 billion, $0.6 billion or less than 0.2 per cent below the estimate. The difference is negligible since it is far smaller than what may result from later revisions of the now available data for 1956.[4]

The shortcoming of the analysis as a basis for policy in 1956 was the failure to place sufficient emphasis on the prospects for continued price rises, although the analysis of the 1956 *Economic Report* pointed out that some experts anticipated these. And about six weeks later, on April 18, 1956, in a memorandum to the Committee, the staff stressed the inflationary aspects of the situation. But this discussion illustrates an advantage of the projections—they are published in a quantitative form with enough detail and statement of assumptions to make possible later testing in the light of events.

Our experience with the use of forecasts of various types for policy decisions in both business and government suggests that the essential theoretical problem is that of specifying the characteristics required for a particular type of decision in a particular set of historical circumstances. Furthermore, in practical circumstances one cannot ignore the probability that the functional relationships between the instruments and the uncontrolled variables may vary according to the specific conditions which require a decision. It is not clear that the existing body of theory, including the interesting contribution by Theil, provides a suitable framework for laying out the specifications for the required predictions and for the analytical structures in which they are to be used in reaching the decisions.

REPLY BY MR. THEIL

Replying to Lehman's and Knowles' comments, I shall confine myself to the following points:

1. Predicted percentage changes were defined as deviates from the previous year's levels as these were known at the moment of prediction. This was done because the equation system yields estimates of relative changes, not of (absolute) levels. The prediction of next year's level is obtained by adding the predicted change to the available estimate of the previous year's level. Any adjustment of the forecast for estimated effects of predicted changes in policies resulting from the forecast (cf. point 5 of the Comment) is highly uncertain and dubious. But it seems plausible that it would in general ameliorate rather than deteriorate the quality of the forecasts.

[4] Since this was written, the Department of Commerce has revised its estimate of GNP for 1956 to $419.2 billion.

2. It is not correct to say that the model produces a tendency toward consistent underestimation of changes. This tendency is produced, not by the model itself, but by the underestimation of changes in exogenous variables (see pages 34 to 35 of my paper).

3. As to the comparison with "naïve" forecasting models, the passage where Lehman and Knowles stated that in about 20 per cent of all cases the model is as effective as the naïve method, the remaining 80 per cent being fairly evenly distributed over more favorable and less favorable cases, is not fully clear to me. I thought that the picture of Charts 1, 2, and 3 was sufficiently clear, but for the sake of completeness I present a table containing the mean absolute extrapolation error (i.e. the average of $A_{-1} - A$, disregarding signs) and the mean absolute forecasting error, both for the unconditional forecasts and for the conditional ones. The data for the former forecasts are derived from Table 1 of my paper. It is clear that four variables are better predicted by the naïve forecasts than by the unconditional forecasts, that the opposite is true for eighteen variables, and that there is one case of a tie; further, that the mean absolute forecasting error is less than one-half of the mean absolute extrapolation error in seven cases. As is to be expected, the conditional forecasts show a still better picture: the median ratio of the mean absolute forecasting error to the mean absolute extrapolation error over all fourteen variables is about a third. See table on page 52.

ſ

Variables	Mean Absolute Error of		Comparison of Mean Absolute Errors		
	Extra-polation (1)	Fore-casting (2)	(1)<(2) (3)	(1)>(2) (4)	½(1)>(2) (5)
			UNCONDITIONAL FORECASTS[a]		
Price indexes:					
Commodity exports	8.9	3.6		*	*
Commodity imports	9.6	1.0		*	*
Consumption	2.2	2.2	tie	tie	
Quantities and volumes:					
Commodity exports	8.6	11.3	*		
Commodity imports	19.0	8.2		*	*
Consumption	2.5	1.7		*	
Industrial production	8.1	5.0		*	
Construction activity	16.3	3.0		*	*
Available labor force	1.0	0.6		*	
Labor productivity	3.5	2.0		*	
Employment in private sector	1.9	1.2		*	
Employment in public sector	5.1	1.9		*	*
Money values:					
Commodity exports	3.5	7.6	*		
Commodity imports	21.0	8.7		*	*
Consumption	3.6	2.1		*	
Net investment (incl. inventories)	67.0	25.7		*	*
Value added in private sector	3.2	5.6	*		
Government wage bill	7.2	5.4		*	
Government commodity purchases	8.8	10.8	*		
Indirect taxes minus subsidies	13.7	3.0		*	*
Exports of services	15.2	13.8		*	
Imports of services	18.2	13.7		*	
Surplus on the balance of services	25.4	14.4		*	
Number of cases			4½	18½	8
			CONDITIONAL FORECASTS[b]		
Price indexes:					
Commodity exports	11.4	2.9		*	*
Consumption	4.0	3.0		*	
Investment goods	8.6	3.2		*	*
Inventories	13.0	2.0		*	*
Government commodity purchases	8.4	3.1		*	*
Quantities and volumes:					
Commodity imports	21.2	4.3		*	*
Consumption	2.1	2.9	*		
Gross fixed investment	10.4	2.3		*	*
Gross national product	5.4	1.8		*	*
Employment in private sector	1.4	0.7		*	
Money values:					
Indirect taxes minus subsidies	15.8	2.6		*	*
Income taxes paid by wage-earners	4.5	1.6		*	*
Income taxes paid by others	11.7	3.8		*	*
Nonwage income	4.0	3.8		*	
Number of cases			1	13	10

a 1949-51 and 1953-55.
b 1950-54 (1949 is omitted because some of the actual changes in 1948 are not available).

PART II

Changes in Consumer Expectations and Their Origin

GEORGE KATONA

SURVEY RESEARCH CENTER, UNIVERSITY OF MICHIGAN

Attitudes matter. The first task of psychological economics is to determine the circumstances under which certain attitudes, or changes in them, affect economic behavior. Several papers and comments in this volume are devoted to an analysis of whether economic behavior reflects attitudes. But to evaluate the quality of data on attitudes, expectations, and plans, one must also find out why the same people express different attitudes at different times.

The studies presented here deal mainly with short-run economic expectations.[1] Economic expectations, defined as subjective notions of things to come, are attitudes about the future rather than reports on information or reflections of deep-seated attitudes which tend to endure in spite of changing circumstances.[2]

Three major circumstances may account for changes in successive answers given by the same sample of respondents to attitudinal questions.

MISCLASSIFICATIONS

In addition to clerical errors, interviewing errors, misunderstanding of questions, and reporting errors, the term may include effects of a person's change in mood and changes resulting from a previous guess or *ad hoc* opinion given in reply to a question to which he did not know the answer.

[1] Most of the data presented here are results of a study carried out at the Survey Research Center under a grant to the Center from the Ford Foundation for studies, to be directed by the author, analyzing the origin and effects of economic attitudes. The sample used in these panel studies has been described in the paper, "Panel Mortality and Panel Bias," by Marion Gross Sobol, *Journal of the American Statistical Association*, 1959, Vol. 54, pp. 52–68. A greatly expanded version of this paper has been published under the title "Attitude Change: Instability of Response and Acquisition of Experience," in *Psychological Monographs*, Vol. 72, No. 10, American Psychological Association, 1958.

[2] George Katona, "Business Expectations in the Framework of Psychological Economics," in M. J. Bowman, ed., *Expectations, Uncertainty, and Business Behavior*, Social Science Research Council, 1958, pp. 59-74.

PERSONAL EXPERIENCES

A person may change his answer because he has learned something since he was last asked the question. Loss of job or a promotion are examples of personal experiences that may change opinions and attitudes. These are "true changes," and important for the individual. Yet such changes may be unimportant in the aggregate because they often cancel out. Therefore personal experiences frequently do not alter the distribution of attitudes obtained in successive studies. The reverse was also found to be true: When two successive measurements of subjective notions yield similar aggregative distributions, then it is likely that many individuals have changed their attitude in one direction, and many others in the opposite direction.

SOCIAL LEARNING

Personal experiences must be distinguished from the acquisition of information by broad groups of people who receive, for example, widely circulated news about general price or wage increases or other new developments in their environment. Such widely transmitted information is comprehended by many people in a similar manner, is reinforced through personal contacts and discussions, and induces similar changes in attitudes. Even people with contrary personal experiences find it difficult to swim against the current. Therefore, when in the aggregate there is a substantial change in subjective notions, it is likely that individual changes will be predominantly in one direction, with the population composed of those who shifted in that direction and those who did not change at all. Then the total number of changers will be close to the minimum number required to bring about the aggregative change.

Forms of Attitude Change

When at two successive dates two different representative samples, drawn from the same universe, are asked the same question or given the same test, we will find that changes in attitude have been either none or insignificant (Table 1, case 1) or substantial (case 2). If several questions are asked both times, we can see whether the changes are internally consistent or related to the demographic or economic characteristics, such as age or income, of the persons answering. If, however, we wish to find out why the changes took place and what their consequences were, the same individuals should be asked the questions both times. The second procedure has disadvantages for measuring changes in distribution because of panel mortality and panel bias, but it has the great advantage of yielding information on the turnover of individuals.[3]

[3] George Katona, "Federal Reserve Board Committee Reports on Consumer Expectations and Savings Statistics," *Review of Economics and Statistics*, Vol. 39, 1957, pp. 40-46; and George Katona and Eva Mueller, *Consumer Expectations*, Survey Research Center, University of Michigan, 1956.

TABLE 1

Models of Marginal Change and Turnover of Individuals
(*per cent*)

RESPONSE	CASE 1: INSIGNIFICANT MARGINAL CHANGE *Measurement*		CASE 2: SUBSTANTIAL MARGINAL CHANGE *Measurement*	
	I	II	I	II
	MARGINALS			
A	50	55	50	70
B	50	45	50	30
	100	100	100	100

	Initial A	*Initial B*	*Total* II	*Initial A*	*Initial B*	*Total* II
	TURNOVER OF INDIVIDUALS					
	Minimum					
Second *A*	50	5	55	50	20	70
Second *B*	0	45	45	0	30	30
Total I	50	50	100	50	50	100
	Intermediate					
Second *A*	35	20	55	35	35	70
Second *B*	15	30	45	15	15	30
Total I	50	50	100	50	50	100
	Maximum					
Second *A*	5	50	55	20	50	70
Second *B*	45	0	45	30	0	30
Total I	50	50	100	50	50	100

I=first measurement, II=second measurement, *A*=frequency of response *A*, and *B*=frequency of response *B*.

Change in the distribution as a whole (marginal change), whatever its size, may arise from a few changes, all in the same direction, or from many changes, some offsetting others.[4] For example, the 5 per cent marginal change in *A* responses in case 1 may be the result of 5 per cent of the people in the sample having changed their answers (minimum turnover) or of 95 per cent having done so (maximum turnover). Similarly,

[4] This possibility has also been pointed out by Paul F. Lazarsfeld ("The Use of Panels in Social Research," reprinted in *Reader in Public Opinion and Communication*, B. Berelson and M. Janowitz, eds., Free Press, Glencoe, Ill., 1953) and Charles Y. Glock ("Some Applications of the Panel Method to the Study of Change," in *The Language of Social Research*, Paul F. Lazarsfeld and Morris Rosenberg, eds., Free Press, Glencoe, Ill., 1955, pp. 242-259).

in case 2, the 20 per cent marginal change may result from 20 to 80 per cent individual changes. This scheme applies to a great variety of situations, among them experiments in the psychology of learning.

Is it possible to characterize the situations when a small or large marginal change will result from a "small" turnover (close to the minimum required to produce the marginal change) or from a "large" or "unnecessary" turnover (much larger than that minimum)? Changes in answers are a function of misclassifications or of true changes which reflect either personal experiences or social learning, as the three categories were defined at the beginning of the paper. In four possible relationships of marginal change and individual turnover, the factors making for change are likely to operate in the following ways.[5]

CASE 1a: SMALL MARGINAL CHANGE AND SMALL TURNOVER

This result may be expected when simple and easily understood questions call for well-established facts or attitudes, and when there is no true change in the period between the two measurements. For example, a question about their education to adults should yield almost the same marginal distributions in two successive surveys conducted a few months apart, with relatively few individuals changing their answers.

CASE 1b: SMALL MARGINAL CHANGE AND LARGE UNNECESSARY TURNOVER

When there has been no true change, but the question calls for guesses and hunches rather than for a well-established answer, many people may shift their guesses to the opposite of whichever way they had guessed originally. Presumably there are other instances of case 1b. True changes in both directions due to personal experiences where no guesses are involved may likewise bring forth small marginal change and large turnover.

CASE 2a: LARGE MARGINAL CHANGE AND SMALL TURNOVER

When there has been a significant environmental change and consequently social learning between two survey dates, case 2a is the probable result. Suppose people are asked once before and once after a general price increase, "Have prices of things you buy gone up, remained the same, or gone down during the last year?" The responses are likely to show a considerable increase in the proportion of people answering "gone up," and hardly any in the cell that represents shifts in the opposite direction except for misclassifications.

Will case 2a occur under other less obvious circumstances? This is a crucial question for attitude research. Substantial aggregate shifts in intentions and expectations—such as an increase in the proportion of people expecting to vote for a candidate or expecting prices to go up—

---

[5] The following discussion has been based in part on the studies by Patricia Kendall (*Conflict and Mood*, Free Press, Glencoe, Ill., 1954).

are often assigned some predictive value. Do such shifts arise through substantial turnover of individuals in both directions (case 2b)? Or do they involve few countershifts and so can be classified as a result of social learning?

CASE 2b: LARGE MARGINAL CHANGE AND LARGE UNNECESSARY TURNOVER

Unreliable measurements, with true change in one direction or with a preponderance of misclassifications in one direction, may bring about case 2b. One somewhat artificial example would be to ask, once on a beautiful summer day and once on a dark winter day, "A week from today will the weather be cloudy or sunny?" Many shifts in both directions are probable, but shifts from "sunny" in the summer test to "cloudy" in the winter test may predominate.

Alternatively, case 2b may occur even though people are not guessing. Assume that both public and private events take place between the surveys; there is news of an improvement in the business situation and some people have had income increases but others income declines. Will a substantial marginal change occur, together with a large turnover of responses?

Statistical Measures

One must first construct measures for the two crucial variables— marginal change and the rate of unnecessary turnover of individual responses. The measures should be applicable whether or not there is a true change in either or both directions. They should not be restricted to the deceptively simple dichotomous distributions presented so far (Table 1). The measures will be prepared for three-by-three distributions (attitudes measured twice on scales such as up-same-down or better-uncertain-worse) since most of the available data are of that kind. While the measures can be extended to more elaborate data, those used and discussed here will be restricted to the analysis of turnover in two successive tests.

In the following discussion, the marginal changes are denoted by small letters: those obtained in the first measurement by p, in the second, by q. There are three cells for individuals giving unchanged or consistent responses, C; and six for those giving changed responses, G for gain and L for loss. Two represent two-step changes, G_2 and L_2, the others one-step changes.[6]

[6] The letters G and L are taken from information theory. The relation between information transmitted and information received has often been presented in a manner similar to that in our turnover tables (Tables 2 and 3, below). In our case one cannot speak of "true information" (information transmitted and received), but only of consistent information or consistent attitudes. Yet the use in information theory of "gain" for information not transmitted but received, and "loss" for information transmitted but not received, has some similarities to their present use for gaining or losing information over time.

Measurement I

	C_1	G_{1A}	G_2	q_1
Measurement II	L_{1A}	C_2	G_{1B}	q_2
	L_2	L_{1B}	C_3	q_3

| p_1 | p_2 | p_3 |

G is used for changes that bring forth the marginal change, L for changes that detract from it. If the marginal change is viewed as a current, gains represent swimming with the current, losses swimming against it. By definition the gains are larger than the losses; that is, the turnover tables will be constructed to conform to the definition.

By differentiating between two-step changes and one-step changes and arbitrarily assigning a double value to the former, we have:

$$G = 2G_2 + G_{1A} + G_{1B}$$
$$L = 2L_2 + L_{1A} + L_{1B}$$

Marginal change ($M\,Ch$) can be expressed either in terms of marginals or in terms of turnover cells:

$$M\,Ch = G - L = (q_1 - q_3) - (p_1 - p_3) \quad \text{or} \quad (2q_1 + q_2) - (2p_1 + p_2)$$

The formula $100 + q_1 - q_3$ or $100 + p_1 - p_3$ has been frequently used to compute an index of attitudes.[7] Clearly the difference between two successive index values represents the aggregate or marginal change in attitudes.

The proportion of changers ($G + L$) and the proportion of consistent people [$C = 100 - (G + L)$], disregarding the duplication of two-step changes, do not represent useful measures for the purpose of testing the relation of unnecessary turnover to marginal change. Obviously, the larger $M\,Ch$ ($G - L$), the larger is G (and therefore $G + L$). The crucial variable is L, as emphasized first by Lazarsfeld and Kendall. Yet it is not enough to measure turnover by L alone, which is negatively correlated with marginal change. The objective is to find out where, in actual observations, L lies in the continuum between the smallest possible instance (minimum L) and the largest possible instance (maximum L):

$$\text{Min } L \underset{L}{\rule{3cm}{0.4pt}} \text{Max } L$$

The turnover measure, T, represents the relation of the distance between L and Min L to the distance between Max L and Min L. Since Min L is zero in all the distributions, we get:

$$T = (L - \text{Min } L)/(\text{Max } L - \text{Min } L) = L/\text{Max } L$$

[7] See for example, Katona and Mueller, p. 93, and the references given there to other diffusion indexes.

This formula yields the value of 1 if $L = \text{Max } L$, and a value of 0 if $L = 0$. In other words, the smaller T, the smaller the proportion of changers beyond those necessary to bring forth the marginal change.

Given the marginal changes, one can always calculate Max L. In a simple, pragmatic way, Max L is calculated differently when p_1 is larger than q_3 than when it is smaller. In the first case, $2q_3$ represents the maximum possible value for the q_3 row. To this must be added the maximum possible value of L_{1A}, which is either q_2 or the difference between p_1 and q_3, whichever is smaller. Therefore:

$$\text{Max } L = 2q_3 + \min [(p_1 - q_3) \text{ or } q_2] \quad \text{if} \quad p_1 \geqslant q_3$$
$$\text{Max } L = 2p_1 + \min [(q_3 - p_1) \text{ or } p_2] \quad \text{if} \quad p_1 < q_3$$

Our measures do not represent a solution of the complex problem of developing *independent* indicators for extent of change in distributions (trend) and for the number of changers. For relating unnecessary turnover (rather than number of changers) to changes in distributions, T appears to be a useful formula.

TECHNICAL NOTE ON STATISTICAL MEASURES

The formulas can be worked out for three-by-three distributions with no distinction between one-step and two-step changes. Then L equals the sum of the three loss cells, while Max $L = [\min (p_1 + p_2) \text{ or } (q_2 + q_3) \text{ or } (p_1 + q_3) \text{ or } 50 \text{ per cent}]$. The data were also calculated by this method and indicated similar regularities, but the method involves loss of information and is therefore inferior to the first method.

The statistical measures prepared for three-by-three distributions with duplication of two-step changes can be readily generalized for more complex distributions.

$$M \ Ch = [(n-1)q_1 + (n-2)q_2 + \cdots + q_{n-1}]$$
$$- [(n-1)p_1 + (n-2)p_2 + \cdots + p_{n-1}]$$

L can be calculated by multiplying the frequency of observed loss cells by the number of steps between them and the diagonal. Max L can be calculated by preparing a turnover diagram with the maximum number of observations consistent with the given distribution of the two sets of marginal changes in the extreme lower left corner.

The T measure used here is one of several possibilities. For studying stability and instability of response Lazarsfeld developed a turnover index, x, which is applicable to dichotomous distributions only.[8] The index is calculated from the equation $L = x(R - x)$, where R is the sum of the marginal values of the row and the column in which L falls.

[8] Attributed to Lazarsfeld in Kendall, p. 180. Turnover, in Lazarsfeld's terminology, denotes the proportion of changers.

The Lazarsfeld index is derived from latent structure theory. The difference between latent or true and observed values is relevant for what are here called misclassifications. The index is used when there is a true change in one direction but, as expressly stated, not in both directions. However, a true change in one direction only "is not easily defended when talking about attitudes." The Lazarsfeld index is not unrelated to the T measure, which is positively correlated with x when the proportion of consistent cases is relatively stable over a set of items.

Ferber asked a small consumer panel identical questions several times at monthly intervals to determine how often the replies to the same question remained the same over different time periods.[9] He used C, the proportion of people giving consistent responses, as a criterion. Since some C responses are expected by chance, Ferber used $(C/\text{Exp } C)$ as his statistical measure. Exp C is the consistency which, given the frequency of the marginal changes, might be expected by chance if the two responses were entirely independent.

Although C is not a satisfactory measure for the present purposes, use of $(L/\text{Exp } L)$ as the statistical measure of turnover yielded regularities similar to those observed when T was used. But Exp L will not be used as the criterion because the relation of observed frequency of losses to chance frequency is of little interest here, where the stability or change in answers is not random. It can be demonstrated that the second response is not independent of either the first or the developments occurring between the two measurements. The relative distance of observed L from Max L and Min L is more important. In addition, not only L but also Exp L is by necessity negatively correlated with M Ch. Sometimes, then, both L and Exp L are close to Min L; at others, to Max L; a crucial difference not indicated by the measure $(L/\text{Exp } L)$.

The measure T was constructed without taking into account misclassifications, although an observed change is a function both of a true change and misclassifications. Eleanor E. Maccoby recently analyzed misclassifications in a perceptive article. She assumes that misclassifications are random; an error is equally likely to occur for any response.[10] In each test, then, misclassifications are proportional to the number of answers. Since the L cells are smaller than the G cells (by definition), the observed L will always be an overestimate of the true loss (L without misclassifica-

---

[9] Robert Ferber, "On the Stability of Consumer Expectations," *Review of Economics and Statistics*, August 1955, pp. 256-266. Only the part of Ferber's paper dealing with changes in response in two successive tests is considered here. Turnover in the course of several interviews has been discussed in the author's article, "Repetitiousness and Variability of Consumer Behavior," *Human Relations*, 1959, Vol. 12, pp. 35–47.

[10] Eleanor E. Maccoby, "Pitfalls in the Analysis of Panel Data," *American Journal of Sociology*, Vol. 61, 1956, pp. 359-363. Randomness is properly assumed for clerical errors. Reporting errors are known to be biased for certain financial variables (e.g. amounts saved), but there is no evidence of bias for economic attitudes and expectations.

tions).[11] L is farther away from Min L, or zero, than the true loss is. As demonstrated in the next section, the observed L tends to be closer to Min L in particular circumstances. It follows that the difference would be more marked if it were possible to eliminate misclassifications. Because of their presence, the data used represent a strong test of the hypothesis under study.

Marginal Change and Turnover of Individuals

Changes in three kinds of attitudes from one survey to the next can be studied:

1. Attitudes expected to be stable for a long time, such as sociocultural norms or tastes assumed to be innate or acquired in early childhood.
2. Habitual attitudes unlikely to change in the short time between test and retest.
3. Attitudes dependent on changing circumstances and likely to change in the short run.[12]

Miss Kendall studied the first type, the present study concentrates on the last. Fluctuations in economic motives, attitudes, and expectations have been studied by the Survey Research Center for the last ten years to determine their influence on changes in spending and saving. Miss Mueller and I recently constructed an index of consumer attitudes and studied the relationship of changes in that index to changes in purchases of durable goods. Because of their association with changes in behavior, the attitudes included in that index, as well as a few other related attitudes, are particularly suitable here.

In the study sponsored by the Ford Foundation which provided most of the data presented here, a representative sample of the urban population of the United States was interviewed at length in June and December 1954, in June and December 1955, and in February 1957. Members of the sample were asked for their attitudes toward their personal financial situations and toward national economic trends and market conditions, including their opinions on the recent past and short-range or longer-range expectations.[13] The resulting thirty-one turnover tables, constructed from answers given by the same individuals each time, reflect attitudes expressed at different times, different attitudes, and varying time

[11] This is put by E. Maccoby as follows (p. 359 n.): "It will inevitably be true that a higher proportion of a minority group will shift."

[12] See S. M. Lipset, P. F. Lazarsfeld, A. H. Barton, and J. Linz, "The Psychology of Voting: An Analysis of Political Behavior," *Handbook of Social Psychology*, G. Lindzey, ed., Addison-Wesley, 1954, p. 1,150; Kendall, pp. 5ff.; and Katona, "Business Expectations . . . Psychological Economics," Chap. 3.

[13] The reader will find the wording of most questions where data derived from individual questions are presented.

spans between the measurements (from six to twenty months). In addition, parts of the Survey of Consumer Finances samples were interviewed twice at twelve-month intervals. A group of the 1948 sample were asked five attitude questions in 1948 and again in 1949, and a group of the 1952 sample were asked four such questions again in 1953. Thus nine turnover tables derived from the SCF sample are included in the present set of data.

Most of the attitude questions were answered in the respondent's own words, taken down by the interviewer as nearly verbatim as possible. Central office coders classified the answers according to pre-established categories, including "don't know" and "not ascertained." Individuals classified in either of those categories in test or retest were omitted from the turnover tables. Those included were ones classified as (1) up, better, good; (2) same, pro–con, or uncertain; and (3) down, worse, or bad.

CHART I

Relation of Turnover Rates to Percentage Marginal Change

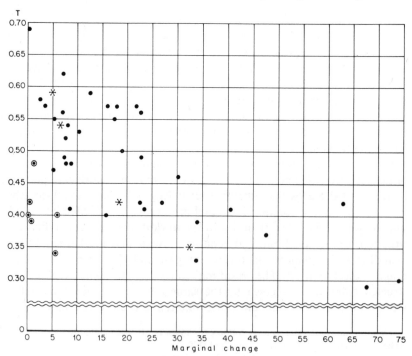

Chart 1 indicates the relation of marginal change to turnover for the forty repeated attitude measurements. Some data approach case 1a (small marginal change and small unnecessary turnover of individual responses). Take, for example, the point on the diagram with a *M Ch* of 0.8 and a

T of 0.39, representing the turnover from June 1954 to June 1955, and the point with a *M Ch* of 0.2 and a *T* of 0.40, the turnover from June 1955 to February 1957. The question read, "A few years from now, do you think you and your family will have a better position and income than you have now, or will you be in about the same situation, or even in a less satisfactory situation?" In all three surveys the distribution of the answers was practically the same, and relatively few individuals shifted. Among the 827 people who gave definite answers to the question in both 1954 and 1955, six shifted from better to worse and four from worse to better (possibly owing to misclassification). Although more shifted from same to better or from better to same, the rate of turnover was small; *L* was 18.5, much smaller than the highest possible *L* of 47.6. The data on the turnover from June 1955 to February 1957 are similar.

Secondly, a number of instances resemble case 1b (small marginal change and large turnover), for example, the point with *M Ch* of 0.3 and a *T* value of 0.69. The question asked in June and December 1955 read, "Do you think that in the country as a whole during the next twelve months we'll have good times financially, or bad times, or what?" The two marginal distributions obtained could hardly be distinguished from each other. Nevertheless, among 757 people approximately a hundred expressed a more pessimistic opinion the second time than the first, and approximately a hundred a more optimistic opinion the second time. *L* was 15.5 and relatively close to the maximum possible *L* of 22.6.

Case 2a (large marginal change and small turnover) is illustrated by the point with *M Ch* of 74.3 and the *T* of 0.30. The question read, "Would you say that at present business conditions in the country as a whole are better or worse than they were a year ago?" In June 1954, 17 per cent said better and 53 per cent worse; in June 1955, 51 per cent said better and 12 per cent worse. Among 818 respondents only eight shifted from better to worse. *L* was 8.7 and relatively distant from the maximum *L* of 29.3.

Similarly, we find a substantial marginal change in price expectations measured in 1948 and 1949 (67.8). Early in 1948 the majority of consumers thought that prices of things they buy would go up during the next year, while early in 1949 the majority thought that prices would go down. *L* was 10.8, Max *L* 37.8, and *T* 0.29.

No instances of very large marginal change coupled with large turnover (high *T*) are found in the turnover tables. But coming close to case 2b is the point with *M Ch* of 21.8 and a *T* of 0.57. The question was, "What do you expect prices of household items and clothing will do during the next year or so, stay where they are, go up, or go down?" Many more said "down" in June 1954 than in June 1955; the shift occurred mainly from "down" to "same." There were also a number of shifts in the

63

opposite direction. L was 16.2 or closer to the Max L of 28.3 than to zero. (The data presented in Table 8, below, with $M Ch$ of 17.9 and T of 0.57 also resemble case 2b.)

What determines the relationship between $M Ch$ and T? Is it the attitude itself? The assumption that responses to certain attitude questions will always be either of case 1b or case 2a can be contradicted. The change in response to the question about expected business conditions in the country as a whole between June and December 1955 was given as an example of case 1b. The same question had also been asked of the same sample in June 1954. The data for June 1954–June 1955 yielded a marginal change of 40.6 (many more people being optimistic about the economic outlook in June 1955 than in June 1954), which was associated with a T value of 0.41, while the absence of a marginal change in the second half of 1955 ($M Ch = 0.3$) was associated with a T of 0.69, as reported above. Thus the same question once yielded a large marginal change and a small turnover, and once from the same people a small marginal change and a large turnover.

Similar findings were obtained with several other questions asked at the same three dates, for example, "Do you think now is a good time or a bad time to buy large household items such as furniture, refrigerator, TV, and things like that?" From June 1954 to June 1955 $M Ch$ was 34.0 and from June to December 1955, it was 2.5. In the first period the T value was 0.39 and in the second 0.58.

On the other hand, there are good reasons to believe that fitting case 1a is a function of the attitude studied. For three questions one could have predicted a priori a yield of small marginal changes and small turnover rates. One was, "How do you people feel about your present income; do you think it is about what you ought to be getting, or not?" Asked three times and yielding two turnover tables, the question is easily understood and relates to relatively permanent or deep-seated notions, as unlikely to change greatly over short periods as are most people's incomes. The same is true of whether people think their position and income will be better or worse a few years from now, and the two resulting turnover tables were cited as instances of case 1a. The same category includes two turnover tables based on short-range personal expectations, "Do you think that a year from now you people will be better off financially, or worse off, or just about the same as now?" (The six observations resulting from the three questions are circled in Chart 1.)

That the three attitudes must be differentiated from the rest can be demonstrated by using the measure of consistency, C, described in the previous section, on the assumption that, unlike the answers to the other questions, the answers to questions on these attitudes are determined more by personality and less by situation. Consequently, the answers should show a higher rate of consistency than the others, and they do, with C

yielding the highest values for the six circled observations and lower values for every one of the other thirty-four.[14]

The data grouped according to the size of marginal change are presented in Table 2. The first part gives a summary of all forty turnover tables, the

TABLE 2

Data on Marginal Change and Turnover

Marginal Change	SUMMARY OF ALL (40) TURNOVER TABLES			
	Average of L	Average of Max L	Average of T	Number of Attitudes
Less than 3.5	23.8	48.2	0.503	7
5 to 12.5	23.9	48.2	.509	14
16 to 30.5	17.8	37.5	.494	12
34 and larger	12.9	37.1	.358	7
				40
	SUMMARY OF TURNOVER TABLES (34) RELATING TO SHORT-RUN ATTITUDE[a]			
Less than 3.5	23.8	39.8	0.613	3
5 to 12.5	24.8	48.5	.518	12
16 to 30.5	17.8	37.5	.494	12
34 and larger	12.9	37.1	.358	7
				34

For an explanation of the units in this table and in Table 3, see text.

[a] Rank correlation between M Ch and T: -0.689.

second of thirty-four. By omitting the six observations assigned to case 1a we can see that the larger the marginal change, the smaller the unnecessary turnover of individual responses on short-run attitudes. Subsets of the data (e.g. the 1954-55 or 1955-57 turnover tables considered separately) yield the same regularities.

Investigators analyzing attitude changes have often argued that changes in answers to individual questions are less reliable than changes derived from clusters of questions. Three such clusters were computed from the material available in June 1954 and June 1955: (1) six questions asking for *evaluations of present conditions*, (2) four questions for *one-year expectations*, and (3) three questions for *five-year expectations*. To these were added (4) the turnover in the *index of consumer attitudes* consisting

[14] A statistical measure of repetitiousness yields the highest values for these six observations. The measure was presented in a paper published in *Human Relations* dealing with changes in attitudes over several surveys (see footnote 9) and with changes in action (spending, saving) over several years. The measure derives from a computation of coefficients of intraclass correlations. It reaches its maximum value when the frequency of identical answers (or of identical behavior) is maximized, a zero value when the actual observations correspond to what would be expected if the consecutive observations were independent of each other, and a minimum value when the frequency of identical answers (or behavior) is minimized. The measure has been developed by Leslie Kish of the Survey Research Center.

of six questions, some of which fall into each of the three clusters.[15] Table 3 contains the data on the turnover of the four group measures. Again the larger the marginal change, the smaller is T.

TABLE 3

Marginal Change and Turnover for Clusters of Attitudes

	M Ch	M Ch[a]	L	Max L	T
Five-year expectations[b]	12.7	5.0	354	602	0.588
One-year expectations[c]	36.1	6.6	534	996	.536
Present conditions[c]	179.4	32.6	325	929	.350
Index of consumer attitudes[c]	102.0	18.5	365	878	.416

[a] M Ch recalculated to make it comparable with 3×3 tables. The data presented on the size of marginal change in the first column are not comparable to those presented in Table 2. In a 12×12 table the maximum number of steps with which changed responses are multiplied is 11; in a 3×3 table it is 2. If, then, we divide M Ch as presented in the first column of the table by $\frac{11}{2}$ (or in one instance by $\frac{5}{2}$), we obtain a M Ch of 5.0 for five-year expectations, of 6.6 for one-year expectations, of 18.5 for the index, and of 32.6 for present conditions. These data with their respective T values have been added to Chart 1 in the form of asterisks.
[b] 6×6 Table.
[c] 12×12 Table.

Thus the following generalization is applicable to subjective notions and expectations not representing deep-seated and enduring convictions. If two successive measurements yield similar aggregate distributions, it is likely that many individuals changed their attitudes in one direction and many others in the other. If in the aggregate there is a substantial change in attitudes, it is likely that the changes will be predominantly in one direction, the population tending to be divided between those who changed in one direction and those who did not change at all. These findings accord with the hypotheses formulated before embarking on the study, which were derived from assumptions about contagion and social learning and from earlier findings obtained without the use of the panel technique.[16]

From the point of view of using survey research, the present findings indicate, first, that small changes from one survey to the next in the distribution of subjective notions and expectations must be viewed with caution because they do not imply that only a few people changed their opinions. On the other hand, substantial shifts may be viewed less skeptically even without recourse to panel data to make certain that most individual shifts were in the same direction.

[15] See the discussion of the index of attitudes in Katona and Mueller.
[16] In earlier studies, when consumer attitudes showed large changes in the aggregate (as in 1950-51), all subgroups of the population showed similar changes. When, however, measurements with two successive samples indicated substantially unchanged distributions of attitudes (as in 1952), some occupational, regional, or income groups showed a shift in one direction and some other groups in the opposite direction.

66

To clarify the generalization, contrast it with the views of Lazarsfeld and Miss Kendall. In Lazarsfeld's theoretical scheme, "turnover," that is, the proportion of changers, is an index of uncertainty or instability.[17] If large, it shows that clarification and education are required. Similarly Miss Kendall identifies "turnover" with instability of response due to vacillation by respondents.

No doubt the authors correctly describe one type of change in response. But the findings here indicate that response changes also occur under circumstances that suggest they may be due to acquisition of experience or learning on the part of many people at about the same time. If a high proportion of changes is associated with uncertainty or with contradictory developments of a personal nature, the data will resemble case 1b (relatively high T value). If a high proportion of changes is associated with social learning, the data will resemble case 2a (relatively low T value).[18]

On the Origin of Changes in Attitudes

When some people change their attitudes from one survey to the next and others do not, there are two approaches to finding out *why* they differed. Data from the first survey may show initial differences in the characteristics of the two groups that account for what happened to their attitudes later. And data from the second may show that there were developments in the interval that differentiated them. (Naturally questions to elicit the appropriate information must have been included in each survey.)

Observed changes in attitudes may be due to incorrect recording in one or the other survey, or, more important, to the firmness with which a given attitude was held. Among people who say "better" the first time, some may have quite different attitudes from those who say "same," but others may have true attitudes relatively close to those answering "same." If the attitudes are distinguished somewhat arbitrarily in a crude system of measurement, a recorded shift from "better" to "same" may not represent a significant change.[19]

17 P. F. Lazarsfeld, B. Berelson, and H. Gaudet, "Introduction," *The People's Choice* (2nd ed., 1948) reprinted in *The Language of Social Research*, Free Press, Glencoe, Ill., 1955, p. 232.

18 Turnover due to true changes rather than to vacillations has been considered by Lazarsfeld and his associates in connection with before-and-after experiments. In discussing, for instance, the showing of a film on anti-Semitism to people whose level of anti-Semitism was measured both before and after seeing the film, Glock speaks of "the effect of a stimulus in producing change" in attitudes (pp. 243ff.). The findings about the rate of turnover were often similar to our findings on attitude changes without experimental stimuli. Sometimes, however, even though the experimental stimulus brought forth a substantial marginal change, reverse changes were also observed and were called the "boomerang effect."

19 Eleanor Maccoby calls attention to this possibility and illustrates it with a graph (p. 361). Procedures similar to the first approach have been used in analyzing shifts by election panels. For instance, those whose intended vote shifted from the Republican

The two approaches are not alternatives. A person who holds an attitude with little conviction may be more likely than others to have experiences that result in his changing that attitude. Thus we should expect to find circumstances in which both approaches contribute to an "explanation." Yet, interestingly enough, at least one case will be found in which the first will not result in an explanation and the second will.

ORIGIN OF CHANGES IN SPECIFIC ATTITUDES

Basic data for detailed studies carried out on two of the thirty-four turnover tables summarized in Table 2 are presented in Table 4. Both

TABLE 4

Basic Data for Studies of Origin of Changes in Expectations
(*per cent*)

EXPECTED PERSONAL FINANCIAL SITUATION DURING NEXT YEAR
June 1954

June 1955	Better(O)	Same(M)	Worse(P)	
Better(O)	20.5	14.7	1.3	36.5
Same(M)	13.3	40.6	3.6	57.5
Worse(P)	1.2	3.9	0.9	6.0
	35.0	59.2	5.8	100.0

$M\,Ch = 1.3 \qquad N = 850$
$T = 0.48$

OO group, 20.5 per cent, in first measurement to be compared with *OM* group (including *OP*) of 14.5 per cent. *MM* group, 40.6 per cent, in first measurement to be compared with *MO* group of 14.7 per cent.

EXPECTED NATIONAL BUSINESS CONDITIONS DURING NEXT YEAR
June 1954

June 1955	Good(O)	Pro–con(M)	Bad(P)	
Good(O)	46.8	20.0	13.5	80.3
Pro–con(M)	6.0	7.0	3.2	16.2
Bad(P)	1.5	0.6	1.4	3.5
	54.3	27.6	18.1	100.0

$M\,Ch = 40.6 \qquad N = 844$
$T = 0.41$

OO group, 46.8 per cent, in first measurement to be compared with *OM* group (including *OP*) of 7.5 per cent. *MM* group, 8.4 per cent (including *PP*), in first measurement to be compared with *MO* group of 23.2 per cent (including *PM*).

to the Democratic candidate were studied regarding their "class interest" (see Glock, p. 247). It was found that people who planned to vote for one candidate were much more likely to abandon their candidate if their class interest was in conflict with their vote intention than those where such conflict did not arise. Such initial differences were sometimes called cross-pressures (Lazarsfeld, p. 512).

questions were asked of the same sample, in June of 1954 and 1955. One
was, "Do you think that a year from now you people will be better off
financially, or worse off, or just about the same as now?" It resulted in a
very small marginal change. The other resulted in a substantial marginal
change, "Do you think that in the country as a whole during the next
twelve months we will have good times financially, or bad times, or
what?"

Table 5 contains the data obtained by applying the two approaches to

TABLE 5

Personal Financial Expectations, June 1954–June 1955

	GROUP			
CHARACTERISTIC	OO	OM	MO	MM
First Approach: Condition at Time of First Test				
1954 median income ($)	6,570	5,500	5.300	4,870
Median age (years)	39	44	42	51
Education (%):				
Grade school	20	33	24	48
High school	48	51	53	35
College	32	16	23	17
Personal finances (%):				
Better off previously	56	39	32	21
Worse off previously	20	21	26	20
Difference	+36	+18	+6	+1
Average evaluation of current conditions (index)	7.2	5.7	6.1	5.9
Second Approach: Change in Year between Two Tests				
Personal finances (%):				
Better off	67	32	36	18
Worse off	8	21	18	18
Difference	+59	+10	+18	0
Income (%):				
Making more	55	29	40	22
Making less	9	21	19	12
Difference	+46	+8	+21	+10
Conditions in respondent's industry (%):				
Better	54	30	49	27
Worse	7	17	13	18
Difference	+47	+13	+36	+9
Correct information on developments in economy received (%):				
Hardly any	11	32	26	32
Some	60	52	54	50
Much	29	16	20	18
Mean questions answered correctly (no.)	4.45	3.44	3.89	3.48

the first question. Groups *OO* and *OM*, as well as groups *MM* and *MO*, expressed the same attitudes in June 1954. Nevertheless, there were substantial differences between the pairs of groups. Those who became more pessimistic (*OM*) were poorer, had lower average incomes, were older, less educated, and less hopeful about present conditions than those who remained optimistic (*OO*). Similarly, those who became optimistic (*MO*) were richer, had somewhat higher incomes, were younger and more educated than those who remained pessimistic (*MM*). Thus data from the first survey help considerably to account for the difference between stable and changing expectations.

Additional explanations are provided by the second approach. The proportion of those of the *OO* group whose income rose and whose evaluation of their personal financial situation improved is much higher than the *OM* group's proportion. Between groups *MM* and *MO* we likewise find differences, but less pronounced, in the expected direction. People's opinions about conditions in the industries in which they worked also show differences indicating that results for the two pairs of groups are related to stability or change in their personal expectations.[20]

To obtain the data in Table 5 on acquisition of information about business conditions in the nation, the members of the panel were asked several questions to determine how much "correct information" they had received.[21] It appears that group *OO* was somewhat better informed than group *OM*. There are hardly any such differences between groups *MM* and *MO*.

[20] It must be stressed that the differences discussed and explained are group differences. As seen in Table 5, there are individuals in the *OM* group, which as a group became more pessimistic, who said they were better off and whose income increased. Accounting for changes in attitudes by individuals is a task not undertaken here; it would require a different kind of interviewing.

[21] A printed card was handed to each respondent with the following instructions: "This card contains some answers we received when we asked people about what had happened during the last twelve months in the American economy. Please check those items which you agree have happened." One of three columns, labeled "happened," "did not happen," and "don't know," had to be checked for each statement. The answers were scored for correctness, "don't know" being taken as not having correct information.

The seven statements—some true, some false—given to the respondents in June 1955 were: "What happened during the last twelve months? (1) Business conditions improved. (2) The cost of living was stable. (3) Unemployment increased. (4) People have less money to spend than a year ago. (5) Stock prices went up. (6) Defense spending by the government declined. (7) The federal budget was balanced last year." Altogether, 27 per cent of the sample answered 0, 1, or 2 items correctly ("hardly any correct information"); 53 per cent, 3, 4, or 5 items ("some correct information"); and 20 per cent, 6 or 7 items ("much correct information"). The mean number of questions answered correctly was 3.73. Since the economy improved greatly in the year prior to June 1955, correct information refers to favorable developments.

The percentage of correct information received was highest for the cost of living (2) and relatively high also for four other items. Least was known about stock prices (5), which the majority checked "don't know," and about defense spending (6) with a frequency of "happened" and "did not happen" answers quite similar.

TABLE 6

One-Year Economic Outlook, June 1954–June 1955

	GROUP			
CHARACTERISTIC	OO	OM	MO	MM
First Approach: Condition at Time of First Test				
1954 median income ($)	6,250	5,000	4,600	4,400
Median age (years)	46	49	46	48
Education (%):				
Grade school	29	39	42	44
High school	42	45	42	42
College	29	16	16	14
Average evaluation of current conditions (index)	7.1	5.7	5.8	5.5
Second Approach: Change in Year between Two Tests				
Personal finances (%):				
Better off	39	25	30	23
Worse off	14	25	15	28
Difference	+25	0	+15	−5
Income (%):				
Making more	37	22	32	23
Making less	10	25	12	33
Difference	+27	−3	+20	−10
Conversations on economic trends (%):				
Optimistic	15	6	8	6
Pessimistic	6	17	12	16
Difference	+9	−11	−4	−10
Correct information on developments in economy received (%):				
Hardly any	14	40	27	63
Some	56	55	55	33
Much	30	5	18	4
Mean questions answered correctly (no.)	4.39	3.04	3.64	2.15

In Table 6, an analysis of stability or change in the one-year economic outlook, the first approach reveals consistent differences between groups *OO* and *OM*. The small deviant group who became more pessimistic had lower incomes, and were somewhat older, less educated, and less hopeful about prevailing conditions than the group who remained optimistic. But the differences in income, age, and education between groups *MO* and *MM* were extremely small or nonexistent. The same is true of changes in personal financial conditions before the first test (not shown in the table). Thus improvement in the general economic outlook, which in this case brought about a substantial marginal change, cannot be accounted for by initial differences between the changers and nonchangers.

The second approach reveals that between the two surveys changes occurred in income and in people's evaluation of their personal financial situations which seem to help explain the attitude change. More pronounced still are the differences in how much correct information on economic developments each group received between the two tests. In the *OO* group many more people answered most questions correctly than answered hardly any correctly; in the *OM* group the reverse was true. Similarly, the *MO* group was much better informed than the *MM* group, the differences being more pronounced than those obtained in Table 5. More important still, one may discount the differences in information in Table 5 by assuming that they reflect primarily differences in education, but there is little difference in education between the groups *MM* and *MO* of Table 6 to account for the larger differences.

Further data pointing in the same direction are differences in answers to the question, "During the last few months have you discussed with other people whether business conditions are getting better or worse?" About the same proportion in each group said yes, but a follow-up question on the content of the conversations showed that the groups varied, in the expected direction, on how many of the conversations were optimistic or pessimistic.

Since correct information about developments in 1954-55 was all favorable, the findings may be restated as follows: The *OO* and *MO* groups acquired information between the surveys about favorable developments in the economy. Such learning, apparently reinforced through conversation, is a current hard to swim against. The acquisition of information by the *MO* group corresponds with a change in their attitudes. It probably also corresponds with a change in group *OO* attitudes, but our crude measurements cannot show this because they had already given the most optimistic answer in the first survey ("good") that the survey recognized.[22]

Thus somewhat different explanations emerge for the frequent improvement in attitudes toward national business conditions (group *MO* in Table 6) and the less frequent improvement in attitudes of the same people at the same time toward their personal financial situation (group *MO* in Table 5). A further step in the analysis is possible, comparison of the changes in the two attitudes. Of particular interest are people whose personal financial expectations deteriorated from June 1954 to June 1955 (the *L* group in Table 4, 18.5 per cent of the sample). How did the business expectations of these people change between the same two dates?

1. In cell *OO*, 8 per cent fell (remained optimistic about business conditions).

---

[22] What has been said about group *MO* also applies to group *PO* (13.5 per cent). Data on *PO* are not shown in Table 6 and are not conclusive because the corresponding *PP* group is too small for comparisons. Yet according to the first approach, *PO* did not differ from *MM*; income gains were less frequent among *PO* than among *MO*; but *PO* had a substantial amount of correct information.

2. In cells *MO, PO,* or *PM,* 6.5 per cent fell (became more optimistic).
3. In cells *MM* and *PP,* 2 per cent fell (remained relatively pessimistic).
4. In cells *OM, OP,* or *MP,* 2 per cent fell (became more pessimistic).

Among people classified under (4) and possibly under (3) we can discern a correspondence between the two changes, or even an influence of personal financial expectations on business expectations. In (1) and (2), however, fell most people whose personal financial attitudes deteriorated; they maintained or even strengthened their optimistic business opinions. A pessimistic turn in opinions about personal finances lost out in competition with good business news.

Of those whose personal financial expectations remained unchanged in their lack of optimism (groups *MM* and *PP* in Table 4, 41 per cent of the sample), 17.5 per cent were optimistic about the national business outlook both times, 16.5 per cent became more optimistic, and only 7.5 per cent remained or became pessimistic. Again business attitudes developed differently from personal financial attitudes. The same conclusion is reached by studying personal financial experiences rather than changes in personal financial expectations. The business expectations of most people who said they were worse off financially were unaffected by their personal experiences.

INDEX OF CONSUMER ATTITUDES

The answers to the six questions that make up the cluster of attitudes represented in the index of consumer attitudes, including the two questions analyzed separately in Tables 5 and 6, were studied to find out which factors made for stability, which for change. Each optimistic answer was given a value of two; a pro-con or "middle" answer, one; and a pessimistic answer, zero; giving a twelve-point scale with twelve the most optimistic value. The turnover from the first to the second survey was classified in eight groups:

1. Three groups were made up of people who were consistent, with consistency defined as a change of 1 point or less from the June 1954 to the June 1955 survey; for example, a change from 8 to 7 or 9 as well as no change. Group *OO* had scored 10, 11, or 12 in the first survey; group *MM,* 7, 8, or 9; and group *PP,* 6 or less.

2. Three groups were made up of people who became more optimistic. In group *PM* people increased by 2 to 4 points from 6 or less in the first survey; in group *PO* by 5 or more points. Group *MO* was made up of people who increased by 2 or more points from the middle position. As before, those who were *O* initially could not show gains.

3. Two groups were made up of people who became more pessimistic by 2 or more points: group *OM* from original values of 10, 11, or 12; group *MP,* a small one, from original values of 7, 8, or 9.

73

TABLE 7

Index of Economic Attitudes, Six Questions, June 1954–June 1955

	GROUP							
CHARACTERISTIC	OO	OM	MO	MM	MP	PO	PM	PP
Number of cases	136	64	140	160	28	55	87	30
Per cent of sample	19.9	9.2	19.8	22.9	3.9	7.9	12.2	4.2

First Approach: Condition at Time of First Test

1954 median income ($)	7,750	5,950	5,900	5,220	4,600	4,450	4,450	3,970
Median age (years)	49	46	43	47	50	40	49	53
Education (%):								
Grade school	21	32	18	40	50	26	47	53
High school	45	44	53	40	26	65	38	44
College	34	24	29	20	14	9	15	3
Average evaluation of current conditions (index)	8.5	7.9	6.4	6.5	6.0	2.9	4.0	3.7

Second Approach: Change in Year between Two Tests

Income (%):								
Making more	46	29	53	27	11	44	22	13
Making less	6	17	6	13	46	16	16	43
Difference	+40	+12	+47	+14	−35	+28	+6	−30
Conditions in respondent's industry (%):								
Better	46	35	43	33	11	32	22	10
Worse	8	21	4	12	25	14	13	17
Difference	+38	+14	+39	+21	−14	+18	+9	−7
Conversations on economic trends (%):								
Optimistic	23	15	10	10	0	11	10	3
Pessimistic	6	9	11	7	29	5	10	17
Difference	+17	+6	−1	+3	−29	+6	0	−14
Correct information on developments in economy received (%):								
Hardly any	10	14	13	24	64	35	42	40
Some	53	62	63	55	29	58	39	53
Much	37	24	24	21	7	7	19	7
Mean questions answered correctly (no.)	4.68	4.29	4.35	3.82	2.13	3.32	3.29	2.77

Initial characteristics help to explain stability or change (Table 7). The differences in income are especially large among those who were either *O* or *M* in the first survey, and in age among the *P* groups. Wide educational differences are found among all the groups, yet the differences in the evaluation of present conditions are small or, for the *P* groups, contrary to expectations.

The data obtained in the second survey show that personal income changes during the interval and respondents' appraisals of changes in the condition of their industries both were substantial and always contribute to an explanation of stability or change in attitudes. Differences in the nature of conversations on economic trends indicate that loss groups had more pessimistic conversations than consistent groups or gain groups. Finally, the data on information received show large differences in the three initial *M* groups.

Thus the data in Table 7 indicate that initial differences among the groups, personal developments in the interval, and information obtained on national economic developments may account for stability or change in the index of consumer attitudes. Some differences, such as some originally pessimistic people becoming more optimistic, others not, seem to hinge primarily on income changes and related personal developments. Other changes seem to result more from the interaction of various influences. This is not surprising because the index is constructed from questions about both personal finances and expected economic conditions.

Some Effects of Attitude Change

Attitudes are predispositions to action, and their relation to actual behavior is a major purpose of studying opinion and expectations data. A few comparisons of purchases by people who were or became optimistic with those by people who were or became pessimistic will be presented in this section. Individual tests can be expected to show a weaker relation of attitudes to purchases than aggregative tests, partly because factors that may cancel out in an aggregative test will not do so here.[23]

The simple and crude measure of durable goods purchases used in the test, described in detail by Miss Mueller in her paper in this volume, was the number of transactions by each family between the June 1954 and June 1955 surveys and during the second half of 1955. Transactions included purchases of one or more automobiles, major household goods, certain luxury or hobby items, and extensive house repairs or additions. On a scale ranging from zero to five, the average family made about one and a half transactions in the year, about one in the following half year.

If we assume that changes in attitudes were evenly distributed over the twelve-month period, or even occurred chiefly near its beginning, we should expect that a group that became more optimistic (for example, *MO*) will have made more purchases during the year than a group that did not change its attitudes (*MM*). ("Expected purchases" were calculated by

---

[23] For an analysis of aggregative tests, see especially Katona and Mueller; for individual tests, see Eva Mueller, "Effects of Consumer Attitudes on Purchases," *American Economic Review*, December 1957, pp. 946ff.; and Katona, "Federal Reserve Board Committee Reports. . . ."

income level to eliminate the effect of income on number of purchases.) And we should expect the *MO* group also to have made more purchases in the following half year since their attitudes were more optimistic than those of the *MM* group in June 1955, although in so doing we are disregarding the influence of possible changes in attitudes between June and December.

Table 8 shows that changes in personal financial expectations did affect purchases in both periods. Group *OO* purchased more than *OM*, group

TABLE 8

Number of Durable Goods Purchases

	JUNE 1954–JUNE 1955		SECOND HALF OF 1955	
	Actual	Actual as Percentage of Expected	Actual	Actual as Percentage of Expected
Personal Financial Expectations (*see Table 5*)				
Group *OO*	1.82	110	1.20	114
Group *OM*	1.45	94	0.93	94
Group *MO*	1.69	109	1.05	105
Group *MM*	1.46	93	0.88	92
General Business Expectations (*see Table 6*)				
Group *OO*	1.53	99	1.09	105
Group *OM*	1.49	104	0.80	85
Group *MO*	1.42	103	0.99	106
Group *MM*	1.45	105	0.85	90

MO more than *MM*. The differences in the second half of 1955 indicate that attitudes did matter. The differences in the year 1954-55 may be related also to the data in Table 5 that show that indications for the forthcoming attitude changes were already available in June 1954, which suggests that some attitude changes took place shortly after the first measurement.

As to the effect of changes in general business expectations, the purchases of the four groups were substantially the same in 1954-55, but there were sizable differences in the second half of 1955. The first finding is explained if one assumes that the information about the changes in business conditions came late in the twelve-month period, an assumption supported by evidence from surveys conducted toward the end of 1954 and from an analysis of business-cycle developments. Also pertinent is the finding of a lack of initial differences between groups *MO* and *MM* in Table 6, which points toward a relatively late shift in attitudes.

According to Table 8, the 1954-55 purchase rates of the initial *O* groups were no higher than those of initial *M* groups. But the more comprehensive index of consumer attitudes shows that in the same period the initial *O* groups had a purchase rate of 107 per cent, the initial M groups of 102 per cent, and the initial P groups of 86 per cent (see Miss Mueller's Table A-2 in this volume).

Implications of the Findings

Writers on business cycles constantly refer to waves of confidence or waves of distrust. And in analyzing specific developments—the great crash of 1929, the upswing in the postwar years—they frequently discuss psychological forces. Usually economists have not considered the optimism or pessimism of businessmen or consumers as major causal forces but rather as reinforcing factors compatible with any economic theory of business cycles.[24] But changes in those attitudes have often been invoked to explain how relatively minor causes have had major effects or to account for the timing of turning points in cyclical fluctuations. Yet the treatment of attitudes has usually been a priori or anecdotal.

A contribution of research in economic psychology to business-cycle studies is the demonstration that changes in the economic attitudes of consumers and businessmen are measurable. Through surveys such as those described here information has been obtained about the direction of changes in sentiment or their absence.[25] Sometimes such information has served only as confirmation of what was generally known or widely expected from data on national income, retail sales, production rates, and the like. But at other times observed changes in consumer attitudes have contradicted trends derived from economic data that reflected past activities of the economy. Three times during the past ten years—in 1949, 1951, and 1954—changes in consumer sentiment proved to be advance indications of otherwise unforeseen changes in consumer buying behavior.

The present studies go beyond previous contributions in two ways. First, they add a second measure to our store of tools, the measure T, which indicates whether the marginal change in attitudes coincides with frequent offsetting shifts or results from similar influences that have affected most people similarly. The finding of a tendency toward an association between large marginal changes and small T rates strengthens the reliability of the first measure—the presence or absence of substantial marginal changes in the distribution of attitudes.

Secondly, investigation of the origin of substantial changes in consumer sentiment indicates that uniform acquisition of experience is possible and may be effective. Lord Keynes argued that consumer income expectations are likely to average out for the country as a whole.[26] If this should be

[24] See, for example, Gottfried Haberler, *Prosperity and Depression*, Geneva, League of Nations, 1937, Chap. 6.

[25] See Katona and Mueller.

[26] J. M. Keynes, *General Theory of Employment, Interest, and Money*, Harcourt Brace, 1936, p. 95.

generally true, the economist's neglect of consumer expectations would be justified, for he is not interested in explaining the antecedents of action by individuals unless the number who increase their rate of consumption is much larger than the number who reduce it. Only then will the economy be affected and the factors inducing changes in the behavior of the masses concern economists.

I have argued before that changes in consumer sentiment usually do not cancel out but rather resemble a contagious disease, tending to spread widely, an argument derived from general socio-psychological principles and not based on specific studies of the origin of economic attitudes.[27] The empirical research reported here confirms the occurrence of non-offsetting changes in economic attitudes. Its aim is the identification of circumstances under which it is probable or not probable that changes in the attitudes of some people in one direction will cancel the changes in the attitudes of others in the opposite direction. Cancellation is not to be expected when—to oversimplify—uniform acquisition of information has taken place.

This finding leads to new questions the consideration of which will help to clarify the finding. First, why bother with attitudes? Why not rely on the information that changed the attitudes? If attitude change is the result of the transmission of information about economic or political developments, consideration of those developments may be more rewarding. This notion must be rejected. Even complete knowledge of all events and developments would amount to only a listing of possible stimuli; we would still not know which items of news are effective or how they are apprehended. Such knowledge can be gained only by starting with the prevailing attitudes and their recent changes and connecting them with events and developments. Then we will be in a position to select the relevant stimuli.

Possible exceptions are developments of overwhelming significance, especially catastrophes, although consumer and business reactions to the outbreak of war have not always been correctly assessed. But aside from radical changes that we know a priori will affect people in a definite manner, measurement of information cannot serve as a substitute for measurement of attitudes. For example, we cannot conclude that income increases will necessarily make people feel "better off," or that they will view price increases as a "good thing" or "bad thing."

From the conclusion that measurement of attitude changes is needed, it does not follow that such measurement always yields significant new insights for business-cycle studies. It is not possible to discover a priori whether attitude changes are autonomous or reflect past trends. Only after determining that prevailing attitudes indicate no significant new developments can one conclude that the measurement contributed no new knowledge and that one can rely on extrapolation of past trends.

[27] George Katona, *Psychological Analysis of Economic Behavior*, McGraw–Hill, 1951.

78

Before World War II, business and government were usually viewed as the sectors of the economy responsible for changes in economic activity. If business investment or government spending generate higher national income and thereupon consumers add to their expenditures, the consumer sector cannot be considered autonomous. Three times, however, during the last few years, autonomously caused changes in consumption were observed. In 1949 a moderate decline in economic activity originating outside the consumer sector failed to influence consumers, who maintained their optimistic attitudes and, by their increased rate of spending, pulled the economy out of the slight recession.[28] In 1951, at a time of rapidly increasing incomes, consumer resentment against price increases and their uncertainty or anxiety about the cold war resulted in restrained buying.[29] And in 1954 a plateau in economic activity ended because consumers were impressed by the small damage done by the widely advertised recession of 1953, by price stability, and by the availability of "good buys."[30] Consumer optimism then led to upgrading of possessions even if this meant increasing their installment debt burden. On the other hand, late in 1955 consumer sentiment and behavior reflected improved business conditions and growing income and did not provide new incentives to the economy.[31]

These experiences lead to the conclusion that the consumer sector, like the business sector, may act autonomously—a finding that gives rise to further questions.

Two new facts confront us today: the increase in the availability of information about even minor difficulties or tendencies and the increase in the number of decision-makers whose actions may influence economic development. Is mass communication conducive to exaggerated and excessive reactions and therefore to a spread and snowballing of either inflationary or deflationary tendencies? And does it make a difference that several million household units, rather than a few thousand large business units, may influence economic activity? In sum, will too much information received by too many people be detrimental to economic stability?

It has often been said that expectations may spread rapidly and become self-reinforcing and self-justifying. In the early thirties banks were said to fail because they were expected to fail; even strong banks could not resist rumors about their difficulties. In the same period a slight reduction

---

[28] See *ibid.*, Chap. 13.

[29] George Katona and Eva Mueller, *Consumer Attitudes and Demand*, Survey Research Center, University of Michigan, 1953.

[30] Katona and Mueller, *Consumer Expectations*.

[31] Consumer attitude surveys conducted by the Survey Research Center in December 1955 as well as in December 1956 indicated optimistic sentiment and a fair rate of buying intentions yet no gains in either respect as against previous measurements. The conclusion from these findings was, "The consumer sector cannot be counted upon to provide any new strength or impetus to the economy." The conclusion was substantiated by subsequent economic developments. According to a survey conducted in June 1957 consumer optimism was weakening at that time.

in demand led to cutbacks in production, then to fear of unemployment and the expectation of lower incomes, which in turn made more and more people reduce their expenditures, and incomes declined because of curtailed demand. Conversely, when inflationary fever affected Germany, France, and other countries, people expected prices to go up, therefore spent their money rapidly, and so prices rose. Finding their expectations fulfilled, they expected further price increases and hastened to hoard goods, and the cumulative process of self-realization of expectations was again set in motion.

But we also have experience with recessions and inflationary movements that were arrested early. Indeed during the past ten years in the United States small recessions and small inflationary movements were the rule rather than the exception. The theory of self-justifying expectations does not represent typical human reactions to common situations; it applies to only a rather rare type of experience and does not help to explain reversals of expectations.

Although present evidence is fragmentary, it appears justified to set forth the assumption that the economic thinking of the masses is fundamentally conservative and sane, with cumulative and self-justifying expectations a form of catastrophic behavior. People resist speculative fever as well as despondency unless their sanity is shaken by repeated shocks. News and rumors without foundation may be accepted for a short while by some but will not sustain action by many for long.

Mass sanity rests upon the desire to understand the reasons underlying events. Expectations may originate from either projecting past trends or seeing good reasons for new trends.[32] Expectations of price increases may arise not only following price increases but also in periods of price stability when people perceive underlying factors that would give rise to a new development. When the expectations are fulfilled—that is, when prices go up—people may note that what was called for has happened and that the forces are exhausted. Similarly, when expectations are based upon simple projections, people search to understand why, and if they do not find reasons, will change their expectations.

Obviously "understanding," as used here, does not involve sophisticated knowledge about economic relationships but rather a feeling about what leads to what. This sort of understanding not only is within the capacity of broad middle-income groups, but is also a prerequisite for the discussions of economic events essential to the spreading of opinions and attitudes. When interviewed, most people who express opinions about the prospective trends of prices or economic activity also promptly answer such questions as, "Why do you say so?" or "Why do you think so?" The answers are frequently simple statements: "everybody is buying," "there is more demand than supply," "the buyers are in control," "there's

[32] Katona, *Psychological Analysis of Economic Behavior*, Chap. 4.

lots of money around." The explanations may not satisfy economic analysts, but those who make them see a connection between their experience and their expectations. One fundamentally conservative notion held by broad groups of people is that the forces that generate trends are not inexhaustible. Often the longer a trend continues, the more people are inclined to look for reversals. Thus, in the economic area, mass reactions may tend toward self-regulation rather than toward excess.

Since World War II, in a period when most people have been confident that their personal financial situations and standards of living would improve, purchases of new cars or television sets have stimulated a desire for further purchases rather than saturation among people quite well off already. Are these expectations and desires without limit? Will they necessarily result in overbuying and subsequent collapse?

Consumer purchases are dependent both on felt needs or desires and on ability to buy. For many years economic forecasts of saturation have proved to be wrong because younger consumers in middle and upper income brackets were willing to enlarge their installment debt burden for the sake of upgrading their possessions. When in 1955 the proportion of incomes mortgaged for debt repayment rose substantially, government experts called for a regulation of installment credit. No regulation was enacted, and the next two years showed it to have been unnecessary—the consumers themselves regulated their financial positions. No doubt some families overreached themselves, and many more figured their permissible debt burdens on the basis of expected future income rather than on current income, thereby exposing themselves and the economy to serious risks if the expected income increases had failed to materialize. But as the slower rate of automobile purchases in the very good years 1956 and 1957 showed, consumers on the whole realized there were limits to how heavy their monthly contractual charges could be. They also kept in mind the possibility of unexpected developments; their desire to save remained strong at the same time when great emphasis was placed on improving their standards of living.[33]

Thus many millions of decision-makers who obtain prompt and similar information about economic developments may add to the stability rather than the instability of the economy. Possibly the more decision-makers there are, the less probable are excessive reactions. It can be argued that dynamic forces may more easily sway an entire group when the group is small—as, for instance, big business—and has the power to control economic activity. With the much more diffuse mass of consumers, early reactions and reversals are more probable.

[33] In my "Attitudes toward Saving and Borrowing" (in *Consumer Instalment Credit*, Part II, National Bureau of Economic Research and Board of Governors of the Federal Reserve System, 1957, Vol. 1, pp. 450-487) I showed that the importance attached to saving and the desire to save did not decline at all during the ten prosperous years following World War II.

The fact that many groups of consumers may acquire the same new economic information at the same time and may accordingly change their attitudes and behavior all at once can occasionally lead to the vicious circle of deflation or the mass hysteria of runaway inflation. Yet knowledge of what influenced consumer attitudes aids our understanding of developments of the past ten years, when consumers contributed to economic stability either by serving as a brake on inflationary trends by refraining from buying or by increasing their demand when the economy needed new incentives.

Summary

THE MODEL

Change in expectations results from (1) the acquisition of widely transmitted information of a general nature, (2) personal experiences, or (3) errors of measurement.

At any given time there will be individuals with whom variables 2 and 3 operate in one direction, and individuals with whom they operate in the opposite direction. On the other hand, most commonly, variable 1 is either noninfluential or operates in the same direction with many people.

DERIVATIONS FROM THE MODEL MADE PROBABLE BY EMPIRICAL FINDINGS

If variable 1 is not influential, aggregate changes in expectations will be small because most changes in individual expectations cancel out. When substantially unchanged distributions are observed, one may not assume that most individuals have maintained their previous expectations. On the contrary, it is probable that among individuals there have been frequent changes in both directions. (This statement does not hold for relatively deep-seated and enduring attitudes, when very small changes in aggregate distributions were observed together with infrequent cross-shifts by individuals.)

If variable 1 is effective and substantial, aggregate changes in expectations will likewise be substantial. Under these circumstances contrary effects of variables of type 2 are suppressed or lessened. Substantial aggregate changes in expectations should then be attributed to variables of type 1. This final derivation from the model, implying causal relations, is suggested (rather than demonstrated) by data on information acquired by different groups as well as by an association between high marginal change rates and low rates of unnecessary turnover.

COMMENT

ROBERT EISNER, Northwestern University

George Katona here discusses a problem of importance to economic analysis as well as to forecasting. His inquiry is into the structure of aggregates or distributions of individual consumer expectations and into some of the factors that effect changes in the distributions.

Except for a few obiter dicta, the paper does not touch on the economic *behavior* of consumers or the possible role of consumer expectations or changes in expectations in recent economic theory about the consumption function. The Modigliani-Brumberg models of consumption, for example, raise searching questions with regard to the relationship between consumers' present and expected future income and the role of this relationship in consumption. It seems a pity that attitude surveys are not better coordinated with the questions raised by economic theory. But in fairness to Katona, everything cannot be done in one paper, or by one man.

Katona's focus is that of a social psychologist interested in the learning process and in statistical tools and data with which to examine it. His data are answers to the same or similar questions on successive surveys of panels of identical respondents. It is thus possible to compare not only shifts in aggregate distribution of attitudes (what Katona denotes as "marginal" distribution), but also shifts in the attitudes of individuals.

Katona's interest is the stability and changeability of individual attitudes, in relation to and apart from shifts of the aggregates. To measure the changeability he constructs a concept of "unnecessary turnover," T, defined as the ratio of the actual frequency of shift in attitudes of individuals in a direction *opposite* to the aggregate shift (L, "losses") to the greatest such frequency possible consistent with the aggregates. In writing $T = L/\text{Max } L$, Katona specifically rejects the variable $L/\text{Exp } L$, where Exp L is the value of L which "might be expected by chance if the two responses were entirely independent given the frequency of the marginals" (p. 60). And here, if I understand Katona, I have a fundamental difference.

For Katona devotes much of his analysis to relating T to the marginal (aggregate) change in attitudes. He generalizes on page 65, "The larger the marginal change, the smaller the unnecessary turnover of individual responses." And further (p. 66), "If in the aggregate there is a substantial change in attitudes, it is likely that the changes will be predominantly in one direction, the population tending to be divided between those who changed in one direction and those who did not change at all." These "hypotheses were derived from socio-psychological assumptions about contagion and social learning, as well as from earlier findings obtained without the use of panel technique." I believe I can demonstrate, however, that the nature of Katona's T is such that his data would *appear* to confirm these hypotheses whether they really do so or not.

Specifically, I can show that if the distribution of attitudes on successive surveys involving independent responses were a purely random function of the marginal probabilities, T would manifest the negative relationship to "marginal change" ($M\ Ch$) that Katona ascribes to "socio-psychological assumptions about contagion and social learning." To do this

I define $E(L)$ as the expected probability of losses or expected value of L, when individuals' responses on the second survey are unrelated to their responses on the first survey and $E(T)$, accordingly, as $\dfrac{E(L)}{\text{Max } L}$. I shall illustrate the point first with simplified tables (in effect reducing Katona's 3×3 tables to 2×2 tables) and for these we can easily draw a few striking exact formulations of the relationship between $E(T)$ and $M\ Ch$. In all of the tables the expected probability of loss within a cell is shown above the cell's diagonal and the maximum possible loss contribution of the cell below it.[1] Expected probabilities within a cell are the products of the

TABLE 1

Expected (Random) Value of "Unnecessary Turnover," $E(T)$, and Marginal Change ($M\ Ch$): Hypothetical Marginal Probabilities, $P_2 = Q_2 = 0$

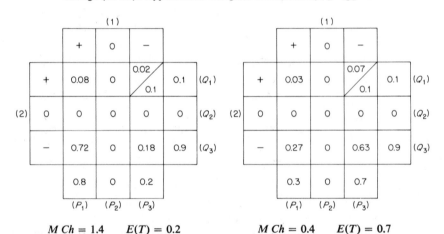

$$M\ Ch = 1.4 \qquad E(T) = 0.2 \qquad\qquad M\ Ch = 0.4 \qquad E(T) = 0.7$$

General assumptions and relations:

Assume $P_1 > Q_1$; $\quad P_2 = Q_2 = 0$; $\quad Q_1 < P_3 = 1 - P_1$.

Then
$$E(T) = 1 - P_1 = P_3,$$
$$M\ Ch = 2|P_3 - Q_3|$$
$$E(T) = Q_3 - \frac{M\ Ch}{2}$$
$$\frac{dE(T)}{dM\ Ch} = -\frac{1}{2}$$

[1] The form of these tables differs from Katona's presentation both in these double entries and in the use of the upper-right boxes as loss cells. Katona, for reasons not clear to me, would have us always arrange the rows and columns so that losses would appear in the lower left-hand cells. It seems better to preserve similar ordering of the rows and columns regardless of the direction of the marginal change, as I have done, and allow the loss cells to appear where they may. This accounts, however, for the inapplicability to our tables of Katona's computational formulas for deriving the value of Max L from the marginals. There is of course no difference between Katona's definitions of L and Max L and mine.

probabilities of occurrences falling in the cell's row and the cell's column. The maximum possible loss contribution is the cell probability entry which would maximize the value of L.

In Table 1, as $M\ Ch$ declines from 1.4 to 0.4, the *expected* value of T, which would be generated on a random probability basis (with no psychology or learning), rises from $E(T)=0.2$ to $E(T)=0.7$. And at the bottom appear the specific assumptions under which we can derive an exact relationship between $E(T)$ and $M\ Ch$, with a slope of -0.5, strikingly similar to the slope in Katona's Chart 1. With less special assumptions (a non-zero 3×3 distribution) a similar relationship between marginal change and the expected value of T is illustrated in Table 2. Katona's data

TABLE 2

Expected (Random) Value of "Unnecessary Turnover," $E(T)$ and Marginal Change $(M\ Ch)$: Non-zero Hypothetical Marginal Probabilities

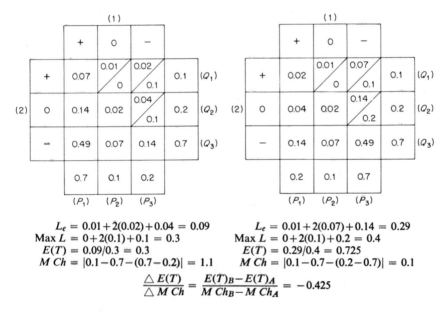

$$L_e = 0.01 + 2(0.02) + 0.04 = 0.09 \qquad L_e = 0.01 + 2(0.07) + 0.14 = 0.29$$
$$\text{Max } L = 0 + 2(0.1) + 0.1 = 0.3 \qquad \text{Max } L = 0 + 2(0.1) + 0.2 = 0.4$$
$$E(T) = 0.09/0.3 = 0.3 \qquad E(T) = 0.29/0.4 = 0.725$$
$$M\ Ch = |0.1 - 0.7 - (0.7 - 0.2)| = 1.1 \qquad M\ Ch = |0.1 - 0.7 - (0.2 - 0.7)| = 0.1$$
$$\frac{\triangle\ E(T)}{\triangle\ M\ Ch} = \frac{E(T)_B - E(T)_A}{M\ Ch_B - M\ Ch_A} = -0.425$$

may well possess the characteristics he asserts. I submit that he can hardly claim to demonstrate it with the turnover variable he defines.

I have indeed another quarrel with T, in how it is likely to respond to variations in the proportion of "same" or "no change" answers. Table 3 illustrates that two distributions with the same marginal change yield different expected values of T when the non-extreme marginals (P_2 and Q_2) change. In this example, where the same or no-change categories are higher, the *expected* value of T is higher for distributions with equal marginal changes.

TABLE 3

Effect on $E(T)$ of Increasing Middle Row and Middle Column Probabilities
(Effect of same and no-change answers on expected value of
"unnecessary turnover")

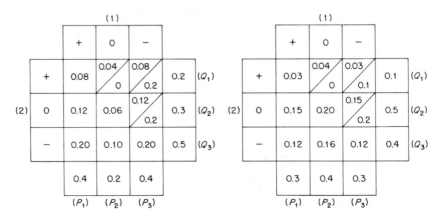

$$E(L) = 0.04 + 2(0.08) + 0.12 = 0.32 \qquad E(L) = 0.04 + 2(0.03) + 0.15 = 0.25$$
$$\text{Max } L = 0 + 2(0.2) + 0.2 = 0.6 \qquad \text{Max } L = 0 + 2(0.1) + 0.2 = 0.4$$
$$E(T) = 0.32/0.6 = 0.533 \qquad E(T) = 0.25/0.4 = 0.625$$
$$M\,Ch = |0.2 - 0.5 - (0.4 - 0.4)| = 0.3 \qquad M\,Ch = |0.1 - 0.4 - (0.3 - 0.3)| = 0.3$$

I shall close on a general methodological note. Katona argues, with pardonable professional pride, that information on consumer attitudes has proved particularly useful on several recent occasions in warranting predictions of consumer spending that were not obvious in terms of economic theory. He implies that economists tend to treat consumption as an endogenous, nonautonomous variable in their system and hence miss critical developments and turning points that are caused by changing human behavior. But however useful surveys of consumer attitudes may be for *forecasting*, they cannot substitute for economic theory in *explaining* economic phenomena. As a practical man of affairs I may have to admit that we can at times make better predictions by treating consumption, or any other variable, as "autonomous" and determined outside of my system of economic variables. But to the extent that, as economists, we make important variables "autonomous," we are abandoning areas of our science. And perhaps we are setting back the fundamental goal of all scientific inquiry, the goal of embracing more and more phenomena in a unified theory developed from a minimum of "autonomous" axioms.

REPLY BY MR. KATONA

Eisner objects to my not using the measure L/L_e (which is the same as T/T_e) or, generally, A/R (A = actual value, R = random expectancy). Naturally, there are many problems the solution of which requires that the relation of A to R should be taken into account. Even then we should use formulas other than A/R, for instance, coefficients of intraclass correlation. This will be done in a forthcoming study of repeat behavior over three years (see footnote 9 to my paper).

What is wrong with the formula A/R? Take as a simple example the following identical data obtained in two tests:

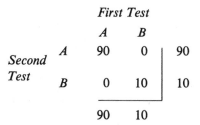

		First Test		
		A	*B*	
Second	*A*	90	0	90
Test	*B*	0	10	10
		90	10	

The A/R value for AA is 1.11 and for BB it is 10.0, although both instances are perfectly repetitious. The measure A/R has an undesirable relation to the size of percentages involved. Or take measurements of unnecessary turnover. In both of the following two cases the unnecessary turnover is maximized. Yet L/L_e is 1.67 in the first case and 1.11 in the second case.

50	40	90		0	60	60
10	0	10		40	0	40
60	40			40	60	

The statistic used depends on the purposes for which it is used. Mine was to find out whether unnecessary turnover was close to its minimum or its maximum possible value. Therefore I wished to consider the relation of L to the entire distance from Min L to Max L. L_e is by necessity smaller than Max L. If we use the measure L/L_e we consider only the distance from Min L to L_e. Furthermore, L and L_e are intercorrelated. The relation between the two does vary some. But most commonly, when L is close to Max L, L_e is also close to Max L; and when L is close to Min L, L_e is also close to Min L. Thus L/L_e may have the same values, once when both are rather high and another time when both are rather low. If my purpose is to differentiate between these two cases, I must use a different measure.

To illustrate this point I may refer to the turnover in the replies to the same question obtained at different times (complete data concerning the 1954-55 turnover were presented in Table 4 of my paper). The relevant data are:

Turnover in Business Expectations

	From June 1954 to June 1955	From December 1955 to March 1957
M Ch	40.6	17.9
Max L	23.2	23.6
L	9.6	13.4
L_e	13.6	17.3
L/L_e	0.706	0.775
T	0.41	0.57

The measure T serves certain purposes, for which it is used, and does not warrant other inferences. Eisner is, of course, right in pointing out that L_e is negatively correlated with marginal change. (So is L, as I noted, and both correlations are in the nature of arithmetical necessities.) Therefore he argues that I would have got negative correlations with M Ch if I had two sets of random throws rather than two sets of measurements of expectations. L_e is the standard of *independence* between the two successive tests. It may be questioned whether L_e should be regarded as the appropriate criterion for "random change" since it is not reasonable to expect that two identical tests of identical respondents should be in fact independent. What is true of random independent throws of a coin need not be true of measurements of expectations of the same people in two successive testings.

In spite of these objections to L_e I have calculated the values for L/L_e and present them, in the manner used in my Table 2 (Part B):

M Ch	L/L_e
Less than 3.5	0.802
5 to 12.5	.762
16 to 30.5	.749
34 and larger	.696

Comparison of this table with my Table 2 indicates that there is somewhat more relation between M Ch and L than between M Ch and L_e.

Central issues of psychological economics are raised by Eisner when he says that I imply that "economists tend to treat consumption as an endogenous, nonautonomous variable in their system and hence miss critical developments and turning points that are caused by changing human behavior." This argument has been expressed fully, though in somewhat different terms, in *Consumer Expectations*, where Miss Mueller and I used the following definitions by Alvin Hansen: "Autonomous investment means investment unrelated to income changes or income levels. Similarly, autonomously caused changes in consumption relate not to income changes, but to changed attitudes of consumers."[1] Disregarding other variables (some of which should not be disregarded) and error terms, one may then differentiate between a theory postulating $C=fY$ or $C=fY_{-1}$ (where C stands for consumer expenditures on durable goods, Y for income, and Y_{-1} for last year's income) and a theory postulating $C=f(Y_{-1}, A)$ (where A stands for attitudes). At the Survey Research Center we adhere to the second type of theory because we believe that attitudes are significant, nonrandom variables necessary for an explanation and prediction of human behavior. Is it correct to say that by making "important variables autonomous we are abandoning areas of our science" and "setting back the fundamental goal of all scientific inquiry"? Motives, attitudes, expectations, and related psychological variables are not fully determined within a narrowly conceived system of economic interrelationships, but contrary to the notion of some (I believe, today, few) students it is not correct to treat them as given, as not susceptible to scientific analysis, or even as mysterious. In psychological or behavioral economics, which is part of "our science" (to repeat Eisner's expression), an attempt is made to measure these variables and to establish functional relationships between them and financial variables.

One aim of economics as a behavioral science is, then, to account for variations in economic behavior which have remained unexplained at earlier times, rather than to increase the number of "autonomous axioms." Through such a procedure we come closer to the goal of establishing a "unified theory," which can hardly be accomplished by disregarding socio-psychological variables.[2]

The greatest difference between Eisner's views and mine is his statement that "surveys of consumer attitudes . . . cannot substitute for economic theory in explaining economic phenomena." I do not know anybody who conducts economic surveys who has this aim. I, myself, have repeatedly shown that psychological economics derives hypotheses from economic theory. Yet I do not regard economic theory as something finished, which has to be either accepted or discarded, but as an integrated body of principles and validated generalizations which need to be made more general, more complete, and more applicable.

[1] Pp. 108ff. Also earlier in Chapter 7 of my *Psychological Analysis of Economic Behavior*, where the wanderings of the consumption function were discussed.

[2] Eisner's point may also be viewed as an application of the law of parsimony. I discussed this "counter-argument" to psychological economics in my appendix to Howard R. Bowen's *The Business Enterprise as Subject for Research*, Social Science Research Council, 1955, pp. 42ff.

The Formation of Business Expectations About Operating Variables

MILLARD HASTAY

STATE COLLEGE OF WASHINGTON

This paper is a report on one phase of a general exploratory study of the Dun and Bradstreet quarterly surveys of businessmen's expectations. The aim of the study has been to find out what use can be made of data on business expectations about operating variables, in distinction from the more familiar data on planned capital expenditures compiled in the Department of Commerce–Securities and Exchange Commission and McGraw–Hill surveys. The present phase of the research has been organized around two basic problems:

1. The rationality of business expectations about operating variables
2. Realized business behavior under conditions of uncertainty.

The first problem involves such questions as whether business expectations disclose self-consistent relations between prospects and plans and whether they are significantly related to past experience. Appraising the results of an attempt to fit models of business expectations to the Dun and Bradstreet data offers a way of looking into this question of rationality.

Under the second heading the central question is whether incorrect expectations have a binding effect on subsequent behavior. Businessmen must act on estimates of the future that often prove wrong, and they are more or less hampered in adjusting to revised estimates as the errors are discovered. What is the evidence that this uncertainty leads to different actions than a correct forecast would have done, and how important are the effects of the uncertainty? The complex of questions involved here is being investigated by trying to fit to the data models of realized behavior in which expectations figure as explicit determinants.[1]

It need hardly be argued that models of the two types are closely related. In fact, answers to questions about the influence of expectations on realized behavior depend critically on the character of the findings about the formation of expectations. Nevertheless, as a technical matter, the two

---

[1] The work of Franco Modigliani on expectations theory ("The Role of Anticipations and Plans in the Economy of the Firm and their Use in Economic Analysis and Forecasting," Mary Jean Bowman, ed., Expectations, Uncertainty, and Business Behavior, conference sponsored by the Social Science Research Council at the Carnegie Institute of Technology, October 27-29, 1955), and of Henri Theil on statistical methodology ("Forecasts and Economic Policy," Amsterdam, 1959) encouraged the pursuit of this line of research.

types of models permit of separate study and can be estimated independently. The priority of the subject of expectation formation has dictated the decision to take it up first. This paper is a report on what has been learned concerning the rationality of business expectations about operating variables. Apart from certain by-products of the expectations study, a discussion of the findings on realized behavior under conditions of uncertainty is left to a subsequent report.

Concepts and Data

In analyzing business expectations, a basic consideration is whether the expectations refer to "action parameters" (also called "instruments") or to data. The distinction depends upon how far the relevant variables are under the control of the individual firm. In this context, business expectations can be classified as *intentions*—plans for action in matters where the firm can make binding decisions; *market anticipations*—expectations about events that result from the interplay between the firm's actions and its environment; and *outlook*—expectations about general business conditions which the firm cannot perceptibly influence but which will help to determine the strength of its markets.[2]

THE DUN AND BRADSTREET SURVEYS[3]

The Dun and Bradstreet "Surveys of Businessmen's Expectations" are quarterly surveys of short-run intentions (for employment, inventories, and perhaps prices) and of anticipations (for new orders, sales, and profits). Since the third quarter of 1951 the sample has never fallen below 1,000 firms and today includes around 1,400. Although the data refer wholly to activity within individual firms, they are aggregated into four broad industrial groups: durable goods manufacturers, nondurable goods manufacturers, wholesalers, and retailers. Each survey yields evidence on sales, employment, inventories, prices, and profits for all four groups, plus new orders for the two manufacturing groups.

The business firms interviewed are a sample drawn from about 54,000 medium-to-large firms of sufficient credit interest to justify re-investigation roughly twice a year. During a two-week period around the close of each calendar quarter the expectations survey is grafted on to the regular credit interviews. The reporters are instructed to prepare a questionnaire for each firm contacted until certain pre-established quotas are met.

Each questionnaire asks for expectations for a period terminating two

[2] The terminology used here is consistent with that used in *An Appraisal of Data and Research on Businessmen's Expectations about Outlook and Operating Variables*, Report of the Consultant Committee on General Business Expectations, Board of Governors of the Federal Reserve System, September 1955; see especially Chap. II, pp. 8-9.

[3] For a more complete description of the surveys, together with evidence bearing on the quality of the data, see *ibid.*, Chap. III, pp. 25-34.

quarters ahead and for actual developments for a period terminating in the quarter just closed. Thus a check on expectations is provided by the reports on actual experience compiled in the survey taken two quarters later, but the two sets of data come from different samples. Consequently problems of sampling variability make comparison of expectations with actual outcomes difficult.

The published Dun and Bradstreet reports show, for each variable and industrial group, the percentage distribution of sampled firms that actually experienced a rise, no change, or a fall in the one-year period just concluded, and a similar distribution describing their expectations for the overlapping one-year period ending two quarters hence. This technique of making comparisons with the corresponding quarter of the previous year and the timing of the surveys for the last quarter covered, blur the distinction between reported expectations and reported realized experience. Such ambiguities are the price paid for the rapid availability of the reports—typically within three weeks of the close of the final quarter covered—and for the elimination of seasonal variations. Further, qualitative reports on direction of change are not only quicker, but they may appeal to executives who might be reluctant to give absolute figures.

Three criticisms of the Dun and Bradstreet surveys are that the sample is haphazard, that the reports are biased because of the credit-rating connection of the compiler, and that uninformed subordinates give the answers. There are various possible answers to the criticisms,[4] but final judgment will depend on the success of efforts to use the data the surveys provide. The population sampled—whatever it is—may behave much like the business population at large, and a more or less constant bias in the answers can be allowed for statistically.

DIFFUSION INDEXES[5]

Qualitative results of the sort tabulated by Dun and Bradstreet are called "diffusion data" since they indicate the number of firms sharing in, or the scope of, a given movement, expressed as a percentage of the total number of firms in the collection. Particular changes in a set of individual-firm variables are frequently called "microchanges"; the change in the corresponding aggregate, a "macrochange." Diffusion data comprise the distribution of signs of microchanges. To analyze the movements, a

---

[4] *ibid.*, pp. 28-32.
[5] For more complete discussions of diffusion indexes, see Geoffrey H. Moore, "Diffusion Indexes: A Comment," *American Statistician*, October 1955, pp. 13-17 and 30; Henri Theil and J. S. Cramer, "On the Utilization of a New Source of Economic Information: An Econometric Analysis of the Munich Business Test," a paper presented at the 16th European Meeting of the Econometric Society, Uppsala, Sweden, August 1954; and Millard Hastay, "The Dun and Bradstreet Surveys of Businessmen's Expectations," *Proceedings of the Business and Economic Statistics Section*, 114th Annual Meeting of the American Statistical Association, 1955, pp. 93-123.

"diffusion index" is used, which measures the net excess of the percentage of rising movements over the percentage of declining movements, usually well within the possible range of −100 per cent to +100 per cent. Though no explicit account is taken of the percentage of series undergoing no change, it is allowed for implicitly since the diffusion index formula implies that any instance of reported no change has a 50:50 chance of being a rise or a decline.

The results of various studies suggest that weighting diffusion data enhances their value as proxies for conventional economic aggregates. Since the second quarter of 1953 Dun and Bradstreet has compiled information on the net tangible assets of the firms interviewed, by means of which it classifies them into ten size groups (Table 1). These data make possible two weighting schemes:

TABLE 1

Percentage Distribution of Respondents by Capital Rating Groups, Dun and Bradstreet Surveys of Businessmen's Expectations, 1953-1956

ESTIMATED TANGIBLE NET WORTH	DURABLE GOODS MANU-FACTURERS		NONDURABLE GOODS MANU-FACTURERS		WHOLESALERS		RETAILERS	
	Firms	Net Worth	Firms	Net Worth	Firms	Net Worth	Firms	Net Worth
$1,000,000 and over	29	91.9	23	90.1	12	58.0	13	84.9
750,000–$999,999	6	1.9	5	1.9	4	5.5	4	2.4
500,000– 749,999	11	2.2	10	2.5	8	9.4	8	3·5
300,000– 499,999	15	2.0	15	2.5	15	10.5	13	3.6
200,000– 299,999	11	0.9	14	1.4	16	7.3	12	2.0
125,000– 199,999	13	0.7	15	1.0	19	5.6	17	1.9
75,000– 124,999	9	0.3	12	0.5	15	2.7	15	1.0
50,000– 74,999	4	0.1	4	0.1	6	0.6	8	0.3
35,000– 49,999	2	a	1	a	2	0.2	5	0.1
Under $35,000	2	a	1	a	2	0.1	5	0.1
Total	100	100.0	100	100.0	100	100.0	100	100.0

In this and the following tables, detail may not sum to totals because of rounding.
Respondents are those replying to questions on sales expectations, excluding a small number of firms for which capital ratings were not reported.
a Under 0.05.

Type I Weights—This scheme merely standardizes the samples for firm-size coverage. A simple diffusion index is computed for each class, and these are combined with weights proportional to the average percentage of firms in each class. Such indexes were calculated for the fifteen surveys made in the period II 1953–IV 1956.

Type II Weights—The second scheme achieves the objective of the first and also a rough weighting of diffusion experience according to the economic importance of each respondent. Each asset class is represented by its mid-value, except for the open-end class of largest firms, for which average values based on a more than 5 per cent random sample of firms with net tangible assets over $1 million is used. Since no breakdown between durable goods and nondurable goods manufacturers was available, the same average net worth is assumed for both manufacturing groups. Such indexes were calculated for the same period as for the Type I weights.

Unweighted—Simple indexes were also calculated for the thirty surveys made in the period II 1949–I 1957.

In the following discussion Theil's notation will be used. The macro-variable under consideration will be denoted X, the diffusion index of *realized* microchanges will be denoted $b(X)$, and the diffusion index of *expected* microchanges, $b(\overline{X})$. The diffusion index is necessarily dated. If it refers to an interval terminating in the present, it bears no subscript; if to an interval terminating in the previous quarter, it will be written $b(X)_{-1}$ for realized diffusion, $b(\overline{X})_{-1}$ for expected diffusion. Since Dun and Bradstreet expectations refer to a situation two quarters after the survey compared with the corresponding situation a year earlier, $b(\overline{X})$ refers to expectations formed two quarters earlier, while the diffusion of *current* expectations must be denoted $b(\overline{X})_{+2}$. Thus today's survey yields a diffusion index of expected sales $b(\overline{S})_{+2}$ and another of realized sales $b(S)$. The latter index is to be compared with the diffusion of sales expected two surveys ago $b(\overline{S})$, and two surveys hence we shall have a diffusion index of realized sales $b(S)_{+2}$ to compare with today's expectations.

Models of the Formation of Expectations

The hypothesis that expectations have an essential role in shaping realized behavior makes most sense for variables over which firms have a measure of control. From this standpoint, the chief candidate for attention is inventory investment—the inventory adjustments which businessmen intend to make and the factors which shape these intentions. While expected inventory change in the very short run may be "given," over two quarters it will represent a target to be reached through procurement and production adjustments. We will thus be primarily concerned with the formation of expectations rather than of anticipations, seeking to explain changes in the instruments of decision-making, and concerned with data only as they influence the decisions about instruments.

INTENDED INVENTORY INVESTMENT

The main elements in inventory planning are fairly well understood. The influence of the following factors on inventory planning can be measured through the behavior of one or more variables in the Dun and Bradstreet surveys:

"*Acceleration principle*" (varying inventory with the expected rate of change in sales) through the diffusion of expected sales, $b(\bar{S})$

"*Purchase-price speculation*" (hedging for expected buying-price rises) through the diffusion of expected buying prices, $b(\bar{p}_h)$

"*Risk aversion*" (allowing for possible market deterioration) through the diffusion of expected selling prices, $b(\bar{p})$

"*Stock appraisal*" (equating current inventories to current needs) through a comparison of the diffusion of prior inventory intentions with the diffusion of corresponding outcomes, $[b(H)-b(\bar{H})]$.

In constructing a model of inventory intentions for diffusion data, we can draw on the close connection between diffusion and aggregate change and think of inventory investment as varying in proportion to inventory diffusion, $b(H)$; of the change in sales as varying in proportion to sales diffusion, $b(S)$; of unintended inventory change as varying in proportion to the excess of realized inventory diffusion over the prior diffusion of inventory intentions, $[b(H)-b(\bar{H})]$; and so on. Then analogy suggests the following equation as an explanation of the diffusion of inventory intentions:

$$(1) \quad b(\bar{H}) = a_1 b(\bar{S}) + a_2 b(\bar{p}) + a_3 b(\bar{p}_h) + a_4[b(H)_{-2} - b(\bar{H})_{-2}] + a_0 + u_1$$

The terms $a_1 b(\bar{S}) + a_4[b(H)_{-2} - b(\bar{H})_{-2}]$ provide a fairly realistic representation of an acceleration principle that makes allowance for pre-existing stocks. The term $a_3 b(\bar{p}_h)$ measures the speculative impact on inventory investment of expected changes in buying prices. And $a_2 b(\bar{p})$ allows for the influence of expected selling-price variations on the appraisal of speculative risk. The linearity of the relation is a practical approximation. It may be thought to hold within a range of moderate fluctuations about an underlying position of stock equilibrium. The term u_1 is an acknowledgement that the relation holds stochastically, and we assume—with some justification for time series akin to quarterly first differences—that successive values of u_1 are statistically independent.

Though Dun and Bradstreet do not compile data on buying prices, manufacturers' selling prices may be treated as proxy for wholesalers' buying prices, and wholesalers' selling prices as proxy for retailers' buying prices, but no buying prices for manufacturers can be inferred. However, because of doubts about this proxy, and to facilitate comparisons between manufacturers and traders, we employ, for the present, for both groups, an equation omitting buying prices:

$$(2) \quad b(\bar{H}) = a_1 b(\bar{S}) + a_2 b(\bar{p}) + a_4[b(H)_{-2} - b(\bar{H})_{-2}] + a_0 + u_1$$

The price of thus truncating the inventory equation may be less than it at first seems. Theil showed that in the hides-leather-shoe production sequence in West Germany, selling prices, both actual and planned, were almost wholly dominated by actual and expected buying prices; and United States manufacturers' buying prices may also vary much as their selling prices do.[6] Combined with the fact that the coefficients a_2 and a_3 may be expected to have the same sign, the truncated manufacturers' equation may reflect much of the influence of buying-price anticipations in the coefficient of the selling-price variable. Whether this argument applies with equal force to traders is uncertain, but it seems reasonably in accord with what we know about price behavior in the trade field.

The theory outlined above clearly implies that a_1, a_2, and a_3 are intrinsically positive, though a high degree of collinearity between $b(\bar{p})$ and $b(p_h)_{-2}$ may make it difficult to estimate a_2 and a_3 with precision. The sign of a_4 is less certain. We can, in fact, distinguish three cases:

1. Substantial production plan inertia, so that the production plan based on $b(\bar{H})_{-2}$ is substantially carried out. Then over-optimism implies $[b(H)_{-2} - b(\bar{H})_{-2}] > 0$, and conversely; whence a_4 negative.

2. Production plans are flexible, but not sufficiently so to keep up with changed intentions. Then overoptimism implies that $b(H)_{-2}$ is cut back below $b(\bar{H})_{-2}$ so that $[b(H)_{-2} - b(\bar{H})_{-2}] < 0$, and conversely; in this case a_4 is positive. This may happen even with perfect adjustment of realized inventory accumulation to "final" intentions, reflecting a revision of general economic appraisals in line with changed inventory requirements; but $a_4 = 0$ may also occur, with the changed outlook appraisal affecting $b(\bar{S})$ and $b(\bar{p})$ for the next period.

3. Just sufficient plan flexibility so that $[b(H)_{-2} - b(\bar{H})_{-2}]$ remains in the neighborhood of zero. Then a_4 will tend to be nonsignificant *without* carrying the implication that inventory adjustment is typically in short-run equilibrium.

COMPLETION OF MODELS OF EXPECTATION FORMATION

The equation for inventories contains two variables that must be regarded as determined along with inventory intentions: expected sales and expected selling prices. Since the buying-price variable used in the traders' model represents the *ex post* diffusion of selling prices of the preceding stage of business activity, it can be treated as predetermined in the same sense as $b(H)_{-2}$ and $b(\bar{H})_{-2}$ are predetermined. To complete the models of expectation formation, equations for sales and price expectations must be adjoined, with buying prices still omitted from the traders' model as well as from the manufacturers' model.

[6] Henri Theil, "Recent Experiences with the Munich Business Test," *Econometrica*, April 1955, pp. 184-192.

Sales Anticipations. The equation for manufacturers' sales anticipations differs from that for traders in two respects: in providing for the role of new orders, and in allowing for the possibility that manufacturers' prices are instruments of deliberate control. We thus have:

Manufacturers

(3) $\qquad b(\bar{S}) = b_1 b(\bar{p}) + b_2[b(p)_{-2} - b(\bar{p})_{-2}] + b_3 b(N)_{-2} + b_0 + u_2$

Traders

(4) $\qquad b(\bar{S}) = c_1 b(S)_{-2} + c_2[b(S)_{-2} - b(\bar{S})_{-2}] + c_0 + u_3$

Treating traders as price takers reduces the equation for their sales anticipations to a simple learning model. By contrast, recognizing that manufacturers may defer making intended price adjustments and that this deferment may affect their sales outlook, requires the introduction of a term in $[b(p)_{-2} - b(\bar{p})_{-2}]$. The use of new orders as a barometer of prospective sales needs no argument, but the choice of realized rather than anticipated new orders does. The economic justification is that new orders lead sales; thus it is orders in hand that dominate next period's sales, rather than orders in prospect. Moreover, in the Dun and Bradstreet surveys, anticipated new orders fail to show a reasonable lead over anticipated sales, suggesting that businessmen base their new order and sales anticipations on essentially the same evidence. Inclusion of anticipated new orders would merely have complicated the model and introduced a possible indeterminacy.

Selling-Price Expectations. The differing degree of control over prices by manufacturers and traders is recognized also in the equations for expected price diffusion. In both equations, expected price changes depend on anticipated changes in sales, but the effect of deferred price adjustments by manufacturers is admitted as an added factor. As price takers, traders are also assumed to base their anticipations on the recent trend of prices. Finally, both manufacturers and traders are assumed to adjust their price expectations to an appraisal of current stocks. The role of disequilibrium stocks seems sufficiently important to warrant the use of the variable $[b(H)_{-2} - b(\bar{H})_{-2}]$ despite its inherent ambiguity. The equations of price expectations thus become:

Manufacturers

(5) $\qquad b(\bar{p}) = d_1 b(\bar{S}) + d_2[b(p)_{-2} - b(\bar{p})_{-2}] + d_3[b(H)_{-2} - b(\bar{H})_{-2}] + d_0 + u_4$

Traders

(6) $\qquad b(\bar{p}) = g_1 b(\bar{S}) + g_2 b(p)_{-2} + g_3[b(H)_{-2} - b(\bar{H})_{-2}] + g_0 + u_5$

AN ALTERNATIVE MODEL FOR MANUFACTURERS

The three equations which comprise the traders' model, equations 2, 4, and 6, have the interesting property of "recursiveness." By this is meant that the interdependence of current expectations can be viewed as a causal chain: $b(\bar{S})$ depends only on predetermined variables, $b(\bar{p})$ depends additionally on $b(\bar{S})$, while $b(\bar{H})$ depends on predetermined variables and both $b(\bar{S})$ and $b(\bar{p})$. Thus each equation can be given a unilateral causal interpretation. The formation of traders' expectations is viewed as beginning with a sales forecast, passing to a price anticipation, and terminating with an inventory objective.

Recursive models of this sort have a strong appeal as representations of intellectual processes. Static equilibrium theory has conditioned economists to think of amount of sales and price as being determined by a pair of simultaneous equations, but it is implausible to suppose that *expectations* about sales and prices result from the mental solution of equations of the same sort. Consequently there is reason to be dissatisfied with the manufacturers' model, equations 2, 3, and 5. Equation 3 tells us that sales expectations depend on price expectations, whereas equation 5 tells us that price expectations depend on sales expectations. Logic is not thereby violated, but our intuitive experience of intellectual processes is. A recursive model of manufacturers' expectations therefore follows:

(2) $$b(\bar{H}) = \text{same as above}$$

(7) $$b(\bar{S}) = b_1 b(\bar{p}) + b_2 b(S)_{-2} + b_3 b(N)_{-2} + b_0 + u_2$$

(8) $$b(\bar{p}) = d_1 b(p)_{-2} + d_2 b(N)_{-2} + d_3 [b(p)_{-2} - b(\bar{p})_{-2}] + d_4 [b(H)_{-2} - b(\bar{H})_{-2}] + d_0 + u_4$$

The choice of $b(\bar{p})$ instead of $b(\bar{S})$ as the initial variable in the causal chain reflects the view that manufacturers tend to treat prices as instruments of control rather than as data. The required change of equation 5 is accomplished by substituting $b(N)_{-2}$ for $b(\bar{S})$ as a measure of demand strength, and by adding $b(p)_{-2}$ as a reflection of price trends. The modification of equation 3 is not strictly necessary for recursiveness. It arises from the belief that recent sales experience as well as new orders received affects sales anticipations. It also reflects the feeling that $[b(p)_{-2} - b(\bar{p})_{-2}]$ is redundant since its effect on demand should be reflected in $b(N)_{-2}$, while its impact on price intentions should show up in $b(\bar{p})$. As finally modified, the model implies that the process of expectation formation for manufacturers begins with a price expectation, passes to a compatible sales estimate, and ends with an inventory objective.

Statistical Evaluation of the Models

When we come to empirical testing, the first consideration is whether the models are "identified." Given sufficient empirical information, would it be possible to determine unique values for the coefficients of the various equations?

99

The Dun and Bradstreet data comprise a set of "solutions" of the model. Since there are generally more solutions than unknown parameters, and since the solutions differ in part for unexplained reasons, some principle of reconciliation, such as least squares, must be employed. However, the principle cannot be depended on to yield unique estimates unless the equations of the model are suitably restricted. Though the stochastic character of the problem admits of other possibilities, the restrictions employed are that certain coefficients in each equation shall be zero, or (what amounts to the same thing) that certain variables shall be absent from each.

Modern statistical theory establishes a close connection between the notion of identification and valid techniques of estimation. A nonidentified equation admits of no valid method of estimation. An exactly identified equation can be evaluated by an indirect application of least squares known as the reduced form method. The equations of a recursive model are always identified, and can be evaluated by least squares either directly or by a suitable process of serial application. The methods of estimation used in this paper are wholly based on least squares because the models involved are either recursive (traders' model and alternative manufacturers' model) or exactly identified (original manufacturers' model).[7]

MANUFACTURERS' EXPECTATIONS

Exactly Identified Model. The nonrecursive model of manufacturers' expectations illustrates the problems that arise in using the technique of indirect least squares to estimate the coefficients of diffusion models, manifested as a disturbing instability in the pattern of findings. Consider, for example, Table 2, which presents the results of evaluating the manufacturers' model in terms of diffusion data.

Different weighting schemes and the industrial contrasts between durable and nondurable goods manufacturers, bespeak the probability of substantial differences between the four models shown. Moreover, with the possible exception of the acceleration coefficient (-0.26) for durable goods manufacturers (Type II Weights), there is no weighted estimate that is clearly inconsistent with the manufacturers' model under consideration. Production and procurement policy seem sufficiently flexible so that the departure of realized inventory accumulation from prior intentions is usually in the right direction, though probably not in the right amount. Price policy shows comparable flexibility among durable goods manufacturers, but not among nondurables manufacturers. Also

[7] For more complete discussions of the methods of estimation used, see Tjalling C. Koopmans, "Identification Problems in Economic Model Construction," and Tjalling C. Koopmans and William C. Hood, "The Estimation of Simultaneous Linear Economic Relationships," both in *Studies in Econometric Method*, Cowles Commission Monograph 14, Wiley, 1953; Herman Wold, *Demand Analysis: A Study in Econometrics*, Wiley, 1953, pp. 49-53; and Lawrence R. Klein, *A Textbook of Econometrics*, Wiley, 1953, pp. 80-92.

TABLE 2

Formation of Manufacturers' Expectations as Reflected in Diffusion Data,
Exactly Identified Model

COEFFICIENTS OF EXPLANATORY VARIABLES

EXPECTATIONAL VARIABLE	Expectation		Actual minus Expected, Lagged		Actual, Lagged	Constant
	Sales	Selling Prices	Inventory	Prices	New Orders	
TYPE I WEIGHTS						
Durable Goods Manufacturers						
Inventories	+0.59	+0.05	+0.18			−0.18
Sales		−0.15		+0.39	+0.62	+0.26
Selling prices	+0.70		+0.20	+0.28		−0.18
Nondurable Goods Manufacturers						
Inventories	+0.51	+0.40	+0.08			−0.22
Sales		+1.42		−1.52	+0.21	+0.28
Selling prices	+0.48		+0.09	+1.01		−0.13
TYPE II WEIGHTS						
Durable Goods Manufacturers						
Inventories	−0.26	+1.20	−0.19			−0.08
Sales		−1.74		+0.79	+1.30	+0.31
Selling prices	+0.43		+0.49	+0.23		−0.03
Nondurable Goods Manufacturers						
Inventories	+0.18	+0.58	+0.15			−0.09
Sales		−2.30		+2.30	+1.02	+0.39
Selling prices	+0.34		−0.06	+0.87		−0.06
UNWEIGHTED						
Durable Goods Manufacturers						
Inventories	+1.22	−0.35	+0.21			−0.44
Sales		−0.49		+0.30	+0.75	+0.28
Selling prices	+0.94		+0.22	+0.35		−0.30
Nondurable Goods Manufacturers						
Inventories	+0.28	+0.73	−0.20			−0.14
Sales		−0.80		+0.50	+1.10	+0.21
Selling prices	+1.01		+0.66	−0.10		−0.45

In this and the following tables the following descriptions apply: *Type I Weights*—a simple diffusion index was computed for each class shown in Table 1, and these were combined with weights proportional to the average percentage of firms responding in each class. The period covered was II 1953–IV 1956. *Type II Weights*—simple class indexes were combined with weights, proportional to the total value of net tangible assets attributable to reporting firms in each class. The period covered was II 1953–IV 1956. *Unweighted*—the period covered was II 1950–III 1957.
The figures in the tables have been rounded.
The equations involved in the present table are 2, 3, and 5.

the largest manufacturers in both groups tend to show responses like those of durable goods manufacturers as a whole. But why should the acceleration coefficients be so low for the largest firms? And why should price expectations seem so generally more important, especially in sales forecasting?

101

Further questions arise when we look at the coefficients based on unweighted data for a period over twice as long as that covered by the weighted data. Type I weighting produces only minor changes in diffusion data, and apart from the influence of the differing periods covered, the unweighted results should be in reasonable accord with the Type I results. Instead durable and nondurable goods manufacturers seem less similar in their control of inventories, more similar in their control of prices; and the contrast in acceleration coefficients is unconvincingly large. Many of the coefficients are probably not statistically significant, given the few degrees of freedom on which the estimates must be based. Nevertheless, a more stable pattern of results seems a reasonable requirement on the basis of earlier work with diffusion data.[8]

Recursive Model. The recursive model of manufacturers' expectations affords an opportunity to test many of these reactions. Table 3 is based on the independent application of least squares to each equation separately, Table 4 on a sequential application of least squares in which current values of the explanatory variables in each equation are computed from the prior equation or equations in the recursive chain. The latter process begins with the direct application of least squares to the price equation, which depends only on lagged values of explanatory variables; so that the coefficients of this equation in each section of Table 3 are identical with the coefficients of the equation in the corresponding sections of Table 4. Both tables also show the estimated standard errors of the several coefficients (in parentheses), together with standard errors of estimate and coefficients of multiple correlation adjusted for degrees of freedom. These measures provide crude indications of the statistical significance of the estimated equations, but neither the assumptions of the model nor the number of quarters covered justify the application of exact tests.

Since the model embodies a different theory of expectation formation than the exactly identified one, it naturally yields different findings even about the formation of inventory intentions (Table 3). Thus we note no marked contrast between the models for durable and nondurable goods manufacturers, or even between models based on Type I and Type II weighting. The larger firms again have lower Type II acceleration coefficients, and their sales anticipations give less weight to new orders and lagged sales. However, new order diffusion and sales diffusion show similar variations over time, implying that their estimated coefficients in the equations for sales anticipations have low precision (note the standard errors in the first two sections of Table 3).

The pattern of Type I results is borne out by the unweighted results, except for the suggestion that inventory control was less complete over the longer period—a finding compatible with our knowledge of inventory behavior during the Korean war. The evidence of collinearity between new

[8] Hastay, pp. 93-123.

TABLE 3

Formation of Manufacturers' Expectations as Reflected in Diffusion Data, Recursive Model

EXPECTATIONAL VARIABLE	COEFFICIENTS OF EXPLANATORY VARIABLES							Constant	STANDARD ERROR OF ESTIMATE	MULTIPLE CORRELATION
	Expectation		Actual minus Expected, Lagged		Actual, Lagged					
	Sales	Selling Prices	Inventory	Prices	Sales	Prices	New Orders			
TYPE I WEIGHTS *Durable Goods Manufacturers*										
Inventories	+0.34 (0.10)	+0.30 (0.11)	+0.27 (0.18)					−0.12	0.04	0.96
Sales		+0.49 (0.35)		+0.23 (0.19)	−0.94 (0.48)	+0.42 (0.12)	+1.28 (0.51)	+0.23	.12	.82
Selling prices		+0.28 (0.23)	+0.54 (0.28)	+0.23 (0.19)			+0.23 (0.13)	a	.06	.95
Nondurable Goods Manufacturers										
Inventories	+0.54 (0.10)	+0.34 (0.10)	+0.12 (0.19)					−0.23	.04	.97
Sales		+0.28 (0.23)			−1.17 (0.57)	+0.51 (0.05)	+1.77 (0.62)	+0.28	.08	.84
Selling prices			+0.44 (0.12)	+0.23 (0.14)			+0.15 (0.05)	+0.02	.02	.99
TYPE II WEIGHTS *Durable Goods Manufacturers*										
Inventories	+0.25 (0.15)	+0.25 (0.27)	+0.34 (0.25)					−0.13	.08	.86
Sales		+0.54 (0.49)			−0.19 (0.57)	+0.36 (0.13)	+0.57 (0.63)	+0.15	.17	.75
Selling prices			+0.12 (0.16)	+0.07 (0.17)			+0.23 (0.09)	+0.03	.06	.95

[table continues on next page

103

Table 3, *continued*

COEFFICIENTS OF EXPLANATORY VARIABLES

EXPECTATIONAL VARIABLE	Expectation		Actual minus Expected, Lagged		Actual, Lagged			Constant	STANDARD ERROR OF ESTIMATE	MULTIPLE CORRELATION
	Sales	*Selling Prices*	*Inventory*	*Prices*	*Sales*	*Prices*	*New Orders*	*Constant*		
Nondurable Goods Manufacturers										
Inventories	+0.13 (0.13)	+0.45 (0.14)	+0.28 (0.15)					−0.05	.05	.91
Sales		+0.41 (0.23)			−0.30 (0.41)		+0.75 (0.48)	+0.28	.11	.76
Selling prices			+0.14 (0.18)	+0.22 (0.24)		+0.57 (0.12)	+0.05 (0.09)	+0.04	.06	.95
UNWEIGHTED *Durable Goods Manufacturers*										
Inventories	+0.38 (0.09)	+0.23 (0.08)	+0.16 (0.12)					−0.14	.06	.88
Sales		+0.16 (0.14)			−0.82 (0.28)		+1.30 (0.30)	+0.26	.09	.84
Selling prices			−0.03 (0.17)	+0.39 (0.10)		+0.41 (0.08)	+0.17 (0.12)	+0.03	.80	.93
Nondurable Goods Manufacturers										
Inventories	+0.45 (0.10)	+0.46 (0.07)	−0.01 (0.10)					−0.20	.06	.94
Sales		+0.12 (0.10)			−0.36 (0.28)		+0.92 (0.28)	+0.29	.08	.84
Selling prices			−0.10 (0.16)	+0.36 (0.11)		+0.59 (0.06)	+0.18 (0.10)	+0.01	.07	.96

In this and the following tables, the figures in parentheses are the estimated standard errors of the coefficients. The equations involved are 2, 7, and 8.   [a] −0.003.

TABLE 4

Formation of Manufacturers' Expectations as Reflected in Diffusion Data, Recursive Model, Sequence Estimation

EXPECTATIONAL VARIABLE	COEFFICIENTS OF EXPLANATORY VARIABLES								STANDARD ERROR OF ESTIMATE	MULTIPLE CORRELATION
	Expectation		Actual minus Expected, Lagged		Actual, Lagged			Constant		
	Sales	Selling Prices	Inventory	Prices	Sales	Prices	New Orders			
	TYPE I WEIGHTS									
	Durable Goods Manufacturers									
Inventories	+0.43 (0.18)	+0.27 (0.17)	+0.17 (0.26)					−0.15	0.06	0.92
Sales		+0.01 (0.45)			−0.73 (0.52)		+1.37 (0.52)	+0.23	.12	.83
Selling prices			+0.05 (0.28)	+0.23 (0.19)		+0.42 (0.12)	+0.23 (0.13)	a	.06	.95
	Nondurable Goods Manufacturers									
Inventories	+0.61 (0.15)	+0.32 (0.14)	+0.03 (0.26)					−0.27	.05	.94
Sales		+0.08 (0.21)			−0.94 (0.48)		+1.65 (0.50)	+1.28	.06	.90
Selling prices			+0.44 (0.12)	+0.23 (0.14)		+0.51 (0.05)	+0.15 (0.05)	+0.02	.02	.99
	TYPE II WEIGHTS									
	Durable Goods Manufacturers									
Inventories	+0.37 (0.14)	+0.08 (0.20)	+0.80 (0.19)					−0.22	.06	.94
Sales		−0.69 (0.60)			−0.03 (0.54)		+1.07 (0.63)	+0.24	.15	.83
Selling prices			+0.12 (0.16)	+0.07 (0.17)		+0.36 (0.13)	+0.23 (0.09)	+0.03	.06	.95

105

[table continues on next page

Table 4, continued

EXPECTATIONAL VARIABLE	Expectation		Actual minus Expected, Lagged		Actual, Lagged			Constant	STANDARD ERROR OF ESTIMATE	MULTIPLE CORRELATION
	Sales	Selling Prices	Inventory	Prices	Sales	Prices	New Orders			
Nondurable Goods Manufacturers										
Inventories	+0.30 (0.12)	+0.42 (0.11)	+0.18 (0.12)					−0.13	.04	.95
Sales		+0.26 (0.24)			−0.36 (0.37)		+0.92 (0.40)	+0.27	.09	.85
Selling prices			+0.14 (0.18)	+0.22 (0.24)		+0.57 (0.12)	+0.05 (0.09)	+0.04	.06	.95
UNWEIGHTED **Durable Goods Manufacturers**										
Inventories	+0.44 (0.14)	+0.24 (0.10)	+0.09 (0.14)					−0.17	.07	.85
Sales		−0.04 (0.19)			−0.70 (0.30)		+1.32 (0.30)	+0.25	.09	.83
Selling prices			−0.03 (0.17)	+0.39 (0.10)		+0.41 (0.08)	+0.17 (0.12)	+0.03	.08	.93
Nondurable Goods Manufacturers										
Inventories	+0.51 (0.17)	+0.48 (0.09)	−0.06 (0.12)					−0.24	.07	.91
Sales		+0.05 (0.12)			−0.27 (0.31)		+0.91 (0.30)	+0.28	.08	.83
Selling prices		[a] (0.16)	−0.10 (0.11)	+0.36		+0.59 (0.06)	+0.18 (0.10)	+0.01	.07	.96

The equations involved are 2, 7, and 8.   [a] −0.003.

106

order diffusion and sales diffusion is not so marked in the unweighted coefficients, so that the generally strong influence of current new order experience on sales anticipations suggested by the Type I data is confirmed.

Table 4 provides a check of the pattern of findings in Table 3, based on a technique of estimation that involves less stringent assumptions about the stochastic properties of the recursive model. In particular, the disturbances u_1 in the several equations need not be regarded as uncorrelated within a given time period. Under these more realistic conditions the estimates will still be "consistent," but replacing current explanatory variables by their predicted values in the estimation process may enhance the collinearity of the revised set of explanatory series and reduce the stability of the estimated coefficients. However the results summarized in Table 4 broadly agree with those in Table 3. Only the following differences are noteworthy:

1. Current new orders are more important in shaping the sales anticipations of the largest firms.

2. The role of selling-price expectations in shaping sales anticipations is substantially reduced.

3. The weighted data are less clear-cut on the respective roles of selling-price expectations and inventory maladjustments in shaping inventory intentions.

The second point may reflect only the collinearity of *predicted* selling-price expectations with realized new orders, and the third only the similar collinearity of such expectations with the measure of inventory maladjustments, although there is no marked increase in standard errors such as would be implied by enhanced collinearity.

The pattern of results found in Tables 3 and 4 is fully interpretable in terms of the recursive model of expectation formation provided we infer (1) that inventory accumulation seldom moves in an undesired direction for as long as two quarters, and (2) that prices, where they are an instrument of deliberate control, are at least equally adaptable to the evolving estimates of market strength. By the test of multiple correlation coefficients, sales anticipations are least successfully explained by the model, price expectations most successfully explained, and inventory intentions only slightly less successfully explained. Except for sales anticipations, the explanations are uniformly more successful than are explanations provided by a scheme of direct extrapolation.[9] The advantage is greatest for inventory intentions.

Charts 1 and 2 exhibit the predictive ability of the models presented in the Type I weighting results in Table 3. The two top curves in each figure represent expected diffusion as actually reported in the Dun and Bradstreet surveys, $b(\overline{X})$, and the corresponding predictions of expected diffusion

[9] Compare Hastay, p. 118.

based on the equation under consideration, $b'(\overline{X})$. The remaining curves represent the contributions of the various explanatory variables to the

CHART I

Durable Goods Manufacturers, Expected Diffusion, Recursive Model

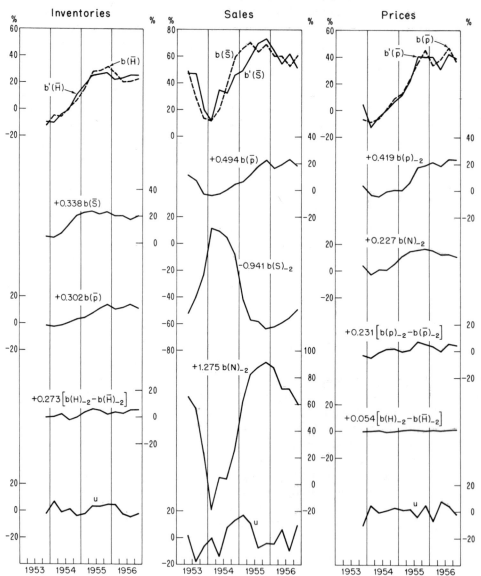

predicted series, together with the divergence of the actual from the predicted series.

Methodological Implications. The rather unfavorable showing of the simultaneous-equation model of expectation formation appears to have methodological, as much as substantive, implications. Because the model

CHART 2

Nondurable Goods Manufacturers, Expected Diffusion, Recursive Model

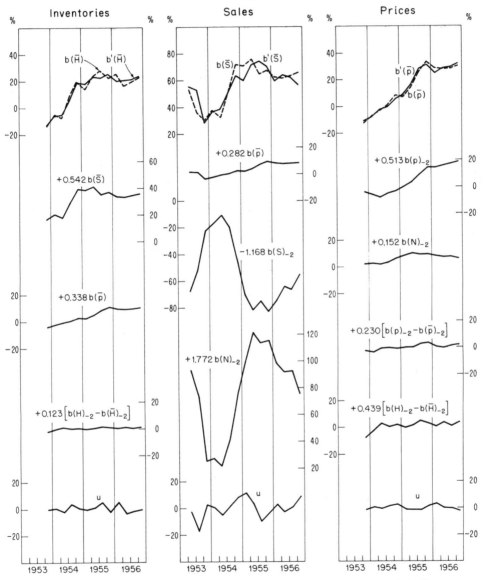

is exactly identified, it can be evaluated by the technique of indirect least squares. In practice, this means that each of the endogenous variables—sales anticipations, price expectations, and inventory intentions—

is independently regressed on all three of the lagged variables of the model. The coefficients in these auxiliary regression equations are unique functions of the unknown coefficients of the model, sufficient in number to permit of an exact solution for the model coefficients. But the solution depends practically on the identifiability of the model being "strong" enough so that sampling variability of the regression coefficients does not cause them to take on values characteristic of the regression coefficients of underidentified models.

The instability in the computed coefficients for our simultaneous-equation model may thus have one or more sources:

1. The models may not be strongly identified. This explanation seems unlikely, as direct examination of the identification question does not suggest that the identifiability of the model is sensitive to the numerical values of the unknown coefficients for quite wide ranges of possible variation.

2. The regression coefficients determined in the first round of the indirect least-squares technique may be subject to wide sampling variability. This explanation holds for the Type I weighting results in Table 2, where there are only 10 degrees of freedom, but applies with less force to the unweighted results where 27 degrees of freedom exist. A factor here may be that the diffusion data, being based on samples, are subject to measurement errors which add to the sampling variability of the regression coefficients without showing up in the computed standard errors. This explanation must therefore be classed as possible.

3. Collinearity among the endogenous variables may be the source of coefficient instability. The collinearity is notably high between sales anticipations and price expectations in every industrial group, and is fairly high even between these variables and inventory intentions. The third explanation therefore seems the most important one in accounting for the instability of the findings on the nonrecursive model of manufacturers' expectations. Combined with the possible influence of the second explanation, it seems to rule out any practicable test of the model until the supply of statistical data is expanded or the precision of the diffusion estimates can be improved.

TRADERS' EXPECTATIONS

The traders' model of expectation formation, being recursive, presents no new statistical problems. It embodies, however, a different theory of expectations. Because the typical trader is imagined to have no effective control over prices, future sales rather than future prices are assumed to mark the first stage in his forward thinking. He predicts that sales will continue to change about as they did in the previous period, adjusting for any mistake in his last prediction. He next forecasts the change in selling

110

TABLE 5

Formation of Traders' Expectations as Reflected in Diffusion Data, Recursive Model

EXPECTATIONAL VARIABLE	COEFFICIENTS OF EXPLANATORY VARIABLES						Constant	STANDARD ERROR OF ESTIMATE	MULTIPLE CORRELATION
	Expectation		Actual minus Expected, Lagged		Actual, Lagged				
	Sales	Selling Prices	Inventory	Sales	Sales	Prices			
TYPE I WEIGHTS *Wholesalers*									
Inventories	+0.58 (0.08)	-0.01 (0.07)	+0.69 (0.15)				-0.26	0.03	0.97
Sales	+0.30 (0.08)			+0.69 (0.22)	+0.27 (0.11)		+0.44	.06	.92
Selling prices			+0.11 (0.20)			+0.67 (0.06)	-0.09	.04	.99
Retailers									
Inventories	+0.48 (0.10)	+0.19 (0.09)	+0.22 (0.15)				-0.22	.06	.90
Sales	+0.14 (0.10)			+0.62 (0.28)	+0.33 (0.15)		+0.45	.10	.83
Selling prices			-0.24 (0.17)			+0.91 (0.09)	-0.04	.06	.96
TYPE II WEIGHTS *Wholesalers*									
Inventories	+0.25 (0.11)	+0.16 (0.14)	+0.62 (0.28)				-0.17	.06	.90
Sales	+0.14 (0.11)			+0.96 (0.33)	+0.08 (0.16)		+0.52	.09	.88
Selling prices			+0.16 (0.30)			+0.65 (0.11)	-0.02	.06	.96

[table continues on next page

111

Table 5, continued

EXPECTATIONAL VARIABLE	COEFFICIENTS OF EXPLANATORY VARIABLES						Constant	STANDARD ERROR OF ESTIMATE	MULTIPLE CORRELATION
	Expectation		Actual minus Expected, Lagged		Actual, Lagged				
	Sales	Selling Prices	Inventory	Sales	Sales	Prices			
Retailers									
Inventories	+0.42 (0.21)	+0.50 (0.23)	−0.64 (0.30)				−0.21	.16	.64
Sales				+0.31 (0.30)	+0.41 (0.21)		+0.46	.17	.69
Selling prices	+0.24 (0.13)		−0.27 (0.21)			+0.77 (0.13)	−0.12	.10	.87
UNWEIGHTED Wholesalers									
Inventories	+0.40 (0.13)	+0.21 (0.10)	+0.04 (0.17)				−0.18	.08	.81
Sales				+0.31 (0.16)	+0.28 (0.10)		+0.37	.11	.71
Selling prices	+0.65 (0.08)		+0.28 (0.13)			+0.51 (0.05)	−0.25	.06	.97
Retailers									
Inventories	+0.33 (0.10)	+0.39 (0.06)	+0.13 (0.09)				−0.20	.07	.92
Sales				+0.16 (0.12)	+0.39 (0.08)		+0.36	.11	.70
Selling prices	+0.37 (0.13)		+0.28 (0.12)			+0.65 (0.06)	−0.17	.09	.95

The equations involved are 2, 4, and 6.

112

TABLE 6

Formation of Traders' Expectations as Reflected in Diffusion Data, Recursive Model, Sequence Estimation

EXPECTATIONAL VARIABLE	COEFFICIENTS OF EXPLANATORY VARIABLES							STANDARD ERROR OF ESTIMATE	MULTIPLE CORRELATION
	Expectation		Actual minus Expected, Lagged		Actual, Lagged		Constant		
	Sales	Selling Prices	Inventory	Sales	Sales	Prices			
TYPE I WEIGHTS *Wholesalers*									
Inventories	+0.56 (0.18)	a (0.15)	+0.78 (0.32)				−0.26	0.05	0.89
Sales	+0.31 (0.11)			+0.69 (0.22)	+0.27 (0.11)		+0.44	.06	.92
Selling prices			+0.19 (0.24)			+0.66 (0.08)	−0.10	.04	.98
Retailers									
Inventories	+0.61 (0.14)	+0.13 (0.11)	+0.12 (0.18)				−0.27	.06	.87
Sales	+0.17 (0.14)			+0.62 (0.28)	+0.33 (0.15)		+0.45	.10	.83
Selling prices			−0.27 (0.18)			+0.90 (0.10)	−0.04	.06	.95
TYPE II WEIGHTS *Wholesalers*									
Inventories	+0.12 (0.14)	+0.34 (0.18)	+0.42 (0.34)				−0.11	.06	.89
Sales	+0.14 (0.13)			+0.96 (0.33)	+0.08 (0.16)		+0.52	.09	.88
Selling prices			+0.20 (0.31)			+0.64 (0.12)	−0.02	.06	.96

[table continues on next page]

113

Table 6, *continued*

EXPECTATIONAL VARIABLE	Expectation		Actual Minus Expected, Lagged		Actual, Lagged		Constant	STANDARD ERROR OF ESTIMATE	MULTIPLE CORRELATION
	Sales	Selling Prices	Inventory	Sales	Sales	Prices			
Retailers									
Inventories	+0.58 (0.20)	−0.05 (0.21)	−0.03 (0.23)				−0.18	.13	.56
Sales	+0.28 (0.16)			+0.31 (0.30)	+0.41 (0.21)		+0.46	.17	.69
Selling prices		+0.26 (0.16)	−0.21 (0.20)			+0.77 (0.13)	−0.15	.10	.86
UNWEIGHTED Wholesalers									
Inventories	+0.38 (0.29)	+0.26 (0.16)	−0.08 (0.22)				−0.17	.10	.69
Sales	+0.60 (0.25)			+0.31 (0.16)	+0.28 (0.10)		+0.37	.11	.71
Selling prices		+0.32 (0.10)	+0.25 (0.23)			+0.50 (0.09)	−0.22	.11	.91
Retailers									
Inventories	+0.54 (0.19)	+0.32 (0.10)	+0.16 (0.12)				−0.29	.08	.88
Sales	+0.28 (0.23)			+0.16 (0.12)	+0.39 (0.08)		+0.36	.11	.70
Selling prices			+0.33 (0.14)			+0.64 (0.08)	−0.13	.10	.93

COEFFICIENTS OF EXPLANATORY VARIABLES

The equations involved are 2, 4, and 6.   a Less than 0.005.

114

prices by projecting conservatively the recent trend of prices, estimating the effect of the already predicted trend of sales, and making allowance for any disequilibrium in his current inventory position. Finally, he sets his inventory-investment objective on the basis of his sales and price forecasts and his appraisal of his current inventory position. Tables 5 and 6 summarize the results of fitting this model to diffusion data for wholesalers and retailers in a form parallel to Tables 3 and 4.

Thus Table 5 is based on the independent application of least squares to each equation separately. As in the case of manufacturers, few coefficients seem puzzling in the light of the model tested, except perhaps the two coefficients of the inventory-appraisal variable in the retailers' model (Type I weighting) which offer contradictory evidence on the flexibility of inventory accumulation. But then the largest retailers show consistent evidence of having less effective control over inventories than do retailers as a whole (compare the Type II data with the other two sets). Speaking generally, the sizes of coefficients, relative to their standard errors, attest to the genuine influence of all the factors embraced by the model. However, inventory appraisal may have little influence on the price expectations of both classes of traders and, for wholesalers, selling-price expectations little influence on inventory objectives. The influence of the period studied can be seen in the unweighted results, where the reduced effect of stock appraisal on the inventory intentions of wholesalers may be traceable to the Korean war period.

Table 6 is based on a sequential application of least squares. Though an increase in standard errors pushes several coefficients into the doubtfully significant class, the pattern of results closely parallels that of Table 5, except for less contrast between large wholesalers and large retailers in their control over short-run inventory accumulation (compare the Type II results).

Charts 3 and 4 show the predictive ability of the traders' models based on Type I weighted data. They bear out the testimony of the multiple correlation coefficients, that price expectations are most successfully explained and sales anticipations least successfully explained by the models. As in manufacturing, except for sales anticipations, the models are superior to explanations of expected diffusion based on extrapolation, and the advantage is greatest for inventory intentions.[10]

Refinements of the Expectations Models

Several features of the models so far discussed are less than satisfactory. The dependence of inventory planning on buying prices has been omitted from the statistical work, and the distinction between manufacturers' stocks of purchased materials and their stocks of finished goods has not

[10] Hastay, *op. cit.*

been explicitly recognized. Also, the measures of *ex post* disequilibria of inventories and selling prices are too crude to yield confident insight into

CHART 3

Wholesale Traders, Expected Diffusion, Recursive Model without Buying Prices

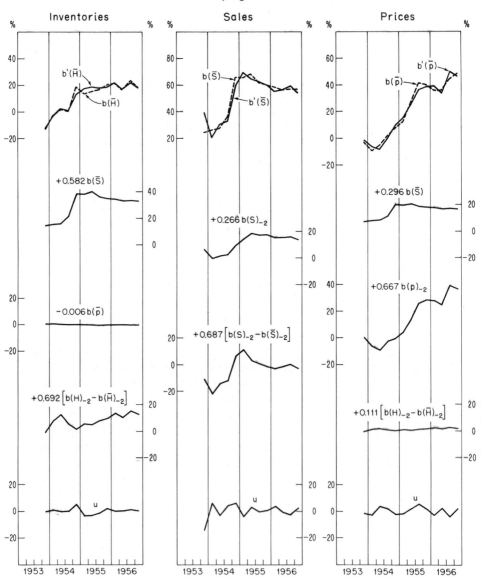

the role of this factor in planning. Now we will consider several experiments designed to remedy these shortcomings.

116

THE REFINEMENTS

Buying-Price Expectations. The role of buying-price expectations can be investigated only for the traders' model, using the selling-price diffusion

CHART 4

Retail Traders, Expected Diffusion, Recursive Model without Buying Prices

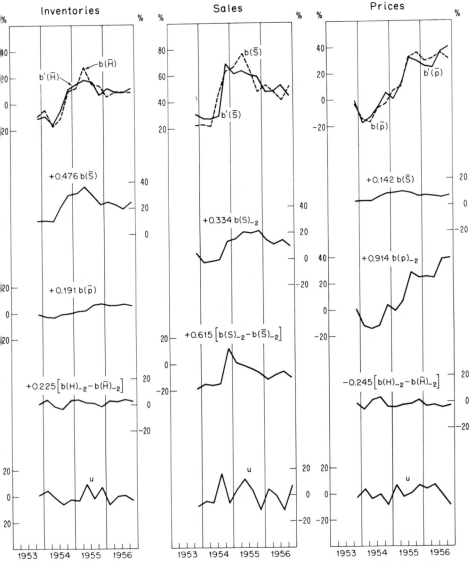

of manufacturers as proxy for the expected buying-price diffusion of wholesalers, and the selling-price diffusion of the latter as the expected buying-price diffusion of retailers.

Since firms are not acquainted with the *expectations* of their suppliers, the most recent diffusion of actual selling prices of the earlier processors are taken as the expected buying-price diffusion. In symbols, $b(p_h)_{-2}$ serves as proxy for $b(\overrightarrow{p_h})$. Restated in terms of this proxy, the general inventory equation for traders becomes:

$$(9) \quad b(\overline{H}) = a_1 b(\overline{S}) + a_2 b(\bar{p}) + a_3 b(p_h)_{-2} + a_4 [b(H)_{-2} - b(\overline{H})_{-2}] + a_0 + u_1$$

Expected buying prices affect not only inventory intentions but also sales and price anticipations. The nature of the influence on sales anticipations is uncertain. A rise in expected buying prices should depress sales anticipations. But since price rises are frequently associated with improved business, the final impact may be negligible or even positive. On selling-price anticipations, however, the influence should be predominantly positive. Thus the traders' model, expanded to allow for buying-price expectations, takes the form:

$$(10) \quad b(\overline{H}) = a_1 b(\overline{S}) + a_2 b(\bar{p}) + a_3 b(p_h)_{-2} + a_4 [b(H)_{-2} - b(\overline{H})_{-2}] + a_0 + u_1$$

$$(11) \quad b(\overline{S}) = c_1 b(S)_{-2} + c_2 [b(S)_{-2} - b(\overline{S})_{-2}] + c_3 b(p_h)_{-2} + c_0 + u_3$$

$$(12) \quad b(\bar{p}) = g_1 b(\overline{S}) + g_2 b(p)_{-2} + g_3 b(p_h)_{-2} + g_4 [b(H)_{-2} - b(\overline{H})_{-2}] + g_0 + u_5$$

Although the realized diffusion index $b(p_h)_{-2}$ figures as a measure of expectations in this model, it is a predetermined variable with respect to its statistical properties and does not require explanation within the model. Thus the number of explanatory equations remains three.

Manufacturers' Purchased Materials. The Dun and Bradstreet questionnaire does not plainly call for inventories of finished goods. Moreover, running in dollar terms, the responses may well include purchased materials. Fortunately, there is evidence to suggest that the acquisition of purchased materials tends to follow new orders with a lag that depends on average delivery time. The lag is probably less than two quarters, but in view of the close association of expected sales and expected new orders in the Dun and Bradstreet reports, the relation is expressed in terms of the diffusion of realized new orders, $b(N)_{-2}$. The resulting equation for manufacturers' inventory intentions takes the form:

$$(13) \quad b(\overline{H}) = a_1 b(\overline{S}) + a_2 b(\bar{p}) + a_3 b(N)_{-2} + a_4 [b(H)_{-2} - b(\overline{H})_{-2}] + a_0 + u_1$$

Since $b(N)_{-2}$ is a predetermined variable within the model, the remaining equations of the manufacturers' model are unaltered.

Ex post Disequilibria. Because of decisions based on erroneous expectations, businessmen often find that matters under their control, such as inventories and selling price, are not in appropriate adjustment to their current environment. Decisions for the future must take account of such maladjustments. So far they have been measured as the difference between attained positions at a given time, $b(X)$, and the corresponding positions

118

expected or planned two quarters earlier, $b(\overline{X})$. But this approach would be fully appropriate only if the planning period were two quarters (i.e. only if decisions taken were not subject to review or modification before two quarters had elapsed). However, nearly all the results suggest that the planning period is typically shorter, for the coefficients of the disequilibrium measures are usually positive, as might be expected if departures of attained positions $b(X)$ from prior intended positions $b(\overline{X})$ were typically in the direction deemed appropriate in the light of revisions of expectations during the two quarter period.

The problem, therefore, is to express the fact that, at the planning date, equilibrium positions of the instrument variables, $b(\hat{X})$, generally differ from the positions expected two quarters earlier, $b(\overline{X})$. In this proposed notation, measures $[b(X)-b(\overline{X})]$ representing divergence from expectations are to be replaced with measures of divergence from equilibrium $[b(X)-b(\hat{X})]$.

Now, it seems probable that planned reactions to uncertain expectations will differ from the reactions that would be planned if the same data were known with *ex post* accuracy. In general, the coefficients expressing planned reactions should be smaller than those expressing the reactions deemed appropriate to the same data by hindsight. Let us call an equation expressing planned reactions to uncertain data the "planning function," the corresponding equation expressing "retrospective" reactions the "equilibrium function." (The kind of equilibrium implied is of course dynamic.) The equations should have the same form and, to the degree that they depend on retrospective data, the same coefficients. To illustrate these ideas in connection with inventory planning by manufacturers, we have for the planning function:

$$(14) \quad b(\overline{H}) = a_0 + a_1 b(\overline{S}) + a_2 b(\bar{p}) + a_3 b(N)_{-2} + a_4 [b(H)_{-2} - b(\hat{H})_{-2}] + u_1$$

and for the equilibrium function:

$$(15) \quad b(\hat{H}) = a_0 + \hat{a}_1 b(S) + \hat{a}_2 b(p) + \hat{a}_3 b(N) + a_4 [b(H)_{-2} - b(\hat{H})_{-2}] + v_1$$

Use of the identity $b(H)-b(\hat{H})=[b(H)-b(\overline{H})]-[b(\hat{H})-b(\overline{H})]$ now easily establishes as the definition of attained disequilibrium for inventories:

$$(16) \quad b(H)_{-2} - b(\hat{H})_{-2} = [b(H)_{-2} - b(\overline{H})_{-2}] - \hat{a}_1 [b(S)_{-2} - b(\overline{S})_{-2}]$$
$$- \hat{a}_2 [b(p)_{-2} - b(\bar{p})_{-2}] - \hat{a}_3 [b(N)_{-2} - b(N)_{-4}]$$
$$- (\hat{a}_1 - a_1) b(\overline{S})_{-2} - (\hat{a}_2 - a_2) b(\bar{p})_{-2}$$
$$- (\hat{a}_3 - a_3) b(N)_{-4}$$

An obvious substitution of $b(p_h)$ for $b(N)$ yields a corresponding result for attained disequilibrium in the traders' model that includes buying prices. Alternatively, elimination of the terms in $b(N)$ establishes the form of the definition for the simpler version of inventory planning with new orders and buying prices absent.

119

Since prices are also treated as instrument variables in the manufacturers' models, we require corresponding measures of attained price disequilibrium. An exactly parallel argument yields the formulas:

(17) $$b(p)_{-2} - b(\hat{p})_{-2} = [b(p)_{-2} - b(\bar{p})_{-2}] - \hat{d}_1[b(S)_{-2} - b(\bar{S})_{-2}]$$
$$- (\hat{d}_1 - d_1)b(\bar{S})_{-2}$$

in the exactly identified, nonrecursive model, and:

(18) $$b(p)_{-2} - b(\hat{p})_{-2} = [b(p)_{-2} - b(\bar{p})_{-2}] - \hat{d}_2[b(N)_{-2} - b(N)_{-4}]$$
$$- (\hat{d}_2 - d_2)b(N)_{-4}$$

in the recursive model.

The refinement of the models of expectation formation envisaged here can now be accomplished by substituting for the formal definitions of attained disequilibria $[b(X)_{-2} - b(\hat{X})_{-2}]$ the operational measures worked out above, in which the parameters $\hat{a}$ and $\hat{d}$ become unknowns to be estimated from the data. The substitutions are required only for instrument variables since the problem arises only in connection with variables over which the firm is assumed to have direct control. It follows that in all models the difference $[b(S)_{-2} - b(\bar{S})_{-2}]$ will remain unaltered, as will the difference $[b(p)_{-2} - b(\bar{p})_{-2}]$ in the model of traders' expectations.

As subjected to statistical test in the following section, the definitions of attained disequilibria are somewhat truncated by the omission of the correction terms in lagged expectations: $(\hat{a}_1 - a_1)b(\bar{S})_{-2}$, $(\hat{a}_2 - a_2)b(\bar{p})_{-2}$, $(\hat{d}_2 - d_2)b(N)_{-4}$, and so forth. The omission is necessary to conserve degrees of freedom by cutting down on the number of predetermined variables in the various models. The resulting measures of disequilibria are thus only approximations, but they suffice for a rough check of the logic of the refinement.[11]

STATISTICAL EFFECTS OF THE REFINEMENTS

The first refinement can be studied only for traders, the second applies only to manufacturers, while the third applies to both. For traders, the first and third refinements are discussed separately, then together; for manufacturers, the third refinement is taken up separately, but the second only with the third. The statistical examination is therefore not logically complete for manufacturers, but it need not be. It is made so for traders only to be sure of isolating the effect of buying prices on expectations, since we need to gauge the consequences of omitting such prices from the manufacturers' models.

Traders' Buying Prices. The first model under examination is defined by equations 10, 11, and 12. Table 7 shows the results of fitting the model to the weighted and unweighted diffusion data. The method of single-equation least squares was used to estimate all the coefficients.

[11] See, however, the reservation expressed on page 129.

EXPECTATIONS ABOUT OPERATING VARIABLES

TABLE 7

Formation of Traders' Expectations as Reflected in Diffusion Data, Recursive Model with Buying Prices

EXPECTATIONAL VARIABLE	Expectation Sales	Expectation Selling Prices	Actual Minus Expected, Lagged Inventory	Actual Minus Expected, Lagged Sales	Actual, Lagged Sales	Actual, Lagged Selling Prices	Actual, Lagged Buying Prices	Constant	STANDARD ERROR OF ESTIMATE	MULTIPLE CORRELATION
TYPE I WEIGHTS *Wholesalers*										
Inventories	+0.66 (0.09)	−0.25 (0.19)	+0.69 (0.14)				+0.20 (0.15)	−0.28	0.02	0.97
Sales				+0.73 (0.29)	+0.22 (0.22)		+0.04 (0.16)	+0.45	.06	.92
Selling prices	+0.30 (0.09)		+0.11 (0.21)			+0.64 (0.32)	+0.04 (0.35)	−0.09	.04	.98
Retailers										
Inventories	+0.48 (0.11)	+0.18 (0.38)	+0.23 (0.17)				+0.01 (0.29)	−0.22	.06	.88
Sales				+0.57 (0.34)	+0.38 (0.24)		−0.04 (0.18)	+0.44	.10	.81
Selling prices	+0.13 (0.09)		−0.15 (0.16)			+0.15 (0.40)	+0.62 (0.32)	−0.06	.05	.96
TYPE II WEIGHTS *Wholesalers*										
Inventories	+0.28 (0.10)	−0.03 (0.18)	+0.38 (0.30)				+0.27 (0.17)	−0.16	.05	.92
Sales				+0.94 (0.39)	+0.10 (0.23)		−0.02 (0.17)	+0.52	.09	.86
Selling prices	+0.14 (0.12)		+0.16 (0.36)			+0.65 (0.18)	−0.01 (0.23)	−0.02	.06	.96

COEFFICIENTS OF EXPLANATORY VARIABLES

121

[table continues on next page]

Table 7, continued

COEFFICIENTS OF EXPLANATORY VARIABLES

EXPECTATIONAL VARIABLE	Expectation		Actual Minus Expected, Lagged		Actual, Lagged			Constant	STANDARD ERROR OF ESTIMATE	MULTIPLE CORRELATION
	Sales	Selling Prices	Inventory	Sales	Sales	Selling Prices	Buying Prices			
Retailers										
Inventories	+0.60 (0.18)	+0.21 (0.41)	-0.09 (0.25)				-0.02 (0.31)	-0.26	.13	.72
Sales				+0.47 (0.35)	+0.27 (0.25)		+0.22 (0.23)	+0.50	.16	.73
Selling prices	+0.07 (0.14)		-0.17 (0.18)			+0.44 (0.18)	+0.36 (0.16)	-0.05	.08	.91
UNWEIGHTED Wholesalers										
Inventories	+0.66 (0.17)	-0.17 (0.19)	+0.05 (0.16)				+0.26 (0.11)	-0.27	.07	.84
Sales				+0.11 (0.18)	+0.62 (0.18)		-0.27 (0.13)	+0.28	.11	.75
Selling prices	+0.63 (0.09)		+0.29 (0.14)			+0.66 (0.20)	-0.16 (0.21)	-0.25	.06	.97
Retailers										
Inventories	+0.33 (0.10)	+0.41 (0.16)	+0.13 (0.10)				-0.02 (0.11)	-0.19	.07	.92
Sales				+0.37 (0.13)	+0.30 (0.12)		+0.02 (0.08)	+0.41	.10	.76
Selling prices	+0.33 (0.12)		+0.28 (0.11)			+0.12 (0.23)	+0.55 (0.23)	-0.20	.09	.95

The equations involved are 10, 11, and 12.

122

By the test of multiple correlation coefficients, the introduction of buying-price diffusion produces little change in the traders' models. There is no improvement for models fitted to weighted data of Type I, improvement only in the case of retailers for models fitted to weighted data of Type II, and but slight improvement for models fitted to unweighted data (compare Tables 5 and 7). For buying-price coefficients, however, the case is less clear. The coefficients are generally negligible, but they are of material size and possibly significant in the equations for retailers' selling-price anticipations and wholesalers' inventory intentions. The equations for retailers' sales anticipations (Type II weighted data) and wholesalers' sales and price anticipations (unweighted data) also show substantial coefficients, but the exceptions are probably too unsystematic to argue for a clear influence of buying prices on sales anticipations in general or on wholesalers' price anticipations in particular.

Some insight into this conflict of testimony is gained by examining the effect of buying prices in the two groups of equations where they seem important. Consider, first, the equations for selling-price anticipations, equation 12. To a good approximation, the coefficients of realized buying-price diffusion and realized selling-price diffusion in the expanded equations sum to the value of the realized selling-price coefficient alone in the original equations without buying prices, equation 6. This sum of coefficients is not quite large enough in the retailers' models applied to weighted data, but the rule holds for wholesalers in all cases and for retailers in the model applied to unweighted data. Moreover, though the buying-price coefficient is frequently small, both coefficients have substantially larger standard errors in the expanded models. These facts attest to the close correspondence of realized selling prices and realized buying prices in trade, and suggest why an apparently significant expectational variable can have so little explanatory value in a model that already includes realized selling prices.

Consider, next, the equations for inventory intentions, equations 10 and 2. Comparison of Table 7 with Table 5 discloses a strong tendency for the influence of selling-price anticipations to be reduced when realized buying prices are taken into account, strong enough to produce negative values for the coefficient of anticipated selling prices in every wholesalers' model. It also produces small to substantial reductions in the same coefficient in the retailers' models applied to weighted data, though the model applied to unweighted data provides an exception. The explanation appears to lie in the marked collinearity of realized buying prices and expected selling prices. Because of this collinearity, the change in the coefficient of anticipated selling prices tends to be offset by the coefficient of realized buying prices, the sum of the coefficients being of the order of the single coefficient of anticipated selling prices in the inventory equation having no buying-price variable. The rule holds quite well for models fitted to weighted data of Type I and to unweighted data, especially for retailers; but it holds poorly or not at all for models fitted to weighted data

CHART 5

Wholesale Traders, Expected Diffusion, Recursive Model with Buying Prices

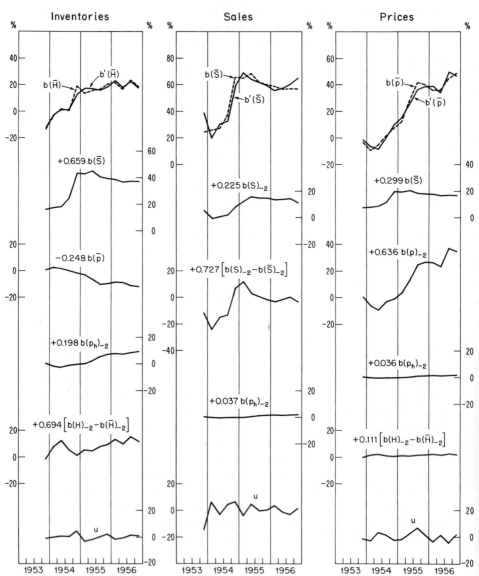

of Type II. A further consequence of collinearity is that, without exception, the standard error of the coefficient of anticipated selling prices is larger in inventory equations containing a buying-price variable than in corresponding equations without it. Thus the net gain from incorporating

CHART 6

Retail Traders, Expected Diffusion, Recursive Model with Buying Prices

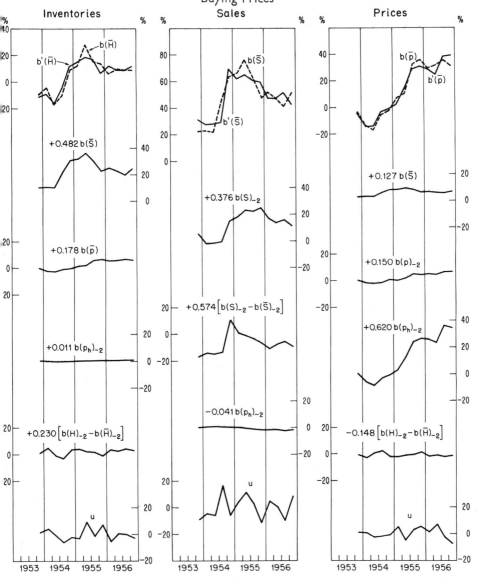

buying prices, as we can measure them, in the explanation of inventory intentions is small.

Other tendencies stand out in comparing Table 7 with Table 5.

1. The equations for anticipated sales, though variously altered by the inclusion of buying prices, show possible improvement only in the models fitted to unweighted data.

2. In the expanded models sales expectations appear to exert more influence on the inventory intentions of wholesalers, less on the price anticipations of retailers.

3. A tendency emerges in the buying-price models for coefficients of the stock-appraisal variable to decline in numerical value. The tendency is clearest in the models fitted to weighted data of Type II, being particularly conspicuous in the reduced size of the negative coefficients in the retailers' model. This finding conflicts with the evidence of Table 5, which suggested that the largest retailers have less effective control over inventory accumulation than either wholesalers or the smaller retailers.

To round out this preliminary treatment of buying prices, Charts 5 and 6 illustrate the Type I weighted model summarized in Table 7. They bring out sharply the generally small influence of the buying-price variable except in the equations for inventory intentions of wholesalers and selling-price anticipations of retailers.

Amended Measures of Divergence from Equilibrium. Tables 8 and 9 present the results derived from recalculations of the various models of expectation formation using amended measures of attained disequilibrium in place of the observational ones. The parallels with earlier tables will be exploited to interpret the results. However, because the present investigation is confined to unweighted diffusion data, only models previously fitted to such data, and of these only recursive models, provide an appropriate basis for comparison.

The method of estimation used was the sequential application of least squares. This method seemed suitable because of the generality of the assumptions on which it is applicable. But the danger of enhanced collinearity between explanatory variables to which it is prone turned out to be particularly troublesome and led to some wildly unstable results. Combined with the use of somewhat truncated measures of attained disequilibrium, this instability makes the interpretation of the statistical findings unusually hazardous.

Before looking into the consequences of employing the amended measures of disequilibrium, it will be well to ask whether the new calculations bear out the earlier findings about the role of buying prices in the traders' model. The question can be answered by comparing the two sections of Table 8. With allowances for the differing techniques of estimation, the contrasts here are remarkably similar to those between the unweighted data in Tables 5 and 7. Both inventory intentions and selling-price anticipations seem to be influenced by buying prices, yet in the first case the effects are largely offset by a contrary change in the influence of expected

TABLE 8. Formation of Traders' Expectations as Reflected in Unweighted Diffusion Data, Amended Recursive Model

EXPECTATIONAL VARIABLE	COEFFICIENTS OF EXPLANATORY VARIABLES								STANDARD ERROR OF ESTIMATE	MULTIPLE CORRELATION
	Expectation		Attained Disequilibrium	Actual Minus Expected, Lagged	Actual, Lagged			Constant		
	Sales	Selling Prices	Inventory	Sales	Sales	Selling Prices	Buying Prices			
WITHOUT BUYING PRICES										
Wholesalers										
Inventories	+0.50 (0.17)	+0.57 (0.13)	-0.21 (0.23)					-0.25	0.09	0.75
Sales				+0.31 (0.16)	+0.28 (0.10)			+0.37	.11	.71
Selling prices	+0.80 (0.66)		+0.21 (0.24)			+0.43 (0.14)		-0.33	.10	.92
Retailers										
Inventories	+0.29 (0.18)	+0.48 (0.07)	+0.14 (0.14)					-0.15	.08	.89
Sales				+0.16 (0.12)	+0.39 (0.08)			+0.36	.11	.70
Selling prices	+0.33 (0.31)		+0.09 (0.14)			+0.62 (0.09)		-0.18	.09	.95
WITH BUYING PRICES										
Wholesalers										
Inventories	+0.26 (0.20)	+0.68 (0.26)	-0.11 (0.23)				-0.12 (0.17)	-0.15	.08	.79
Sales				+0.11 (0.18)	+0.62 (0.18)		-0.27 (0.13)	+0.28	.11	.75
Selling prices	-0.35 (0.39)		-0.10 (0.27)			+1.53 (0.44)	-0.94 (0.44)	+0.24	.90	.94
Retailers										
Inventories	+0.08 (0.17)	+0.95 (0.36)	+0.02 (0.15)				-0.30 (0.26)	-0.04	.08	.88
Sales				+0.37 (0.13)	+0.30 (0.12)		+0.02 (0.08)	+0.41	.10	.76
Selling prices	+0.59 (0.40)		+0.13 (0.15)			+0.13 (0.32)	+0.47 (0.29)	-0.34	.08	.96

The equations involved here are: *Top half*—Equations 2, 4, and 6 as amended to incorporate measures of divergence from equilibrium, $[b(H)_{-2} - b(\bar{H})_{-2}]$, in place of divergence from expectations, $[b(H)_{-2} - b(\hat{H})_{-2}]$. *Bottom half*—Equations 10, 11, and 12 similarly amended.

127

TABLE 9. Formation of Manufacturers' Expectations as Reflected in Unweighted Diffusion Data, Amended Recursive Model

EXPECTATIONAL VARIABLE	Expectation Sales	Expectation Selling Prices	Attained Disequilibrium Inventory	Attained Disequilibrium Selling Prices	Actual, Lagged Sales	Actual, Lagged Selling Prices	Actual, Lagged New Orders	Constant	STANDARD OF ESTIMATE	MULTIPLE CORRELATION
INVENTORY INTENTIONS NOT DEPENDENT ON NEW ORDERS										
Durable Goods Manufacturers										
Inventories	+0.57 (0.16)	+0.39 (0.12)	+0.06 (0.15)					−0.26	0.06	0.88
Sales		−0.02 (0.19)			−0.86 (0.29)		+1.48 (0.32)	+0.23	.09	.84
Selling prices			−0.21	−0.50		+0.54	−0.01	+0.13		
Nondurable Goods Manufacturers										
Inventories	+0.38 (0.22)	+0.51 (0.12)	−0.19 (0.17)					−0.14	.07	.92
Sales		+0.10 (0.10)			−0.45 (0.28)		+1.05 (0.29)	+0.28	.08	.85
Selling prices			−0.22	+0.28		+0.70	+0.03	+0.07		
INVENTORY INTENTIONS DEPENDENT ON NEW ORDERS										
Durable Goods Manufacturers										
Inventories	+0.40 (0.35)	+0.51 (0.26)	+0.16 (0.18)				+0.05 (0.25)	−0.24	.07	.87
Sales		−0.02 (0.19)			−0.86 (0.29)		+1.48 (0.32)	+0.23	.09	.84
Selling prices			−0.21	−0.14		+0.54	−0.01	+0.13		
Nondurable Goods Manufacturers										
Inventories	−0.23 (0.90)	+0.52 (0.17)	−0.17 (0.18)				+0.39 (0.52)	+0.02	.08	.91
Sales		+0.10 (0.10)			−0.45 (0.28)		+1.05 (0.29)	+0.28	.08	.85
Selling prices			−0.22	+0.27		+0.70	+0.03	+0.07		

The equations involved here are: *Top half*—Equations 2, 7, and 8 as amended to incorporate measures of divergence from equilibrium $[b(H)_{-2} - b(\overline{H})_{-2}]$ and $[b(p)_{-2} - b(\bar{p})_{-2}]$, in place of measures of divergence from expectation $[b(H)_{-2} - b(\overline{H})_{-2}]$ and $[b(p)_{-2} - b(\bar{p})_{-2}]$, respectively. *Bottom half*—Equations 13, 7, and 8 similarly amended.

selling prices and in the second by a compensating change in the influence of realized selling prices. The rule for coefficient addition formulated for Tables 5 and 7 holds less well for Table 8, but the reason appears to be the enhanced collinearity of realized buying prices with anticipated sales and anticipated selling prices that results from the sequential method of estimation. Consistent with this interpretation is the sharp increase in standard errors of the latter two variables in the second half of Table 8. Also traceable to marked collinearity are the negative coefficient of sales anticipations in the wholesalers' equation for anticipated selling prices, and the implausibly large coefficient of anticipated selling prices in the retailers' equation for inventory intentions. By and large, therefore, the contribution of buying prices, as we can measure them, does not seem any greater in the amended traders' models than it did in the models treated earlier.

The introduction of realized new orders into the equations for manufacturers' inventory intentions is even less successful (Table 9). As measured by the adjusted coefficient of multiple correlation, the explanatory value of the inventory equations is unimproved, and the equations themselves are less plausible. Particularly unconvincing is the negative coefficient of sales anticipations in the model for nondurable goods manufacturers. Also doubtful is the apparently stronger influence of new orders on the inventory intentions of nondurable goods manufacturers than on those of durables manufacturers. Nevertheless, for the present, the results must be classed as inconclusive because of the extreme collinearity of realized new orders and anticipated sales (see their standard errors).

Turning to the amended measures of disequilibrium, we are concerned whether their introduction into the various models leads to improvements either in explanatory power or in theoretical plausibility. The amended variables are meant to be measures of disequilibria that exist at the time expectations are formed and that must be corrected for in the intentions being worked out for the future. Insofar as the measures are successful, they should carry negative coefficients in the models of expectation formation. As a practical matter, this need only be the tendency of the findings. Since the equilibrium measures are only approximations to those suggested by theory, and since the method of estimation enhances the uncertainties created by collinearity between explanatory variables, any stronger validation is not to be expected.

To study the role of the new measures in the traders' model in isolation, other aspects of the model should be held constant as well as the technique employed in its estimation. Subject to these conditions, the only comparison possible is that of Table 8 with Table 6, both of which involve the traders' model *without* buying prices and the sequential use of least squares. Corresponding equations of sales anticipations are identical, but other equations differ because they depend on alternative measures of the disequilibrium in inventory positions. The following bear on the success of the amended measures of disequilibrium:

1. Multiple correlation coefficients, adjusted for degrees of freedom, are only slightly improved by use of the new measures, except for inventory intentions of wholesalers.

2. Coefficients of the new measures of disequilibrium are always algebraically smaller than corresponding coefficients of the original measures.

3. None of these coefficients, however, is negative except in the equation for wholesalers' inventory intentions, and it was negative even in the original evaluation of the model (Table 6).

On balance, the resulting improvement of the traders' models of expectation formation is slight. The showing of the amended measures in the manufacturers' models is somewhat better. Here the appropriate comparison is between Tables 9 and 4. Note the following points:

1. Correlation coefficients for the expected selling-price relations are not available in Table 9, but all other correlations, including those for the equations of anticipated sales, are slightly higher than in Table 4.

2. Every coefficient of price and inventory disequilibrium in Table 9 is algebraically smaller than the corresponding coefficient in Table 4.

3. Most of the coefficients of these measures are negative in Table 9. One—the coefficient of selling-price disequilibrium in the equation for expected selling prices of durable goods manufacturers—is positive in Table 4. However, the coefficients of inventory disequilibrium in the equation for inventory intentions of durable goods manufacturers, and that of selling-price disequilibrium in the equation for selling-price expectations of nondurable goods manufacturers is positive in Table 4 and remains so.

4. Realized new orders have virtually no influence on selling-price expectations in Table 9, although they seem to play a substantial role in all previous applications of the recursive manufacturers' model (see, especially, Tables 3 and 4).

Thus, while the use of the amended measures of disequilibrium in the manufacturers' model is broadly successful, there remain inconsistencies which may be traceable to the technique of estimation or to the approximations used in casting these measures in observational form.

Evidence on the Equilibrium Function. One implication of the observational form given to the amended measures of disequilibrium is that they contain implicitly the coefficients of the equilibrium function, representing desired adjustments of instrument variables *ex post.* Evidence on the nature of the function is marshaled in Tables 10 and 11 for manufacturers and traders.

Manufacturers are assumed to dispose of two intentions variables,

TABLE 10

Implied Coefficients in Equilibrium Functions for Manufacturers' Inventory and Selling-Price Intentions

INDUSTRIAL GROUP	ESTIMATED COEFFICIENTS IN FUNCTION FOR INVENTORY INTENTIONS				ESTIMATED COEFFICIENTS IN FUNCTION FOR SELLING-PRICE INTENTIONS			
	Diffusions of:				Lagged Selling Prices d_1	Diffusions of:		
	Sales $\hat{a}_1$	Selling Prices $\hat{a}_2$	New Orders $\hat{a}_3$	Inventory Maladjustments a_4		New Orders $\hat{d}_2$	Maladjustments Prices d_3	Maladjustments Inventory d_4
WITHOUT NEW ORDERS AS A DETERMINANT OF INVENTORY PLANS								
Durable goods manufacturers	+2.34[a]	+3.58		+0.06	+0.54	+0.03	−0.50	−0.21
Nondurable goods manufacturers	+1.17[b]	+0.20		−0.19	+0.70	−0.59	+0.28	−0.22
WITH NEW ORDERS AS A DETERMINANT OF INVENTORY PLANS								
Durable goods manufacturers	+2.41[a]	+1.84	−0.86	+0.16	+0.54	+1.41	−0.14	−0.21
Nondurable goods manufacturers	+0.98[b]	+0.25	+0.28	−0.17	+0.70	−0.39	+0.27	−0.22

The equations involved are 19 and 20.
[a] As implied in equation for expected selling prices, $\hat{a}_1 = +2.00$.
[b] As implied in equation for expected selling prices, $\hat{a}_1 = +0.13$.

TABLE 11

Implied Coefficients in Equilibrium Function for Traders' Inventory Intentions

| EQUATION FROM WHICH ESTIMATES ARE DERIVED | ESTIMATED EQUILIBRIUM COEFFICIENTS | | | |
	Sales $\hat{a}_1$	Selling Prices $\hat{a}_2$	Buying Prices $\hat{a}_3$	Inventory Maladjustments a_4
WITHOUT BUYING-PRICE VARIABLE				
Wholesalers				
Inventory intentions	+0.53	−1.35		−0.21
Selling-price anticipations	+1.68	−1.32		+0.21
Retailers				
Inventory intentions	−1.98	+0.75		+0.14
Selling-price anticipations	+3.27	−4.23		+0.09
WITH BUYING-PRICE VARIABLE				
Wholesalers				
Inventory intentions	+1.09	−3.42	+0.88	−0.11
Selling-price anticipations	+4.52	−5.34	+5.04	−0.10
Retailers				
Inventory intentions	−7.16	+6.16	−0.01	+0.02
Selling-price anticipations	+3.19	−2.13	−0.16	+0.13

The equation involved is 19 as modified according to text footnote 12.

inventories and selling prices. Their planning is therefore characterized by two equilibrium functions:

(19) $\quad b(\hat{H}) = a_0 + \hat{a}_1 b(S) + \hat{a}_2 b(p) + \hat{a}_3 b(N) + a_4[b(H)_{-2} - b(\hat{H})_{-2}] + v_1$

(20) $\quad b(\hat{p}) = d_0 + d_1 b(p)_{-2} + \hat{d}_2 b(N) + d_3[b(p)_{-2} - b(\hat{p})_{-2}]$
$\quad\quad\quad + d_4[b(H)_{-2} - b(\hat{H})_{-2}] + v_2$

where coefficients without carets are assumed to be the same as in the corresponding planning functions. Their coefficients, as inferred from Table 9, are presented in Table 10.

The equilibrium function for inventory diffusion turns out plausibly for nondurable goods manufacturers, but less so for durable goods manufacturers. In particular, the finding that $\hat{a}_3 < 0$ and $a_4 > 0$ for the latter contradicts the theory of inventory planning with which we have been working. On the other hand, it is the durable goods manufacturers group which yields the plausible forms of the equilibrium function for selling-price diffusion. For nondurable goods manufacturers, the results $\hat{d}_2 < 0$ and $d_3 > 0$ are inconsistent with the model. The findings thus seem at a standoff. However, the tendency of the suspect coefficients, when compared with those of earlier models, is uniformly in the right direction, and the worst contradictions are clearly associated with high collinearity of explanatory variables. The weight of the evidence thus appears to favor the general model of expectations advanced for manufacturers.

The equilibrium functions for traders is summarized in Table 11. Only a single function for inventories is involved because traders are assumed to behave as price takers.[12] Lines labeled "Inventory intentions" and "Selling-price anticipations" thus represent *alternative* estimates of the same equilibrium coefficients, derived from different equations in the expectations model. Ideally, the alternative estimates should agree, and the extent to which they do so is a test of the adequacy of the measures of disequilibrium, or of the method of estimation, or both.

The most striking feature of the table is the contrast between wholesalers and retailers. For wholesalers, alternative versions of the equilibrium function have coefficients of the same sign though of substantially different magnitude. For retailers, alternative versions are sharply contradictory in sign as well as magnitude. The contrast is the more surprising because the correlations for the retailers' models in Table 8 seem somewhat better than those for the wholesalers' models. However, some of the coefficients in Table 11 are unacceptably large, indicating the instability found in estimates from highly collinear data; others are unbelievably small, indicating the obverse side of the collinearity problem. Though collinearity affects the wholesalers' models, it affects the retailers' models more severely and produces unintelligible findings on the level where indirect estimates must be sought. Such collinearity may be an inescapable feature of expectational diffusion at the retailers' level, but more likely it springs from the use of overly crude approximations to the proposed measures of disequilibrium, combined with an inappropriate technique of estimation.

Despite the unfavorable showing of the estimates on the analytical level, Charts 7 through 10, which show the explanatory value of the models summarized in Tables 8 and 9, provide good explanations of the expectations actually reported by businessmen, and surpass the performance of models based on extrapolating the most recent actual diffusion of the variable in question.[13] This superiority over "naïve" models extends not only to correlations but, more significantly, to matters of timing.

Summary

Research in business expectations about operating variables is a new field. It has required the invention of a new type of survey yielding a novel form of statistical information that imposes considerable strain on the technical tools developed for work with more conventional data. The findings of the paper are therefore partly methodological and partly substantive.

[12] The form of the function is strictly analogous to equation 19 except that $b_{(P_h)}$ replaces $b(N)$.
[13] Compare Hastay, pp. 118–119.

133

ESTIMATION TECHNIQUES

Linearity. All of the models proposed to explain the generation of expectations, no less than the techniques employed to estimate them, depend for their plausibility on the analogy between diffusion data and rates of change in corresponding aggregates. In this paper the change in

<table>
<tr><td>CHART 7</td><td>CHART 8</td></tr>
<tr>
<td>Expected Diffusion and Estimates Derived from Amended Manufacturers' Model with New Orders a Determinant of Intended Inventory Investment, Durable Goods Producers</td>
<td>Expected Diffusion and Estimates Derived from Amended Manufacturers' Model with New Orders a Determinant of Intended Inventory Investment, Nondurable Goods Producers</td>
</tr>
</table>

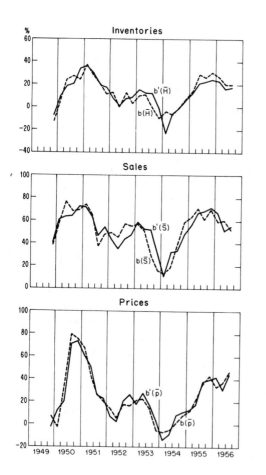

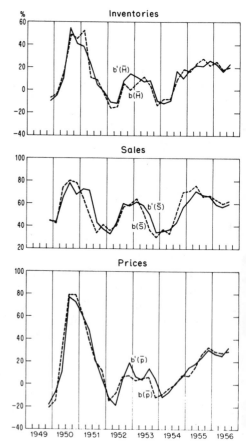

an aggregate such as finished goods inventories—say, ΔH—was held to be a stochastic function of the net percentage of firms experiencing increases in finished goods inventories—say, $b(H)$. Or, in symbols, $\Delta H = f[b(H), u]$, where u is a chance variable distributed independently in time. Further, the relation was held to be essentially linear in the observed ranges of variation of $b(H)$.

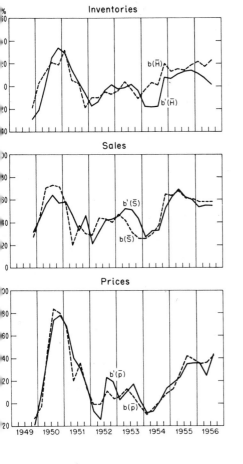

CHART 9

Expected Diffusion and Estimates Derived from Amended Traders' Model with Buying Prices, Wholesalers

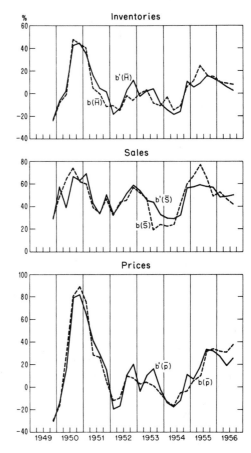

CHART 10

Expected Diffusion and Estimates Derived from Amended Traders' Model with Buying Prices, Retailers

135

The theoretical considerations sufficient to justify the linear hypothesis rigorously are fairly restrictive, and some of the problems encountered may attest to their occasional breakdown, particularly when expectations change sharply. So far, however, I have hit on no nonlinear scheme that notably improves the relationship between measures of aggregate change and the Dun and Bradstreet data. Moreover, the importance of non-linearities in the diffusion–aggregate change relation should be considerably reduced in models where changes are represented entirely by diffusion data.

Reliability of Estimates. More serious are the sources of instability in the coefficients estimated for the several expectation models. These include the high degree of collinearity shown by diffusion series, the sensitivity of identification in exactly identified models, and perhaps also measurement errors in the reported diffusion indexes considered as representations of diffusion in the underlying business population. All of these problems are present in the exactly identified model of expectation formation proposed for manufacturers. Even when identification is strong, the method of indirect least squares appropriate for estimating the coefficients of such models is peculiarly sensitive to multicollinearity among the endogenous variables.

Even the analysis by means of recursive models is not immune to estimation troubles. Though the models are overidentified and may be estimated by the application of least squares one equation at a time, the technique that rests on the least restrictive assumptions about the disturbances in the models is highly vulnerable to the presence of multi-collinearity among the variables. This technique recognizes the interdependence of equations in each model, since current values of the explanatory variables in a given equation are derived from earlier equations in the recursive chain, beginning with the equation that depends only on exogenous variables. But such a process, while "consistent" under quite general conditions, enhances the collinearity of explanatory variables at each successive stage and may yield coefficient estimates with very large standard errors.

More stable results can be achieved by the alternative technique of estimating each equation independently. However the coefficients may be biased, for conditions on the stochastic properties of the disturbances in such models sufficient to rule out bias are quite restrictive. Since in the end the paper places chief reliance on the latter technique, the possibility of bias must be kept in mind in putting interpretations on the findings.

FORMATION OF EXPECTATIONS

Rational Interdependence of Anticipations and Intentions. While it would be an exaggeration to claim that the results of the present study reverse the prevailing impression that expectation formation is characterized by a low degree of rationality, they unmistakably call for corrections. Based on the interrelations of only a few key operating variables, the following findings stand out:

1. Theoretical analysis suggests that intended inventory investment depends on expected change in sales, anticipated price changes, and an appraisal of the current position of stocks. None of these influences can be measured perfectly with the data available. Inventories and sales are measured in current rather than constant dollars, and while such data are adequate to investigate the existence of an intended inventory–sales ratio, they may exaggerate the covariation of intended inventories and anticipated prices. Moreover, data on anticipated buying prices are unavailable for manufacturers, so appeal must be had to the close covariation of anticipated buying and selling prices found in other studies. Finally, the measure of the current position of stocks is indirect and requires interpretation. Yet the evidence for rationality in inventory planning remains. The assumption that businessmen plan to vary their inventories in step with anticipated changes in sales and prices provides a better explanation of the intentions they report than a more or less direct projection of past experience.

2. Theory suggests that selling-price expectations will vary in step with sales anticipations or related variables and with buying-price anticipations. Sales anticipations (for traders) or recent new order experience (for manufacturers) provide a regular, and frequently significant, determinant of selling-price expectations. And where they can be measured roughly (for traders), buying-price anticipations appear to be a sometimes influential determinant. There is also some evidence that unwanted inventories may occasionally compel a downward adjustment of price anticipations. But a far more consistent finding is that price anticipations are sluggish, depending strongly on the immediate past trend of change. None of these findings contradicts the presumption of rationality, nor can a simple scheme of extrapolation explain current price expectations so well. By the test of multiple correlations, the account of the formation of selling-price expectations is better than that for any other expectational variable, although because of their inertia they are easiest to explain.

3. The explanation of sales anticipations is least successful chiefly because of a lack of evidence on the appropriate demand determinants. For traders, a simple learning model that runs entirely in terms of past sales experience or anticipations has to be used. For manufacturers, there is evidence on price intentions and realized new orders but none on how businessmen view the general business situation or conditions in their own industries. Thus the present paper does not materially advance the explanation of sales anticipations beyond what can be accomplished by a simple extrapolation of past experience. This does not imply that sales anticipations are merely naïve projections, for results obtained by that

method are not good either. Since our interest focuses chiefly on inventory intentions, the weakness of the analysis of sales anticipations is not serious. It hampers statistical techniques which attempt to take account of the stochastic interdependence of business expectations, but it is irrelevant to the application of single-equation least squares to the recursive structures of expectation formation, on which chief reliance was placed.

Suggestive Contrasts in the Findings. Less conclusively established by the models are certain contrasts in business behavior or anticipations:

1. In the formation of price intentions, durable goods manufacturers appear to give more weight to new order experience than do nondurables manufacturers. This reasonable result is clearest for large firms, but is not confirmed by the analysis of the unweighted data.

2. The general impression that two quarters is long enough for manufacturers to achieve a desired reversal of inventory policy may not hold in a period such as that following the start of the Korean war. More fully developed models of expectation formation will need to take account of factors limiting production in boom times.

3. Wholesalers and retailers appear to differ notably in the flexibility of inventory control. The evidence suggests that retailers often cannot reverse unwanted inventory accumulation within two quarters. However, such inertia may characterize only the largest firms, since the evidence for the contrast is considerably weaker or absent altogether when unweighted data are used.

Open Questions. Among the issues raised in this paper, but still open questions, three deserve mention:

1. The results fail to establish that new orders are a determinant of manufacturers' inventory intentions. This result would be acceptable if those answering the survey reported on finished inventory only, but the probability is that purchased materials are also considered. The failure appears to be a consequence of the extreme collinearity of new order experience and sales anticipations, both of which figure in the general equation for inventory intentions, a collinearity exaggerated by the recursive application of least squares. What is required is more data to reduce the standard errors of coefficient estimates. Beyond this, perhaps further research will yield techniques of working with diffusion data by which collinearity can be reduced. Less drastic aggregation is probably a first step, perhaps along the lines of vector techniques.

2. The effort to illuminate indirectly the equilibrium function implicit in business planning suggests that more appropriate techniques of estimation might yield conclusive findings. Given the uncertainty attending business expectations and the inevitability of disappointments, neither

reported plans nor realized behavior can be interpreted as characterizing the equilibrium of the firm. In principle one could ask questions about such positions directly. Short of this, we must consult indirect evidence reflecting desired positions in the light of what has happened *ex post*. The approach suggested in the discussion of the equilibrium function is an avenue we might use.

3. Since reports on expected and realized changes in inventories, sales, and new orders run in value terms, they have a common element, which undoubtedly contributes to the collinearity found in the Dun and Bradstreet data and confuses the interpretation to be put on certain of the coefficients found in the models. The price factor also reduces the autonomy of the relationships found, making them dependent in some measure on a particular postwar history of chronic mild inflation. The most natural way around the difficulty is to ask businessmen for reports on changes in physical quantities. But such data are not readily obtainable, especially for multiple-product firms; and the increased difficulty of answering might cause top management to delegate the questions to less informed or responsible personnel. The choice, then, is between a subordinate's judgment of an optimum question and management's judgment of a less appropriate one. Particularly for the purpose of studying entrepreneurial expectations, the correct choice is not an obvious one.

COMMENT

ROBERT EISNER, Northwestern University

Millard Hastay concerns himself in this rich and admirable paper with the search for functions which generate expectations. He asks whether "business expectations disclose self-consistent relations between prospects and plans and are . . . meaningfully related to past experience." The skill with which he has marshaled his data and the high technical quality of his statistical analysis should be so apparent that I may perhaps be forgiven in confining myself to offering certain critical comments.

Hastay's basic data are "diffusion indexes," from the second quarter of 1950 to the third quarter of 1957, of the Dun and Bradstreet quarterly surveys of the expectations of individual firms. His underlying variables are actual and expected changes in the volume of sales, level of inventories, and level of selling prices, and, for manufacturers only, new orders received. Hastay fits linear equations designed to explain or predict, for firms in four broad industrial groups, the diffusion indexes of expected changes in the current dollar value of inventories and sales and in selling prices. His estimates are based on least-squares procedures, both direct and sequential, on the ground that his models are either exactly identified or recursive.

First I shall concentrate on the economic content and value of Hastay's model. Hastay's focus is inventory investment—the inventory adjustments businessmen intend to make and the factors that shape these intentions. Expecting the diffusion of expected inventories to be positively related to sales (because of the acceleration principle), positively related to prices (because of motives of "speculation" and "risk aversion"), and negatively related to the difference between past actual and anticipated inventories (because of the stock appraisal and plan-adjusting process), Hastay gets, in fact, a number of "significant" positive coefficients for expected sales and for expected selling prices. But he gets very poor results with his stock appraisal variable and is not able to improve matters significantly by introducing a stock disequilibrium variable in its place.

I would question Hastay's formulation of the acceleration principle for inventories. As Abramovitz has emphasized, the role of the acceleration principle in explaining inventory investment is a subtle one, differing with each type of inventory. Thus while we may expect stocks of *goods in process* to be related positively to output and, probably, to sales, *stocks of finished goods* probably are negatively related to sales. Clearly the first effect of an increase in sales is to drain down existing stocks of finished goods. And as output increases, there will also be a draining down of liquid raw materials (the finished goods of suppliers) until production can be increased. Such an "anti-acceleration" effect is likely to be especially important for expectations data. For one salient fact emerging from most of the empirical investigations (explained by theoretical models of the planning process such as those of Modigliani) is that businessmen are conservative (if not reactionary) in their expressed expectations and slow to act upon expectations, which are necessarily uncertain. My own interviews with businessmen confirm that a businessman's most typical reaction to even an actual change in sales is to wait and see if it is temporary or permanent. Indeed the carrying of inventories is designed in large part to afford flexibility and allow compartmentalization of the planning horizon and delay of final decisions and action until reasonably definite information is available. Inventories give the firm time to change its rate of production if the expected change in sales actually occurs. Under this interpretation, a businessman expecting an increase in the physical volume of sales must also expect a drop in the physical volume of inventories. Hastay regards inventory expectations as *intentions* expressing changed production plans. To me such expectations are *anticipations* based upon the current production plan and anticipations of future sales which have not generally affected current production plans.

Hastay's positive regression coefficients might appear to confirm his view of inventory expectations, but because of the nature of the underlying data I am not convinced by his findings. The data out of which Hastay's variables are constructed are not physical volumes but dollar volumes.

The significance of this fact is that price is a factor in the expression of expectations, a factor unrelated to the acceleration principle. During most of the period under review, businessmen had reason to anticipate price increases. Since when prices rise, almost everything measured in dollars also rises, they also anticipated a dollar rise in inventories and sales. This fact largely accounts for the substantial positive entries shown by the diffusion indexes and produces the marked collinearity which Hastay noted frequently and thus vitiates the reliability of most of Hastay's estimates of regression coefficients. In view of the role played by price changes, it is interesting that Hastay's coefficients of "expected" on "actual, lagged" sales for manufacturers are persistently negative (see, for example, his Tables 3 and 4). This is perhaps another confirmation (against heavy odds) of the regressive or reactionary character of short-run expectations.

The anomaly of not correcting for price changes in models conceived in real terms also accounts for several of the inconsistencies and failures of Hastay's variables. For example, Hastay suggests that "a rise in expected buying prices should depress sales anticipations" but he fails generally to verify this conclusion. Surely, though, if a rise in buying prices is associated with a general price rise, the physical volume of sales would have to fall sufficiently to outweigh the effect of an increase in selling price for such a result to be obtained.

Hastay's paper also raises some statistical issues. His data are not the economic variables with which we are ultimately concerned but diffusion indexes, an unknown and possibly changing nonlinear transformation of relevant economic variables. I have suggested elsewhere that McGraw–Hill data on sales expectations indicate that the magnitudes of expected changes, as distinct from their direction, show surprisingly little relation to the magnitudes of actual changes and to other variables, thus confirming the relative usefulness of diffusion indexes for some purposes. I certainly do not wish to be construed as dismissing recent ingenious use of diffusion data. Theil, Hastay himself, and others have contributed elsewhere rigorous and perceptive analyses of some of their statistical properties and potentialities and requirements for their use. But what is the usefulness of linear regression coefficients relating one diffusion index to another? Even if I am told, as in Hastay's Table 5, that a 10 per cent increase in the difference between the diffusion indexes of actual and expected sales, lagged, is associated with an increase of 6.9 per cent in the diffusion index of expected sales, I do not know anything about the regression coefficients for the data underlying these indexes.

There is, I submit, a difficulty even more basic than the fact that Hastay gives us no parameters of the transformation of economic data into diffusion indexes, for there can hardly be a unique transformation for all variables and all periods. In the example just mentioned, the diffusion index for actual sales—involving presumably almost exclusively positive and negative entries—and the diffusion index for expected sales—a variable with a large "same" category—are not even remotely similar transformations of the underlying data. Yet the two are combined in one variable for which a regression coefficient is calculated. A similar combination is involved in the "inventory, actual minus expected, lagged" variable.

An associated issue relates to the meaning of standard errors of regression coefficients for small samples in which there is little or no evidence that the desired conditions for least-squares estimates are met. There is no evidence here that the variables are normally distributed or that error terms are independent, either within or between equations. Indeed, the nature of the serially correlated series of historical price changes leads me to expect high serial correlation among all of the variables and the error terms. All least-square regression coefficients relating to data extending back to 1949 would be dominated by the extreme values of the first few quarters of the Korean war (see Hastay's Charts 7 through 10). In series of twenty-seven items it will not take many pairs of extreme values to give regression coefficients that are pleasing ratios of their own "standard errors."

Finally, the overlapping and lack of independent identity of the variables contributes to the collinearity and difficulty of making reliable estimates of parameters. One special case involves the use in the sales expectations equations of one independent variable defined as "sales, actual minus expected, lagged" and another defined as "sales, actual, lagged." Actual dollar sales change for the same period thus appears as one variable and as a (probably major) element of another. More generally, Hastay relates variables that are half identical. For example, if businessmen were interviewed in July, one of the sales expectations equations would relate the change in dollar value of sales expected from the fourth quarter of the previous year to the fourth quarter of the current year with the change that occurred from the second quarter of the previous year to the second quarter of the current year. The change in actual sales from the fourth quarter of the previous year to the second quarter of the current year is thus a common element in both variables. On this count alone it would be hard again to avoid positive coefficients. This common element in variables appears also in actual, lagged, and expected inventories in the inventory expectations equations, and in actual, lagged, and expected prices in the price expectations equation. It is probably present too, indirectly, in the relation between lagged new orders and sales expectations, as well as in all relations among current expectations variables where the actual price changes of the previous six months are a common factor. This raises the serious and basic question whether positive relationships among Hastay's "expectations" variables reflect more than this common element of already realized behavior.

REPLY BY MR. HASTAY

Robert Eisner's comments on my paper are a vivid demonstration of the power of negative thinking. In trying to nail down his objections in brief compass, I feel like the vulture gnawing at Prometheus' liver—the job is never finished. To set limits to the task, I shall sort his criticisms into two categories: the substantive, which I shall discuss in detail, and the methodological, which I shall deal with more briefly. Under the first heading are (1) his objection to the accelerator mechanism in my inventory model, (2) his proposal of an alternative model, and (3) his denial of the suitability of diffusion data based on current dollar magnitudes to investigate my hypothesis. Under the second heading are (1) his questions about the nature of diffusion data, (2) his denial of the formal applicability of my statistical procedures, and (3) his contention that the relationships I find among diffusion data are largely spurious.

METHODOLOGICAL CRITICISMS

Now, plainly, if the methodological criticisms are valid, the substantive ones are irrelevant or inadmissible. But the demonstration that they are not valid rests largely on earlier work cited in my paper and cannot be recapitulated here. I shall therefore restrict my remarks to a few considerations designed to assure that methodological issues will be considered responsibly.

Nature of Diffusion Data. Several basic investigations, both theoretical and empirical, have dealt with the relation between diffusion data and more familiar economic aggregates. These suggest that, to a first approximation, diffusion data vary stochastically as the first difference in a corresponding aggregate, for example, that the diffusion of retailers' sales varies as the rate of change in aggregate retail sales. Sufficient conditions for this relation to hold are rather stringent, but I have published results, and have made unpublished tests, suggesting that they are tolerably well fulfilled for the Dun and Bradstreet data (see the references in footnote 5 of my paper).

Applicability of Statistical Procedures. Considering the origin of diffusion data in first differences of microvariables, it should not come as a great surprise that the *stochastic* aspect of the relation of diffusion data and rates of change involves apparently independent disturbances. But this fact, together with the foregoing, suffices to establish that diffusion models of economic behavior based on analogy with certain standard rate-of-change models will yield simultaneous, linear, stochastic difference-equations with serially independent disturbances. To such models, when properly identified, least-squares procedures are applicable. In denying this, in suggesting that the disturbances must be Gaussian, in confusing serial correlation with multicollinearity, in suggesting that a parametrically unique transformation of microvariables into diffusion data is necessary for all variables and all periods, Eisner seriously misrepresents the methodological issues of dealing with diffusion data. Moreover, in rejecting results based on small samples, Eisner misses the point of the systematic replication of experimental models presented in my paper, the aim of which is precisely to reinforce judgment from small samples. I cannot take the reader to a significance table in an elementary textbook, but the statistical world had Tchebycheff before it had Karl Pearson, and people made inductive inferences before they had either. Regrettably, the evidence leaves room for difference of opinion; but what it calls for is hard thought, not a throwing up of hands.

Spuriousness of Diffusion Relations. But what about the point that Dun and Bradstreet expected and realized diffusion data overlap in time and thus contain a common element of realized experience? This is admittedly a source of part correlation, or what Karl Pearson labeled pejoratively "spurious" correlation. If none of his other criticisms hold up, Eisner suggests that this property alone may account for all or most of the apparent relationships I have exhibited. I submit that this objection is insupportable in the light of my paper of September 1954, where I demonstrate the independent predictive value of the part of expected diffusion data that is *not* included in overlapping data on realized diffusion. Moreover, the expected magnitude of the "spurious" correlation implied is, on any realistic assumptions, significantly less than any of the correlations found. I agree, however, that it would be useful to be able to break down the Dun and Bradstreet diffusion data into nonoverlapping segments; and a beginning has been made with a special question on manufacturers' new orders recently adjoined to the Dun and Bradstreet questionnaires. Since the resulting two-quarter diffusion series are potentially affected by seasonal variations, it is not yet possible to present empirical estimates of the magnitude of part correlation between expected and realized diffusion as currently compiled by Dun and Bradstreet, but a provisional examination of the data bears out my earlier findings that the purely forward-looking part of Dun and Bradstreet expectations is significantly and substantially correlated with subsequent realized behavior. (See *Basic Research and the Analysis of Current Business Conditions*, 36th Annual Report, National Bureau of Economic Research, May 1956, pp. 29-31.)

SUBSTANTIVE CRITICISMS

Acceleration Principle. Eisner contends that the evidence is all against a model of inventory expectations based on an accelerator mechanism, even when modified by allowance for the current position of stocks. The evidence cited is (1) Abramovitz' monograph on inventories, (2) the claim that Dun and Bradstreet inventory expectations cannot be treated as "intentions," or goals of action, but only as supine "anticipations" of

144

the outcome of impersonal market forces, and (3) the fact that business-men are conservative in their diagnoses of the future.

1. Now, the appeal to Abramovitz is beside the point. I deal with inventory plans, he with realized inventories. What actually happens to inventory–sales ratios is irrelevant in view of the widely attested result that businessmen's *desired* inventory adjustments are frequently unrealized because of business-cycle developments. Eisner would have us disregard this evidence and assume that the realized behavior of inventories is what businessmen plan—surely a novel view of the matter, but one for which he will find little support in Abramovitz.

In short, Eisner's is a model of realized inventory behavior masquer-ading as a model of expectations. Producers of finished staples may, in fact, be able to tolerate substantial departures from planned inventory goals; but it is not very plausible to assume that they cooperate with the inevitable to the extent of planning things that way.

2. Eisner, however, contends that Dun and Bradstreet expectations have nothing to do with plans or intentions, and it must be admitted that the question whether they do is a reasonable one. For periods of a few weeks to a month, it is probable that inventory expectations are, in fact, anticipations about changes over which the firm has little deliberate control. But over six months, for firms whose average stocks are three months' sales, the element of deliberate intention must be dominant in inventory expectations, and it is these which are reported in the Dun and Bradstreet surveys.

3. Nothing in this view of expectations, or in my models, is hostile to the idea that businessmen are conservative in their inventory planning. I expect them to underrespond to uncertain data by the test of what would seem right in retrospect, though I do not follow Eisner in expecting them not to respond at all. But the question of conservatism cannot be answered by expectational models alone. It is a matter not only of the signs of coefficients, but also of their size; and questions of size require investiga-tions along the lines of my "equilibrium hypothesis."

Diffusion in Current Dollars and Inventory Planning. It will be con-venient to discuss the second and third of Eisner's substantive criticisms together. Eisner contends that the acceleration principle does not apply to current dollar magnitudes, and that the assumption that it does masks my failure to see that an alternative inventory model really characterizes businessmen's expectations. I propose to upset both contentions.

1. My defense of an acceleration model for dollar magnitudes rests on the interesting work of Henri Theil and his associates, which shows that actual and expected selling prices are largely determined by actual and expected buying prices, respectively, for the same period, and that little

else in the way of significant determinants of selling prices is to be found in diffusion data (see the reference in footnote 6 of my paper). Let us assume, therefore:

  a. That equilibrium physical stocks, H, are intended to be a constant proportion, β, of the physical quantity of sales, Q
  b. That finished stocks are priced at market
  c. That raw materials and finished goods prices vary in step.

By the simple acceleration principle we have

(1) $$H = \beta Q$$

(2) $$H_1 - H_0 = \beta(Q_1 - Q_0)$$

Let price in time 0 be denoted P; in time 1, $P + \Delta P$. Then in dollar terms $H_1 - H_0$ becomes

(3) $$(P + \Delta P)H_1 - PH_0 = P(H_1 - H_0) + (\Delta P)H_1$$

and $Q_1 - Q_0$ becomes

(4) $$(P + \Delta P)Q_1 - PQ_0 = P(Q_1 - Q_0) + (\Delta P)Q_1$$

But if the acceleration principle applies, we have

$$P(H_1 - H_0) = \beta P(Q_1 - Q_0), \text{ with } P \text{ a common multiplier}$$
$$(\Delta P)H_1 = \beta(\Delta P)Q_1, \text{ with } \Delta P \text{ a common multiplier.}$$

Adding gives

(5) $$P(H_1 - H_0) + (\Delta P)H_1 = \beta[P(Q_1 - Q_0) + (\Delta P)Q_1]$$

or

(6) $$(P + \Delta P)H_1 - PH_0 = \beta[(P + \Delta P)Q_1 - PQ_0]$$

i.e. the acceleration principle applies to dollar magnitudes for finished inventories. A similar argument holds for purchased materials in view of the close relation of buying and selling prices.

2. Consider the alternative model proposed by Eisner, viz. inventories a passive shock absorber of sales variations. In physical terms, this can be written

(7) $$H_1 - H_0 = -1(Q_1 - Q_0)$$

where equilibrium stocks are meant to satisfy $H = \beta Q$. In dollar terms, we have to re-evaluate equation 3. Employing the equilibrium assumption and (7), we can write

(8) $$H_1 = H_0 + (H_1 - H_0) = \beta Q_0 - (Q_1 - Q_0)$$

thus

(9) $$(\Delta P)H_1 = (\Delta P)\beta Q_0 - (\Delta P)(Q_1 - Q_0)$$

146

From (7)

(10) $$P(H_1 - H_0) = -P(Q_1 - Q_0)$$

Adding (9) and (10) gives

(11) $$(P + \Delta P)H_1 - PH_0 = -(P + \Delta P)(\Delta Q) + (\Delta P)\beta Q_0$$

Now, Eisner contends that the negative shock-absorber relation (7) becomes a *positive* relation in the form (11). But let us recall that, in terms of the questions asked by Dun and Bradstreet, the survey variables are based on first differences in four-quarter moving averages *at annual rates*. Thus the flow variables Q are of annual magnitude and the accelerator may be supposed to average about $\beta = 1/4$; that is, average stocks about three months supply. Then for "Eisner's effect" to be overshadowed by price effects, we must have

$$(\Delta P)\beta Q_0 > P_1(\Delta Q)$$

that is,

$$(\Delta P)/P_1 > (1\Delta/\beta)[(Q)/Q_0]$$

which requires that price change must be $1/\beta = 4$ times quantity change. In other words,

$$\text{Amplitude ratio} = \frac{\Delta P}{P} : \frac{\Delta Q}{Q} = 4:1$$

But, generally speaking, this degree of price flexibility does not exist in manufacturing and trade. I conclude, therefore, that Eisner's alternative inventory model implies *negative* acceleration coefficients in the Dun and Bradstreet data except under assumptions known to be contrary to fact.

To summarize, we see that:

a. If the acceleration principle applies to physical quantities, it will hold as between dollar magnitudes as well.
b. If Eisner's counterprinciple applies—that is, ΔH is the inverse of ΔQ—then negative coefficients should hold even between dollar magnitudes unless (i) average stocks are a large fraction of one year's supply, or (ii) price flexibility is very great.

3. On one point, Eisner's observations on the price factor in Dun and Bradstreet inventory and sales data must be accepted: it does contribute to the multicollinearity that afflicts certain of the models involving buying and selling prices. It does not, however, "vitiate" the reliability of my estimates of regression coefficients; it increases their standard errors in a way that is fully registered in their reported sizes. The more important point is one that I make in my summary: it reduces the autonomy of my expectational relations, making them in some degree dependent on a particular history of chronic postwar inflation. But some coefficients are more affected by this loss of autonomy than others, the acceleration

coefficients least of all. I submit, therefore, that Eisner's case against my acceleration hypothesis falls to the ground.

Relation of Buying-Price and Sales Anticipations. A final point is interesting as a matter of tactics. Eisner quotes me as saying that "a rise in expected buying prices should depress sales anticipations." He does *not* quote my next sentence: "But since price rises are frequently associated with improved business, the final impact may be negligible or even positive." My expectation of an initial depressive effect of expected buying-price increases on anticipated sales revenue is based on the belief that most business firms conceive their demand curves to be elastic; this is why they meet competition. It would imply negative marginal revenue if they did not so believe. And without any direct experience of the sort, it is hard to see why they should imagine total revenue for the industry to go up in consequence of a cost-induced rise in prices—unless in a general expansion of the volume of business, which is recognized in my unquoted sentence.

The positive relations generally found between expected buying prices and anticipated sales is thus not unanticipated in my comments, which in fact cover Eisner's explanation as a special case of increasing aggregate demand.

Consumer Attitudes: Their Influence and Forecasting Value

EVA MUELLER
SURVEY RESEARCH CENTER, UNIVERSITY OF MICHIGAN

That measurements of consumer attitudes can help to explain and predict changes in discretionary consumer spending which cannot be accounted for by income changes is a belief basic to the work of the Economic Behavior Program of the Survey Research Center.[1] Psychological factors are frequently mentioned by writers on the business cycle, but usually as influencing primarily investment decisions. In regard to consumer spending the state of optimism and confidence has at best been treated as a secondary factor which may reinforce prevailing trends. The proposition that consumer attitudes may at times exert an autonomous influence on consumer spending clearly assigns to them a greater importance than they have traditionally enjoyed.

Since the war we have experienced short-run variations in consumer spending which cannot be explained by changes in income. For example, in 1951 discretionary consumer spending declined while personal incomes were rising. In the winter of 1954-55 consumer spending increased more sharply than did personal incomes. In late 1957, many analysts again referred to the consumer as the big question mark in the economic outlook. The possibility that variations in consumer confidence may help to account for fluctuations in consumer spending therefore has important implications for economic forecasting.

Empirical tests of the role of attitudes can be made at two levels: the aggregative and the individual. "Aggregative" tests start with the construction of time series based on the expressed attitudes of representative samples of American consumers at successive time points. These can then be checked against time series for total consumer purchases or purchases of specific goods. For example, if people were more optimistic at one date

NOTE: The author is greatly indebted to George Katona for his advice throughout all phases of this study as well as for many helpful ideas. She also wishes to thank James N. Morgan who made a number of valuable suggestions and Robert Hsieh who participated in the statistical analysis. The collection of the re-interview data as well as the analysis reported here were made possible by a grant from the Ford Foundation to the Survey Research Center for studies of the "Origin and Effects of Economic Attitudes."

[1] "Discretionary" consumer spending denotes spending on such items as consumer durable goods, vacations, and luxuries. Expenditures may be discretionary because they are for nonessentials or because they are postponable (i.e. replacement of durable goods). Relevant to the analysis of fluctuations in discretionary spending are attitudes and opinions responsive to short-run changes in the economic environment rather than personality traits or attitudes evolved over a long time.

149

than at another, were consumer purchases higher relative to disposable income after the first than after the second? "Individual" or "re-interview" tests require interviewing the same people at least twice. They tell us whether individuals who were optimistic were more likely to make major expenditures in the subsequent period than those who were pessimistic.

Evidence derived from the aggregative test of the relation between consumer attitudes and fluctuations in consumer spending was presented in several previous publications.[2] The analysis there, though not quantitative in a rigorous statistical sense, indicated that consumers' attitudes and their rate of discretionary spending exhibited similar movements over time, with changes in attitudes sometimes leading changes in spending. Here I shall first attempt to carry the aggregative test one step further by means of time-series correlations between consumer attitudes and spending on durable goods. Most of the data come from the periodic surveys which have been conducted by the Survey Research Center several times a year since 1951. Data for early 1953 and early 1954 come from the annual Survey of Consumer Finances.

The second and third sections present data on the relation between consumer attitudes and spending based on re-interviews. An extensive panel study was begun by the Survey Research Center in June 1954, when a representative cross section of 1,150 urban families in all parts of the country was interviewed. Additional interviews were scheduled in December 1954, June 1955, December 1955, and February 1957. Four complete interviews were obtained from 800 families during the first year and a half, and the fifth from about 700 families.[3]

In the last section the results of both tests are compared and evaluated.

Two attitude measures are related to consumer purchases in this paper. The primary measure is an index of consumer attitudes constructed experimentally from people's answers to questions on their:

1. Economic status relative to the preceding year
2. Personal financial expectations for the coming year
3. One-year expectations regarding business conditions
4. Long-range economic outlook
5. Appraisal of buying conditions for household goods and clothing
6. Price expectations.

Tentatively, the six components of the index have been given equal weight.[4]

[2] See George Katona and Eva Mueller, *Consumer Attitudes and Demand, 1950-52* (1953) and *Consumer Expectations, 1953-56* (1956), both published by the Survey Research Center, University of Michigan. The most recent data are contained in periodic reports by the Foundation for Research on Human Behavior, Ann Arbor, Michigan.

[3] See Marion Gross Sobol, "Panel Mortality and Panel Bias," *Journal of the American Statistical Association*, March 1959, pp. 52–68.

[4] An index including the six components has been computed and published by the Survey Research Center for the past four years (described in detail in Katona and Mueller, *Consumer Expectations, 1953-56*, pp. 91-105). Based on six questions, and scoring optimistic replies as 2, medium (same, pro-con) replies as 1, and pessimistic replies as 0,

The second measure is a newly constructed index of buying intentions. In the panel study, data were collected on expressed intentions to buy houses, cars, durable household goods, to make home improvements or repairs, and to make major nonhousehold expenditures. Only plans which families thought had at least a fair chance of fulfillment were considered. Each family was scored 0 = no such expenditure plan, 1 = any one type of plan, or 2 = two or more categories of plans. The index of buying intentions indicates willingness to spend rather than predicts specific purchases. It was used for the re-interview test but not for the aggregative test, since only some of the necessary data were available for all dates. For the aggregative test, a buying plans index referring only to car and house purchases was used, an index used in recent years together with the index of consumer attitudes to obtain a general evaluation of consumer sentiment. In the combined index, consumer attitudes have a weight of three-quarters, buying intentions one-quarter, as of the base period, November 1952.

Although the two indexes are still in a developmental stage, current tests may provide useful guides for future research. However, it should be noted that both the theory that consumer attitudes affect spending and a particular measure of attitudes are being tested here. If the results are disappointing, the question will arise whether theory or measure is at fault.

The Aggregative Test

Chart 1 shows durable goods sales, disposable personal income (both deflated Department of Commerce series), and consumer attitudes including and excluding buying intentions for November 1952–December 1957. Fluctuations in the index of consumer attitudes resemble fluctuations in durable goods spending. Changes in disposable income are somewhat less consistent in this respect. Movements of the buying-intentions component of the attitude index (see Appendix Table A-2) correspond only in part to movements in durable goods sales, possibly because buying intentions, which here cover only cars and houses, are subject to some seasonal variations. For the time being there are too few observations to make a seasonal correction.

With time-series correlation I shall first compare the effectiveness of attitude data and disposable income as advance indicators of spending on consumer durables. The following simple model must suffice because of the few observations:[5]

$$(1) \qquad D = a(A) + b(Y_{-1}) + c$$

---

a score was computed for each respondent from his six answers. The scores can range from 0 for extreme pessimism to 12 for extreme optimism. People who repeatedly gave "I don't know" or similar answers were excluded from the present analysis. The remaining expressions of uncertainty were scored 1.

[5] The computation of such regressions at this early stage was prompted by Arthur M. Okun's paper in this volume.

where D = durable goods spending in the two quarters following the quarter in which the attitude survey was made (in current dollars)

A = a measure of consumer attitudes

Y_{-1} = disposable personal income in the two quarters preceding the quarter in which the attitude survey was made (in current dollars).

Past income is used since only data available at the time of the forecast

CHART I

Durable Goods Sales, Personal Income, and Consumer Attitudes, 1952–1957

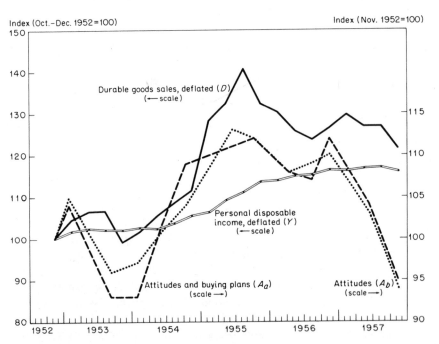

can legitimately be employed. Conceivably this treatment gives the attitudes an advantage, since they are closer in time than past income to the dependent variable. Therefore an alternative equation can be formulated:

(2) $D = a(A) + b(Y) + c$

where Y = disposable personal income in the two quarters following the quarter in which the atitude survey was made (in current dollars), that is, in the same period for which durable goods spending is being predicted.

This is obviously not a forecasting equation, but it may throw light on the relative influence of attitudes and income on spending.

TABLE 1

Correlations between Levels of Spending on Durable Goods, Three Measures of Consumer Attitudes, and Income, November 1952–November 1956

| | REGRESSION COEFFICIENTS | | | | | PROPORTION OF VARIANCE EXPLAINED[a] | |
| Measures of Attitudes | | | Income | | | Unadjusted Deflated | |
Attitudes and Plans to Buy (A_a)	Attitudes (A_b)	Plans to Buy (A_e)	Past (Y_{-1})	Current (Y)	Constant	Data	Data[b] $(\bar{R}^2$ or $\bar{r}^2)$
			EQUATION 1				
$D=$ +0.30 (0.07)			+0.05 (0.03)		−12.54	0.84	0.82
$D=$	+0.41 (0.06)		+0.03 (0.02)		−18.86	.91	
$D=$		+0.08 (0.05)	+0.10 (0.04)		−1.50	.57	
$D=$			+0.13 (0.04)		−0.85	.50	.35
			EQUATION 2				
$D=$ +0.25 (0.06)				+0.07 (0.02)	−11.55	.88	.86
$D=$	+0.36 (0.07)			+0.04 (0.02)	−17.24	.93	
$D=$		+0.06 (0.04)		+0.11 (0.03)	−3.90	.75	
$D=$				+0.13 (0.03)	−3.20	.70	.71

In this and the following tables, the figures in parentheses are the estimated standard errors of the coefficients (needless to say, they do not provide a valid significance test).

a Corrected for degrees of freedom in each case.

b Based on deflated data adjusted for changes in the number of families. Source: Appendix Table A-2.

Table 1 summarizes the results of the test, using eleven observations from November 1952 to November 1956. (Observations for June and December 1957 had to be omitted, since durable goods expenditures in the following half-year were not yet available.) For each equation three alternative attitude measures are tested: the combined index of consumer attitudes and buying intentions and its two components. Ideally, we should test attitudes and buying intentions in the same question as separate independent variables, but with only eleven observations, testing the three measures alternatively is preferable. The data are presented merely for descriptive purposes. They cannot be subjected to a valid significance test, since the statistical requirement that all observations must be independent from one another is clearly not met. Moreover, the period of observation is short; the consistency of the relation between attitudes and

CHART 2
Actual and Estimated Durable Goods Sales, 1952–1957

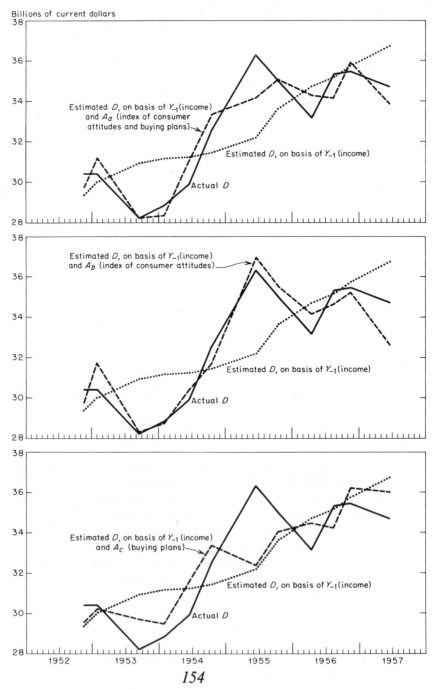

Billions of current dollars

Estimated D, on basis of Y_{-1}(income) and A_a (index of consumer attitudes and buying plans)

Estimated D, on basis of Y_{-1} (income)

Actual D

Estimated D, on basis of Y_{-1}(income) and A_b (index of consumer attitudes)

Estimated D, on basis of Y_{-1}(income)

Actual D

Estimated D, on basis of Y_{-1} (income) and A_c (buying plans)

Estimated D, on basis of Y_{-1} (income)

Actual D

154

spending at the aggregative level can be evaluated only as additional observations become available in the future.

Table 1 presents the regression coefficients for each of the six equations and compares the percentage of the variance explained by income alone and by income jointly with each of the three attitudinal measures. Chart 2 shows actual expenditures on consumer durables in the half-years following the survey dates, compared with the expenditures that would have been predicted (1) solely on the basis of income in the past half-year, and (2) on the basis of past income and each alternative measure of consumer attitudes.

For the period under study, income together with attitudes and plans to buy or with attitudes alone explained a substantial part of the variance in durable goods spending. Forecasts based on the latest available figure for disposable income together with consumer attitudes would have done substantially better than forecasts based on income alone. When future income (Y) is substituted for past income (Y_{-1}) the attitudes variables still contribute to the explanation of D. However, one cannot determine the net contribution of A relative to that of Y_{-1} or Y, since both are highly correlated with A. The results are substantially the same, whether deflated or current dollar figures are used.

Because of the small number of observations, we cannot be sure which measure of A is most closely related to D. In particular, we cannot decide whether the index of consumer attitudes has a greater explanatory value with or without buying plans, since both explain a very high proportion of the total variance, although the buying-plans component taken alone clearly contributed less to the explanation of durable goods spending than the attitudes component.

Another equation can be formulated expressing the notion that *changes* in attitudes should predict *changes* in spending, other factors being equal:

$$(3) \qquad \Delta D = a(\Delta A) + b(\Delta Y_{-1}) + c$$

where ΔD = the change in durable goods spending in the two quarters following the quarter in which the attitude survey was made

ΔA = the change in attitudes since the previous survey

ΔY_{-1} = the change in income between the quarter in which the survey was made and the previous two quarters (in current dollars).

Again, ΔY (change in income in the half-year following the survey as compared with the previous half-year) may be substituted for ΔY_{-1}:

$$(4) \qquad \Delta D = a(\Delta A) + b(\Delta Y) + c$$

This formulation may have the advantage that the few observations are more independent of one another than in the first test. Its disadvantage

TABLE 2

Correlations between Changes in Spending on Durable Goods, Three Measures of
Consumer Attitudes, and Income, November 1952–November 1956

	REGRESSION COEFFICIENTS						PROPORTION OF VARIANCE[a] EXPLAINED ($\bar{R}^2$ or $\bar{r}^2$)
	Changes in:						
	Measures of Attitudes			Income			
	Attitudes and Plans to Buy ($\triangle A_a$)	Attitudes ($\triangle A_b$)	Plans to Buy ($\triangle A_c$)	Past ($\triangle Y_{-1}$)	Current ($\triangle Y$)	Constant	
			EQUATION 3				
$\triangle D=$	+0.28 (0.10)				+0.12 (0.14)	−0.72	0.45
$\triangle D=$		+0.32 (0.14)			+0.05 (0.16)	−0.29	.35
$\triangle D=$			+0.06 (0.04)		+0.12 (0.19)	−0.50	.00
$\triangle D=$					+0.08 (0.20)	−0.09	.00
			EQUATION 4				
$\triangle D=$	+0.26 (0.10)			+0.08 (0.14		−0.46	.42
$\triangle D=$		+0.33 (0.16)		−0.01 (0.17)		−0.11	.30
$\triangle D=$			+0.06 (0.04)	+0.18 (0.18)		−0.79	.07
$\triangle D=$				0.15 (0.19)		−0.50	.00

[a] Corrected for degrees of freedom in each case.
Source: Appendix Table A-3.

is that it relies essentially on paired comparisons.[6] The results of the
second test are presented in Table 2. Neither short-run changes in income
nor changes in buying plans contribute to the explanation of changes in
consumer spending. This is true whether past or current income changes
are used in the equation. Changes in consumer attitudes explain 30 to 45
per cent of the variance in changes in consumer spending. Here the index
of consumer attitudes including buying intentions does somewhat better
than the index excluding buying intentions, although the differences are
minor considering the small number of observations.

A third test has been applied by Arthur Okun and James Tobin, which
may be formulated as follows:[7]

$$(5) \qquad D/Y = a(A) + b$$

[6] This point is discussed in the paper by Okun in this volume.
[7] Ibid., and James Tobin, "On the Predictive Value of Consumer Intentions and
Attitudes," The Review of Economics and Statistics, February 1959, pp. 1–11.

Although in the past, the Survey Research Center has compared graphically the trend of attitudes with the trend of the ratio of durable goods sales to income, I question the use of D/Y for testing the forecasting value of attitudes. The index of consumer attitudes is correlated not only with future durable goods spending but also with future income. Answers to several of the questions in the index may be influenced directly or indirectly by whether or not the breadwinner expects a raise in the next few months. Over short periods such expectations usually are quite accurate. Thus when the index rises, D and Y are likely to follow suit. If favorable attitudes have a positive effect of their own on spending, D/Y should also rise, but this fraction is difficult to predict in the short run since changes in D and Y will not be perfectly synchronized. This criticism is less relevant when A is represented by buying plans only. For the period under study the simple time-series correlation (adjusted for number of degrees of freedom) between income in the half-year following the survey and consumer attitudes alone is 0.76, between subsequent income and buying plans only 0.38. Equation 5 cannot do justice to these complicated interrelationships. Hence it is not surprising that both indexes of consumer attitudes explain only about 39 per cent of the variance in D/Y for the following half-year (i.e. $\bar{R}^2 = 0.39$); the buying-plans component alone explains about 22 per cent.[8]

The Re-interview Test

THE INFLUENCE OF ATTITUDES

Influence, unlike forecasting value, may be studied in retrospect. Thus we may take account of initial attitudes as well as of attitude change. We can also take account of *current* income. Buying plans can be disregarded, since they can hardly be thought of as having an independent influence on spending.[9]

The dependent variable here will be the *number* of major purchases of a family rather than the dollar amounts spent. This choice was made in part because number of purchases could be determined readily for half-year periods for a comprehensive list of items, while dollar figures were collected only on a calendar year basis and for fewer expenditures. However, it also has a conceptual basis. The state of consumer confidence may influence primarily the decision whether or not to go ahead with a desired expenditure rather than the amount spent.

[8] These figures differ slightly from those presented by Okun in this volume (his equation 3); this discrepancy is discussed in my comment on Okun's paper.

[9] Measures of buying plans represent an attempt to intercept the decision-making process for forecasting purposes. Presumably, they reflect the current influence of many variables relevant to spending decisions, including income and a wide range of attitudes. It has been suggested that it might be interesting to hold buying plans constant while examining the influence of income and attitudes on purchases. Such a test could only obscure the real influence of attitudes and income.

Included in the number of purchases are expenditures for cars, large household goods, additions or repairs to the home, and major non-household expenditures (for power lawnmowers, musical instruments, speedboats, typewriters, etc.). Excluded are medical and educational expenditures—which are largely nondiscretionary—and vacations—which are strongly seasonal and do not necessarily involve a major expense.[10] The major independent variables are income and the index of consumer attitudes (excluding buying intentions).

Our data cover three periods: June–December 1954, June–December 1955, and December 1955–February 1957. An analysis of some data for the first two has already been published.[11] Otherwise the material is presented here for the first time.

In the first period there was a pronounced divergence between income and attitude trends. The economy was recovering from a mild recession and disposable income in the second half of 1954 was only 2 per cent above the previous year. On the other hand, consumer attitudes as well as intentions to buy cars and houses already showed substantial improvement in June 1954, and attitudes reflected even greater optimism by December.[12]

By the second half of 1955 the divergence had narrowed. Income rose sharply in 1955, and in the second half of that year it was 8 per cent above 1954. Attitudes continued to improve during the first half of 1955, and in the second half showed stability at a very high level. Thus it would not be surprising if the relative influence of income and attitudes varied between the two periods.

During the third phase neither income nor attitudes changed precipitately, but some divergence was apparent. Between the last quarter of 1955 and the first quarter of 1957 personal disposable income rose by 7 per cent, but real income by only 4 per cent. Yet consumer attitudes grew decidedly less optimistic. However, independent nonpanel surveys conducted at three different times in 1956 and again in the spring of 1957 show that while some weakening occurred in 1956, the most pronounced deterioration took place in early 1957. Hence many purchases must have been made before the major downturn of attitudes, a factor which

[10] Five categories of expenditures were counted: (1) buying one car, (2) buying a second or third car, (3) buying one or more major household goods, (4) making major repairs or improvements on one's house or apartment, (5) making major nonhousehold expenditures (as defined above). For each family the number of categories which applied in each half-year was computed. Thus the maximum number that could be obtained in any half-year was 5, in an entire year 10. Actually, no family scored more than 4 for a half-year, nor more than 6 for a whole year. The average number of purchases per family in our urban sample was 1.52 for the year June 1954–June 1955, and 1.02 for the half-year June–December 1955.

[11] Eva Mueller, "Effects of Consumer Attitudes on Purchases," *American Economic Review*, December 1957, pp. 946-965.

[12] See Appendix Table A-1.

handicaps the test of the effect of attitude change on purchases for that period.

The re-interview test involved classifying families according to attitudes and attitude change and comparing purchases made by the various attitude groups. The index of consumer attitudes was used to distinguish among people who were initially optimists (scoring 10 to 12 on a 12-point attitude scale), medium (scoring 7 to 9), and pessimists (scoring 0 to 6); and also among those whose attitudes remained "the same" (i.e. changed by 1 point or less), "improved" (by 2 or more points), and "deteriorated" (by 2 points or more).

The analysis proceeded in two stages. First the income effect was "eliminated," because optimists tend to have higher incomes than pessimists. The average number of purchases was determined for each of nine income groups, which gave an "expected" number of purchases for each family based on its current income, and the re-interview gave its actual number of purchases. After adding up actual and expected purchases for all the families within any one attitude group, the ratio of its actual to expected purchases was computed.

The method is a rigorous test of the influence of attitudes on purchases, in that it gives priority to income. The method determines how much consumer attitudes contribute toward the explanation of purchase decision over and above the explanation provided through current income. To the extent that differences in purchases between income groups are due to differences in attitudes, the influence of attitudes is understated. The method also is flexible, facilitating examination of crucial subgroups of the sample.

Table 3 shows the average number of purchases made by families within each of seven attitude groups in the second half of 1954 and in the first half of 1955. Considerable differences appear—all in the expected direction. However, the data overstate the influence of attitudes because no account was taken of income differences between the attitude groups. Therefore in the second half of the table, ratios of actual to expected purchases are presented for the same seven groups classified according to initial attitudes in June 1954 and attitude change during the following twelve months.[13] The total columns show the ratio of actual to expected purchases by initial attitude groups, irrespective of later attitude change. In the first half-year initial attitudes appear to have a pronounced effect on subsequent purchases. A variance analysis of these differences shows them to be significant at better than the $2\frac{1}{2}$ per cent level. In the second half-year the group whose attitudes in June 1954 were medium had a higher actual to expected purchases ratio than either the optimists or the pessimists, but the observed differences between the three groups were not

---

[13] Examination of the partial correlation coefficient indicates that eliminating the income effect also eliminates most of the effect of age on purchases.

TABLE 3

Initial Attitudes, June 1954, and Attitude Change, June 1954–June 1955, Related to
Actual Purchases and to Ratios of Actual to Expected Purchasers

INITIAL ATTITUDE	ATTITUDE CHANGE				TOTAL NO. OF FAMILIES[a]
	Improved	*Same*	*Deteriorated*	*Total*	
ACTUAL AVERAGE NUMBER OF PURCHASES PER FAMILY					
In Second Half of 1954					
Optimist		1.24	1.05	1.18	209
Medium	1.00	0.83	0.73[b]	0.89	295
Pessimist	0.77	0.63[b]		0.75	170
All	0.88	0.99	0.96		
In First Half of 1955					
Optimist		0.70	0.59	0.67	
Medium	0.80	0.65	0.50[b]	0.70	
Pessimist	0.51	0.27[b]		0.46	
All	0.65	0.64	0.56		
RATIO OF ACTUAL TO EXPECTED PURCHASES WITHIN ATTITUDE GROUPS[c]					
In Second Half of 1954					
Optimist		1.17	1.09	1.15	
Medium	1.04	0.90	0.82[b]	0.95	
Pessimist	0.91	0.76[b]		0.88	
All	0.97	1.00	1.01		
In First Half of 1955					
Optimist		1.00	0.89	0.97	
Medium	1.23	1.04	0.85[b]	1.10	
Pessimist	0.89	0.48[b]		0.82	
All	1.05	0.97	0.88		
Total No. of Families[a]	269	320	85		674

[a] The numbers are the same for both half-years and both parts of the table. Given over 650 cases, the fact that the sample was clustered has practically no effect on the significance tests presented in this section.

[b] Less than thirty-five cases.

[c] Figures within cells represent ratios of actual to expected number of purchases in each of the two half-years. Expected number of purchases were calculated separately for each cell on the basis of its income distributions. Simple variance analysis showed that for the second half of 1954 differences in the seven-way classification were significant at the 5 per cent level, with an F-ratio of 2.13 (2.10 at the 5 per cent level); for the first half of 1955 only at 10 per cent level, with an F-ratio of 1.89 (1.77 at the 10 per cent level).

statistically significant. That is, there was little carryover of the effect of June 1954 attitudes to purchases beyond December 1954. A further check was made by relating June 1954 attitudes to purchases in the third half-year period (June–December 1955), but no significant differences emerged.

160

Among the people whose attitudes improved there was a disproportion-
ate number of initial pessimists, and among those whose attitudes deteriorated initial optimism was relatively frequent. The bottom row of Table 3
("all") therefore understates the impact of attitude change. To isolate the
net effect of attitude change on purchases, initial attitudes must be held
constant. Accordingly, in the following tabulation the average number of
purchases was computed for each income group within the three attitude
groups. "Expected" purchases as used here thus take account of both
income and initial attitudes.

Ratios of Actual to Expected Purchases

| | ATTITUDE CHANGE, JUNE 1954–JUNE 1955 | | |
	Improved	*Same*	*Deteriorated*
Second half of 1954	1.04	0.99	0.95
First half of 1955	1.11	0.95	0.87
Number of cases	269	320	85

Undoubtedly people whose final attitudes differed from their initial
attitudes changed at different times during the year. Probably the number
whose sentiment changed increased as the year progressed. Therefore a
stronger relationship of attitude change to purchases in the second half-
year is to be expected. For the first half-year the differences are not
statistically significant, although they are in the expected direction. For
the second half-year there are at least three chances in four that the three
groups differ with regard to number of purchases.

We may conclude that between June 1954 and June 1955 consumer
attitudes exerted a significant influence on spending decisions. However,
after extensive attitude changes, as during the second half of 1954, the full
impact of the state of consumer confidence becomes apparent only when
account is taken of the attitude change as well as of the initial attitudes.
And apparently the influence of a given set of attitudes extends primarily
over the half-year preceding and the half-year following the measurement,
rather than the full year after the expression of attitudes.

There was less divergence between income and attitudes in the second
half of 1955, and the data show that attitudes made a smaller net contribution to the explanation of consumer purchases than in 1954. Table 4
relates purchases in the second half of 1955 to initial attitudes in June 1955.
The data are less complete than for the previous year so the relationship
with attitude change could not be analyzed. No difference appears in the
ratio of actual to expected purchases between the optimist and the medium
groups. The pessimists show a somewhat lower ratio, but they had shrunk
to 10 per cent of the sample by June 1955. The differences are not statistically significant.

TABLE 4

Initial Attitudes, June 1955, Related to Actual Major Purchases, June–December 1955, to Expected Purchases, and to Ratios of Actual to Expected Purchases

| INITIAL ATTITUDE | PURCHASES | | | TOTAL NO. OF FAMILIES |
	Actual[a]	Expected[b]	Ratio of Actual to Expected[c]	
Optimist	1.10	1.09	1.01	292
Medium	1.00	0.99	1.01	317
Pessimist	0.77	0.84	0.92	65

[a] Observed average number of major purchases per family.
[b] Expected on the basis of income distribution within each of the three attitude groups.
[c] Differences are not statistically significant.

TABLE 5

Initial Attitudes, November–December 1955, and Attitude change, December 1955– February 1957, Related to Ratios of Actual to Expected Purchases

| INITIAL ATTITUDE | ATTITUDE CHANGE | | | | TOTAL NO. OF FAMILIES[b] |
	Improved	Same[a]	Deteriorated	Total	
RATIO OF ACTUAL TO EXPECTED PURCHASES WITHIN ATTITUDE GROUPS[c]					
In First Half of 1956					
Optimist		1.20	1.10	1.14	285
Nonoptimist	1.13	0.93	0.68	0.91	324
All	1.13	1.06	0.96		
In December 1955–February 1957					
Optimist		1.17	1.04	1.10	
Nonoptimist	0.95	0.97	0.87	0.94	
All	0.95	1.07	0.98		
Total No. of Families[b]	88	277	244		609

[a] By definition, most of those who were initially optimistic (scoring 10 to 12 on a scale ranging from zero to 12) could not improve (by 2 or more points). However, some of these people probably did in fact feel more optimistic at the time of the second interview.
[b] The numbers are the same for both periods.
[c] Figures within cells represent ratios of actual to expected number of purchases in each of the two periods. Expected number of purchases were calculated separately for each cell on the basis of its income distribution. Differences in the five-way classification were significant only at the 10 per cent level for the first half of 1956, with an F-ratio of 2.07 (1.94 at the 10 per cent level); at 5 per cent for December 1955–February 1957, with an F-ratio of 2.44 (2.37 at the 5 per cent level).

Table 5 relates initial attitudes in late 1955, and attitude change from late 1955 to early 1957, to number of purchases.[14] Because attitudes have

[14] The index for December 1955 was computed by substituting the corresponding June 1955 figure for the one component which was not available.

their maximum effect during the first half-year following the measurement, we so far have analyzed purchases during half-years. In this third period the time which elapsed between the initial interview (December 1955) and the final interview (February 1957) was so long that many respondents had difficulty recalling the approximate date of their purchases.[15] Since the data for the whole period are better and more complete than data for the two halves, Table 5 shows the relation between attitudes and purchases for the first half of 1956 as well as for the fourteen months from December 1955 to February 1957. Because the number of pessimists in December 1955 was very small (52 families), the medium and pessimist groups were combined.

For the first half of 1956 substantial differences appear in the ratios of actual to expected purchases among the five attitude and attitude change categories—all in the expected direction. For the whole period Table 5 shows somewhat smaller variations, and the ratios for the nonoptimists who improved and for those whose attitudes did not change are about the same. However, the differences for the first half fall short of being significant at the 5 per cent level, unlike the differences for the entire period.

Examining again the separate effects of initial attitudes and attitude change, we find that differences between the two initial groups are in the expected direction. But for the first half-year they again fall short of being significant at the 5 per cent level. For the whole period they are significant at the $2\frac{1}{2}$ per cent level. Differences in the ratio of actual to expected purchases for attitude change groups were computed holding constant initial attitudes. Although the differences were largely in the expected direction, no statistically significant results emerged for either half. Since much of the attitude change during this period occurred rather late this finding is not surprising.

THE PREDICTIVE VALUE OF DATA ON CONSUMER ATTITUDES

Although we shall now speak of predictive value, this is not forecasting in the aggregative sense. Rather, we wish to determine whether groups of consumers who differ with respect to certain initial variables differ also with respect to later purchases.

Since we are interested in forecasting, only data available at the beginning of the period under study can be used: the past year's income, not current income; and initial attitudes, but not attitude change during the year being forecast. In view of the findings reported in the previous section, the predictive value of data on consumer attitudes over half-year periods rather than for entire years was analyzed, by a multiple correlation technique, using re-interview data.

[15] During the first year and a half of the study interviews were taken at half-year intervals. Therefore the dating of purchases by half-years presented no problem.

Certain variables may be held constant in analyzing the relation between attitudes A and purchases P:

1. Variables which affect A as well as P. Previous studies have indicated that income and age fall into this category. Optimism increases with income. The number of purchases also increases with income, and this relation is by no means due entirely to the greater optimism prevailing among the upper income groups. Young people are more optimistic than older people. They also make more purchases, partly because of their greater optimism, but also because usually they must equip a newly formed household.

2. Variables which affect P but show no significant relation to A (after account has been taken of income and age), for example, marital status, number and age of children, education, place of residence, home ownership status. If the sample is sufficiently large, groups homogeneous with respect to income and age but differing in attitudes should have similar distributions of this second type of characteristic. These variables may then be disregarded without biasing the relationship between A and P, although some random variations may arise from the presence of small subgroups in the sample.

By contrast, variables which determine attitudes should *not* be held constant. These include a wide variety of stimuli originating in the economic and political environment as well as more personal experiences. However, they also include age and income. So when we relate attitudes, income, and age to purchases in a single equation, we do not know how much of the effect of income and age is brought about indirectly through their impact on attitudes.[16]

Keeping this problem of interpretation in mind, we present two regression equations for each of our three periods (Table 6). The first relates income (Y_{-1}), age (X), and the index of consumer attitudes excluding buying intentions (A_b) to purchases in the subsequent half-year. In the second the index of buying intentions (A_c) is added to the independent variables.

The results bear out the previous findings. Equation 6 indicates that for the second half of 1954 the index of consumer attitudes made a significant contribution to the forecast of P. For the second half of 1955 (equation 8), on the other hand, the coefficient of A_b is smaller than its standard

---

[16] Given the following equations, the "pure" relation between P and A is not identifiable:

$$A = f_1(Y, X, O)$$
$$P = f_2(A, Y, X)$$

where A=attitudes, Y=income, X=age, O=a short-cut expression for other determinants of attitudes, and P=purchases.

TABLE 6

Predictive Equations Relating Consumer Purchases to Attitudes, Plans to Buy,
Income, and Age, Selected Periods, June 1954–February 1957

EQUATION		Attitudes (A_b)	Plans to Buy (A_c)	Income (Y_{-1})	Age (X)	Constant	COEFFICIENT OF MULTIPLE CORRELATION (R)
			SECOND HALF OF 1954				
6	$P =$	+0.031 (0.015)		+0.060 (0.017)	−0.066 (0.024)	+0.708	0.23
7	$P =$	+0.022 (0.015)	+0.131 (0.044)	+0.052 (0.016)	−0.053 (0.024)	+0.624	.25
			SECOND HALF OF 1955				
8	$P =$	+0.015 (0.018)		+0.085 (0.017)	−0.063 (0.025)	+0.758	.25
9	$P =$	+0.011 (0.019)	+0.157 (0.048)	+0.073 (0.018)	−0.050 (0.026)	+0.655	.28
			FIRST HALF OF 1956				
10	$P =$	+0.013 (0.014)		+0.052 (0.012)	−0.050 (0.019)	+0.315	.24
11	$P =$	+0.013 (0.014)	+0.108 (0.032)	+0.041 (0.013)	−0.040 (0.019)	+0.240	.28
			DECEMBER 1955–FEBRUARY 1957				
12	$P =$	+0.023 (0.021)		+0.143 (0.019)	−0.097 (0.029)	+0.777	.37
13	$P =$	+0.023 (0.021)	+0.220 (0.049)	+0.121 (0.019)	−0.078 (0.030)	+0.625	.40

The column header group is: REGRESSION COEFFICIENTS spanning Attitudes, Plans to Buy, Income, Age, Constant.

error.[17] In 1956 (equations 10 and 12), the predictive value of data on consumer attitudes was less significant than in the second half of 1954, but greater than in the second half of 1955.

The addition of the index of buying intention (A_c) to the predictive equations raises the multiple correlation coefficients only slightly, although buying intentions show a highly significant relation to consumer purchases in each period. The reason is that since buying intentions are correlated with our other three independent variables, their introduction reduces the contribution of the latter. In particular, the contribution of consumer attitudes in the second half of 1954 now appears of less importance.

This result is not surprising, nor does it contradict the notion that attitudes influence purchases. The influence of consumer attitudes should express itself in part through their relation to buying intentions; in part it should be independent, affecting the likelihood of unplanned purchases. It appears reasonable that in the second half of 1954, when income was

[17] The standard errors provide an unsatisfactory test of significance, partly because of the interdependence of the independent variables mentioned above, and also because we are dealing with a clustered sample.

fairly stable, the high level of buying intentions should stem in part from the high level of consumer optimism. Yet if we are concerned with the practical problem of forecasting (as opposed to questions of influence or causation), we must conclude that, at the individual level, buying intentions have proved to be a better predictive device than data on consumer attitudes.[18]

This conclusion is reinforced by Table 7, which shows the intercorrelations between our variables as measured by the simple and partial correlation coefficients. In all three periods the simple correlations (zero order) of purchases with income and buying plans are somewhat higher than the correlations of purchases with age and attitudes. Several of the intercorrelations between the independent variables are stronger than the correlations of any one of them with purchases. Particularly strong are the correlations between income and attitudes, income and buying plans, and, in 1954, attitudes and buying plans.

The net correlation between attitudes and purchases (third order) is decidedly lower for the second half of 1955 than for 1954. The first half of

TABLE 7

Interrelationships among Purchases, Income, Age, Consumer Attitudes, and Buying Plans, Selected Periods, June 1954–February 1957

$1 = $ Purchases(P) $2 = $ Income(Y_{-1}) $3 = $ Age(X) $4 = $ Attitudes(A_b)
$5 = $ Buying plans(A_c)

PERIOD	ZERO ORDER CORRELATION COEFFICIENTS									
	R_{12}	R_{13}	R_{14}	R_{15}	R_{23}	R_{24}	R_{25}	R_{34}	R_{35}	R_{45}
Second half of 1954	0.18	−0.13	0.14	0.19	−0.08	0.31	0.25	−0.12	−0.22	0.28
Second half of 1955	.23	−.15	.12	.19	−.21	.30	.26	−.28	−.22	.18
First half of 1956	.21	−.16	.11	.20	−.25	.30	.31	−.18	−.22	.11
December 1955–										
February 1957	.34	−.21	.16	.28	−.26	.30	.31	−.18	−.21	.11

	THIRD ORDER CORRELATION COEFFICIENTS			
	$R_{12 \cdot 345}$	$R_{13 \cdot 245}$	$R_{14 \cdot 235}$	$R_{15 \cdot 234}$
Second half of 1954	0.12	−0.08	0.06	0.11
Second half of 1955	.16	−.08	.02	.13
First half of 1956	.13	−.09	.04	.13
December 1955–				
February 1957	.24	−.10	.06	.18

	MULTIPLE CORRELATION COEFFICIENTS		
	$R_{1.23}$	$R_{1.45}$	$R_{1.2345}$
Second half of 1954	0.21	0.21	0.25
Second half of 1955	.25	.21	.28
First half of 1956	.24	.22	.28
December 1955–			
February 1957	.37	.30	.40

[18] How purchases shortly *before* the survey (when most people must have had the same attitudes) varied between optimists and pessimists is not considered here (see the comments by Katona on Okun's paper in this volume).

166

1956 occupies an intermediate position. The higher the attitude coefficient, the lower the income coefficient. Income was a less important determinant of consumer spending in the second half of 1954 (when attitudes diverged from income trends) than in the second half of 1955 (when both income and attitudes had risen substantially).[19] The correlation between buying plans and purchases is generally of about the same magnitude as the correlation between income and purchases.[20]

The third part of Table 7 compares the joint explanatory value (multiple) of income and age with that of attitudes and buying plans. In 1954 about equally accurate forecasts could have been obtained from either of the pairs of variables (disregarding the other pair). For the first half of 1956, income and age would have done slightly better than attitudes and buying plans; and for the second half of 1955 the superiority is more marked. Consumer attitudes make only a small net contribution to the joint forecasting potential of attitudes and buying plans. These conclusions apply, however, only to cross-sectional forecasting. When we draw inferences about forecasting at the aggregative level, the cyclical behavior of our variables must be taken into account.

Also included in Table 7 are correlation coefficients for the period from December 1955 to February 1957. The correlations of all the variables with purchases are higher for these fourteen months than for the half-year periods. The multiple correlation coefficient is 0.40 as compared with 0.28 for the first half of 1956. The difference reflects the fact that purchases over a year are more easily explained than purchases over shorter periods, which are more strongly affected by accidents of timing. It is also noteworthy that while for the first half of 1956 the explanatory value of income

---

[19] The difference between the second half of 1954 and the second half of 1955 appears even more clearly if we substitute current income (Y) for the past year's income (Y_{-1}). This is done in (7A) and (9A), which otherwise correspond to (7) and (9):

		A_b	A_c	Y	X	R
			SECOND HALF OF 1954			
(7A)	$P =$	$+0.021$	$+0.126$	$+0.056$	-0.041	$+0.564$	0.26
		(0.015)	(0.044)	(0.016)	(0.024)		
			SECOND HALF OF 1955			
(9A)	$P =$	$+0.002$	$+0.143$	$+0.092$	-0.039	$+0.557$	.30
		(0.019)	(0.048)	(0.018)	(0.026)		

Current income here means income of the entire calendar year in progress. The "forecast" is being made in June for the second half of that year. It appears that for the second half of 1954 the regression coefficient of A_b is not affected appreciably by this substitution. A_b has only a slightly closer relation to Y than to Y_{-1}: the correlation between Y and A_b is 0.315, between Y_{-1} and A_b, 0.308. For the second half of 1955, however, the regression coefficient of A_b is reduced considerably as a result of this substitution, while the importance of income is increased further. For this period the correlation between Y and A_b is 0.354, between Y_{-1} and A_b 0.315.

[20] For the second half of 1955 the buying plans coefficient is somewhat lower. But buying plans there were measured as of the previous December instead of June 1955.

and age is only slightly greater than that of attitudes and buying plans, for the whole fourteen months income and age have a decided advantage —a result consistent with the finding that the influence of a given set of attitudes extends primarily over the half-year before and after the attitude measurement. It is also consistent with a similar finding on buying plans. The percentage of all car purchases which were planned is much higher for the half-year immediately following a survey than for the subsequent half-year.[21]

We have found that the relative influence of income and attitudes on consumer purchases varied between periods. Attitudes showed the strongest autonomous influence in the second half of 1954. In 1956 their influence was less significant, and in 1955 it was negligible. The importance of income varied in the opposite direction, being smallest in the second half of 1954 and largest in the second half of 1955. If we define "autonomous" variations in consumer spending as variations which are unrelated to changes in income, there is every reason to believe that at times no such variations will occur. We conclude from our data that autonomous variations in consumer spending, indicated in advance by attitude changes, did occur in the second half of 1954 and to a lesser extent in 1956, but not in the second half of 1955.

How can forecasters know when consumer attitudes will have an autonomous effect on spending? Measurements are needed because the answer depends upon how much changes in attitudes diverge from changes in income. Information on consumer attitudes is most valuable when there is a marked divergence such as occurred in the second half of 1954. The divergence may be due to people's reactions to economic news about price changes, tax changes, employment opportunities, sales trends, recession or recovery prospects. Or it may be due to political developments such as the outcome of an election or international disturbances. When there is less divergence, attitudes may also be influential. However, since financial and demographic factors play a greater role as determinants of attitudes at such times, attitudes data can add little to the explanation of consumer behavior provided by these factors. Additional studies conducted under varying economic conditions are needed to substantiate this hypothesis.

The Relationship between the Aggregative and the Re-interview Test

We have found that data on consumer attitudes showed a close relation to consumer spending at the aggregative level for 1952-56. At the individual level the net impact of attitudes appeared rather small and varied from period to period.

---

[21] See Charles Lininger, Eva Mueller, and Hans Wyss, "Some Uses of Panel Studies in Forecasting the Automobile Market," *Proceedings of the Business and Economic Statistics Section* of the American Statistical Association, 1957, pp. 409-421.

The apparently contradictory findings are to be expected and apply to other anticipations data as well.[22] Group characteristics will almost always yield demonstrably higher correlations with group behavior than the corresponding cross-section variables relating to individuals because a much larger number of factors affect individual behavior than can be taken into account in the analysis.[23] In the present case personality traits, past experience, recent illness, and quantity and quality of durable goods owned are examples of relevant "omitted" characteristics. The larger the groups analyzed, the less likely it is that these factors will vary between groups. In the entire population these characteristics vary little, or not at all, in the short run. With this sort of "noise" eliminated, the relationship between anticipations and behavior emerges more strongly.

The investigation also revealed that at the aggregative level consumer attitudes were more highly correlated with spending than were buying plans, while the reverse was true at the individual level. Again these findings need not be in conflict.

The cross-section analysis presented here is essentially static, while the time-series analysis is dynamic. For example, differences in income over time are quite different from cross-section differences in income (which reflect primarily people's position on the income scale). Conceivably there are variables which affect spending behavior appreciably only when they change to a significant extent (in the population). Price expectations may be a case in point.

More important, some variables vary more over time than others. There are variables such as age or thrift which vary considerably between individuals, producing correlations with spending behavior in a cross section without varying appreciably over time; their value to business cycle analysts or forecasters is almost nil. Hence any conclusions about the significance and relative importance of attitudes and buying plans must be drawn in the light of their cross-section relation to behavior *and* their variation over time.

Appendix Table A-4 presents data on the variability of attitudes, buying plans, and income over the course of the panel study. It shows that attitudes varied more than income and buying plans, absolute changes in proportions of the population with a given characteristic being relevant here, rather than their percentage changes. In the panel study the proportion having no buying plans varied between 39 and 45 per cent and the proportion with pessimistic attitudes between 8 and 25 per cent. Thus the contribution of buying plans to aggregative prediction could equal the contribution of attitudes only if the buying plans had a considerably higher correlation with individual behavior. Clearly, if several variables

[22] See for example the paper by Murray F. Foss and Vito Natrella in this volume.
[23] W. S. Robinson, "Ecological Correlations and Behavior of Individuals," *American Sociological Review*, June 1950, pp. 351-356.

are ranked according to the strength of their relation to spending first at the individual and then at the aggregative level, the two rank orderings need not correspond closely.

Consideration of the bias imparted by omitted variables leads to similar conclusions. Kuh has demonstrated that "the biases from excluded variables are likely to be of strikingly different nature in the two cases, time series and cross sections. Therefore, the propriety of applying estimated behavior relations for prediction purposes in one context that were estimated in another context is highly questionable."[24] The time-series error is likely to be caused by *dynamic* excluded variables, which vary to some extent with the business cycle; the cross-section error primarily to *static* excluded variables such as demographic characteristics, personality traits, stocks of durable goods owned. Conceivably consumer attitudes, having a clear business cycle reference, are correlated with the dynamic excluded variables and reflect some of their impact on spending, while buying plans may be more closely related to the static excluded variables. If this assumption is correct, time-series tests would have a tendency to overestimate the influence of attitudes and cross-section tests a tendency to overestimate the influence of buying plans.[25]

Another relevant consideration relates to the concept of marginal or borderline decisions. Some variables, notably income and certain demographic characteristics, may have a pervasive influence on consumer spending patterns. Other variables, such as small price changes, presumably affect only the marginal decisions. Yet the latter variables may account for a considerable part of all fluctuations in spending. Conceivably the influence of attitudes on purchases is limited to marginal decisions. Since we have no way of distinguishing between marginal and nonmarginal decisions among the survey population, and must test the influence of attitudes across the board, it is not surprising that the relationship between attitudes and purchases at the individual level appears rather weak. Buying plans, on the other hand, may predict the nonmarginal purchases more accurately than the marginal purchases and therefore make a good showing in the cross-section test. For example, the man who always trades cars every second year, the man who has just advanced a major step in his career, or the man whose car needs a complete overhaul can probably state his buying plans very accurately; but these are not the marginal buyers whose purchases explain the ups and downs in car sales.

These theoretical considerations show that neither the aggregative nor

[24] Edwin Kuh, "The Validity of Cross-Sectionally Estimated Behavior Equations in Time Series Applications," paper delivered in December 1957 at the Philadelphia meeting of the Econometric Society.

[25] If the correlation between the error due to excluded dynamic variables and consumer attitudes is fairly stable, it may detract little from the observed forecasting value of consumer attitudes. The period of observation is too short, however, to provide information on the stability of that relation.

the re-interview test is sufficient by itself for testing the influence of consumer attitudes on spending. Both tests are needed. The results of the tests described here are not yet conclusive. On the positive side were (1) the strong relationship between attitudes and purchases obtained in the aggregative test over the short period for which data were available, and (2) the finding that at the individual level attitudes exhibited a pronounced influence on purchases in two of the three periods studied (as long as buying plans were disregarded). On the negative side is the finding that data on consumer attitudes consistently made only a small *net* contribution to forecasts of consumer spending at the individual level, when income, age, and buying plans were also taken into account. However, theoretical considerations suggest that a small net contribution by the attitudinal data at the individual level is not inconsistent with a considerably greater contribution to forecasting at the aggregative level. More definite conclusions must wait upon additional data.

One clear need for further research is in connection with the aggregative test. Data collection must continue over a longer time so that we can make aggregative tests on the index of consumer attitudes and the index of buying plans based on larger numbers of observations. With additional observations seasonal adjustment factors could be worked out for various types of buying plans.[26] More research also is needed at the individual level. We have seen that the influence of consumer attitudes on purchases, after account is taken of income differences, varies considerably from period to period. The next goal is to learn more about the conditions under which attitudes do, or do not, have influence.

Several further studies, based on the Ford Foundation Re-interview Project, are under way and may yield clarification of the relation between the attitudes and spending behavior of individuals. One of these will use an alternative approach—relating *changes* in expenditures to *changes* in attitudes. Instead of number of purchases, changes in dollar amounts spent will be used as a dependent variable. Another study will analyze in more detail than was possible here the relation of consumer buying plans to purchases.

Most important, however, is the challenging problem of seeing whether closer correlations with purchases can be established by constructing a more refined index of consumer attitudes. The index used here was constructed several years ago on an experimental basis. Since then additional measures of attitudes and buying plans have been developed, some of which should be incorporated into the index. Also the question of what attitudes are most influential under what circumstances and for what kinds of people should be analyzed with the aim of improving the weighting

[26] Since this paper was prepared in the fall of 1957 four additional time series observations have become available for the aggregative test. Equations (1) and (2), when recomputed including these four new observations, in every case yield values of $\bar{R}^2$ as high as those shown in Table 1, in some cases slightly higher.

and composition of the index. For example, certain complexes of attitudes, or of attitudes and financial developments—such as the expectation of rising prices accompanied by an expectation of stable income—may have a particularly strong impact on behavior. Finally there is the difficult task of improving the underlying attitude measurements themselves.

TABLE A-1

Data Underlying Chart 1

	DOLLAR AMOUNT (BILLIONS)				INDEX OF:	
Year and Quarter	Durable Goods Sales[a] (current) (1)	Durable Goods Sales[b] (deflated) (2)	Personal Disposable Income[a] (current) (3)	Personal Disposable Income[b] (deflated) (4)	Consumer Attitudes Including Buying Intentions[c] (5)	Consumer Attitudes Excluding Buying Intentions[c] (6)
1952:						
IV	29.0	25.5	244.3	214.1	100	100
1953:						
I	30.2	26.6	247.9	218.2	104	105
II	30.6	27.1	251.0	219.2		
III	30.5	27.2	251.7	218.5	93	96
IV	28.0	25.3	251.0	218.5		
1954:						
I	28.5	25.9	252.3	219.8	93	97
II	29.2	26.9	252.3	219.2	102	101
III	29.4	27.7	254.6	222.0		
IV	30.4	28.4	258.4	226.1	109	104
1955:						
I	34.7	32.7	260.1	227.6		
II	35.3	33.7	267.8	234.1	111	113
III	37.2	35.9	273.2	237.8		
IV	35.4	33.7	278.6	242.9	112	112
1956:						
I	34.6	33.2	279.6	243.8		
II	33.3	32.1	285.8	246.0	108	108
III	33.0	31.5	288.8	246.6	107	109
IV	34.8	32.2	294.0	249.2	112	110
1957:						
I	35.9	33.1	296.1	249.0		
II	35.0	32.3	300.4	249.9	104	103
III	35.0	32.3	303.3	250.5		
IV	34.4	31.0	302.1	248.4	95	94

[a] In this and the following tables, from *Survey of Current Business*, Dept. of Commerce, July 1957, May 1958. Figures are seasonally adjusted annual rates.

[b] Obtained by deflating the figures in cols. (1) and (3) respectively, on the basis of the Department of Labor Consumer Price Index, reclassified, *Survey of Current Business*, October 1957, Table 4. For disposable income the deflator is the "all items" index; for durable goods sales the deflator is the "durables" index.

[c] In this and the following tables, from Survey Research Center, University of Michigan. The series through October 1955 have been published in George Katona and Eva Mueller, *Consumer Expectations 1953-1956*, Survey Research Center, 1956.

TABLE A-2

Data Underlying Table 1 and Chart 2

Survey Date	AMOUNT (BILLIONS OF CURRENT DOLLARS)			INDEX OF:		
	Actual Durable Goods Sales[a] (1)	Past Income[b] (2)	Current Income[c] (3)	Consumer Attitudes Including Buying Intentions (4)	Consumer Attitudes Excluding Buying Intentions (5)	Buying Intentions (6)
Nov. 1952	30.40	237.3	249.5	100	100	100[d]
Jan.–Feb. 1953	30.40	242.3	249.5	104[e]	105[e]	100
Sept. 1953	28.25	249.5	251.7	93	96	85
Jan.–Feb. 1954	28.85	251.4	252.3	93	97	80
June 1954	29.90	251.7	256.5	102	101	106
Oct. 1954	32.55	253.5	259.3	109	104	125
June 1955	36.30	259.3	275.9	111	113	106
Oct. 1955	35.00	270.5	279.1	112	112	113
April 1956	33.15	279.1	287.3	108	108	108
Aug. 1956	35.35	282.7	294.8	107	109	101
Nov. 1956	35.45	287.3	297.5	112	110	120
June 1957[f]	34.70	295.1	302.7	104	103	108

[a] Durable goods spending in the two quarters following the survey. Where the survey fell into the later part of a quarter, the two following quarters were used. Where the survey was taken at the beginning of a quarter, the current quarter and the following quarter were used. Figures are seasonally adjusted annual rates.

[b] Personal disposable income in two quarters preceding the quarter in which the survey was conducted. Figures are seasonally adjusted rates.

[c] Personal disposable income in two quarters following the survey (concurrent with the figures in col. (1)).

[d] Estimated since data not available in November 1952 survey.

[e] Several components estimated since they were not available in the January–February 1953 survey.

[f] Data for June 1957 not included in computation of regression equations.

173

TABLE A-3

Data Underlying Table 2

	CHANGE IN:					
	AMOUNT (BILLIONS OF CURRENT DOLLARS)			INDEX OF:		
Survey Date	Actual Durable Goods Sales[a] (1)	Past Income[b] (2)	Current Income[c] (3)	Consumer Attitudes Including Buying Intentions[d] (4)	Consumer Attitudes Excluding Buying Intentions[d] (5)	Buying Intentions[e] (6)
Sept. 1953	−2.30	+3.8	+0.3	−7	−4	+15
Jan.–Feb. 1954	−0.40	+0.6	+1.0	0	+1	−5
June 1954	+1.05	+1.3	+4.2	+9	+4	+26
Oct. 1954	+3.25	+6.1	+5.8	+7	+3	+19
June 1955	+1.30	+9.4	+12.0	+2	+0	−19
Oct. 1955	−1.25	+10.8	+8.6	+1	−1	+7
April 1956	−1.85	+7.2	+8.2	−4	−4	−5
Aug. 1956	+2.20	+9.2	+7.5	−1	+1	−7
Nov. 1956	+1.55	+8.2	+6.1	+5	+1	+19

[a] Change in durable goods spending between the two quarters following the survey and the two preceding quarters. Where the survey fell into the later part of a quarter, the two following quarters were used. Where the survey was taken at the beginning of a quarter, the current quarter and the following quarter were used. In either case change is measured from the two preceding quarters. Figures are based on seasonally adjusted annual rates.

[b] Change in personal disposable income between quarter in which survey is made and two quarters earlier. Figures are based on seasonally adjusted rates.

[c] Change in personal disposable income between the two quarters following the survey and the two preceding quarters (concurrent with the figures in col. (1)).

[d] Change in September 1953 is from November 1952, since the attitude indexes for January–February 1953 are partly interpolated (only a few attitudes were available for January–February 1953).

[e] Change in September 1953 is from January–February 1953, since buying plans were not included in the November 1952 survey.

TABLE A-4

Variations in the Distribution of Attitudes, Buying Plans, and Income,
June 1954–February 1957 among Panel Members

(*per cent*)

	INDEX OF CONSUMER ATTITUDES[a]			
	June 1954	*June 1955*	*Dec. 1955*	*Feb. 1957*
Optimistic (10-12)	31	43	47	30
Medium (7-9)	44	47	45	47
Pessimistic (0-6)	25	10	8	23
All	100	100	100	100

	INDEX OF BUYING INTENTIONS[a]			
	June 1954	*Dec. 1954*	*Dec. 1955*	*Feb. 1957*
Two or more plans	26	19	27	
One plan	35	39	28	not
No plan	39	42	45	available
All	100	100	100	

	INCOME DISTRIBUTION		
	1954 Income	*1955 Income*	*1956 Income*
Under $3,000	23	21	19
$3,000-4,999	30	29	24
5,000–7,499	31	31	34
7,500 and over	16	19	23
All	100	100	100

[a] The data here are derived from the panel study. They relate to the urban population only and are not strictly representative for the later interviews (because of panel losses). The data in Tables A-1 and A-3, on the other hand, are derived from successive independent cross sections and relate to the entire population—urban as well as rural. Also the index of buying intentions constructed for the panel differs from that shown in Tables A-2 and A-3 (see discussion at the end of the introductory section of the paper).

COMMENT

IRWIN FRIEND, University of Pennsylvania

Eva Mueller has written an extremely interesting paper on the effects of consumer attitudes on purchases which concludes that "under certain

NOTE: Since these comments were written, two years ago, Miss Mueller has revised her paper rather drastically, but has made only one major substantive change—the addition of an aggregative test of the relative effectiveness of an index of attitudes, an index of buying intentions and deflated disposable personal income (Commerce) in predicting or explaining deflated durable goods sales (Commerce), based on eleven observations from November 1952 to November 1956. In this test, attitudes (but apparently not buying intentions) do add significantly to the prediction or explanation of durable goods spending. Some of the questions that might be raised are implied in my earlier comments relating to the form of the relationship tested, objective variables not introduced into the analysis and—perhaps most important—the comparative predictive ability of projections of the most recent rate of expenditure.

175

conditions attitude variables do contribute significantly toward an explanation of fluctuations in consumer spending." Though Miss Mueller makes some remarks on the contribution of attitudes to the understanding and prediction of short-term trends in aggregate expenditures, the core of her paper is devoted to cross-section analyses of the relationship between the number of major (or large) expenditures per family and key objective and attitude variables characterizing the family.

The first type of analysis Miss Mueller presents is essentially devoted to tests of the significance of differences in the number of actual expenditures of families with different attitudes at the beginning and end of various periods after elimination of income effects. She finds that initial attitudes as distinct from intentions or plans to buy did have a statistically significant influence on purchases for at least a six-month period ahead in two of the three periods tested, those beginning in mid-1954 and the end of 1955 but not that beginning in mid-1955. Changes in attitudes had a significant influence on purchases only in the first of these periods. Since this is perhaps the most impressive evidence to date that data on consumer attitudes may under certain conditions help to explain variability in expenditures which cannot be explained by objective variables such as income, these results merit close examination. One question which arises is how to tell in advance when data on consumer attitudes will be a useful supplement to objective data and when they will not be. However, a more fundamental question is whether consumer attitudes are not correlated with objective variables other than income which have an important influence on expenditures. This latter question leads directly to the second and probably most interesting set of results in Miss Mueller's paper.

In this second type of analysis, Miss Mueller presents multiple linear regressions between the number of major family expenditures as the dependent variable, and family income, age of head, an index of initial consumer attitudes, and an index of buying intentions as the independent variables. Family income and age of head are selected as the key objective variables influencing both expenditures and attitudes (and presumably also buying intentions). Initial attitudes seem to have a clearly significant influence on the number of major expenditures only in the first of the periods tested (viz., that beginning in mid-1954) and only when buying intentions are not included in the regression. Income, age, and buying intentions seem to be significant in all periods. When all four independent variables are included in the regression, the regression coefficient of attitudes is about one and a half times its standard error for the period beginning in mid-1954 but equal to or less than the standard error in the other periods. Consequently, Miss Mueller's conclusion as to the significant contribution of attitudes under certain conditions (as distinct from objective variables or intentions) seems to be based largely on the 1954 regression results, and perhaps to a lesser extent on the first, less com-

176

prehensive analysis referred to earlier. In 1954 attitudes seem definitely significant when buying intentions are not held constant, much less so when buying intentions are held constant.

The question naturally arises whether these results contradict findings by other analysts—including Arthur Okun's paper in this volume and one by James Tobin[1]—that whereas buying intentions (as Miss Mueller also finds) have predictive value, other attitudinal questions do not. Tobin presents new cross-section results for 1952 which reaffirm this negative conclusion as to the predictive value of attitudinal questions. The apparent discrepancy between Tobin's and Miss Mueller's findings might reflect the difference in time periods; initial attitudes might have been useful in explaining expenditures in 1954 and not in 1952. Moreover, Miss Mueller gets somewhat better results with a six-month period than with the year period Tobin uses. The discrepancy may also simply reflect the fact that Tobin is attempting to explain variation in the dollar amount of expenditures (on cars and major household goods), Miss Mueller variation in the number of expenditures. Clearly, we are more interested in amounts than in number, but Miss Mueller points out that her paper is simply the first step in a more comprehensive analysis.

I think however that a more important reason for the discrepancy in the two findings may be the difference in the independent variables and in the forms of the relationships tested. Tobin introduces three independent objective variables—liquid assets and personal debt (both as ratios of income) and marital status—in addition to income and age, and uses a rather different mathematical form, attempting to eliminate heteroschedasticity in the dependent variable and allowing for interaction between income change and other explanatory variables. Tobin's findings suggest, but do not of course prove, that Miss Mueller may be attributing to attitudes in 1954 an influence on expenditures which really reflects either objective variables—such as assets and debts—omitted from her analysis or departures from linearity in the assumed linear relationship between the number of expenditures and income and age.

One final comment is in order. Miss Mueller and both Okun and Tobin present evidence that consumer buying intentions have predictive value in the sense that they explain, in advance, variability in cross-section and aggregate expenditures which cannot be explained by objective variables. It seems to me that three qualifications should be noted. First, the expenditures involved are largely major durables, and an obvious objective variable which has not yet been introduced into these analyses is the initial stock of durables. Second, it is possible at least in some of these analyses that the test used introduces a timing bias in favor of intentions data. This would be true in Tobin's test, for example, if the intentions data

[1] James Tobin, "On the Predictive Value of Consumer Intentions and Attitudes," Cowles Foundation Discussion Paper No. 41, mimeographed, October 8, 1957.

collected in early 1952 to help predict expenditures during 1952 reflected to any significant extent expenditures in the opening months of the year. Third, these papers do not show how at the aggregate level consumer-expenditures intentions—either alone or supplemented by objective information on income and related economic, social, and demographic characteristics—compare in predictive ability with simple projections of the most recent rate of expenditure (again if desirable supplemented by additional objective information). At the cross-section or individual family level, the family's expenditures in the preceding period may also serve as a highly useful "objective" variable in explaining or helping to predict expenditures in the next period, though obviously the correlation between the two periods might be direct or indirect depending on the nature of the item.

To summarize, I think the weight of evidence including the new data presented by Miss Mueller suggests that consumer-intentions data in the major household expenditures or durable goods area do have predictive value, whereas the evidence for consumer attitudes as distinct from intentions is mostly negative though not conclusive. However, unlike the situation for fixed capital expenditures planned by business, blow-ups of consumer intentions give extremely poor forecasts of expenditures and, even when supplemented by objective data, do not as yet give very reliable forecasts of expenditures.

ROBERT FERBER, University of Illinois

Evaluation of the use of intentions and attitude data in predicting consumer durable goods purchases should be improved by approaching the problem with a broader perspective. In the context of such surveys, durable goods purchases during a given period can be segregated into two broad groups, purchases for which (1) a plan had been previously reported, and (2) a plan had not been previously reported.[1]

Plans for type 1 purchases were not only known in advance but were also fulfilled. In predicting such purchases, the value of intentions or plans-to-buy data clearly depends on our ability to discriminate between those that will be and those that will not be fulfilled during the given period. Preliminary indications are that, at least in the aggregate, such discrimination is possible.[2]

Type 2 purchases can be divided for analytical purposes into three major groups, (2a) those for which a plan had existed but was not reported to the interviewer, (2b) those unplanned at the time of the interview but

[1] For an earlier version of this model, see Robert Ferber, "Sales Forecasting by Sample Surveys," *Journal of Marketing*, July 1955, pp. 10-12.

[2] Robert Ferber, *Factors Influencing Durable Goods Purchases*, Bureau of Economic and Business Research, University of Illinois, 1955.

made later because of necessity, and (2c) those unplanned and not needed but purchased largely on impulse.

Type 2a purchases are undoubtedly a function of the interviewing approach and the survey technique, and may well be constant from one interviewing wave to another. But a correction factor or equation for this understatement in the aggregate should not be difficult to obtain.

For predicting necessity purchases (type 2b) survey data are likely to be of little value, except perhaps the data on the age distribution of specific durables. These data would serve as a determining variable in predicting necessity purchases (given an operational definition of them) with the aid of multivariate techniques.

It is in the prediction of impulse purchases (type 2c) that attitude data may well be most useful. The extent of purchases made on the spur of the moment, at a given level of economic circumstances (income, prices, etc.), probably depends on consumer attitudes at the time. But an impulse to purchase can arise under many different kinds of circumstances. It seems desirable, therefore, to subclassify this category before attempting to assess the net effect of attitudes or even attempting to devise prediction techniques for such purchases.

This rather sketchy outline of the proposed model will, I hope, be sufficient to indicate its potential general usefulness as a means of integrating survey techniques with aggregate techniques and of predicting consumer purchases of either specific durable goods or all durable goods.

The Railroad Shippers' Forecasts and the Illinois Employers' Labor Force Anticipations: A Study in Comparative Expectations

ROBERT FERBER

UNIVERSITY OF ILLINOIS

How comparable are different types of anticipations data with each other? It is not yet clear to what extent one set of anticipations is representative of others for similar magnitudes, mainly because of the difficulty of locating comparable sets. Invariably, differences are found in questioning procedures, reporting practices, compilation of data, industry coverage, distance in the future to which the anticipation applies, period covered, and other factors.

This paper reports an analysis of two sets of anticipations data: the Illinois employers' labor force anticipations and the Midwest region railroad shippers' carloadings forecasts. Both sets of data—although not exactly comparable—are issued as actual figures as well as anticipations, from which a rough estimate can be made of how much the differences between the two series reflect actual diverse trends or inherent differences in the characteristics of the anticipations data. For example, the railroad shippers' forecasts for the region are issued quarterly by thirty-two major industry classifications, several of which are directly comparable with the labor force industry breakdowns.

After a brief outline of the way the labor force anticipations and the railroad shippers' forecasts are prepared, to see sources of similarity and dissimilarity between them, the two sets of data are examined for:

1. Similarities between anticipations made at about the same time
2. Degree of correspondence over time between errors in the two series
3. Similarities between the factors that appear to influence each series.

Nature of the Forecasts

LABOR FORCE ANTICIPATIONS

Since 1946, Illinois employers have been asked by the Illinois Department of Labor (as part of a federal Bureau of Employment Security

NOTE: This study is an outgrowth of the project on expectations and business fluctuations sponsored by the Merrill Foundation and conducted at the University of Illinois under the direction of Franco Modigliani. The author is indebted to the University Research Board and to the Bureau of Economic and Business Research of the University of Illinois for assistance which made this study possible. He would also like to thank Nai Ruenn Chen and Fadil Zuwaylif for aid with the statistical analysis.

program) to report at the end of each month the actual size of the labor force employed that month and the anticipated size two months and four months in advance. For the Chicago labor market area the Labor Department compiles and publishes the data by firm and by industry group every second month.

Coverage. All business firms in Illinois with twenty-five or more workers are asked to cooperate except in the Chicago–Calumet labor market area, where coverage is restricted to firms with sixty-five or more employees (about 80 per cent of all manufacturing employment).

Response Rates. While exact records are not kept on response rates, considerably more than half of the firms report labor force anticipations. For sales volume, employment, and other indicators of economic importance, the rate of return is much larger because reports are obtained from practically all leading firms in the Chicago area—by mail or, failing that, by telephone or personal interview. But the tendency of many firms to skip an occasional month creates perplexing gaps in both the anticipated and actual employment data.

Representativeness of Replies. How far the anticipations represent the official outlook of a firm where such exists, and what level of management is responsible for them, is difficult to tell. Because of the confidential nature of the replies, only circumstantial evidence is available; the titles of those to whom questionnaires are addressed suggest that data are usually supplied by a personnel manager or his assistant, and only occasionally by a production manager or vice-president. The signatures on returns are often not those of the person addressed but of someone of lower rank, such as a clerk. In the opinion of the Department of Labor analysts, if a low-ranking signer has worked up the data, the personnel manager or another higher official is invariably consulted. But concrete evidence on the matter is lacking.

Meaning of Anticipations. The anticipations reported by the respondents are not forecasts in the sense of predicting what is likely to happen. Rather they are more in the nature of conditional expectations, as suggested by the question used: "Provided an adequate supply of labor will be available, what will your total employment be on: (a) [15th of month two months hence]? (b) [15th of month four months hence]?"

The conditional aspect is most important during labor shortages, as in the immediate postwar years, or during and shortly after a strike, when replies are of little value for gauging actual business conditions. On the other hand, when manpower supplies are adequate, the anticipations would seem to be equivalent to predictions of future employment. This is true for nearly all of the period covered by the present study (July 1952 to the end of 1955) except for periods of major work stoppages.

182

THE RAILROAD SHIPPERS' FORECASTS[1]

United States railroad shipping is served by thirteen regional boards, each "shippers' advisory board" composed of representatives—usually traffic managers—of the firms which ship heavily by rail. The boards advise the Association of American Railroads (AAR) on shipping problems, bring grievances to its attention, and, among other functions, since 1927 they have prepared quarterly forecasts of railroad carloadings for the AAR. Because the procedure varies among the regional boards, only the methods used by the Midwest Shippers' Advisory Board will be described here.

The Board covers the states of Iowa, Wisconsin (excluding the northwestern tip near Minneapolis), Illinois (excluding the St. Louis area), and the western part of Indiana. The Chicago metropolitan area is the chief center of the region's industrial activity.

About six weeks before the beginning of each calendar quarter, the Board asks the shippers of the region to forecast their freight-car requirements for the next quarter and to transmit their forecasts promptly to the chairman of the appropriate commodity group (thirty-two in all) for their products. Commodity-group totals are sent by the secretary of the Board (a paid AAR official) to the AAR office in Washington for publication with the forecasts of the other regional boards.

Response to the forecast requests in the Midwest region appears to be generally good, and emphasis on securing data from the larger shippers has made the representation in each commodity group well over half of total shipments. Indirect evidence suggests that the forecasts are sincere attempts at accuracy without deliberate bias even though the commodity-group chairman is a shipper himself. (The forecasts for other regions are sent directly to each board's secretary.) For two commodity groups, automobiles and coal, the forecasts are reported by the industry associations, though presumably after consultation with the individual firms.

Unlike the question on labor force anticipations, the shippers' forecast question is phrased to refer specifically to the level of carloadings in the corresponding quarter of the preceding year. In some cases commodity-group chairmen ask for forecasts, not in absolute figures, but as the expected percentage change from the corresponding quarter of the previous year. By this means shippers apparently try to avoid corrections for the sharp seasonal oscillations characteristic of most types of railroad shipments. Employment anticipations are not a part of the railroad shippers' forecasts, which are nearly always made by the traffic managers of the firms.

[1] This section is based on Robert Ferber, *The Railroad Shippers' Forecasts* (Studies in Business Expectations and Planning, No. 1, Bureau of Economic and Business Research, University of Illinois, 1953), which contains a more detailed discussion of the data.

INDUSTRIES SELECTED FOR COMPARISON

Eight industry classifications used for the labor force anticipations are listed with seven apparently closely corresponding Midwest shippers' forecasts:[2]

No. of Firms	LABOR FORCE ANTICIPATIONS Title	RAILROAD SHIPPERS' FORECASTS Title
4	Food, excluding meat packing	Food products
5	Meat packing	Livestock
12	Iron and steel	Iron and steel
2	Cans	} Other metals
4	Other fabricated metals	
7	Nonelectrical machinery	Machinery and boilers
8	Transportation equipment, excluding farm machinery	Vehicles and parts
3	Automobiles and parts	Automobiles and trucks

Exact correspondence cannot be established because the shipper members of each commodity group are not publicly identified. Their number in most of the commodity groups is, however, undoubtedly many times larger than the number of firms in the corresponding labor force–industry classifications. The one saving feature is that the discrepancy in coverage for most industries is probably offset by the large size of the firms— generally the largest in an industry—whose labor anticipations were analyzed in this study. The largest firms in the labor market area and the Midwest shippers' region are usually in the Chicago area, except for the meat packing and automobile industries. Two of the biggest meat packing firms could not be included in the study because of lack of data. Only three firms (plants) are included from the automobiles and parts industry. How well these firms represent trends and outlook of the industry in the area—around Chicago, made up of many small and medium-sized plants —is open to question. Nevertheless, all seven industries were used in the analysis.

Comparison of the actual aggregated employment of the member firms in the seven industries with the total carloadings reported for each industry is shown in Chart 1. At best only rough correspondence can be expected, partly because of the differing coverage in the two series and partly because of the fundamental differences between fluctuations in carloadings and in

[2] Correspondence between the meat packing and livestock categories is based on the fact that activity in both categories is centered in the big meat packing plants in Chicago. Shipments made by these plants are included under "livestock" (with the exception of canned meat products), but an appreciable portion of the total is undoubtedly accounted for by other sources.

CHART I

Aggregated Employment of Sample Firms and Railroad
Carloadings in the Midwest Region, by Industry, 1951–1956

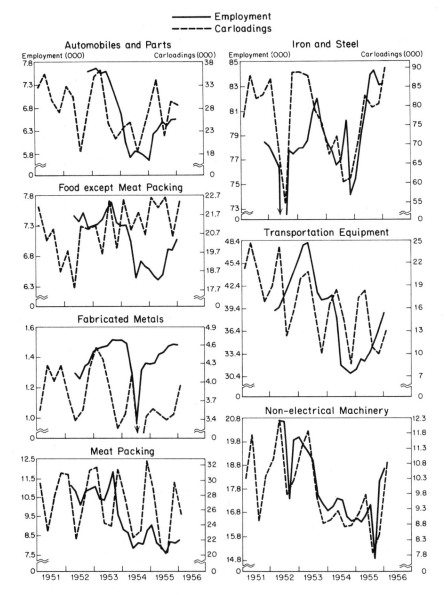

employment. Fluctuations arise from inventory changes and from sharp
seasonal variations, particularly marked in railroad carloadings. Good
correspondence between the two series is exhibited in four industries—

iron and steel, nonelectrical machinery, meat packing, and transportation equipment. Some rough correspondence is shown in automobiles and parts, whereas very little if any is displayed in food or other metals.

Data are not available to explain the differences in correspondence. However the four industries with good correspondence are all highly oligopolistic, and the few firms in the employment anticipations sample could constitute a much larger portion of their industries and be more representative of them than do the firms in the industries with poor correspondence. In any event, lack of correspondence between actual magnitudes does not preclude correspondence in direction between the anticipations and forecasts.

Similarities and Correspondence

DIRECTION OF THE ANTICIPATIONS

The direction of movement of the two sets of anticipations can be determined by comparing the level of actual employment and carloadings in one year either with the level at the corresponding time the year before or with the immediately preceding actual figure (i.e. the most recent available to the forecaster at the time of reporting an anticipation). The first method will eliminate the seasonal factor insofar as this does not change from year to year and will be more realistic, for carloadings at least, because railroad shippers' forecasts are based on the level of carloadings a year earlier.

The second method would seem worth using only if the industries exhibited relatively little seasonal variation during the period in question. Otherwise misleading indications of correspondence would result because of the strong underlying seasonals in both series (e.g. meat packing, Chart 1). All industries in the sample exhibit sharp seasonal variation in carloadings, and it is impracticable to study movements for individual months or quarters of the few years covered by the study. Hence, only the first method is used here even though it may exaggerate the extent of agreement between the two series, which may differ little relative to the previous year but substantially relative to current levels. Chart 2 indicates the extent of correspondence between the two sets of anticipations.

For most of the industries, Chart 2 shows that the carloadings forecasts do correspond with the employment anticipations. For food, iron and steel, fabricated metals, automobiles and parts, and nonelectrical machinery, the general trend is much the same for both sets of expectations data. But the minor fluctuations do not often coincide and some of the more dramatic instances of correspondence are due primarily to abnormal levels of operation in those industries in the preceding year (such as the steel strike in the summer of 1952) causing the denominators of all three ratios for the same period to be unusually low. Almost no correspondence between the expectations data is apparent in the meat packing industry,

186

CHART 2

Anticipated Changes in Carloadings and Employment Relative to
Actual Levels at the Corresponding Time of
the Preceding Year, by Industry, 1952–1956

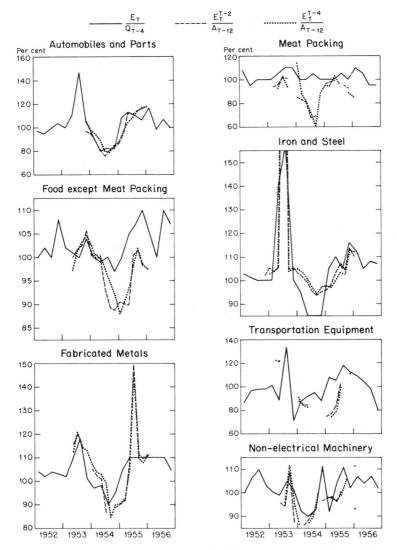

and the relatively few observations available for transportation equipment
make that comparison inconclusive.

The close correspondence between the two-month and four-month
employment anticipations indicates that the four-month ones, usually
identical with the two-month anticipations, do not contribute much useful

187

information. More precise measures of correspondence between the two sets of expectations data are provided in Table 1. It presents simple determination coefficients between the shippers' forecasts and the two-month employment anticipations for the closest periods to which the expectations pertain and the closest times at which the expectations were prepared.

TABLE 1

Coefficients of Determination between Anticipated Change in Carloadings and Two-Month Employment Anticipations by Industry, 1951-1955

| | OBSERVATIONS | COEFFICIENTS OF DETERMINATION | |
| | | *Pairing Time:* | |
		To Which Anticipations Pertain[a]	*At Which Anticipations Made*
Food, except meat packing	11	0.07	0.10
Meat packing	10	.10	.13
Iron and steel	11	.62[b]	.45
Fabricated metals	10	.71[b]	.50
Nonelectrical machinery	9	.38	.43
Transportation equipment	6	.01[c]	.05[c]
Automobiles and parts	9	.75[b]	.60[b]

[a] Where one expectation based on time of preparation was equidistant between two expectations of the other magnitude, an average of the two was used as the corresponding observation. For example, the time to which forecasts pertain was obtained by averaging the January and March employment anticipations to yield a figure comparable to that of the shippers' expectations for the first quarter.

[b] Significantly different from zero at the 0.05 probability level.

[c] Negative correlation.

As the table shows, the results of the two comparisons are much the same. Fairly close correspondence between the two sets of anticipations is apparent in iron and steel, fabricated metals, and automobiles and parts, though the correlations are not always statistically significant. The correspondence in nonelectrical machinery is no greater than what could result from chance, and none is apparent for the other three industries.

ACCURACY OF THE ANTICIPATIONS

The labor force anticipations appear to be noticeably more accurate than the railroad shippers' forecasts when the four-month anticipations are compared with the three-month shippers' forecasts, as in Table 2. For only one of the seven industries (transportation equipment) is the average absolute percentage error larger for the four-month labor force anticipations than for the shippers' forecasts. For the other six industries, the four-month anticipations turn out to be more accurate, and for three of them considerably so. The two-month anticipations are more accurate still, with average percentage errors ranging between one-half and one-

TABLE 2

Average Absolute Percentage and Naïve Forecast Model Error of Labor
Force Anticipations and of Railroad Shippers' Forecasts by Industry,
July 1952–December 1955

	OBSERVATIONS			AVERAGE ABSOLUTE PERCENTAGE ERROR[a]		
	Labor Force Anticipations		Shippers'	Labor Force Anticipations		Shippers'
	2-mo.	4-mo.	Forecasts	2-mo.	4-mo.	Forecasts
Food, except meat packing:						
Actual	21	21	14	2.4	3.7	4.9
Naïve model				2.3	5.6	7.4
Meat packing:						
Actual	17	17	14	5.5	8.2	9.3
Naïve model				5.9	13.6	8.2
Iron and steel:						
Actual	20	19	11	1.9	2.9	9.0
Naïve model				2.1	3.8	17.8
Fabricated metals:						
Actual	19	21	13	2.0	3.0	12.2
Naïve model				4.6	7.8	16.0
Nonelectrical:						
Actual	16	16	14	2.8	6.4	8.5
Naïve model				4.6	6.7	7.6
Transportation equipment:						
Actual	14	10	13	2.8	5.7	4.0
Naïve model				8.5	19.9	27.0
Automobiles and parts:						
Actual	19	17	12	4.2	6.6	16.6
Naïve				3.2	9.2	19.6

Errors clearly influenced by work stoppages were excluded.

[a] See text footnote 5.

sixth of the errors in the corresponding shippers' forecasts. Both series do better, generally, than "naïve model" extrapolations of level.

That the phenomena are not due to a few extreme errors here and there but are fairly representative of the situation is supported by the data in Table 3. Here the comparison between the two series is of the extent of overestimation and the prevalence of relatively large errors (over 5 per cent) in each direction. With few exceptions, errors of the latter type are far more frequent among the shippers' forecasts than among the labor force anticipations of either length. Although the sample sizes in each case are small (Table 2), the results are sufficiently uniform to be fairly conclusive. Thus, all four instances in which all the errors in one direction exceeded 5 per cent occurred in shippers' forecasts; six of the seven instances in which none of the errors in one direction exceeded 5 per cent occurred in labor force anticipations; and the seventh instance, in the shippers' forecasts, was the only one based on a sample of only four observations.

189

TABLE 3

Direction of Errors of Labor Force Anticipations and of Railroad Shippers' Forecasts by Industry, July 1952–December 1955 [a]

	PERCENTAGE OF OVERESTIMATES, TOTAL			PERCENTAGE OF OVERESTIMATES EXCEEDING 5%			PERCENTAGE OF UNDERESTIMATES EXCEEDING 5%		
	Labor Force Anticipations		Shippers' Forecasts	Labor Force Anticipations		Shippers' Forecasts	Labor Force Anticipations		Shippers' Forecasts
	2-mo.	4-mo.		2-mo.	4-mo.		2-mo.	4-mo.	
Food, except meat packing	57	48	29	17	30	50[b]	11	18	40
Meat packing	59	41	64	30	57	100	72	50	40[b]
Iron and steel	55	68	45	0	0	60	0	33	50
Fabricated metals	58	48	62	9	10	62	0	20	100[b]
Nonelectrical machinery	69	75	72	18	33	80	0	25[b]	25[b]
Transportation equipment	43	40	77	33	25[b]	30	0	40[b]	0[b]
Automobiles and parts	90	76	42	41	38	100[b]	50[b]	50[b]	100

[a] Based on the same observations as in Table 2. [b] Based on five observations or less.

Table 3 also indicates some slight tendency toward overestimation in both sets of forecasts. The phenomenon varies considerably by industry and also by source of anticipation, but it tends to bear out the "permanent optimism" hypothesis advanced in the previous study of the railroad shippers' forecasts.[3] The uniformly negative signs resulting from averaging the percentage error of each set of anticipations for each industry attest to the prevalence of overestimation (Table 4). The values are not high (for the shippers' forecasts somewhat lower than those obtained in the

TABLE 4

Average Percentage Error of the Two Sets of Anticipations by Industry, July 1952–December 1955

	Labor Force Anticipations		Shippers' Forecasts
	2-month	4-month	
Food, except meat packing	−1.0	−0.8	1.3
Meat packing	−1.1	−1.7	−6.2
Iron and steel	−0.5	−0.5	−2.5
Fabricated metals	−0.9	0.1	−3.9
Nonelectrical machinery	−2.2	−3.6	−6.4
Transportation equipment	−1.0	−1.3	−3.1
Automobiles and parts	−3.3	−4.9	−1.2

The percentage error is based on the formula: (actual minus anticipation) divided by actual.

[3] Ferber, pp. 46ff.

earlier study)[4] but they are negative even for the transportation equipment labor force anticipations and for the shippers' forecasts of automobiles and parts carloadings, both characterized most frequently by underestimates (Table 3).

Influential Factors

EFFECT OF AMPLITUDE

Do the foregoing findings suggest an inherently greater accuracy in the labor force anticipations than in the railroad shippers' forecasts, or is there some other explanation for them? The absence of paired data by individual firms precludes testing various hypotheses, but one important

CHART 3

Scatter Diagram of Amplitude of Actual
Magnitudes and Average Absolute Percentage
Error of Anticipations, by Industry
1951–1956

× Employment
● Carloadings

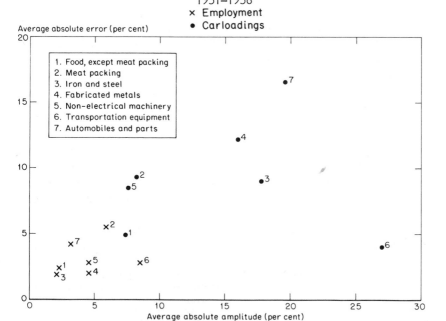

possibility can be tested—that the observed differences are largely if not wholly explainable by the differential amplitudes of fluctuation in employment and in carloadings. Chart 1 suggests the existence of such differentials, and in Chart 3 the scatter diagram between the amplitudes and the corresponding average absolute percentage errors of the anticipations lends strong support to the hypothesis.

4 *Ibid.*, Table 5, p. 50.

The amplitudes were based on estimates of the absolute average percentage change in the actual figures during the period of observation for each industry (Chart 1).[5] The average absolute percentage errors were taken from Table 2; the two-month anticipations were used for the labor force data.

Chart 3 leads to three conclusions:

1. The amplitude of fluctuations in carloadings, even after allowance for the two-month span, is generally considerably larger than that of employment in the same industry.

2. For both employment and carloadings, the average error of the forecasts tends to be positively correlated with amplitude. But the influence of changes in amplitude seems to be considerably greater for the railroad shippers' forecasts than for the labor force anticipations.

3. The difference in accuracy exhibited between the two sets of anticipations data is therefore explainable in large measure by the different amplitudes of the actual magnitudes.

Because of the small number of observations (industries), no attempt was made to adjust the errors of the forecasts for differences in amplitude. Chart 3 suggests that there would remain some differences in accuracy in favor of the employment anticipations, but they would lend slight, if any, support to an assumption of "inherent" superiority for the employment anticipations.

CORRESPONDENCE BETWEEN ERRORS

Correspondence between the two sets of anticipations, abundantly evident in the direction of the anticipations, is not evident in the direction of their errors. Only for the food industry does any correspondence appear in Chart 4, and even here it is not close.

The results of an attempt to compare the direction of errors in the shippers' forecasts with that in the two-month employment anticipations

---

[5] The exact measure of amplitude varied with the extent of seasonality in each series. If relatively little seasonal variation was present (as defined below), the measure used was $\sum[(A_t - A_{t+2})/NA_{t+2}]$ for employment in month $t+2$, where N is the number of observations; this is the naïve model forecast error presented in Table 2. If seasonal variation was substantial, a crudely adjusted extrapolation of level was substituted for A_t, namely, $A_t(A_{t-10}/A_{t-12})$—so that the measure of amplitude of employment becomes: $\sum[(A_t/A_{t+2})/(A_{t-12}/A_{t-10}) - 1]$. This is also the seasonally corrected naïve model forecast error presented in Table 2. Corresponding forms were used for carloadings.

Seasonal variation in a series was considered "relatively little" if the relative amplitude of the seasonal index derived for that series by link relatives was less than 10 per cent. This was true of all the employment series except transportation equipment, and of none of the carloading series. For further details, see my *Employer Forecasts of Manpower Requirements* (Studies in Business Expectations and Planning, No. 3, Bureau of Economic and Business Research, University of Illinois, 1958).

CHART 4

Percentage Errors of Railroad Shippers' Forecasts and
of Labor Force Anticipations, by Industry, 1951–1957

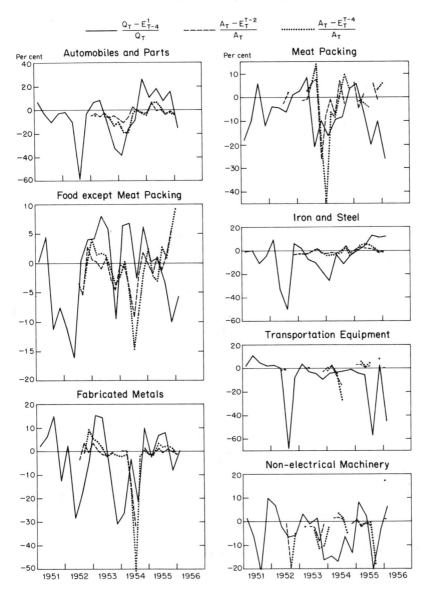

$$\frac{Q_T - E^1_{T-4}}{Q_T} \qquad \frac{A_T - E^{T-2}_T}{A_T} \qquad \frac{A_T - E^{T-4}_T}{A_T}$$

show little similarity between them (Table 5). None of the percentages are significantly different from 50 per cent at the 0.05 probability level, even if the two types of error are combined for each industry or for all seven industries.

193

TABLE 5

Correspondence between Direction of Errors of Labor Force Anticipations
and of Railroad Shippers' Forecasts, July 1952–December 1955

	ANTICIPATIONS ERRORS		PERCENTAGE OF TIME SHIPPERS' FORECAST ERROR IN SAME DIRECTION	
	Over-estimates	Under-estimates	Over-estimates	Under-estimates
Food, except meat packing	8	6	25	67
Meat packing	7	5	71	20
Iron and steel	8	5	50	60
Fabricated metals	6	4	83	75
Nonelectrical machinery	9	3	67	33
Transportation equipment	4	4	75	0
Automobiles and parts	10	2	40	50

These results were to be expected. For one of the two principal determinants of error in a forecast is the level of the actual magnitude, and the previous analyses showed little correspondence, in the short run, between fluctuations of carloadings and of employment by industry during the period studied.

Structure of the Anticipations

The railroad shippers' forecasts have shown a striking tendency to regress toward the past level of carloadings. In my earlier study it was shown that the shippers' forecasts for the prewar and early postwar years could be closely approximated by two terms: the level of shipments in the corresponding quarter of the preceding year (Q_{t-4}); and the year-to-year change in carloadings for the most recent quarter (Q_{t-1}/Q_{t-5}). It was also found that shippers' expectations were contrary to what one would expect. When carloadings had risen for twelve months, the shippers' expected carloadings in the next quarter to decline more than halfway back to the previous year's level. When carloadings had fallen, they expected a reversal of the movement and a rise more than halfway back again. The phenomenon characterized total national carloadings as well as those of all five industries studied.

The same hypothesis was tested with the labor force anticipations to see whether the regressive tendency is characteristic of other types of anticipations and with the Midwest shippers' forecast data, since only national aggregates had been used in the earlier study. The basic functions to be fitted for testing the hypothesis were, for the railroad shippers' forecasts:

(1) $$E_t = a + bQ_{t-4} + cQ_{t-4}\left(\frac{Q_{t-1} - Q_{t-5}}{Q_{t-5}}\right)$$

194

and for the labor force anticipations:

$$(2) \qquad E_t = a + bA_{t-12} + cA_{t-12}\left(\frac{A_{t-2} - A_{t-14}}{A_{t-14}}\right)$$

where Q_t represents actual carloadings in quarter t, and A_t represents actual employment in month t.

In the absence of any trend, the discussion makes it evident that if c exceeds one, extrapolation is indicated; if less than one, a reversal. Assuming a straight line trend over the preceding year, if an upward trend is present, a value of c as low as 0.75 in (1) and 0.83 in (2) would be consistent with an extrapolation hypothesis, because extrapolation of just the latest level for the railroad shippers' data would require adjusting Q_{t-4} for the increase in carloadings from Q_{t-4} to Q_{t-1}. By the above assumption this would be three-fourths of the distance from Q_{t-5} to Q_{t-1}, the modifying element in (1). A similar argument holds for the employment anticipations.

The results obtained from fitting (1) and (2) to the two sets of anticipations are shown in Table 6. They may be summarized as follows:

1. On the whole, the hypotheses fit the data well for both sets of anticipations (column 4). More than three-quarters of the variance in the anticipations is explained by one or both of the independent variables for six of the seven industries in each case. The exceptions are the iron and steel carloading forecasts and the nonelectrical machinery employment anticipations, for which the explained variance is no larger than would be expected as a result of chance.

2. In several instances, the hypothesis appears to be unnecessarily complicated inasmuch as the anticipations appear to be based solely on the actual level of operations a year earlier (columns 2 and 3). This is true of the shippers' forecasts in the food, meat packing, and transportation equipment industries.

3. The regression phenomenon remains in evidence for all the carloadings functions for which equation 1 is valid but not for any of the labor force anticipation functions. This is evident from column 3, which shows all the estimates of c of (1) to be well below 0.75, the minimum for extrapolation in the presence of an upward linear trend. Only two estimates of c in (2) are consistent with the corresponding minimum of 0.83 (at the 0.05 probability level). Furthermore, the estimate of $b - c$, which reflects the extent to which the present trend is reversed in preparing the anticipations, significantly exceeds zero (at the 0.05 probability level) for all industries where (1) holds, but not for any instance in which (2) has been fitted.[6] Indeed, the estimates of $b - c$ in (2) are mostly negative, which could indicate a sharp extrapolation of the current trend.

[6] The reflection of extent of the reversal depends on the assumption that b is approximately one, in which case (1) becomes:

$$E_t = a + Q_{t-1}\frac{Q_{t-4}}{Q_{t-5}} - (b - c)(Q_{t-1} - Q_{t-5})\frac{Q_{t-4}}{Q_{t-5}}$$

TABLE 6

Test for Regression Hypothesis on Labor Force Anticipations and
Railroad Shippers' Forecasts

	ESTIMATES OF PARAMETERS OF EQUATION 1 OR 2			R^2 USING AS DEPENDENT		ESTIMATES OF REVERSAL COEFFICIENTS
	a (1)	b (2)	c (3)	E_t (4)	A_t (5)	$b-c$ (6)
Food, except meat packing:						
Employment	787	0.90	0.84	0.83	0.69	(0.06)
Carloadings	424	1.00	(0.07)	0.77	0.40	0.93
Meat packing:						
Employment	1,661	0.81	0.88	0.80	0.72	(−0.07)
Carloadings	(636)	1.00	(−0.03)	0.92	0.77	1.03
Iron and steel:						
Employment	99,033	−0.25	0.56	0.83	0.59	−0.81
Carloadings	28,986	0.63	0.20	0.68	(0.25)	0.43
Fabricated metals:						
Employment	1,394	(0.03)	0.42	0.94	0.66	−0.39
Carloadings	(−61)	1.06	0.31	0.89	(0.14)	0.75
Nonelectrical machinery:						
Employment	11,312	(0.36)	(0.33)	(0.21)	(0.04)	(0.02)
Carloadings	2.562	0.77	0.37	0.83	0.65	0.39
Transportation equipment:						
Employment	13,957	0.65	0.87	0.96	0.95	(−0.22)
Carloadings	2,852	0.82	(−0.08)	0.79	0.63	0.90
Automobiles and parts:						
Employment	2,354	0.66	0.77	0.90	0.70	(−0.11)
Carloadings	4.597	0.85	0.37	0.77	(0.22)	0.48

NOTE: The regressions shown are based on somewhat fewer observations than the number noted in Table 2, mainly because earlier data were not available to permit calculation of the change terms for the entire period of observation.

All numbers are significant at 0.01 probability level except those with rules, which are significant at 0.05 probability level; and those in parentheses, which are not significant at the 0.05 probability level.

4. Pronounced differences between the estimates of the parameters of the two functions are evident also for b. For the shippers' forecasts, five of the estimates are not significantly different from 1.0 and one only barely. For the labor force anticipations, only two of the estimates are consistent with a true value of 1.0 for b. In general, deviations of the estimates of b from 1.0, as well as significant estimates of a, may point to the need for modifications in the original formulation of the hypothesis.

5. The hypothesis implicit in (1) and (2) appears a more valid explanation of actual (aggregate) structure of the shippers' forecasts than of the labor force anticipations. In fact, it is doubtful whether (2) provides a really adequate explanation of the formation of the labor force anticipations. It follows both from the preceding observations and from a

comparison of columns 4 and 5, which shows when (1) and (2) are fitted alternately to E_t and to A_t, as dependent, that the closeness of fit varies much more for carloadings. The high correlations obtained with (2) may reflect, for example, primarily extrapolation of current levels. In the same vein, for all the labor force anticipations industry functions, the estimate of a particular parameter based on E_t, as dependent, was similar to that based on A_t, as dependent, whereas this was true of only one of the carloading functions (transportation equipment). Then too, the hypothesis advanced in the next section to explain the regression phenomenon would, if valid, negate (2).

Thus the main conclusion emerging from this part of the study is that the regression phenomenon, so typical of the railroad shippers' forecasts, is not present in the labor force anticipations—at least not when the actual level in the corresponding period of the preceding year is used as the base.[7]

EXPLANATION OF THE REGRESSION PHENOMENON

Why should the regression phenomenon appear so strikingly in the railroad shippers' forecasts and yet not be apparent in the labor force anticipations? The available evidence suggests that the answer may well lie in the different phrasing of the questions used in the two surveys.

The traffic managers are asked for two figures: the *actual percentage change in carloadings over the past year*, and the *expected change in carloadings next quarter relative to the same quarter for the preceding year*. Whatever their absolute percentage changes may have been during the past year (Q_{t-1}/Q_{t-5}), most traffic managers are inclined to deflate the change in the belief that carloadings are not likely to rise, or fall, as much at an annual rate in the next quarter as in the preceding quarters. Hence, they predict E_t/Q_{t-4} invariably lower than Q_{t-1}/Q_{t-5}, and seemingly with little awareness of the full extent of the change that has already taken place, Q_{t-2}/Q_{t-4}. Since Q_{t-2}/Q_{t-4} is common to both terms, their prediction of E_t relative to A_{t-1} seasonally adjusted—which is in effect $A_{t-1}(A_{t-4}/A_{t-5})$—tends in the aggregate to run counter to the prevailing trend.

The two figures requested from the employers are very different from those just discussed: the *current level of employment* (A_t) and the *expected level two months hence* (E_{t+2}).[8] When employers prepare their labor force anticipations, they are not confronted with any past actual change as a

[7] One could modify the basic hypothesis to allow for rate-of-change factors and for use of different bases for preparing the anticipations. As shown in the earlier study on the railroad shippers' forecasts, however, such refinements are likely to have negligible effect on the main results, and hence were not attempted here. A detailed exploration of the factors that seem to influence the labor force anticipations will be found in the monograph on the subject published by the Bureau of Economic and Business Research of the University of Illinois.

[8] The same applies to the four-month anticipations.

basis for modification but use solely the current levels, to which they are asked to add or subtract the next expected change in their labor force. As a result, the value of the employers' E_{t+2} is far less likely to be deflated relative to past trends than is the value of the railroad shippers' E_t. In other words, the regression phenomenon appears to be the product largely of a forecast requested (1) for year-to-year changes, (2) in percentage terms, and (3) by comparison with the actual change over the past year, when most of the period of the forecast is already over.

Summary

Comparison of two sets of anticipations for the same industries, area, and time period resulted in the following main findings:

1. The degree of correspondence in direction between the two series of anticipations varies sharply by industry.
2. No correspondence is evident between the errors in the two sets of anticipations for any particular industry.
3. The labor force anticipations, particularly the two-month but also the four-month, are considerably more accurate than the railroad shippers' forecasts. Much if not all, of the difference would be removed if allowance were made for the higher amplitude of fluctuations of carloadings and for the generally positive relationship between amplitude and predictive accuracy.
4. A tendency toward overestimation is apparent in both sets of anticipations. The "permanent optimism" hypothesis, proposed and supported by the earlier study of the railroad shippers' forecasts, receives further support here from the evidence that larger errors are made on the downswings than on upswings.
5. The basic hypothesis on the structure of anticipations, formulated in the earlier study, is more effective for explaining the formation of the shippers' than for the employers' expectations. For the two sets of anticipations, the form of the correlation functions for the same industry differs substantially. Particularly noticeable is the absence in the labor force anticipations of the regression phenomenon so typical of the railroad shippers' forecasts.
6. The regression phenomenon in the railroad shippers' forecasts seems to stem from the request for an expected annual (usually percentage) change relative to the actual annual percentage change during the past year. The question appears to elicit use of some deflated value of the past change in carloadings as the basis for forecasts. The question asked employers, on the other hand, calls for use of the current level of employment as the base for anticipations with little tendency to consider or modify recent percentage changes.

7. Incidentally, for the labor force anticipations little additional information is provided by the four-month figures over that contained in the two-month anticipations, both usually being the same.

Whether the instances of lack of correspondence between the two sets of anticipations can be explained by differences in outlook of the people who prepare them remains open. Replies to the two questionnaires by the same firm are probably prepared independently. Within the same firm short-run changes in employment are not necessarily related to short-run changes in carloadings. They occur in different divisions of the firm's operations, and often may be partly caused by inventory changes in handling storable goods. On the other hand, the differences do not rule out the possibility of a similarity in outlook.

COMMENT

Douglas G. Hartle, University of Toronto

By applying the same statistical technique to anticipations and to actual data for the same period and for roughly the same plants, Robert Ferber has made an interesting contribution to the discussion of the nature and significance of anticipations data. Although a substantial body of particular findings has resulted from earlier studies, too many employed differing variables, periods, and techniques; and thus it has been extremely difficult to draw general conclusions.

I am pleased to be able to add to the generality of some of Ferber's findings by noting similar results secured in a study I made of the Employment Forecast Survey (EFS) conducted by the Canadian Department of Labour.[1] After examining the individual establishment forecasts and the predictions derived from them, I came to the following conclusions:

1. For 1952-56 the "permanent optimism" hypothesis proposed by Ferber was borne out quite conclusively by the six-month but not the three-month forecasts.

2. A close relationship existed between the average absolute percentage errors of an industry's predictions and the amplitude of the year-to-year changes in its actual employment. Like Foss and Natrella, I found an inverse relationship between size of firm (employment) and the relative errors of their forecasts.

3. Like Ferber, I gained little information from the six-month forecasts not provided by the three-month ones (or vice versa), because so many were identical for both periods.

4. Although the predictions derived from the establishment forecasts tended to lag the nonseasonal changes in the aggregate actual employment

[1] The EFS is a quarterly mail-interview survey of a fixed sample of seven hundred establishments asked to forecast their employment three and six months ahead and to report their actual employment during each of the three preceding months.

of an industry and of the sample, I found no consistent evidence of the regressive tendency Ferber found in his analysis of the shippers' forecasts.

The reason for the presence of the regressive phenomenon in the shippers' forecasts but not in the labor force anticipations (or in the EFS predictions) was suggested by Ferber in an earlier paper. He proposed that the regression phenomena, observed in his original study of the shippers' forecasts "might conceivably have resulted from the extrapolation of the level of the corresponding quarter of the previous year by a large group of respondents and the extrapolation of trend by another large group."[2] Because the shippers' data were available only in aggregate form Ferber was unable to test this hypothesis, but I believe his explanation is substantially correct.

Following his line of reasoning, we know also that if a large proportion of respondents forecast "no change" in the current level of a variable for the next two to four months, we will not find the consistent regression phenomena which his analysis of the shippers' anticipations unearthed. Rather the results will be consistent with Ferber's for the labor force anticipations. I believe that the difference in structure between the two sets of anticipations can be attributed to a strong tendency on the part of the shippers to forecast no change from the same quarter last year, and an equally strong tendency among the establishments to forecast no change from the current level (i.e. from two or three months earlier).

This view is strongly supported by Ferber's results, and by mine in both the investigation of the EFS establishment forecasts and an earlier study of the labor force anticipations of firms in the broadwoven textile industry in North Carolina, as reported to the state employment security agency there. In all of these, approximately half the labor force anticipations were for no change from the current level.

Why do so many shippers forecast no change in the level of shipments from that same quarter of the previous year at the very time many employers are forecasting no change from the current level of employment? Partly, I believe, because the greater seasonality of the shipments series makes a no-change forecast from the current level obviously wrong, partly because the shippers and employers are asked to use different sorts of base figures. The shippers are specifically asked to look at the year-to-year level, the employers to report their latest actual employment.

Other probable explanations of the many no-change forecasts, regardless of the base of the comparison, are:

[2] Robert Ferber, "Measuring the Accuracy and Structure of Businessmen's Expectations," *Journal of the American Statistical Association*, September 1953. This hypothesis was also expounded in Report of Consultant Committee on General Business Expectations, *An Appraisal of Data and Research on Businessmen's Expectations about Outlook and Operating Variables*, Board of Governors of the Federal Reserve System, September 1955.

1. Some respondents really expect no change.

2. Some think a no-change answer the best one when they are uncertain.

3. Some think a no-change answer is the easiest way to get rid of a questionnaire while appearing to cooperate.

I do not wish to give the impression that I think the difference in base of the no-change anticipations is the only source of differences between the shippers' and the labor force anticipations. As Don Daly suggested at the conference, the greater seasonality of the industry may itself be a cause of a higher rate of error in the shipments series. My point is simply that, if one could apply Ferber's analysis to the data after excluding establishments reporting no-change anticipations from both the actual and anticipations series, the gross difference between the structures of the two sets of anticipations would probably disappear. If my views are correct, I think one can draw certain conclusions about predictions derived as the sum of reported anticipated shipments or employment that include many no-change answers:

1. The predictions will lag the actual changes they purport to predict except in the unlikely event that the anticipations of change always compensated for the no-change anticipations.

2. If the weight of the no-change responses remained fairly constant, the average error of the predictions probably could be reduced by use of corrective factors. But whether the corrected predictions would catch turning points is doubtful.

3. Elimination of firms that consistently forecast no change, or adoption of an aggregation technique to give less weight to no-change forecasts might improve the reliability of predictions.

The possibility of improvement in reliability by use of the elimination procedure gained only little encouragement from my work with the EFS. In several tests I found that the number and size of the eliminated establishments created sampling errors that usually more than offset the reductions in forecast errors. The net effect of the elimination was a deterioration in reliability.

In an experiment with different aggregation procedures, I converted the quantitative EFS establishment forecasts into forecasts of the direction of year-to-year change and computed an index based on the percentage of firms expecting year-to-year employment gains as a percentage of all reporting establishments.[3] The diffusion approach has its own problems, and my findings are far from complete. But I can report that the method seemed to reduce the lag of the predictions in virtually all instances and

[3] In this I followed a lead suggested by Millard Hastay ("The Dun and Bradstreet Surveys of Businessmen's Expectations," *Proceedings of the Business and Economic Statistics Section*, 114th Annual Meeting of the American Statistical Association, 1955, pp. 93-123).

eliminated it altogether in some although no establishment forecasts (no change or other) were eliminated. These results suggest the trial of other aggregation procedures as means of circumventing the difficulties posed by the prevalent no-change anticipation.

Ferber left open the question whether predictions of different variables secured from the same firm can be explained by "differences in outlook of the people who prepare them. Replies to the two questionnaires by the same firm are probably prepared independently." But he thinks similarity in outlook is not ruled out. Because I am not convinced about the significance of the difference between the structures of the two sets of anticipations, although I agree there is a difference, I must also bring in the Scottish verdict of "not proven." In the EFS interviewing program we encounter so much response variation on employment anticipations within the same firm that inconsistent anticipations of other variables reported to different surveys by the same firm would not be surprising.

I wish that Ferber had dealt more fully with another aspect of his study—the correspondence between the two sets of anticipations compared with the correspondence between the two actual series. I have the impression that he thinks that there was a closer relationship between the anticipations than the actual series, although I am not entirely convinced of this by an examination of Charts 1 and 2. It would have been useful if he had given us the coefficient of determination between the actual year-to-year changes in carloadings and in aggregate actual employment.

Also it is to be hoped that further work by Ferber and others will consider in greater detail the relationship between the anticipations and the actual data of different variables derived from the same firms. Such an investigation should throw light on the sources and character of business anticipations. It would be extremely interesting to know, for example, which anticipations lead and which anticipations lag, and which anticipations are dominant.

I conclude with a plea for more work on anticipations data at the establishment or firm level. If we find, as I believe we will, that much of the anticipations data gathered from business firms have little predictive value, we will be forced to give more consideration to the problem of how firms make predictions, and how they use them in the decision-making process.

I think the inadequacy of much of our anticipations data stems from asking the wrong questions of the wrong people at the wrong time. For example, after interviewing about fifty of the respondents in the EFS survey to learn how they made their forecasts, who made them, and why they were as good or as bad as they were, we had the outstanding impression that a firm rarely forecast its own future employment for its own purposes, presumably making current employment decisions without regard to future requirements or the cost of labor turnover. Whatever the reason, firms clearly only thought about employment needs three and six months ahead because we asked them to! It is hardly surprising that the answers were often of doubtful value. Perhaps we should have asked for forecasts of other variables about which the firm held anticipations of operational significance and derived from them our employment predictions. Also the dating of our questionnaires may have been entirely out of phase with the planning periods of the firms; and the three- and six-month target dates may have undershot or overshot their time horizons for employment.

To secure better anticipations data I think we must begin to look for answers to questions of the kind I have raised. The developments in decision theory, ably represented by Charles Holt's interesting paper in this volume, may provide a fruitful approach. Although an expensive, roundabout way to improve our predictions, it will increase our knowledge of the firm and the cycle—possibly of more significance in the long run.

Quantitative Evidence for the Interwar Period on the Course of Business Expectations: A Revaluation of the Railroad Shippers' Forecast

ALBERT GAILORD HART

COLUMBIA UNIVERSITY

Of the many sins of method with which economists are charged, few should concern us more than the accusation that when facts are hard to explain, we take refuge in irrefutable allegations. A widely accepted rule for avoiding this sin calls for dealing only in "observable" magnitudes. But following the rule has tended to exclude the intuitively attractive possibility of interpreting events in terms of expectations, on the ground that expectations were not observable.

For the postwar period, the discipline of confrontation with evidence has been extended to many interpretations that rest on expectations, since the rapid growth of expectational statistics has greatly broadened the range of empirical testing. But the postwar data arise from surveys that tap the informant after his expectations are framed and before the anticipated events take place. Expectations not picked up currently can be reconstructed only as we can find documentary traces. And while many traces exist, most of the evidence about expectations held in the past is so scattered and fragmentary as to defy analysis. Thus it seemed until recently that explanations through expectations of events before World War II must remain in the limbo of the unobservable.

However, one broad expectations survey, at least, goes back as far as 1927. In years when economists regarded anticipations as only a matter for speculation, practical men concerned with railway traffic were already collecting and publishing a quarterly survey of the freight-car requirements foreseen by traffic managers for each oncoming quarter year.[1] The survey by the railroad shippers' advisory boards seems to have preserved a high degree of comparability, with slight and infrequent changes in commodity classification and methods of compilation, over most of its thirty-year span—the longest span incidentally of any expectations series

[1] *National Forecast of the Regional Shippers' Advisory Boards Concerning Freight-Car Requirements: Estimated Percentage Increase or Decrease as Compared with Actual Carloadings Same Quarter Last Year*, Association of American Railroads, Car Service Division. The bulletin appears quarterly a week or two after the opening of the quarter for which estimates are made.

Note the reference in the title to a percentage-change comparison with the corresponding quarter of the previous year; this is crucial to the argument of the present paper.

surveyed by the students of the subject so far. And with its thirteen regions and fairly detailed commodity breakdown, the survey offers over two hundred separate nonagricultural series for analysis. While a far from perfect substitute for a sample of returns from individual informants, this richness of structure gives us some prospect of getting inside the aggregates and tracing changes in the dispersion of anticipations.[2]

Previous Studies

DISCOURAGING RESULTS OF FERBER AND HULTGREN

The pessimistic findings of the pioneer studies by Hultgren and Ferber have discouraged an intensive study of this body of evidence.[3] Hultgren was concerned primarily with the predictive value of the forecasts for estimating actual railway traffic. He concluded that working merely from observed seasonal patterns of the actual carloadings "a simple mechanical procedure yields estimates of total traffic that are somewhat less erroneous on the average than the estimates obtained by the elaborate advisory board procedure."[4] Ferber was more concerned with the relation of antici- pations to the experience out of which they grow, and he found that "in effect the shippers in the aggregate expect a sharp reversal of trend which will erase more than half of the gain (or loss) from A_{t-5} to A_{t-1}."[5] As to direct forecasting value, like Hultgren he found that estimates made by extrapolation alone systematically showed smaller errors than did the shippers' forecasts themselves, in the interwar period.[6]

On the face of these findings, the shippers' forecasts for the interwar period would seem of little value. If they really embody the expectations by which business operated, they ought to show coherent relationships both to antecedent and to ensuing events. We dare not be too utopian in our standards of "coherence": reported expectations cannot be both a good image of what businessmen expected and a good forecast of actual events unless businessmen were good prophets. The well-known fact that

[2] The National Bureau's array of current diffusion indexes includes a carloadings index computed from the nineteen national totals for nonfarm commodities in the post- war bulletins. If the clerical effort were thought worthwhile, the number of items could be expanded to rather over two hundred (19×13 less a few blanks) by using regional figures in detail; and the time span could be carried back to 1927.

[3] Thor Hultgren, "Forecasts of Railway Traffic," *Short-Term Economic Forecasting*, Princeton University Press for the National Bureau of Economic Research, 1955; and Robert Ferber, *The Railroad Shippers' Forecast*, University of Illinois Press, 1953.

[4] P. 377.

[5] P. 91. In Ferber's convenient notation, A_t is an actual magnitude of period t, E_t an expected magnitude for the same period. E_t is viewed as *framed* in period $t-1$. (The Appendix to this paper contains all the symbols used and their definitions.)

[6] P. 60. Ferber did find (pp. 61 and 131–132) that the postwar data showed more predictive value. But this is cold comfort. We have alternative sources of postwar expectations data. It is for the interwar years that the shippers' forecast, if a valid measure of expectations, would be uniquely valuable, because for those years we have only fragments from other sources.

inventory expansion runs past peaks into downswings and its contraction past troughs into upswings shows major errors of foresight. And so does the substantial influence of business fluctuations upon stock prices. Yet if the shippers' forecasts were really segments of business operating plans, how could they be so completely devoid of forecasting value (Hultgren) or so paradoxically related to past experience (Ferber)? Did the firms lack coherent operating plans? Or if they had such plans, did their traffic managers fail to transmit them through their forecasts?

Motivated perhaps by a vested interest in expectations, I went behind the results of the pioneer studies and restudied the data by methods which reflect the structure of the advisory board surveys.[7] While I have been able to process too little of the data to obtain conclusive results, my revaluation suggests that the forecasts did embody valid information about coherent operating plans, and that we can bring this information to the surface by correcting for certain standing biases. I find that the shippers' forecasts for the interwar period:

1. Predicted well at times when it is reasonable to suppose that operating plans could be executed.

2. Failed to predict at turning-points in just the way a true measure of the expectations of fallible businessmen should.

3. Embodied a coherent and reasonable extrapolative relation to antecedent experience, together with valid nonextrapolative elements.

My general conclusion is that we seem to have here a body of data which may enable us to test against evidence many hypotheses that have been regarded as nonrefutable.

BASIS FOR THE PESSIMISTIC FINDINGS

The pessimistic findings of the two pioneer studies, it should be pointed out at once, have evidence behind them. By a simple graphical technique (Chart 1), we can see their basis in the original data.

The continuous curve at the top of the chart shows Ferber's compilation of actual carloadings for all manufactured products from 1927 through 1941 with my seasonal adjustment.[8] Comparison with the Federal Reserve Board index of manufacturing production (lower curve) shows extremely close conformity of shape most of the way across the chart, with two exceptions:

1. At the beginning of the series, the high level of carloadings shown for I 1927 seems to have no warrant in the production series—perhaps because the survey did not shake down at once to its permanent pattern.

---

[7] For an account of the way the surveys are made, see Ferber, pp. 15-21.

[8] I adjusted the data for seasonal fluctuations using a moving seasonal derived from ratios to moving averages. The coefficients used, together with data before and after seasonal adjustment, are shown in Appendix Table A-1.

CHART I

Actual and Shippers' Forecast Carloadings, All Manufactured Products and Manufacturing Production, Quarterly, Seasonally Adjusted, 1927–1941

2. At the end of the interwar period, reported actual carloadings fail to share the vigorous rise of production in 1940-41. There may well have been a marked relative shift, in view of the intensified level of fabrication of manufactures and the relative growth of products which were self-transporting. Yet we cannot rule out the possibility that the "actual" carloadings of 1940-41 lacked comparability with those of 1927-39.

Consequently I limited my analysis to data from II 1927 through IV 1939.

Each forecast (for the same total of carloadings with the same seasonal adjustment) is shown as a point—tied back by a thin line to the actual level of the previous quarter. Each thin line can be seen as an abortive projection of the solid curve, showing how it would have continued had the results of the survey added up to a perfect forecast.

If our only concern were the general level of carloadings, we might view the stub lines merely as a bit of fuzz clinging to the continuous curve of actual carloadings, and assert that the forecasts give a fairly good picture of the actual level.[9] Obviously there is a high correlation ($r^2 = 0.84$) between the estimated level ^sE_t and the actual level ^sA_t in the seasonally adjusted series. Unfortunately for the value of the raw forecasts, however, the correlation is considerably weaker than the one obtained on the naïve-model hypothesis that ^sA_t is related to the preceding observation $^sA_{t-1}$ ($r^2 = 0.94$). Furthermore, a *joint* use of ^sE_t and $^sA_{t-1}$ to predict ^sA_t yields an imperceptible partial correlation ($r^2_{{^sA_t}{^sE_t} \cdot {^sA_{t-1}}} = 0.02$) for ^sE_t. We are forced to conclude that the raw forecast has no *net* predictive value for the level of carloadings.[10]

As forecasts of quarter-to-quarter changes, the thin lines indicate an almost perfect record of failure. It almost looks as if the shippers had followed the cheap but infallible rule for being right at turning-points (at the expense of being wrong all the rest of the time) by always predicting a turning opposite to the last turn observed. During recessions, the raw forecasts not only are too high, but they keep saying, "Beginning next quarter we will be on the upgrade again." Conversely during upswings, almost all the thin lines point downward. Thus the forecasts seem "regressive" in the classical sense, as Ferber points out. Instead of recognizing that a swing in progress may continue, they seem uniformly to point to some sort of reversion toward a norm.

The Shippers' Forecasts as Four-Quarter Estimates

Before we write off the shippers' forecasts as useless, however, we must examine them for what they purport to be. To look at them as estimates of quarter-to-quarter change may misrepresent them. For the whole emphasis of the survey is on comparison of the oncoming quarter with the same quarter in the previous year. What we have before us is a body of consistently biased four-quarter-change estimates.

[9] This fact presumably explains the failure of the compilers of the survey to identify and correct the biases analyzed below. The *Proceedings* of the regional Shippers' Advisory Boards show great interest in a quarterly "accuracy check" matching the latest available actual figures (ordinarily two or three quarters back) against forecasts for the same date. But the check concentrates on *levels*, while it is analysis of *rates of change* that enables us to measure the biases.

[10] If we run the same correlations on data *without* seasonal adjustment, we get results somewhat more favorable to the forecasts. A simple correlation of A_t with A_{t-1} yields an r^2 of about 0.85; a joint regression of A_t on A_{t-1} and E_t yields an R^2 of about 0.89. The implied partial r^2 of A_t on E_t, taking account of A_{t-1} is about 0.24.

This result suggests that E_t does contain an element of valid allowance for seasonal fluctuations, although the root of the bias in the E's is lack of confidence in shippers' ability to allow for seasonality! But in this type of comparison, we are penalizing our naïve hypothesis for having a shape which embodies no seasonal allowance. If we started from A_{t-1} *and* an estimate of seasonally-to-be-expected change, there would probably again be no trace of net predictive value for E_t.

CHART 2

Actual and Forecast Four-Quarter Changes in Carloadings, All
Manufactured Products, 1927–1939

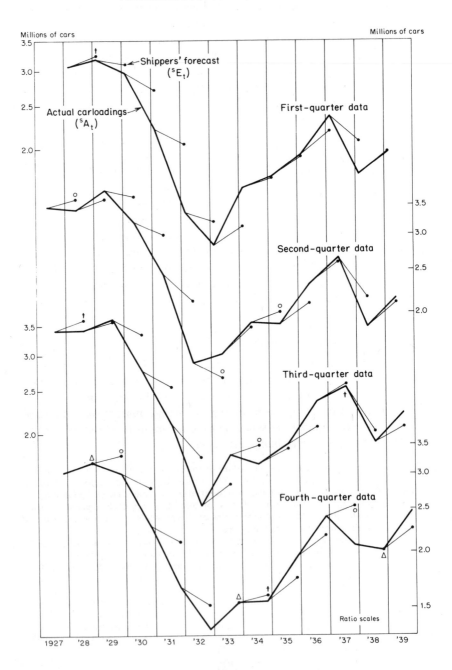

The coherence of the four-quarter estimates is shown in Chart 2. Since we are interested in four-quarter changes, I drew a separate curve for each time of year. As in Chart 1, I linked the actual carloadings in a continuous curve, showing forecasts as points connected with the corresponding previous actual data by thin lines. In only 6 instances (marked on the chart by ○) does the thin line fail to move in the same direction as the actual data—that is, the forecast E_t/A_{t-4} fails to give the same direction of change as the actual A_t/A_{t-4}. Only in 5 (marked by †) does the estimate give the right direction but overstate the change. In 3 instances (marked by △) the estimate and outcome coincide.[11] In the other 33 instances, the forecast four-quarter change is right in direction but too small—too small, typically, by rather more than half.

The failures to point in the right direction, furthermore, are not only few but interestingly dated. Of the 6, 3 (at IV 1929, II 1933, and IV 1937) suggest the missing of major turns in activity.[12] As the facts on inventory accumulation indicate, such major turns involve major surprises for the business community. Thus the discrepancies do not conflict with the hypothesis that we are looking at reports rooted in the actual plans of business. On the contrary, what is really disconcerting is the failure of the forecast to *miss* the upturn in 1938, for which the special explanation may be that this was an extremely well-advertised revival, in view of the lively concern of the public with the government's antirecession policy. In addition, the fact that the upturn first registers as an actual four-quarter gain, in I 1939 shows that information had unusually good opportunity to be right.

CORRECTION FACTORS

Confronted with such a systematic bias, the natural response of the analyst who wants to forecast is to counter it by a systematic correction.[13] The logic of such a correction will be different if instead we aim to reconstruct an image of what businessmen thought would happen. But before

---

[11] For details, see Table A-2.

[12] Two of the remaining 3 (at III 1934 and III 1935) represent the missing of sharp interruptions of a major upswing. Note that the 3 errors of direction in the forecast that are linked with major turning-points come *after* turns (at III 1929, I 1933, and II 1937) in the seasonally adjusted actual data shown in Table A-1. In each case, the quarter of the error in direction is that in which the swing of business took on momentum after a start which might have been felt as a mere wobble.

[13] See the strictures of the Consultant Committee on Business Expectations on the failure of the Illinois study to make such adjustments, in *Reports of Federal Reserve Consultant Committees on Economic Statistics*, Joint Committee on the Economic Report, 1955, pp. 533-534. As the Committee pointed out, the desirability of a correction was recognized by Franco Modigliani, the director of the Illinois study which included Ferber's monograph. But Modigliani's tests of such adjustments applied them to the forecasts treated as one-quarter-change estimates (E_t/A_{t-1}) rather than as four-quarter estimates. See Franco Modigliani and O. H. Sauerlender, "Economic Expectations and Plans of Firms," *Short-Term Economic Forecasting*, pp. 283-286, and 308.

facing these difficulties, we should pause to see what correction factors the data yield.

Actual four-quarter changes are graphed as a scatter against raw shipper-forecast changes in Chart 3. Four points on the chart are left floating. The two marked D represent the two quarters (IV 1929 and IV 1937) when major downswings took on momentum; the two marked U represent the quarters (II 1933 and III 1938) when major upswings took on momentum. The slopes of the lines joining the remaining points to the center of gravity of the scatter may be seen as estimates from individual observations of the degree of understatement in four-quarter change forecasts. It is plain from the scatter that the estimates are averageable.

Regression analysis using all quarters except those marked D and U suggests that our best estimate of the actual change from a given E_t is given by the equation:

$$\text{Estimate of } {}_aY_t = {}_hY_t = 0.997 + 2.269 \, ({}_eY_t - 1.026)$$

where ${}_aY_t$ is the actual four-quarter change (that is, A_t/A_{t-4}) and ${}_eY_t$ is the change indicated by the raw forecast (that is, E_t/A_{t-4}). The constant terms 0.997 and 1.026 introduce a correction for the over-optimism in level of the forecast change (which averages $+2.6$ per cent whereas actual change averaged -0.3 per cent); the multiplier 2.269 introduces a correction for the understatement of change.[14]

For the forty-two quarters used to fit the regression, the predictive value of this estimating equation is impressive. It yields an r^2 of about 0.89. Contrary to our finding for the raw forecasts of level, this correlation far exceeds that of comparable naïve-model hypotheses. The hypothesis that ${}_aY_t$ can be predicted from ${}_aY_{t-1} = A_{t-1}/A_{t-5}$ yields an r^2 of only 0.756. This naïve-model hypothesis cannot be perceptibly improved by bringing in also the previous value ${}_aY_{t-2} = A_{t-2}/A_{t-6}$; for the resulting R^2 is only 0.764. Thus the shippers' forecast shows a considerable superiority to naïve-model hypotheses in predicting four-quarter change, by the test of its gross predictive value.[15] Combining ${}_hY_t$ with ${}_aY_{t-1}$, gives an R^2 of 0.89— no better than the simple r^2 for ${}_hY_t$ alone. Thus the net predictive value

[14] This coefficient is the reciprocal of the regression of ${}_eY_t$ on ${}_aY_t$. I preferred this to the alternative regression (2.024) of ${}_aY_t$ on ${}_eY_t$ primarily to minimize deviations in the direction of presumed error, because the actual data should be less subject to error than the raw-forecast E's.

[15] If we were concerned with forecasting for its own sake rather than as a test of our ability to reconstitute a picture of expectations, the case for the shippers' forecast would be still stronger. For the actual shipments A_{t-1} cannot be measured with any precision till several weeks after the forecast E_t is available. A practical forecast of ${}_aY_t$ from data observable in advance, therefore, could use only ${}_hY_t$ and ${}_aY_{t-2} = A_{t-2}/A_{t-6}$. But $\bar{r}^2$ for ${}_aY_t$ on ${}_aY_{t-2}$ is only 0.45. And of course since ${}_aY_{t-1}$ shows no net predictive value when combined with ${}_hY_t$, the same is and must be true for ${}_aY_{t-2}$. So for practical purposes, the record suggests that the shippers' forecast is useful, and the available extrapolative data useless.

of the forecast, when we add it to extrapolative evidence, is to reduce unexplained variance from about 0.24 to about 0.11, with a partial r^2 of about 0.55. We must infer that the reconstituted forecast ratio $_hY_t$ contains valid evidence over and above what a simple extrapolation would yield.[16]

Turning to the formation of expectations, the greater part of the *gross* forecasting value of $_hY_t$ does seem to trace to its extrapolation content. We find an r^2 of 0.83 between $_eY_t$ (which of course must have the same correlation as $_hY_t$) and the previous actual change $_aY_{t-1}=A_{t-1}/A_{t-5}$. This can be raised to an R^2 of 0.86 by including $_aY_{t-2}=A_{t-2}/A_{t-6}$ as a second independent variable.[17] Since the extrapolation can explain more of the forecast than it can of the actual data, while the forecast has substantial

---

[16] My precautions of lopping off the suspect 1940-41 figures and omitting the four quarters most affected by major turns in activity turn out to have been needless for getting unbiased estimates of the degree of understatement and of the predictive power of the forecast. On four alternative standards of coverage, results are as follows:

Basis	Excluding Four Major-Turn Quarters		All Quarters	
	1928-39	1928-41	1928-39	1928-41
Number of quarters	42	50	46	54
Understatement correction:				
$1/b_{ea}$	2.28	2.24	2.28	2.24
Simple r^2's:				
$_ay_t$ on $_ey_t$	0.90	0.82	0.87	0.81
$_ay_t$ on $_ay_{t-1}$	0.76	0.72	0.76	0.70
$_ey_t$ on $_ay_{t-1}$	0.83	0.83	0.79	0.80
$_ay_t$ on $_ay_{t-2}$	0.46	0.42	0.46	0.43
$_ey_t$ on $_ay_{t-2}$	0.44	0.46	0.45	0.48
$_ay_{t-1}$ on $_ay_{t-2}$	0.69	0.71	0.70	0.71
Multiple R^2's:				
$_ay_t$ on $_ey_t, _ay_{t-1}, _ay_{t-2}$	0.90	0.83	0.88	0.82
$_ay_t$ on $_ay_{t-1}, _ay_{t-2}$	0.77	0.74	0.76	0.74
$_ey_t$ on $_ay_{t-1}, _ay_{t-2}$	0.86	0.85	0.81	0.81
Partial r^2:				
$_ay_t$ on $_ey_t$, with				
$_ay_{t-1}, _ay_{t-2}$ constant	0.57	0.34	0.47	0.32

Regardless of coverage, the forecast four-quarter change shows stronger *gross* predictive value than the last two experienced changes (singly or in combination), and has a strong partial r^2 (while the gain from r^2_{ae} to $R^2_{ae \cdot a_{t-1}, a_{t-2}}$ is so trifling as to yield insignificant partial correlations for the extrapolative series).

[17] Though $_aY_{t-2}$ makes only a modest net contribution to the prediction of the forecast $Y(r^2_{e_t a_{t-2} \cdot a_{t-1}} = 0.17)$, the partial regressions look sensible. We obtain:

$$_ey_t = 0.59(_ay_{t-1}) - 0.15(_ay_{t-2})$$
$$= 0.44(_ay_{t-1}) + 0.15(_ay_{t-1} - _ay_{t-2})$$

Remembering that the percentage change shown by $_eY_t$ has to be amplified by about 2.27 to correct for understatement, this is to be interpreted as saying that the forecast has as its basic element the change from $t-5$ to $t-1$, tempered by the recent rise or fall in the rate of change.

213

CHART 3

Four-Quarter Link Relatives of Actual and Shippers' Forecast
Carloadings, All Manufactured Products, 1928–1939

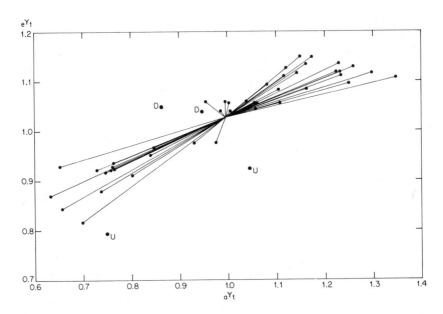

net predictive value, we must infer that extrapolation injected a certain amount of error into the forecast—more than offset by nonextrapolative elements in the forecast.

If we included the four D and U quarters in the analysis, the apparent relation of actual to forecast four-quarter change would be weaker. On this basis, the r^2 for actual changes in carloadings on shippers' forecast changes would be only 0.87 instead of 0.90, and the partial r^2, taking account of the two previous changes $_aY_{t-1}$ and $_aY_{t-2}$ would be only 0.47 instead of 0.57. But this is as it should be: the hypothesis that we are looking at forecasts based on the actual plans of fallible businessmen *requires* that including these quarters should weaken the relationship. On the other hand, it *is* somewhat damaging to the hypothesis that including the D and U quarters changes the relation of the forecast to antecedent experience: the R^2 for the forecast $_eY_t$ on the previous actual changes $_aY_{t-1}$ and $_aY_{t-2}$ drops from 0.86 to 0.81.

INTERPRETATION OF UNDERSTATEMENT

While a correction for understatement along these lines is statistically plausible, is it economically and psychologically plausible? If the correction were only a small fraction, there would be no problem. Instead it is embarrassingly large. Suppose for example that a 20 per cent increase over the quarter $t-4$ is in prospect for the quarter t. Then the seasonally adjusted level at the time the forecast is framed (toward the end of quarter $t-1$) is likely to be perhaps 15 per cent above that of quarter $t-4$. How then can we explain the shippers saying that A_t will be only 8 per cent above A_{t-4}—i.e. putting their estimate ^sE_t (say) 7 per cent *below* the seasonally adjusted level $^sA_{t-1}$ which exists as they frame their forecast?

A number of interpretations have been suggested, notably:

1. Mixed in with four-quarter-change forecasts from one group of informants are one-quarter or two-quarter forecasts from another group.

2. Mixed in with four-quarter-change forecasts from one group of informants are "no-change" forecasts from another group who do not really mean what they say.

3. The four-quarter-change forecasts are scaled below the change informants actually expect out of "statistical conservatism."

Probably each interpretation has some validity, but the main weight falls upon the third.

Mixture of One-Quarter and Four-Quarter Forecasts. The first possible interpretation may be inferred from a suggestion by Modigliani and Sauerlender, though they would clearly never have offered it as the major explanation of the discrepancies in the shippers' forecast.[18] If for example one-quarter changes averaged one-fourth of the four-quarter changes that include them, and if half the informants substituted one-quarter forecasts, this would explain an understatement of actual change by three-eighths. A scattering of such responses is clearly possible, since survey procedures have never been standardized. Yet there are strong indications that the collectors of the survey and their informants do in fact aim to compare with the same quarter a year previous. The *National Forecast* bulletin, which shippers receive quarterly, refers in its title to a year ago, and from the beginning has printed its results in four columns—actual cars loaded a year ago (at $t-4$), cars to be loaded in quarter t, percentage increase (for industry groups estimating a rise), and percentage decrease (for those estimating a fall). Ferber's survey of the way data are procured suggests that all the various procedures used lead the informant to look at last year's figures and that none call upon him to look at figures for intervening quarters.[19]

---

[18] *Op. cit.*, p. 303: "Respondents are not really replying to the question as worded, but . . . (perhaps subconsciously) [to] a question" about change over a shorter period. Their suggestion is addressed specifically to discrepancies in the Dun and Bradstreet survey, where there seem to be ambiguities in the reference dates the informant is supposed to use. They put much the same stress as does the present paper on the strong emphasis placed by the shippers' survey on the previous-year reference point, which should reduce the frequency of short-period forecasts in the returns of individual informants.

[19] *Ibid.*, p. 17. The lack of standardization is of course the reason Ferber fails to reproduce any questionnaire forms.

Furthermore, an interesting piece of numerological evidence indicates that shippers do aim their forecasts to refer to four-quarter changes— the prevalence of rounded four-quarter-change percentages. Offhand, since we are supposedly looking at the ratio of a summation of estimated cars in quarter t to actual cars in quarter $t-4$ for a number of shippers, it would seem fantastically unlikely that we should often find such percentages for $_e Y_t = E_t/A_{t-4}$ as 100.0 or 90.0. Yet in fact such round numbers are decidedly common in the printed figures. Many of the items for particular commodities in particular regions must not in fact be survey results, but "single-voice responses." By this I mean that some single spokesman is taking it upon himself either to substitute his judgment for that of his commodity group or at least to round the figures yielded by the survey. In the Alleghany district, where such responses have been relatively common, the roughly 760 entries of estimated change $_e Y_t = E_t/A_{t-4}$ in 1928-39 include 128 which are multiples of 5.0 per cent.[20] If we may take it that the single-voice responses that crop up in print have much the same character as individual responses buried in the aggregates, it would seem clear that it is normal to relate the forecast to the same time last year as suggested by those who collect the figures. There does not seem to be any greater frequency of round-figure estimates for one-quarter changes than could arise by chance.[21] While these figures relate to only one district, and to a district where round-figure published entries may be unusually common, it apparently is not a district where understatement is unusually mild. If anything, preliminary analysis suggests more than average understatement in the Alleghany district. Thus inclusion of one-quarter-change

[20] Specifically:

	Per Cent	Number
Items of	100.0	44
Other multiples of	25.0	20
Total multiples of	25.0	64
Multiples (other than 50, 100, and 150 per cent) of	10.0	36
Total multiples of	10 or 25	100
Multiples (other than 25 and 75 per cent) of	5.0	28
Total multiples of	5.0	128

In addition, we find a few multiples of 33.3 per cent, and many of 2.5 per cent, 2.0 per cent, and 1.0 per cent. Also several commodities often show estimates diverging in a uniform direction from a round figure by an amount of 0.1 or 0.2 per cent—suggesting a single voice covering most of the industry, with a few informants filing separate returns. Thus the figure of 128 understates the number of round-figure responses by an amount that is hard to specify.

[21] This impression may be unreliable. The *National Forecast* is not published in a form to facilitate one-quarter comparisons; two numbers must be collated to match E_t with A_{t-1}. In any event, figures for A_{t-1} are incomplete by several weeks as each respondent frames his E_t, so the published totals for A_t would not be accurate sums of the estimates informants would use if they tried to estimate one-quarter changes.

estimates erroneously processed as four-quarter estimates does not seem to account for much of the understatement.

Mixture of Change and No-Change Forecasts. The second explanation would be that the published figures may be an averaging together of relatively realistic estimates of four-quarter change by some respondents with unrealistic estimates of no change submitted by or on behalf of other respondents.[22] An estimate of no change (that is, $_eY_t = E_t/A_{t-4} = 100.0$ per cent) would on its face mean, "I forecast that A_t will be the same as A_{t-4} within 1 or 2 per cent." Often, this is what it does mean. But a no-change estimate could also be a code message meaning, "Estimation for date t has to be on such a shaky basis that I refuse to forecast and enter last year's figure not because I think it will really be repeated but because my answer must be arbitrary." A postwar example of such a code message is the filing by the mine operators' association in the Ohio Valley district of no-change estimates in 1946 and in 1949 when there were strikes *in the quarter when the estimate was framed.* No-change estimates are surprisingly common. Some seem to be code messages of the type just described. Others are entered as a clerical routine in regional offices when data are not at hand for a real forecast, especially for commodities so unimportant in the district that there is no commodity chairman.

This second hypothesis was my favorite when I prepared the original draft of my paper. But I was able to devise a few tests, and the results suggest that it does not account for the bulk of the understatement. Scrutiny of the forty-four no-change entries for nonfarm commodities in 1928-39 in the Alleghany district shows that a large proportion come at stages when it seems likely that almost-no-change may have been the informant's real meaning; that is, they come between an estimate of increase and an estimate of decrease. Furthermore, for a group of nine commodities with no-change estimates in the Alleghany district in 1935-39, I tried replacing no-change figures with the average estimated change in the remaining series. This procedure, which should remove understatement resulting from no-change code messages, had remarkably little effect on the size of estimated changes.[23] I must conclude that this factor

[22] This hypothesis was drawn to my attention by Millard Hastay (see his comment at p. 571 of the committee report on general business expectations, *Reports of Federal Reserve Consultant Committees on Economic Statistics,* Joint Committee on the Economic Report, 1955). It develops that the same suggestion was made by Geoffrey Moore in correspondence and by Robert Ferber in a paper in the *Journal of the American Statistical Association,* September, 1953, pp. 385–413.

[23] For all nine industries, the average without regard to signs of the twenty forecast four-quarter changes in 1935-39 is 7.3 per cent. Calculating change to each quarter t only for those of the nine industries which *do not* estimate $E_t/A_{t-4} = 100.0$ per cent raises the average to 8.1 per cent. This is for a period including two major turns. If the two quarters (IV 1937 and III 1938) excluded from calculations in the text are excluded here, the average forecast change becomes 6.6 per cent for all nine industries, 7.6 per cent for those which do not estimate "no change" in the quarter in question. The selection of industries in which single-voice responses seem to be normal should make this a reasonable test of the quantitative importance of coded no-change estimates.

as well as the admixture of one-quarter-change estimates is incapable of explaining the bulk of the understatement.

Statistical Conservatism. We are left, then, with statistical conservatism, which may take any of several different forms.[24] The traffic manager may suspect the production and sales departments of the firm of furnishing exaggerated estimates of change. Or having framed estimates in line with theirs, he may tone them down before he submits them to the advisory board. (He may think that if he had the direction of change right, he will not lose credit for sagacity by understating the size of the four-quarter change. And if by any misfortune he turns out to be wrong about direction, he will look wiser if he has not said the change will be large.) Or the compilers in the office of the advisory board or commodity chairman may tone down estimates which look extreme to them.[25]

If the procedure of the survey was such that the informant always had the full benefit of the record of the year so far in deciding what figure to submit, statistical conservatism could scarcely yield regressive forecasts which show a change from quarter $t-4$ to quarter t smaller than has already taken place from quarter $t-4$ to quarter $t-1$. But apparently businessmen still rarely keep their records on a seasonally adjusted basis; even fewer did so in the interwar period. The whole same-time-last-year basis of comparison expresses a lack of confidence in the informant's ability to sort out seasonal from nonseasonal changes in the events of the last few months. If the informant consults his records for any quarter other than $t-4$, the likeliest figures to use for orientation will be either the recently completed ratio $_aY_{t-2}=A_{t-2}/A_{t-6}$ or the almost-completed ratio $_aY_{t-1}=A_{t-1}/A_{t-5}$, using a forecast for the results (A_{t-1}) of the quarter which is in process when the forecast $_eY_t=E_t/A_{t-4}$ must be framed. If, say, the ratio $_aY_{t-1}=A_{t-1}/A_{t-5}$ bids fair to be 115 per cent, it may seem conservative to put $_eY_t=E_t/A_{t-4}$ at 110 per cent.

We must choose among the three hypotheses if we wish to assert that the respondent at the back of the survey really has a carloading expectation in line with a coherent operating plan, an expectation somehow given a biased report in the survey. If we deny this proposition, there are two other possible interpretations of the data:

4. The traffic manager really expects much what is reported—for example, he really expected each quarter in 1930-32 to see the downswing reversed immediately—but has no coordination with the rest of his firm. (If the firm as a whole really expected an upturn in each of these quarters, it would have maintained employment and produced to inventory, which we know from the history of the period most firms did not.)

5. The traffic manager was really not talking about the plans of his

---

24 A possibility also adumbrated by Modigliani and Sauerlender.
25 Michael Lovell tells me he has found indications in one regional office of a systematic leveling down of individual responses which suggest drastic change.

firm, but merely "participating" in the activity of his regional advisory board by playing a numbers game. In this case, his figure was designed simply to fit into a pattern, which implies that it will be purely a figure, for which there is no source but extrapolation of recent carloading figures.

These two hypotheses have one crucial element in common. They imply that the traffic manager has no evidence to go on from other aspects of his firm's operation and works only from the record of carloadings—supplemented perhaps by evidence from outside the firm on general business conditions, of which he can scarcely be an expert analyst.

The present analysis of the predictive value and apparent genesis of forecasts is reasonably selective between these two families of hypotheses. Hypothesis 4 or 5 requires that extrapolative naïve-model hypotheses should match or better the performance of the shippers' forecast, whether raw or corrected for bias. Hypotheses 1, 2, and 3 require that the forecast (raw or corrected) should perform so well that we must infer the use of valid nonextrapolative evidence, and scrutiny of the four-quarter-change estimates has supported this view. The next step is to correct for understatement of change, treat the results *as if* they represented realistic operating intentions, and see whether they can outperform naïve hypotheses in "explaining" levels of shipments and one-quarter changes.

THE RECONSTITUTED H-PREDICTION OF LEVEL

Given our regression for four-quarter changes, it is simple to reconstitute an implied series of estimated levels of carloadings. For each quarter t, we have a raw forecast of four-quarter change $_eY_t = E_t/A_{t-4}$. We can transform this into a forecast purged of change understatement and level optimism by writing:

$$_hY_t = 1.00 + 2.27 \, (_eY_t - 1.03).$$

If we use the symbol H_t for the implied expectation of the level of carloadings, we can simply write $H_t = (_hY_t \cdot A_{t-4})$, or with seasonal adjustment $^sH_t = (_hY_t \cdot {}^sA_{t-4})$. We can then graph the ^sH_t's against actual carloadings (Chart 4) on the same convention we used for the raw-forecast ^sE_t's in Chart 1. Against a solid curve of seasonally adjusted ^sA_t's, the seasonally adjusted ^sH_t's are shown as points, each connected by a thin line to the point representing $^sA_{t-1}$.[26] A glance at the chart shows that our

[26] An alternative procedure for deriving H-predictions would be to seek an understatement coefficient that would minimize squared deviations for levels of carloadings or for one-quarter changes, rather than for four-quarter changes. In correlation terms, what we minimize in the procedure used in the text is the sum of squares $(_ay_t - B_e y_t)^2$ when $_ay$ and $_ey$ are deviations from the means of $_aY_t$ and $_eY_t$. To get the minimum squared deviation of levels or one-quarter changes, we would minimize a *weighted* sum of the squares of such terms. The weights are base-period shipments (A_{t-4}'s) for the estimate of levels, and ratios (A_{t-4}/A_{t-1}) for one-quarter changes. An experiment on the latter basis yields to three significant figures the same understatement coefficient we obtained from the unweighted sum, so that in the present case it probably matters little

CHART 4
Actual and Forecast Carloadings, All Manufactured Products, Quarterly, Seasonally Adjusted, 1927–1939

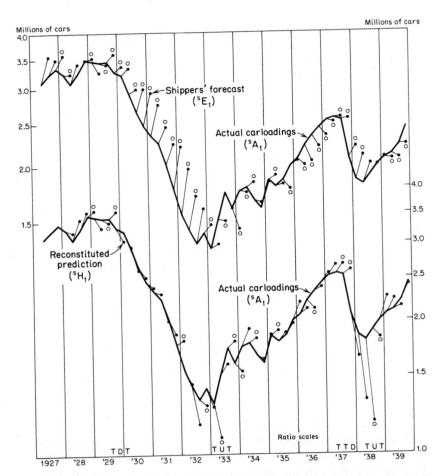

simple adjustment has shaken out almost all the nonsense that appeared in Chart 1. The levels shown by the H-predictions diverge much less from the actual carloadings. Into the bargain, the slopes of the thin lines agree most of the time with the slopes of corresponding segments of the actual carloadings curve.

A regression analysis of the reconstructed H-prediction in relation to the actual data is thoroughly compatible with the hypothesis that the H-prediction represents genuine expectations. On a seasonally-adjusted basis, for the forty-three quarters when it is reasonably likely that plans

which procedure we use. The logically simpler method of the text happens not to be at any statistical disadvantage.

could be fulfilled, there is an r^2 of 0.949 between the actual level ${}^sA_t$ and the reconstituted forecast ${}^sH_t$. This is slightly superior to the r^2 of 0.943 for ${}^sA_t$ on the previous actual level ${}^sA_{t-1}$ over the same forty-three quarters. True, both these coefficients can be bettered by a slightly more refined extrapolative hypothesis: ${}^sA_t$ has an R^2 of 0.956 over the forty-three quarters with ${}^sA_{t-1}$ and ${}^sA_{t-2}$ combined. But if we take a multiple correlation which combines these two pieces of extrapolative evidence with ${}^sH_t$, the R^2 for forty-three quarters goes up to 0.969, implying a partial r^2 of 0.30 for the H-prediction. This result squares very well with the hypothesis that the reconstituted forecast combines extrapolative evidence with valid nonextrapolative evidence in the minds of informants.[27]

This impression is strengthened if we exclude also the testimony of the eight quarters marked T on the chart—quarters so linked with major turning points that substantial surprises are likely (though not so highly probable as for the D and U quarters). For the remaining thirty-five quarters, the first naïve model (correlating ${}^sA_t$ with ${}^sA_{t-1}$) yields an r^2 of 0.931, and the second (correlating ${}^sA_t$ with a combination of ${}^sA_{t-1}$ and ${}^sA_{t-2}$) an R^2 of 0.947. Both correlations can be bettered by the simple correlation of ${}^sA_t$ with ${}^sH_t$, which yields an r^2 of 0.960. Furthermore, the inclusion of ${}^sH_t$ with the two previous actual figures raises the R^2 from 0.947 to 0.970, implying a partial r^2 of 0.45 for the H-prediction.[28]

As to the formation of expectations, the regression analysis shows the reconstituted forecast ${}^sH_t$ in a sensible relation to preceding experience. We get essentially the same relation of the forecast to preceding experience whether we do or do not exclude the quarters when intentions must or may have been frustrated.[29] On a forty-seven-quarter basis, we arrive at the regression equation:

$$ {}^sh_t = 1.01{}^sa_{t-1} + 0.65({}^sa_{t-1} - {}^sa_{t-2}) $$

[27] For all forty-seven quarters (including the D and U quarters where our hypothesis requires the informants to be in error), the simple and partial correlations for the H prediction are lower; the partial r^2 is only about 0.18.

[28] As before, if our central interest were forecasting as such, we would have to rule out ${}^sA_{t-1}$ on the ground that it was not available as soon as ${}^sH_t$. The latest previous actual figure which could definitely be used (${}^sA_{t-2}$) has a much lower correlation with ${}^sA_t$ than does the unavailable ${}^sA_{t-1}$. If we use all forty-seven quarters (to take the basis least favorable to the H-prediction), a simple correlation of ${}^sA_t$ with ${}^sA_{t-2}$ yields an r^2 of only 0.83, as against r^2 of 0.91 for ${}^sH_t$ and an R^2 of 0.93 for both variables combined. Thus for practical forecasting, availability of ${}^sH_t$ would have been a great improvement. On the other hand, we used some hindsight in estimating ${}^sH_t$, because both the seasonal adjustment and the understatement coefficient rest on data for the entire period; a current estimate of ${}^sH_t$ would presumably have been inferior.

[29] Regression results are as follows:

Number of Quarters	Joint Regression Equation		Alternative Form	R^2
35	${}^sh_t = 1.54{}^sa_{t-1} - 0.58{}^sa_{t-2}$	=	$0.96{}^sa_{t-1} + 0.58({}^sa_{t-1} - {}^sa_{t-2})$	0.938
43	${}^sh_t = 1.60{}^sa_{t-1} - 0.62{}^sa_{t-2}$	=	$0.98{}^sa_{t-1} + 0.62({}^sa_{t-1} - {}^sa_{t-2})$	0.937
47	${}^sh_t = 1.66{}^sa_{t-1} - 0.65{}^sa_{t-2}$	=	$1.01{}^sa_{t-1} + 0.65({}^sa_{t-1} - {}^sa_{t-2})$	0.932

This implies that our putative "real expectation" (for which H_t is a synthetic substitute) is built up by starting with the last quarter's actual carloadings (on a seasonally adjusted basis), and adding about two-thirds as large an increment as occurred between quarter $t-2$ and quarter $t-1$. There is then presumably a further addition or subtraction for non-extrapolative indications, as indicated by the fact that the reconstructed forecast outperforms the extrapolative naïve models in the quarters when it appears that the outcome was likely to be close to the expectation.

The Shippers' Forecasts as One-Quarter Estimates

THE RECONSTITUTED H-PREDICTION OF CHANGE

It is demanding a great deal of the reconstituted H-prediction to ask it to predict one-quarter changes. Our basic supposition is that the shippers had reasonably well integrated operating plans, but that the signals they sent in through the shippers' forecast about their plans were garbled in transmission. The adjustment in deriving $_hY_t$ from $_eY_t = E_t/A_{t-4}$ may be looked at as a device for filtering out noise picked up in transmission and thus approximating the original signal. But it is scarcely likely that the optimism about level and the size-of-change understatement which constitute the noise were so uniform through time as we imply by using a single constant to correct for each.[30]

Inspection of Chart 4, however, shows that in fact the H-prediction gives a rather sensible picture of quarter-to-quarter changes. Notably, the long series of regressive one-quarter-change forecasts shown by the raw figures of Chart 1 for 1930-32 and 1935-37 is replaced by an almost continuous series of forecasts that match the actual direction of one-quarter change. Whereas the raw forecast gave the wrong direction 28 times out of 47 quarters in 1928-39, the reconstituted forecast gives the wrong direction only 14 times. Furthermore, the 14 disagreements include 4 (at IV 1929, II 1933, IV 1937, and III 1938—our D and U quarters) which are required by hypothesis, and 3 more (at IV 1932, III 1937, and IV 1938) which have a similar relation to the major turning points. Out of the 35 quarters (including IV 1932) not tagged with D, U, or T and excluded from some analyses on grounds that, near turns, plans could very likely not be executed, the H-prediction on a seasonally adjusted basis disagrees with

[30] I experimented to see whether $_aY_t = A_t/A_{t-4}$ could be more closely estimated by an equation that lets the understatement coefficient be a function of the date and of the size of the four-quarter change to be estimated. Results were negative. Consequently, the simple equation used may be taken as my best estimate of the way to adjust the raw forecast with allowance for smooth changes over time and over differences in size of forecast. But any attempt to allow for less continuous changes in the degree of understatement of change would have to rest on correlation of the shippers' series with outside data (for example, with orders), which I have not attempted.

the actual direction of one-quarter change 7 times, compared with 25 times for the raw forecast.

A closer look reveals that almost all the disagreements in direction of one-quarter change are of a single type. In only 2 (in I 1932 and III 1936) does the H-prediction forecast a turn which fails to happen. In the other 12 the H-prediction forecasts a continuation of the previous direction of change while the actual data exhibit a reversal of direction. Of the 15 actual changes of direction in the seasonally adjusted figures, only 4 (at III 1928, I 1933, I 1935, and III 1935) were picked up by the H-prediction. Thus if this reconstitution is correct, it says that almost without exception the shippers expected continuation of the recent direction of movement and were surprised by turning points.[31]

Our chief interest must be in the one-quarter-change forecasts with seasonal adjustment, because this adjustment gives more scope for inquiries into extrapolative patterns of forecasting. But since the seasonal adjustment unavoidably brings in an arbitrary element, it is worth pausing to look at the relation of one-quarter changes without seasonal adjustment.

Without Seasonal Adjustment. On an unadjusted basis for 46 quarters[32] the series of actual changes (denoted by $_aX_t=(A_t/A_{t-1})$ shows 22 changes of direction between II 1928 and IV 1939, of which no less than 15 are picked up by the H-prediction $_hX_t=(H_t/A_{t-1})$, X being the one-quarter equivalent of Y. Besides missing 7 turns, the H-prediction calls for turns which did not happen in 7 of the 24 quarters when the direction of quarter-to-quarter change continued.

For the 34 quarters when it seems reasonably likely that expectations could be fulfilled, the correlation of one-quarter actual and H-predicted changes is fairly high ($r^2=0.72$). This is much better than we can do on the naïve-model hypothesis that $_aX_t$ can be explained by the year-previous change $_aX_{t-4}=A_{t-4}/A_{t-5}$; for this yields an r^2 of only 0.45. An alternative naïve-model hypothesis would be that the actual change $_aX_t$ can be explained by the seasonally-to-be-expected change $_sX_t=S_t/S_{t-1}$; this yields an r^2 of 0.56. Thus the gross predictive value of the H-prediction for one-quarter change is appreciably better than that of either naïve hypothesis. Furthermore, combining the seasonally-to-be-expected and H-predicted

---

[31] In the original version of this paper, I was inclined to view the shippers as missing major turns but picking up minor ones. This impression seems to go back to the roughness of my original seasonal adjustment. In view of Ruth Mack's finding that the mechanism of "sub-cycles" seems to be a reversal of the inventory band wagon (an event one would naturally interpret as surprising), it is much more reasonable that expectations should miss minor as well as major turns. (See Mrs. Mack's paper in *American Economic Review*, Supplement, May 1957, pp. 161-174).

[32] We lose one quarter as against the previous basis of calculations because we need to compare actual changes with previous-year changes at the same season (that is, with $_aX_{t-4}=A_{t-4}/A_{t-5}$); and the lack of a reliable A_t for quarter I 1927 means that our first estimate of $_aX_{t-4}$ applies to quarter III 1928.

change in a joint regression for the actual change gives an R^2 of 0.76. The gain over the simple correlation for the seasonally-to-be-expected change is large enough to give a partial r^2 of about 0.44 for the H-predicted change.

The H-predicted change shows a strong relation to the seasonally-to-be-expected change—as of course it must in order to be a good predictor of actual change without seasonal adjustment in our thirty-four quarters. The correlation of $_hX_t$ with $_sX_t$ yields an r^2 of 0.55. In addition, the H-predicted change shows a significant element of extrapolation from a year previous. If we take a joint regression for $_hX_t$ on $_sX_t$ and $_aX_{t-4}$ it yields an R^2 of 0.64, indicating a partial r^2 for $_aX_{t-4}$ of about 0.21. That is, there are some signs that *nonseasonal* change a year previous helps shape the forecast, in addition to seasonal allowances. Since $_aX_{t-4}$ has no net predictive value for $_aX_t$ when seasonality is taken into account,[33] this element in the forecast can only be a source of error. If therefore the H-predicted change $_hX_t$ is more highly correlated with actual change $_aX_t$ than is the seasonally-to-be-expected change $_sX_t$, it can only be because $_hX_t$ includes valid evidence on nonseasonal changes in prospect.

This view is confirmed by the fact that the predictive value of the H-prediction falls (while that of the seasonally-to-be-expected change does not) as we bring into our calculations the quarters when expectations were less likely to be fulfilled. If we recalculate for forty-two quarters (still excluding the four quarters of most drastic change, denoted by D and U), the r^2 for $_aX_t$ on $_hX_t$ drops to 0.60, while the r^2 for $_aX_t$ on $_sX_t$ stands almost unaffected at 0.54. If we go all the way to forty-six quarters, the r^2 for $_hX_t$ drops to 0.34—now markedly below that for $_sX_t$, which is still substantially the same ($r^2 = 0.56$).

Finally does the H-predicted change continue to conform to the actual at the appropriate points (i.e. for quarters on our list of thirty-four) if we make separate comparisons for each time of year? This test denies the H-prediction the benefit of knowing what time of year it is, as the correlation rests on *divergence* from the seasonal pattern in the actual and estimated changes. Since our thirty-four quarters are now split into four groups, individual statistical results from the four calculations rest on too few observations to carry any statistical weight. But the uniformity of

---

[33] The correlation of $_aX_t = A_t/A_{t-1}$ with $_sX_t = S_t/S_{t-1}$ and the previous-year change $_aX_{t-4} = A_{t-4}/A_{t-5}$ yields an R^2 of only 0.587, compared with an r^2 for $_sX_t$ alone of 0.562 over the thirty-four quarters.

This result should not surprise us. If the seasonal adjustment is unbiased, the residue of previous-year change after allowing for seasonality would exhibit a correlation with the current change only if the series exhibited either long runs of seasonally adjusted change in one direction or cycles close to a year in length (five or three quarters). The present series has neither characteristic; so our expectation is that the systematic element in the relation of $_aX_t$ to $_aX_{t-4}$ will all be incorporated in the seasonal adjustment.

results from the four tests is entitled to be taken seriously. For each of the four times of year:[34]

1. Actual change has a positive correlation with H-predicted change.

2. Correlation of actual change with previous-year change, though positive, is much smaller.

3. In a joint regression of actual on previous-year and H-predicted change, the latter accounts for the bulk of the variance "explained."

With Seasonal Adjustment. Analysis of seasonally adjusted data has the advantage that it makes the changes in recent quarters most comparable with current change. Thus it lends itself to a search for extrapolative influences on forecasts.

For this analysis, in addition to the current actual and H-predicted changes:

$$
{}^{s}_{a}X_t = {}^{s}A_t/{}^{s}A_{t-1}
$$
$$
{}^{s}_{h}X_t = {}^{s}H_t/{}^{s}A_{t-1}
$$

we can represent recent history by:

$$
{}^{s}_{a}X_{t-1} = {}^{s}A_{t-1}/{}^{s}A_{t-2}
$$
$$
{}^{s}_{h}X_{t-2} = {}^{s}A_{t-2}/{}^{s}A_{t-3}
$$
$$
{}^{s}_{a}X_{t-3} = {}^{s}A_{t-3}/{}^{s}A_{t-4}
$$
$$
{}^{s}_{a}X_{t-4} = {}^{s}A_{t-4}/{}^{s}A_{t-5}
$$

For the thirty-four quarters when intentions are most likely to have been carried out, an extrapolative estimate of the actual change ${}^{s}_{a}X_t$ from all four pieces of recent experience yields an R^2 of 0.35.[35] This is weaker than the

[34] The seasonally-to-be-expected change does not figure in the calculations because in comparisons for a single time of year it varies only with its trend. For the two remaining predictive variables, and excluding the eight T quarters and four D and U quarters, the relevant correlations are as follows:

QUARTERS RELATED

	I with IV	II with I	III with II	IV with III
$_aX_t$ on $_hX_t$:r^2	0.34	0.21	0.53	0.78
$_aX_t$ on $_aX_t$:r^2	.03	.02	.11	.40
$_aX_t$ on $_hX_{t-4}$ and $_aX_{t-4}$: R^2	.34	.25	.54	.84
$_hX_t$ on $_aX_{t-4}$:r^2	.06	.34	.34	.74

Compare the first three lines with the negative correlations obtained for raw forecasts at three of the four times of year by Ferber (p. 77). And in the last line, the four time-of-year calculations agree also in finding a positive correlation between $_hX_t$ and the previous-year change $_aX_{t-4}$, confirming the impression that the previous year's events enter (irrationally) into forecasts. Except for changes from the third to the fourth quarter, where $_aX_{t-4}$ happens to have a fairly strong correlation with $_aX_t$, this influence on the prediction $_hX_t$ must be a source of error (or at best of random differences).

[35] This could just as well be described as an estimate based on the last three pieces of experience, excluding $_aX_{t-4}$, for the multiple correlation is just the same whether we do or do not introduce this variable. This absence of predictive value for the previous-year change, as we saw in footnote 34, indicates the success of our seasonal adjustment.

r^2 of 0.44 which we find when we correlate $_a^s X_t$ with $_h^s X_t$. Furthermore, a compound prediction using the H-predicted change together with all the extrapolative elements yields a considerably improved correlation: $R^2 = 0.56$. The margin by which this exceeds the R^2 obtained on a purely extrapolative basis leaves a partial r^2 for $_h^s X_t$ of 0.33. Thus it is plain that $_h^s X_t$ has net as well as gross predictive value.[36]

The relation of the prediction to previous experience seems to show a fairly reasonable pattern. A multiple regression of $_h^s X_t$ on the four elements of recent experience yields an R^2 of 0.39. The greater part of the predictive value of recent experience for the reconstituted forecast seems to spring from the most recent history: for $_h^s X_t$ on $_a^s X_{t-1} = {}^s A_{t-1}/{}^s A_{t-2}$ alone, the $r^2 = 0.32$.[37]

When we take in quarters when expectations were less likely to be fulfilled, the admixture of surprises pulls the forecasting correlation down rapidly. For forty-two quarters, though an extrapolative estimate still produces an R^2 of 0.37, the simple correlation of actual on H-predicted change is reduced to an r^2 of 0.35, and the partial r^2 falls to 0.22. On a forty-six-quarter basis, the extrapolative estimate is much weaker ($R^2 = 0.18$), and the simple correlation ($r^2 = 0.09$) and partial r^2 (0.01) for $_h^s X_t$ become negligible. On the other hand, the apparent relation of H-prediction to antecedent experience remains much the same.[38]

FORECASTS AND SURPRISES

How seriously can we take the H-predicted change as a measure of the specific changes at specific times? The fact that for our thirty-four quarters the r^2 for $_a^s X_t$ on $_h^s X_t$ is rather modest (0.44) might suggest either that the original plans were loose or that much random noise remained in the signal even after our rectification. But the correlation itself is inconclusive; once more we must ask whether the deviations as well as the similarities have a story to tell.

Actual one-quarter changes, seasonally adjusted, are graphed as a time series in the upper curve of Chart 5. The curve below shows the H-pre-

---

[36] As usual, we could make a better showing for the H-prediction if our central concern were forecasting with data available as soon as the shippers' forecast becomes available, ruling out A_{t-1} and hence $_a^s X_{t-1}$. A forecast of $^s X_t$ from the other more remote elements of experience yields an R^2 of only 0.09 compared with the r^2 of 0.44 from $_h^s X_t$ alone. Thus the forecast would at the very least be useful as a way of mobilizing evidence on $_a^s X_{t-1} = {}^s A_{t-1}/{}^s A_{t-2}$ before it would ordinarily be available.

This comparison, however, is biased slightly in favor of the H-prediction by its use of two elements of hindsight: both the seasonal adjustment and the change–understatement coefficient are estimated from data for the entire period 1928-39.

[37] By some fluke, the calculations show no net predictive value for the second-most-recent item of experience, $_a^s X_{t-2}$.

[38] For the prediction $_h^s X_t$ on the most-recent-experience item $_a^s X_{t-1}$, r^2 over forty-six quarters is 0.26—slightly less than for thirty-four quarters. But R^2 using all four items of experience goes up to 0.41. The year-previous change $^s X_{t-4}$ shows a positive regression throughout, but a negligible partial correlation.

CHART 5

Carloadings of All Manufactured Products,
Seasonally Adjusted Levels, Actual and Predicted, 1927–1941

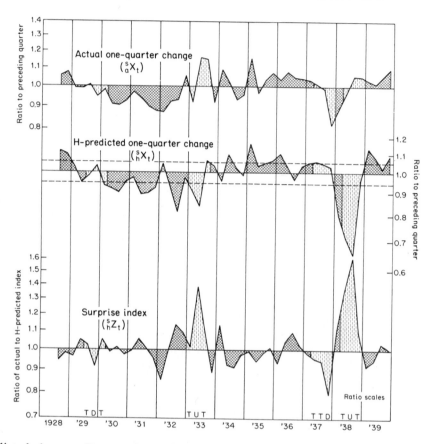

dicted changes. For our best thirty-four quarters (dark-shaded areas) the general family resemblance on which the correlation rests is clearly visible; so is the appropriate disagreement around the main turns (light-shaded areas). But for present purposes, the main interest attaches to the bottom curve, which traces the ratio of actual to expected one-quarter changes $^s_hZ_t = {}^s_aX_t/{}^s_hX_t$. This may be read as an index of surprise—upward-pointing teeth on the curve showing quarter-to-quarter changes more favorable than our index says was expected (agreeable surprises), and downward-pointing teeth less favorable (disagreeable surprises). The surprises registered at the four main turns are appropriate on the hypothesis that we have a valid index of expected changes.[39] But whether the wobble during

[39] However the allegedly expected adverse changes in 1938 (and the apparent disagreeable surprise) are unplausibly large. As with forecast four-quarter changes, the

CHART 6

Surprise Index and Acceleration Index, Quarterly, 1928–1939

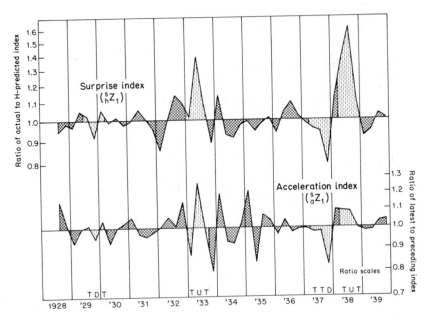

the thirty-four best quarters (dark-shaded parts of the chart) is appropriate, we cannot say without further examination.

By the same logic which makes it appropriate for the *H*-prediction to miss major turns of activity, the index of surprise should be related to the *acceleration* of seasonally adjusted actual carloadings (that is, to an index $_a^s Z_t = _a^s X_t / _a^s X_{t-1}$). This is indeed the case, as may be seen from Chart 6. Here the top curve (carried forward from Chart 5) is our index of surprise $(_h^s Z_t = _a^s X_t / _h^s X_t)$, the lower curve the index of acceleration. The relation of surprise to acceleration at the major turns is shown by the parallel saw-teeth in the dotted parts of the curves. Besides, there is a marked family resemblance between the parts of the two curves (dark-shaded areas) which report on our best thirty-four quarters. Of the 6 sharp points of disagreeable surprise (at I 1932, IV 1933, III 1934, II 1935, I 1936, and I 1939), only 1 (at I 1932) lacks a counterpart on the acceleration curve. The 5 peaks of agreeable surprise (at II 1929, III 1932, I 1934, and III 1939) do not fare so well: only 2 (at I 1934 and III 1939) have definite counterparts, while the highest rate of acceleration on the chart (at I 1935) fails to induce agreeable surprise. Thus the relation between surprises and acceleration is one of the weaker ones in the complex we are investigating,

---

upturn of 1938 was unusually well advertised and was in fact the only one of the four major turns *not* missed by the four-quarter-change estimates. Perhaps here the correction for understatement of four-quarter changes was overdone.

yet apparently significant: over thirty-four quarters $r^2 = 0.25$, over forty-six quarters $r^2 = 0.29$. Broadly speaking, we may say that of the variance in the one-quarter forecast $_h^s X_t$ within the best thirty-four quarters, 44 per cent is accounted for by valid forecasting of actual change and about a quarter of the remainder by identifiable failures to register forces accelerating or decelerating the actual carloadings. Thus on the hypothesis that the original signals registered coherent actual expectations, some 42 per cent of the variance in our reconstituted one-quarter forecasts must be attributed to noise picked up in the process of coding and decoding the message.

Such a result is scarcely surprising given the degree of arbitrariness in the way the figures were processed. It implies a standard error for H-predicted one-quarter changes of about 5.4 per cent. A zone of this width around unity is marked off on Chart 5. Taking one standard error as the margin beyond which an H-prediction probably registers an actual expectation that carloadings will move in the indicated direction, we may classify our H-predictions as follows:

	Probably Registering Expectation of Increase	Doubtful	Probably Registering Expectation of Decrease
1928	II, IV		
1929		I[a], III[b], IV[a]	II
1930		IV	I, II, III
1931		I, II	III, IV
1932		I[a], IV[a]	II, III
1933	III[b]	IV[a]	I, II[a]
1934	II	I[a], III[a], IV	
1935	I, IV	II[a], III	
1936	I	I[b], III[a], IV	
1937	II	I, III[a], IV[a]	
1938		IV[a]	I, II, III[a]
1939	I, II, IV	III[b]	

[a] Quarters where actual change was in the opposite direction from H-predicted change.
[b] Quarters where a small change was indicated but a large change in the predicted direction eventuated.
For specific figures, see Table A-2.

It is plain that a large proportion of the most interesting quarters must be classified as doubtful. On the other hand, some generalizations at least of a negative character can be offered. From the beginning of 1929 till mid-1933, there was not a single quarter (unless we count I 1932, with an H-predicted increase of 4.3 per cent) when expansion was probably expected. Similarly, from mid-1933 until early 1938, there was not a single quarter (unless we count III 1936, with an H-predicted drop of 3.7 per cent) when contraction was probably expected. On the whole, then, expectations appear to have reinforced rather than braked the major swings of business. Hesitation in 1929 and 1937 may have facilitated the downturns, but the two upturns seem to have happened despite strong expectations to the contrary.

Further Uses of the Shippers' Forecasts

From this examination, it appears likely that by simple adjustments to filter out bias we can transform the shippers' forecast into a workable source of data on what businessmen expected about the physical volume operations, and thus can go a long way toward rescuing expectational interpretations of the past from the limbo of the unobservable. As measures of both four-quarter changes and future level, the reconstituted forecast behaves just as it should if it represents actual expectations. As a measure of one-quarter change, it shows some weaknesses, inevitably impaired by the noise which the adjustment procedure fails to remove. But then much of the time the most skilled business cycle analysts are in some doubt about which way the economy is currently moving.

Even as they stand, the data afford a testing ground for some hypotheses about fluctuations. In particular, they can test the hypothesis that changes of expectations trigger major turning points in business—it flunks the test disastrously. Much more can be done by dealing with component series. Reweighting the components by value added instead of shipping-space requirements is likely to yield a more revealing aggregate. Furthermore, collation of these data with evidence on orders may cast a good deal of light on the relationship of orders to business operating decisions.

The analysis of component series will also provide strong tests for hypotheses on the formation of expectations. For example, we can test how much expectations in a given industry are shaped by the general state of business, how much by the industry's own experience. And comparison of postwar and interwar data can give clues to the stability of estimation patterns.

Finally, a good deal of data from which expectations can be reconstructed seems to exist, but it is probably fragmentary. However, the shippers' forecast may provide a framework by which the other series can be calibrated. And the apparent coherence of the shippers' forecast should encourage us to search for other data and to develop theories that can illuminate the data and be tested by them.

APPENDIX

SYMBOLS USED AND THEIR DERIVATIONS

Symbols Used in Equations

- A indicates actual carloadings
- a indicates deviations from mean of actual carloadings
- a as a subscript indicates the symbol refers to actual carloadings
- E indicates expected carloadings (shippers' forecast)

e as a subscript indicates the symbol refers to expected carloadings

F indicates the Federal Reserve Board index of manufacturing production

H indicates reconstituted prediction (corrected for bias)

h indicates a deviation from mean of the reconstituted prediction

h as a subscript indicates a symbol refers to the reconstituted prediction

S indicates the seasonal adjustment coefficient

s as a superscript indicates that a symbol has been seasonally adjusted

s as a subscript indicates that a symbol refers to the seasonal adjustment

t, $t-1$, $t-4$, etc., as subscripts indicate the quarter to which the figure refers (current quarter, previous quarter, four quarters or a year previous, etc.)

X indicates one-quarter change

Y indicates four-quarter change

y indicates deviation from mean of four-quarter change

Z indicates acceleration of change

Their Derivations and Examples

A_t and E_t are the basic data, transcribed from Ferber

^sA_t indicates actual carloadings in the current quarter, seasonally adjusted

^sE_t indicates expected carloadings in the current quarter, seasonally adjusted

$_aY_t = A_t/A_{t-4}$ = actual four-quarter change

$_eY_t = E_t/A_{t-4}$ = expected four-quarter change

$_hY_t$ = best estimate of $_aY_t$

$H_t = {}_hY_t \cdot A_{t-4}$ = implied expectation of level of actual carloadings for a given quarter

$^sH_t = {}_h^sY_t \cdot {}^sA_{t-4}$ = the same, seasonally adjusted

$_sX_t = S_t/S_{t-4}$ = the seasonally to be expected change

$_aX_t = A_t/A_{t-1}$

$_hX_t = H_t/A_{t-1}$

$_a^sZ_t = {}_a^sX_t/{}_a^sX_{t-1}$

$_h^sZ_t = {}_a^sX_t/{}_h^sX_t$

Indicators in Charts and Tables

O indicates forecast in the wrong direction

† indicates a forecast in the right direction but an overestimate

△ indicates the forecast and outcome coincide

D indicates a quarter in which a major downswing took on momentum

U indicates a quarter in which a major upswing took on momentum

T indicates a quarter (other than a D or U quarter) containing or just following a major turning point

TABLE A-1

Actual and Estimated Carloadings, All Manufactured Products, Seasonal Adjustment
Coefficient, and Index of Manufacturing Production, 1927-1939
(*carloadings in millions of cars*)

YEAR AND QUARTER	NO SEASONAL ADJUSTMENT			WITH SEASONAL ADJUSTMENT			SEASONAL COEF-FICIENT (S_t)	MANU-FACTURING PRODUCTION, SEASONALLY ADJUSTED (^5F_t)
	Actual Car-loadings (A_t)	*Shippers' Forecast* (E_t)	*Recon-stituted Pre-diction* (H_t)	*Actual Car-loadings* (^5A_t)	*Shippers' Forecast* (^5E_t)	*Recon-stituted Pre-diction* (^5H_t)		
1927:								
II	3.47	—	—	3.09	—	—	1.12	51
III	3.41	3.77	—	3.21	3.55	—	1.06	50
IV	3.01	3.15	—	3.33	3.49	—	0.90	48
1928:								
I	3.06	3.27	—	3.24	3.57	—	0.92	50
II	3.42	3.61	3.58	3.07	3.24	3.19	1.12	51
III	3.42	3.60	3.64	3.24	3.41	3.42	1.06	53
IV	3.18	3.18	3.20	3.48	3.48	3.55	0.91	56
1929:								
I	3.18	3.24	3.28	3.46	3.52	3.58	0.92	57
II	3.79	3.61	3.04	3.43	3.26	3.27	1.11	59
TIII	3.62	3.57	3.55	3.44	3.40	3.36	1.05	60
DIV	3.01	3.30	3.25	3.26	3.58	3.56	0.92	55
1930:								
T I	2.96	3.10	2.80	3.21	3.36	3.05	0.92	52
II	3.21	3.66	3.26	2.92	3.33	2.95	1.10	50
III	2.77	3.34	2.76	2.65	2.99	2.62	1.05	45
IV	2.29	2.79	2.32	2.46	2.99	2.52	0.93	42
1931:								
I	2.21	2.71	2.22	2.34	2.93	2.39	0.92	42
II	2.45	3.00	2.32	2.25	2.75	2.31	1.09	42
III	2.10	2.55	2.10	2.02	2.45	2.01	1.04	38
IV	1.67	2.11	1.74	1.77	2.24	1.87	0.94	34
1932:								
I	1.44	2.05	1.71	1.55	2.21	1.81	0.93	33
II	1.55	2.13	1.58	1.43	1.97	1.44	1.08	29
III	1.38	1.77	1.23	1.33	1.71	1.17	1.04	28
IV	1.34	1.52	1.23	1.41	1.60	1.29	0.95	30
1933:								
T I	1.21	1.37	1.19	1.30	1.47	1.28	0.93	29
U II	1.62	1.43	1.18	1.51	1.33	1.09	1.07	35
TIII	1.79	1.54	1.71	1.74	1.50	1.60	1.02	43
IV	1.54	1.54	1.71	1.60	1.60	1.80	0.97	36
1934:								
I	1.63	1.34	1.43	1.75	1.44	1.54	0.93	39
II	1.90	1.86	2.06	1.78	1.74	1.92	1.07	42
III	1.71	1.88	1.88	1.67	1.83	1.83	1.02	37
IV	1.55	1.60	1.58	1.60	1.65	1.64	0.97	38
1935:								
I	1.73	1.72	1.73	1.85	1.84	1.86	0.94	44
II	1.89	2.01	2.03	1.79	1.90	1.90	1.06	44
III	1.89	1.85	1.92	1.85	1.81	1.88	1.02	46
IV	1.95	1.75	1.90	1.99	1.77	1.97	0.98	50

[table continues on next page

TABLE A-1, *continued*

| YEAR AND QUARTER | NO SEASONAL ADJUSTMENT | | | WITH SEASONAL ADJUSTMENT | | | | MANUFACTURING PRODUCTION, SEASONALLY ADJUSTED |
	Actual Car-loadings (A_t)	Shippers' Forecast (E_t)	Recon-stituted Pre-diction (H_t)	Actual Car-loadings (^sA_t)	Shippers' Forecast (^sE_t)	Recon-stituted Pre-diction (^sH_t)	SEASONAL COEF-FICIENT (^sS_t)	(^sF_t)
1936:								
I	1.93	1.92	2.05	2.06	2.05	2.20	0.94	49
II	2.33	2.10	2.25	2.22	2.00	2.13	1.05	53
III	2.36	2.07	2.18	2.33	2.04	2.13	1.02	57
IV	2.40	2.18	2.35	2.43	2.20	2.38	0.99	60
1937:								
I	2.37	2.19	2.40	2.52	2.33	2.56	0.94	63
T II	2.66	2.60	2.70	2.55	2.50	2.67	1.04	64
TIII	2.55	2.58	2.71	2.53	2.56	2.68	1.01	63
DIV	2.07	2.54	2.56	2.07	2.54	2.60	1.00	50
1938:								
I	1.75	2.08	1.57	1.85	2.20	1.66	0.94	43
T II	1.86	2.17	1.39	1.80	2.10	1.32	1.03	42
UIII	1.91	2.02	1.19	1.90	2.01	1.18	1.00	47
TIV	2.02	2.02	1.83	2.00	2.00	1.81	1.01	52
1939:								
I	1.96	1.97	2.14	2.07	2.08	2.26	0.95	53
II	2.16	2.11	2.31	2.11	2.06	2.23	1.03	53
III	2.22	2.07	2.15	2.22	2.07	2.15	1.00	57
IV	2.47	2.26	2.44	2.43	2.22	2.41	1.02	45

For the meaning of the symbols used, see the list in this appendix.

Source: *Cols. A_t and E_t*—Robert Ferber, *The Railroad Shippers' Forecasts*, University of Illinois Press, 1953, p. 138. *Col. H_t*—From correlations described in the text. *Col. S_t*—Fitted by the author to actual carloadings for 1947-51 by ratios to moving average. *Col. F_t*—Federal Reserve index, 1947-49 = 100, *Federal Reserve Bulletin*, Board of Governors of the Federal Reserve System.

TABLE A-2

Link Relatives of Actual and Predicted Carloadings,
All Manufactured Products, 1927-1939

| YEAR AND QUARTER | ON SAME QUARTER IN PREVIOUS YEAR | | | ON PREVIOUS QUARTER | | | | |
| | No Seasonal Adjustment | | | No Seasonal Adjustment | | | With Seasonal Adjustment | |
	Actual Car-loadings $(_aY)$	Shippers' Forecast $(_eY)$	Recon-stituted Prediction $(_hY)$	Seasonal Coef-ficient $(_sX)$	Actual Car-loadings $(_aX)$	Recon-stituted Prediction $(_hX)$	Actual Car-loadings (^s_aX)	Recon-stituted Prediction (^s_hX)
1927:								
III	—	—	—	0.945	0.983	—	1.040	—
IV	—	—	—	0.851	0.883	—	1.037	—
1928:								
I	—	—	—	1.015	1.017	—	1.002	—
II	0.986	1.040 ○	1.028 ○	1.217	1.118	—	0.919	—
III	1.003	1.056 †	1.064	0.948	1.000	1.061	1.055	1.115
IV	1.056	1.056 △	1.064	0.864	0.930	0.939	1.076	1.096
1929:								
I	1.039	1.059 †	1.071	1.007	1.000	1.031	0.993	1.027 ○
II	1.108	1.056	1.064	1.204	1.192	1.145	0.990	0.945
TIII	1.058	1.044	1.037	0.950	0.955	0.937	1.006	0.981 ○
DIV	0.947	1.038 ○	1.023 ○	0.877	0.832	0.901	0.947	1.035 ○

[table continues on next page

TABLE A-2, *continued*

	ON SAME QUARTER IN PREVIOUS YEAR			ON PREVIOUS QUARTER				
	No Seasonal Adjustment			No Seasonal Adjustment			With Seasonal Adjustment	
YEAR AND QUARTER	Actual Car-loadings (aY)	Shippers' Forecast (eY)	Recon-stituted Prediction (hY)	Seasonal Coef-ficient (sX)	Actual Car-loadings (aX)	Recon-stituted Prediction (hX)	Actual Car-loadings $(\tfrac{s}{a}X)$	Recon-stituted Prediction $(\tfrac{s}{h}X)$
1930:								
T I	0.931	0.975	0.881	1.000	0.983	0.930	0.984	0.933
II	0.847	0.966	0.860	1.192	1.084	1.101	0.910	0.919
III	0.765	0.923	0.763	0.952	0.863	0.860	0.906	0.899
IV	0.761	0.927	0.772	0.891	0.827	0.838	0.926	0.951
1931:								
I	0.747	0.916	0.750	0.993	0.965	0.965	0.972	0.973
II	0.763	0.935	0.722	1.179	1.109	1.050	0.941	0.891
III	0.758	0.921	0.759	0.955	0.857	0.857	0.898	0.895
IV	0.729	0.921	0.759	0.905	0.795	0.829	0.879	0.924
1932:								
I	0.652	0.928	0.774	0.986	0.862	0.124 ○	0.875	1.043 ○
II	0.633	0.869	0.643	1.167	1.076	1.090	0.923	0.924
III	0.657	0.843	0.584	0.957	0.890	0.787	0.931	0.816
IV	0.802	0.910	0.736	0.918	0.971	0.884	1.057	0.973 ○
1933:								
T I	0.840	0.951	0.826	0.979	0.903	0.888	0.923	0.911
U II	1.045	0.923 ○	0.763 ○	1.155	1.339	0.975 ○	1.160	0.841 ○
T III	1.297	1.116	1.199	0.959	1.105	1.025	1.152	1.062
IV	1.149	1.149 △	1.276	0.932	0.860	0.955	0.923	1.035 ○
1934:								
I	1.347	1.107	1.179	0.972	1.058	0.929 ○	1.089	0.549 ○
II	1.173	1.148	1.274	1.143	1.166	1.266	1.021	1.099
III	0.955	1.058 ○	1.050 ○	0.962	0.900	0.990	0.936	1.025 ○
IV	1.006	1.039 †	1.025	0.946	0.906	0.924	0.958	0.986
1935:								
I	1.061	1.055	1.062	0.965	1.116	1.116	1.156	1.161
II	0.995	1.058 ○	1.068 ○	1.131	1.093	1.173	0.966	1.032 ○
III	1.105	1.082	1.123	0.964	1.000	1.016	1.038	1.050
IV	1.258	1.129	1.229	0.960	1.032	1.011	1.074	1.062
1936:								
I	1.116	1.110	1.186	0.959	0.990	1.051 ○	1.033	1.102
II	1.233	1.111	1.188	1.119	1.207	1.166	1.079	1.034
III	1.249	1.095	1.152	0.976	1.013	0.936 ○	1.048	0.963 ○
IV	1.231	1.118	1.204	0.974	1.107	0.966 ○	1.044	1.033
1937:								
I	1.228	1.135	1.242	0.952	0.988	1.000	1.037	1.052
T II	1.142	1.116	1.199	1.107	1.122	1.181	1.014	1.059
T III	1.081	1.093 †	1.141	0.969	0.959	1.019 ○	0.989	1.046 ○
D IV	0.863	1.048 ○	1.068 ○	0.989	0.812	1.008 ○	0.821	1.028 ○
1938:								
I	0.738	0.878	0.664	0.946	0.845	0.759	0.894	0.800
T II	0.699	0.816	0.523	1.095	1.063	0.789 ○	0.971	0.713
U III	0.749	0.792	0.467	0.972	1.027	0.640 ○	1.057	0.654 ○
T IV	0.976	0.976 △	0.883	1.003	1.058	0.958 ○	1.054	0.964 ○
1939:								
I	1.120	1.126 †	1.222	0.940	0.970	1.059 ○	1.032	1.132
II	1.161	1.134	1.240	1.084	1.102	1.179	1.017	1.080
III	1.162	1.084	1.125	0.974	1.113	0.995 ○	1.055	1.019
IV	1.223	1.119	1.208	1.018	1.113	1.099	1.093	1.090

For the meaning of the symbols used, see the list in this Appendix.
Source: calculated from Table A-1.

COMMENT

DAVID C. MELNICOFF, The Pennsylvania Railroad

The focus of Albert Hart's paper is not on forecasting as such, but rather on the role of forecasts as indicators of businessmen's expectations. If expectations can be measured and related to business fluctuations, we might, indeed, have a "powerful testing device" for cyclical analysis and theory—provided, of course, that expectations and their fulfillment or denial engender a consistent pattern of stimulus and response over time. The shippers' advisory board forecasts seem a likely source of data, but it is not yet clear just how useful these data can be.

Hart was dissatisfied with earlier analyses of the shippers' forecasts not only because the results just did not *feel* right in view of his theoretical predilections, but also because of some other experience with the behavior of anticipations data and the testing of survey results. His new analysis and his statistical results—though even rougher than he concedes—are impressive. His hypothesis, which follows suggestions of Ferber, Hastay, and others, has much to recommend it. At least, it jibes with some of my own experience. The correction for what appears to be a systematic bias yields the kind of results that make sense: that is, they do not violate most conceptions of what expectations ought to be. It is impressive—but not completely convincing.

An old story, told with many variations, is apropos. Once a lion tamer who had just received a large and ferocious beast from the African jungles was preparing to enter the lion's cage, in purple tights and armed only with a short stick. A friend tried to stop him, but the trainer insisted he would have no trouble. "You see," he said, "my theory is that purple tights set up an emotional disturbance for the lion which renders him incapable of any violence so long as I hold the stick. I have great confidence in this theory, and I know it will work out." "Yes," said the friend, "you know the theory—but does the lion?"

Now, in contrast with the lion tamer's foolish theory, Hart sets forth an eminently reasonable hypothesis. I am sure, however, that the traffic managers who report to the advisory boards do not know that this is the way they are supposed to operate! And I question whether the assumed conditions remained stable during the entire period under review. We cannot know to what extent they prevailed without reviewing the procedures and forecasts of individual firms and of the chairmen of commodity groups. Given the age distribution of traffic managers, few of the individuals involved in the interwar forecasts are still available for interview. But one might interview those who are currently making the forecasts and compare current performance with that of the interwar years. This might provide not only some insight into the problem by analogy but also direct evidence on whether the forecasting procedures used today are the same as those of thirty years ago.

The tests suggested by Hart are helpful but not conclusive. In particular, the second, which relates shippers' forecasts to changes in the earlier part of the year, is subject to varying interpretation, and even the calculated regression coefficients do not seem to tell a consistent story.

Of course, the statistical correction for understatement of year-to-year change does not depend on or grow out of the assumptions of the hypothesis. Though it is probably essential to the analysis that the forecasts were made in relation to the level of carloadings of the previous year rather than to that of the previous quarter, the hypothesis is only one possible explanation of why the data behave as they do. One can readily agree on the probability of the year-to-year forecast yet not believe that there are only two large groups of forecasters with only two forecasting patterns. The forecasts are made by many highly diversified groups and thus exhibit a large variety of errors and many different types of bias.

What the data show is that forecasters—in the aggregate—make year-to-year predictions in the right direction, but usually go only about half as high or low as they should. On correcting for bias the results come close enough to the "actual" outcome to appear reasonable. But even aside from the omission of turning-point situations, the statistical results allow one to say only, "These are the expectations of one large group—the only group we need consider because the other group is not registering its expectations at all." In fact, uninformed guesses of year-to-year changes with no relationship to the decision-making process of the firm can come so close to the actual results that Hart's statistical methodology cannot differentiate them. The shippers' expectations could be completely without rhyme or reason, rather than neatly divided, and the statistics alone would not disclose this.

The corrected forecasts lag, they do not lead; there is little in these data which guarantees to the railroads a better tool for forecasting car requirements. Nevertheless, they may show sufficient promise to warrant looking for predictors among some of the individual series. More rigorous and detailed tests should be undertaken. In the meantime, one must be wary of taking the adjusted forecasts as firm expectations of a significant group of business firms and using them as though they were a reliable tool in business cycle analysis. We do not yet have such a tool, but Hart's paper suggests that we may someday be able to fashion one.

DONALD J. DALY, Canadian Department of Trade and Commerce

Albert Hart gives no serious attention to Hultgren's study, an unfortunate omission because Hultgren's excellent brief article made an important contribution to the subject.[1] His essential point was that the shippers'

[1] Thor Hultgren, "Forecasts of Railway Traffic," *Short-Term Economic Forecasting*, Studies in Income and Wealth, Vol. 17, Princeton University Press for the National Bureau of Economic Research, 1955.

unsatisfactory view of nonseasonal changes over the recent three-quarters of a year had adverse effects on their comparisons of freight car requirements one quarter ahead with those of the same quarter in the previous year.

Professional economists and statisticians generally accept the advantages of using seasonally adjusted data when analyzing recent changes in the economy. Such data show up underlying changes more clearly than unadjusted data do and are essential if changes in a six-month period, in particular, are to be evaluated at its close.[2] Yet in my experience business firms rely heavily on comparisons of current operating statistics with those of the same month a year previous and tend to draw conclusions on recent changes in them. For the individual firm and industry, however, such comparisons can frequently lead to incorrect conclusions and contribute to incorrect anticipations. Thus to the shippers who make rather accurate forecasts and to the many who estimate "same as last year" should probably be added a group of companies whose forecasts are poor because their conclusions are based on an incorrect assessment of recent developments, and there is some evidence that the last group is significant. Seasonal variations, which are relatively more important for individual firms and industries than for industry as a whole, can affect the views of businessmen on the recent past and, therefore, their short-run outlook.

Hart raised this point, but it is also relevant to the volume as a whole. It contains no serious discussion of seasonal factors in business operating statistics, of whether the treatment of seasonal factors by businessmen has been adequate, and of whether, if inadequate, the inadequacy had any effect on businessmen's expectations. However previous studies have recognized the problem, and Ferber has indicated that further empirical data are being gathered that may throw light on it.

ROBERT EISNER, Northwestern University

Whatever the implications of Ferber's data or Hart's revaluation of them, it is interesting to note the grounds on which truly "regressive" expectations may be rationalized. These relate to possibilities of intertemporal substitution and suggest that there should be at least a component of expectations which is regressive.

Data collected from one large shoe manufacturer in the course of a study of expectations and investment revealed a sharp negative correlation between preseason or early season orders and those of the balance of the season. A ready explanation lies in the stability of shoe demand—more early buying means less later buying. Thus where sales were higher during

---

[2] For an excellent article covering this point and giving some results from the use of electronic computers to compute seasonal adjustments, see Julius Shiskin, "Electronic Computers and Business Indicators," *Journal of Business*, October 1957, reprinted as Occasional Paper 57 by the National Bureau of Economic Research.

the first two months of a season than in the corresponding two months the year before, they would tend to be lower in the ensuing months than in the same period the year before. If actual sales changes proceed in this regressive fashion, a similar regressive character in expectations would hardly be surprising.

An opportunity to observe this relationship again was found in the McGraw–Hill data at my disposal. In late 1949, McGraw–Hill respondents were asked for the percentage figure by which they expected 1950 sales to depart from 1949 sales. When the expectations were related to actual 1948-49 percentage sales changes, the simple linear correlation was found to be virtually zero. However, some nonlinear correlation was apparent. Higher sales were expected in greater proportion both by firms whose sales had increased the most (10 per cent or more) and by those whose sales had decreased the most (more than 20 per cent). Among firms expecting some change in sales, increases were expected by 75 per cent of the above "extremes" as against only 47 per cent of those with moderate sales-change experience. (Tschuprow's T was 0.25, significant at the 1 per cent level, and the tetrachoric coefficient of correlation was 0.42.)

If one assumes that a high proportion of firms with large 1948-49 sales changes were also long-run growth firms, data on past capacity changes can be used to enlighten this relationship. And the relation between sales-change expectations and prior changes in capacity was found to be strongly positive. For the 1939-48 changes in capacity ($T=0.36$) and 1947-48 changes ($T=0.25$) the correlations were significant at the 1 per cent level.

More and better data will certainly be needed to formulate more than a tentative hypothesis. But the findings touched upon here are at least not obviously inconsistent with a theory I have proposed elsewhere that short-term sales expectations are compounded of two elements, the long-term trend (with which short-term sales expectations are positively correlated) and short-term deviations from the long-term trend (with negative correlation). Whatever the direction of the long-term trend, a short-term sales change that deviates markedly from the long-term expectations may be seen as essentially stochastic and thus lead to expectations of a reversal back toward the trend in the following year.[1]

[1] Robert Eisner, "Expectations, Plans and Capital Expenditures: A Synthesis of Ex Post and Ex Ante Data," *Expectations, Uncertainty and Business Behavior*, Mary Jean Bowman, ed., Social Science Research Council, 1958, esp. p. 162.

The Source of Regressiveness in Surveys of Businessmen's Short-Run Expectations

JOHN BOSSONS

HARVARD UNIVERSITY

FRANCO MODIGLIANI

CARNEGIE INSTITUTE OF TECHNOLOGY

Analyses of several surveys of businessmen's short-run expectations have consistently revealed a surprising degree of inaccuracy in the forecasts. Accordingly economists have tended to write them off as containing little useful information. As a result, the resources allocated to several such surveys have been sharply reduced. The analysis of one survey, the Canadian Employment Forecast Survey, has for instance been all but abandoned. When judged against this background, Hart's gallant attempt at rehabilitating the railroad shippers' forecasts undoubtedly represents an original and significant undertaking. However, we feel that his analysis, for all its ingenuity, has merely succeeded in scratching the surface of a very complex and interesting problem: why are the reported anticipations of all these surveys so systematically yet preposterously regressive? We propose to show that an answer to this question will have to be found along lines quite different from those suggested by Hart, and that this redirection in turn raises serious questions concerning the appropriateness of Hart's correction and the interpretation of his corrected series.

The Issues that Need to be Explored

The essence of Hart's approach is that since the poor forecasting record of the shippers' survey can be traced to the reasonably stable systematic understatement of the change over the four quarters previous to the time for which the forecast is made, we can more closely approximate future change by correcting the original forecasts for this understatement. The resultant series—Hart's "reconstituted" anticipations—is, by construction, free of the systematic bias. The most obvious use would be as an improved predictor of future changes, and we shall test whether such series provide better forecasts than can otherwise be obtained. But Hart proposes that, whether or not the corrected series can provide good predictions, they have a second use of possibly even greater potential value as measures of businessmen's short-run expectations. For a knowledge of prevailing business anticipations can be used to predict changes in other

NOTE: This paper originated as a comment on Albert Hart's paper in this volume. For useful and stimulating assistance, we are greatly indebted to James W. Harpel. We also wish to express our thanks to Michael C. Lovell for reading the manuscript and making many valuable suggestions.

production and investment variables which depend on plans made in the light of these anticipations. Here, however, an explanation must be furnished to show why a manipulation of the original series provides a more accurate picture of businessmen's expectations than the original forecasts themselves.

Hart's justification for his "correction" arises from his unwillingness to believe that the regressive anticipations which surveys report could possibly be the expectations on the basis of which current operating decisions are made. He therefore has suggested several hypotheses which attempt to explain regressiveness as the consequence of distortions picked up in the transmission and aggregation of the individual responses. We shall examine these hypotheses, and shall then test the underlying assumption made by Hart and other previous analysts that the source of the regressive behavior of the aggregate forecasts is to be found in the collection and collation of the survey responses rather than in the respondents' anticipations themselves. In so doing, we shall attempt to isolate the source of the regressiveness to be explained.

The Forecasting Value of "Reconstituted" Anticipations

Hart's paper provides the reader with a bewildering array of statistics bearing on the forecasting quality of the H-series. There are several different tests, whose relation to each other is not always clear, and for each test several results are usually given, each result being based on a different subsample of the observations, selected according to various criteria. We have therefore endeavored to sift out the relevant results and to present them in a systematic and compact form in Table 1. There is only one test for which all the data available for the interwar period have been used. In every other case we are forced to rely on the results of tests which omit the last two years, 1940 and 1941, and trust Hart's judgment that the omission does not significantly affect the outcome.

Like previous analysts of the shippers' forecasts, Hart tests predictive value by verifying whether his "corrected".series gives a more accurate prediction than is provided by simple extrapolative formulas based exclusively on the past behavior of the variable to be forecasted. As can be seen from Table 1, Hart has carried out basically four tests, differing from each other in terms of the variable to be predicted (column 2) and of the variables used in the extrapolative formula (column 6). For each test, two measures of predictive accuracy are provided. The first consists of a comparison of the simple correlation between the variable to be predicted and the H-prediction (column 5) with the correlation between the same dependent variable and the extrapolative forecast (column 7)—a comparison, in other words, of the gross predictive values of the two types of forecast. The second measure (column 8) is the partial correlation of the

240

TABLE 1

Tests of the Predictive Value of Hart's "Reconstituted" Shippers' Forecasts

Test Number (1)	Variable to Be Predicted (2)	Form of H-predictor (3)	Number of Observations (4)	Gross Predictive Value of H-forecast (r^2) (5)	Variables Used in Naïve Model (6)	Gross Predictive Value of Naïve Model Forecast (r^2 or R^2) (7)	Net Forecasting Value of H-prediction (8)
1	A_t/A_{t-4}	H_t/A_{t-4}	46	0.82	A_{t-1}/A_{t-5}	0.72	0.343
			54	.81	$A_{t-1}/A_{t-5}, A_{t-2}/A_{t-6}$	.74	.32
					A_{t-1}/A_{t-5}	.71	
					$A_{t-1}/A_{t-5}, A_{t-2}/A_{t-6}$	.74	
2	^sA_t	$(H_t/A_{t-4})^sA_{t-4}$	47	.921	$^sA_{t-1}$	.936	.18
3	A_t/A_{t-1}	$(H_t/A_{t-4})(A_{t-4}/A_{t-1})$	46	.34	normal seasonal variation	.56	
4	$^sA_t/^sA_{t-1}$	$(H_t/A_{t-4})(^sA_{t-4}/^sA_{t-1})$	46	.09	$^sA_{t-1}/^sA_{t-2}, \; ^sA_{t-2}/^sA_{t-3}$	.18	.006

Sources in Hart's paper: Test 1—pp. 212-213, especially footnote 16; Test 2—pp. 219-221; Test 3—pp. 223-224; Test 4—pp. 225-226.

H-prediction in a multiple correlation involving both the extrapolative variables and the H-prediction as independent variables—an index, in other words, of the net forecasting value of the H-prediction.[1]

The outcome of the first test (in which the variable to be predicted is the four-quarter change) is quite favorable to the H-prediction. The figures of column 5 are appreciably higher than those of column 7, and the figures of column 8 are fairly impressive, implying a partial correlation of close to 0.6.

Similar results have been obtained by Douglas Hartle in a study of the Canadian Employment Forecast Survey.[2] While his analysis is primarily concerned with the important question of separating the sampling errors in the survey from the forecast errors in the population, it does provide evidence on the regressiveness of the survey forecasts. The substantial underestimation of actual four-quarter change by the forecasts is indicated by the following regression equation of forecasted on actual change:[3]

$$(1) \qquad (E_t/A_{t-4}) - 1 = 0.29[(A_t/A_{t-4}) - 1] + 0.008$$

The corresponding equation reported by Hart for the railroad shippers' forecast is:[4]

$$(2) \qquad (E_t/A_{t-4}) - 1 = 0.44[(A_t/A_{t-4}) - 1] + 0.27$$

It is evident that the underestimation of forthcoming change is, if anything, even more pronounced in the Canadian survey than in the shippers' survey.[5] When the coefficients of equation 1 are used to correct this systematic bias in reported expectations, the correction appreciably improves the original predictions of employment, raising the correlation with actual change from 0.26 for the unadjusted data to 0.47 for the "reconstituted" forecasts.[6] Furthermore, a test analogous to the first

---

[1] The figures in column 8 are partial determination coefficients—that is, partial correlation coefficients squared.

[2] Douglas Hartle, "Predictions derived from the Employment Forecast Survey," Canadian Dept. of Labor, May 1957, mimeographed. (This paper has since been published in the August 1958 issue of the *Canadian Journal of Economics and Political Science*, but all references here are to the mimeographed version.)

[3] The Canadian survey requested respondents to make two four-quarter change forecasts of employment, one for three months ahead and one for six months ahead. Equation 1 is computed from a scatter of 31 six-month forecasts made in quarter t-2, plotted against the corresponding actual changes in Hartle, Chart 2.

[4] Computed from Hart's equation on p. 212 and footnote 14.

[5] The higher regression coefficient of equation 2 may partly reflect Hart's exclusion of observations at or near major turning points. More important, however, a large standard error is associated with the regression coefficient of equation 1. The correlation coefficient is small, even though significant at the 0.001 level, so that the two estimates of the regression coefficient of (E_t/A_{t-4}) on (A_t/A_{t-4}) obtained by alternately minimizing the variation of (E_t/A_{t-4}) and (A_t/A_{t-4}) are materially divergent from one another. By using the computation procedures of the principal components technique a more accurate representation of the average understatement of four-quarter change could be obtained; this procedure would yield a regression coefficient closer to that obtained for the shippers' forecasts.

[6] Coefficients of determination for 31 observations.

test in Table 1 shows that the correlation between actual change and the corrected forecasts is substantially higher than for the predictions obtained by extrapolating the previous actual change.[7]

Clearly the "reconstituted" series represent a great improvement over the unadjusted anticipations, for the uncorrected published forecasts perform appreciably worse than even the naïve-model forecasts. At the same time, however, it should be remembered that the naïve model used in this test is indeed naïve. The extrapolative prediction is roughly equivalent to forecasting shipments or employment in the next quarter by an extrapolation of the level of the current quarter, adjusted for seasonal variation by the ratio of the levels of the corresponding quarters of the year before.[8] This is obviously a most primitive way to adjust for seasonal variation. The favorable results of the first test can thus be of limited significance at best.

The results of the second test indicate that a forecast based on a projection of the seasonally adjusted level of shipments of the previous quarter (A_{t-1}) has appreciably higher gross predictive value than Hart's H-prediction. And column 8 shows that even the net forecasting value, though significant, is modest. These conclusions are confirmed by the last two tests, which are in effect variations of the second. The third test shows that normal seasonal variation accounts for a greater part of the unadjusted quarter-to-quarter fluctuations of shipments than does the H-prediction. The last test shows that the H-series is of little use in predicting quarterly change arising from forces other than the recurrent seasonal variation. The simple correlation between the seasonally adjusted quarterly change and the H-prediction is only 0.3, somewhat less than that for an extrapolative model based on a projection of previous seasonally adjusted changes; the partial correlation confirms that the H-forecast has essentially no net predictive value.

It is evident that the series manufactured by Hart represents a considerable improvement over the published anticipations. However, its

[7] The coefficient of determination of the relation between actual change and the corrected forecasts is 0.38 (for 39 observations), compared with 0.13 for the extrapolative predictions. The past change in this instance is $[(A_{t-2}/A_{t-6})-1]$, rather than $[(A_{t-1}/A_{t-5})-1]$ as in Table 1, since the employment forecasts corrected are six-month forecasts.

[8] Using the superscript f to denote a forecast, the extrapolative formula used as a naïve model prediction in Hart's first test is basically of the form $A_t^f/A_{t-4}=A_{t-1}/A_{t-5}$ which implies $A_t^f=A_{t-1}(A_{t-4}/A_{t-5})$. By the same token, when the extrapolative model relies on A_{t-2}, the adjustment for seasonal variation is performed by the ratio, A_{t-4}/A_{t-6}. To the extent that A_{t-4}/A_{t-5} (or A_{t-4}/A_{t-6}) does reflect a trend in addition to purely seasonal and random factors, the forecast is not, strictly, a seasonally adjusted projection of the level of the current quarter. However, projecting the trend which existed between two quarters a year ago is hardly a sensible procedure. This interpretation of the naïve forecast used as an alternative in the first test is, of course, only approximately valid. The extrapolative forecast is not strictly of the above form since the regression of A_t/A_{t-4} on A_{t-1}/A_{t-5} will in actuality involve a constant term and slope coefficient which are not precisely zero and one, respectively.

243

record does not appear to necessitate a significant revision of the conclusion of Hultgren, Ferber, and other previous analysts that, at least in the interwar period, the shippers' forecasts are of little use in predicting shipments.[9]

It should be recognized that the fact that E_t is known substantially earlier than A_{t-1} means that the tests hitherto discussed underestimate the usefulness of the H-index as a forecasting device. However, since the tests of Table 1 indicate that E_t contains little information about forthcoming changes in shipments from the current rate, the practical forecasting usefulness of any "reconstituted" anticipations must lie primarily in its being a proxy for information on current developments.[10] Not that the forecasts merely mirror the rate of activity at the time of the survey. Indeed, as Hart has pointed out, the movement of the shippers' forecast cannot be fully accounted for by the previous course of shipments. It appears, however, that the nonextrapolative element in the forecast, whether or not it is a reliable indication of the mood of the respondents, does not on balance contain much information of significant net forecasting value.

"Reconstituted" Anticipations as Measures of Expectations

We now turn to Hart's claim that a "corrected" series can represent a truer measure of businessmen's expectations than the original published anticipations. Hart's reasoning is that the systematic regressive bias in the forecasts is picked up during the collection and aggregation of the individual responses. The most direct test of this hypothesis would be to examine Hart's presumption that the anticipations of individual responding firms are nonregressive. Unfortunately no information about the forecasts made by individual firms is available for the shippers' survey. We do have such information, however, for a number of surveys conducted by Dun and Bradstreet, and we propose to rely rather heavily on the evidence thus provided.

---

[9] We have not made tests analogous to the last three of Table 1 for the Canadian Employment Forecast Survey. However, in a forthcoming book to be published by the University of Toronto Press, Hartle has tested the forecasting value of the survey when compared to naïve models using seasonally adjusted data. His preliminary results indicate that our conclusion also applies to his survey.

[10] Hartle has advanced some interesting evidence on this point. He found that the size of the understatement of actual changes in the Canadian employers' survey seemed to be a function of cyclical changes in employment. When $[(A_t/A_{t-4})-1]$ was increasing between surveys, the magnitudes of the four-quarter changes were understated by the forecasts. Conversely, even though the forecasts understated $A_t/A_{t-4}-1$ on the average (as indicated in equation 1), E_t/A_{t-4} tended to become larger than A_t/A_{t-4} when the rate of change of A_t/A_{t-4} was negative. (Hartle, pp. 16-18 and Chart 2.) This behavior corresponds to expecting change in employment to be a fraction of actual four-quarter changes lagged one to two periods—or, in other words, to recognizing only part of recently occurred changes. (Cf. Kenneth J. Arrow and Marc Nerlove, "A Note on Expectations and Stability," *Econometrica*, April 1958, pp. 297–300.)

The Dun and Bradstreet survey is similar to the shippers' and employers' surveys in several essential respects. Respondents are asked to report anticipations for the forthcoming quarter in terms of the change expected from the corresponding quarter of the year before.[11] The same dismal forecasting record is displayed.[12] Most significantly, the predictive record

CHART I

Monthly Manufacturers' Sales in the Fabricated Metal Products
Industry, 1948–1949

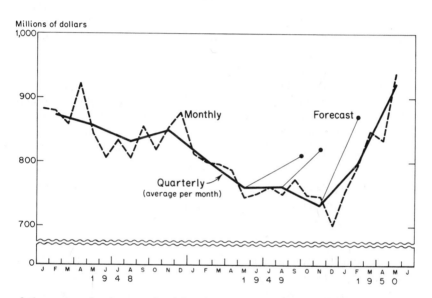

of the survey is characterized by the same occurrence of regressive one-quarter forecasts arising from systematically downward-biased predictions of four-quarter change.

Chart 1, collated from the responses of the fabricated metal products industry, illustrates this regressiveness. The dash line indicates monthly

[11] In the early surveys, including two of those analyzed below, the Dun and Bradstreet survey experimented with asking respondents to forecast for periods other than simply the forthcoming quarter. Respondents were asked, in the April 1948 survey, to forecast sales for the year 1948 and, in the May 1949 survey, to forecast sales for the next six months. In every case, however, the reference point was the corresponding period of the year before. The form in which $[(A_{t-1}/A_{t-5})-1]$ was reported also varied. In the April 1948 survey respondents reported the change in sales between the first quarter of 1947 and the first quarter of 1948; in all other surveys, respondents reported current sales in the month in which the survey was made over sales in the same month of the preceding year.

[12] Cf. Franco Modigliani and Owen H. Sauerlender, "Economic Expectations and Plans of Firms in Relation to Short-Term Forecasting," *Short-Term Economic Forecasting*, Studies in Income and Wealth, Vol. 17, Princeton University Press for the National Bureau of Economic Research, 1955, pp. 299-303.

245

sales adjusted for seasonal variation; the solid continuous line super-
imposed on the monthly indicator shows the movement of average sales
per month in each quarter, also seasonally adjusted. Each of the three
forecasts available is shown as a floating point tied back by a thin line to
the average level of sales in the previous quarter.[13] These forecasts, all
made following a sustained fall in sales, exhibit the same trend-reversing
patterns characteristic of the shippers' forecasts: the expected change in
sales from the level of the year before $[(E_t/A_{t-4})-1]$ is smaller than the
seasonally adjusted change that has already occurred $[(^sA_{t-1}/^sA_{t-4})-1]$
so that the forecast implies the expectation of a sudden reversal of the
existing trend. Such regressiveness was characteristic of the forecasts of
other industries covered by the surveys.[14] This is illustrated in Chart 2
which shows, for each industry covered by the survey, the average four-
quarter change in sales expected by the respondents in August 1949
plotted against the average past change reported by them.[15]

If the average past change reported by the respondents were the change
that had occurred between the reference date of the forecast and the time
the forecast was made, then Chart 2 would clearly indicate the regressiveness of the survey. Recall that extrapolation of level means

(3) $$^sE_t = {}^sA_{t-1}$$

where, as in Hart's paper, the s is used to denote seasonally adjusted data.
From this it is evident that if (3) holds, then

(4) $$(^sE_t/^sA_{t-4})-1 \equiv (E_t/A_{t-4})-1 = (^sA_{t-1}/^sA_{t-4})-1$$

where the first identity follows from the obvious fact that quarters t and
$t-4$ represent the same season of the year. Extrapolation of trend, on the
other hand, means $^sE_t > {}^sA_{t-1}$ when $^sA_{t-1} > {}^sA_{t-4}$, and conversely, or

(5) $$(E_t/A_{t-4})-1 \gtreqless (^sA_{t-1}/^sA_{t-4})-1 \text{ as } (^sA_{t-1}/^sA_{t-4})-1 \gtreqless 0$$

By the same token, reversal of trend, or regressiveness, means $^sE_t < {}^sA_{t-1}$
when $^sA_{t-1} > {}^sA_{t-4}$, and conversely, or

(6) $$(E_t/A_{t-4})-1 \lesseqgtr (^sA_{t-1}/^sA_{t-4})-1 \text{ as } (^sA_{t-1}/^sA_{t-4})-1 \gtreqless 0$$

[13] The floating point tied back by a thin line follows Hart's usage.

[14] For nondurable goods industries, the results of an additional survey conducted in
April 1948 is available. In spite of the fact that any regressiveness in this survey is
obscured to some extent because respondents were asked to forecast sales for the entire
year (as a ratio to 1947 sales), the regressive pattern held in this survey as well.

[15] The points in the scatter of Chart 2 are weighted averages of the individual responses
in each industry. One industry, the primary metal producers, is omitted. This industry
was sharply "antiregressive" in the August survey, forecasting a decline in sales of
36 per cent for the last quarter of 1949 from the last quarter of 1948—more than double
the 16 per cent decline from August 1948 to August 1949 reported by the responding
firms. This unusual forecast, however, was obviously shaped by the impending steel
strike which began on October 1. As a result of the work stoppage, steel output dropped
from about 85 per cent of rated capacity in late September to close to 8 per cent in the
first two weeks of October, and seasonally adjusted manufacturers' sales of iron and
steel declined 40 per cent. (Cf. *Survey of Current Business*, Dept. of Commerce, October
and December 1949.)

CHART 2

Forecast Change and Past Change in Sales in Each Industry
in the August 1949 Survey

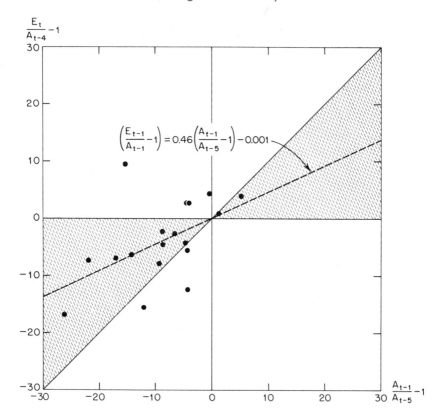

Thus, plotting $[(E_t/A_{t-4})-1]$ against $[(^sA_{t-1}/^sA_{t-4})-1]$, equation 4 would be represented by a straight line at 45° through the origin. Points falling on or close to this line would represent industries which, on the average, anticipate a continuation of the present level. Similarly, since the region defined by equation 5 is the portion of the plane falling between the 45° line and Y-axis in the northeast and southwest quadrants, points falling in this region would represent industries which anticipate a continuation of the previous trend. All remaining points would correspond to industries anticipating a reversal of trend.[16]

[16] More precisely, those observations falling between the 45° line and the X-axis (corresponding to the shaded area in Chart 2) represent regression in the original sense of wiping out some of the increase or decrease which occurred between $t-4$ and $t-1$. Those falling in the northwest and southeast quadrants also represent anticipated reversals of trend—reversals so sharp as to more than offset the movement recorded in the preceding quarters.

Unfortunately we do not know the average value of $[(^sA_{t-1}/^sA_{t-4})-1]$ for the sample of firms responding in each industry. However, the survey did request each respondent to report the change which had occurred between $t-1$ and $t-5$, and we may reasonably suppose that (A_{t-1}/A_{t-5}) will not, as a rule, differ significantly from $(^sA_{t-1}/^sA_{t-4})$. As a first approximation, then, we can use $[(A_{t-1}/A_{t-5})-1]$ as a proxy for the change occurring between the benchmark date of the forecast and $t-1$. Chart 2 can therefore be interpreted much as if $[(^sA_{t-1}/^sA_{t-4})-1]$ were plotted on the horizontal axis. But we must now be somewhat more cautious in our interpretation.

In the first place, even though $[(A_{t-1}/A_{t-5})-1]$ should be close to $[(^sA_{t-1}/^sA_{t-4})-1]$, the difference between the two is not likely to be purely random. Because trends typically last well over a year, it follows that change over four consecutive quarters will often be larger than the change which occurred over three of those quarters, so that the relation between the two will be of the form

$$(7) \qquad (A_{t-1}/A_{t-5})-1 = (1+k)[(^sA_{t-1}/^sA_{t-4})-1]$$

where k is a positive number. If trends were linear and of indefinite length, the four-quarter change would be $\frac{4}{3}$ as large as the three-quarter change so that the value of k would be $\frac{1}{3}$. But since in fact trends are far from continuous—especially for individual firms or small aggregates of firms—k is likely to be, on the average, a good deal smaller than $\frac{1}{3}$, though almost certainly positive. Solving equation 7 for $[(^sA_{t-1}/^sA_{t-4})-1]$ and substituting the result in equation 4, the condition for extrapolation of the existing level—the borderline, in other words, between extrapolation and reversal of trend—becomes

$$(8) \qquad (E_t/A_{t-4})-1 = [1/(1+k)][(A_{t-1}/A_{t-5})-1]$$

The line dividing the regions will thus be inclined at somewhat less than 45 degrees.[16a]

[16a] It should be reiterated that whether any given observation should be classified as either extrapolative or regressive depends upon the relative level of that firm's sales in $t-5$ and $t-4$. Not having this information for each firm, we are forced to draw a boundary line corresponding to the average relationship between $^sA_{t-5}$ and $^sA_{t-4}$ in each industry. Our proposition is thus that, on the average, this *average* boundary line is inclined at not much less than 45°. It should be noted, however, that the slope of the borderline can in certain circumstances be greater than unity—or even negative. In the usual case described above, $^sA_{t-4}$ is between $^sA_{t-5}$ and $^sA_{t-1}$, and k is positive. If, however, $^sA_{t-5}={}^sA_{t-4}$, then k is zero and the boundary line is the 45° line. Again, if $^sA_{t-4}$ is outside rather than between $^sA_{t-5}$ and $^sA_{t-1}$, k will be negative and, providing that $^sA_{t-5}$ is between $^sA_{t-4}$ and $^sA_{t-1}$, the slope of the boundary will be greater than unity. In the rare case where $^sA_{t-5}$ and $^sA_{t-4}$ are on opposite sides of $^sA_{t-1}$, $k<-1$ so that the borderline corresponding to extrapolation of level is actually negatively sloped. Such exceptions frequently occur at or shortly after major turning points in the business cycle, since at such times the change which occurred from $t-4$ to $t-1$ may well be in the opposite direction to what occurred between $t-5$ and $t-4$.

The second point to be kept in mind in interpreting this chart, is that, once we replace $(^sA_{t-1}/^sA_{t-4})$ with (A_{t-1}/A_{t-5}), the position of an observation no longer tells us with certainty whether the anticipations are extrapolative or regressive. A dot falling in the trend reversal area is likely to represent a regressive expectation, especially if it is far from the boundary, but it might on occasion correspond to an extrapolative anticipation if it happens that the seasonally adjusted change from $t-5$ to $t-4$ were abnormally large compared with the change from $t-4$ to $t-1$. Similarly, a dot in the extrapolative region might occasionally correspond to a regressive anticipation if the change from $t-5$ to $t-4$ were in the direction opposite to that from $t-4$ to $t-1$ and sufficiently large. But such pathogenic instances seldom occur. Though inferences about individual observations must be subject to some uncertainty, it is clear that if most of the dots fall in one particular region we can be confident that the anticipations are prevailingly of the type thus indicated.

Looking at Chart 2 in the light of these considerations, there can be little doubt that the anticipations are prevailingly regressive. Out of 18 observations only 3 fall in the extrapolative region as against 15 falling in the trend reversal region, 11 of which are regressive in the original, narrow sense. This count would be essentially unchanged if the boundary had a slope as low as 0.85.

This visual impression is fully confirmed by regression analysis. The regression of expected four-quarter change on recent past change is:[17]

$$(9) \qquad (E_t/A_{t-4}) - 1 = 0.46[(A_{t-1}/A_{t-5}) - 1] - 0.001$$

This result is representative of the relation between the average expected change and the average past change for individual industries in the other Dun and Bradstreet surveys.

Equation 2 indicates that, on the average, the anticipated change is only about half as large as we should expect if anticipations tended to represent an extrapolation of the recent level. The regression coefficient is strikingly similar to that reported by Ferber for the shippers' forecasts and to the systematic downward bias estimated by Hart.[18] There seems therefore, to be ample ground for confidence that evidence from the Dun and Bradstreet surveys can be utilized to test Hart's hypothesis and, more generally, to throw light upon the source of regressiveness in the shippers' and similar surveys.

[17] The coefficient of determination is 0.51, which is significant at the 5 per cent level.

[18] Both coefficients were about 0.44. Robert Ferber, *The Railroad Shippers' Forecasts*, Bureau of Economic and Business Research, University of Illinois, 1953, pp. 70-71, equations 4.1.6 and 4.1.7; and *supra* equation 2.

Previous Explanations of Regressiveness

In suggesting that the systematic, regressive bias in surveys of short-run business expectation is picked up in the transmission and aggregation of the individual responses, previous analysts have had to advance hypotheses to explain how such a "transmitting error" might have arisen. The explanation which historically has received the most favorable review is that advanced by Robert Ferber and Millard Hastay, who suggested that the understatement of four-quarter change in the published shippers' forecasts arose from the inclusion of a large group of respondents in the sample who arbitrarily reported an anticipation of "no change." For this hypothesis to be operationally valid, the proportion of individual respondents arbitrarily forecasting "no change" should be roughly constant from survey to survey and should be at least as large as the size of the downward bias in the surveys.[19] The available evidence indicates that this proportion is neither large nor constant. A breakdown of the respondents in each Dun and Bradstreet survey into the proportions expecting an increase in sales, a decrease in sales, and no change, is available since the inception of the surveys. Over this period the proportion of respondents who forecasted no change in sales never exceeded 30 per cent and varied substantially from survey to survey, reaching a minimum of 12 per cent.[20] Thus, even if all the respondents who reported "no change" had been doing so arbitrarily, the proportion of such forecasts would still be much too small and variable to account for the known understatement of the survey. Moreover, an analysis of the four surveys for which we have data on individual responses indicates that many respondents who make such a forecast also report no change in actual sales over the preceding four quarters. The fact that the proportion of respondents reporting "no change" in the past is a sensible function of the business cycle suggests that such respondents do expect that sales will continue to be unchanged from the previous year's level. Since the size of the rest of the group forecasting "no change" also fluctuates with the movement of seasonally adjusted sales, it is likely that a number of these forecasts are also not just arbitrary responses. Although a number of "no change" forecasts are probably made arbitrarily from time to time, all the available evidence

[19] This is of course a necessary but not a sufficient condition. As it happens this condition seems to be satisfied in both the Canadian and the Illinois employment forecast surveys, and it has been suggested that the Ferber–Hastay hypothesis therefore applies to these surveys. Hartle has in fact used this hypothesis as the basis of his intriguing explanation of the lesser degree of understatement in the employment anticipations (see Ferber's paper and Hartle's comment in this volume). But in addition to this condition, the Ferber-Hastay hypothesis requires that the nonarbitrary forecasts in each survey be nonregressive. This we shall later show is not true for the Canadian survey.

[20] The figures quoted are based on an analysis of data through April, 1954, which were made available to the authors in convenient summary form through the courtesy of Millard Hastay. A less systematic examination of later surveys does not suggest significantly different conclusions.

suggests that such forecasts do not represent a significant fraction of the total. For the Dun and Bradstreet survey, the Ferber–Hastay hypothesis thus does not appear to provide an explanation of even just an important part of the downward bias and regressiveness of the forecasts, and there seems little ground for supposing that this ingenious hypothesis might fare better when applied to the shippers' forecasts.

Hart has suggested that the aggregate industry forecasts published by the shippers' survey are regressive because the original four-quarter expectations of firms—expectations which are themselves nonregressive— get repeatedly squashed and distorted as they pass through the various stages preceding publication. Michael Lovell's evidence indicates that such purposeful understatement does occur in the aggregation of the replies, and it is probable that this "sin of commission" also arises in the replies of the traffic managers themselves. Anticipated carloadings seldom are the basis for operating decisions, and there may in some cases be little communication between the traffic manager and executives responsible for planning and forecasting.[21] In such an event, it is questionable whether the traffic manager's forecast would reflect the operating expectations; his forecasts might be made simply as a "conservative" extrapolation of recent shipments tempered by what he hears about the outlook for his firm.[22] Even in those cases where information on his firm's operating expectations is furnished to the traffic manager, considerable distortion might still arise, since the traffic manager wishing to be conservative quite conceivably might cut down his forecast as he translates the firm's operating expectations into a forecast of carloadings.[23]

[21] Interviews conducted by the Merrill project with executives directly or indirectly responsible for forecasting and planning activity in their firms revealed that, in many instances, these executives were not aware of the shippers' forecasts or of the participation of the traffic manager in the survey. Modigliani still has a vivid recollection of one instance in which the president of a medium-sized company summoned the traffic manager in the midst of the interview and castigated him for not telling him about his participation in the shippers' survey.

[22] That the forecasts might be made in this fashion need not imply that the traffic manager had no evidence about his firm's operations other than a record of carloadings, which is what Hart seems to suggest. Nor need such an explanation—even if it purported to explain all the regressiveness of the survey—require for its validity that extrapolative naïve-model projections better the predictive performance of the shippers' forecasts, corrected or uncorrected. (However, cf. Hart's last two paragraphs of the section "Statistical Conservatism.")

[23] As Hart has pointed out, this "conservative" editing of the original anticipations can give rise to regressive forecasts and at the same time be "reasonable" only if the editors confuse one-quarter change with four-quarter change through an inability to differentiate between seasonal fluctuations and nonseasonal movements. An interesting though scarcely conclusive test of the importance of this will be provided by an examination of the April 1948 Dun and Bradstreet survey, which asked respondents to forecast sales for the entire year. Since some of the confusion about the seasonal component of change should thus be avoided, we should expect that the April survey should be significantly less regressive than the others if "conservative" editing were an important cause of regressiveness.

The hypothesis thus has an appealing a priori plausibility. Can it explain a significant part of the regressiveness of the survey forecasts? To answer this question, we must analyze the anticipations of the individual respondents. If these expectations exhibit little of the regressiveness associated with the published forecasts, then we can safely conclude that the regressiveness is introduced during the transmission and aggregation of the individual responses. But if the individual firm's anticipations are themselves significantly regressive, then, to the extent that they are, any distortions which arise in the survey procedures must be that much less significant in accounting for the bias in the aggregate forecasts.

Are the Expectations of Individual Firms Really Nonregressive?

Information on individual responses is not available for the shippers' survey. However, the forecasts of individual establishments together with a record of actual changes in their employment were available to Hartle in his analysis of the Canadian employers' survey. He reports that the signs of the errors in the forecasts of employment made by each establishment tended to be the same at each target date, which implies that the errors in the aggregate forecasts were a reflection of similar errors in the individual responses. Even more revealing, he found that the establishments sampled at each time persistently underestimated the magnitudes of the non-seasonal changes in their future employment.[24] These findings are not by themselves conclusive evidence that the expectations of the respondents are biased. Hartle made a survey of firms in the employment survey's sample which suggests that many of the firms do not use predictions of their future employment in making their operating plans.[25] The forecasts of employment made by personnel managers consequently may often reflect operating expectations only to a limited extent, so that distortions could conceivably be introduced by personnel managers in their transmission of the anticipations of their firms.

Fortunately a much more conclusive test can be carried out with data available for some of the Dun and Bradstreet surveys.[26] Of all current variables, expectations about future sales are the most likely basis of businessmen's operating plans as well as the source from which forecasts of shipments and of employment are most likely to be derived. The anticipations of sales collected by Dun and Bradstreet are obtained by personal

[24] Hartle, pp. 43-46.
[25] See Hartle's comment in this volume.
[26] The data consists of a complete record of the individual responses to all questions asked in the surveys taken in April of 1948 and in May, August, September, October, and November of 1949, made available to the Merrill project through the courtesy of Dun and Bradstreet. The identity of the individual respondents was not disclosed, each firm being identified only by a code number. The responding firms were, however, classified by a two digit SIC classification and, in some cases, were further broken down by approximate sales volume.

interview, reportedly from persons responsible for their firm's plans and expectations about the future, and we may consequently be confident that most of the reported forecasts represent the original operating expectations of the respondents.

Chart 3 shows a scatter of the four-quarter change in sales anticipated by 39 firms in the machinery industry which were sampled by the Dun and Bradstreet survey of October 1949, plotted against the past change reported

CHART 3

Forecast Change and Past Change in Sales for Individual
Respondents in the Machinery Industry in the
October 1949 Survey

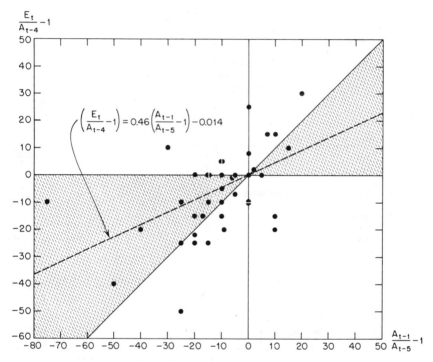

to the survey by these respondents. One thing that is immediately apparent from this graph is that the individual anticipations do not bear a common mechanical relation to past change. The scatter is substantial: the correlation coefficient is only 0.51 which, though highly significant, is still small. In spite of this wide scatter, the trend-reversing tendency of the anticipations is immediately apparent. Out of 39 observations only 10, about a quarter, fall in the clearly extrapolative region—a proportion even larger than is typical. By contrast, 21 observations fall in the trend reversal region, 16 of which are regressive in the classic sense. Of the remaining 8,

3 fall on the borderline represented by the 45° line; the remaining five are unclassifiable since they report no change in the past. The overall impression engendered by this distribution is fully confirmed by the regression equation:

$$(10) \qquad (E_t/A_{t-4})-1 = 0.46[(A_{t-1}/A_{t-5})-1]-0.014$$

The regression coefficient is much less than unity and is quite close to the value recurring in the analysis of the relation between anticipated and actual change.

Graphs similar to Chart 3 could be exhibited for all the industries and surveys for which the required information is available. That such graphs would all reveal much the same relation between anticipated and past change is indicated by Table 2, which presents the constant terms, slope

TABLE 2

Parameters of the Regressions of $[(E_t/A_{t-4})-1]$ on $[(A_{t-1}/A_{t-5})-1]$
in Selected Industries and Surveys

| INDUSTRY | | DATE | | REGRESSION EQUATION: | |
SIC No.	Description	OF SURVEY	CORRELATION COEFFICIENT	Slope Parameter	Constant Term
28	Chemicals	5–49	0.52	0.74	−0.004
		8–49	.55	.47	+ .012
		11–49	.72	.45	+ .030
34	Fabricated metal products	8–49	.78	.72	− .013
		11–49	.43	.44	+ .075
35	Machinery	8–49	.75	.63	− .037
		11–49	.54	.37	+ .004
36	Electrical machinery	8–49	.52	.44	− .022

parameters, and correlation coefficients of the regressions of $[(E_t/A_{t-4})-1]$ on $[(A_{t-1}/A_{t-5})-1]$ among individual respondents for a sample of some of the large industry subsamples.

A useful summary view of the regressive nature of the response is provided in Table 3, which presents for each survey a cross-tabulation of the expected four-quarter change in sales against the direction of the past change in sales for all respondents who provided a quantitative answer to both questions. It includes four of the six surveys for which such information was available to us. One of the remaining surveys was conducted in September 1949 and asked the same anticipatory question as the August survey; the other was made in October and asked the same question as the November survey. It seemed unlikely that the replies to these surveys could provide much useful additional evidence, and they were therefore not tabulated. The industries covered are all those available.

There is a correspondence between the entries in Table 3 and the

254

TABLE 3
Cross-Tabulation of Individual Responses

DATE OF SURVEY	NUMBER OF RESPONDENTS	DIRECTION OF PAST 4-QUARTER CHANGE REPORTED BY RESPONDENTS	4-QUARTER CHANGE FORECAST BY RESPONDENTS:						
			DOWN			NO CHANGE	UP		
			More Than Past	Equal to Past	Less Than Past		Less Than Past	Equal to Past	More Than Past
			(PERCENTAGES OF RESPONDENTS)						
April 1948	145	Up		8.3		11.7	16.6	16.6	9.7
		No Change		1.4		17.2		4.8	
		Down	2.8	2.1	1.4	5.5		2.1	
May 1949	240	Up		5.8		6.7	9.2	6.3	6.7
		No Change		4.2		4.2		3.8	
		Down	17.1	9.6	7.5	11.3		7.9	
August 1949	467	Up		3.6		5.6	6.4	9.2	8.8
		No Change		2.4		4.1		3.9	
		Down	11.6	11.8	13.1	9.0		10.7	
November 1949	417	Up		3.4		8.4	10.1	6.5	8.4
		No Change		2.2		8.4		6.7	
		Down	3.1	5.5	9.8	12.2		15.3	
All Surveys Combined	1,269	Up		4.4		7.4	9.3	8.6	8.4
		No Change		2.5		7.0		4.9	
		Down	8.8	8.2	9.6	10.1		10.7	

255

regions of Charts 2 and 3, which we have attempted to make clear in our arrangement of Table 3. For instance, the entries in the upper right and lower left corners of each component table correspond to the regions bounded by the 45° line and the vertical axis in the northeast and south-west quadrants of Chart 3. These entries indicate the number of respond-ents who reported that $[(E_t/A_{t-4})-1]$ would have the same sign and be of greater magnitude than $[(A_{t-1}/A_{t-5})-1]$. The sum of these figures (9.7 per cent plus 2.8 per cent in the April 1948 survey) thus represents the total number of responses which are clearly extrapolative.

The frequency of such extrapolative forecasts is rather small, ranging from a minimum of 11.5 per cent in the November survey to a maximum of 24 per cent in the May survey and averaging about 17 per cent. Much larger is the frequency of respondents who expect a reversal of the recent trend. These respondents, whose responses are tabulated in six entries in each table making up Table 3, account for an average of 51.5 per cent of the respondents in the samples.[27] Of these responses, about three quarter are regressive in the classic sense of the word: the expected four-quarter change is in the same direction as past change but of a lesser (though not necessarily nonzero) magnitude.

The remaining five entries in each table, which generally account for somewhat over 30 per cent of the total respondents, fall into two groups. First is a group for whom $[(E_t/A_{t-4})-1]$ and $[(A_{t-1}/A_{t-5})-1]$ are equal, corresponding to responses on the 45° boundary line in Chart 3. Although by no means negligible, the number of such respondents seems small, ranging from 12 per cent of the sample in November to 21 per cent in August. One might have anticipated that this type of response would be frequent, both because it corresponds roughly to an extrapolation of level and because it is the easiest response for a respondent who, whether from uncertainty or lack of interest, prefers to make an arbitrary projection of his record of past four-quarter change. The fact that a number of respond-ents report expected change equal to past change for all the variables surveyed by Dun and Bradstreet indicates that some of these responses do originate in "psychological inertia." But the frequency of such responses is evidently not large; the great diversity of the patterns of responses

---

[27] The six entries are: (1) up in the past, less up expected; (2) up in the past, no four-quarter change expected; (3) up in the past, decrease expected; (4) decrease in the past, less down expected in the future; (5) decrease in the past, no four-quarter change expected; (6) decrease in the past, increase expected. Actually, the proportion of responses which are regressive may be even greater than 51.5 per cent. Both the surveys of May 1949 and August 1949 were made several quarters after an important cyclical turning point so that, particularly in the industries most widely represented in each survey sample, the movement in sales between $t-4$ and $t-1$ was in the opposite direction to that which had previously occurred between $t-5$ and $t-4$. As a conse-quence, a number of forecasts which we have classified as extrapolative or non-classifiable are, in these two surveys, probably regressive. (Cf. *Survey of Current Business*, December 1953, Tables 2 and 5, pp. 21–28).

strongly suggests that the respondents customarily endeavor to give honest and thoughtful answers to the questions of these surveys.[28]

The last remaining group of respondents are those who report no change over the previous year and who therefore cannot be classified in terms of extrapolation or reversal of trend. There is a strong tendency for these respondents to expect no change in the future. Firms reporting no past change account for nearly 30 per cent of the no change expectations even though they represent only 14 per cent of the total responses. This should scarcely be surprising. Evidence from Table 3 on the variation of the proportion of total respondents reporting no past change also suggests that such reports—and the forecasts associated with them—are very seldom arbitrary. The largest frequency of reports of no past change occurred in the first survey, when the level of activity of nondurable industries had increased only moderately over the previous year. In the surveys of May and August, 1949, when the level of manufacturing activity had declined rather severely from the previous year, the proportion fell to 12 and 10 per cent. And, as the rate of decline in manufacturing activity leveled off, the proportion of respondents reporting no past change increased to 17 per cent in the November survey.

The regressive tendency of individual anticipations indicated by Table 3 can be made even more vividly apparent by analyzing the entries of the table in a somewhat more summary fashion. Table 4 presents this summary by contrasting the past change reported by the respondents with the anticipated direction of change from current levels implied by their four-quarter expectation. The relation of the difference between ^sE_t and $^sA_{t-1}$ to that between $[(E_t/A_{t-4})-1]$ and $[(A_{t-1}/A_{t-5})-1]$ has to be qualified by the considerations discussed in Section 4, but, subject to these qualifications, the impression given by this table is clear. Of the 1,086 respondents in all four surveys for whom such a division is relevant, somewhat more than 60 per cent report anticipations which are regressive.

---

[28] Some more direct evidence is available on this point. Modigliani has had occasion to talk to some of the Dun and Bradstreet interviewers and was assured, in every case, that the respondents took the questionnaire seriously and frequently looked up figures from their records. Respondents have the option of not answering a question at all, or of indicating the expected direction of change but not quantifying the answer, and a number avail themselves of this opportunity. A cursory analysis of the number of refusals yields patterns which correspond to what one would expect from businessmen who took the questionnaire seriously. The smallest refusal rate is typically for the price question: refusals to answer run about 5 per cent or less, and refusals to quantify are only slightly more frequent. For the sales question, the rate of refusal is somewhat higher, about 15 per cent, but the difference is mostly due to the greater frequency of "no answer." The largest refusal rate occurs for new orders in nondurable goods industries, where it comes close to 50 per cent, for the fairly obvious reason that the question is often not relevant. The fact that almost as many respondents do not report the past change in new orders bears this out. Finally, a high and variable number of firms, ranging from 20 to 40 per cent, refuse to give definite answers to the profit question, though a large proportion of these refusals represent an understandable reluctance to quantify.

TABLE 4

Implied Expected Change in Sales from Current Level in Relation to
Past Four-Quarter Change, All Dun and Bradstreet Surveys

	DIRECTION OF PAST CHANGE:	
	Up	*Down*
PERCENTAGE OF RESPONDENTS EXPECTING DIRECTION OF $[(^sE_t/^sA_{t-1})-1]$ to be:		
Same as past, or no change	44	36
Opposite to past	56	64
Number of respondents	484	602

Both the limited information available for the Canadian employers' survey and the extensive evidence available for the Dun and Bradstreet survey point clearly to only one conclusion. The short-run anticipations which individual firms report to surveys of businessmen's expectations of the four-quarter change in operating variables tend, on the average, to be quite strikingly regressive.[29]

This is a surprising result. It evidently contradicts the presumption upon which Hart and other previous analysts have based their attempts to explain the regressiveness in these surveys. For if we accept Hart's claim that the operating expectations of businessmen cannot possibly be regressive, we are forced to conclude that what people claim to expect is not what they "really" expect. This distinction between real and reported anticipations seems, when viewed in the light of the evidence on the care with which respondents generally reported their anticipations, to be more an invitation to metaphysical dispute than an operationally significant proposal. Yet if we reject this distinction, we must accept the implication that individual anticipations really are regressive. This implication in turn seems to contradict common sense notions about the relationship between operating plans and expectations.

We thus seem to have reached an impasse. How can the evidence we have introduced be reconciled with our a priori notions of what businessmen's expectations should be? In a forthcoming article we shall show that

[29] It should be reiterated that one of the Dun and Bradstreet surveys which provide evidence for this striking regressiveness asked respondents to predict sales for the entire year (compared, of course, to those of the previous year). Indeed, there are some indications that regressiveness may prevail even for expectations of yearly sales, which do not involve comparison with same time last year. For instance, Robert Eisner, analyzing the relation between the expected change in sales from 1949 to 1950 and the actual change from 1948 to 1949, for a sample of some 160 firms, found that the correlation was negative (though not significant at the 5 per cent level). (See "Expectations, Plans and Capital Expenditures: A Synthesis of Ex Post and Ex Ante Data" in *Expectations, Uncertainty and Business Behaviour*, Social Science Research Council, 1958, Table 2, p. 172.)

it is primarily our prior conceptions of what constitute reasonable anticipations, and not the implications of the evidence, which must be modified. We shall show, in fact, not only that it is reasonable to regard individual firms' anticipations as regressive but also that such regressive expectations conform to the movement of those firms' sales. The change consequently necessary in our conception of the way in which individual anticipations are formed raises significant questions about the way in which the forecasts provided by surveys of businessmen's short-run anticipations can be utilized and improved. These questions, too, will have to be discussed elsewhere.

COMMENT

ALBERT G. HART AND MARSHALL KOLIN, Columbia University

On several of the points raised by John Bossons and Franco Modigliani, we may open by recording our agreement.

1. The net predictive value of the "reconstituted" *H*-prediction (except as this may serve as a proxy for *ex post* information which is published only with a lag) is admittedly modest.

2. The "rolling-mill hypothesis" fails to fit the Dun and Bradstreet survey. Thus we need either an independent special explanation for the regressiveness of the Dun and Bradstreet results or some explanation which will cover the regressiveness of both sets of figures.

3. The suggestion that regressiveness in individual forecasts may have roots in regressiveness of individual experience brings an important new element into the discussion, though we see very different applications than Bossons and Modigliani indicate.

SIGNIFICANCE OF PREDICTIVE VALUE

The central point of the paper to which Bossons and Modigliani are reacting is not the use of shippers' forecasts to find out what was going to happen, but their use to find out what shippers' "really" expect to happen. The basic hypothesis that the reconstituted *H*-prediction pictures what they "really" expect *requires* "failures" of forecasting at turning points. To give an analogue, suppose we set up a poll of certain unfortunate commuters, asking them how many minutes they predict morning trains will take between Stamford and Grand Central Station. We will expect their forecasts to have predictive value—better than that of the official time table, and comparable to that of a naïve-model hypothesis based on the previous day's running time, though perhaps with systematic biases. We will expect the forecasts to be related to recent experience, becoming more pessimistic when the New Haven Railroad goes into one of its spells of late arrivals.[1] But we will not expect the commuter forecasts to tell us on which days the New Haven will outdo itself by having a string of derailed freight cars block the tracks for several hours, or how great the delays will be on such days. If we want to test the bias of commuter forecasts, we should compare forecasts with outcomes only for days when there are no derailments. We should not ignore derailments. They may affect, for example, the way forecasts are framed for the ensuing week. But we should give them separate treatment: merely lumping the two kinds of delay-experience together will obscure rather than clarify our analysis.

THE DUN AND BRADSTREET EVIDENCE

Transforming the four-quarter forecasts reported by Dun and Bradstreet into one-quarter forecasts from the date of estimation yields regressive aggregates. These aggregates, however, are probably dominated by responses from small firms, whereas the shippers' forecast aggregates are dominated by responses from large firms. A special explanation for the Dun and Bradstreet regressiveness—which would not apply to the shippers' forecast, and which would leave us in need of still another special explanation for the employment-intentions surveys—might be based on the presumption that small firms are much more likely than large firms to have frequent quarter-to-quarter reversals of direction in their sales. We are finding evidence of such a difference by size of firm in a study of sales experience in the steel industry now in progress at Columbia University.

The fact of a general tendency of forecasters to underestimate the change from a base date in the past to a reference date in the future is well established, and a general explanation for this tendency has been well roughed out by Theil.[2] But the grossness of the understatement, leading to implicit forecasts of reversal of the recent movement, remains puzzling. We are unconvinced by the Bossons–Modigliani suggestion that this result rests on regressiveness of individual-firm experience. But this debate must be adjourned to an occasion when a sufficient body of data on individual-firm experience is on the table.

BUSINESS-CYCLE IMPLICATIONS OF "REGRESSIVENESS"

Bossons and Modigliani seem to imply that any preference for an extrapolative over a regressive model of what businessmen "really" expect can only be sentimental. But have they considered the implications of the

[1] A more fundamental test of whether commuters "really" expect the trip to take abnormally long is whether at least some of them act upon their forecasts by leaving the house abnormally early for the station (or by arranging to avoid early appointments at the office). If current expectations are "really" more pessimistic than last month, there will be an increased proportion of commuters making such provision for extra slow commuting.
[2] H. Theil, *Economic Forecasts and Policy*, North–Holland Publishing Company, Amsterdam, p. 154.

hypothesis that expectations are "really" regressive? By "really expect," we might appropriately mean "place bets upon" through forward-looking action, whatever verbalizations may be found in a survey.

Now if expectations are really regressive in this sense, we must infer that the whole course of a business upswing is a series of agreeable surprises, which keep things going up despite a tendency of business to reverse the upswing by decisions to cut back inventory, staffing, procurement, and the like. Admitting that it is hard to systematize the use of business-cycle evidence in this connection, we assert that our preference for nonregressive models is not sentimental. Rather, it reflects the large body of facts which lead most analysts of fluctuations to give much weight to "cumulative" elements in expansion and contraction, and to doubt the inherent stability of the business process. In the light of these facts, how can expectations simultaneously be regressive and be linked up with the decision processes which generate business fluctuations?

REPLY BY MR. BOSSONS AND MR. MODIGLIANI

It is true that small firms are somewhat more likely than large firms to have frequent quarter-to-quarter reversals of direction in their sales, and it is generally recognized that the forecasting errors of smaller firms are larger than those of large firms. We doubt, however, that the "extra" regressiveness in forecasts made by smaller firms is sufficient to provide an explanation of the regressiveness of the aggregate Dun and Bradstreet forecasts. An examination of several of the larger industries in the August 1949 survey—which in its reporting of responses and its position in the cycle is the most "typical" survey for which we have individual data—indicates no obvious systematic tendency for forecasts to become more regressive as the size of firm decreases. For the August survey as a whole, roughly 55 per cent of the responses of firms in the largest size-class in each industry were regressive—a somewhat greater proportion, in other words, than the 48.4 per cent of all responses in the survey sample which were regressive. Although we have not tallied the responses by size group for other surveys, a cursory investigation indicates that the responses of the larger firms are equally regressive in the April 1948 and November 1949 surveys.

Hart's attempt at avoiding a metaphysical dispute over what respondents mean by their forecast, by defining "real" expectations as what businessmen would place bets upon, is interesting though perhaps less operational than it sounds. Unfortunately, a survey of verbalized expectations cannot help us measure the distribution which is attached to a point forecast by the respondent or the utility function with which he evaluates this distribution. It cannot, therefore, help us measure what bets the respondents will place as a result of their stated anticipations. Because of the limited space here available, we shall have to leave to a later article a discussion of the relationship of regressive expectations to operating decisions through the course of the business cycle. We should state that we have considered the implications of truly regressive expectations, and that we do not regard such expectations (even defined as point forecasts a la Hart) as incompatible with the actual movements of inventories and other operating variables. But this we will have to substantiate in another place.

PART III

The Predictive Value of Consumers Union Spending-Intentions Data

F. THOMAS JUSTER

AMHERST COLLEGE AND THE NATIONAL BUREAU OF ECONOMIC RESEARCH

Autonomous variations in the rate of consumer expenditures are now widely recognized as an integral part of any analysis of short-term fluctuations in general economic activity. To gain insight into the reasons behind the variations and to predict their direction and extent, researchers have used survey methods extensively and have tried to link data from replies with household income, purchases, liquid assets, and debt. The best known body of data in this area is provided by the Survey of Consumer Finances (SCF), obtained by personal interviews from a widely representative sample of approximately 3,000 households.[1]

The other large and unusually interesting body of data dealing with household intentions and purchases is supplied by Consumers Union of the United States (CU), a product testing and rating organization. Its annual questionnaire (mailed to some 700,000 subscribers, with replies in recent years from over 100,000 or 20 per cent) is designed to obtain information of value to the CU testing program.[2] Replies over the period 1945 to date have included a good deal of intentions data. Respondents

NOTE: This paper has been materially improved by careful review and criticism from Albert G. Hart of Columbia University and Geoffrey H. Moore of the National Bureau of Economic Research. Consumers Union of the United States, Mount Vernon, New York, made its records of questionnaire resources freely available, and supplied additional tabulations at its own expense. The Relm Foundation, Ann Arbor, Michigan, contributed generously to the support of further work in process on the Consumers Union data.

[1] Conducted for the Board of Governors of the Federal Reserve System by the Survey Research Center, University of Michigan, and the results published regularly by the Board.

[2] The usual CU procedure is to tabulate the summary results for a sample of 5,000 of the returned questionnaires and discard the others after a few years. But returns from the questionnaire are available for 1953 and 1954 (incomplete), and for 1955 and 1956 (complete). The punch cards prepared from annual samples are available for 1951, and for 1954 through 1956; summary tabulations of the punch card data are available for all years from 1946 through 1955.

have been asked (every year but 1953) about automobile and household durable goods buying plans for a twelve-month forward period, about income prospects (occasionally), and about house buying plans. Information has been obtained not only about purchases of these major durable goods, but also about income, education, age, and ownership of financial assets. Despite their usefulness, the reader must remember that the CU data have many statistical shortcomings:

1. Most of the analytically interesting questions were not asked every year, some only once. Although the spending-intentions question was asked except in 1953, only about seven major durable goods items were systematically included.

2. The mailing date for the questionnaires and the closing date for returns have varied.

3. The CU subscriber group is quite obviously not a random sample of the population as a whole. The median income is almost double that of the population median; the percentage of college-educated people is several times higher; and CU membership itself suggests that the household is likely to be atypical in its purchasing and planning habits.

The Predictive Value of Spending-Intentions Data

INTENTIONS DATA AND FORECASTING

Before examining the evidence, a discussion of the assumptions (or hypotheses) implicit in tests of the predictive value of intentions data is in order.[3] My purpose is the development of a model useful for making accurate forecasts of aggregate expenditures by economic units—including business and government as well as households. And how data on household intentions to purchase durable consumer goods can contribute to forecasting such totals is by no means obvious, since changes in the purchase of durables may tend to be systematically offset by compensating changes elsewhere in the economy.

Among plausible hypotheses about behavior—unsupported by solid empirical evidence—which would imply net forecasting value for data on purchases of consumer durables, three examples are:

1. The acquisition of durables competes with personal saving for what income remains after customary (habitual) expenditures for rent, food, small clothing items, services, and so forth. The pattern of habitual expenditures is determined by tastes, preferences, and relative prices; the aggregate amount can be predicted fairly easily from income data. The

---

[3] Usefulness in prediction is not the only function of these data. Analysis of how people formulate plans, of how the plans emerge from attitudes and expectations, and of how the plans evolve—or fail to evolve—into actions may further our understanding of economic and other social phenomena.

uncommitted income—if any—may then be either saved or spent on durables,[4] with its distribution determined by a complex set of attitudes and expectations, partly by the asset, debt, and demographic character- istics of the household, and partly by the same factors that determine customary expenditures.[5]

2. Purchase intentions for durables are related to aggregate consumer expenditures though not necessarily to expenditures on durables. That is, the consumption–income ratio would tend to be relatively high when intentions to purchase durables are relatively high, and vice versa. Actual purchases of durables would not necessarily be high at the same time, since a household planning to buy a refrigerator might instead take an extra two-week vacation or buy more food. The hypothesis implies that purchase intentions really indicate a general willingness to buy, and that purchase decisions for all categories of goods are arrived at in much the same way regardless of how costly the item or how often bought.

3. A change in the level or composition of durable goods purchases, even though it does not affect consumption expenditures, affects total expendi- tures via its influence on the level of private investment. This proposition rests on the notion that gross investment tends to be greater when the composition of output is changing than when it is stable, other things being equal. Advancing industries will undertake positive net investment, while declining ones cannot have gross investment of less than zero. On balance, a positive amount of net investment will usually be forthcoming even if the aggregate growth rate of consumption is equal to zero.

Each hypothesis suggests a different kind of empirical test to determine whether or not household intentions data have any predictive value as part of an aggregate model. Even if all were found to be seriously deficient, such data would still have some forecasting value for more modest objectives—for example, for economists analyzing particular industries or groups of industries and for the business community. But I shall now

---

[4] An alternative formulation of the hypothesis would be that customary household purchases are differently motivated and more easily predictable than discretionary purchases. The latter comprise such items as vacations and clothes, for example, in addition to major durables—which certainly make up the bulk of the discretionary purchase category.

[5] George Katona and Eva Mueller (*Consumer Attitudes and Demand, 1950-1952*, Survey Research Center, University of Michigan, 1953, p. 4) said that when consumer durable goods outlays are concentrated in one period, the rate of liquid saving declines and total spending by consumers rises, but that when they are made in several periods, the reverse is true. See also "Report of Consultant Committee on Consumer Survey Statistics" (*Hearings on Economic Statistics*, Subcommittee of the Joint Committee on the Economic Report, 84th Cong. 1st sess., July and October, 1955, p. 308) where it is pointed out that consumer expenditures for durable goods as a percentage of disposable income are virtually the inverse of personal liquid saving as a percentage of disposable income. The choice between the two is an important factor determining the inflationary or deflationary impact of the household sector, a choice on which attitudinal data should throw light.

turn to the main purpose of this paper—the analysis of the relationship between purchase intentions and purchases of durables.

INTENTIONS DATA AND PREDICTION

The nature of the empirical tests employed here—comparison of changes in intentions with changes in purchases of durables—implies acceptance of the first hypothesis in order to use the data as an ingredient in an aggregate model.[6] Thus, it is assumed that purchases of major durable goods compete mainly with liquid saving and that the distribution of income between the two is related to the attitudes and expectations of the household, their asset, debt, and demographic position, and to the usual factors of income, tastes and preferences, and relative prices.

In principle, one could construct an empirical model containing expressions for all variables that form the basis for purchase decisions.[7] The task would be formidable, involving perhaps impossible problems of quantification and weighting. Alternatively, the households could be asked, in effect, to do the quantification and weighting by answering whether or not they planned to purchase major durable goods.

The latter approach has the merit of simplicity and concreteness, but it requires sophistication on the part of the responding households.[8] It may be less difficult, however, to use explicit spending plans as indicators of the net interaction of attitudes and expectations than to ask about attitudes and expectations and attempt to deduce future purchases from these. Both kinds of data are subject to the same difficulties. While spending plans do not represent the sum of rationally calculated decisions to purchase particular goods, capricious plans are balanced to some extent by equally capricious and unrealistic attitudes and by unrealized expectations. And explicit spending plan data have the further advantage of reflecting the household's own criteria for the weighting and quantification of the basic variables that influence spending decisions.

[6] The second hypothesis suggests a comparison of changes in intentions to purchase durables with changes in aggregate consumer expenditures.

[7] Up to now, only tentative attempts have been made to use attitude and expectation data as ingredients in a forecasting model, although researchers have used them as permissive, modifying, or intensifying adjuncts to the explicit spending plans. (See Katona and Mueller, *Consumer Attitudes and Demand*; John B. Lansing and Stephen B. Withey, "Consumer Anticipations: Their Use in Forecasting Consumer Behavior," *Short-Term Economic Forecasting*, Studies in Income and Wealth, Vol. 17, Princeton University Press for National Bureau of Economic Research, 1955; and Lawrence R. Klein and John B. Lansing, "Decisions to Purchase Consumer Durable Goods," *Journal of Marketing*, October 1955.) Klein and Lansing investigated the degree to which a large number of attitude and expectation variables, including explicit spending plans, could discriminate between buyers and nonbuyers of durables.

[8] It can be argued that households in general are better able to answer questions about their attitudes and expectations than about what they intend to do. I may know that I am pessimistic about relevant economic events without being able to say concretely what difference this attitude will make in what I will buy.

Whatever the merits of the two procedures, clearly there are knotty analytical problems involved in making *joint* use of attitude and expectation data and spending-intentions data.[9] One can argue that, in principle, the two are redundant. A serious plan to purchase a particular commodity must take into account the probable course of whatever future events influence the household's purchase decisions. Thus knowledge of the buying plan should be equivalent to knowing the end result of the interactions among all factors that shape the plan. However, this does not necessarily imply that attitude and expectation data are redundant to an explanation of actual purchases, though they may be. Information about expectations, in particular, would be necessary in order to know whether plans will be carried out or modified. For example, if the income expectations accompanying buying plans were less favorable than the income actually received, purchases should be high relative to plans and vice versa.[10]

Given the nature of the average household, it is unrealistic to suppose that intentions are always formulated with the degree of care and foresight just described. Thus, we may be able to use the attitude data to discriminate between legitimate and fanciful purchase intentions, or to decide in advance that intentions are likely to prove unreliable for a particular period. And when the spending-plan data are ambiguous, attitude data may show factors that should be included, in principle, in the purchase plan, but often are not.

In the last analysis, the ultimate test is empirical. If spending plans provide an adequate basis for forecasting, they serve the purpose. If they do not, we must develop a model based either on the causal factors that underlie purchase decisions or on some combination of explicit intentions and causal factors.[11]

---

[9] This is the procedure most frequently followed. For example, the SCF indicates that it employs attitude and expectation data to check the reasonableness of spending plans; and in the actual forecast it makes substantial use of these data to modify or amplify the magnitude of changes suggested by the spending plan data (see, for example, SCF, *Federal Reserve Bulletin*, June 1949.)

[10] It is not entirely clear to me where attitude (as distinguished from expectation) data fit into this picture. Attitudes are either generalized notions about economic status and conditions (better off or worse off than last year, good time or bad time to buy a car, etc.) or they are rather long-run speculations (a major depression likely within the next five years). One cannot speak of attitudes being fulfilled or not fulfilled, but only as being changed or not changed. Whether or not expectations have been fulfilled can hardly be inferred from knowing whether or not attitudes have changed. If this is so, attitudes would still be, in principle, redundant to a knowledge of spending plans, and they or their changes could not be brought to bear on the question of plan fulfillment. Expectations would be redundant to analysis of purchase plans, but not to analysis of purchases.

[11] Much current thinking stresses the desirability of devoting more resources to gathering and interpreting attitude information, since a framework of attitudes and expectations must form the basis for the purchase plans of households. Almost no mention is made of buying-plan data by Katona and Mueller (especially Chapters 3 and

Obviously, there is no simple means of testing the predictive value of spending-intentions data. Nevertheless, if household spending intentions have any real significance there should be some rough correspondence between plans and purchases, or, at least, reasons why plans and purchases diverged for a particular period.

EMPIRICAL TESTS OF DATA

In this section, year-to-year changes in the level of expressed spending intentions are compared with year-to-year changes in the level of purchases. As noted previously, the CU data are employed for the analyses, and SCF data are included for comparison.[12] In both, spending intentions for the respective samples are tested against purchases for the entire population to explore their value as indicators of aggregate purchases. For the CU data, the working hypothesis is that, although the sample is obviously nonrandom for the entire population, it is a fairly good sample of the durable goods-buying population. In addition, the bias toward a better educated and more articulate population in the CU sample may be a net advantage in prediction for the whole population.[13]

Of several possible kinds of empirical tests, comparisons of the direction and extent of year-to-year changes in purchase intentions with actual purchases are useful but somewhat imprecise (see Appendix Tables A-1 and A-2). Although with so few observations, results of correlation tests are subject to a wide margin of error, they give a basis for some tentative conclusions.[14] Table 1 shows squared correlation coefficients (corrected for the number of observations) relating the year-to-year changes in the aggregate value of purchase intentions for the two samples to a similar change in purchases for the population as a whole.

The correlations for the CU data are all significant (at the 5 per cent level), while for the SCF data only total purchases in constant prices show statistical significance. None of the differences between CU and SCF

---

4) who examine a half-dozen attitude–expectation indicators and their interrelationships. On the other hand, the Consultant Committee on Consumer Survey Statistics (page 64) found that intentions data (buying plans) had considerable predictive value for durable goods purchases, but that the attitude and expectation indicators—with two minor exceptions—made little contribution to an explanation of purchases. Klein and Lansing arrive at much the same conclusion.

12 The CU and the SCF periods are about the same length, twelve months, but CU data start with the date for the required return of questionnaires and cover roughly fiscal years; the SCF data cover calendar years.

13 A more complete discussion of the CU sample and an analysis of the biases will be found in the next section.

14 Data for the full 1946-55 period are incomplete for the following reasons: (1) because in 1945-46 supply restrictions limited purchases, yet wartime price controls prevented price increases, 1946 purchase intentions were not usable, and the year-to-year comparison between 1946 and 1947 was eliminated; and (2) because purchase intentions are lacking in the CU 1953 data when the intentions question was omitted from the questionnaire. We are thus left with only six observations for the CU data and eight for the SCF data.

TABLE 1

Correlation Coefficients and Slopes of Regression Equations Derived from a
Comparison of Changes in CU and SCF Spending Intentions with Changes
in Actual Purchases by the Population as a Whole, 1946-1955

Expenditure Category	r^2 (corrected)		b_{yx}	
	(current prices)	(constant prices)	(current prices)	(constant prices)
Automobiles:				
CU	0.75	0.66	0.64	0.62
SCF	.35	.29	.58	.61
Household furnishings:				
CU	.58	.79	.39	.59
SCF	.00	.00	.19	.16
Total durables:				
CU	.84	.85	.58	.64
SCF	.22	.44	.38	.66

In this and the following tables, figures underlined are significantly different from zero
at the 5 per cent level; zeros represent small (positive) correlations that were washed out
by the correlation.

a Change in planned purchases is the independent variable; change in actual purchases
the dependent variable.

b The SCF data show the effect of the Korean War, unforeseen at the time consumers
reported to it their 1950 intentions; the CU questionnaire went out shortly after the war
had begun. Recalculating SCF correlations without 1950 data yields r^2's of 0.42 for
automobiles, 0.00 for household furnishings, and 0.30 for total durables, in current
prices. The r^2's in constant prices become 0.26 for automobiles, 0.00 for household
furnishings, and 0.45 for total durables. None of the correlations is significant at the
5 per cent level, since the loss of one observation more than compensates for the gain
in degree of relationship for the total durables (constant price) category, and the others
do not gain enough from the elimination of 1950 data.

Source: Tables A-4 to A-7. The regression equations are of the form $D_t/D_{t-1} = a + bX_t/X_{t-1}$, where D_t is the value in current (constant) prices of durable goods
purchases and X_t is the value in current (constant) prices of spending plans for durable
goods.

correlations show statistical significance, even though some—particularly
for the household furnishings category, which includes all major durables
except automobiles—are quite sizable. The correlation for total durables
in the CU data is higher than that for either subcategory in both current
and constant price data; a result to be expected if there is any tendency to
substitute one kind of durable for another when purchase intentions are
translated into decisions. The SCF data are ambiguous in this regard.

As for the slopes of the regression equations, they are all less than unity,
which suggests that changes in purchases are generally some fraction of
changes in plans.[15] This finding suggests that consumers are apt to show

[15] Since the constant terms are all positive, the statement is true only when the changes
in both are relatively large. Thus, if there is no change in plans, purchases tend to be
somewhat larger than in the preceding year. This result should not be attributed simply
to growth in population or other trend factors, since the index of planned purchases
includes an allowance for increase in number of households.

269

greater changes in attitudes and plans than in actions, in contrast to business planners who show the reverse tendency—changes in actual investment expenditure are generally larger than changes in planned expenditures.[16] It seems plausible that household planning is less systematic than business planning, which often employs last year's results as a first approximation to this year's planning.[17] Such systematized planning might produce a built-in bias toward reporting smaller changes than are really contemplated.

The results obtained with CU data appear to justify their serious consideration as spending-intentions data with considerable forecast value. Despite the severe handicap of so few observations, the CU data can be said to have passed one of the relevant tests with comparatively high marks.

INCOME CHANGES INTEGRATED INTO THE MODEL

Although spending intentions were significantly related to purchases, the existence of a net impact of intentions on purchases, after allowance for other variables, has not been demonstrated. If foreseen, income changes and other events should already be accounted for in the plans; if unforeseen, they will have an independent influence on purchases. In general, we have no way of knowing whether particular economic events were expected by households, although some people apparently were able to make accurate, though crude, forecasts about their own income prospects.[18]

Even if some households anticipate changes correctly, many are certainly pleasantly or unpleasantly surprised, and consequently some net effect of additional variables on purchases should be found. Since income changes are probably one of the most sensitive variables influencing consumer decisions, a relationship first suggested by Duesenberry[19] was employed— the ratio between current real per capita income and the highest level of real per capita income previously achieved. Table 2 summarizes the correlation coefficients for multiple regression equations relating actual purchases to CU and SCF planned purchases and real income changes and

[16] Cf. "Report of Consultant Committee on Consumer Survey Statistics."

[17] Cf. the interesting results obtained by Robert Ferber in "The Railroad Shippers' Forecasts" (*Studies in Business Expectations and Planning*, University of Illinois Press, 1953).

[18] The SCF shows how many people expect their income to rise and how many expect a fall. Aggregate income has tended to move in the direction expected by the majority of those who registered an expectation, thus giving assurance of some correct anticipations of changes. But the inflationary nature of the postwar period over which these surveys have been gathered suggests that the accuracy of such household forecasts may be a pure happenstance.

[19] James Duesenberry, *Income, Saving, and the Theory of Consumer Behavior*, Harvard University Press, 1952.

shows correlations for the two simple regressions. The value of $r^2(R^2)$ was used (corrected for the number of observations).

TABLE 2

Correlations Relating Changes in Purchases to Changes in Spending Plans
and Real Income, CU and SCF Data, 1946-1955

| | Square of Correlation Coefficients for Regression Equations[a] | | | | | |
| | (current prices) Independent Variables | | | (constant prices) Independent Variables | | |
Expenditure Category	X, Y[b]	X	Y	X, Y[b]	X	Y
Automobiles:						
CU	0.73	0.75	0.68	0.67	0.66	0.63
SCF	.48	.35	.15	.38	.29	.16
Household furnishings:						
CU	.65	.58	.70	.73	.79	.63
SCF	.63	.00	.67	.36	.00	.43
Total durables:						
CU	.83	.84	.74	.80	.85	.65
SCF	.58	.22	.50	.58	.44	.35

[a] The regression equations have the following form: X, Y: $D_t/D_{t-1} = a + b(X_t/X_{t-1}) + c[(Y/NP)/(Y/NP)_0]$, X:$D_t/D_{t-1} = a + b(X_t/X_{t-1})$, and Y: $D_t/D_{t-1} = a + b[(Y/NP)/(Y/NP)_0]$, where D=purchases of major durable goods, X=spending plans for major durable goods, and Y/NP=real disposable per capita income.

[b] Multiple correlation coefficients among plans, income, and purchases are sometimes lower than simple correlation coefficients because the improvement in relationship does not compensate for the loss of an additional degree of freedom.

Source: Tables A-4 to A-9.

Clearly real income changes were closely related to purchases, especially of household furnishings, but, surprisingly, in different degrees for the CU and SCF data. Recalculation of the material (in both cases relating purchases of the population as a whole to changes in per capita real income) for SCF calendar years indicated that much of the discrepancy arose from a difference in time periods rather than in coverage.[20]

Addition of the income variable did not much improve the correlations for the CU data. This finding cannot be due to a lack of relationship between purchases and real income, which was generally stronger for the CU data, but rather to the close relationship for that data between the *independent* variables—spending intentions and income changes where the impact of the same variable appears to be measured twice. The same problem did not arise with the SCF data, where the correlations between

[20] The coverage of purchases is somewhat different because CU time periods do not run over either a calendar or a fiscal year. I had to aggregate quarterly CU data, and the available breakdowns are less finely detailed (e.g. automobile parts are included in purchases of automobiles).

271

independent variables—spending intentions and real income changes—are quite low:

Expenditure Category	r^2 (corrected)			
	Current Price Data		Constant Price Data	
	CU	SCF	CU	SCF
Automobiles	0.61	0.00	0.35	0.00
Household furnishings	.73	.18	.70	.28
Total durables	.66	.00	.70	.01

The existence of the relationship for the CU data makes it impossible to determine the net influence of either spending plans or income changes on purchases. In the following tabulation, $r^2_{12.3}$ gives the relationship between actual purchases (dependent) and planned purchases (independent), real income changes being held constant, and $r^2_{13.2}$, that between actual purchases (dependent) and real income changes (independent), planned purchases being held constant:

Expenditure Category	r^2 (not corrected)			
	Current Price Data		Constant Price Data	
	$r^2_{12.3}$	$r^2_{13.2}$	$r^2_{12.3}$	$r^2_{13.2}$
Automobiles				
CU	0.40	0.23	0.35	0.27
SCF	.49	.32	.38	.27
Household furnishings				
CU	.12	.37	.45	.01
SCF	.07	.70	.06	.52
Total durables				
CU	.52	.23	.58	.03
SCF	.31	.56	.46	.37

The net correlations for the CU data are erratic, since whichever of the two independent variables has the higher correlation with purchases tends to dominate. (Compare the current and constant price net correlations for household furnishings.) The net correlations for automobiles are the most significant since the relationship between independent variables is least powerful. Net correlations for the SCF data are considerably more significant and conform generally to what would be expected on a priori grounds. Automobile purchases are more dependent on spending plans than on real income changes, and purchases of household furnishings show the reverse tendency. Actually, income changes dominate the household furnishings category in the SCF data because of lack of relationship between plans and purchases.

In general, the attempt to integrate real income changes into the analysis of CU data proved unsuccessful. The changes are closely related to purchases though not so closely as spending intentions are. However, a close relationship also exists between spending intentions and income changes, vitiating any endeavor to isolate the net effects of the two factors.

The most striking aspect of the data is the disparity between the CU and SCF spending intentions–real income change relationships. If we postulate that (1) household spending intentions are an indicator of household purchases, (2) spending intentions are formulated within a framework of anticipated income change, with intentions being high when income is expected to rise and vice versa, and (3) household anticipations of income changes are generally correct, then intentions and income changes should be highly correlated. If (1) and (2) are correct, but (3) is wrong, then we would expect little or no correlation. The CU sample may show a high correlation between the independent variables because its members successfully predicted changes in their own income. But these conclusions are based on few observations, and alternative (and less complimentary) explanations are not precluded by the data.

SUMMARY

The empirical test demonstrates that the CU data are a most promising body of information. All correlations between the purchase intentions of the sample and actual purchases of the whole population show statistical significance at the 5 per cent level. This result is especially noteworthy for the household furnishings category of durables, where purchase intentions data from other surveys have proved unreliable. The net forecasting value of the CU intentions data after allowance for the effect of real income changes on purchases could not be accurately measured since the independent variables were highly correlated. Nevertheless, the improvement of all but one of the simple correlations between real income changes and purchases when the intentions variable was added indicates that such value exists.[21] Indeed the high correlation between the independent variables is suggestive in itself, since purchase intentions and income changes should be highly correlated under certain conditions.

Certain reservations bear repeating. All the generalizations are based on exceedingly few observations within a prosperous period conducive to reasonably accurate forecasting. The nature of the CU sample gives added pause for thought. Why should a sample of this kind, with its obvious biases and peculiarities, yield as good results as it did during this period, and is it likely to continue to perform well?

---

[21] See Table 2. In contrast, the simple correlation between intentions and purchases is generally not improved, after correction, by adding the income-change variable.

Characteristics of the Consumers Union Sample

SOME CONSIDERATIONS ON SAMPLING

If intentions data are to be used to forecast consumer expenditures, a random probability sample of the total population may not be the best one. If the sample is random, then the average rate of purchase intentions in the sample is an estimate of the average rate for the population as a whole. Changes in the rate from one year to the next are taken to signify more purchase plans and hence more purchasing than in the preceding year.

Suppose, however, that the sample deviates from the average in income and age distribution but deviates in the same way and about equally during consecutive years. Any change in the level of purchase intentions for a wholly random sample, provided it was systematic (i.e. proportional) for all groups, would be reflected by the biased sample. The *level* of intentions would be different, being higher or lower depending on the nature of the biases.[22]

Since our concern is with intentions to purchase durables, a sample with income and age distribution biases might actually provide *better* estimates of change in the level of purchase intentions for the population than a random sample of the same size could. The objective is really a random sample of the durable goods buying population rather than of the entire population. The younger, higher-income groups purchase durable goods more often, relative to disposable income, than the older, lower-income groups do. Thus, a consistently biased sample of the first group might be a better sample of the relevant population, and therefore have a smaller sampling error.[23]

[22] If a change in the frequency of intentions occurred in one class of people and not in others, the biased sample would not necessarily show movements exactly comparable from year to year with those shown by a random sample, although the movements would be generally similar. The two samples might even show movements in different directions. For example, if high income people planned to purchase many more durables and lower income people many less, a sample biased toward high incomes could show a higher average rate of purchase intentions at the same time that a random sample of the population showed a lower average rate.

The level of the intentions would usually differ. For example, in a sample with high income and younger age for the household head relative to the population average, the level of purchases would be considerably higher than for a random sample. However, in a sample with relatively high income but relatively *older* age for the household head, the level of purchases might not differ from the population average, despite the biases. In any event, changes in the population would be reflected in the sample, provided the biases were consistent and all subgroups showed proportionate changes.

[23] What matters is not only the sampling error for intentions but also (1) the relationship between intentions and fulfillment for the sample, and (2) the relationship between sample purchases and population purchases. If the members of a biased sample, such as the CU subscriber group, show a closer relationship between their own purchase plans and purchases than does the population, and in addition there is a stable relationship between the purchases of the sample and population purchases, then the biased sample might predict population purchases better than any conceivable random probability sample could. I am indebted to Mary Jean Bowman for this point.

Another facet of the sampling problem is the possible advantage of concentrating on series that are thought to move in advance of the rest of the economy or whose reactions are more volatile than the average, in the hope of predicting changes in general conditions by observing changes in supposedly critical areas. Are there households whose patterns of behavior are likely to precede (and perhaps influence) the behavior of other households? Economists frequently assert that the consumption patterns of higher-income groups—certainly patterns of what goods are purchased and perhaps also of what is saved or spent—"trickle down" to the rest of the economy.[24] By the same logic, the more perceptive and articulate members of the population may exert an influence on behavior out of proportion to their numbers; and changes in their attitudes, expectations, and plans may foreshadow similar changes for the population as a whole.

Such an argument cannot be tested since there is little empirical evidence that can be brought to bear on it, and so must be used with caution. However, the results obtained with the CU data suggest its validity.

DESCRIPTION OF THE SAMPLE

Table 3 shows that median income for the CU sample was markedly higher than that for the whole population. There was some tendency for

TABLE 3

Comparison of Income Distributions for the CU and SCF Samples,
1948, 1951, and 1953

| MONEY INCOME BEFORE TAXES | PERCENTAGE OF SPENDING UNITS DURING | | | | | |
| | 1948 | | 1951 | | 1953 | |
	CU	*SCF*	*CU*	*SCF*	*CU*	*SCF*
	(per cent)					
Less than $2,000	4	30	1	28	1	23
2,000–2,999	16	23	3	18	2	14
3,000–3,999	24	20	13	18	7	16
4,000–4,999	19	12	18	15	14	16
5,000–7,499	22	10	35	14	35	21
7,500–10,000	8	2	14	4	19	5
10,000–over	8	3	15	3	21	5
	(dollars)					
MEDIAN INCOME	4,337	2,840	5,992	3,200	6,818	3,780

The time periods are not equivalent because the CU data do not cover calendar years, and they are not reported in every year. Accordingly, the time difference in the CU data between the columns marked 1948 and 1951 in the table, is really 49 instead of 36 months. The correspondence between 1951 and 1953 is better, with a 26-month gap for the CU data. See Table A-3 for the time periods actually covered.

Source: For CU data, Table A-10. For SCF data, as a random sample of the population, "Survey of Consumer Finances," *Federal Reserve Bulletin*, September 1952, Table 1; and July 1954, Table 2. Details may not add to totals due to rounding.

[24] Cf. Duesenberry.

the spread *between* the median incomes to increase slightly, since median CU income increased by about 6 per cent per year from 1946 to 1955, the population median by a little under 5 per cent. The CU sample has particularly small representation of income groups below $2,000, and for recent years poor representation of the $2,000-2,999 group relative to its estimated size in the population. The higher income groups are, of course, strongly overrepresented.[25]

The geographical distribution of the CU sample for two periods, indicates that major underrepresentation occurs only in sparsely populated areas:[26]

		PERCENTAGE RESIDING IN REGION			
		1947		*1950*	
CU REGION	CENSUS REGION	*CU Sample*	*Total Population*	*CU Sample*	*Total Population*
1	New England and Middle Atlantic	36	27	33	26
2	South Atlantic and East South Central	10	21	11	22
3	East North Central and West North Central	31	30	30	30
4	West South Central and Mountain	7	13	8	13
5	Pacific	18	10	17	10
6	Outside Continental United States	0	—	2	—

Two census regions have half the share of CU subscribers required for full representation of their populations, but the representation is not really poor. The geographic overconcentration of CU subscribers seems to be primarily in the New England and Middle Atlantic area and on the Pacific Coast.

Geographical underrepresentation in the CU sample is apparently related to the size of the communities in which subscribers reside. The following tabulation shows the distribution of CU subscribers and of the

[25] An average of over 96 per cent of all CU respondents answered the income question on the questionnaire every year.

[26] The CU data are from Table A-11. Data on the United States population are from *Statistical Abstract of the United States, 1949*, p. 31; and *1953*, p. 18. CU period 6— roughly fiscal 1952—was used for comparison with the 1950 population figures, because geographical information was not requested in the previous year. Census regions were grouped to conform with CU classification in regions.

population as a whole by size of community and size of urban community, for selected years:[27]

	PERCENTAGE OF TOTAL POPULATION				PERCENTAGE OF URBAN POPULATION		
	CU Sample			U.S. Population	CU Sample		U.S. Population
	1949	1953	1954	1950	1953	1954	1950
Over 1 million	27	18	21	12	19	22	18
1 million to 100,000	28	29	29	18	31	30	28
100,000 to 25,000	15	18	18	12	19	19	18
25,000 to 2,500	20	22	19	18	23	20	28
Less than 2,500	11	12	12	41			
Farm		5	5	36			
Nonfarm		7	7	5	8	8	8

The major gap is in towns of less than 2,500 population in which only about 11 per cent of the CU sample reside, compared with about 41 per cent of the whole population, and in rural areas. The distribution of urban CU subscribers is close to that of the U.S. urban population. Surprisingly enough, there is little overconcentration in large cities.[28]

The education of CU subscribers may give some indication of how "planning minded" they are. In replies of 1948-49 and 1954-55, over 70 per cent of the sample indicated some college education, and 17 per cent high school or an equivalent. The corresponding percentages for the United States adult population in 1950 are 13 and 37.[29] The two sets of figures are not strictly comparable. The CU data may refer to only one adult in each family, while the census data indicate the percentage of all adults having a particular degree of education. If the CU percentages for the "some college" group are halved, the percentage of CU college educated persons is still close to three times that of the population, a disparity that cannot be dismissed on grounds of a possible tendency to exaggerate on the part of CU respondents.[30]

[27] The CU data are from Table A-12. Data for the United States population are from *Statistical Abstract, 1949*, p. 12; and *1954*, p. 27. Details may not add to totals because of rounding.

[28] The data may be misleading because communities classified as under 25,000 frequently turn out to be suburbs of nearby larger cities.

[29] *Statistical Abstract of the United States, 1953*, Bureau of the Census, p. 121.

[30] The occupational status of CU respondents is similar. While roughly 55 per cent of the CU sample from the 1954-55 questionnaire are either professional or self employed, about 10 per cent of the whole population are classed as professional and another 15 to 20 per cent as managerial or self employed ("Survey of Consumer Finances," *Federal Reserve Bulletin*, July 1954, Supplementary Table 2). Thus the percentage of CU respondents classed in the two categories is about double the percentage for the whole population.

PURCHASING HABITS OF THE CU SAMPLE

Of perhaps greater significance than the characteristics of the sample are its purchasing habits. In the last section, it was argued that the under-representation of low income groups in the sample is not necessarily a disadvantage for its use in forecasting durable goods purchases. As Table 4 shows, an average of more than 80 per cent of all major durables are purchased by household spending units with incomes higher than $3,000 per year.[31] This confirms the belief that the CU sample was a better sample of the major durable goods buying population over most of the period than a random sample of the population as a whole was.[32] This conclusion may not be valid for recent years, however.

TABLE 4

Cumulative Income Distributions of the CU and SCF Samples,
and Purchasers of Major Consumer Durable Goods,
by Income Groups, 1952, 1953, 1954

	PERCENTAGE OF UNITS WITH INCOMES GREATER THAN:[a]				
YEAR	$2,000	$3,000	$4,000	$5,000	$7,500
1952:					
CU	99	96	85	67	31
SCF	75	59	41	26	9
Purchasers of major durables	92	83	67	52	23
1953:					
CU	99	97	90	75	41
SCF	77	63	47	31	10
Purchasers of major durables	93	83	69	54	25
1954:					
CU	99	97	91	77	42
SCF	77	63	46	32	11
Purchasers of major durables	89	80	68	53	22

a The percentage for greater than zero is 100, and for infinity it is zero.
Source: Tables A-13 to A-15. The figures for purchasers of major durables are averages for the two categories, new automobiles, and furniture and major household appliances, in Table A-15.

A limited amount of data can be used to test differences between the purchase habits of the CU sample and the population as a whole in

[31] The percentage is even higher for the crucial "purchases of new automobiles" category.
[32] That is, the match between the share of major durable goods purchases made by households with incomes greater than x dollars per year and the share of CU subscribers with incomes greater than x dollars is closer than the match between the shares of purchases by households with incomes greater than x and the share of the total population with incomes greater than x dollars per year. Also the CU sample contains many more households that make purchase plans, relative to households of the population in keeping with their higher income composition (see Robert Ferber, "Planning in Consumer Purchases—Durable Goods," *American Economic Review*, December 1954).

comparable income groups. A detailed breakdown of the population income distribution of durable goods purchasers is available only for automobiles and television sets.[33] From Table 5 it is evident that far more automobiles, particularly new ones, were purchased by the CU sample than by comparable income groups in the population. The disparity is clearly marked for income groups below $5,000 per year, becoming less clear above that level. For the highest income group shown ($7,500 and up) the percentages are quite close. Prospective purchasers are also much more numerous in the CU sample than in comparable population groups.

Since the CU publication, *Consumer Reports*, stresses its analyses of automobile performance and characteristics, people purchasing automobiles (or planning to purchase them) naturally tend to subscribe to it at an average above that of the population in general. Since the greater frequency of actual (and prospective) automobile purchasers among CU subscribers is a recurring phenomenon, it should cause no bias in the use of CU automobile spending plans to forecast purchases of the population. Instead, the high concentration of new car buyers may enhance the accuracy of forecasting changes in the level of purchases.

Similar comparisons for television sets (Table 5) show only actual purchasers by income class, since prospective purchasers are not obtainable from published SCF data. In contrast to the automobile data, there appears to be little or no systematic tendency in the data for the frequency of purchases in the CU sample to exceed that of the SCF sample, except in the lowest income groups.[34] The differences are not statistically significant at the 5 per cent level of probability in most cases, and none are at the 1 per cent level.

Estimates were made of purchases of other durable goods items by the population by assuming their purchasing habits to be comparable to those of the CU subscriber sample if the percentage of purchasers among CU subscribers at each income level was multiplied by the number of spending units at that income level in the population. The results indicate that the average CU subscriber purchases more of most durables (especially freezers) relative to income, than the average for the population.[35]

Work Planned on CU Project for 1957-1958

At present the National Bureau of Economic Research is analyzing tabulations from a pilot study of about 5,000 CU questionnaires for 1955. The study is designed to test the usefulness of certain cross relationships

[33] The data are published in the *Survey of Consumer Finances*. In addition, the SCF publishes the income distribution for purchasers of furniture and major household appliances, but a comparable category cannot be extracted from the CU data.

[34] The percentages for the lowest income groups are unreliable because their representation in the CU sample is extremely small.

[35] For details of the computation, see Appendix C of Juster, in source note to Table 5.

279

TABLE 5

Prospective and Actual Purchasers of Automobiles, and Actual Purchasers of
Television Sets, CU and SCF Samples, by Income Group, 1952 and 1953
(*percentage of spending units*)

PURCHASER	Under $3,000	$3,000– 3,999	$4,000– 4,999	$5,000– 7,499	$7,500 and over	All Spending Units
New and Used Automobiles						
Prospective, 1952:						
CU	13	18	19	18	20	18
SCF	a	8	9	13	15	8
Prospective, 1953:						
CU	17	20	22	20	24	21
SCF	a	10	10	15	20	10
Actual, 1952:						
CU	22	25	28	32	37	31
SCF	a	28	27	27	33	22
Actual, 1953:						
CU	20	32	36	34	39	35
SCF	a	23	26	29	39	24
New Automobiles						
Prospective, 1953:b						
SCF	a	4	5	10	7	4
Actual, 1953:						
CU	10	17	22	23	30	25
SCF	a	7	6	14	29	9
Television Sets						
Actual, 1951:						
CU	13	19	19	23	29	23
SCF	a	14	14	24	26	12
Actual, 1952:						
CU	10	15	17	17	19	16
SCF	a	13	17	16	16	11
Actual, 1953:						
CU	11	17	16	18	18	17
SCF	a	18	19	19	21	14

See Table A-3 for details on the CU time periods, which do not correspond exactly
to the calendar years shown.

a Less than 0.5 per cent.

b CU not available.

Source: *Purchasers of automobiles*—CU percentages, F. Thomas Juster, "Expectational Data and Short-term Forecasting" (unpublished doctoral dissertation, Columbia
University, 1956), Appendix C; SCF data, "Survey of Consumer Finances," *Federal
Reserve Bulletin*, July 1953, Supplementary Table 3; June 1954, Supplementary Tables
7 and 22. *Purchasers of television sets*—CU data, basic data sheets prepared by Consumers Union; SCF data, "Survey of Consumer Finances," *Federal Reserve Bulletin*,
June 1954, Supplementary Table 11.

for the analysis of purchase decisions. For example, exhaustive cross tabulations of questions dealing with income expectations and with budgeting habits may yield previously unavailable information bearing on purchase decisions and plans. Questions were included on where subscribers live, their education, and their living arrangements to test whether the data are systematically related to purchases or plans. The pilot study should also yield more information on how many questionnaires must be tabulated to provide statistically significant relationships among the variables.

In addition to the pilot study, between 16,000 and 25,000 of the 1955 questionnaires are now being coded, punched, and tabulated to give information both more detailed and of higher quality. For example, it will be possible to analyze and cross classify aggregate purchases and purchase plans for some thirty major consumer durables by household and by commodity, which should extend our knowledge about the net impact of many variables on the structure and magnitude of durable goods purchases, on the formation of purchase intentions and decisions, and on the use of mail surveys of this kind to gather information about consumer intentions and actions.

In the near future, tabulation will begin on the 1957 questionnaire designed, partly for the analytical needs of the project, to elicit more information about purchases, plans, and characteristics of the households than previous CU questionnaires. Comprehensive demographic information and comprehensive data on ownership of durable goods are being gathered for the first time. A distinction being made between plans to purchase within six months and plans to purchase later than that should help to separate concrete plans with good prospects of fulfillment from rather vague hopes or wishes and thereby improve the predictive value of the spending-intentions data.

Important data will still be lacking, particularly on a household's debt and liquid asset structure, but the 1957 questionnaire provides an opening for future gathering of this kind of information. Subscribers are asked to indicate willingness to answer future questionnaires for the sole purpose of contributing information for research purposes. A preliminary review shows an impressive number of positive replies, possibly promising a sample of 30,000. Provided the sample proves reasonably unbiased in other characteristics—which can easily be determined—rather complete information should be obtained on debt and liquid asset structure, expectations and attitudes, income changes, buying plans for different forward time periods, and so forth. Further, it may be possible to use this sample as the basis for a re-interview study, which would require matching returns from the same respondent in successive surveys.

Appendix

TABLE A-1

Predictive Value of CU Spending Plan Data, Seven Observations,
1947-1953 and 1955

| | CATEGORY OF SPENDING PLANS | | | | | |
| | Automobiles | | Household Furnishings | | Total | |
	(value)	(volume)	(value)	(volume)	(value)	(volume)
Criterion: Direction of Change						
Successful prediction	6	5	3	5	6	5
Unsuccessful prediction	1	2	4	2	1	2
Criterion: Difference between Planned and Actual Changes						
Less than 10%	3	3	2	3	4	4
10%–20%	2	1	3	3	1	1
More than 20%	2	3	2	1	2	2

Source: Tables A-4 and A-5.

TABLE A-2

Predictive Record of SCF Spending Plan Data, Nine Observations,
1947-1955

| | CATEGORY OF SPENDING PLANS | | | | | |
| | Automobiles | | Household Furnishings | | Total | |
	(value)	(volume)	(value)	(volume)	(value)	(volume)
Criterion: Direction of Change						
Successful prediction	8	7	5	5	8	6
Unsuccessful prediction	1	2	4	4	1	3
Criterion: Difference between Planned and Actual Link Relatives						
Less than 10%	4	2	3	3	1	3
10%–20%	0	3	3	4	5	5
More than 20%	5	4	3	2	3	1

Source: Tables A-6 and A-7.

282

TABLE A-3

Time Period Equivalent for CU Data, 1946-1955

Calendar Time Span	Planning Period	Purchasing Period
July 1, 1946–June 30, 1947	P-1	A-1
July 1, 1947–June 30, 1948	P-2	A-2
July 1, 1948–June 30, 1949	P-3	
Nov. 15, 1948–Nov. 14, 1949		A-3
Nov. 15, 1949–Nov. 14, 1950	P-4	
Oct. 1, 1949–Sept. 30, 1950		A-4
Oct. 1, 1950–Sept. 30, 1951	P-5	
Aug. 15, 1950–Aug. 14, 1951		A-5
Aug. 15, 1951–Aug. 14, 1952	P-6	
July 1, 1951–June 30, 1952		A-6
July 1, 1952–June 30, 1953	P-7	
Oct. 1, 1952–Sept. 30, 1953		A-7
Oct. 1, 1953–Sept. 30, 1954	P-8	A-8
Oct. 1, 1954–Sept. 30, 1955	P-9	

Planning period (P) is the time span of data on quantity of consumer durables CU subscribers planned to buy.

Purchasing period (A) is the time span of data on quantity of consumer durables CU subscribers actually purchased.

Source: Memorandum from Consumers Union.

TABLE A-4

Year-to-Year Changes in the Value of Planned Purchases, CU Sample, and in Total Purchases of Durable Goods, Department of Commerce Data, Current Dollars, 1947-1955

(*previous period = 100*)

	CONSUMER PURCHASES IN CURRENT DOLLARS					
	Automobiles		*Household Furnishings*		*Total*	
PERIOD	Plan	Actual	Plan	Actual	Plan	Actual
P-2	88	117	76	115	84	116
P-3	100	120	121	94	107	104
P-4	126	142	139	119	131	130
P-5	94	97	102	96	99	96
P-6	58	86	73	90	63	89
P-7	128	120	98	106	114	113
P-8	n.a.	104	n.a.	104	n.a.	104
P-9	140[a]	130[b]	131[a]	112[c]	137[a]	121[d]

n.a. = not available.

See Table A-3 for analysis of the time span of each CU time period in this and the following tables.

[a] P-7 = 100, since P-8 data are not available.

[b] 135, if P-7 = 100.

[c] 117, if P-7 = 100.

[d] 126, if P-7 = 100.

Source: *Planned purchases*—Juster, Tables B-13 through B-18. *Actual purchases*—Table A-26.

TABLE A-5

Year-to-Year Changes in Volume of Planned Purchases, CU Sample, and
in Volume of Durable Goods Purchases, Department of
Commerce Data, Constant Prices, 1947-1955
(*previous period* = *100*)

| | CONSUMER PURCHASES IN CONSTANT PRICES | | | | | |
| | *Automobiles* | | *Household Furnishings* | | *Total* | |
PERIOD	*Plan*	*Actual*	*Plan*	*Actual*	*Plan*	*Actual*
P-2	80	n.a.	69	n.a.	75	n.a.
P-3	85	110	103	93	92	102
P-4	116	134	134	121	125	128
P-5	99	92	87	88	93	90
P-6	53	82	71	89	60	86
P-7	117	115	102	108	110	112
P-8	n.a.	104	n.a.	105	n.a.	105
P-9	138[a]	131[b]	127[a]	114[c]	132[a]	123[d]

n.a. = not available.
The total for the actual purchases data is the average of the year-to-year changes in
the two components shown.
[a] P-7 = 100, since P-8 data are not available.
[b] 135, if P-7 = 100.
[c] 120, if P-7 = 100.
[d] 127, if P-7 = 100.
Source: *Planned purchases*—Juster, Tables B-13 through B-18. *Actual purchases*—
Table A-29.

TABLE A-6

Year-to-Year Changes in Total Value of Planned Purchases of Durables,
SCF Sample, and in Purchases, Department of Commerce Data,
Current Dollars, 1947-1955
(*previous year* = *100*)

| | CONSUMER PURCHASES IN CURRENT DOLLARS | | | | | |
| | *Automobiles* | | *Household Furnishings* | | *Total* | |
YEAR	*Plan*	*Actual*	*Plan*	*Actual*	*Plan*	*Actual*
1947	127	175	73	136	104	148
1948	116	120	123	105	118	111
1949	130	134	108	93	123	110
1950	104	129	125	127	110	127
1951	62	86	82	91	69	89
1952	124	92	93	97	111	95
1953	138	133	139	102	138	117
1954	87	94	89	102	87	98
1955	114	137[a]	85	114[a]	104	126[a]

[a] Based on only three quarters.
Source: *Planned purchases*—Juster, Tables B-13 through B-18. *Actual purchases*—
Table A-23.

TABLE A-7

Year-to-Year Changes in Number of SCF Spending Units Planning to Buy
Selected Durable Goods, Survey of Consumer Finances Data, and
in Volume of Durable Goods Purchased, Department of
Commerce Data, Constant Prices, 1947-1955
(*previous year = 100*)

	NUMBER OF SPENDING UNITS PLANNING TO BUY AND TOTAL PURCHASES					
	Automobiles		*Household Furnishings*		*Total*	
YEAR	*Plan*	*Actual*	*Plan*	*Actual*	*Plan*[a]	*Actual*[a]
1947	109	n.a.	77	n.a.	94	n.a.
1948	95	107	107	99	101	103
1949	126	126	111	96	119	111
1950	116	126	109	127	113	127
1951	57	80	89	83	73	82
1952	121	86	91	99	106	93
1953	119	130	137	101	128	116
1954	94	96	87	105	91	101
1955	110	138[b]	103	114[b]	107	126[b]

[a] Simple average of automobile and household furnishings index.
[b] Based on first three quarters only.
Source: *Spending units planning to buy*—Juster, *op. cit.*, Table A-20. *Actual purchases*—Table A-28.

TABLE A-8

Derivation of Income Change Variables Covering CU Time Periods

	1935-39 DOLLARS PER CAPITA			CURRENT DOLLARS PER CAPITA		
PERIOD	Y/NP	$(Y/NP)_0$	$\dfrac{Y/NP}{(Y/NP)_0}$	Y/N	$(Y/N)_0$	$\dfrac{Y/N}{(Y/N)_0}$
P-2	740	738.5[a]	100.3	1,223	1,148	106.5
P-3	750	740	101.4	1,288	1,223	105.3
P-4	782	750	104.3	1.333	1,288	103.5
P-5	788	775	101.7	1,440	1,333	108.0
P-6	789	790	99.9	1,489	1,440	103.4
P-7	811	790	102.7	1,546	1,489	103.8
P-8	813	816.5	99.6	1,563	1,546	101.1
P-9	838	818	102.4	1,606	1,563	102.8

The Y/NP and Y/N are averages for the period covered, with quarterly data being divided in half where necessary to insure accuracy. The $(Y/NP)_0$ and $(Y/N)_0$ data are the highest level of real per capita disposable income and per capita disposable income, respectively, for any four consecutive quarters prior to the spending period under consideration (except as noted). It can be seen that the highest previous income level is not necessarily the income level during the immediately preceding period, even during periods when income is steadily rising. The reason is that the CU time periods do not

TABLE A-9

Derivation of Income Change Variables Covering Calendar Year
Time Periods, 1948-1955

	1935-39 DOLLARS PER CAPITA			CURRENT DOLLARS PER CAPITA		
PERIOD	Y/NP	$(Y/NP)_0$	$\dfrac{Y/NP}{(Y/NP)_0}$	Y/N	$(Y/N)_0$	$\dfrac{Y/N}{(Y/N)_0}$
1948	748	737	101.5	1,281	1,174	109.1
1949	746	748	99.7	1,261	1,281	98.4
1950	787	748	105.2	1,359	1,281	106.1
1951	791	787	100.8	1,464	1,359	107.7
1952	797	791	100.5	1,508	1,464	103.0
1953	819	797	102.8	1,568	1,508	104.0
1954	815	819	99.5	1,569	1,568	100.1
1955	839[a]	819	102.4	1,615[a]	1,569	102.9

$(Y/NP)_0$ and $(Y/N)_0$ are the highest levels of real disposable per capita income and disposable per capita income, respectively, for any year previous to the one under consideration. The 1941-46 period is not included in the calculations for the highest level of per capita disposable income achieved previous to the given year, since the apparent real income level during this period was badly overstated because of shortages of goods and the existence of price controls.

[a] First three quarters.

Source: Y/NP and Y/N data, Juster, Table A-35.

---

always start and stop at the same date. Thus, the highest level of income prior to period 5 is $775 per capita, while period 4 showed a higher average income level—$782 per capita. Period 5 begins on October 1, 1950, while period 4 ends on November 15, 1950; thus, the high income level during October and November, 1950, is not part of the highest level of income previous to period 5. Several other periods show similar results for the real income computation, though none does for the per capita money income data.

[a] Taken as the average for the first two quarters of calendar 1947, the period just prior to the P-2 spending period. This period is used rather than the preceding four quarters because the latter include the last part of 1946, where the real income level is badly overstated due to disequilibrium on the supply side of the market. Prices had risen sufficiently during the first part of 1947 to make the real income figures for that period reasonably accurate (cf. Robert Ferber, *A Study of Aggregate Consumption Functions*, National Bureau of Economic Research, Technical Paper 8, 1953).

Source: Juster, Table A-36; time periods as shown in Table A-24.

TABLE A-10

Income Distribution of Households, CU Sample

CU TIME PERIODS[a]	MONEY INCOME BEFORE TAXES								Don't Know or No Answer	Median Income
	0–$1,999	$2,000–2,999	$3,000–3,999	$4,000–4,999	$5,000–7,499	$7,500–9,999	$10,000–24,999	$25,000 and over		(dollars)
	(number)									
P-1	130	437	615	432	469	132	161	17	107	4,034
P-2	208	738	1,129	928	1,037	364	333	38	225	4,336.7
P-4	116	373	907	1,001	1,348	494	497	60	204	5,002
P-6	66	167	636	880	1,709	676	624	96	146	5,992
P-7	57	140	533	858	1,793	749	653	97	120	6,188
P-8	36	119	363	687	1,700	947	889	142	117	6,818
P-9	38	103	293	638	1,676	905	958	130	259	6,937
	(per cent)									
P-1	5	18	25	17	19	5	6	1	4	
P-2	4	15	23	19	21	7	7	1	4	
P-4	2	8	18	20	27	10	10	1	4	
P-6	1	3	13	18	34	14	12	2	3	
P-7	1	3	11	17	36	15	13	2	2	
P-8	1	2	7	14	34	19	18	3	2	
P-9	1	2	6	13	34	18	19	3	5	

In this and the following tables, details may not add to totals because of rounding.

[a] In Tables A-10–A-14, the omission of a period means that the appropriate data were not requested in that period.

Source: in Tables A-10–A-12, the basic data were obtained from CU questionnaires. The sample was 2,500 in P-1, and 5,000 in the other periods. The dates of the periods are given in Table A-3.

287

TABLE A-11

Geographical Distribution of Households, CU Sample
(*per cent*)

CU TIME PERIODS	CU REGION[a]					
	1	*2*	*3*	*4*	*5*	*6*
P-2	36	10	31	7	18	b
P-3	34	10	32	6	18	1
P-4	38	10	32	7	13	1
P-6	32	11	30	8	17	2
P-7	31	12	29	7	18	1
P-8	33	11	30	8	16	2

[a] The CU regions correspond to census regions, as follows: 1, New England and Middle Atlantic; 2, South Atlantic and East South Central; 3, East North Central and West North Central; 4, West South Central and Mountain; 5, Pacific; 6, Outside Continental U.S.

[b] Less than 0.5 per cent.

TABLE A-12

Distribution of Households by Size of the Community, CU Sample, 1946-1955
(*per cent*)

CU TIME PERIODS	PERCENTAGE OF TOTAL IN CU SAMPLE LIVING IN COMMUNITIES WITH POPULATION OF				
	Over 1 million	*100,000 to 1 million*	*25,000 to 100,000*	*2,500 to 25,000*	*Less than 2,500*
P-1	27	24	16	21	12
P-2	26	24	17	22	11
P-4	27	28	15	21	10
P-8	18	29	18	22	12a
P-9	21	29	18	19	12a

[a] Farm, 5 per cent; nonfarm, 7 per cent.

TABLE A-13

Income Distribution of Households, CU Sample 1946-1955
(*cumulative percentages*)

CU TIME PERIODS[a]	INCOME BEFORE TAXES GREATER THAN[a]						
	$2,000	$3,000	$4,000	$5,000	$7,500	$10,000	$25,000
P-1	95	76	51	33	13	7	1
P-2	96	80	57	37	15	8	1
P-4	98	90	71	50	22	12	1
P-6	99	95	82	64	29	15	2
P-7	99	96	85	67	31	15	2
P-8	99	97	90	75	41	21	3
P-9	99	97	91	77	42	23	3

[a] The percentage for greater than zero is 100, and for infinity it is zero.
Source: from Table A-10.

TABLE A-14

Income Distribution of United States Population, 1948-1954
(*cumulative percentages*)

	INCOME BEFORE TAXES GREATER THAN[a]						
YEAR	$1,000	$2,000	$3,000	$4,000	$5,000	$7,500	$10,000
1948	88	70	47	27	15	5	3
1949	86	67	46	27	16	5	3
1950	87	70	51	32	20	6	3
1951	87	72	54	36	21	7	3
1952	89	75	59	41	26	9	4
1953	90	77	63	47	31	10	n.a.
1954	90	77	63	46	32	11	n.a.

[a] The percentage for greater than zero is 100, and for infinity it is zero.
Source: "Survey of Consumer Finances," *Federal Reserve Bulletin*, September 1952, Table 1; July 1954, Table 2; and May 1955, Supplementary Table 2.

TABLE A-15

Cumulative Purchases of Major Consumer Durable Goods by Incomes
of Purchasers, 1952-1954

	PERCENTAGE OF TOTAL PURCHASES BY SPENDING UNITS WITH INCOME BEFORE TAXES GREATER THAN[a]					
COMMODITY	$1,000	$2,000	$3,000	$4,000	$5,000	$7,500
Automobiles:						
1952	98	91	78	55	36	14
1953	97	90	77	61	44	18
1954	98	89	77	59	44	15
Furniture and major household furnishings:						
1952	96	87	72	53	35	12
1953	95	86	75	59	39	14
1954	94	84	73	56	41	14
Television sets:						
1952	98	94	78	58	36	12
1953	99	94	85	64	43	16
1954	98	91	78	57	31	13
New automobiles:						
1952	100	97	93	81	68	33
1953	100	99	91	79	68	36
1954	98	94	88	79	64	29

[a] The percentage for greater than zero is 100, and for infinity it is zero.
Source: "Survey of Consumer Finances," *Federal Reserve Bulletin*, May 1955, Supplementary Table 2.

COMMENT

MARY JEAN BOWMAN, University of Chicago

Thomas Juster's analysis of the forecasting value of the Consumers Union data on intentions to purchase durable goods is extremely interesting, and his presentation is both cautious and well organized. But his findings are perhaps even more valuable for raising questions that affect other kinds of social and economic analysis than they are for forecasting.

JUSTER'S HYPOTHESES

Juster suggests three "hypotheses about behavior . . . which would imply net forecasting value for data concerned with purchases of consumer durables." He specifies that hypothesis 1, the comparison of changes in intentions with actual changes in purchases of consumer durables, is the only one suited to his particular test. I think the part of hypothesis 3 that is on the same analytical plane with 1 is equally suitable. The confusion arises because he shifts when he comes to 3, and considers the adjustments of the whole economic system to a change in consumer durables outlays. This aspect of 3 cannot, of course, be tested by his study, but 1 and 2 might also have been elaborated similarly. Evidently 3 was selected for special treatment so that consumer durables spending intentions could be used as an indicator of total consumer spending and gross national product and not merely of consumer durables expenditures. But this broader goal is given no further explicit attention in Juster's study.

At the simplest and most limited level one might set up all three of Juster's hypotheses with an initial assumption of no change in income. Hypothesis 1 involves a shift from savings to consumer durables with no change in expenditures on other consumer goods. Hypothesis 2 involves a change in what might be called spending mood, leading to a shift from saving to consumption, with part of the expressed intentions to buy durables diverted to consumer nondurables. Finally, the first part of hypothesis 3 involves an increase in purchases of consumer durables matched by a corresponding decrease in expenditures on nondurables. This is supplemented by the proposition that gross investment would thereby be increased because of the change in the composition of consumer goods output. If one ignores this supplementary aspect of 3, the hypothesis fits just as well as 1 into his empirical study. With appropriate modifications, all three hypotheses can be set up to conform to a situation in which income is in fact changed, partly because of changes in consumer durable goods purchases or intentions. Such a model could distinguish between expected and unexpected income changes in deriving the components of total spending (and saving) as functions of consumer durables buying intentions. Elaborating still further, one could introduce stochastic

290

variables into equations for each component of spending (both consumer and investment expenditures) and savings.

ATTITUDE DATA AND FORECASTING

Juster next discusses the use of attitude and associated expectations data in conjunction with intentions data. With a number of qualifications, he takes a position essentially contrary to that of the Survey Research Center, discarding attitude data as inefficient for forecasting and largely redundant when combined with intentions data. He appears to justify this position partly by a limited but clear deductive logic (enlarged in the revision of his paper), partly on the basis of the crude empirical evidence suggested by the superiority of CU over Survey of Consumer Finances predictions even when the latter are modified by attitude data. However, testing the forecasting value of attitude materials was not a principal objective of Juster's study.

Even if we assume that results to date are negative, it is curious that Juster stopped here, for his findings on the superior predictive value of the CU data suggest fresh approaches to the content and uses of attitude surveys—including value attitudes that have no particular time dimension and no orientation to the future per se. I believe that Juster's concept of attitudes is too narrow when he says, "Attitude data may show factors that should be included, in principle, in the purchases plan, but often are not." Two examples of possibilities that Juster appears to ignore are (1) attitudes and expectations in conjunction with conditional intentions data; and (2) the use of attitude data in sample evaluation.

The first possibility implies a prior or simultaneous refinement in the intentions data by the introduction of explicit "if" conditions. Questions on durable goods buying intentions might, for example, include some on income expectations and their firmness, on anticipated shifts in purchase plans in the event of specified shifts in income, prices, commodity models, and so forth, together with questions concerning attitudes and expectations about such changes.[1] While care must be taken in formulating "if" questions and in interpreting the answers, intentions data are implicitly "if" data. Experiments to make the "if" questions and the judgments of answers to them more explicit are worth considering.

While my suggestions are consistent with Juster's basic analytical framework, they point to a somewhat different set of research problems and lead to a different conclusion about the potentialities of attitude and expectations data for forecasting consumer purchases. The kinds of attitude–expectations data I have in mind are in the main fairly conventional. But the methods of using them differ. This approach seems a logical step

[1] The experiences of the Survey Research Center with income expectations data do not, in my judgment, justify discontinuing this line of questioning. They do indicate that the approach should be revised.

following upon the work of Katona and Mueller with consumption surveys, and that of Okun with survey data on assumptions about external variables that underlie reported intentions.

One specific use of expectations data could be to determine whether an event such as a general increase or decrease in income was foreseen. Juster recognizes this in passing, but with no attention to its relevance in connection with degrees of uncertainty and their role in behavior. With a proper project design, income (and some other) expectations data would provide a possibility of testing the effects on consumer behavior of increased sureness or the "spread of sureness" and the effects of the realization of expectations versus surprise. These problems have been noted in connection with business behavior by a number of economists.[2]

The second possibility—the use of attitude data for sample evaluation —would require fresh concepts of the kinds of attitude material to be investigated. Here the emphasis is on attitudes with no clear time dimension or future orientation, as distinct from expectations. Attitude data, some of them with an "ought" character, would be used with information about past spending patterns, shopping practices, household budgeting and economic planning, and other household attributes (e.g. demographic traits and income). Its potential value for improving forecasting would justify only a small part of the expense and technical difficulties involved in gathering such information; the main justification would probably lie in its contribution to the study of human behavior and decision-making processes. Can we measure degrees of planning? When and to what extent do impulsive and residual spending displace weighing of alternatives, and vice versa? What are the time lags between thinking about a major purchase and acting? Do different groups of people have distinctive patterns? How close are the associations between attitudes and behavior in the decision-making process? Can certain attitude and behavior patterns be identified objectively in different sectors of the population? These and other questions could have ultimate, even if incidental, value for the interpretation of intentions data and the improvement of predictions based upon them.

FORECASTING VALUE OF THE CU SAMPLE

Juster's defense of the CU sample for forecasting purchases of consumer durables must stand on four pegs, the first three of which he considers at some length:

1. Better representation of the population that buys consumer durables than a random sample of the same size

---

[2] Among them Ruth P. Mack and Robert Eisner in their papers for the 1955 Social Science Research Council conference proceedings, *Expectations, Uncertainty, and Business Behavior*, ed. M. J. Bowman, SSRC, 1958.

2. More accurate prediction of both spending by CU members and associated variables (such as changes in income)

3. Stability in the bias of the sample in representation of the actual population buying durable goods, i.e. stability of bias in representation of actual purchases

4. Stability in the bias of predictions versus actual buying at least as great as in the population as a whole.

Juster finds support for the first two of these points in his empirical material, though he is commendably cautious in his discussion of it. But the most problematic and vital of the pegs are the third and fourth—stability in the sample biases with respect to actual purchases and to discrepancies between predicted and actual purchases.

A likely advantage of the CU sample (point 1) that Juster passes by is that it may represent new households better than the SCF does. The Survey Research Center is fully aware of the problem of forecasting expenditures on household furnishings because the newest families and those about to be formed are missed or seriously underrepresented. Is the SCF less successful in dealing with new households than the self-selected CU sample? Perhaps the 1957 CU questionnaire will enable Juster to answer this question more directly.

Attempts to assess any possible changes in the bias of the CU sample vis-à-vis the total consumer durables buying population (point 3)—not mentioned by Juster in discussing his plans for future research—might include an analysis of turnover and change in composition in CU membership. How do intentions of new members compare with those of old ones? Such information, together with data on occupation, income, age, household composition, date of marriage, and so forth, could throw light on a number of important questions; and it is good news that the 1957 questionnaire will provide some of the basic demographic information hitherto unavailable.

Unfortunately there are no simple relations between economic or demographic attributes and consumer durable purchases. For example, a change in the income bias of the CU sample would not necessarily imply a change in the bias for representation of actual purchases; it might even be a necessary condition of stability in the purchases bias. This could be the case if CU members are younger, if younger people make up most of the durable goods buying population, and if incomes of younger people have risen more than those of the rest of the population.[3] Relations among

[3] Because of the time periods covered in the CU data in Juster's Table 3, the increase in upward income bias of the CU sample between 1948 and 1951 is exaggerated. As he notes in his Appendix Table A-3, the "1951" CU data are in fact for the period August 15, 1951 to August 14, 1952 and his "1948" CU data are for July 1, 1947 to June 30, 1948. A rough test of the hypothesis of stability in income bias over this period is only possible by comparing the change in the CU membership income distribution with the 1947 to 1951 and the 1948 to 1952 changes in the SCF sample. This was done, plotting

household size and composition, income, and consumer goods purchases, and changes in these relations, introduce even more awkward problems. Nevertheless, if we are to have better insight into possible changes in the actual purchases bias of the CU sample it is necessary to have a better understanding of these relationships.

In evaluating the hypothesis of a stable bias, the big question is what would happen in a severe downturn. It cannot be denied that the scientific validity of evaluations of forecasting data inevitably suffers from lack of sufficiently severe economic experience since the beginning of forecasting efforts. Until, as scientists, we are granted the dubious good fortune of a dismal dish of economic experience, we can only speculate on its taste and appearance to the would-be forecaster. Like Shackle, I see ghosts at the table.

Juster raised the question about economic climate in connection with the sampling problem in use of CU data for forecasts: Has the relatively continuous prosperity since World War II brought accidentally good predictions from CU versus other data? But he goes no further. It is plausible to speculate that a downturn of any real severity would increase planning and care in spending for the large items, and that a larger proportion of prospective purchasers would then take the precaution of joining CU.[4] A less likely result could be a selective dropping out of old members who definitely intended no important purchases and were saving pennies. In any case, the CU sample vis-à-vis the durable goods buying population as a whole could be seriously distorted. This and other possible hypotheses point once again to the importance of regularly analyzing both buying intentions and demographic and income attributes of the CU sample by membership categories—new and old members, and if possible

---

[4] It should be noted that a cyclical pattern of this sort might be associated with a rising income bias of the CU sample in a period of prosperity and a decreasing income bias of the sample in a major downturn. However, other aspects of selectivity in the CU sample would probably be more important in their effects on cyclical income bias.

---

the curves on log-probability paper and interpolating for the quartile and median incomes. The resulting income ratios were estimated to be as follows:

	SCF		CU	SCF	CU
	1951	*1952*	*8/15/51–8/14/52*	*1953*	*10/1/53–9/30/54*
	1947	*1948*	*7/1/47–6/30/38*	*1951*	*8/15/51–8/14/52*
Bottom quartile	1.27	1.14	1.34	1.17	1.14
Median	1.24	1.20	1.33	1.19	1.15
Top quartile	1.19	1.22	1.31	1.18	1.14

Some increase in the upward income bias of the CU sample between 1947 and 1952 is indicated. Why Juster used the 1953 SCF figures for comparison with the CU data for the period 10/1/53–9/30/54 is not clear, but the difference in dates is certainly sufficient to explain any small reversal of the apparent bias that might be suggested by the figures shown here; in fact, the upward bias in the CU sample could even have continued to increase from 1951 to 1954.

drop-outs. Changes in any or all of these relationships among subgroups or between the CU membership and the population as a whole, or both, would signal warnings about the interpretation of CU data for predictions in a changing general economic climate.

While the likelihood of a highly variable bias in the prediction sample (nonrealization of point 4, above), as distinct from that in the actual purchase sample bias, appears to me to be low, the possibility remains. Two questions are pertinent:

1. How accurate are predictions by individual CU members, and what clues do they give us about what might be expected in a changing economic climate?

2. Is there a distinctive cyclical pattern in the prediction accuracy of CU members, reflecting the nature of their household economic planning?

The second question merges in part with the question of sample bias in actual purchases. For example, there is obviously a motivation to join CU when major durable goods outlays are contemplated. If CU membership is selective for those with firmer plans, and if, when economic conditions worsen, the ratio of total actual outlays to firmly planned outlays changes versus its ratio to vaguer intentions, then there would be a cyclical factor in CU sample prediction bias. This factor would be over and above changes in the bias as an actual-purchase sample. There can be no adequate test of this distinctly plausible hypothesis in advance, but some hints may be found by considering the first question.

Instead of attempting a systematic estimate of what can be learned from analysis of prediction accuracy of individuals within the CU sample, and of comparable panel studies by the Survey Research Center, I shall again rely on an illustration. What can such material contribute to the problem raised in discussing question 2? Maximum insights would be obtained (depending on the scope of the information) by including expectations–attitude materials, and data on conditional intentions and "firmness of intentions or plans." Actual behavior, in the face of pleasant and unpleasant surprise, observed subsequently in the same spending units, would then be analyzed. Such a study could serve as a partial proxy—inadequate but extremely illuminating—for aggregative observations in a changing general economic climate. This would of course be an ambitious program, but it would be amply justified for nonforecasting as well as forecasting use.

Juster mentions study of individual prediction accuracy as a possibility in analyzing future CU questionnaires. Perhaps some method can be derived for identifying individual respondents by number in subsequent CU questionnaires to facilitate a panel study approach. For such a purpose the CU sample has unusual advantages because of membership accruals and drop-outs, which almost automatically solve many of the usual sampling problems in survey panel technique, at far less cost, and permit introduction of limited revolving features. Also comparison of buying intentions and their realization rates for relatively new versus old members might increase understanding of the meaning of the intentions data. For example, are plans of new members firmer because of the relative prosperity of recent years, and is this a major factor in the comparative success of the CU forecasts to date? If so, would this advantage persist in the future, or would it, with a significant worsening of the general economic situation, introduce a distortion? Full-scale analysis to include expectations, and so forth, would be a special study, requiring interviews with a subsample of the CU membership.

WARNING SIGNALS IN ANTICIPATIONS DATA

At this point, perhaps a brief digression from the problem of forecasting consumer expenditures to a more general question of anticipations data may be justified. Several authors have mentioned the effects of the no-change responses on forecasting from intentions data. Hartle set up a three-part classification of reasons for such a reply: (1) it may be the easiest way of getting rid of the interviewer or the questionnaire; (2) people may really mean it; and (3) people may be uncertain about the future and think that there is nothing better to say. The first category should be fairly stable, lending a conservative bias to predictions. But the relative weights of the other two could be highly significant for forecasting purposes. A sizeable increase in the proportion reflecting uncertainty should be at least a warning signal to the forecaster concerning the viability of the situation. It is worth a try to develop techniques for sorting out these types of no-change responses, even by interviewing a sample if necessary.

Often the analysis of no-change responses would fail to reveal the nature or extent of the "spread of uncertainty," but other techniques for "building in" measures of this phenomenon are possible and should be explored. Recent experience with the McGraw–Hill survey, as reported by Keezer, showing that more follow-ups were required, and that the firms failing to reply as usual to the questionnaires explained that their predictions this time would be less reliable than formerly, should surely be taken into account in interpretation of the McGraw–Hill forecasts of capital expenditures. It would be interesting to know whether any significant differences between the forecasts for these firms and others (both analyzed relative to their previous behavior) shows up in the data. Also, this recent experience suggests the introduction of questions to evaluate the degree of firmness of plans or intentions this year versus last year.

SAMPLE SELECTION AND LEAD SERIES

Whether or not the biases of the CU sample remain stable, Juster's findings are fertile with suggestions for improving and supplementing research on the SCF and related studies. As for the forecasting use of these studies, their contribution is not only toward improving predictions based on responses from any given sample of the population but also toward sample selection. The CU sample, as a self-selected group, has performed remarkably well. Can this performance be matched, or even bettered, by development of criteria for selective sampling, or the selective weighting of returns from a random sample?

I should like to conclude with a few suggestions for research other than or complementary to work with CU data. As a first step in determining criteria of sample selections and weighting, some of the questions to be proposed here should be asked of panels so that attributes of the household can be directly related to its prediction accuracy record. Other questions might aim at trying to develop a lead series sample in consumer durable goods buying, by identifying the kinds of households that change actual purchases or purchase plans, or both, ahead of the rest of the population.

Among attributes that might be investigated on both counts are the obvious demographic ones—income, occupation, and education. Also, as a check on both the accuracy selection and lead series elements, a distinction, as in the 1957 CU questionnaire, might be made between plans or intentions for the immediate future, for the second half of the year, and possibly intentions with no definite time specifications.

On the prediction accuracy side, there is a strong case for looking into shopping habits and household account keeping—if any—along with attitudes toward planning. Incidentally, it might be interesting to know how many and who of a random sample have ever heard of Consumers Union.

In attempts to identify a lead series subsample, rough indexes of social mobility and social participation might prove illuminating. But a word of warning is needed. Statistical evidence of diffusion requires a sophisticated interpretation that must take into account distinctive economic and psychosocial constraints and precipitating conditions. Also, a shift in the composition of durable goods purchases can alter the apparent diffusion pattern and the identity of the lead households, as Juster's figures on home freezers versus television clearly attest.[5] Moreover, either stability in the statistical diffusion rate or some kind of predictability of it is necessary for the effective use of a lead series. Here, again, there is wide scope for research that would incorporate but go far beyond the type of analysis reported in this volume by Katona, and its contributions to basic problems in human behavioral sciences might far exceed those to economic forecasting, as such.

[5] I am highly skeptical of his suggestion that the CU sample may be a lead sample for actual purchases. Examination of characteristics of a consumer lead sample might incidentally contribute insights into changes in the CU sample vis-à-vis the durable goods buying population as a whole.

The National Industrial Conference Board Survey of Capital Appropriations

MORRIS COHEN

NATIONAL INDUSTRIAL CONFERENCE BOARD

My paper is a progress report on the quarterly survey of capital appropriations by large manufacturing companies conducted by the National Industrial Conference Board, under the financial sponsorship of *Newsweek* magazine. The project, less than two years old, may furnish significant insights into the capital spending decision. However, here I shall dwell only on the forecasting potentialities of the data.

First, I shall set the role of the appropriations survey in the complex of expenditure intentions surveys which have come into being with the postwar development of business statistics and the parallel trends in growth of business planning. Second, I shall discuss our coverage, and the problems peculiar to an appropriations approach. Third, there is an outline of the battery of statistical indicators made available by the survey. In conclusion, I shall present the findings of the quarterly data for 1953-58 and some new dimensions of the 1955-56 capital spending boom.

Foreshadowing Series and Business Planning

The quarterly survey of capital appropriations is a newcomer among collections of expectations information. Over the past decade, the short-term forecasting emphasis has shifted to indicators of this type.

The movement to foreshadowing data has its basis in a parallel trend toward business planning. Since the war, the progressive company has turned to the budgeting process as an important tool of scientific management.[1] The founding and growth of the National Society for Business Budgeting, with some eight hundred members, chapters in twenty-two cities, and annual and regional meetings attended by hundreds of staff technicians, attest to the growing importance of business planning.[2] This

---

NOTE: The author hereby expresses his appreciation to Jane Were-Bey for her assistance in the preparation of this paper.

[1] A survey of the historical development of business budgeting by date when the budget, especially the capital budget, was first instituted would be interesting and might reveal how recently the forecasting aspect of scientific management has really taken hold in medium and larger-scale business. For example, I was surprised to learn that in a very large public utility the capital budget was less than twenty years old.

[2] See Morris Cohen, "An Economist Looks at Budgeting," *Business Budgeting*, September 1957, pp. 20-25. (This is the bimonthly publication of the National Society for Business Budgeting.)

development has made available to statisticians a growing body of information concerning the future.

The Department of Commerce and the Securities and Exchange Commission surveys of expected capital expenditures and those of the McGraw–Hill organization have become widely accepted as a basic tool of short-term forecasting. What, then, has the new appropriations survey to offer?

Comparison with Expenditure Intentions

The appropriations survey is linked to the expenditure intentions surveys via the capital budgeting process. The government and McGraw–Hill surveys report expected annual capital expenditures based upon the annual capital budget. The SEC–Commerce survey also reports historical and prospective quarterly figures. The latter are reported early in the third month of the quarter for the following quarter. The basic rationale of our survey is the need to gauge changes in trends before they show up in these statistics. For this we require a frequent measure of decisions and changes in decisions to spend for plant and equipment.

Such a measure is the capital appropriation. Each time a board of directors approves a capital appropriation it makes a decision which can corroborate the capital budget or change it. The capital budget is thus tested project by project through the appropriations procedure.[3] In a sense, our survey represents a second stage of development in tapping the formalized business planning process.

The approval of the capital appropriation formalizes the top management planning decision for each block of capital spending and unlocks the company's vaults so that the money can be committed and spent. Of course, the actual expenditure may not show up on the books for months.

Like other expenditure expectations surveys, our emphasis is on the company making the decision. Here the company is the active agent. We started out with the hope of constructing a new order expectations series but discovered that this was not feasible. Other surveys focus on the company receiving the order. For example, both McGraw–Hill and *Fortune* magazine have conducted surveys on the order expectations of machinery producers. In these cases, the company is more or less passive. Both points of view, that of the producer and that of the company placing the order, should complement each other.

Pilot Studies

A review of some of the pilot studies carried out at the Conference Board suggests why the appropriations approach was followed and some

---

[3] For a comprehensive discussion of company practices in this field, see *Controlling Capital Expenditures*, National Industrial Conference Board, *Studies in Business Policy* 62, 1953.

of the future lines our research may take. Early in 1956, a questionnaire was addressed to a hundred members of the Conference Board's Council of Financial Executives, Council of Marketing Research Directors, and West Coast Marketing Research Council.[4] Forty-two formal replies were received, as classified in Table 1.

TABLE 1

Replies to NICB Questionnaire on the Availability of Data on Capital Appropriations and New Capital Orders, Early 1958

	NUMBER OF COMPANIES REPORTING			
	Total	*Data Available*	*Data Could Be Available*[a]	*Data Not Available*
Total capital appropriations:[b]				
Reply not detailed	12	4		8[c]
Reply detailed	30	29	1	
Appropriations breakdown:				
Plant versus equipment	30	18	8	4
New plant versus modernization	30	20	6	4
Equipment by type	30	12	8	10
New capital goods orders				
expected to be placed	30	9		21

[a] With added effort, e.g., capital appropriations could be consolidated.

[b] Three informal replies were also received: one company had the information readily available; two had it on a divisional basis so it would require added effort to comply.

[c] Includes one sales division and one service organization where the data were inapplicable.

It was clear that the information on capital appropriations was available, but relatively few companies prepared schedules of new capital goods orders expected to be placed. Plant could be separated from equipment in the appropriations approach by the majority of companies, new plant could be distinguished from plant modernization by fewer companies, and equipment could be classified by type, though with added effort. In view of the newness of the approach we decided to confine the opening survey to total capital appropriations on a quarterly basis, although breakdowns along the lines indicated are on the agenda for the future.

In undertaking a regular appropriations survey, we brought into reality the recommendation of the Terborgh Committee, one of the five consultant committees organized in 1954 by the Federal Reserve Board at the request of the Subcommittee on Economic Statistics of the Joint

[4] For a list of these councils, see *Annual Report 1956*, NICB.

Committee on the Economic Report (now the Joint Economic Committee).[5] We have learned that, by and large, the results are consistent and comparable. There are exceptional companies, now numbering six, that cannot be included in our survey while others cannot participate because they do not follow the appropriations procedure. However, we feel that we have sufficient coverage to warrant serious attention.

The Universe: The 1,000 Top Companies

Unlike other capital spending surveys, the appropriation survey is limited to large companies. This limitation is inherent in our purpose. We are necessarily confined to organizations large enough to have a formal appropriations procedure. We chose to concentrate on the 1,000 largest manufacturing companies in terms of total assets; the cut-off point was roughly $15 million.[6] Experience has shown that this group comes close to exhausting the present universe.

Although we are debarred from investigating all manufacturing, the area we cover is significant. Our 1,000 top companies account for about 55 per cent of manufacturing employment and about two-thirds of manufacturing assets. They account for about three-quarters of manufacturing investment and contribute substantially to all business investment. Since satellite and other lesser companies often gear their investment programs to those of major companies, the activities of the latter should provide important clues to trends in these totals.

Because we focus on companies where spending is subject to the discipline of capital budgeting and appropriation, the information we obtain is objective and a matter of record. Also our approach is the more

[5] *Statistics on Business Plant and Equipment Expenditure Expectations*, Report of the Consultant Committee on Business Plant and Equipment Expenditure Expectations, July 1955, pp. 5-6. "The present question is the feasibility of compiling a current series of authorizations. . . .

"This question can be answered definitely only by a more extended investigation than we have been able to make. This is true also of the possibility of defining authorizations in such a way as to get consistent and comparable results from different companies. It is probably desirable to explore these questions further, but on the basis of our present knowledge we favor an alternative approach, a compilation of equipment orders placed.

"*There should be further exploration of the possible advantages and the feasibility of a series on authorization for the purchase of equipment.*"

[6] The universe of the individual top 1,000 manufacturing companies was developed primarily from Moody's *Industrials, 1955*. This was supplemented by Standard and Poor's *Register of Directors and Executives, 1956*, annual company reports, and other private trade sources. An effort was made to compile as accurate a listing as possible. Comparison with the Federal Trade Commission's *A List of 1,000 Large Manufacturing Companies, Their Subsidiaries and Affiliates, 1948* (June 1951) discloses that the great majority of companies are found to be on both registers. Comparison has not yet been made with the latest, *Report of the Federal Trade Commission on Industrial Concentration and Product Diversification in the 1,000 Largest Manufacturing Companies, 1950*, published in 1957.

practical for being back-stopped by the government survey which covers thousands of companies regardless of their size or planning practices.

Survey Coverage

Our basic published tables are based upon a continuous sample of 500 companies for all quarters of 1955 to date. These surveys provide the basis for the comparisons over time. In addition, 86 companies reported only for 1956, 1957, and 1958. The resulting 586 company data for 1956-58 are "blown up" to yield estimated results for the 1,000 company universe.[7]

TABLE 2

Ratio of Assets of NICB Respondent Companies to Assets of the
1,000 Largest Manufacturing Companies, by Industry, 1954
(*per cent*)

	586 Company Sample	500 Company Sample
All manufacturing	75	70
Durable goods industries	75	67
Primary iron and steel	96	94
Primary nonferrous metals	96	95
Electrical machinery and equipment	85	79
Machinery, except electrical	72	64
Transportation equipment[a]	52	39
Stone, clay, and glass products	93	86
Fabricated metal products	71	52
Other durable goods industries[b]	51	43
Nondurable goods industries	75	72
Food and beverages	59	52
Textile mill products	74	66
Paper and allied products	82	80
Chemicals and allied products	92	88
Petroleum and coal products	74	74
Rubber products	97	97
Other nondurable goods industries[c]	53	45

NOTE: The assets are from balance sheets for year-end 1954 or the closest fiscal year to it. The 586 companies furnished information for 1956, 1957, and the first quarter of 1958 (nine quarters); the 500 companies also furnished information for 1955 (thirteen quarters).

[a] Includes motor vehicles.

[b] Includes lumber products, furniture and fixtures, instruments, ordnance, and miscellaneous manufactures.

[c] Includes apparel and related products, tobacco, leather and leather products, and printing and publishing.

In Table 2, the coverage of our latest report is expressed as the ratio of the assets of our respondents to those of the top 1,000 manufacturing

[7] The data reported by the 586 companies were blown up by the ratio of total industry assets (of the 1,000 top companies) to the industry assets of the reporting companies, for each of three size classes: under $50 million; $50 to under $100 million; and $100 million and over.

companies. The assets of the basic 500 sample group represent 70 per cent of the assets of the top 1,000 manufacturing companies. Coverage rises to 75 per cent for the 586 company sample, with the highest ratios in the iron and steel; nonferrous metals; stone, clay, and glass; chemicals; and rubber industries. Aside from transportation equipment, coverage is weakest in groups characterized by a relatively small scale of operations, even at the apex of the manufacturing pyramid. For example, in both the "other" durables and "other" nondurables, coverage is only about 50 per cent; lumber and furniture in the hard-goods group, and apparel, leather, and printing in the soft-goods group are the least represented. These figures indicate that the survey is sufficiently broad in scope to reflect the activities of the manufacturing sector.

The capital expenditures reported by the NICB–cooperating companies represent over half of the capital spending estimated by Commerce–SEC

TABLE 3

Distribution of Capital Expenditures Reported in NICB and Commerce–SEC
Surveys, by Industry, 1957

	CAPITAL EXPENDITURES			
	As percentage of All Manufacturing		As percentage of Durables and and Nondurables	
		Commerce–		Commerce–
	NICB[a]	SEC	NICB[a]	SEC
All manufacturing	100.0	100.0		
Durable goods industries	49.6	50.3	100.0	100.0
Primary iron and steel	17.6	10.8	35.4	21.5
Primary nonferrous metals	7.6	5.1	15.3	10.1
Electrical machinery and equipment	5.3	3.8	10.6	7.5
Machinery, except electrical	4.9	8.0	10.0	15.9
Transportation equipment[b]	6.5	10.0	13.1	20.0
Stone, clay, and glass products	4.6	3.6	9.2	7.1
Other durable goods industries[c]	3.2	9.0	6.4	17.9
Nondurable goods industries	50.4	49.7	100.0	100.0
Food and beverages	3.1	5.3	6.2	10.7
Textile mill products	1.7	2.6	3.4	5.1
Paper and allied products	4.7	5.1	9.3	10.2
Chemicals and allied products	14.4	10.8	28.5	21.7
Petroleum and coal products	23.7	21.6	47.2	43.5
Rubber products	2.1	1.2	4.2	2.5
Other nondurable goods industries[d]	0.6	3.1	1.2	6.2

[a] Based upon capital expenditures reported by the basic sample of 500 companies.
[b] Including motor vehicles.
[c] Includes fabricated metal products, lumber products, furniture and fixtures, instruments, ordnance, and miscellaneous manufactures.
[d] Includes apparel and related products, tobacco, leather and leather products, and printing and publishing.

for all manufacturing companies. A comparison of the composition of the appropriations survey sample with that of the total Commerce–SEC survey is shown in Table 3 in terms of the distribution of 1957 capital expenditures by industries. The proportion accounted for by durables and nondurables is roughly similar, but the weighting of the constituent series varies.

The NICB emphasis on large companies naturally underweights the miscellaneous groups which consist predominantly of smaller companies. The same emphasis, as well as excellent coverage, accounts for the importance of iron and steel in our survey. The lower proportion accounted for by transportation equipment reflects the lower coverage of the NICB sample. The higher proportion accounted for by the petroleum industry is a result of the NICB definition which includes more of the industry in manufacturing than does Commerce–SEC.

Limitations

First, the appropriations survey differs from other expenditure intentions surveys in that no specific time dimension is attached to an approved capital appropriation. At mid-1957 the backlog of approved appropriations represented between three and four quarters of spending at the II 1957 spending rate, so that the time dimension does not stretch out indefinitely. What cannot be foretold is the specific quarter or quarters in which appropriated money will be spent. For the present the link between an appropriation and ensuing expenditures will have to be constructed through correlation and other statistical methods.

Second, capital appropriations may contain an allowance for overstatement and understatement, such as plus or minus 10 per cent. Relatively small changes in total capital appropriations are thus not to be sifted too finely. Since movements in the series over the past five years have been generally large in either direction, this does not detract from its usefulness.

Third, the capital appropriations survey is limited by the problems inherent in an attempt to develop a foreshadowing series. No matter how carefully a company plans and appropriates for capital spending, factors such as supply limitations, price changes, unexpected engineering and construction problems, and financial difficulties may affect the amount and timing of expenditures.

Fourth, there are problems involved in attempting to fit capital appropriation procedures into one consistent pattern. There is a question of what constitutes an appropriation. In some companies, only major expenditures are appropriated. In others, fortunately few, expense items associated with capital expenditures (capital items otherwise charged to current expense) are included in capital appropriations.

305

Another complication arises because some companies (among industries, most important in size is petroleum) make a lump sum appropriation for the year as a whole. If all companies did this, the appropriations survey would be identical with the survey of annual capital budgets. However, of the 500 companies in the basic sample, only thirty-four generally follow this practice and half of these find it necessary to make supplemental appropriations during the year. Since twenty-five make their major appropriations in the first quarter (almost all the rest make them in the fourth quarter), these practices contribute to a first-quarter seasonal peak in new appropriations as opposed to a first-quarter seasonal trough in expenditures. In our judgment, at least for the manufacturing sector, such complications present less of a problem than originally thought. While considerable correspondence marked the opening stages of the survey, the present reports contain comparable and consistent information.

More troublesome is the question of postponements which was raised by technicians and by some public pronouncements in early 1957. These can represent a problem in the context of the annual capital budget, as well as in the appropriations approach. The decision to postpone may take place when the capital appropriation is up for review in which case they could show up as a decline in approved capital appropriations.

Postponements may also occur after the formal approval by the board of directors. Then, as the survey is presently constituted, we would not be formally aware of it. However, if such a development were to become widespread, as in a recession, for example, it would show up as a relative rise in the backlog of appropriations with declining expenditures and commitments.

Lastly, questions arise in the definition of manufacturing. These are particularly troublesome for the nonferrous metals and the petroleum industries, where extraction, transportation, and distribution are sometimes included in the industry total. The NICB and government surveys are not comparable in this respect.

Appropriation Indicators

A battery of statistical indicators is made available by the quarterly survey of capital appropriations. We start out with the capital appropriations outstanding at the beginning of the quarter. These are the appropriations, previously approved, that have not yet been used. To this we add the capital appropriations approved during the quarter. The sum of the backlogs and the appropriations newly approved gives us the total appropriations available for use during the quarter.

We next take into account the capital appropriations either committed or spent during the quarter. By commitment, we mean the actual placing of the order for new plant and equipment. From one point of view this is when the company's capital spending decision has its initial impact on other firms. If all companies were able to report their commitments, the survey would be even more forward looking. Unfortunately, only about 35 per cent of the companies are able to report on this basis.[8]

We use the information on capital expenditures to expire the appropriations of companies unable to report commitments.[9] We also take into account the cancellation of appropriations. This may serve as an indicator of the level of business optimism in the field of capital spending decisions. If you subtract from the total appropriations available for use during the quarter those appropriations that were either committed or spent, and those appropriations that were canceled, you arrive at the total outstanding and available for use in future quarters.[10]

To illustrate, we estimated that at the beginning of 1957 the top 1,000 manufacturing companies had an appropriations backlog of $9.5 billion. To this is added the $4.5 billion in new appropriations approved during the first quarter making a total of $14 billion in appropriations available for use. During the first quarter, these companies either spent or committed $2.9 billion and canceled a little over $100 million. This left a backlog of $10.9 billion in outstanding appropriations at the end of the first quarter.

Thus far, we have published in fifteen, two-digit industry detail, this battery of quarterly appropriation information for 1955, 1956, 1957, and the first quarter of 1958. We have presented estimated figures for the 1,000 top manufacturing companies, in total, and for durables and non-

---

[8] The count refers to II 1957 for the basic sample of 500 companies. Actual dollar commitments reported by these companies amounted to 36 per cent of the total commitments and expenditures published for the quarter. Thus the survey is mostly on an expended basis.

[9] Albert Hart, in correspondence with the author, called attention to the series of appropriations committed but not yet spent obtained by subtracting capital expenditures from the total of appropriations committed or spent.

[10] In practice, the relationships do not add exactly. For example, in some companies all capital expenditures are not covered by appropriations. Subtracting total capital expenditures from the sum of outstanding appropriations plus net new appropriations would, therefore, not yield exactly the total outstanding at the end of the quarter. However, in the aggregate, such differences are small.

To illustrate, consider the II 1957 information for all manufacturing companies (*Conference Board Business Record*, September 1957, p. 411). The arithmetic sum of the total outstanding capital appropriations at the beginning of the quarter, plus new appropriations during the quarter, less commitments or expenditures during the quarter, less cancellations, is $7,870 million. The actual reported backlog at mid-1957 was $7,891 million, a difference of only $21 million, or a fraction of one per cent.

There are other small differences between the backlog at the end of a quarter and the backlog at the beginning of the following quarter. Some companies find it necessary to make some technical adjustments such as the change of a particular appropriation from capital to expense, or vice versa. Again, these technical accounting adjustments so far as the total survey is concerned represent a small discrepancy. Thus, at the end of I 1957, the backlog was $8,498 million. At the beginning of II 1957, the backlog was reported as $8,494 million.

The reported figures are always shown with these minor discrepancies.

durables.[11] More recently, we collected quarterly information for 1953 and 1954 from the basic sample of 493 companies. Of these, we have thus far tabulated 353 companies, which account for 89 per cent of new appropriations in 1955 as reported by the larger sample of 500.[12]

My analysis will be based upon the basic sample of 500 companies reporting for the quarters of 1955 to date, linked to the subsample of 353 companies also reporting for 1953-54. The subsample returns were blown up to the level of the 500 companies by applying the ratio prevailing in 1955 for each appropriation measure (e.g. for appropriations, backlogs, etc.).

Seasonal Fluctuations

New appropriations reported by the petroleum industry have a pronounced seasonal fluctuation, dominated by annual appropriations in the first quarter. Data for iron and steel, electrical and nonelectrical machinery, and the fabricated metal products industries also show evidence of seasonality. Recognizing the obvious dangers of constructing seasonal indexes for less than twenty quarters, we nevertheless made separate adjustments for these industries. The data for the other industries have not been adjusted.

The problem of seasonal adjustment for expenditures is less troublesome, since the basic factors at work are the accounting convention which siphons proportionately more expenditures into the fourth quarter, and cold weather which limits first-quarter construction activity. Our seasonal indexes for capital expenditures were calculated for the durables and nondurables groups as a whole. Cancellations also have a seasonal peak in the fourth quarter, probably associated with the year-end closing of company books, and adjustment has been made for this.

Appropriation Cycles

The seasonally adjusted data on new appropriations for all manufacturing for 1953-57 are given in Table 4. According to Commerce–SEC, capital expenditures by all manufacturers and by nondurable goods manufacturers were fractionally higher in 1953 than in 1952. Outlays by durable manufacturers declined in 1953. A peak in capital appropriations occurred in III 1953. From this peak to the trough in I 1954, new appropriations dropped 15 per cent. If correction is made for cancellations, appropriations declined 19 per cent from a III 1953 peak to a I 1954 trough.

[11] The results of the surveys so far conducted were published in *Conference Board Business Record*, October 1956, December 1956, March 1957, June 1957, September 1957, December 1957, March 1958, and June 1958.

[12] Additional returns for 1953-54 are still being received. The data presented for 1953-54, therefore, are preliminary and subject to revision.

TABLE 4

Appropriations, Cancellations, and Capital Expenditures of
Manufacturing Companies, by Quarters, 1953-1958
(*millions of dollars*)

	New Appropria-tions	Cancellations	Net New Appropria-tions	Capital Expenditures	Changes in Backlogs (3) − (4)
	(1)	(2)	(3)	(4)	(5)
1953					
I	1,162	66	1,096	1,504	−408
II	1,412	111	1,301	1,492	−191
III	1,459	68	1,391	1,491	−100
IV	1,260	106	1,154	1,463	−309
1954					
I	1,243	116	1,127	1,428	−301
II	1,255	89	1,166	1,369	−203
III	1,284	83	1,201	1,327	−126
IV	1,595	71	1,524	1,335	189
1955					
I	1,878	89	1,789	1,302	487
II	2,121	80	2,041	1,389	652
III	2,426	82	2,344	1,469	875
IV	2,648	76	2,572	1,565	1,007
1956					
I	2,910	78	2,832	1,755	1,077
II	2,888	96	2,792	1,967	825
III	2,297	130	2,167	2,116	51
IV	2,288	127	2,161	2,239	−78
1957					
I	2,728	93	2,635	2,380	255
II	2,126	185	1,941	2,371	−430
III	1,665	119	1,546	2,477	−931
IV	1,668	232	1,436	2,216	−780
1958					
I	1,448	332	1,116	2,009	−893

NOTE: All data are seasonally adjusted and based upon reports from 500 companies for 1955-58, linked to a subsample of 353 companies for 1953-54. In 1953-54 each measure has been raised by the appropriate ratio between the 353 company sample and the 500 company sample prevailing in 1955.

From a peak in I 1953 to a trough in I 1955, spending fell 13 per cent. As shown in Table 5, the peak in new appropriations for durables was reached in II 1953. From peak to I 1954 trough, new appropriations fell 28 per cent. On a net basis, the decline was 34 per cent. In contrast, capital spending fell 20 per cent from the I 1953 peak to the III 1954 trough.

309

TABLE 5

Appropriations, Cancellations, and Capital Expenditures of Durables
Manufacturing Companies, by Quarters, 1953-1958
(*millions of dollars*)

	New Appropria-tions (1)	Cancellations (2)	Net New Appropria-tions (3)	Capital Expenditures (4)	Changes in Backlogs (3)−(4) (5)
1953					
I	485	12	473	689	−216
II	602	36	566	679	−113
III	590	32	558	643	−85
IV	566	43	523	596	−73
1954					
I	435	63	372	570	−198
II	477	42	435	583	−148
III	533	33	500	550	−50
IV	530	26	504	552	−48
1955					
I	933	31	902	551	351
II	1,095	28	1,067	550	517
III	1,364	29	1,335	634	701
IV	1,365	41	1,324	701	623
1956					
I	1,512	30	1,482	819	663
II	1,540	43	1,497	968	524
III	934	55	879	1,039	−160
IV	1,180	47	1,133	1,140	−7
1957					
I	1,155	34	1,121	1,200	−79
II	1,002	85	917	1,201	−284
III	689	55	634	1,219	−585
IV	653	67	586	1,063	−477
1958					
I	463	122	341	933	−592

NOTE: Seasonally adjusted; see footnote to Table 4.

Table 6 shows that the peak in new appropriations by nondurables manufacturers occurred in III 1953 with the trough in III 1954. The peak to trough decline was 14 per cent. From the IV 1953 peak in capital spending to the I 1955 trough, the drop was 13 per cent.

The evidence for 1953-54 must be considered separately for durables and nondurables. New appropriations net of cancellations is the series most likely to foreshadow future expenditures. For the durables the peak in net appropriations followed the peak in spending by one quarter. In

TABLE 6

Appropriations, Cancellations, and Capital Expenditures of Nondurables
Manufacturing Companies, by Quarters, 1953-1958

(*millions of dollars*)

	New Appropria- tions	Cancellations	Net New Appropria- tions	Capital Expenditures	Changes in Backlogs (3)−(4)
	(1)	(2)	(3)	(4)	(5)
1953					
I	677	54	623	815	−192
II	810	75	735	813	−78
III	869	36	833	848	−15
IV	694	63	631	867	−236
1954					
I	808	53	755	858	−103
II	778	47	731	786	−55
III	751	50	701	777	−76
IV	1,065	45	1,020	783	237
1955					
I	945	58	887	751	136
II	1,026	52	974	839	135
III	1,062	53	1,009	835	174
IV	1,283	35	1,248	864	384
1956					
I	1,398	48	1,350	936	414
II	1,348	53	1,295	999	296
III	1,363	75	1,288	1,077	211
IV	1,108	80	1,028	1,099	−71
1957					
I	1,573	59	1,514	1,180	334
II	1,124	100	1,024	1,170	−146
III	976	64	912	1,258	−346
IV	1,015	165	850	1,153	−303
1958					
I	985	210	775	1,076	−301

NOTE: Seasonally adjusted; see footnote to Table 4.

nondurables, the peak in net appropriations preceded by one quarter the peak in spending. For durables the appropriations decline was significantly greater than the spending decline. For nondurables the two declines were roughly comparable.

However, in the absence of information prior to 1953, it is not possible to appraise fully the relationships between the magnitude and timing of appropriations versus expenditures for this period.

The evidence from the trough to the peak of the next cycle should convince even the skeptics. Capital spending by manufacturing companies (see Table 4) reached a trough in I 1955, as in the Commerce–SEC series. Meanwhile new appropriations were rising from the I 1954 trough. By I 1955, new appropriations had increased 51 per cent; net appropriations, 59 per cent.

How does this compare with the findings of the capital spending intentions approach? In November 1954, the first McGraw–Hill survey of annual capital budgets foreshadowed a 7 per cent decline in manufacturers' capital outlays in 1955 compared with 1954. In mid-March 1955, Commerce–SEC reported that annual 1955 manufacturers' capital spending was expected to be down 3 per cent from 1954. Actual 1955 spending was almost 4 per cent higher than a year earlier.

It is noteworthy that the second McGraw–Hill survey of annual capital budgets published in the spring disclosed that 1955 annual capital outlays by manufacturers were now expected to be 4 per cent higher. Thus the shift in expectations from −7 per cent to −3 to +4 per cent occurred over the period when substantial I 1955 capital appropriations were being approved. The appropriations survey would have noted the fact of this increase and probably the implication of higher outlays in 1955.

The full half cycle in appropriations from the I 1954 trough to a peak in I 1956 reveals the magnitude of the investment boom of 1955-56. New appropriations rose 134 per cent and net appropriations rose 151 per cent. The increase in spending from the I 1955 trough to the I 1957 peak was only 83 per cent, implying an increase in backlogs.

Since mid-1956, the trend in net new appropriation approvals has been generally downward. The rate of net appropriations during the four quarters beginning with III 1956 was almost a fifth lower than the three peak quarters of late 1955 and the first half of 1956, and about a sixth less than the average rate of the four quarters beginning with III 1955. Net appropriations in the three quarters beginning with III 1957 were almost 40 per cent below the average rate of the four quarters.

Changes in Appropriation Backlogs

The pattern of change in unspent appropriation backlogs (see Table 4) parallels the course of newly approved appropriations. During 1953 and 1954, backlogs were whittled down while expenditures declined.

In I 1955 the trend was sharply reversed. Backlogs increased while actual spending was rising gradually. By the end of the third quarter, the average 1955 rate of net appropriations was 64 per cent higher than during 1954. The initial shock which greeted the first McGraw–Hill announcement of preliminary plans for 1956 capital spending might have been tempered had these figures been available. During the second half of 1956, the change in backlogs was negligible. There was an increase in I 1957 (entirely in nondurables, discussed below) but this was followed, in the remaining quarters of 1957 and I 1958 by a decline amounting to almost 60 per cent of the cumulative change in backlogs which had taken place between I 1955 and I 1957.

Backlogs of durables companies surged ahead during 1955 and the first half of 1956 (Table 5). By the end of III 1955, the average 1955 rate of net appropriations was 143 per cent higher than the 1954 average. Here is evidence of the upsweep of capital spending plans as they were unfolding during a period when capital spending was rising moderately. Since mid-1956 appropriation backlogs have declined in the durables group. Beginning with III 1956 and continuing through I 1958, backlogs were whittled down to about one-third of the total accumulated over 1955 and the first half of 1956.

The cutback in backlogs during 1953-54 and the increase in backlogs in 1955-56 were more moderate for nondurables than for durables (Tables 5 and 6). Furthermore, nondurables appropriation backlogs were still increasing in III 1956 and I 1957. It was only in II 1957 that these backlogs fell appreciably. The fall from II 1957 through I 1958 was just under 50 per cent of the cumulative change in backlogs from IV 1954 through I 1957.

The patterns outlined for the durables and nondurables groups are reasonable on a priori grounds. One would expect the former to react more quickly and violently to outside stimuli affecting the strategic capital goods sector.

Year-to-Year Patterns

Further perspective on the patterns of new appropriations, backlogs, and spending is available by comparing year-to-year changes in each series, as shown in Table 7. For all manufacturing, in the 1953-54 comparison, changes in backlogs were greater than in new appropriations. In the 1954-1955 comparison the relationship was reversed. During 1955-56, gains in new appropriations became a loss, while gains in backlogs narrowed. In the 1956-57 and 1957-58 comparisons, new appropriations declined more than backlogs.

The fluctuations in appropriations and backlogs parallel the cycle of spending, but lead by two quarters in the 1954-55 upswing. Thus, the gains in new appropriations and backlogs in the I and II of 1955 compared with 1954 were reflected in the gain in spending beginning in III 1955. A similar two-quarter lead is evident for durables and nondurables.

The evidence for the full downswing of the cycle is still incomplete. Yet, the first year-to-year decline in new appropriations occurred in the III 1956 to III 1955 comparison, while spending first slowed up in I 1957 as compared with I 1956. This relation held for all manufacturing and for durables. For nondurables, the I 1956 to I 1957 gain in new appropriations

TABLE 7

Changes in New Appropriations, Backlogs, and Capital Expenditures,
Manufacturing Groups, by Quarters, 1954-1953 to 1958-1957
(*per cent*)

	ALL MANUFACTURING			DURABLES			NONDURABLES		
	New Appropriations	*Backlogs*	*Capital Expenditures*	*New Appropriations*	*Backlogs*	*Capital Expenditures*	*New Appropriations*	*Backlogs*	*Capital Expenditures*
1954-53									
I	10	−18	−5	−10	−18	−18	21	−17	6
II	−12	−18	−8	−21	−17	−15	−6	−19	−3
III	−11	−16	−11	−10	−13	−15	−12	−20	−8
IV	19	−7	−9	−7	−11	−8	46	−4	−9
1955-54									
I	41	13	−10	109	14	−4	14	11	−13
II	74	28	1	138	36	−7	32	20	6
III	93	47	10	164	62	14	43	31	7
IV	80	67	16	156	90	26	30	42	9
1956-55									
I	46	64	35	60	82	49	35	46	24
II	33	63	41	35	73	76	31	52	19
III	−4	47	44	−35	41	64	37	54	28
IV	−14	23	44	−12	21	63	−15	26	28
1957-56									
I	−3	12	37	−21	6	49	12	19	27
II	−28	−1	22	−34	−7	26	−19	7	18
III	−33	−11	19	−29	−15	19	−35	−6	18
IV	−33	−20	−1	−47	−25	−6	−13	−14	5
1958-57									
I	−43	−31	−16	−59	−35	−23	−33	−26	−9

NOTE: Based upon unadjusted figures. Data for 1955-58 relate to reports by 500 companies. Data for 1953-54 relate to 353 companies raised to the level of the 500 company sample by the ratio for the particular measure prevailing between the two samples in 1955.

represents a complication in this two-quarter relationship; nevertheless, the drop in appropriations in the fourth-quarter comparison was followed by a narrowing of the gain in expenditures in II 1957 compared with the same period a year previous.

Appropriation Diffusion

Perspective is added to the year-to-year percentage changes by considering the diffusion of appropriation changes. Accordingly, the 500 companies reporting quarterly information for 1955-58, and the 353 companies reporting information for the quarters of 1953-55, have been placed in three categories: those with increases from year to year in new appropriation approvals, those with decreases, and those reporting no changes. The percentage distribution of the number of companies in each category is given in Table 8.

NICB SURVEY OF CAPITAL APPROPRIATIONS

TABLE 8

Distribution of Companies by Direction of Change in Appropriations,
Manufacturing Groups, by Quarters, 1954-1953 to 1958-1957
(*per cent*)

	ALL MANUFACTURING			DURABLES			NONDURABLES		
	Higher	Lower	No Change	Higher	Lower	No Change	Higher	Lower	No Change
1954-53									
I	48	47	5	46	48	6	50	47	3
II	44	49	7	39	53	8	51	44	5
III	41	51	8	37	53	10	47	47	6
IV	49	44	7	53	39	8	44	50	6
1955-54									
I	59	38	3	63	34	3	53	44	3
II	61	33	6	63	29	8	57	39	4
III	64	30	6	68	26	6	60	35	5
IV	68	28	4	68	27	5	66	30	4
1956-55									
I	64	34	2	65	33	2	63	36	1
II	55	41	4	52	43	5	58	39	3
III	50	44	6	47	46	7	55	41	4
IV	47	50	3	49	47	4	44	53	3
1957-56									
I	48	50	2	45	53	2	51	47	2
II	42	54	4	42	54	4	43	54	3
III	39	54	7	35	57	8	45	51	4
IV	39	57	4	37	60	3	41	54	5
1958-57									
I	31	65	4	28	69	3	37	59	4

NOTE: The 1956-55, 1957-56, and 1958-57 comparisons are based upon 500 reporting companies, the 1954-53 and 1955-54 comparisons upon 353. Examination of the percentages for the overlap period, 1956-55 for the smaller sample shows no substantial difference from the above data.

Changes in the diffusion of company behavior generally parallel changes in new dollar appropriations (Table 7), but there is some evidence of a lead in the former. (All changes specified in this section are on a year-to-year basis. For example, changes in 1954 refer to 1954-53 data, although this will not be spelled out.) The increase in new appropriations in I 1954 was followed by two quarters of losses. This corresponds to a decline in the number of companies reporting higher appropriations (from 48 per cent to 41 per cent) from I to III 1954.

In IV 1954, there was an increase in dollar appropriations, while the number of companies reporting higher appropriations rose sharply, foreshadowing a further rise in appropriations. In I 1955, dollar appropriations actually were substantially higher and the number of companies reporting higher appropriations increased from 49 to 59 per cent, the largest absolute gain in the series.

In II and III 1955, dollar appropriations increased substantially while the number of companies reporting higher appropriation levels rose modestly. Both series peaked in IV 1955. In the first half of 1956, the rate of increase in dollar appropriations slowed down. There was a small

315

decline in the number of companies registering increases in I 1956, and a much sharper decline in the second quarter. While dollar appropriations reached a peak in the first half of 1956, the number of companies lowering their rate of appropriations increased, a lead corresponding to a cyclical pattern discovered in the business cycle research of the National Bureau.

The first absolute declines in dollar appropriations occurring in III and IV 1956 were matched by a further fall in the number of companies reporting increases. The absence of dollar change in I 1957 was paralleled by stability in the number of companies reporting lower appropriations. However, the sharp dollar drop in II 1957 was accompanied by a decrease in the number of companies reporting higher appropriations. The appropriation declines in the balance of 1957 and early 1958 were matched by further deterioration in the percentage of companies with higher approvals.

The comparisons between year-to-year changes in dollar appropriations and the number of companies reporting higher or lower approvals also generally hold true for durables and nondurables. Of interest is the rise in the number of durables companies reporting higher appropriations in IV 1954 along with a reduction in the appropriation decline during that quarter. The spectacular increase in the dollar approvals in I 1955 was accompanied by a larger percentage of durables companies with higher levels, but the absolute increase in these percentages from III 1954 (37 per cent) to IV 1954 (53 per cent) was greater than the increase from then to I 1955 (63 per cent). The slowing down of the rate of the dollar increase during II 1956 was matched by a sharp reduction in the number of durables companies reporting higher levels.

Nondurables again complicate the analysis. In IV 1954 they reported a higher dollar rate of appropriations while the number of companies with higher appropriations declined. On the other hand, a modest increase in the I 1955 appropriations was accompanied by a sharp increase in the number of companies reporting higher approvals.

In the first half of 1956, nondurables followed the pattern of the durables group. In particular, the second-quarter drop in the number of companies with higher appropriations supported the thesis of the lead underlying the diffusion approach. The rebound in nondurables appropriations in I 1957 was matched by an increase in the number of companies with higher levels. Again, the sharp dollar drop in II 1957 paralleled the decline in the number of nondurables companies reporting higher approvals.

While the relationship between changes in the diffusion of company behavior and changes in total dollar appropriations needs more analysis, the evidence thus far tends to bear out the Mitchellian-based hypothesis of a lead in the former.[13]

[13] Thor Hultgren has demonstrated a similar hypothesis with profits data. See *Cyclical Diversities in the Fortunes of Industrial Corporations*, National Bureau of Economic Research, Occasional Paper 32, 1950, p. 12.

Cancellations

A feature of the appropriations survey is the separate information available on the cancellation of appropriations. In Table 9 cancellations are shown as a ratio of new appropriations. Although erratic, the course of the ratio is related to trends in new appropriations. For example, the trough in appropriations occurred in the first half of 1954, as did the peak in the cancellation ratio. The peak in new appropriations was reached in the first half of 1956, along with the trough in the cancellation ratio. Finally, the sharp cutback in appropriations in II 1957 was associated with a higher cancellation ratio. The further reductions in appropriations

TABLE 9

Ratio of Cancellations to New Appropriations, Manufacturing
Groups, by Quarters, 1953-1958
(*per cent*)

	All Manufacturing	Durables	Nondurables
1953			
I	5.7	2.5	8.0
II	7.9	6.0	9.3
III	4.7	5.4	4.1
IV	8.4	7.6	9.1
1954			
I	9.3	14.5	6.6
II	7.1	8.8	6.0
III	6.5	6.2	6.7
IV	4.5	4.9	4.2
1955			
I	4.7	3.3	6.1
II	3.8	2.6	5.1
III	3.4	2.1	5.0
IV	2.9	3.0	2.7
1956			
I	2.7	2.0	3.4
II	3.3	2.8	3.9
III	5.7	5.9	5.5
IV	5.6	4.0	7.2
1957			
I	3.4	2.9	3.8
II	8.7	8.5	8.9
III	7.1	8.0	6.6
IV	13.9	10.3	16.3
1958			
I	22.9	26.3	21.3

Source: Based upon data shown in Tables 4, 5, and 6.

317

in late 1957 and early 1958 brought with them a peak in the cancellation ratio.

This matching of peaks and troughs in appropriations and cancellations also held for durables. Furthermore, the sharp drop in the III 1956 rate of appropriation approvals was paralleled by a rise in the cancellation ratio.

For nondurables, however, the low point in appropriations came in the middle quarters of 1954 while the peak in cancellations occurred in 1953. More recently, the rise in the cancellation ratio paralleled the IV 1956 drop in new appropriations. The further drop in appropriations in II 1957 was associated with a greater rise in the ratio.

Backlog Rates

A backlog rate shows how many quarters the appropriations backlog will last at the present rate of spending or commitment. Backlog rates for all manufacturing, durables, and nondurables, are shown in Table 10. Since a seasonally adjusted total backlog cannot be readily calculated, comparison is restricted to year-to-year changes.

Corresponding to the trough in appropriations and deep backlog losses, backlog rates showed large year-to-year declines in the first half of 1954. In the second half of 1954 these year-to-year losses disappeared. The backlog rate rose in succeeding quarters, reaching a peak, in terms of absolute advance over the year-ago quarter, in II 1956. By IV 1956, the backlog rate was below the same quarter of the previous year, and still further below II 1957.

The time shape of these developments for durables and nondurables differed slightly. The durables backlog rate rose during 1954 when compared to 1953, starting with the second quarter. The subsequent trend was generally the same as for all manufacturing.

For nondurables, the rise in appropriations began with IV 1954, but while backlogs were still lower than a year previously, the backlog rate was a shade over the 1953 level. However, with I 1955, the backlog rate evidenced a sharp gain over the 1954 figure. The trend since that time parallels that for durables and for the total. Thus we have an additional measure which can corroborate developments in capital goods expectations.

Forecasting and Analysis

The quarterly survey of capital appropriations is a multi-dimensional approach. The battery of statistical indicators provided by the survey strengthens the analysis of capital goods anticipations. When they all point in the same direction, the analyst can have increased confidence in his forecast.

TABLE 10

Appropriation Backlog Rates, Manufacturing Groups,
By Quarters, 1953-1958

	All Manufacturing	*Durables*	*Nondurables*
1953			
I	3.9	4.2	3.6
II	3.1	3.3	2.8
III	3.0	3.4	2.6
IV	2.4	2.9	2.0
1954			
I	3.1	4.2	2.5
II	2.8	3.6	2.3
III	2.9	4.0	2.3
IV	2.6	3.2	2.2
1955			
I	3.6	4.2	3.1
II	3.1	3.7	2.5
III	3.4	4.3	2.7
IV	3.2	3.6	2.7
1956			
I	4.3	4.8	3.8
II	3.8	4.3	3.2
III	3.8	4.6	3.1
IV	2.9	3.2	2.5
1957			
I	4.1	4.4	3.7
II	3.4	3.8	3.0
III	3.2	3.6	2.8
IV	2.5	2.9	2.2
1958			
I	3.7	4.3	3.3

NOTE: Backlog rate is defined as the number of quarters of commitments or expenditures represented by outstanding appropriations at the end of the quarter. The underlying data are unadjusted and based upon reports from 500 companies for 1955-58, and reports by 353 companies for 1953-54 which were raised to the level of 1955-58 by the ratio between the two samples in 1955 for appropriations, committed or spent, and backlogs, respectively.

In our continuing commentary in the *Conference Board Business Record*, we can compare simultaneously changes in new appropriations with changes in profits, profit margins, and liquidity. Such interrelationships can be traced on a quarterly basis. One major step forward in our analysis of this new body of data is to make such simultaneous comparisons on a formal statistical basis, through correlation and other techniques. We also plan to do this on a company basis. With over 7,500 quarterly observations at hand, many hypotheses can be tested relating the decision to spend with other variables.

The quarterly survey of capital appropriations is a short-run forecasting tool. The backlog rates suggest that, *on the average*, the formal planning period is about one year. For some industries, such as iron and steel, electrical machinery, and chemicals, it may be a year and a half. There are instances in which companies have long-range budgets running as far ahead as twenty years. But the appropriations survey suggests that these long-range budgets are merely guides to thinking.

As an indicator of prospective short-run trends in plant and equipment spending, the appropriations survey foreshadowed the 1955-56 capital spending boom. It provided the first quantitative indication of a leveling off in 1957 outlays, and the capital spending decline in 1958.

The series on appropriation approvals, and the ancillary measures contribute to a richer understanding of the flow of capital spending dollars. It may help us to discover whether, in a downturn, a decline in business investment takes the form of cancellations of existing projects, stretching out of existing appropriations, a sharp drop in newly approved capital appropriations, or a combination of all three. The evidence for 1953-54, however, does not reveal any mass cancellation. The drop in new appropriations was mostly moderate, and backlogs declined even more than appropriations. In view of the relatively mild decline in capital spending during this period, these developments are not surprising. With a more severe cycle, the role of these factors may become clearer.

The survey is not intended to supersede the surveys of capital spending budgets; they are companion measures with differing perspectives. For the short-term forecast which goes beyond the end of the calendar year, the appropriations data provide the first clue to prospective changes in manufacturers' spending for plant and equipment. In addition, this new series may disclose changes in direction in spending decisions during the year which are not clear from expected expenditure figures.

COMMENT

JOHN R. MEYER, Harvard University

Undoubtedly the National Industrial Conference Board's capital appropriation series represents a substantial addition to the available information on anticipations. It increases our knowledge of the time pattern of the capital budgeting process and should enable us to improve predictions of future capital spending patterns. Furthermore, the information on cancellations of capital appropriations and the extent of the appropriations backlog should provide information about how the capital budgeting process may change at different stages of the business cycle and under various external business conditions. Certainly, the first results are most hopeful and suggestive. It is possible, however, to be overly optimistic about how much additional information on investment decisions the appropriations series will provide. Information on appropriations will add mainly to our knowledge of short-run reversals or changes in investment policies. It will provide little new knowledge of exogenous or longer-run investment determinants. Moreover, the appropriations series does not eliminate other serious data deficiencies that now impede investment studies based on time periods of less than one year.

The predictions obtained from anticipations data also would seem susceptible to improvement. A principal concern of this conference was, in fact, trying to improve predictions based on anticipations data by placing these predictions in a conditional format; that is, by trying to specify in advance the correct eventual value of explanatory variables other than anticipations.[1] The obvious next step in utilizing conditional estimation procedures is to "close" the system by specifying those functions that relate the future endogenous values not only to one another but also to predetermined variables that are either exogenous or present values of endogenous variables. This would remove in effect the restraints or limitations on the conditional predictions.

Full specification of the economic structure in this fashion is the correct formal, or ultimate objective. However, the record to date indicates that empirical realization of the objective is extremely difficult. When predictions obtained from fully specified economic models are compared with ones obtained from simple (e.g. one equation, least squares estimated) models, the latter as often as not yield superior predictions. The basic rationale of the simple approach is to discover as many regularities as possible in previous economic behavior and then to assume that these regularities persist into the future.

A similar reliance on established regularities could be used to improve the unconditional forecasts[2] with which anticipations surveys are usually concerned. The regularities could be well established empirical generalizations discovered by methods other than surveys, or additional discoveries made by analyzing the data generated as part of the survey procedure.

The basic analytical problem in utilizing the results of any survey is the proper weighting of the responses. As a rule, two-stage weighting

[1] Examples of this viewpoint will be found in Arthur Okun's paper in this volume; see also Franco Modigliani and H. M. Weingartner, "Forecasting Uses of Anticipatory Data on Investment and Sales," *Quarterly Journal of Economics*, February 1958; and James Tobin, "On the Predictive Value of Consumer Intentions and Attitudes," *Review of Economics and Statistics*, February 1959.

Suggestions on how to improve unconditional predictions similar in some ways to mine will be found in the papers by Robert A. Levine, Eva L. Mueller, George Katona, and Murray F. Foss and Vito Natrella, also in this volume.

[2] An unconditional forecast will be defined as one that ignores (or at least minimizes the importance of) interactions occurring between predicted variables and other variables during the prediction period that modify the predicted values.

procedures are used. First, a simple unitary weighting of the individual responses is employed to obtain the sums within specified sample groups. (By group is meant an industry, product group, income class, or similar category.) Next, the simple sums of sample results usually are "blown up" according to some ratio relationship.

This scheme might be improved by modifying unitary weighting to take into account any historical reportorial biases. Firms that consistently underestimate should be appropriately marked up and firms that consistently overestimate should be marked down.[3] The implicit assumption of traditional weighting procedures is that errors of estimate cancel out. However, experience suggests that there is more underestimation than overestimation. Illustrative of this is the tendency of survey aggregates to be underestimates of actual developments on cyclical upswings and to be reasonably accurate on downswings.[4] On the downswing, the underestimation apparently is eliminated by the revision of plans as the extent of the decline becomes better known. One possible explanation of consistent individual differences in response patterns is the wish to provide for contingencies. Cohen notes that "capital appropriations may contain an allowance for overstatement and understatement, such as plus or minus 10 per cent." Other circumstances that might bear on the question of bias are whether or not the report is based on solid, well established capital budgeting procedures; whether the report is completed by one who is high or one who is low in the managerial hierarchy; and whether the report is completed early or late in a firm's budget preparation period.

The ratio markup of sample results can also be performed too casually. For example, no allowance usually is made for differences in investment patterns for different size firms at different points in the business cycle. Such an approach discards available information. As a rule, the small firms' percentage of total investment in an industry falls in a recession. This suggests that it might be useful to stratify firms by size within industry groups,[5] as is done, for example, in the SEC–Commerce survey.

---

[3] Such a weighting for consistent reportorial bias would appear to be equivalent to the γ term in Levine's equation 2.

[4] Modigliani and Weingartner think that much of this underestimation on the upswing is attributable to the failure of business planners to allow for future price increases. They present some reasonably convincing empirical evidence to this effect (Tables 1-A and 1-B). However, two objections to their conclusion and findings might be offered. (1) The rather long delay that often occurs between the actual ordering of materials and equipment and the recording of such acquisitions suggests that the records should be corrected by a price index that is a weighted average of previous prices rather than a current value index as used by Modigliani and Weingartner. The use of a "distributed lag" index would reduce the amount of reduction effectuated by price deflation of the investment values in inflationary periods. (2) There is good evidence that business planners often make a contingency allowance for price increases in times of inflation, so price deflation again would understate the final results. Still, it seems highly probable that price changes account for some inaccuracies in investment anticipations.

[5] If industry groups are stratified according to exhibited differences in investment

However, survey samples often have very little or no coverage of smaller firms.[6] This is clearly the case, for example, with the NICB survey. Consequently, the relationship between the firms included and excluded from the survey is likely to change with the business cycle and the final adjustment between the sample and total groups should take this into account.

Available information about interdependencies within the economic system also might be used to improve the adjustment between the survey and overall totals. Although the firms not included in the basic surveys are usually small, Cohen points out that "satellite and other lesser companies often gear their investment programs to those of major companies." Again the question arises of why this information shouldn't be used to obtain better forecasts. The plans of some small and medium-sized firms are probably more closely related to those of some large firms than to others. For example, the capital equipment needs of small automobile parts producers in the transportation equipment industry are probably more closely tied to the investment plans of large automobile parts producers than they are to the plans of large rail equipment and aircraft producers. This suggests a modified input-output approach in marking up sample totals to industry totals.

Unfortunately, any effort to apply these suggested improvements to the NICB estimates will encounter special problems. The greatest weakness of the appropriation series is its lack of time dimension without which it is impossible to predict actual capital outlays in some future period. The cancellation series provides a partial solution to this problem but it is questionable how complete that series is.

What is needed, of course, is a determination of the lead time between the making of an appropriation and the actual outlay. In other words, it is necessary to find the distributed lag function relating capital outlays to lagged appropriations. Of course, other variables—like material shortages, money market conditions, changes in expectations—may influence this relationship and must be taken into account. In addition to this econometric or statistical approach, respondent firms should be asked to estimate, to the best of their ability, the time that elapses between appropriation and outlay. At a minimum, these responses would provide a check on the results obtained from the more formal statistical procedures.

A special type of weighting problem, seasonal adjustment, arises when

---

patterns, the differences would be reflected in the industry total. Without such stratification, the industry totals are likely to be biased, the extent of the bias depending on how similar the year chosen for determining the ratio benchmark is to the year to be estimated.

[6] The greater variability of small firm investment plans raises serious questions about the legitimacy of the much heavier weighting given large firms in most survey samples. The basic tenet of stratified sampling is that sample size in a stratum should increase both with the stratum's variance and its importance in the total to be estimated.

time periods of less than a year are employed, as they are in the NICB study. Cohen notes that appropriations data apparently have a different seasonal pattern than investment outlays. There are no special problems created by these differences if the two seasonals are reasonably stable. However, there are signs in the NICB data that the seasonality in the appropriations series has been changing, and rather drastically, in the last few years. The evidence can be found by inspecting Tables 4, 5, and 6. Such changes are not too surprising since capital budgeting procedures, like most new techniques, are being rapidly improved. Those compiling questionnaire responses based on these procedures therefore must be especially alert.

There are, in sum, substantive and difficult problems to be solved before the full potential of the NICB appropriations survey, or any other survey, can be fully utilized. The most promising source of improvement would appear to be the integration of established empirical regularities into the estimation procedure. Such an integration would also illustrate the basic complementarity between the survey technique and other empirical methods in economics.

Forward Investment Commitments of Life Insurance Companies

JAMES J. O'LEARY

LIFE INSURANCE ASSOCIATION OF AMERICA

The purpose of my paper is to consider whether data on the forward investment commitments of life insurance companies and other investing institutions can be of aid in anticipating general business developments. Therefore, the bulk of my comment will be devoted to the coverage of life insurance commitment figures and their behavior during 1951-56. A necessary preliminary is the definition of a forward commitment.

What Are Forward Investment Commitments?

A "forward investment commitment" is a binding agreement on the part of a lending institution to make available a given amount of funds, upon given credit terms, at specified dates or over an agreed-on period of time varying from just over a month to two or three years. The agreement gives the interest rate, maturity, redemption privileges, and so forth, and sets forth a schedule of disbursement or "takedown" of the funds. Whether it is written or oral, the lender regards it as morally binding, and the borrower, too, is obligated. To an increasing extent in recent years, particularly as the bargaining power of the lender has become stronger, the agreement has involved a commitment fee to provide some assurance that the borrower will abide by the agreement.

A large percentage of commitments are made in connection with the direct placement of corporate securities. For example, the Prudential Insurance Company of America may agree to purchase $50 million of the bonds of International Business Machines at given credit terms and on a prearranged takedown schedule. Over 90 per cent of the industrial bonds purchased by life insurance companies today are direct placements and involve the forward commitment process. Business and industrial mortgage loans are also arranged this way. Thus, a mortgage loan to a real estate developer to build an office building would involve a forward commitment. In residential mortgage loans, too, the lending institution may bind itself to advance funds to a builder or a prospective owner-occupant on prearranged terms. This commitment is in turn the basis for construction credit by a bank. Other major types of financing involving the forward commitment are purchase-lease deals and state and local government financing. Many toll roads were financed by life insurance companies with the funds committed for two to three years in advance of the final takedown.

Our data include some commitments to bond houses to purchase a given amount of a public issue. Normally however, public issues of corporate securities do not give rise to a forward commitment partly because, to appear in our data, the commitment must have a life of over one month.

Life insurance companies are not the only type of financial institution making forward commitments. Commercial banks have made forward commitments regularly for many years, and their term loans involve a procedure practically identical with that employed by life insurance companies in direct placements of corporate securities. Uninsured pension funds, to the extent that they acquire direct placements of corporate securities, also make forward commitments. Similarly, mutual savings banks and savings and loan associations are active in the mortgage field in arranging their financing on this basis. But to the best of my knowledge only the life insurance business has obtained regular reports on commitments for any length of time. Recently the savings and loan associations have begun to collect these data, and I hope that other lender groups will soon follow suit.

What Do the Commitment Data of the Life Insurance Association of America Cover?

The collection of forward commitment data by the LIAA began in April 1951 under the Voluntary Credit Restraint Program. As participants in the program the life insurance companies submitted monthly commitment data to the Federal Reserve Board as an evidence of whether their current lending activities were in keeping with the VCRP. The monthly data, with suitable modifications, have been obtained regularly ever since. Originally, the canvass included companies holding about 85 per cent of total life insurance assets, but after the VCRP was terminated in March 1952 the ratio was reduced to about two-thirds. This coverage is very satisfactory for blowing up the total forward commitments of the life insurance business but less so for estimating the component parts of the series.

Our monthly reports show two major types of forward commitments, those involving securities and those involving real property and mortgages. Under securities are classified business and industrial bonds, public utility bonds, railroad bonds, state, municipal, and local securities, and all other securities. Business and industrial commitments in turn are broken down according to the Standard Industrial Classification. Real property and mortgage loans include business and industrial mortgages, real property for lease or rental, home office buildings, farm mortgages, and nonfarm residential mortgages. The latter are in turn broken down into Federal Housing Administration–insured, Veterans Administration–guaranteed, and conventional.

The tables show new commitments made during the month and the total amount outstanding at the end of the month in each category. The reports further indicate how large an amount within each category of outstanding commitments is expected to be taken down within one month, two months, and six months. Until recently the breakdown was simply within six months and over six months. The tables also reveal takedowns during the month, and cancellations.

Behavior of Forward Commitment Data, 1951-1956

Chart 1 shows, in index number form, the changes which have taken place in total outstanding commitments, and in outstanding commitments to purchase securities and real property and mortgage loans from April 1951 through December 1956. To make the series consistent over time I included only those companies which reported throughout the entire period.

Commitments immediately before the base month, April 1951, were at a very high level because there had been a sharp build-up in the second half of 1950 and early in 1951 before the Federal Reserve–Treasury "accord." Anticipation of Regulation X, instituted in October 1950, was a great inducement to builders and mortgage bankers to obtain immediate mortgage commitments. The ability of investing institutions to dispose of federal government securities at pegged prices above par also encouraged the build-up.

By April 1951 total commitments outstanding had begun a decline which carried the index to 80 in August 1951. It fluctuated about this level until February 1954 when a steady rise began which carried it to 125 in November. After a decline to 116 in December 1954, the index displayed considerable stability during 1955 but 1956 saw a steady rise from 117 in January to 139 in October and November, with a falling back to 133 in December.

During the same period, the two major component series showed widely divergent movements. Commitments to purchase real property and mortgages of all types declined steadily from an index of 100 in April 1951 to 59 in July 1952. Commitments to purchase securities declined from the April base to 88 in August 1951, but rose spectacularly to 142 in September 1952. This build-up gave some clue to the pronounced rise in business and industrial expenditures which occurred in the first several months of 1953 on a seasonally adjusted basis.

The index of commitments for real property and mortgage loans, having reached a low in July 1952, remained stationary through December. It

CHART I

Outstanding Commitments, Total and for Securities and Real Property and
Mortgage Loans, Monthly Index, April 1951–December 1956

Source: The data were compiled by the Life Insurance Association of America.
Commitments of only those life insurance companies which reported throughout
the entire period are included. These companies represented more than 60 per cent
of the total assets of all United States life insurance companies.

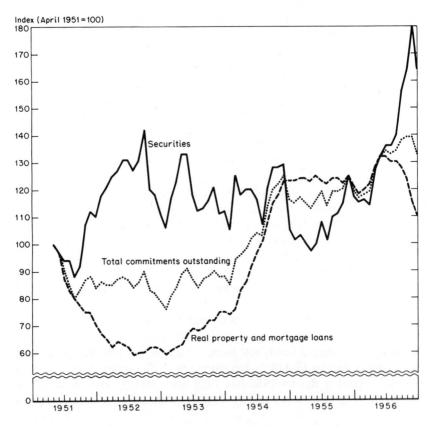

drifted upward to 76 in February 1954 and then rose more rapidly to 125
in May 1955. It held this position for the remainder of 1955 and then rose to
132 by May 1956, then fell back to 110 by December 1956. In connection
with these movements, it is important to note that within the general
category of real property and mortgage commitments there are important
divergent movements between commercial and industrial mortgage loans
(which behave more like securities commitments) and residential mortgage
loan commitments.

Returning to commitments to purchase securities, the index fell off in
October 1952 through January 1953, and then rose from 106 in January to

133 in April 1953. After a decline to 118 in June, the commitments moved within a somewhat narrower range the rest of 1953 and 1954. The index declined in December 1954 through April 1955, but August 1955 saw the beginning of an upswing which was particularly pronounced between March and November 1956 when the index jumped from 114 to 180. This rise may have anticipated the boom in business and industrial plant and equipment expenditures which got under way in 1956 and continued in 1957.

Chart 2 shows the percentage of total outstanding commitments for securities compared with those for real property and mortgages from September 1952 through 1956. The relationship between the two sets of figures remained fairly stable from October 1952 through May 1953, whereupon the securities percentage showed a steady decline through May 1955 and the real property and mortgage percentage a corresponding rise. The shift from Federal Reserve credit restraint to ease beginning in

CHART 2

Outstanding Commitments for Securities and Real Property and Mortgage Loans as Percentages of Total Commitments Outstanding, Monthly, September 1952–December 1956

the spring of 1953 contributed to this shift in commitments. Beginning in June 1955 the securities proportion of the commitments rose steadily through 1956 and the real property and mortgage proportion declined.

Chart 3 presents index numbers showing changes from April 1951 through 1956 in commitments to purchase business and industrial bonds, business and industrial mortgages, and nonfarm residential mortgages. The index of commitments to purchase business and industrial bonds declined from 100 in April 1951 to 84 in August, and then rose more or less steadily to

CHART 3

Outstanding Commitments for Business and Industrial Bonds and Mortgages
and Nonfarm Residential Mortgages, Monthly Index,
April 1951–December 1956

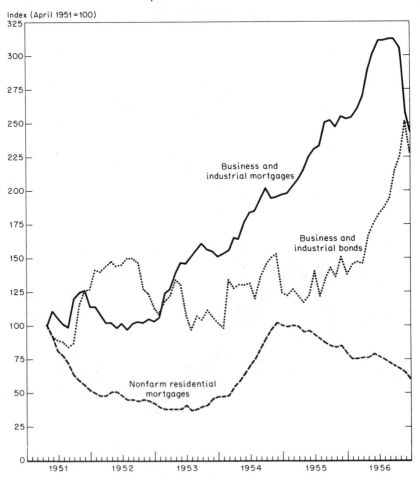

150 in July and August 1952. Here again may be an indication of the business plant and equipment boom which occurred in the latter part of 1952 and during 1953. Beginning in September 1952 a decline occurred which placed the index at 108 in January 1953. After a rise to 134 in April 1953, the index dropped suddenly to 108 in June and 97 in July and hovered around these points through January 1954. In February the index jumped to 133, where it stabilized until it began to rise again in September. It reached 153 in November 1954 but suddenly shifted to 124 in December and remained at about that level through May 1955. The index then rose, at first moderately then spectacularly, to 251 in November 1956, a rise which may have suggested that the boom in capital spending by business and industry would be sustained throughout 1957.

The sudden changes from one level of commitments to another, particularly characteristic of this index, are probably explained by one or a few large new commitments or takedowns in a given month. Also, it is worth noting that it seems to be a regular pattern for commitments to decline in December of each year, a pattern probably due to peculiarities in the operation of life insurance company investment departments.

Turning to the index of business and industrial mortgage commitments, the prolonged and great rise from 106 in January 1953 to 312 in August and September 1956 reflects the tendency for life insurance companies in recent years to concentrate more of their mortgage investments in the business and industrial field for portfolio balance. It also reflects the boom in industrial and business financing of the past few years. The mortgage loan has especially been used to finance small business enterprises and particular types of construction such as shopping centers.

The index of commitments to purchase nonfarm residential mortgages is particularly interesting. This index declined steadily from 100 in April 1951 to 37 in July 1953. Just before July 1953, the Federal Reserve moved to a policy of credit ease and the VA mortgage interest rate was raised from 4 to $4\frac{1}{2}$ per cent. The shift to residential mortgages followed like night the day. From July 1953 to November 1954 the index rose from 37 to 102—an indication of the resurgence of the residential construction boom in 1955. Commitments stayed at close to peak levels until March 1955 and then declined to 60 in December 1956, anticipating the decline in residential construction in 1956 and 1957.

Chart 4 shows the percentage of total outstanding commitments in the form of business and industrial bonds, business and industrial mortgages, and nonfarm residential mortgages from September 1952 through 1956. A familiar picture emerges. The percentage of total outstanding commitments in the form of business and industrial bonds declined slightly from 39 per cent in September 1952 to 33 per cent in January 1953. There followed at first a moderate rise, then a decline, to below the 30 per cent level, and then relative stability. After a jump to 33 per cent in February

CHART 4

Outstanding Commitments for Business and Industrial Bonds and Mortgages and Nonfarm Residential Mortgages as Percentages of Total Commitments Outstanding, Monthly, September 1952–December 1956

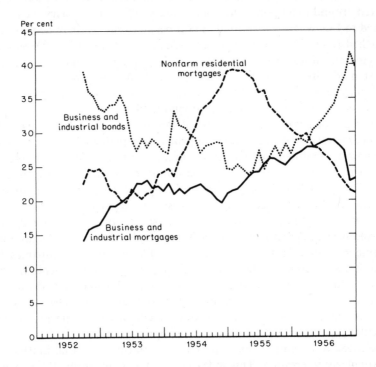

1954, the percentage declined to 25 by year-end. There was little change until August 1955 when the percentage began a climb which took it to 42 in November 1956.

The percentage represented by business and industrial mortgages rose more or less steadily from September 1952 through September 1953, whereupon it was stable for over a year. It rose gradually from 20 per cent in November 1954 to 29 per cent in July 1956, and then declined to 23 per cent in December.

The percentage of total outstanding commitments in the form of nonfarm residential mortgages rose slightly in the last quarter of 1952 and then flattened out at a lower level during most of 1953. Beginning in the last quarter of 1953 the percentage rose from 21 to 39 in January 1955. At that point a decline set in which persisted during the remainder of 1955 and throughout 1956.

Chart 5 shows a breakdown of the component parts of nonfarm residential mortgages: FHA–insured, VA–guaranteed, and conventional. The

CHART 5

Outstanding Commitments for FHA-Insured, VA-Guaranteed, and
Conventional Residential Mortgages, Monthly Index,
April 1951–December 1956

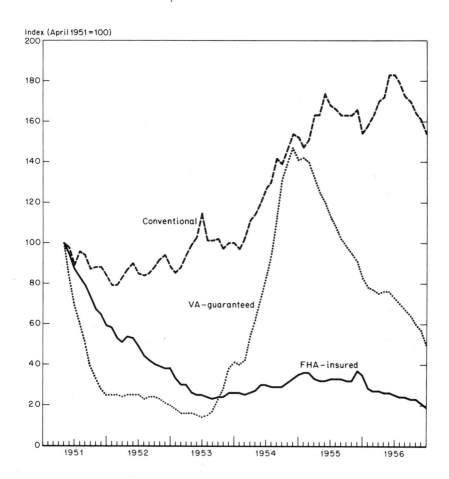

Index (April 1951 = 100)

highly volatile series are commitments to purchase VA mortgages, which
declined sharply from April 1951 through December, as a result of two
forces. After their big build-up in 1950 there was a natural tendency to let
them decline for portfolio balance. Also as demand for corporate funds
increased, and corporate bond yields rose, funds were attracted away
from the VA mortgage field where the gross rate was pegged at 4 per cent.
The index displayed unusual stability at a low level until September 1952
but then sagged to a low of 14 in June 1953. In late April and early May
two events of great importance to the capital market occurred. The
Federal Reserve shifted rather abruptly from a policy of credit restraint

333

to one of ease and then later in the year "active ease", and the VA interest rate was raised to $4\frac{1}{2}$ per cent. The Federal Reserve's action accentuated the force of a reduced demand for corporate funds which occurred at that time. The combination of a rise in the VA rate (belatedly and just when it was not needed) and the decline in corporate yields produced a rise in VA commitments beginning in July 1953. The index rose from 14 in June 1953 to 42 in February 1954, and then gathered momentum to reach a peak of 147 in November. Despite the accelerating flow of funds, the yield on VA mortgages was not driven downward. During the second half of 1953 and throughout 1954 discounts were readily available on $4\frac{1}{2}$ per cent VA mortgages. Apparently, as the supply schedule of VA funds shifted to the right, it induced a counterbalancing shift in the demand schedule. What happened was that lending institutions eased other terms in VA loans. In early 1954 the no-downpayment thirty-year VA loan became common and by the late spring builders were offering all kinds of special inducements to prospective owners. Since homes are purchased today with a downpayment and monthly carrying charges, in which the interest rate is not a major factor, the no-downpayment and long amortization terms actually created a demand for housing which accommodated the expanded flow of funds into VA mortgages at relatively attractive net yields.

Turning to Chart 5 again, one can see that at the end of 1954 the VA commitment index started a steady decline which carried it from 147 in November to 83 in December 1955 and to 50 in December 1956. The decline occurred because of a shift in commitments primarily to industrial securities, industrial and business mortgages, and conventional residential mortgages. The shift took place because of a resurgence in business and industrial demand for capital funds and a change in Federal Reserve policy to one of credit restraint. Yields on business and industrial securities rose to the point where the VA mortgage at a gross rate of $4\frac{1}{2}$ per cent (net of $3\frac{3}{4}$ per cent) was no longer attractive, especially on overly liberal downpayment and amortization terms. Increasing discounts on these mortgages were largely ineffective in holding the flow of funds from life insurance companies because the latter were reluctant on public relations grounds to purchase VA mortgages at other than rather moderate discounts. The flow of funds into conventional mortgages was maintained because rates were flexible and thus competitive. Just as the sharp build-up in VA commitments in the latter part of 1953 and in 1954 anticipated the boom in residential construction which took place in the latter part of 1954 and in 1955, so the decline in these commitments beginning in early 1955 signaled the decline which occurred in late 1955 and throughout 1956 and 1957 in houses financed with VA mortgages.

Throughout most of the period life insurance companies generally preferred VA to FHA mortgages, probably because of more favorable redemption terms on the former in case of default. Although the two indexes tended to fall and rise together, after September 1953 FHA commitments were consistently much lower in dollar amounts than VA commitments and also were lower than their own level in 1951 and the first half of 1952. From April 1951 the index declined steadily to 23 in August 1953. It rose to 36 in January and February 1955, exhibited considerable stability through December, and then declined to 19 in December 1956.

The index of conventional mortgage commitments moved to a lower level in early 1951 and then fluctuated generally within a narrow range until early 1953. The index rose from 85 in January 1953 to 115 in June, and then declined to 101 in July where it held through December. January 1954 saw the start of a build-up which, with minor setbacks, continued until the index reached 183 in May 1956. By the end of 1956 it had fallen back to 154.

One would expect to find the greatest stability in conventional mortgage commitments because (1) the contract rates of interest are flexible and remain in line with competing rates in other sectors of the capital market; and (2) institutional investors such as life insurance companies desire to regularize their flow of funds into residential mortgages because of the need of their home office and field organizations to do a mortgage business. The latter fact means that conventional residential mortgages naturally get a large and increasing share of funds such as was apparent, generally speaking, from 1954 through 1956. The build-up of conventional commitments in 1954, 1955, and 1956 perhaps gives a clue to the changing type of residential construction of 1956 and 1957, and the fairly well maintained volume. The build-up in conventional residential commitments came later than did the VA build-up, and so did the takedowns.

Chart 6 shows the variations which have taken place in the structure of nonfarm residential commitments. Of particular interest is the movement of VA commitments as a percentage of total nonfarm mortgage commitments. These commitments declined from 21 per cent in September 1952 to 14 per cent in June 1953, rose to 54 per cent in September and October 1954, and then gradually declined to 32 per cent in December 1956.

Also shown is the sharp rise in conventional commitments from 43 per cent of total residential commitments in September 1952 to 62 per cent in June 1953. This was to be expected in view of the rise in interest rates in the bond market in that period and the ability of conventional mortgage rates to move upward flexibly at the expense of administered rates in the government-insured and guaranteed mortgage field. Conventional commitments declined steadily beginning in July 1953 to reach 32 per cent in January and February 1955. This likewise was to be expected in view of the softening in corporate bond and conventional mortgage rates which occurred beginning in the spring of 1953 and the relative attractiveness of VA mortgages at $4\frac{1}{2}$ per cent. Again, beginning in March 1955 the

CHART 6

Outstanding Commitments for FHA-Insured, VA-Guaranteed, and
Conventional Residential Mortgages as Percentages of Total
Nonfarm Residential Mortgage Commitments, Monthly,
September 1952–December 1956

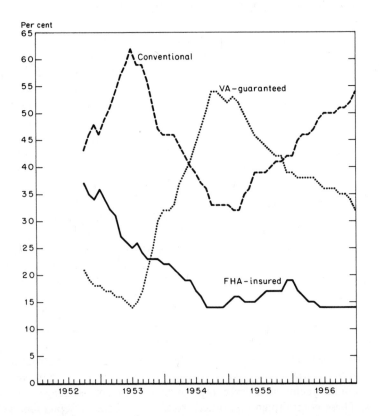

percentage of conventional commitments rose from 35 to 54 in December
1956 because of a rise in corporate bond yields and a concomitant increase
in conventional mortgage rates.

The percentages for FHA mortgages show the somewhat more stable
but lower level of these commitments. Starting from a high level of 37 per
cent in September 1952, FHA commitments showed little change through
January 1953 and then underwent a prolonged decline to 14 per cent in
August-November 1954. They then began to reflect the push toward
higher-yielding government-insured and guaranteed mortgages and rose
moderately from 15 per cent in December 1954 to 19 per cent in November
and December 1955. During 1956 they declined gradually.

Chart 7 shows, in index numbers, changes in total new commitments
made each quarter, and changes in the two major components, securities

CHART 7

New Commitments, Total and for Securities and Real Property and
Mortgage Loans, Quarterly Index,
Fourth Quarter 1951–Fourth Quarter 1956

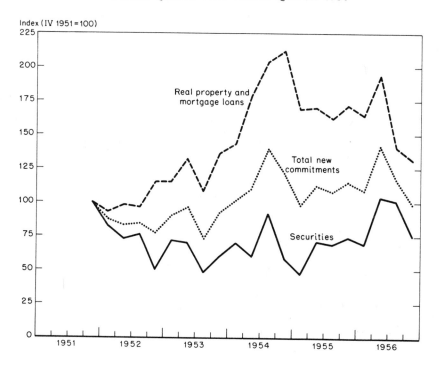

and real property and mortgages, from IV 1951 through 1956. New
commitments are perhaps more useful than *outstanding* commitments in
connection with business anticipations because they are a better measure
of current investment policy.

As before, it is most instructive to analyze these data in terms of movements in the constituent series. Chart 8 provides quarterly data on new
commitments to purchase business and industrial bonds, business and
industrial mortgages, and nonfarm residential mortgages. For business and
industrial bonds, the new commitment index declined in each quarter of
1952. Although it rose in I and II 1953, it fell back again in III and IV.
In 1954 new commitments fluctuated at a higher level and in 1955 fluctuated around a somewhat lower level. Perhaps most interesting is the sharp
rise in 1956, possibly anticipating the 1957 boom in plant and equipment
expenditures.

New commitments to purchase business and industrial mortgages
showed a strong tendency to rise in II 1952 through I 1953, and then
declined the rest of 1953. In 1954-56 they rose and held at very high levels

CHART 8

New Commitments for Business and Industrial Bonds and Mortgages
and Nonfarm Residential Mortgages, Quarterly Index,
Fourth Quarter 1951–Fourth Quarter 1956

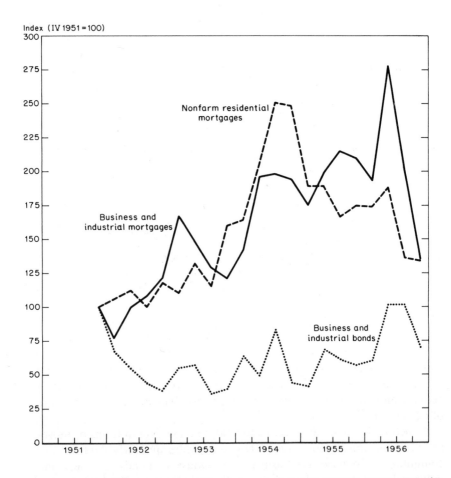

until a sharp decline occurred in the second half of 1956. New commitments to make residential mortgage loans were higher in 1953 than in 1952. They rose sharply in 1954 but fell back in 1955 and 1956. Here again, the broad categories make generalization difficult.

Chart 9 shows, in index numbers, a breakdown of the changes in new commitments to make residential mortgage loans. New commitments to purchase VA mortgages have undergone spectacular changes. After a steady decline from 165 in I 1952 to 56 in I 1953 they rose in II 1953 to 74 and then climbed dramatically to 948 in III 1954. Beginning in IV 1954 a decline began which carried the index to 230 in IV 1956. Both the rise and

CHART 9

New Commitments for FHA-Insured, VA-Guaranteed, and Conventional
Residential Mortgages, Quarterly Index,
Fourth Quarter 1951–Fourth Quarter 1956

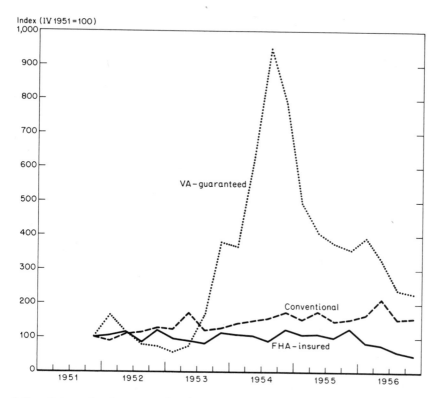

fall anticipated subsequent developments in residential construction. New commitments to make conventional residential mortgage loans displayed an upward trend over the period and in 1955 and 1956 foreshadowed the nature of residential construction. As expected, new FHA commitments showed a great deal of stability, although they declined considerably in 1956.

Charts 10-12 complete my review of the behavior of commitments. They show the percentage of outstanding commitments within the various categories expected to be taken down within six months. The figures highlight the time lag between the date of the new commitments and their subsequent takedown and use in economic activities such as home building or plant and equipment construction. According to Chart 10 over 60 per cent of outstanding mortgage commitments are generally taken down during the following half year while securities commitments tend to remain outstanding for much longer.

339

CHART 10

Percentages of Outstanding Commitments Expected to Be Taken Down within Six Months, Total and for Securities and Real Property and Mortgage Loans, Monthly, September 1952–December 1956

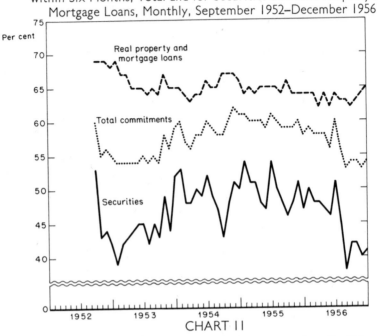

CHART 11

Percentages of Outstanding Commitments Expected to Be Taken Down within Six Months for Business and Industrial Bonds and Mortgages and Nonfarm Residential Mortgages, Monthly, September 1952–December 1956

CHART 12

Percentages of Outstanding Nonfarm Residential Mortgage Commitments, by Type, Expected to Be Taken Down within Six Months, Monthly, September 1952–December 1956

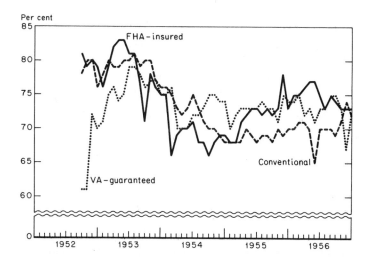

The data on expected takedowns also help explain trends in the commitment figures. For example, Chart 10 shows that the percentage of all outstanding commitments expected to be taken down within six months declined from some 60 per cent in 1955 to 54 per cent in December 1956. The decline was tied to the shift from mortgage commitments to commitments for securities, but it also apparently reflected a tightening cash flow position of the life insurance companies. Interpreted in conjunction with cash flow data, it apparently foreshadowed the decline in outstanding commitments during 1957.

Some Factors Affecting Commitment Policy

Prior to the "accord" between the Federal Reserve and the Treasury in March 1951, life insurance companies and other institutional investors were largely free to make forward commitments without regard to their cash flow because of the availability of federal government securities which could be readily sold at predictable prices above par supported by Federal Reserve purchases. With the unpegging of the prices of governments, however, this situation changed. Uncertainty about the prices at which government securities could be sold at some future time when commitments would be taken down required life insurance companies to pay stricter attention to cash flow when making commitments. As time has

341

gone on, not only have the bulk of government securities held by life insurance companies gradually been liquidated, but also heavy losses have been involved, which serve as a strong deterrent to sales unless new investments can be obtained at high enough rates to amortize the losses over relatively short periods of time.

Much time and effort have been devoted by companies in the last few years to obtaining detailed and reliable information about projected cash flow. Since I 1957 many of the companies which report commitment data to the LIAA have also been reporting total cash flow for the quarter just ended and expected cash flow for the ensuing two quarters. This information enables us to relate outstanding investment commitments scheduled to be taken down within six months to total cash flow expected in the same six-month period. At the end of both the first and second quarters of 1957 this relationship was fairly steady at about 75 per cent. Thus, the cash flow figures, in conjunction with the commitment figures, are helpful in providing a clue to future developments in the capital markets.

Investment expectations also influence commitment policy. Generally speaking, when interest rates are declining or are expected to decline, companies will probably strive to build up their commitment accounts, thereby tending to offset a decline in commitments which one might expect from a reduced demand for capital funds. On the other hand, when interest rates are rising or are expected to rise, some companies undoubtedly avoid becoming heavily committed in order to reserve funds for even better investment opportunities. Their reluctance tends to retard the natural build-up of commitment positions in a period of heavy capital demand. Thus not only cash flow but also forces based on investment psychology lend stability to the volume of investment commitments at any given time. Of course the commitment position of most institutional investors probably reflects expectations in only a marginal way.

The commitment and cash flow data of the life insurance business are available regularly to the Treasury, the Federal Reserve, and government agencies in the housing field. The commitment position of the life insurance companies, and the trends in these commitments, have played a part in Treasury decisions on how successfully a long-term bond issue could be sold at any given time.

Forward Commitments as an Aid in Anticipating Business Developments

Much more thought and careful study need to be given to the forward commitment data, but it seems that they are of possible aid in forecasting (1) the outlook for the capital market and interest rates, (2) developments in residential construction, and (3) business plant and equipment expenditures.

First, the degree to which life insurance companies and other investors have built up a backlog of commitments relative to cash flow provides a clue to probable developments in the capital market and accordingly in interest rates. For example, if commitments are at a very high level relative to cash flow, this situation, of itself, would seem to rule out any sharp decline in long-term interest rates. However, these data are useful only in conjunction with other information. Data on investment expectations, such as those provided by the McGraw–Hill and Commerce Department–Securities and Exchange Commission surveys of capital expenditure plans, the National Industrial Conference Board survey of capital appropriations, and information on sources and uses of capital funds, are essential elements in a forward looking analysis of capital markets.

Secondly, data on forward commitments to make residential mortgage loans seem to have special predictive value. Although many of these commitments have been on existing homes, a large part have been to finance new construction, particularly in the government-insured and guaranteed category. It seems quite clear that the sharp rise in residential mortgage commitments in the second half of 1953 and in 1954 anticipated the rising tide of residential construction in the second half of 1954 and the well-sustained high level in 1955. Likewise, the decline in residential mortgage commitments in 1955 and 1956 seems to have anticipated the drop in residential construction of the past two years. As noted earlier, the causal force leading to the shift of commitments to and then away from residential mortgages is the rigidity of government-insured and guaranteed mortgage interest rates in the face of changing capital market conditions.

One reservation about the predictive value of commitment data in this area is that we must assume that the commitments actually lead to construction. In the period under consideration the rate of attrition on residential mortgage commitments has generally been stable at about 10 per cent. Economic conditions (of which the rate of residential construction is a highly important part) have been such as to encourage builders and individuals to go through with construction plans after having received financing commitments. Possibly we shall encounter conditions which will bring a sharp increase in the rate of attrition on residential mortgage commitments.

Thirdly, forward investment commitment data are helpful in anticipating changes in business and industrial plant and equipment expenditures. Here data are much less conclusive than for residential construction, probably because of the greater complexity of the industrial and business financing market, but they suggest that forward commitment build-ups anticipated the plant and equipment boom of late 1952 and first half of 1953, as well as the boom of 1956 and 1957. However, the same reservation needs to be

343

made about the assumption of a continued low level in the rate of attrition on outstanding commitments.

In conclusion, commitment data can probably be useful in forecasting general business conditions. Their value can easily be exaggerated, but the possibilities are great enough to justify careful study of the forward commitment process about which we still know too little. In this connection there is a special aspect of the process which merits consideration. Those who have studied the direct placement of corporate securities on a forward commitment basis with life insurance companies, uninsured pension funds, and other investors are firmly convinced that this procedure lends encouragement to long-run planning of investment expenditures by business concerns, such as programs for pipeline expansions or large scale housing developments. There is, of course, no assurance that the rate of attrition on these programmed investments will not increase in the event of a recession. But the greater tendency toward long-range planning should contribute to the predictability and, perhaps, the stability of general business conditions.

COMMENT

SAUL B. KLAMAN, National Association of Mutual Savings Banks

As one who has previously had the privilege and responsibility of access to the data on investment commitments of life insurance companies, I am delighted that James O'Leary and the Life Insurance Association of America have decided to release the data publicly. This will enable users with varying interests to exchange views on the meaning and value of commitments figures in economic and financial analysis. And perhaps interest in the data will lead to improvements in reporting and coverage and stimulate other types of financial institutions to make similar information available.

As the first available analysis of investment commitments of life insurance companies, O'Leary's paper substantially advances our knowledge and understanding of the commitment technique and its use in various investment sectors. It tells us much about the behavior of the various types of new and outstanding commitments during a period of important changes in capital market conditions and in Federal Reserve and Treasury policies. It does not, however, provide much analysis of the relationship of commitments to investment flows and to capital formation, nor does it deal with the problems inherent in the commitment process itself, problems which bear directly on the usefulness of the figures in anticipating business developments. It is with such matters that my comments are mainly concerned.

Given the complex behavior of most economic variables, one cannot establish simple standards for judging the predictive value of any particular time series. Certain kinds of data, such as construction contract awards, are inherently endowed with predictive qualities. Other kinds have been found empirically to lead business activity more or less regularly.

The series on new and outstanding commitments of life insurance companies clearly belong in the former category in that they represent agreements to undertake certain kinds of investment just as contract awards represent future construction expenditures. In this framework, a fundamental question is whether the commitments data can indicate anything about the timing, volume, or direction of related investment and business activity, or whether they are useful chiefly as general guides to our understanding of a developing situation. The answer depends on analysis, within each of the various investment sectors, of relationships between new and outstanding commitments, flows of investment funds, and underlying capital formation and expenditures.

For a few areas where the commitment process generally plays an integral role and life insurance companies are an important source of funds—the nonfarm mortgage sector, VA and FHA loan markets, and the manufacturing component of the business securities sector—I have compared, on a quarterly basis, new and outstanding commitments with investment acquisitions of life insurance companies and with broader variables in related financial and product markets. The findings suggest that it is extremely hazardous to try to forecast quarterly or even annual movements in the flow of investment funds, expenditures, or physical volume, solely on the basis of movements in related commitments data in preceding periods.

There is no clear relationship, for example, either in timing or percentage change in volume, between life insurance company commitments to acquire VA loans, their actual acquisition of these loans, the total of all VA loans closed, or total housing starts under VA loans. If someone had used commitments data to predict the direction of change in various types of VA activity, he would have been right in more quarters than he would have been wrong, but he would seldom have been right in all types of activity in the same quarter. Timing patterns are unclear, but a time relationship seems to be more discernible in the comparison of outstanding VA commitments with VA starts than in the other mortgage loan categories tested or in the business finance category.

These comparisons are only a small sample of the kind of investigation which needs to be made on a continuing basis before firm conclusions can be drawn about the predictive value of data on life insurance company investment commitments. Many more relationships need to be examined, various lead and lag patterns tested, and the usefulness of commitment takedown ratios appraised. In some sectors the data may be useful for anticipating investment flows but not capital expenditures, in others for anticipating new work to be undertaken rather than dollar volume of investment. The determination of seasonal behavior, if any, in both new and outstanding commitments series would advance our knowledge and ability to use the data.

O'Leary noted one seasonal trend, an apparently "regular pattern for outstanding commitments to decline in December of each year, a pattern probably due to peculiarities in the operation of life insurance company investment departments." This is interesting in view of my findings about the operation of mortgage companies in a study recently published by the National Bureau.[1] I found a definite complementary relationship between changes in mortgage company inventories and changes in mortgage holdings of life insurance companies, which predominate as purchasers of loans from mortgage companies. The greatest increase in life insurance company mortgage holdings occurred consistently in the fourth quarter of each year, coincident with a regular decline, absolute or in rate of growth, in fourth-quarter holdings of mortgage companies. The implication is that life insurance companies draw down their outstanding commitments at the end of each year as they acquire mortgages from originators in accordance with commitments made earlier in the year.

UNCERTAINTIES INHERENT IN THE COMMITMENT PROCESS

One can hardly expect relationships between commitments of life insurance companies and investment flows and business expenditures to be precise, either in timing or in changes in activity. Variation in the number of life insurance companies included in the commitments series compared with the number in the investment acquisitions series accounts for some of the difference in movements between the two. However, the commitment process itself is subject to uncertainty and change in the lag between outstandings and takedowns, the rate of attrition, techniques employed, and relationship to cash flows. Consequently a given level of commitments in any one period may give rise to a varying pattern of capital investment and expenditures.

Improved data on expected takedowns and cancellations, available since 1957, may help to solve part of the problem. Comparison of expected and actual takedowns from commitments, however, shows considerable divergence, particularly in the mortgage loan categories. In the business securities sector, expected and actual takedowns are in much closer agreement, reflecting the greater certainty of the whole commitments–investment process in this area. In any event we need longer

[1] Saul B. Klaman, *The Postwar Rise of Mortgage Companies*, National Bureau of Economic Research, Occasional Paper 60, 1959.

experience with the new data on expected takedowns before we can fully evaluate their usefulness.

The uncertain meaning of commitments to acquire mortgages reflects the uncertainties of the mortgage and construction markets. For example:

1. Planned construction is sometimes deferred, or not undertaken, or frequently not completed on schedule.

2. The completed mortgage loan may be for a different amount than the commitment.

3. Commitments may not be taken up by borrowers either because they have obtained funds elsewhere on more favorable terms or because of otherwise changed plans.

Because of these and other uncertainties the life insurance companies themselves have difficulty calculating expected cash flows into mortgages.

The uncertainty which attaches to mortgage commitments is illustrated by the situation which developed in 1954 and 1955 when some companies found themselves overcommitted relative to anticipated cash flows. The resort to warehousing at commercial banks during 1955 while funds were accumulated changed the 1955 pattern of mortgage investment substantially from what might have been anticipated on the basis of 1954 and early 1955 commitments.

Translating commitments for corporate securities into cash flows is apparently simpler for insurance companies because arrangements for direct placements are generally more specific about date of payment than mortgage commitments. Also corporations usually carry through their scheduled plans for issuing securities. In contrast to the mortgage market, the use of commitments in the corporate securities area is often more an accommodation to the life insurance company than to the borrower.

The broader problem of anticipating developments in the corporate securities market and in plant and equipment expenditures is complicated by other factors. For one, much corporate financing, especially by public utilities, is done through public offerings, with commitments playing a minor role. When changes in corporate financing and expenditures reflect chiefly that type of offering, rather than direct placement, movements in the commitments figures may have little predictive value and even may be misleading. Secondly, even in the area of direct placement, lack of information on purpose of borrowing restricts the usefulness of the commitments data in anticipating capital expenditures. For example, a changing proportion of outstanding commitments may be associated with corporate borrowing to repay bank debt rather than to finance new expenditures.

The lack of commitments data from other financial institutions is another limiting factor. Shifts in anticipated investment flows from life insurance companies do not necessarily reflect the shifts of other investors. Indeed, when the entire investment community is considered, shifts in various areas may be offsetting. For example, when life insurance companies were pulling out of the VA market after the Federal Reserve–Treasury accord, savings banks were expanding their activities in it chiefly because VA yields were competitive with those on limited alternative investments in Eastern areas where most savings banks are located.

GENERAL USEFULNESS OF COMMITMENTS DATA

While commitments data are apparently of limited usefulness in forecasting changes in timing, volume, and even direction of related investment and business activity, they contribute to our understanding of a developing economic and financial situation. Most important is the direct insight given into the liquidity position and investment policies of life insurance companies and other financial intermediaries.

The volume of commitments outstanding for securities and mortgages relative to cash flows tells a good deal about the liquidity of an institutional investor and its maneuverability in capital markets. The relationship between outstanding commitments in the various investment sectors compared with past periods, and in the light of cash flows, may be indicative of the ability and willingness of companies to shift their investment programs in response to changing market developments. New commitments are more sensitive than outstandings, however, in reflecting current investment programs of life insurance companies, their reactions to changes in monetary and fiscal policies, and to economic developments generally. The timing of changes in new commitment volume, both in total and within investment sectors, may be a useful indicator of lags in the impact of monetary policy changes on capital markets.

Data on new and outstanding commitments are most useful when related to each other. The implication of changes in new commitments in the various investment sectors can be evaluated best only in relation to levels of outstanding commitments. An unusually large build-up of outstandings relative to past levels and to cash flows, for example, may foretell a decline or shift in new commitments and in investment flows almost irrespective of external market influences. We need to know more about the basic relationships to assess the significance of changes in them. Here internal company investment policies play a vital role and vary widely. Some companies like to maintain a certain portfolio balance. Others invest entirely according to yield and ignore any resulting "imbalances."

Because commitments have become such an integral part of the investment process, and because they often precede related investment flows by a year or more, such data have become almost essential for appraising current developments, apart from their usefulness as anticipations data. Whether changes in commitments reflect changes in the available supply of funds or in demands for funds by corporations, governments, and con-

348

sumers can never be established by statistics alone. The various series must be continually appraised in the light of all available knowledge relating to each sector and to financial and commodity markets generally. Regardless of the basic influences, however, clearly the availability of commitments data enhances our understanding of unfolding economic events.

PART IV

Capital Expenditures Forecasts by Individual Firms

ROBERT A. LEVINE
THE *RAND* CORPORATION

The initiation and development over the last decade of statistical series on capital expenditures anticipations of business came about largely because government and business urgently needed accurate short-run investment predictions. In spite of efforts by Clark, Klein, and others, existing series could not be adapted to this purpose.[1] Since there was little evidence that economists could make predictions on a behavioral basis, reasoning from economic magnitudes affecting investment to estimates of investment, recourse was had to businessmen themselves. In its purest form, the investment anticipations survey approach assumes that the businessman takes account of all relevant factors in making his prediction, and that the only task of the economist is to make correct use of sampling theory in deriving aggregate expenditure predictions from individual questionnaire answers. This is the general approach used by the Commerce Department–Securities and Exchange Commission survey, the McGraw–Hill survey, and the Canadian survey of capital expenditures.

Thus far the surveys have produced aggregate forecasts for a year in advance which have been, on the whole, very accurate. There have been many large errors, however, in the constituent company forecasts. These errors may be random in nature, or they may be caused systematically by outside economic factors, in which case they constitute a potential source of bias. The effects of a factor such as deviation of sales from expectations may have balanced out over the last decade, but this cancellation cannot necessarily be projected into the future.

NOTE: The author is indebted to William Fellner, James Tobin, Thomas Schelling, and Harold Watts of Yale University, who saw him through many earlier versions of this paper, and to Bernard Marks and Ralph Bristol of The RAND Corporation, who contributed many suggestions which aided in the preparation of the present version. Thanks are also due to Dexter Keezer of McGraw–Hill who made available the data on which the paper is based.

[1] Colin Clark, "A System of Equations Explaining the United States Trade Cycle, 1921-1941," *Econometrica*, April 1949, p. 93. Lawrence R. Klein, *Economic Fluctuations in the United States, 1921-1941*, Wiley, 1950.

351

The purpose of my paper is to investigate various possible systematic causes of errors in companies' investment predictions, and to suggest some methods whereby the analyst can correct for them, in order to avoid possible gross error in the aggregates. The adjustment of the individual firm's predictions might be carried out within a partially endogenous gross national product model so that at least some of the corrective factors used are estimates, based on the other equations of the model. The objective in this case would be to explain the deviations of actual from predicted investment, regardless of whether the factors causing these deviations occurred before or after the prediction. While this effort would certainly be an important step in the advancement of the science, it seems more urgent and useful at present to develop an adjustment procedure which can serve as a forecasting aid. Consequently the methods evolved here will use only the information available when the forecast is made.

Review of Survey Results

As indicated in Table 1, annual aggregate plant and equipment expenditures predicted by the Commerce–SEC and the McGraw–Hill surveys in the United States, and by the Department of Trade and Commerce survey in Canada, have come close to actual expenditures for 1947-54. The two United States surveys erred badly in 1947, and again in 1950 when business' plans were changed radically by the onset of the Korean war, but they have missed no cyclical turning points and have shown no systematic bias in either direction. Friend and Bronfenbrenner pointed out that the Commerce–SEC surveys have been giving better results than either a projection of actual capital expenditures for the previous year or a seasonally adjusted projection of actual expenditures for the first quarter of the year in question.[2] The Canadian survey tends to underpredict, and it missed the downturn in 1954, but the Canadian effort is more ambitious than ours. Questionnaire answers are gathered in December rather than in March, and cover not only nonfarm business but all public and private investment.

If the accuracy which has characterized the aggregate forecasts were based on accurate company forecasts, the surveys would probably continue to yield reliable results. Table 2 indicates that this is not the case. In the Commerce–SEC and the Canadian surveys close to half of the responding firms missed their predictions by 40 per cent or more. In the McGraw–Hill survey, where the better-predicting large companies are more strongly represented, not quite half of the respondents missed by 30 per cent or more. This individual company inaccuracy is the root of

---

[2] Irwin Friend and Jean Bronfenbrenner, "Plant and Equipment Programs and Their Realization," *Short-Term Economic Forecasting*, Studies in Income and Wealth, Vol. 17, Princeton University Press for National Bureau of Economic Research, 1955, p. 60.

CAPITAL EXPENDITURES FORECASTS BY FIRMS

TABLE 1

Comparison of Actual and Forecast Investment, 1947-1954
(*U.S. and Canadian dollar figures in billions*)

	ACTUAL U.S. INVEST-MENT	COMMERCE–SEC *Fore-cast*	*Error*[a]	MCGRAW–HILL *Fore-cast*	*Error*[a]	ACTUAL CANADIAN INVEST-MENT	CANADA *Fore-cast*	*Error*[a]
YEAR	*(1)*	*(2)*	*(3)*	*(4)*	*(5)*	*(6)*	*(7)*	*(8)*
1947	$20.6	$17.6	+16%			$2.5	$2.6	−3%
1948	22.1	21.4	+3			3.2	3.1	+4
1949	19.3	19.5	−1	$20.1	−4%	3.5	3.4	+2
1950	20.6	17.5	+15	18.5	+10	3.8	3.6	+5
1951	25.6	26.2	−2	24.4	+4	4.6	4.3	+7
1952	26.5	26.2	+1	26.2	+1	5.3	5.2	+2
1953	28.4	27.0	+5	29.0	−2	5.8	5.6	+4
1954	26.7	27.2	−2	27.2	−2	5.5	5.9	−8

[a] Departure of actual investment from forecast.
Source: Col. 1—*Economic Reports of the President*, 1947-1954. Col. 2—Computed from cols. 1 and 3, since published forecasts are not comparable in dollar terms to published fulfillments, due to annual change of base. Col. 3—1947-52 from Irwin Friend and Jean Bronfenbrenner, "Plant and Equipment Programs and Their Realization," in *Short-Term Economic Forecasting*, Studies in Income and Wealth, Vol. 17, Princeton University Press for National Bureau of Economic Research, 1955, p. 59. 1953-54 from mimeographed report of Louis J. Paradiso, Dept. of Commerce, to George Terborgh, Chairman of Federal Reserve Committee on Plant and Equipment Expenditures, 1955, Table 1. Col. 4—computed from cols. 1 and 5. Col. 5—1949-53 from "Planned versus Actual," unpublished McGraw–Hill Dept. of Economics paper. 1954 from change of actual investment in col. 1 and predicted change of investment in *Business' Plans for New Plant and Equipment, 1954-57*, McGraw–Hill, 1954. Col. 6—from *Public and Private Investment in Canada, Outlook*, Dept. of Trade and Commerce, Ottawa, annual series, 1946-54. Col. 7—computed from cols. 6 and 8. Col. 8—1947-51 from O. J. Firestone, "Investment Forecasting in Canada," in *Short-Term Economic Forecasting*, p. 231. 1952-54 computed from col. 6 and from forecast data in *Public and Private Investment in Canada, Outlook*.

the problem. If null hypotheses denying the relationship of individual company predictive errors to other economic factors cannot be rejected, the predictive errors probably represent random drawings from a population with a mean at zero error. If the individuals filling out the questionnaire are careless or too low in the hierarchies of their firms to have full knowledge, this might occur. With the large number of random drawings represented by a sample in the thousands, there would be little chance of aggregate error. If, however, some null hypotheses are rejected, then corrections should be made for the systematic effects of the economic magnitudes represented by these hypotheses.

Data Employed

The method illustrated in the section below entitled "Statistical Findings" is just that—an illustration of a method. The data used had too

353

TABLE 2

Frequency Distribution of Percentage Deviations of Actual from
Forecast Investment, by Percentage of Firms, Selected Years

PERCENTAGE ERROR[a]	MCGRAW–HILL 1949	MCGRAW–HILL 1954	COMMERCE–SEC 1949	CANADA 1949	CANADA 1950
More than −100			0	0	0
−100 to −80			3.0	9.6	9.8
−79.9 to −60	9.5	3.3	3.5	6.5	5.4
−59.9 to −50			7.5	7.2	7.4
−49.9 to −40	7.5	6.2			
−39.9 to −3C	6.1	6.6	12.5	6.9	6.4
−29.9 to −20	8.2	7.3			
−19.9 to −10	8.8	16.0	14.7	5.9	3.6
−9.9 to 0	6.8	12.4			
0 to 9.9	15.6	16.4	12.8[b]	20.8[b]	21.0[b]
10 to 19.9	7.5	6.2			
20 to 29.9	6.8	5.9	11.6	5.6	4.8
30 to 39.9	2.7	2.6			
40 to 49.9	4.1	4.8	6.8	4.2	4.3
50 to 59.9					
60 to 79.9			3.7	3.3	2.6
80 to 99.9	16.3	12.4	2.9	2.2	1.7
100 to 199.9			9.0	7.7	8.2
200 and over			12.0	20.1	24.8
Total	100.0	100.0	100.0	100.0	100.0

[a] Departure of actual investment from forecast.

[b] It is not known whether the Commerce–SEC firms with no change are in the −19.9 to 0 or the 0 to 19.9 category. For the Canadian data these companies are in the latter category. For the McGraw–Hill data they are in 0 to 9.9.

Source: Commerce–SEC data from Irwin Friend and Jean Bronfenbrenner, "Plant and Equipment Programs and Their Realization," *Short-Term Economic Forecasting*, Studies in Income and Wealth, Vol. 17, Princeton University Press for National Bureau of Economic Research, 1955, p. 65. Canadian data from O. J. Firestone, "Investment Forecasting in Canada," *Short-Term Economic Forecasting*, p. 208. McGraw–Hill data computed by the author from raw data. The latter refer to manufacturing and non-manufacturing firms; other data cover manufacturing only.

many deficiencies for it to be claimed that any definitive answers are given to either the question of what specific factors should be corrected for in improving the accuracy of the surveys or the question of what is the mathematical effect of these factors. What is suggested is that those, particularly the surveying organizations themselves, who have access to more and better data, might do well to try this method or a similar one to determine these specific factors and to improve the accuracy of their results.

The data used to test the effect of certain factors on individual firm forecasts were answers to certain of the questions asked by the early winter surveys by 409 companies which were selected from the McGraw–Hill sample. The questions and the years when they were asked are:

1. Size of company by employment (1949-54). (To avoid individual company identification, they were grouped into five size classes in the data given the author.)

2. Actual capital expenditures in the previous year and planned capital expenditures in the current year (1949-54)

3. Actual sales in the previous year (1952-54) and expected sales in the current year (1954)

4. Expected percentage sales change for the company over the next three years (1952-54)

5. Expected percentage sales change for the industry over the next three years (1952-53)

6. Actual percentage capacity change in the previous year (1950-54) and expected percentage capacity change in the current year (1951-54)

7. Actual breakdown of investment into expansion and replacement in the previous year and expected breakdown of investment into expansion and replacement in the current year (1950-54).

From the McGraw–Hill sample 409 companies were selected, but not all of the companies answered all the questions in any one year.

McGraw–Hill could not identify the responding companies by name or industry without violating its pledge of secrecy to the respondents. Had identification been possible, the questionnaire data could have been supplemented with published balance sheets, stock market reports, and other information which would have given a better picture of the economic pressures affecting the firms. The deficiencies due to the lack of identification were threefold:

1. The lack of data on company assets posed a major problem since, in discussing investment by individual firms, it is necessary to express the dollar figures in terms of firm size. I was forced to divide each firm's annual investment by its mean investment for the six years covered. This gives variations from the six-year norm for individual firms, but company investment was probably high relative to fixed assets throughout this period. The deficiency does not affect the equations below which describe factors bearing on the fulfillment ratio of actual to predicted investment, since the ratio comes predeflated. It does affect the attempt to predict actual investment by use of predicted investment and other factors.

2. The questionnaires give no information about liquidity or profits, variables which could be expected to have an important effect on company behavior.

3. No differentiation could be made among respondents by industry.

The data are also deficient in the time period covered. The relatively prosperous years from 1949 to 1954 do not provide an adequate sample of the economic conditions under which companies may have to forecast.

Furthermore, while information on investment forecasts and fulfillments was gathered every year, information on factors which serve as explanatory variables in the analysis was gathered over even shorter time spans. For example, data on actual sales in the previous year were requested only from 1952 to 1954, and expected sales in the current year, only for 1954. Since sales change rather than level of sales is the relevant variable, there are only two usable years of actual sales change and only one of expected change. The data deficiencies obviously make it impossible to apply the equations and parameters developed below directly to the task of improving investment forecasts.

Method of Approach

DEFINITIONS

Strictly speaking, the "accuracy" of a firm's investment predictions defines the closeness of the predictions to actual investment. Accuracy is measured by the proximity of the ratio of actual investment to predicted investment, which I call the "fulfillment ratio," to unity. A 0.95 ratio represents the same degree of inaccuracy as a 1.05 ratio.

Since we are concerned with systematic causes which may bias predictions, we are interested in the direction as well as the size of error. To take account of this, we can define a company's "fulfillment" or "realization" of its anticipated investment as the degree to which it carries through the investment. Fulfillment is measured by the value of the fulfillment ratio, and a 0.95 ratio is, under this definition, of a different character from a 1.05 ratio. The differentiation between accuracy and fulfillment of company predictions is important because the two are not necessarily affected by the same variables. For example, in 1949, predictions of capital expenditures on new equipment were considerably more accurate than predictions of expenditures on new plant in the United States.[3] However, 41.7 per cent of the firms invested less in equipment than anticipated, while 41.8 per cent invested less in plant, indicating no difference between the two categories so far as fulfillment is concerned.

Of more importance is the distinction between "plans" and "anticipations." The two words are not interchangeable, but they are sometimes used interchangeably by the surveying organizations. The Commerce–SEC survey requests "anticipated" expenditures but goes on to explain, "For 'anticipated expenditures' show estimates of cost which according to present *planning* will be incurred during the specified period" (my italics). The definition of the verb, "plan" is "to devise or project a method or a course of action." The difficulty is that a company official may expect, when he fills out his questionnaire, an investment outlay which has not yet reached the status of a projected course of action, the more so because

[3] Friend and Bronfenbrenner, Table 6, p. 75.

planning in a large company may be a fairly formal procedure. The fact of this ambiguity is borne out by the statement of the Federal Reserve Committee on Plant and Equipment Expenditure Expectations that "there is a tendency toward systematic understatement in the plans reported by business, apparently as the result of the partial omission of small or uncertain items."[4] Since the omission of uncertain items is considered an understatement, evidently what is meant by "plans" is "best-guess anticipation." The McGraw–Hill survey asks, "How much do you now plan to invest?" In the past the published aggregate forecasts tended to treat the plans as if they were anticipations, but more recently, this mis-interpretation has been corrected.[5]

The issue here is one of certainty, which may be the key to individual company realization of forecast investment. At the moment the investment questionnaire is filled out, the firm will have in mind for the period concerned various investment projects, to which are attached differing degrees of certainty. The firmest are those for which contracts have already been let. Those which have passed through the formal planning and budgeting process (which differs widely among companies) may also be considered relatively firm. However even for the next year there remains a residue of projects which, while nebulous, nevertheless have a probability greater than zero of being carried out. The difficulty with the wording of the investment questionnaires is that they fail to make clear to the respondents whether they call for answers about projects which have reached a particular stage in company planning or best guesses on total investment.

ADJUSTMENT PROCEDURE

The character of the estimates received by a survey determines the approach used in adjusting the forecast. If the plans concept is used and is well-enough defined so that both questioner and respondent know what sort of plans should be reported (e.g. plans on which contracts have been let or plans provided for in the budget), then the investigator may correct the plans for systematic factors causing deviations from expected expenditures on planned projects, and add his own estimate of investment projects which will take place but have not yet reached the stage of hard plans. If anticipations are requested and it is made clear that what is desired is the best guess at total investment expenditures, no matter what projects have reached what stage in present budgeting and planning, then the

---

[4] *Hearings before the Subcommittee on Economic Statistics*, Joint Committee on the Economic Report, 84th Cong., 1st sess., 1955, p. 33.

[5] Compare the statement accompanying the 1954 forecasts that "Manufacturing industries expect to spend $12.3 billion" (*Business Plans for Plants and Equipment*, McGraw–Hill, 1953, p. 3) with the statement in 1956 that "This new McGraw–Hill survey . . . isn't a forecast but an objective report on what companies say they're now planning for the future" (*Business Week*, May 19, 1956, p. 23).

investigator will correct for factors he may think will affect fulfillment, but he will not add any estimates of other projects. Either concept can be used as a basis for forecasts of aggregate investment.

Since McGraw–Hill uses the plans rather than the anticipations concept, the procedure below both corrects and adds estimates of unplanned investment. I do this, however, with trepidation, since it is by no means clear that the respondents understood what sort of plans they were to report. The statistical results indicate that the division between the planned and unplanned portions of investment is by no means sharp.

MATHEMATICAL RELATIONSHIPS

In my discussion, the following symbols are used:
I = one year gross dollar investment by one firm.
γ = proportion of investment projects planned comparatively firmly.

Subscripts:

a   means that the investment in question is the actual investment for the year in question.

p   means that the investment is the business firm's prediction for the year in question, the prediction appearing on the survey questionnaire at the beginning of the same year.

π means that the investment is that which the firm has planned.

i   means that the planning referred to by the use of π has taken place before the questionnaire is filled out. This is the portion of investment which is comparatively certain at questionnaire time.

ii   means that the planning in question has not occurred until after the questionnaire.

    i and ii are used only in conjunction with π.

Superscripts:

t   is the year in which the investment actually takes place, is predicted to take place, or is planned to take place.

Then

(1-A) $I_a^t = \gamma I_{\pi i}^t + I_{\pi i i}^t$

(1-B) $I_p^t = I_{\pi i}^t$

Equation 1-A states that the actual investment taking place during a year is the sum of some proportion, γ, of the investment projects planned comparatively firmly for that year up to the time of the survey questionnaire; plus the investment which has entered into plans after the questionnaire. Since investment "projects" may be thought of in terms of physical capital rather than money expenditures, p may be less than unity if the previously planned projects turn out to be less elaborate than had been thought. It may be greater if the reverse is true. The coefficient of investment planned after the questionnaire is assumed to be one because the lag time between planning and execution is short enough to preclude changes from plans during the period. Equation 1-B is an identity stating that under the conditions of the McGraw–Hill survey, the business firm records as its prediction the investment which has been planned at the time of the questionnaire.

Substituting (B) into (A), we get:

$$(2) \qquad I_a^t = \gamma I_p^t + I_{\pi ii}^t$$

which states that actual investment during the year t will be some number, γ, times the investment predicted by the company on the questionnaire, plus investment "planned" after the questionnaire.

In the past the surveys have either not attempted to predict I_a^t or have used I_p^t as the best approximation. In the following sections, an attempt is made to discover variables which may affect γ and $I_{\pi ii}^t$. Versions of these variables, which will be available to the investigator at the time that he receives his filled-out questionnaires, are then used together with I_p^t to obtain an improved estimate of I_a^t, by a multiple regression technique.

Statistical Findings

In the statistical work below, each observation is on one company for one year. The symbols used in the equations in this section are as follows:

I = one year gross dollar investment by one firm.

S = one year dollar sales for one firm.

ΔC = one year per cent capacity change for one firm.

Co = one firm's expectation of three year per cent change in its own sales.

Ind = one firm's expectation of three year per cent change in its industry's sales.

ΔGNP = one year per cent change in money gross national product (computed from *Economic Reports of the President*, 1956).

Superscripts:

3, 4, 5, 6   mean that the magnitude in question occurred during or was predicted for 1953, 1954, 1955, 1956.

t means that the magnitude in question occurred during or was predicted for several different years within this particular equation.

m means that the value is the arithmetic mean of the magnitude for the individual firm for as many years out of six as the magnitude was reported.

359

Subscripts:

a　　means that the magnitude in question is an actual or fulfilled one.

p　　means that the magnitude in question is a predicted one.

3, 4　for predicted magnitudes means that the prediction was made at the beginning of 1953, 1954.

t　　for predicted magnitudes means that predictions made in several years were considered within this particular equation.

Thus, I_a^t refers to actual annual investment in several years, not distinguishing among observations on different years, while $Co_{p4}^{4\text{-}6}$ refers to the company's early 1954 prediction of its own sales change from 1954 to 1956.

FACTORS AFFECTING PLANNED INVESTMENT

To avoid as much as possible the problem of having to deflate investment figures by dividing by the six-year mean of investment for the firm, the investigation of the factors which might affect γ was carried on by using regressions of hypothesized explanatory variables against the fulfillment ratio, I_a^t/I_p^t, rather than by using these same variables in regressions of I_a^t/I_a^m against I_p^t/I_a^m. If κ is significant in the relationship $I_a^t/I_p^t = \kappa x_1$, there is at least a presumption that it will be significant in a relationship $I_a^t/I_a^m = \kappa(I_p^t/I_a^m)(x_1)$. Since we are now looking for factors which might be useful in the ultimate predicting equation, this presumption suffices. The very low coefficients of multiple determination in some of the equations below also suffice since they are significant by an F test for the large samples used, and no conclusions are drawn on the basis of these equations alone. The coefficient of the final predicting equation is considerably higher.

That errors in investment predictions should be related to errors in sales anticipations seems a reasonable hypothesis. However, the hypothesis could not be confirmed on the basis of the available data. Only 1954 data were available on predicted sales. No significant connection could be discovered between the variables I_a^4/I_{p4}^4 and S_a^4/S_{p4}^4 either in simple or multiple relationships. However, a significant relationship was discovered between accuracy of sales prediction and the fulfillment ratio for change of capacity, a magnitude closely related to the investment fulfillment ratio. The equation is:

(3)　　　　　$\Delta C_a^4/\Delta C_{p4}^4 = -0.4074 + 1.6083\ S_a^4/S_{p4}^4$

　　F ratio for equation with 1 and 160 degrees of freedom $= 5.7295$

　　R^2 for equation $= 0.0358$

The relationship, although not strong, is statistically significant. While it is of little use in formulating predictions of investment expenditures, it suggests that with large and better bodies of data, the null hypothesis that S_a^t/S_p^t has no effect on I_a^t/I_p^t might be rejected.

Other studies, as well as a previous investigation of mine, suggested that size of company had an effect on the company's fulfillment of planned investment, the smaller firms tending to underpredict and the larger coming closer to perfect prediction.[6] Therefore, another independent variable investigated was company size as measured by number of employees. Data were available in five employment size classes rather than as a continuous variate. I therefore included it in the regression by computing a separate constant term for each of the five classes. The explanation of the variance of the dependent variable, I_a^t/I_p^t, stemming from this technique was tested and found to be significant.

Annual change in sales might also affect the fulfillment ratio and the γ of equation 2 if, as hypothesized above, γ measures in some sense the manner in which a more firmly planned project is carried out. New plant and equipment may be currently planned for next year, but may be more or less elaborate depending on the movement of sales. To put this concept into the terminology of economic theory, it may be certain that a company is operating too far to the right on its short-run average and marginal cost curves, and that therefore some move to a new point on the long-run average cost curve is necessary. The particular point on the long-run curve may be determined on the basis of next year's sales or the trend indicated by next year's sales. Provisions for adaptability and flexibility may depend on the sales change or its trend.[7] Unfortunately, annual sales change data were available only for 1952-53 and 1953-54, and their use would have entailed discarding the statistics on investment fulfillment ratios for 1949-52. Therefore I assumed that change in GNP measures to some extent sales change for all firms. This assumption is not used in the final predicting equation but in the preliminary equation 4, annual change of GNP is used as a variable applied equally to the observations on all firms for a given year.

Finally, it seems reasonable to hypothesize that firms which are growing rapidly will over-fulfill their investment predictions more often than those expanding more slowly. Companies anxious to expand predict investment on the basis of expected constraints and then put more money in if the constraints are less oppressive than anticipated. The inclusion of some measure of company growth may substitute for the liquidity variables excluded from the analysis, since liquidity is an important constraint of the type mentioned. Mean capacity change over the six years was used to

---

[6] See, for example, Friend and Bronfenbrenner, Table 4, p. 70, and Robert A. Levine, "Plant and Equipment Expenditures Surveys, Intentions and Fulfillments," Cowles Foundation Discussion Paper 17, mimeographed, October 26, 1956, Table 1, p. 105.

[7] George Stigler, "Production and Distribution in the Short Run," *Journal of Political Economy*, June 1939, p. 305.

estimate this growth pressure. The major reason for using mean rather than annual capacity change was statistical. Change in capacity in a given year is closely related to actual investment in the same year, but the investment is the numerator of the dependent variable in the regression. Therefore the use of the annual capacity change figure would probably lead to some spurious correlation.

Thus, the three variables tested and found significant are: company size as measured by employment; annual percentage change in money GNP, applied to all companies in a given year; and mean percentage change in capacity, applied to all years for a given company. It must be emphasized that many other variables might have proved useful, had they been available in the data.

The equation as estimated is:

$$(4) \qquad I_a^t/I_{pt}^t = \begin{matrix} 1.0249 \\ 1.1690 \\ 1.1612 \\ 1.0154 \\ 0.8622 \end{matrix} \begin{pmatrix} \text{Firms employing } 0\text{--}500 \\ 500\text{--}1{,}000 \\ 1{,}000\text{--}5{,}000 \\ 5{,}000\text{--}10{,}000 \\ \text{more than } 10{,}000 \end{pmatrix} + 2.0350\Delta GNP^t + 0.0700\Delta C^m$$

F ratio for equation with 6 and 911 degrees of freedom = 8.8738

R^2 for equation = 0.0552

The constant term of 0.8622 for the largest companies would put them close to perfect prediction for years in which GNP increases by about 5 per cent. The smaller companies tend to underpredict (over-fulfill), probably because they engage in less detailed advance planning. There seems no good explanation for the better prediction on the part of the smallest firms. The signs on the coefficients of the other two variables are as postulated above.

FACTORS AFFECTING ADDITIONAL INVESTMENT

The McGraw–Hill data on actual investment did not differentiate between investment projects planned before and after the date of the predicting questionnaires. Therefore the investigation of variables which might estimate the less firmly expected investment, I_{mii}^t, was carried on under the assumption that factors affecting total investment would also affect the specific portion in question. Since no conclusions are drawn from equation 5 alone, the complete validity of the assumption is not vital. The factors available for testing were limited to various accelerator-type sales change variables. I have elsewhere discussed the method of approach, the different variables tested, and some general conclusions relevant to investment theory.[8] I discovered that the equation which

[8] Levine, p. 121.

explains the greatest portion of the variance of one-year investment (divided by mean investment for the firm for reasons discussed above) is:

(5) $\qquad I_a^4/I_a^m = 1.0384 + 1.2159Co_{p\,4}^{4\text{-}6} - 1.5621Ind_{p\,3}^{3\text{-}5}.$

F ratio for equation with 2 and 97 degrees of freedom $= 12.0655$

R^2 for equation $= 0.1992$

Only 1954 data were available for the *Co* and *Ind* variables with the proper lags.

It is important to note that the company's expectations of its own three-year sales change was significant in a simple regression against investment as well as in the multiple relationship, while company expectations of industry sales change was valid only in the multiple computation. It would therefore appear that there is an accelerator relationship between investment and a firm's longer-run sales expectations, but the accelerator is qualified by the expected change of the company's position within its industry. As between two companies which expect the same change in industry sales, the one which expects the greater increase in its own sales will invest more heavily. This conforms to an accelerator hypothesis. However, as between two companies expecting the same change in their own sales, the one expecting to increase relative to its industry will invest more than the one expecting to increase only with its industry.

Here the certainty hypothesis again enters. If a firm is to invest on the basis of sales or other expectations, the investment plans will be firmer, the more certain are the expectations. In the case in point, the firm expecting its sales to increase relative to its industry probably has a better reason for the expectation—a new product or a new sales campaign, for example, than the firm expecting its sales to move up with its industry's. The accelerator component is still present, as evidenced by the positive coefficient of $Co_{p\,4}^{4\text{-}6}$, but the funds invested depend not only on the best guess at expected sales change, but also on the confidence the company has in this guess.

THE PREDICTING EQUATION

In the predicting equation certain changes were made in some of the variables which were found to affect the relationships between actual and planned investment; and in some of those which by affecting total investment indicated that they might also bear a relationship to that portion of investment not yet planned at questionnaire time. The equation was derived from 1954 investment data alone because several of the relevant variables were available only for this year. Since the number of available observations is 90, compared to the 918 in equation 4 for six years of investment, I had to group the data into three rather than five employment classes. In addition, the company growth variable of equation 4, ΔC^m, was found not to add significant explanation in this equation and was dropped out.

Finally, expected sales change for the individual firm for 1953-54 was substituted for the actual GNP change which was inserted into equation 4. Change in GNP could, of course, not be used in an equation using one year of data, since it would have the same value for each observation. I could have substituted actual 1953-54 sales change had I not decided to estimate the equation using only variables available to the analyst at the time of the survey.

It may seem strange that expected sales, a variable reported at the same time as the firm's investment forecast, could explain changes from predicted investment. A first guess might be that *deviations* from expected sales would be a more likely choice, but as shown above these deviations did not have a statistically significant effect. Expected sales is not meant here as a substitute for deviations, but rather the expected sales change variable may sort firms out according to how badly they want to invest in the year in question. A company, in recording its investment predictions, either assumes a certain ability to raise funds or ignores liquidity conditions and assumes that funds will be available as desired. When the question of actually obtaining the investment funds comes up, however, some firms may be unwilling to pay the price and will therefore revise their investment plans.

The sales change variable used here implies that the companies with the most rapid expected sales increases will be the most willing to pay the necessary price for the funds and therefore the most likely to fulfill their plans. This variable may therefore take account of some of the liquidity factors otherwise ignored.

In equation 6 the value of the coefficient of this variable is fairly high (0.8155) and is quite significant (standard error of 0.0863) for 1954, a year of comparatively easy liquidity. The coefficient will not have the same value for all years, since it depends on a complex interaction of actual and expected liquidity. The use of this variable with its coefficient expected to shift from year to year does not conform completely to the objective of formulating an equation which can be used directly at the time for forecast without calling upon the analyst to estimate separately the values of the relevant variables, but it is a valuable forecasting aid.[9]

The predicting equation, estimated by multiplying the variables within the brackets by $I_{p_4}^4/I_a^m$, and using multiple regression on the resulting linear function is:

[9] A variable of this sort (or, preferably, a better variable expressing the effects of liquidity), may, when estimated for a range of years, perform a valuable service by giving different investment forecasts for different levels of liquidity and therefore giving useful information to those who try to affect the level of investment by use of monetary policy.

$$(6) \quad I_a^4/I_a^m = \left[\begin{matrix} +0.0561 \\ -0.1118 \\ -0.1385 \end{matrix} \begin{pmatrix} \text{Firms employing } 0\text{–}5,000 \\ 5,000\text{–}10,000 \\ \text{more than } 10,000 \end{pmatrix} + 0.8155 S_{p4}^4/S_a^3 \atop (0.0863) \right] I_{p4}^4/I_a^m$$

$$+ 0.2022 + 0.7962 Co_{p4}^{4\cdot6} - 0.5940 Ind_{p3}^{3\cdot5}$$
$$(0.2434) \qquad\qquad (0.2523)$$

F ratio for equation (6 and 83 degrees of freedom) = 21.5647
R^2 for equation = 0.6087
F ratio for comparison of this equation with $I_a^4/I_a^m = I_{p4}^4/I_a^m$ (7 and 83 degrees of freedom) = 4.8656
R^2 for $I_a^4/I_a^m = I_{p4}^4/I_a^m = 0.4489$

Despite the imperfections of the data employed, this equation explains 15 per cent more of the variance of actual investment by individual firms than does the equation $I_a^4/I_a^m = I_{p4}^4/I_a^m$, which uses the firms' answers to the investment surveys without any adjustment.

The computations do not, however, confirm the certainty theory I outlined. Under the hypothesis of equation 2, the part of equation 6 within the brackets would represent γ, the relationship between predicted expenditures on the comparatively certain portion of investment planned by the time of the questionnaire, and actual expenditures on the same portion. The part of the equation beginning with the constant term, 0.2022, would then estimate $I_{\pi ii}^t$, the investment expenditures which were less certain at the time of the questionnaire. A simple example shows that these two portions of investment are not separable statistically as easily as they are conceptually. A company employing 5,000-10,000 persons, predicting investment 10 per cent greater than its mean, expecting annual sales increases of 5 per cent (implying a 15.76 per cent increase over the three-year period), and expecting a three-year industry sales increase of 10 per cent, will actually invest 8.2 per cent more than its mean.

This seems reasonable. However, the value of γ would be about 0.74, while $I_{\pi ii}^t$ would be about 25 per cent of total investment, indicating that the firm would reduce expenditures on the more certain projects by about a quarter, while a quarter of final total investment would be on the less certain portion. Not only for the particular example shown here, but also for most of the range of likely values for the independent variables, this interpretation of the two parts of equation 6 would have firms sharply reducing their money expenditures on the certain investment projects planned before the questionnaire and then planning a large portion of investment later on. The two portions of the equation evidently do not represent unambiguously the two hypothesized portions of fulfilled investment.

The hypothesis about planned and unplanned investment is not denied, but the difficulty or impossibility of testing it on the basis of data now available is indicated. The various surveys do not produce data which touch all of a company's investment. Because of the lack of precise definition of the information desired, they also do not produce data on a company's most certain plans alone. It would help us to understand what it is that we are receiving in the annual investment surveys if each firm were requested to answer two investment intentions questions, one on plans which had entered the budget at time of questionnaire and the other on additional expected investment.

Perhaps the major factor ignored in the investment anticipations surveys and in past analyses of them is the question of uncertainty. Some portions of investment are more certain at any given instant than are others, and there is no reason to believe that all portions are affected by the same factors in the same manner. Similarly, some companies' expectations of sales changes are more firmly grounded than others, and there is no reason to believe, in discussing accelerator-like sales-investment effects, that both certain and uncertain sales increases will affect investment in the same way. The consumer surveys of the Survey Research Center have for some time been inquiring not only what the consumer expects to buy, but how strong is the expectation. The investment anticipations surveys should at least try to do as much.

Because of data deficiencies it cannot be claimed that equation 6 is a final predicting equation which can be used by surveying organizations for better prediction. Nevertheless the equation, with all of its imperfections, explained significantly more of the variance of actual investment by individual firms than did the individual firms' own answers to the surveying questionnaires. It clearly indicates that the factors causing the wide variation in company fulfillment ratios illustrated in Table 2 above are not random in nature. Certain of the variables isolated, particularly those representing various sales change expectations, are ones that could severely bias both the individual company forecasts and the aggregates at some crucial turning point in the business cycle. Therefore it would seem worthwhile for those who have access to better and larger bodies of data to undertake a similar study and to obtain a predicting equation which could be used directly for the improvement of forecasts.

C O M M E N T

ROBERT EISNER, Northwestern University

Investment anticipations, as reported on survey questionnaires, are based upon the conditions existing at the time the anticipations are formed and on expectations about future conditions. To the extent that new information becomes available to the respondents and that their plans are flexible, realizations (actual expenditures) may differ from anticipations. The mere confirmation by actual sales and profits of previously uncertain expectations may lead to an increase in expenditures. Thus, if we know the initial conditions and expectations embodied in reported plans or anticipations, we should be able to predict how the plans will be affected by developing information. We should be able to make similar adjustments on the basis of independent forecasts of how conditions and expectations are likely to change as a result, say, of new governmental policies not reflected in the business plans. Tentative confirmation of the usefulness of this approach may be found in data provided by the 1949-50 McGraw–Hill capital expenditure surveys and related financial statements.

From the 1949 surveys I took capital expenditure plans for 1950 and the expected percentage change in dollar volume of sales (for the firm), 1949-50. The 1950 survey told me how much the firm's capital expenditures in 1950 actually were. Income statements and balance sheets yielded 1949 gross fixed assets (used to relate expenditures to the size of firm), and actual sales in 1948, 1949, and 1950. I was thus able to define the following variables:

I = 1950 actual capital expenditures divided by 1949 gross fixed assets.

K = 1950 capital expenditures anticipated in 1949, divided by 1949 gross fixed assets.

A = Actual percentage change in sales, 1948-49.

B = Actual percentage change in sales, 1949-50.

C = Expected percentage change in sales, 1949-50, as indicated in the fall of 1949.

Since virtually no correlation was found between sales expectations and capital expenditure anticipations, as defined above, there remained a consideration of the effect upon capital expenditures of changes in sales which occurred after capital expenditure anticipations were indicated. The prime test here was the improvement of the correlation by adding actual sales changes after anticipations to the linear regression relating actual and anticipated expenditures. The results follow.

The simple or zero order correlation between capital expenditures and anticipations (as deflated by gross fixed assets) was $r_{IK} = 0.685$; the value of r_{IK}^2 was 0.469. But the first order partial correlation between actual capital expenditures and previous sales change, with capital expenditure anticipations in the regression, was $r_{IA.K} = 0.370$. And the second order partial correlation between capital expenditures and current sale change, with anticipations and previous sales change in the regression, was $r_{IB.KA} = 0.396$. Since r_{IC} was only slightly positive and r_{KC} was almost zero, current sales change (B) showed almost as high a partial correlation with actual capital expenditure (I) when prior expectations of that sales change (C) were included in the regression; $r_{IB.KCA} = 0.360$. Thus the multiple correlation of capital expenditures with capital expenditure anticipations *and* current and previous sales changes was $R_{I.BKA} = 0.783$ and the value of $R_{I.KBA}^2$ was 0.613. Since $r_{IK}^2 = 0.469$, the addition of these sales change variables explains some 27 per cent of the variance in capital expenditures left unaccounted for by the anticipatory data.[1]

From the standpoint of forecasting, several observations are appropriate. First, the information on 1948-49 sales changes became available after anticipated 1950 capital expenditures were reported, but before these expenditures were carried out. Therefore, the information could have been used to improve predictions of 1950 investment. Second, information on the 1949-50 change in sales began to accumulate early in 1950, at least to the extent of permitting comparisons between the first and second quarters of the two years. With the commencement of the Korean war in June 1950 the analyst might well have predicted that the total volume of sales would substantially exceed that of the previous year—the actual outcome. It should then have been possible to add estimates of sales changes to the regression (or regressions, for firms categorized by industry or other relevant characteristics), to improve further the forecasting value of the original anticipations.

Of course, ex post knowledge of correlation does not help us to forecast unless we have estimates of regression coefficients that can be used before actual expenditures are realized. However, the positive correlations and regression coefficients derived for the 1948-50 period, as relating to 1950 investment, are consistent with appropriate theoretical models and in particular a sophisticated version of the acceleration principle, involving distributed lags and the relation of output to capacity. It is therefore possible that reliable estimates of fairly stable parameters of an investment "realization" function can be obtained. I am engaged currently in an investigation of the McGraw–Hill capital expenditure surveys data of 1949 to 1957 and related collateral statistics on an individual firm basis, in the hope of discovering such parameters.

---

[1] I reported on this procedure more fully in "Expectations, Plans and Capital Expenditures," in *Expectations, Uncertainty and Business Behavior*, Mary Jean Bowman, ed., Social Science Research Council, 1958, pp. 165-188.

Observations on the Predictive Quality of McGraw–Hill Surveys of Business' Plans for New Plants and Equipment

DEXTER M. KEEZER, ROBERT P. ULIN,
DOUGLAS GREENWALD, AND MARGARET MATULIS

MCGRAW–HILL PUBLISHING COMPANY

Over their ten-year history, the McGraw–Hill surveys of business' plans for investment in new plants and equipment have been remarkably successful in predicting actual performance in this field. The mere making of these surveys seems to have stimulated longer-range investment planning and improved the accuracy of estimates of future capital expenditures.

Of course, their reliability has yet to be thoroughly tested since the past ten years have been characterized by unusual circumstances, including a sustained investment boom. However, their value has been sufficiently well established to make it foolhardy for anyone engaged in forecasting to neglect this source of information.

Such success as the McGraw–Hill surveys of plans have achieved as forecasting devices is incidental to the purposes they are designed to serve: (1) to measure the long-range *potential* for business investment and (2) to shed light on the *underlying forces* shaping the character and volume of such investment.

Origin of McGraw–Hill Surveys

In 1947, two rather inconsistent notions about business investment had impressively wide sponsorship. One was that the post-World War II boom in such investment had pretty well run its course. The other, reflected in proposed legislation, was that the federal government should be generally authorized to purchase and install manufacturing facilities where shortages existed.[1]

The staff of the McGraw–Hill Department of Economics disagreed with both these notions. It was our contention that the postwar boom in new producing facilities still had a long way to go. Also we felt that the right

[1] For example, the Spence Bill (Economic Stability Act of 1949), introduced in the House of Representatives in the first session of the 81st Congress, contained a proposal to provide the President with the power to provide industrial facilities in industries where he found that a shortage was hampering or likely to hamper the economy. However, the government was not to construct new plants if private companies would do it through government loans, or on terms prescribed by the President.

of way in providing adequate industrial equipment properly belonged to private establishments, assuming they had the requisite capacity and inclination.

Factual information to document these positions was notably lacking. The Department of Commerce and the Securities and Exchange Commission had initiated surveys of business plans for new plants and equipment, but these early surveys did not provide detailed information on the plans and there was no breakdown by manufacturing industries. Also they were not available as early as persons concerned with economic policy and business forecasting might have wished.

Therefore, in 1947, our Department undertook the development of surveys that would (1) bring out the full potential for private investment, with enough explanatory detail to make this a tangible goal, and (2) indicate, in some detail, the plans for investment by particular industries. We also undertook to publish the data on a faster schedule than was possible for the government agencies.

We were influenced by the fact that McGraw–Hill periodical publications are, as a group, particularly concerned with the capital goods industries and hence would benefit from more knowledge about capital investment on an industry basis. The information developed by the surveys has been especially helpful in this regard. However the need for greater knowledge for public purposes was also a motivating factor.

Framing the Questions

An important decision concerned the type of questions we could reasonably expect companies to answer. The questions were drawn up to permit simple and definite answers. The McGraw–Hill surveys have always concentrated on *plans* for business investment rather than anticipations or expectations. A plan gives an expectation a dimension of action and reduces its ephemeral character.

In our experience, *plans* reported to us represent varying degrees of finality. Some represent actual construction schedules based on outstanding orders; others, expenditures formally approved by a board of directors. We have not sought to standardize the concept of a plan, but rather to encourage individual companies to be consistent in the concept they use. The first question on the McGraw–Hill surveys has always been simply: "How much do you now plan to spend on new plants and equipment in 19—?"

Originally we limited ourselves pretty much to this one question. We used it in a survey made early in the year of plans for new plants and equipment (1) in the current year, and (2) in the following year. In 1949 the survey was extended to include plans for the next five years and, since 1952, plans for the next four years have been a regular feature of the survey. This extension in time has improved our picture of the potential for capital expenditures.

Surveys since 1952 have also included detailed questions on the purpose of investment (modernization, expansion, new products or processes) and on the potential for investment under varying conditions of capital availability, technical progress, and general business activity. Thus we are gauging the long-range potential (over a four-year period) and the underlying forces that affect investment. These detailed surveys of business' plans are made in the spring of the year for which current plans are reported.

Since 1954 we have also made a preliminary check in the fall on plans for the year just ahead. This was suggested by reporting firms who told us that advance information would be available to them in the budget-making period toward the close of the old year. Thus in the spring of 1957 one would obtain information from the McGraw–Hill survey on advance plans for 1958, 1959, and 1960 to compare with plans for the current year. The October 1957 McGraw–Hill survey provided a closer, though still preliminary, estimate for 1958. However, the Department of Commerce survey for 1958 was not available until early in that year.

We believe that our surveys with their reiterated questions about long-range investment plans have stimulated the development of such plans and imparted an element of stability to them. Initially, only a handful of companies had any definite idea of expenditures more than one year ahead. But in our most recent survey, which included a much larger number of firms, almost 90 per cent could give estimates of capital spending for three years in advance. We feel that business interest in investment planning, as stimulated by the McGraw–Hill and Department of Commerce–SEC surveys, has made it easier for other groups to conduct surveys on special aspects of the problem. Notable among the latter are various regional surveys of plans for capital expenditures,[2] the *Fortune* survey of machinery producers on expected deliveries of new capital equipment and the National Industrial Conference Board survey of capital appropriations by manufacturing companies. Special studies are needed since the McGraw–Hill national surveys do not provide data that are readily applicable to the situation in a particular region or product line.

Predictive Value

In reporting the results of our questionnaires we have always stated that "the McGraw–Hill survey is *not a forecast*. It is a report of what companies

[2] Regional surveys are conducted regularly by the Federal Reserve Bank of Philadelphia for the Philadelphia metropolitan area; the Federal Reserve Bank of Boston for Massachusetts; and the University of Pittsburgh for the Pittsburgh area. In addition, regional surveys have also been carried out by the Federal Reserve Bank of St. Louis for St. Louis, and by the Cleveland Electric Illuminating Company for the Cleveland area.

now plan to spend on new plants and equipment." It was probably inevitable, however, that analysts would use the results of the McGraw–Hill surveys to forecast events in the crucial sector of business investment.

Experience has shown that the dollar expenditures planned for the year immediately ahead are pretty good indicators of the actual level of investment and of the degree and direction of change. Except in 1948, 1950, and 1956, actual capital expenditures, as measured by the Commerce–SEC final figures, were within 8 per cent of planned spending, as measured by the McGraw–Hill surveys (Table 1). We have had the right direction in every year except two: in our first survey carried out early in 1948, and in the one carried out early in 1950, when plans were drastically changed as a result of the Korean war. Our last five surveys indicated changes in the volume of investment which, on the average, differed less than 4 per cent from actual changes as measured by the final Commerce–SEC figures (Table 2).

A comparison of the planned expenditures of reporting companies (Table 3 gives the sample coverage) with what they actually spent shows the performance of the McGraw–Hill surveys to have been remarkably good. Except in 1950, capital expenditures made by industrial firms

TABLE 1

Actual and Planned Plant and Equipment Expenditures,
1948-1956

	Amount (millions of dollars)		Percentage Ratio of Actual to Planned
	Actual	Planned	
1948	$16,904	$14,856	114
1949	14,625	14,130	104
1950	14,934	12,400	120
1951	19,728	21,544	92
1952	20,936	21,175	99
1953	22,012	23,335	94
1954	20,314	21,499	94
1955	28,707	29,486	97
1956	35,080	38,965	90

Source: Actual expenditures as reported by the Dept. of Commerce and the Securities and Exchange Commission in the June 1956 and March 1957 *Survey of Current Business*. Figures include major revisions in the manufacturing and nonmanufacturing series published in the December 1951 and August 1952 *Survey of Current Business*. Planned expenditures as reported in annual reports, *Business' Plans for New Plants and Equipment*, McGraw–Hill. The series were made directly comparable for the years 1948 through 1954. Agricultural business, and commercial capital expenditures, and outlays charged to current account are excluded. For 1955 and 1956 both series include commercial capital expenditures. The McGraw–Hill data for 1955 and 1956 also include outlays of the petroleum industry charged to current account (estimated at $1.0 billion in 1955 and $1.5 billion in 1956).

TABLE 2

Year-to-Year Actual and Planned Changes in Plant
and Equipment Expenditures, 1948-1956
(*previous year* = 100)

	Actual	Planned	Percentage Ratio of Actual to Planned
1948	116.4	92.1	126.4
1949	86.5	95.2	90.9
1950	102.1	86.7	117.8
1951	132.1	145.2	91.0
1952	106.1	112.8	94.1
1953	105.1	106.2	99.0
1954	92.3	96.4	95.7
1955	107.0	105.5	101.4
1956	122.2	129.8	94.1

Source: Actual changes based on actual expenditures listed in Table 1. Planned changes based on data reported by McGraw–Hill in annual reports, *Business' Plans for New Plants and Equipment.*

TABLE 3

Employment Accounted for by Companies Reporting to McGraw–Hill,
by Industry, 1956
(*per cent*)

Iron and steel	70
Nonferrous metals	63
Machinery	44
Electrical machinery	66
Autos, trucks, and parts	95
Transportation equipment	59
Other metalworking	31
Chemicals	73
Paper and pulp	31
Rubber	63
Stone, clay, and glass	30
Petroleum refining	82
Food and beverages	33
Textiles	20
All manufacturing	38
Petroleum industry	83
Mining	35
Railroads	53
Other transportation and communications	43
Electric and gas utilities	59
All business excluding commercial	42
Commercial	11
All business	30

reporting to McGraw–Hill came within 4 per cent of their planned expenditures. In 1955, their actual and planned expenditures were exactly equal (Table 4).

373

TABLE 4

Differences between Actual and Planned Plant and Equipment Expenditures of
Companies Reporting to McGraw–Hill, by Industry, 1949-1956
(*per cent*)

	1949	1950	1951	1952	1953	1954	1955[a]	1956[a]
Chemicals	−14	+19	+11	−1	−4	−9	−16	−4
Food	+4	−12	+3	+11	−1	−7	−10	+2
Steel	−15	+15	−12	−7	−11	−26	+2	−9
Petroleum refining	−15	−9	−3	−15	−15	−1	−4	−14
Machinery	−7	+43	+16	+37	+1	−2	+12	0
Autos	−35	+7	+13	−6	+8	+12	+9	−13
Textiles	+2	+19	+9	+24	+26	+4	+46	+9
Electrical machinery	−10	+4	−13	−37	−16	−22	+2	+1
Transportation equipment	−11	−12	+34	−29	−28	−10	+7	−10
Miscellaneous manufacturing	−11	+41	+21	+27	+4	−2	−4	−8
All manufacturing	−12	+11	+6	0	−5	−5	−2	−5
Mining	+17	+7	−4	0	−30	−18	−3	+12
Railroads	−5	+33	+2	−10	+1	−3	+11	−12
Utilities	+10	+5	+7	−2	−4	−3	−3	+1
Other transportation and communications	+2	+4	+42	+18	−17	+2	+11	+4
All business	−4	+10	+4	+1	−2	−4	0	−1

[a] Not directly comparable with previous years because of differences in classifications.

Table 4 shows that this close correspondence between plans and performance is not characteristic of particular industries. The record in individual manufacturing industries shows variation as large as 46 per cent in one year. The economic temperament of the managers of industry may have a bearing here. Some appear to be chronically optimistic about the amount of new producing facilities they expect to buy; others, chronically pessimistic. The textile industry, for example, has always purchased more than it anticipated. In contrast, the petroleum industry has never, over a decade, managed to make all of its planned purchases.

Also, individual companies generally do not do as well in keeping to plans as the averages for industries would suggest. In every year with the exception of 1956, one-fifth of the companies reporting were off the mark by 40 per cent or more and at least 45 per cent were off by 20 per cent or more (Table 5). To date, the individual errors have offset each other in the totals, but there is no guarantee that it will always work out that way.

Since the surveys were begun there has been an almost continuous boom in business investment in new plants and equipment. This condition may well have had a decisive influence in giving our reports their high predictive value although we can only be sure about this after we experience a recession. At any rate, an assessment of the nature of the economic times is essential to the wise use of the data on plans.

TABLE 5

Difference between Actual and Planned Plant and Equipment
Expenditures of Individual Companies Reporting to
McGraw–Hill, 1949-1956

| | 0 | RANGE OF DIFFERENCE | | |
		1% to 19%	*20% to 39%*	*40% and over*
		(per cent of companies)		
1949	5	38	24	33
1950	2	36	21	41
1951	4	46	25	25
1952	4	41	26	29
1953	3	52	25	20
1954	6	49	23	22
1955	2	47	24	27
1956	4	55	29	12

The Purpose of Investment

To throw light on the *underlying forces* that shape investment in new plants and equipment, we have—over the years—asked a series of questions on capacity, sales expectations, and expansion versus modernization, and many qualitative questions as well. The answers to some of these questions also have an important predictive value.

NEW CAPACITY

Questions on recent and planned additions to capacity have been included in the McGraw–Hill surveys since 1949. The answers, weighted by industrial importance in the same way as the Federal Reserve index of manufacturing production is weighted, are combined in the McGraw–Hill index of manufacturing capacity. This is the only index now available that shows the yearly increase in total manufacturing capacity. (The Federal Reserve Board has developed a capacity index for production of basic materials, but this is only a small part of all manufacturing.) Separate capacity indexes are available for each of the major manufacturing industries.

The McGraw–Hill index of manufacturing capacity has proved to be a valuable forecasting device. The index increased sharply in 1951-53, presaging the downturn in expenditures in 1954. Since 1954 the index has again risen. As reported in the spring 1957 survey, the 1957 year-end index was expected to stand 50 per cent above the figure for 1950. Manufacturing output rose only 30 per cent in the same period. This build-up of extra capacity clearly foreshadowed a decline in manufacturing investment in 1958.

The McGraw–Hill surveys show that companies fulfill their capacity expectations much more accurately than they do their plans for dollar

375

investment in new facilities. Since we began checking the capacity figures, the planned figure for manufacturing has not been off by more than 2 per cent in any year except 1950, when it was off by 4 per cent—presumably because of the unexpected defense build-up (Table 6). Individual com-

TABLE 6

Actual and Planned Changes in Plant Capacity by
Companies Reporting to McGraw–Hill, 1950-1956
(*per cent*)

	Actual	Planned
1950	+7	+3
1951	+7	+9
1952	+9	+9
1953	+7	+7
1954	+5	+4
1955	+7	+5
1956	+6	+8

panies and industries also adhere more closely to their capacity plans than to their dollar investment plans. The reasons for this may include the effects of price increases on dollar outlays, and the fact that dollar payments tend to lag behind physical construction.

Since 1955 we have asked companies at what rate they are operating their capacity and at what rate they would *like* to operate. Apparently, manufacturing companies generally prefer to operate at around 90 per cent of capacity. When operations are at a higher rate, expenditures for new plant capacity probably increase. When operations are much below 90 per cent, it is time to look for a downturn. Anyone who followed these operating figures closely could easily have predicted the rise in manufacturing investment during 1955-56, or the tapering off in 1957. Whereas most companies reported operating above 90 per cent capacity at the end of 1955, the average rate was down to 86 per cent by the end of 1956—and some important industries were well below this. These data—coupled with the very large rise in the index of manufacturing capacity—clearly indicated that manufacturing investment was about to slow down.

DEPRECIATION, REPLACEMENT, AND MODERNIZATION

We have also established certain facts about expenditures for purposes other than expansion. For example, most companies report that they regularly spend their entire depreciation allowance for new plants and equipment (presumably for modernization in most cases) and that depreciation allowances are increasing. This puts a limit on the drop in investment that might occur in any year. We have also learned that over the years about half of the capital expenditure dollar has gone for modernization and replacement but that the ratio generally increases after a capacity

376

build-up has begun to taper off, as after the 1948 build-up and again after the Korean expansion. Thus we can predict with some assurance that modernization and replacement's share in the investment total will increase in 1958, and perhaps in 1959.

The survey findings dispose of the old notion that once capacity reaches a temporary peak, capital investment will decline drastically until a situation of demonstrable undercapacity develops. The modern businessman seems to regard the end of an expansion phase as an opportunity to step up modernization outlays (provided his cash flow including depreciation is adequate). These data permitted the careful analyst to predict the mild nature of the 1949 and 1954 declines in capital investment.

Other questions in the McGraw–Hill surveys have provided data to support the prediction that any drop in expansion outlays will be cushioned by greater expenditures for modernization. In 1948 we asked companies how much it would cost to put all their plant and equipment in "first-class shape." The replies indicated a relatively large backlog of technical improvements ($136 billion at 1948 prices) to be made whenever cash became available.

In several early surveys we also asked, "How soon do you expect an investment in new equipment to pay off?" The typical answer for manufacturing companies was: in three to five years. In other words a return of 20 to 33 per cent was expected. Follow-up interviews revealed that modernization expenditures offered such rich rewards, in terms of cost-saving, that companies could spend all their available funds on projects with short payout periods. With a huge backlog of modernization to be accomplished, and a high rate of return on such expenditures, it is evident that any prediction of total capital investment must allow for a high level of modernization outlays.

RESEARCH AND DEVELOPMENT

When industrial technology is changing rapidly, it is vital to know how quickly technical developments are proceeding and how quickly they can be translated into a practical basis for capital investment. Before 1953 there were no comprehensive data available. In that year the National Science Foundation found that $3.7 billion was spent on research performed by private industry. And since 1956 the McGraw–Hill surveys have included regular questions on expenditures for research and development. The spring 1957 survey indicated that expenditures for research by private industry would reach $7.3 billion in 1957. Even allowing for cost increases since 1953, this is a striking increase.

Exactly when and how these outlays will lead to investment in new plants and equipment is not yet clear. A recheck conducted among a small sample of the participants in the 1957 survey indicated that about seven years—on the average—is required from the start of research on a new product to the time when it is ready for full-scale production. This suggests that the upswing in research spending that got underway in the mid-fifties will begin to show up as a major force in capital investment during the early sixties. Our check also revealed that improvements in *existing* products—which take less time to accomplish—are a major purpose of research outlays, especially where machinery and other capital goods companies are concerned. We can, therefore, expect a substantial impetus to modernization by 1958 or 1959 from the increasing development of improved machinery.

As to the dollar volume of capital expenditure that may be influenced by research, the 1957 McGraw-Hill survey indicated that 32 per cent of all manufacturing companies expected a "substantial" portion of their 1957 capital investment to be for the production of new products. The increase over the 1956 proportion (28 per cent) suggests that as research expenditures rise, more manufacturing investment will be related to new product development—a prediction confirmed by the replies to our question "What per cent of your 1960 sales do you expect to be in new products?" The answers averaged 10 per cent for all manufacturing but more than 15 per cent in the industries making the largest expenditures on research. The present average for manufacturing is only about 8 per cent.

Thus we can expect that an increasing share of total capital investment will be tied not to the business cycle or to a desire to expand capacity but to the independent and steadily rising trend of new product development. Such a shift would add to the stability of capital expenditures. The data on research and new products—like those on modernization—are a warning against projecting into the late fifties the sort of cyclical decline that occurred in the thirties.

A Practical Test

A significant way of gauging the predictive value of the McGraw-Hill surveys is to compare the course of events as indicated by a survey with events as they actually occurred. For this purpose, we refer to the 1954 survey which covered plans through 1957.

The 1954 survey showed that industry was still expansion minded, despite falling sales in that year. (Because of the decline, the 1954 questionnaire included questions on expected *future* sales and comparisons with capacity plans.) Most companies correctly anticipated sales and capacity increases between 1954 and 1957. The survey also indicated that expansion might be overdone, for most companies were counting on sales increases considerably larger than they forecast for the average in their own industries. Because so many companies were planning to outsell their industries, the survey report observed "that more intense competition is in the offing." It also noted an increased emphasis on plant modernization, because "modernization means cost cutting—an essential for many companies that want to prosper in the competitive period they see ahead." This describes what actually took place in 1957.

The respondents were also asked the minimum they would spend on plant and equipment if sales declined substantially and the maximum they would spend if they could take advantage of all the new technical developments. For most industries, the answers indicated the 1954-57 range with remarkable accuracy, even though business fluctuated considerably and the cost of capital goods rose sharply. The chemical industry, despite rapid growth, has not spent more than the $1.8 billion maximum estimated in the 1954 survey. The textile industry, despite severe recession, has not spent less than the $245 million minimum they estimated. For all manufacturing, the estimate of maximum capital spending in 1954-57 was $14.4 billion. Three years later, at the peak of the investment boom, plans for 1957 investment totaled $14.5 billion (actual expenditures turned out to be slightly lower). This and other tests clearly indicate that the survey data, sensibly handled, can be remarkably helpful to those engaged in plotting the economic future.

Appendix: Questions on Investment Plans in McGraw–Hill Surveys, 1948-1957

QUESTIONS ASKED IN ALL YEARS

1. How much did you invest in new plants and equipment in the continental United States in [previous year, $]? (This includes all purchases charged to capital accounts, whether for replacement, expansion, or other purposes.)

2. How much do you now plan to invest in new plants and equipment in [current year, $]?

3. How much do you now plan to invest in new plants and equipment in [each of 3 years ahead, $]?

4. At the end of [previous year] how did your capacity, measured in terms of physical volume, compare with what it was at the end of [a year ago, greater or smaller, %]?

5. If you carry out this program [investment plans for current year], what will be the net change in your company's physical capacity [greater or smaller, %]?

6. If you carry out this program [investment plans for 3 years ahead], what will be the net increase in your company's capacity from the end of [current year] to the end of [3 years ahead, %]?

QUESTIONS ASKED IN CERTAIN YEARS ONLY

Capacity

1. [1949, 1955-57] At the end of [previous year], how much of your capacity were you operating? [%]

2. [1949, 1955, 1957] What do you consider a desirable operating rate at the end of the year in your industry? [%]

3. [1948] Can you break down your capital investment budget to show how important each of the following objectives is in your 1948 budget and in your 1949-53 plans? Your best judgment here, even though precise allocations are impossible, will be of tremendous value. Reasons: To expand capacity? To replace or modernize facilities? Other (please specify)? [% of investment allocated to each for 1948 and 1949-53]

A. Of the money you are spending to expand capacity: How much is going to add capacity for production of present products? How much is going to add capacity for new products? [%, 1948 and 1949-53]

B. Of the money you are spending to replace and modernize facilities: How much is being spent to install entirely new processes for making your present products? How much is going to replace particular buildings or equipment by more efficient types of the same general design? [%, 1948 and 1949-53]

4. [1948] When your postwar expansion is complete, how much greater will your capacity be than it was in 1939? [%]

Sales

1. [1953-57] How much were your company's sales in [previous year, $]?

2. [1954-57] How much do you think the physical volume of sales of your company will increase or decrease between [previous year] and [current year, increase or decrease, %]?

3. [1953-57] How much do you think the physical volume of sales of your *company* will increase or decrease between [current year] and [3 years ahead, increase or decrease, %]?

4. [1953, 1954] How much do you think the physical volume of sales of your *industry* will increase or decrease by the end of [3 years ahead, increase or decrease, %]?

5. [1948] Do you expect sales of your company in 1948 to be higher or lower than in 1947 or the same? If you expect higher sales, how big an increase do you look for? [%]

Research and Development—New Products and Processes

1. [1956, 1957] What was the cost of all research and development performed by your company in [previous year, $]? (Research and development includes basic and applied research and engineering, and also design and development of prototypes and processes. It does *not* include quality control, routine product testing, market research, sales

380

promotion, sales service, geological or geophysical exploration. This definition is the same as used by the Bureau of Labor Statistics in its survey of research and development expenditures for 1953.)

2. [1956, 1957] How much do you estimate your expenditures for research and development will increase (decrease) between [previous year] and [current year] and between [current year] and [3 years ahead, %]?

3. [1954] How much did your company spend on all types of research in 1953, excluding research paid for by the government? [$] How much do you estimate your company will spend for research in [each of 4 years ahead, $]?

4. [1956, 1957] Roughly, what per cent of your [3 years ahead] sales do you think will be in new products (either products not produced in [previous year] or products sufficiently changed to be reasonably considered as new products)? [%]

5. [1956, 1957] Will a significant part (more than 5%) of your [current year] expenditures for new plants and equipment be for facilities to make new products? [yes or no] If yes, how much? [about what % of total expenditures]

6. [1953] Are there any new machines or processes in your *industry* which will require particularly large capital expenditures during the next few years? [yes or no] If yes, please describe briefly.

Expansion versus Modernization

1. [1951-55] Roughly, how was your [previous year] investment in new plants and equipment divided between (a) expansion and (b) replacement and modernization? [%]

2. [1950-55, 1957] Of the total amount you plan to invest in new plants and equipment in [current year] please indicate how much is for (a) expansion and (b) modernization? [%]

3. [1953, 1954, 1957] Roughly, how would your total investment [3 years ahead] be divided between (a) expansion and (b) replacement and modernization? [%]

Employment

1. [1957] How much will this program [research expenditures 3 years ahead] change your employment of scientists and engineers in research and development? [increase or decrease, 1 and 3 years ahead, %]

2. [1951] How many employees do you have? [number] If it is convenient, would you indicate the number of *production workers*: On the first shift? On the second shift? On the third shift?

3. [1954] How much do you expect your company's employment to increase or decrease between 1953 and the end of 1957? [%]

Construction versus Equipment

1. [1951, 1955] Of the total amount you invested in new plants and equipment in [previous year] please indicate how much was for: (a) new construction (buildings) and (b) equipment? [%]

2. [1951, 1955, 1956] Of the total amount you plan to invest in new plants and equipment in [current year], please indicate how much is for (a) new construction (buildings) and (b) equipment? [%]

Depreciation and Accelerated Amortization

1. [1953] How much was your depreciation allowance, including rapid amortization of defense facilities, in [previous year, $]? How much do you estimate your depreciation allowance, including rapid amortization, will be in [each of 4 years ahead, $]? Has it been your policy to spend all or nearly all of your depreciation allowance for new plant and equipment? [yes or no] Do you expect any change in this policy? [yes or no] If so, please list the other uses for these funds.

2. [1954] Has it been your policy to spend all or nearly all of your depreciation allowance for new plants and equipment? [yes or no] If depreciation allowances were substantially increased, what would be the main effect on your company's financial policy? [check] Spend more on new plants and equipment? Rely less on outside funds? Reduce outstanding debt? Other (please specify)?

3. [1951] On what part of your planned 1951 expenditures for plants and equipment will you apply for certificates of necessity authorizing accelerated amortization? [%]

Pay-off Periods

1. [1952, 1955] How soon do you figure an investment in new equipment should pay off? Please give estimate *before taxes.* [years]

2. [1952] How does this compare with the pay-off period you expected two or three years ago? [longer, shorter, or same] If the pay-off period has changed, what is the main reason?

3. [1949] In general, how soon do you think a new investment should pay off to make it worthwhile? In equipment? In buildings? [years]

Source of Funds

1. [1949] Would you tell us (a) where you expect you will raise the money, and (b) where you would like to get the funds to finance the program outlined in your answer to question [investment plans in next 5 years]? What part do you expect you will get from each source? Internal sources including retained earnings, reserves, and depreciation? Bonds or notes? Stock? Others (please specify)? [%] What part would you like to get from each source? Internal sources including retained

earnings, reserves, and depreciation? Stock? Bonds or notes? Others (please specify)? [%]

2. [1948, 1950-52] Where will the money to finance your [1 year ahead] program come from? Retained earnings, depreciation, and reserves? Bonds or notes? New stock? Other (please explain below)? Total [100]. [%]

3. [1952] Where will the money to finance your [3 years ahead] program come from? Retained earnings, depreciation, and reserves? Bonds or notes? New stock? Other (please explain below)? Total [100]. [%]

Advance Planning

1. [1953-55] How far in advance does your company usually plan its capital expenditures? [years]

2. [1955] In what month and year could you first have given a reasonably accurate estimate of your capital spending plans for [current year; month and year]?

3. [1950] Are your 1950 investment plans subject to review and revision? [yes or no] If yes: Monthly? Quarterly? Semiannually? By whom: Officers? Directors? Others? [check]

4. [1952] Is it the usual practice in your company to plan capital expenditures several years in advance? [yes or no] If yes, please indicate how many years.

Value and Cost of Replacing Present Facilities
with Most Modern Facilities

1. [1955] What would be the total cost—approximately—of equipping your company fully with the most up-to-date plants and equipment? [$]

2. [1949] At present prices what do you estimate was the value (reproduction cost in its present condition) of your plant and equipment at the beginning of 1948? [$] What would it cost—approximately—to replace your present facilities with the most up-to-date plant and equipment so far developed? [$]

3. [1949] Assuming that you could get what's needed at present prices, and finance it, how much would you need to invest now to put your plant and equipment in first-class shape? Total? Equipment? Buildings? [$]

If Economic Conditions Were to Change

1. [1953, 1954] What is the *maximum* annual expenditure on new plant and equipment you feel your company could make in the years [3 years ahead] if you were able to take full advantage of all technological developments? [$, per year]

2. [1953, 1954] What is the *minimum* annual expenditure on new plant

383

and equipment you feel your company would make in the years [3 years ahead] even if sales declined substantially? [$, per year]

3. [1950] Would you increase your planned capital expenditures for 1950 if you could sell new common stock at a price 50% above its present market price? [yes or no] If yes, by approximately how much would you increase it? [%]

4. [1950] Would you cut your 1950 capital budget if general business activity declined 20% during the year? [yes or no] If yes, by about how much? [%] Apart from an increase in volume of sales, what single development would cause you to increase your 1950 capital expenditure budget?

5. [1949] Would you increase your 1949-53 investment in new plant and equipment if: Your net profit increased 10%? The corporate income tax rate were reduced to 20% (from 38% today)? You were allowed to depreciate fully new plant and equipment in 5 years for federal income tax purposes? You were able to issue new common stock at a price equal to ten times gross earnings? [yes or no]

6. [1950] If you changed your 1949 capital budget during the year by 10% or more, please indicate: Whether you spent more or less than planned. [more or less] How much more, or less? [%] The principal reason or reasons for the change?

7. [1950] If your 1950 investment will be substantially more or less than your 1949 investment, please indicate the principal reason for the change.

8. [1949] Have you been holding back on plant construction? [yes or no] (a) If so, would you list the major reasons? (b) If construction costs should drop 20% (which is as much as they could be cut, short of a major depression) would you increase your construction budget for the next 5 years? [yes or no]

9. [1949] If you think your expenditure will decline after 1948, what are the major reasons?

10. [1948] If wage rates go up 15-20%, will you increase or decrease your capital budget substantially? [yes or no]

Other Questions

1. [1952] What will be the primary reason for this investment [planned investment for 3 years ahead]? More capacity to make present products? Capacity to make new products? Plant dispersal for security reasons? Plants to serve new market areas? Replacement and modernization of plant and equipment? Other (please specify)? [check]

2. [1951] Do you expect that additional defense orders will raise your needs for new plants and equipment as the year goes on? [yes or no]

3. [1952] Are your plans for new plants and equipment in 1952 limited by prospective shortages of materials or equipment? [yes or no]

If yes, how much would your program be increased if you could get all the materials and equipment you want? [%]

4. [1952] Approximately how much of your 1952 investment do you plan to make in the first half-year and how much in the second half-year? [%]

5. [1948] What proportion of your postwar expansion program is now complete? [%] How much of it will be complete by the end of 1948?

6. [1948] How much of your planned capital expenditures have been placed under contract? [%] How much will be under contract by June 30? [%]

7. [1948] Do you expect to spend more or less for new plant and equipment in 1949 than in 1948? [more, less, same, no plans]

COMMENT

ROBERT M. WEIDENHAMMER, University of Pittsburgh

In the spring of 1955, with the encouragement of Dexter Keezer, we discussed with Pittsburgh companies the possibility of their cooperation with the University in a semiannual survey of estimated plant and equipment expenditures. The results of the first survey were published in November 1955. Later we included in the survey questions on employment and inventory policies and developed adequate sampling methods. The fall 1957 survey went to 452 companies.

A regional survey has certain aspects which may make it of more than local significance. Close personal contacts with respondents may permit evaluation of the motives behind changes in investment decisions (plant, equipment, inventories) and of the role played by changes in profit margins, sales, equipment prices, liquidity, interest rates, and equity prices. Personal contacts may also reveal the nature of planned outlays, that is, whether they represent primarily initial steps (foundations) or completions (machinery). Initial steps are more vulnerable to cancellation than are completions, but they provide a better basis for projecting expenditures into the future. The problem is how to quantify such information obtained from personal contacts.

Knowledge of the activities and anticipations of the Pittsburgh district as a center of capital goods industries may possibly prove valuable for forecasting. To determine whether and to what extent the Pittsburgh district leads or lags in these respects we are comparing the local and national surveys and also the Pittsburgh business index with the Federal Reserve Board index. Our local index, which is published weekly, monthly, and annually, has just been revised backward to 1929 to conform with the FRB index.

I am working with local companies to compare the results in lead time and accuracy that "expectations to spend" data (McGraw–Hill, Commerce Department–Securities and Exchange Commission, and University of Pittsburgh) and "appropriations by boards" data (National Industrial Conference Board) would have yielded during the last decade. We are planning a conference between local company officials who fill out the various questionnaires and those who use the final results with a view to improving our surveys in the light of the questions raised above.

The Structure and Realization of Business Investment Anticipations

MURRAY F. FOSS   VITO NATRELLA

DEPARTMENT OF COMMERCE   SECURITIES AND EXCHANGE COMMISSION

Our paper presents an analysis of the results of the Department of Commerce–Securities and Exchange Commission annual survey of business investment anticipations, giving the data on an aggregative basis by industry division, 1947-57. We also show a cross-sectional analysis in terms of frequency distributions of individual company deviations from anticipations by industry, size of firm, and scale of investment, 1950-56, with some data for 1949 where they were readily available. We hope thereby to highlight some of the basic factors which affect accuracy and the tendency to spend more or less than anticipated. This approach has sometimes been used in the past.[1] But we bring together results for several years to permit a check on earlier findings, to make possible at least a limited comparison of years in different stages of the business cycle, and to give a tentative explanation of the main factors underlying the performance of the survey.

Our findings are subject to the following qualifications:

1. The Commerce–SEC series applies to one-year investment anticipations obtained early in each year. The factors relevant to the realization of such anticipations are not necessarily the same as those most pertinent to the realization of longer-range expectations.

2. The predominant trend since 1947, when the annual series was started, was upward. In 1949 and 1954, investment decreased 5 and 6 per cent in current dollars, and the gross national product less than 1 per cent. While these declines were slightly larger if deflated, and also from the

---

NOTE: The Securities and Exchange Commission and the Department of Commerce, as a matter of policy, disclaim responsibility for any private publication by any of their employees. The views expressed herein are those of the authors and do not necessarily reflect the views of the Commission or Department or of the authors' colleagues on the staffs of the Commission or Department.

[1] See Irwin Friend and Jean Bronfenbrenner, "Business Investment Programs and Their Realization," *Survey of Current Business*, December 1950, and "Plant and Equipment Programs and Their Realization," *Short-Term Economic Forecasting*, Studies in Income and Wealth, Vol. 17, Princeton University Press for the National Bureau of Economic Research, 1955. Also Vito Natrella, "Forecasting Plant and Equipment Expenditures from Businessmen's Expectations," *Proceedings*, *Business and Economic Statistics Section*, American Statistical Association, 116th Annual Meeting, 1956; and Murray Foss and Vito Natrella, "Ten Years' Experience with Business Investment Anticipations," *Survey of Current Business*, January 1957.

highest to the lowest quarter, their mildness limits our assessment of the survey under different economic conditions.

3. There were widespread shortages of particular kinds of labor and materials, and the rise in construction and equipment costs was almost uninterrupted. Delays and shortages may always be encountered in a period of heavy fixed investment when plant construction in particular is important, but they obstruct a statistical analysis of factors governing the demand for investment and particularly the realization of investment expectations.

4. Rapid tax amortization programs, in 1951-53 especially, also introduced abnormal influences on investment.

5. Unweighted data are used in several of the tables. While an individual firm analysis can clarify some underlying relationships, weights are needed to bridge the gap between an essentially atomistic approach and the dollar totals. This is especially important in investment analysis, for firms are not of equal weight, and size of company appears to affect the planning and realization of investment.

6. The breakdowns of the company data are restricted in their scope and do not take into account, except in a limited way, fundamental determinants of investment on the demand side.

Survey Results

Table 1 presents summary results of the survey for the aggregate and for six major industry divisions, 1947-57.

TABLE 1

Business Investment, Actual and Anticipated, by Industry, 1947-1957
(*actual investment in previous year* = 100)

Investment	Manufac- turing	Mining	Rail- roads	Other Transpor- tation	Public Utilities	Commercial and Other	All Industries
1947:							
Actual	126	123	161	a	183	132	134
Anticipated	104	109	175	a	163	112	115
Actual as % of							
anticipated	121	113	92	a	112	118	117
1948:							
Actual	112	116	144	88	141	122	119
Anticipated	104	100	176	98	121	125	115
Actual as % of							
anticipated	108	116	82	90	116	97	103
1949:							
Actual	87	92	102	74	117	95	94
Anticipated	87	102	110	93	117	93	95
Actual as % of							
anticipated	100	90	93	80	100	102	99

[table continues on next page

Table 1, *continued*

Investment	Manufac-turing	Mining	Rail-roads	Other Transpor-tation	Public Utilities	Commercial and Other	All Industries
1950:							
Actual	113	92	84	85	101	96	102
Anticipated	93	88	69	67	94	88	89
Actual as % of anticipated	122	105	123	126	108	110	115
1951:							
Actual	145	131	133	123	111	107	124
Anticipated	145	131	133	141	112	110	129
Actual as % of anticipated	100	100	100	87	99	97	97
1952:							
Actual	107	106	95	101	106	98	103
Anticipated	108	107	100	119	108	90	104
Actual as % of anticipated	99	99	95	84	98	108	100
1953:							
Actual	102	100	94	104	117	113	107
Anticipated	100	103	93	101	114	100	102
Actual as % of anticipated	102	97	101	103	103	113	105
1954:							
Actual	93	99	65	97	93	103	95
Anticipated	93	103	72	96	97	103	96
Actual as % of anticipated	100	96	91	101	95	100	99
1955:							
Actual	104	98	108	106	102	115	107
Anticipated	97	92	89	99	104	107	101
Actual as % of anticipated	107	107	121	107	98	107	106
1956:							
Actual	131	130	133	107	114	117	122
Anticipated	131	119	142	111	116	112	122
Actual as % of anticipated	100	109	94	96	98	104	100
1957:							
Actual	107	100	113	103	127	94	105
Anticipated	110	98	119	107	124	94	106
Actual as % of anticipated	97	102	95	97	102	100	99

NOTE: Actual as percentage of anticipated is based on unrounded indexes.

a Included with commercial and other.

Source: The Department of Commerce–Securities and Exchange Commission annual surveys of plant and equipment expenditure anticipations, for this and the following tables unless otherwise noted.

The record for all industries combined, the survey's emphasis, is quite favorable. Actual expenditures were within 3 per cent of anticipated in seven of the eleven years; only in 1947 and 1950 were deviations large.

The direction of change was correctly anticipated in every year except 1950, including the downturn years, 1949 and 1954.

The results by major industry division also appear good, although deviations are usually larger than for the total. Manufacturing, accounting for about two-fifths of total outlays over the period, shows deviations of 3 per cent or less in seven of the years. Actual expenditures came close to anticipations in 1951-52 and 1956-57 when large increases were projected and carried out. The two years of downturn in total output and plant and equipment expenditures also turned out well. However, predictions for 1950 and 1955, which saw an upward change in direction from the previous year, showed less than average (median) accuracy. The large deviation in manufacturing in 1950 appears to have been attributable mainly to the outbreak of the Korean hostilities in July, although this is not necessarily true for all industries combined.[2]

Railroads exhibit the largest deviations of any of the major industry divisions, while mining, nonrail transportation, and commercial firms show median deviations higher than the average. The record on direction of change shows that manufacturing and mining firms have missed twice each; and rails, other transportation, and public utilities once each.

Underestimates (actual in excess of anticipated) predominate in the total and in manufacturing, mining, and the commercial group, while overestimates are more prevalent in both transportation groups. Public utility estimates reveal no distinct tendency.

Results by Individual Firms

Earlier evaluations of investment anticipations surveys demonstrated that individual firms do not anticipate with anything like the accuracy that characterizes the aggregate, and that individual firm deviations are in large part offsetting. In 1956, for example, when the deviation in manufacturing as a whole was under 1 per cent, actual outlays for only 30 per cent of the manufacturers came within 20 per cent of anticipated expenditures.

These unweighted results reflect the predominance of small firms in the sample. The importance of large firms in the dollar aggregates is indicated

[2] On the basis of the current seasonally adjusted series, actual II 1950 outlays were substantially above the first quarter, and showed an annual rate of expenditure almost the same as the 1949 total, in contrast with the greater than 10 per cent decline that was anticipated for the year. The survey that was reported in June of 1950, moreover, indicated that further increases were being scheduled for the third quarter.

Considered by itself, the annual survey for manufacturing in 1955 missed the direction of change. Viewed in the light of the quarterly information that was simultaneously provided, the survey correctly indicated that the downturn in investment would come to a halt in I 1955 and that a sharp rise would follow. The projected figure for the full year 1955 was about 4 per cent higher than the seasonally adjusted first quarter, which was the sixth successive quarter of decline.

by the fact that in 1956 the 250 largest concerns, with assets over $100 million, accounted for about 60 per cent of total corporate manufacturing assets. Large firms anticipate much more accurately than small companies. Therefore when weights are added to the distribution for 1956, about five-eighths of manufacturers' anticipated expenditures fall within the 20 per cent range of realization and the extremes of the distribution of company deviations are considerably less important.

There still remains an appreciable amount of dispersion, and it is important to determine whether the deviations are random or systematic. We begin our investigation of causal relationships with an examination of the structure of anticipations broken down by asset size of firm.

SIZE OF FIRM

In Table 2 frequency distributions of deviations from planned investment by size of firm, including both Commerce and SEC companies,

TABLE 2

Deviations of Actual Investment from Anticipated, by Size of Firm
and Deviation, Manufacturing, 1949-1956
(as % of all firms)

Deviation and Firm Size[a]	1949	1950	1951	1952	1953	1954	1955	1956	Median
Actual more than anticipated									
Small firms	60	76	63	51	65	62	71	65	64
Medium-sized firms	61	74	64	53	64	58	62	59	61
Large firms	43	51	59	42	48	44	51	46	47
Actual within 20% of anticipated									
Small firms	22	17	23	24	23	20	21	23	22
Medium-sized firms	33	24	35	37	36	33	32	40	34
Large firms	48	40	50	52	47	49	47	55	48
Actual 60% or more above anticipated									
Small firms	32	52	34	35	36	35	43	37	36
Medium-sized firms	18	39	23	19	22	22	26	21	22
Large firms	10	15	17	10	13	8	11	6	11
Actual 40% or more below anticipated									
Small firms	16	11	16	15	14	17	12	16	16
Medium-sized firms	9	6	8	13	8	11	8	8	8
Large firms	9	1	5	7	2	7	6	5	5

[a] In this and the following tables "small firms" are those with total assets of less than $10 million, "medium-sized firms" those with total assets of $10 million to $49.9 million, and "large firms" those with total assets of $50 million and over.

1949-56, are summarized for certain standards of performance. These data reveal that:

1. On the average, large firms (assets of $50 million and over) showed some tendency to overestimate, while more than three-fifths of small (assets under $10 million) and medium-sized firms underestimated their expenditures. Among the former, the proportions are similar in the downturn years of 1949 and 1954 and the steel strike years of 1952 and 1956.

2. In every year the proportion of firms whose actual outlays were within 20 per cent of anticipated expenditures increased as size of firm increased.

3. In every year large positive and negative deviations decreased in importance as size of firm increased. While the extremes of the distributions carry little weight in the dollar aggregates, they are a manifestation of small firm behavior, particularly when such companies definitely alter their views about income and sales, as they did in 1950 and 1955.

One reason for the relatively better performance of large firms is capital budgeting, which becomes more prevalent as size of firm increases. The existence of large deviations among large firms and the information offered by company executives in interviews conducted by Commerce and the SEC and by other investigators make it clear that budgets may be flexible instruments. But their use presupposes some willingness to disregard short-run fluctuations in demand. In response to our 1955 questionnaire large firms less often attributed changes from anticipations to unexpected changes in sales, profits, and working capital requirements than small firms did.[3]

Large firms have an advantage in that their reported expenditures usually involve several projects, where there may be offsetting errors. They are better able to allow for replacement and unexpected breakdowns. Most important, large firms engage in large scale programs more often.

SCALE OF INVESTMENT

Table 3 gives data on deviations from anticipated investment, broken down by size of firm and scale of investment, for 1950-56 for manufacturing, electric and gas utilities, and railroads. A limited amount of information for 1949 is also provided in footnote b of the table.

Scale of investment refers to the ratio of anticipated expenditures to gross fixed assets at the beginning of the year. The anticipated rather than the actual expenditure is used for classifying because we are primarily interested in evaluating the reliability of the figures reported early each year in the annual survey. Some spurious inverse correlation is apparent

[3] Murray Foss and Vito Natrella, "Investment Plans and Realization—Reasons for Differences in Individual Cases," *Survey of Current Business*, June 1957.

TABLE 3. Deviations of Actual Investment from Anticipated, by Size of Firm, Deviation, and Scale of Investment, Manufacturing, Public Utilities, and Railroads, 1950-1956
(as % of all firms)

Industry, Firm Size, and Scale of Investment[a]	Actual More than Anticipated								Actual within 20% of Anticipated							
	1950	1951	1952	1953	1954	1955	1956	Median	1950	1951	1952	1953	1954	1955	1956	Median
Manufacturing[b]																
Small firms:																
Less than 5%	79	70	73	71	68	79	71	71	19	21	16	17	16	13	22	17
5–9.9%	74	57	52	62	64	63	60	64	17	20	29	26	32	33	28	28
10% and over	73	52	49	43	43	51	52	51	34	37	42	33	30	34	48	34
Total	76	60	60	63	63	68	61	63	20	27	27	23	23	24	34	24
Medium-sized firms:																
Less than 5%	80	74	61	78	68	73	75	74	18	16	31	32	24	23	22	23
5–9.9%	72	70	51	62	50	62	64	62	28	43	39	31	33	33	46	33
10% and over	62	51	40	47	50	45	47	47	38	38	33	49	52	48	49	48
Total	74	64	51	63	58	62	59	62	25	34	34	37	35	33	40	34
Large firms:																
Less than 5%	73	70	77	63	60	74	65	70	18	40	14	35	30	30	42	30
5–9.9%	47	71	40	49	42	61	51	49	46	48	63	48	54	51	54	51
10% and over	36	51	35	36	37	29	34	36	50	54	57	54	57	57	54	54
Total	51	60	42	47	45	53	44	47	38	50	52	48	49	48	52	49
All firms:																
Less than 5%	78	72	67	73	67	76	72	72	18	21	22	25	21	20	24	21
5–9.9%	65	66	49	60	53	62	59	60	31	38	40	33	38	37	41	38
10% and over	54	52	42	44	44	43	44	44	42	42	43	45	47	46	49	45
Public utilities																
Less than 5%	34	55	50	38	28	70	45	45	17	64	50	64	58	45	46	50
5–9.9%	50	52	38	41	32	37	46	41	72	64	57	66	78	76	77	72
10% and over	59	25	31	40	31	29	35	31	70	77	71	86	78	71	76	76
Total	51	38	35	40	31	38	42	38	64	72	66	79	76	70	73	72
Railroads[c]																
Less than 2%	80	62	67	83	50	66	70	67	20	11	29	40	31	24	8	24
2–3.9%	64	46	39	64	32	51	58	51	36	54	50	58	62	43	46	50
4% and over	50	30	33	49	22	54	30	49	55	48	58	64	39	46	40	48
Total	69	39	42	62	40	59	49	49	31	43	50	56	43	34	34	43

a In this and the following tables, scale of investment is measured by the ratio of anticipated capital outlays to gross fixed assets at the beginning of the year. The sample includes Securities and Exchange Commission registrants only, because gross fixed asset data were lacking for most of the nonregistered companies.

b In 1949, 61 per cent of the small and medium-sized firms combined and 49 per cent of the large firms had actual expenditures more than anticipated; 26 per cent and 43 per cent, respectively, had actual expenditures within 20 per cent of anticipated.

c Because their outlays were generally lower relative to gross fixed assets, the scale of investment classes used for railroads differs from the other groups in this and the following table.

BUSINESS INVESTMENT ANTICIPATIONS

TABLE 4

Distribution of Firms by Size of Firm and Scale of Investment, Manufacturing,
Public Utilities, and Railroads, 1950-1956
(*as % of all firms*)

Industry, Firm Size, and Scale of Investment	1950	1951	1952	1953	1954	1955	1956
Manufacturing							
Small firms:							
Less than 5%	59	40	49	49	52	47	36
5-9.9%	26	26	23	29	31	29	28
10% and over	15	34	28	22	17	24	36
Total	100	100	100	100	100	100	100
Medium-sized firms:							
Less than 5%	50	24	33	38	41	40	29
5-9.9%	31	34	32	31	33	38	30
10% and over	19	42	35	31	26	22	41
Total	100	100	100	100	100	100	100
Large firms:							
Less than 5%	30	15	14	23	24	26	15
5-9.9%	37	31	30	34	43	38	32
10% and over	33	54	56	43	33	36	53
Total	100	100	100	100	100	100	100
Public Utilities							
Less than 5%	15	12	5	8	7	13	8
5-9.9%	44	35	24	24	44	50	44
10% and over	41	53	72	68	49	37	48
Total	100	100	100	100	100	100	100
Railroads							
Less than 2%	48	17	21	23	48	52	26
2-3.9%	33	25	28	38	34	34	30
4% and over	19	58	51	39	18	14	44
Total	100	100	100	100	100	100	100

in the results since the measure of scale contains in the numerator the same figure that is contained in the denominator of the measure of realization. The designations "small," "medium," and "large" refer to the classifications established in Table 3.

The data for manufacturing are summarized below:

1. Firms reporting large-scale programs invariably show smaller deviations than firms anticipating medium and small-scale programs.

2. In six of the eight years firms anticipating large-scale programs spent less than planned; companies anticipating lesser programs almost always spent more than planned.

3. Size of firm and scale of investment are closely correlated. If Table 3 is read so that size is held constant, companies with large-scale programs had a better record in anticipations in practically every year.

4. In each year, the larger the firm, the more frequent were large-scale programs (see Table 4).[4] This is a major factor in the relatively better performance of large companies and their characteristic of spending less than planned. The size-of-firm effect remains, however. When anticipated scale of investment is held constant, a higher proportion of large firms' deviations usually fall within the ± 20 per cent intervals (Table 3).

5. Regardless of firm size, when small-scale programs were anticipated, they were invariably exceeded. When large-scale programs were antici- pated by small and medium firms they show no particular tendency to exceed or fall short. But large programs of large companies have almost always fallen short of expectations.

The same characteristics of the ratios that were evident in manufacturing appear in utilities and railroads. The medium and large programs of both groups show little difference in the proportion falling within the 20 per cent limits. The utilities almost always spent less than planned, especially when they had large programs. The rails tended to exceed anticipations when the anticipated programs were small; otherwise they exhibit no persistent tendencies.

PLANT AND EQUIPMENT OUTLAYS

Separate plant and equipment data are not currently published by Com- merce and the SEC because of inadequate reporting by a relatively small but important group of the very largest firms. They predominate in steel, petroleum, and chemicals, where the distinction is often not easy to make. The discussion that follows is based on the unpublished reports.

In Table 5 manufacturing firms are classified according to scale of investment and proportion of plant in total anticipated 1956 expenditures. Within each firm-size class the large-scale anticipations contain a much higher proportion of plant than the small-scale programs. For all firms combined, 21 per cent of small-scale programs consist of 25 per cent or more of plant; 28 per cent of medium-scale programs, and 57 per cent of large-scale programs. We could not at this time make a similar investiga- tion for other years. However, unpublished figures for the manufacturing aggregate show that the ratio of construction to total outlays in 1954 and 1955 generally increased with size of firm.

This breakdown suggests why large-scale programs tend to come relatively close to realization. New plants or major additions involve large outlays, considerable advance planning, and extensive forward commitments because they take long to build. Investigators found that

[4] Plant and equipment expenditures refer to gross and not net investment.

TABLE 5

Distribution of Firms by Size of Firm, Scale of Investment, and Proportion
of Plant Outlay to Total Investment, Manufacturing, 1956
(*as % of all firms*)

Firm Size and Scale of Investment	PLANT OUTLAYS AS % OF TOTAL INVESTMENT				
	Zero	Less than 24.9	25–49.9	50 and over	Total
Small firms:					
Less than 5%	47	36	10	7	100
5–9.9%	45	29	20	6	100
10% and over	19	21	29	31	100
Total	36	29	20	15	100
Medium-sized firms:					
Less than 5%	38	38	17	7	100
5–9.9%	19	56	18	7	100
10% and over	7	38	32	23	100
Total	19	44	23	14	100
Large firms:					
Less than 5%	24	48	28		100
5–9.9%	8	55	22	15	100
10% and over	10	31	35	24	100
Total	12	40	30	18	100
All firms:					
Less than 5%	41	38	15	6	100
5–9.9%	28	44	20	8	100
10% and over	12	30	31	26	100
Total	25	37	23	15	100

during the Korean mobilization scheduled construction time for new
plant averaged nine months in manufacturing and mining industries.[5]
The actual time was considerably longer, as construction progress records
under the rapid tax amortization program indicate.[6] Average construction
time exceeds nine months in industries like iron and steel, nonferrous
metals, chemicals, and petroleum refining. In the integrated iron and steel
industry, for example, scheduled construction time for facilities such as
blast furnaces, coke ovens, and open-hearth furnaces was estimated at
approximately fifteen months under very favorable supply conditions.[7]

INDUSTRY COMPARISONS

To judge from the industry averages, manufacturing firms project
outlays more closely than either utilities or railroads. The distribution of
company deviations, however, shows quite a different pattern. Average
experience for 1950-56 shows that 72 per cent of the utilities, 49 per cent

[5] Thomas Mayer and Sidney Sonenblum, "Lead Times for Fixed Investment,"
Review of Economics and Statistics, August 1955.

[6] *Expansion Progress*, Office of Defense Mobilization, various issues, 1952-55.

[7] "Investment Costs and Capacity in Iron and Steel," Office of Business Economics,
Dept. of Commerce, September 1953 (unpublished).

396

of the largest manufacturers, and 43 per cent of the railroads had deviations falling within ± 20 per cent (Table 3).

With scale of investment and size of firm held constant, utilities still rank ahead of railroads and manufacturing for each scale-of-investment class; the latter industries are not much different in the proportion of firms whose deviations fell within the ± 20 per cent band.

Separate breakdowns were prepared for individual manufacturing industries including iron and steel, electrical machinery, machinery except electrical, chemicals, and petroleum. A persistent understatement of anticipated small-scale programs was found in all the above industries except petroleum, in which firms on the average were about equally divided between those exceeding and those falling short of small-scale anticipations. In large-scale programs the steel and petroleum industries showed a distinct tendency to spend less than planned. Electrical machinery and chemicals showed no particular tendency in this regard, and machinery except electrical fell in between the other groups.

REASONS FOR OVER- AND UNDERESTIMATES

Firm size and size of anticipated expenditure were obviously the most important factors associated with how closely firms realize their reported plans. But other characteristics, associated with whether firms spend more or less than planned, were brought to light.

1. The clearest tendency is a characteristic of firms, regardless of size, to spend more than they anticipate when the anticipated outlay is small. Although large firms have not been immune in this respect, small-scale anticipations of large manufacturers have had a very small weight in large company programs. In 1950, for example, anticipated small-scale expenditures accounted for 15 per cent of expected dollar expenditures of large companies, or about half the corresponding proportion of firms shown in Table 4. Because small firms usually report relatively small programs, a comparison of their plans and results generally shows the actual expenditure higher than anticipated.

2. When large manufacturing firms reported anticipations of large programs, they almost always spent less than planned. Because of the predominance of large programs among large manufacturing firms, such companies spent slightly less on the whole than anticipated in four of the five years, 1952-56.

Special questionnaires support the notion that a major reason why the largest manufacturers persistently overestimate their expenditures on large-scale projects is that postwar supply conditions have made it impossible for them to realize the time schedules of construction progress and equipment deliveries that underlie their investment anticipations. The underlying schedules may be unrealistic because they assume conditions of excess capacity in capital-goods industries. Engineers may use such schedules to win executive approval of their projects. Conversely they may be imposed on engineers by management. Or large companies, being cognizant of the unsettled supply conditions, may have included unusually large contingency allowances in their projects. Gort found that electric utilities included contingency allowances in their budgets at the beginning of the year, but we have no direct evidence of this in manufacturing.[8]

The fact that overstatement characterizes utilities and large manufacturing firms, but not railroads, suggests that the longer lead time for the programs of the former makes them more vulnerable to delays. It is significant that large-scale anticipations of small firms, involving presumably shorter construction times, do not fall short on the average.

The tendency of companies to exceed anticipations when the anticipation is relatively small may result from a number of factors. The 1949 and 1955 studies found that the necessity of cutting costs in the face of intensified competition led to unanticipated expenditures, as did unexpected machinery breakdowns. The 1955 study revealed that some firms were submitting anticipations before the board of directors or the executive committee had met, so that only figures for the ensuing few months were available.

The understatement may also arise because of inadequate allowance for price increases. If firms projected a physical volume of investment at prevailing prices, some understatement must have resulted if real spending for capital goods is relatively inelastic, since capital goods prices rose almost steadily after the war.

While unexpected price increases undoubtedly contributed to the understatement, we are not inclined to assign a major role to this factor. In a recent paper[9] Modigliani and Weingartner criticized us for minimizing the role of unexpected price change and took issue with a suggestion made in March 1956 *Survey of Current Business* that the appropriate base period for projecting prices into the year ahead is around the beginning of the year.[10] But such a base period seems reasonable for the typical firm, whose capital outlays are comparatively small. Naturally, where large projects are duly weighted, the appropriate time period must precede the start of the year because of the time requirements in planning, letting contracts and so forth. Actually, the difference in capital goods costs at the start of any of the postwar years and average costs in the final quarter

[8] Michael Gort, "The Planning of Investment: A Study of Capital Budgeting in the Electric Power Industry. II," *Journal of Business of the University of Chicago*, July 1951.

[9] Franco Modigliani and H. M. Weingartner, "Forecasting Uses of Anticipatory Data on Investment and Sales," *Quarterly Journal of Economics*, February 1958.

[10] Murray F. Foss, "Business Expectations for 1956—Investment Outlays and Sales," *Survey of Current Business*, March 1956.

of the preceding year (the rough approximation used by Modigliani and Weingartner) is quite small.

The chief argument against emphasizing the price effect is the amount of the understatement. Actual expenditures by small companies exceeded anticipations by approximately 10 per cent over the past five years, and this is substantially more than can be accounted for by price changes. During the same period, actual aggregate outlays by the largest firms fell slightly short of anticipations, so that a positive price effect, if it exists, must be more than offset by opposing forces.

A final possibility is that firms report as anticipations primarily what has been contracted for, or what remains to be done on projects in process. The 1955 questionnaire showed that some firms, usually smaller ones, have little basis for making a forecast. Actual expenditures are related not to firmly held anticipations but to current income or cash position. These factors appear to explain why aggregate expenditures in the second half of the year have usually been understated, a bias even more evident in anticipations of more than one year.

Cyclical Patterns of Over- and Underestimates

EXPANSION VERSUS CONTRACTION

The relative importance of large- and small-scale anticipations varies over the cycle (see Table 4), so that cyclical patterns of overstatement and understatement may greatly affect the confidence that can be placed in the annual anticipations.

The 1950-56 average experience, expressed in terms of the medians in Table 3 indicates the performance of companies in the years of sharp upturn, 1950 and 1955, and the one year of mild downturn shown, 1954:

1. *Small programs.* In 1950 and 1955 the proportion of manufacturing firms spending more than planned is above the average regardless of size of firm, though the excess is small for the largest firms. All sizes fall below the average in 1954.

2. *Large programs.* Those of small manufacturers appear to vary cyclically, like the small programs just noted. Those of medium and large manufacturers are usually close to the average in 1950, 1954, and 1955; the largest deviation, in 1955, is contracyclical. When firms of all sizes are combined, the proportion of firms anticipating large-scale programs in the downturn year of 1949 and spending more than planned is larger than the average.

3. *Medium programs.* There is some evidence of cyclical variability but no distinct pattern by size of firm.

In terms of scale of investment, patterns of cyclical variability in utilities and rails are less clear than in manufacturing. For rails there appears to be a cyclical pattern.

DIRECTION OF CHANGE

The ability of an aggregate series to forecast direction of change is extremely important, but for the individual firm it is only a rough measure of predictive ability. Direction of change in the aggregate has been missed even though about three out of four manufacturing companies were able to anticipate direction properly. Nevertheless individual firm data provide an indication of small firm behavior and give further evidence of the tendency of companies to spend more than their reported anticipations.

Information on direction of change for 1950-56 is shown in Table 6. At

TABLE 6

Anticipated and Actual Direction of Change from Actual Investment by
Firms in Previous Year, Manufacturing, 1950-1956
(*per cent*)

Firms	1950	1951	1952	1953	1954	1955	1956
Anticipating increase:							
Experiencing increase	29	50	27	36	27	35	47
Experiencing decrease	6	9	8	8	8	7	8
Anticipating decrease:							
Experiencing decrease	38	26	48	38	47	36	30
Experiencing increase	27	15	17	18	18	22	15
Total	100	100	100	100	100	100	100
Correctly anticipating direction of change	67	77	75	73	74	71	77
Anticipating increase	36	59	35	44	35	42	55
Correctly	82	86	77	81	77	83	84
Anticipating decrease	64	41	65	56	65	58	45
Correctly	58	64	74	67	72	62	67

Figures will not necessarily add to totals because of rounding.

no time did the proportion of correct anticipations of direction of change fall below 67 per cent; the proportions are lowest for 1950 and 1955. These data are, of course, dominated by small companies. While large companies are somewhat better at anticipating, there is relatively little difference by size of firm.

Except for 1951 and 1956, when aggregate investment increases of 45 and 31 per cent, respectively, were projected by manufacturers, more than half of the anticipations were expectations of decrease. An examination of large firm expectations would show a much more nearly equal distribution in this respect. Projections of decreases were correct less often than those of increases—another aspect of the tendency of firms to understate anticipations. Expectations of increase were correct most often in 1951 and the turning point year of 1955; least often, in the downturn year of 1954 and the steel strike year of 1952.

Effect of Structural Factors on Survey Results

Like other investigators, we found that departures from sales and profits expectations were the primary influences that gave rise to changes from investment expectations.[11] On an aggregative basis a high coefficient of correlation can be obtained by relating deviations from annual sales anticipations with deviations from annual investment anticipations, for manufacturing as a whole, 1948-56.[12] On an individual industry basis we may note a similar association. Table 7 presents a comparison of the signs

TABLE 7

Comparison of Investment and Sales Deviations, Fourteen Manufacturing Industries, 1952–1956

Industries	1952	1953	1954	1955	1956[a]
Investment higher, sales higher than anticipated	1	9	2	11	3
Investment higher, sales lower than anticipated	6	3	4	1	3
Investment lower, sales higher than anticipated	3	1	0	2	3
Investment lower, sales lower than anticipated	4	1	8	0	3
Number with like signs	5	10	10	11	6

[a] Excludes two industries where one of the deviations was less than 0.5 per cent.

of the deviations for individual two-digit manufacturing industries, 1952-1956. Reasons for the poor associations in 1952 and 1956 are suggested below. The questionnaires analyzing the realization of the 1949 and 1955 investment anticipations of individual firms demonstrated that departures from sales expectations were important causal influences.

While recognizing the importance of sales and profits deviations, we feel that the particular context in which these deviations occur must also be considered. We therefore suggest, on the basis of the discussion in the preceding pages, how departures from sales expectations may be modified.

THE TENDENCY TOWARD UNDERSTATEMENT

The understatement bias works in a contracyclical fashion when business is declining. The tendency of some firms to underestimate their expenditures cushions the negative influence of sales disappointments

[11] See, for example, the previously cited works by Friend and Bronfenbrenner, and by Foss and Natrella.
[12] $r = 0.88$ for the nine observations.

upon the realization of investment plans. However when sales turn out better than expected, the deviation from planned investment is accentuated by this practice.

In 1957, for the first time, a limited attempt was made to correct for understatement by small manufacturers. We quote from the March 1957 *Survey of Current Business*: "The adjustment amounted to a 10 per cent increase, which was roughly the average annual understatement of the small firms, considered as a group, over the past five years. The adjustment was uniformly applied to the planned expenditures of the small size classes in each industry. The correction added $0.3 billion to total anticipated manufacturing investment as reported in this review; this constitutes 2 per cent of manufacturing investment and 0.8 of 1 per cent of aggregate investment this year."

THE PREVALENCE OF LARGE-SCALE PROGRAMS

The cross-sectional data indicate that large-scale programs in manufacturing, when anticipated by large and medium-sized firms, have shown some insensitivity to cyclical change, though the test was necessarily limited by the period under consideration. The insensitivity would be suspect if firms anticipating large outlays experienced consistently smaller sales deviations than firms expecting lesser expenditures. Therefore we ran a comparison test. Companies were classified by two-digit manufacturing industries; firm size had to be disregarded as an independent variable because of the small numbers involved. We found that median sales deviations of firms engaged in large programs were virtually as great as (within 1 per cent) or greater than sales deviations of firms engaged in medium or small programs, in seven out of nine industries in 1954 and 1955, and six out of nine industries in 1956.

PLANT AND EQUIPMENT SUPPLIES

The plant and equipment supply situation is difficult to treat, partly because it does not readily lend itself to measurement under normal circumstances. About the only "supply-requirements" information available is that compiled by the government during war and mobilization periods, when allocations systems are in effect. Also, "aggregate supply" data may be misleading because of the crucial importance of particular kinds of materials or labor.

Supply conditions have less influence on the realization of investment anticipations as the period under consideration lengthens. We are dealing here with anticipations for one year—a comparatively short time given the timing factors relevant to planning and executing of fixed investment, especially in heavy manufacturing industries and public utilities.

Questionnaires have helped to illuminate the role of supply conditions.[13] In the 1955 survey, among firms that spent less than anticipated, delay in deliveries and construction progress was by far the most important factor cited, and its importance increased with size of firm and size of program. Although direct evidence is lacking, materials shortages in 1952 and 1956 largely explain the poor association between investment and sales deviations, as indicated in Table 7. Among firms that exceeded plans, unexpectedly high sales and profits received the most emphasis.

In the 1949 study the relative importance of supply conditions and demand was reversed. Firms that exceeded their plans mentioned better-than-expected supplies more often than better-than-expected profits or sales. Firms that fell short of anticipated investment stressed disappointing sales, profits, and working capital rather than supply difficulties. The changing importance of supply conditions in two different phases of the cycle indicates how they may play a modifying and partially compensatory role in affecting the realization of short-run investment plans.

STAGE OF COMPLETION

The stage of the individual firm's investment cycle, and the amount of work that remains to be done at the start of the year, have a bearing on the extent to which programs are realized. The expenditure anticipation may be thought of as consisting of outlays to complete (or extend) projects started earlier and outlays for new projects. The carryover portion is the more certain, less flexible part. A large volume of work remaining to be done at the start of the year is a stabilizing influence on an investment anticipation, especially when it represents the completion phase of a major project.

At the end of 1953, for example, a sizable allowance for projects carried over from the Korean mobilization period was included in the 1954 anticipations (which constituted a decrease). The necessity for completing such work will not prevent a reduction of outlays below anticipations when sales turn out badly, but it limits the size of the reduction. By way of contrast, the end of 1949 saw postwar low points in unfilled orders and goods-in-process inventories in durable-goods industries, and probably the lowest volume of work carried over in the postwar period. As Table 4 shows, the importance of small-scale programs was then relatively high, and that of large-scale programs relatively low. The anticipation for 1950 was especially vulnerable to a shift in sales from expectations and a large deviation developed, even before the Korean outbreak.

---

[13] The 1955 questionnaire also demonstrated that slow deliveries and construction progress were an important explanation for what appeared to be an anomaly in the individual company data and, oftentimes, industry data: shortfalls in investment coupled with an excess of actual overanticipated sales.

COMMENT

JEAN A. CROCKETT, University of Pennsylvania

On the basis of seven years' experience with investment anticipations, the following pattern emerges for manufacturing firms:

1. Small and medium-sized firms with small or medium-sized programs understate their expenditures in 60 to 70 per cent of the cases, and those with large programs understate about as often as they overstate.

2. Large firms with small programs understate their expenditures in about 70 per cent of the cases, those with medium-sized programs understate about as often as they overstate, and those with large programs overstate in about two-thirds of the cases.

The pattern suggests that, while small and medium-sized firms tend to understate expenditures, large firms do not. Possibly the latter make more adequate provision for routine replacement needs, which are predictable only on the average. Probably a more important reason is that businessmen tend to report only fairly certain projects, and large companies tend to make firm decisions further ahead than do small firms. There is less chance that a large company will make substantial outlays before the end of a year on a project not certain at its beginning. One test of this reasoning would be to note whether small and medium-sized firms are more inclined than large firms to anticipate expenditures for the second half of a year unrealistically lower than those for the first half.

Secondly, there may be a general tendency toward overstatement of large programs, possibly due, as Foss and Natrella argue, to the delays in equipment deliveries and plant construction progress frequently encountered in the postwar capital goods market. If so, an offsetting of biases would occur in large programs of small and medium-sized firms, only the negative bias in their smaller programs, and only the positive bias in the large programs of large firms. But is the superior accuracy of the large programs of small and medium-sized firms entirely due to the netting out of opposing biases? (For large firms the large programs are not significantly more accurate than the medium-sized ones.) I think not. First, a 20 per cent error in estimating the cost of a program is obviously much more serious when the project is large relative to fixed assets than when it is relatively small. More important, a company is less free to exceed a large program by a large percentage, even in response to highly favorable developments, because there is a limit to how far any firm wants to commit itself in a single year. At the same time it is not clear that a large program is more likely to fall short by a large *percentage* than a small program.

Some light can be thrown on the role of supply factors in the overestimation of large programs by examining the behavior of such programs in 1949 and 1954 when the supply situation was somewhat easier than in most of the postwar period.[1] The relative superiority of the large programs appears to be as great for medium-sized firms in these two years as in the other years studied, but somewhat less for small firms. The tendency for large firms to overstate large programs was less in 1949 but not in 1954.

Turning now to the effect of unexpected movements in sales and profits on the realization of investment programs, I suggest that the understatement bias should be eliminated before attempting to measure this effect. In the two years of minor recession, 1949 and 1954, the downward pressure of sales movements was offset by the usual bias toward underestimation and thus largely concealed. In the two years of upturn, 1950 and 1955, the upward pressure of sales movements was exaggerated by the tendency to underestimate. Fluctuations in the supply situation in expansions and contractions have also served to limit sales-induced deviations from investment programs in the postwar period. It is not clear how important this countercyclical force will be under normal supply conditions.

Other factors have a bearing on the precise effect of sales deviations. If programs generally are relatively large, unexpected gains in sales are likely to have less effect (and unexpected declines more) than if programs are small. The work of Robert Eisner with the 1950 McGraw–Hill data and my own work with the 1949 Commerce–SEC data indicate that sales deviations should have stronger effects when expansionary investment represents a high proportion of the total. Finally, while the effect of liquidity is hard to quantify, I believe that high liquidity will accentuate the effects of an unexpected increase in sales, while a tight cash position will accentuate the effects of an unexpected decline. Perhaps the only conclusion to be drawn now with any conviction is that expenditures are likely to exceed anticipations when sales rise unexpectedly if existing capacity is rather fully utilized, if programs are small, and if the supply situation and level of liquidity permit.

[1] Foss and Natrella do not give the appropriate breakdown for 1949, and I am drawing on my own work for that information.

The Value of Anticipations Data in Forecasting National Product

ARTHUR M. OKUN

COWLES FOUNDATION FOR RESEARCH IN ECONOMICS AT
YALE UNIVERSITY

The forecaster of economic activity has access to a variety of series which supply a continuing record of the anticipations of a number of groups in the economy. The present paper seeks to ascertain the value of such data and the requirements for their efficient use in prediction. It explores certain theoretical issues, reviews the empirical record of the aggregative time-series relationships between some of the anticipations data and subsequent realizations, and analyzes the findings of cross-section studies in which the predictive value of anticipations data has been appraised at the level of the individual firm or household.

Since the focus of the study is the problem of forecasting the gross national product and its components, the analysis is restricted to anticipations data which fit fairly neatly into established income and product accounts. Consequently data which may throw light on financial trends, employment levels, and the level of sales and production of particular industries are ignored. It is to be hoped, however, that the task of relating the latter variables to the GNP framework will receive a high priority in future research.

Observations on the Characteristics of Anticipations Data

Data on economic variables are the raw materials from which forecasts are constructed, and each forecaster will select his own preferred set of raw materials and processes. Expressed anticipations may be poor predictors in their raw state and yet be valuable when transformed so as to eliminate bias. If, for example, some group in the economy typically overestimates its prospective income or expenditure, an appropriate adjustment may be made. Expectational data can be useful provided they bear some discernible systematic relationship to forthcoming trends. Also, anticipations relating to one economic variable may provide insight into the future

NOTE: The paper was written as part of the project in Research on Short-Term Economic Forecasting, conducted at the Cowles Foundation for Research in Economics at Yale University and financed by the Rockefeller Foundation. The author is indebted to Professor Thomas F. Dernburg of Purdue University and to Mrs. Wilma Heston for their valuable assistance with the empirical material presented in this study.

407

behavior of another variable. Suppose survey data showed that business-men expected Congress to lower the tax rate on corporate profits a year hence. Even if the economic analyst felt that such legislation was highly unlikely, he might find the anticipation a valuable indicator of the probable course of business spending. Thus, indirect uses of an anticipations variable may prove fruitful even when the series is not helpful in its presumptive primary use. Furthermore, anticipations data should be utilized as comple-ments, rather than substitutes, for nonexpectational data. The objective is to enlarge the fund of information on which forecasts are based, and the forecaster must apply his ingenuity and analytical skill to find useful combinations of the various available series.

Because anticipations have many possible uses, it is exceedingly danger-ous to render an over-all judgment on the predictive value of any ex-pectational variable. Any investigator rash enough to declare that a series has no value is stating merely that he has discovered no fruitful use. He may find himself embarrassed in short order by the research of a more ingenious or more fortunate economist. On the other hand, a favorable verdict may be upset by a demonstration that equally good results can be obtained without reliance on that series. The appraisal of the predictive value of data is inherently a risky business. Any evaluation should be advanced, and interpreted, as tentative and resting on a pragmatic foundation.

DEFINITION OF ANTICIPATIONS

Anticipations data are here taken to consist of series which are forecasts of an economic magnitude directly expressed by decision-makers in operating units in the economy, and which are not usually recorded in the normal course of economic activity. Series on new orders, contract awards, and commitments are excluded by this definition since these are records of bona fide transactions.

Information on anticipations is necessarily collected by direct interview or mail response to questionnaires and is subject to all the problems of sampling error and response errors inherent in the survey technique. It seems highly unlikely, however, that the potential value of anticipations data would be nullified by limitations associated with the collection process. Data on nonexpectational variables have been successfully collected through surveys. The general agreement of results in independent efforts to collect anticipations data on similar variables suggests that usable measures of economic anticipations can similarly be obtained.

ANALYTICAL CONSIDERATIONS

In appraising the predictive value of anticipations data it is useful to distinguish among various types of anticipations. Some concern variables which are *internal*, relating directly to the future experience of the respon-dent, such as the flows of his receipts or outlays. Other expectations are *external*, and record his forecasts of the experience of other producers or consumers or his views on the outlook for the economy as a whole.

One must be skeptical of the direct predictive value of external expectations, despite the statistical appeal of relying on a consensus view. If each individual forecast is slightly superior to a random guess, and if there is a fair amount of independence among the individual predictions, the consensus view obtained from a large sample becomes highly reliable. Unfortunately, neither condition is likely to be fulfilled: the amateur may not be better informed than the naïve model, and the views are likely to exhibit strong interdependence. Forecasting business activity is a technical, complex task; and there is nothing to suggest that a consensus of the views of amateurs would improve on the resources available to the professional analyst. But when the external variables are close to the direct experience of the respondent, he may be able to contribute to their prediction. For example, a businessman's own insight or expert advice from his professional staff may supply him with some ability to forecast the course of activity in his industry.

Expectations about external variables may have profitable indirect uses by providing insight into the probable economic behavior of groups expressing particular expectations. However, plausible cases can often be made for conflicting hypotheses on the probable effect of a particular external anticipation. For example, firms expecting inflation may wish to accumulate inventories for speculative purposes; on the other hand, their present inventories may reflect these price expectations so that, unless inflation materializes, they will reduce their inventories. Thus the role of a priori reasoning is sharply limited, and one must hope for assistance from empirical research.

A far stronger analytical case can be made for the direct predictive value of certain internal anticipations. Expectations about purchases or sales of goods and services by the respondent are the chief internal anticipations considered in this paper. The predictive value of such anticipations depends on:

1. Whether the respondent has an articulated plan of action which he reports accurately in the survey
2. Whether he has the power to fulfill his plan
3. Whether, and how, he is likely to revise his plan voluntarily in the light of later information about the economic environment.

Existence of Plans. All firms have selling and buying plans of some sort. They must forecast, at least for the near future, their expected sales volume, production needs, and input requirements. Households are also likely to make tentative advance decisions about major purchases, other than those of an emergency nature, and about the probable supply of labor services. How much a knowledge of the various expectations will contribute to forecasting will depend on the range, timing, and definiteness with which plans are formulated. Survey data on anticipations and realizations can supply evidence on the extent and character of such planning.

Feasibility of Fulfillment. The ability to realize internal expectations differs considerably with the variable in question. When a household predicts its income, its anticipation implies a compound estimate of: (1) the supply of factor services; (2) the likelihood of their finding employment; and (3) the returns which they will earn. Obviously, the latter two components are external expectations not subject to the household's control. The ability of households and firms to carry out buying plans is likely to be greater but still limited. Excess demand for goods or the unavailability of expected means of financing may frustrate purchase intentions. Otherwise, purchasers presumably have the power to acquire the specific items on their shopping lists; but, because buyers cannot control prices, they can fulfil intentions only by permitting their dollar outlays to diverge from the expected level whenever there are unforeseen movements in prices. Alternatively, buyers can maintain their proposed dollar outlays when prices vary by making substitutions for certain items on their shopping lists. Thus, purchasers can make binding decisions either on amounts they will spend or on the quantity and quality of commodities they will acquire, but not on both.

Where markets have any imperfection, firms can realize their expected physical volume of sales by permitting their prices to vary. Or they can maintain their planned prices, allowing physical sales to diverge from plans. Actual prices and quantities can both correspond with plans only if the firm has accurately forecast demand. Since firms typically treat price as the decision variable, any error in the projection of demand will be initially reflected in a divergence of physical sales from expectations. If data were available on the anticipations of both buyers and sellers of a product, knowledge of the dynamics of supply-demand adjustment in the particular market would be relied on for estimates of the changes in prices, output, and inventories resulting from any disparate expectations. Lacking such a complete record of plans, the analyst will usually find the plans of sellers most helpful in forecasting the short-term course of prices, since producers are price-makers. Plans of buyers will normally assist most in the prediction of sales volume at a given level of prices.

Revision of Plans. Even when the fulfillment of internal anticipations is feasible, buyers and sellers may wish to alter their plans. If the actions of any economic unit were exclusively determined by conditions of preceding periods and if its reported intentions reflected the full impact of the predetermined variables affecting behavior, its feasible intentions would be regularly fulfilled. Over the short-run, actions would be insensitive to contemporaneous events and could be considered exogenous. However, such a pattern of behavior is implausible. Plans are made on the basis of assumptions about the future environment. To a large extent, these assumptions are forecasts of external variables and may well prove wrong. Hence, intentions are subject to change even though the cost of reconsidering and revising plans will produce some inertia in tentative decisions. The possibility of plan-revision detracts from the predictive value of internal anticipations. However, survey data can provide information on the assumptions about external variables underlying intentions. With such information, the forecaster can evaluate the likelihood that plans are based on excessively optimistic or pessimistic expectations. Even when the underlying assumptions of respondents seem wide of the mark, intentions data may be helpful if they are interpreted as revealing a single point on a schedule relating actions to possible states of the environment. The forecaster must then estimate how the economic units are likely to revise their plans when the environment deviates from their expectations. This is not easy, but it holds promise as one means by which insight into the future can be increased.[1]

Consumer Expenditure

In the past twenty years, there have been many quantitative explorations designed to explain and forecast aggregate consumer expenditure in terms of nonexpectational variables. Disposable personal income was generally used as an explanatory variable. Many studies also incorporated predetermined flow variables, such as lagged income and lagged consumption, and various balance-sheet magnitudes of the household sector. Anticipations data are further potential explanatory variables. Their usefulness as predictors depends on their ability to complement the nonexpectational variables in explaining the observed variation in consumer spending.

THE ROLE OF DURABLE GOODS EXPENDITURE

In the intentions data collected from consumers, plans to buy durable goods receive primary emphasis. Most individual durable goods involve a substantial expenditure, are infrequently purchased by any single household, and provide considerable latitude in the timing of their acquisition. These characteristics provide analytical support for the belief that many households plan their purchases of durables well in advance and are able to offer accurate information about their decisions in interviews.[2]

---

[1] For other theoretical explorations, from which the discussion above has benefited, see "Report of Consultant Committee on General Business Expectations," *Reports of Federal Reserve Consultant Committees on Economic Statistics*, 1955, pp. 506-508 and 675-676; Irwin Friend, "Critical Evaluation of Surveys of Expectations, Plans and Investment Behavior," pp. 189-190, and Franco Modigliani and Kalman J. Cohen, "The Significance and Uses of *Ex Ante* Data," both published in *Expectations, Uncertainty, and Business Behavior*, Mary Jean Bowman, ed., Social Science Research Council, 1958.

[2] See the discussion in George Katona, *Psychological Analysis of Economic Behavior*, McGraw–Hill, 1951, pp. 64-69.

Households could perhaps report on other prospective purchases that have a lower unit cost and are made on a recurring basis; for example, the decision to move to a larger apartment must be made some months prior to the move. The major reason that plans to buy durable goods stand almost alone in studies of household intentions is the belief that spending on durables is highly volatile and accounts for a significant portion of the variation in aggregate consumer expenditure that cannot be accounted for by nonexpectational variables.

If a high level of durable goods purchases, relative to income and other variables, were normally associated with an offsetting low level of spending on nondurables, ability to forecast the propensity to buy durables would supply no insight into the prospective behavior of total consumer demand. Thus, in terms of the objectives of forecasting national product, the keen interest in durables is predicated on the hypothesis that a high level of durables spending is associated with a low level of personal saving, relative to the nonexpectational explanatory variables.[3] This proposition may be put formally as follows. Consider personal saving (S) and durable goods expenditures (D) as functions of disposable income (Y) and other non-expectational variables $(X_1, \ldots, X_n)$, and let u_1 and u_2 represent the error terms in the respective relationships. Then,

$$(1) \qquad\qquad S_t = S(Y, X_1, \ldots, X_n) + u_{1t}$$

$$(2) \qquad\qquad D_t = D(Y, X_1, \ldots, X_n) + u_{2t}$$

The ability to forecast durables perfectly would mean that the value of u_2 for some period t could be specified without error at some time prior to t. The assistance that such knowledge can give in the specification of the saving function depends on the degree of relationship between u_1 and u_2. It would be nil if u_1 and u_2 were independent. However, the analytical hypotheses cited above suggest a negative relationship between u_1 and u_2 which, if linear, would take the following form:

$$(3) \qquad\qquad u_{1t} = -au_{2t} + u_{3t}$$

The relative amount of explained variation in u_1 contributed by the fore-knowledge of u_2 depends on the relative size of the variances of u_1 and u_3, the respective errors before and after durables spending is taken into account. This procedure is equivalent to the use of consumer expenditure on durable goods as an added independent variable in the saving function. If equation 2 is used to eliminate u_{2t} from equation 3, and if the resulting

---

[3] See the paper by F. Thomas Juster in this volume; and John B. Lansing and Stephen B. Withey, "Consumer Anticipations: Their Use in Forecasting Consumer Behavior," *Short-Term Economic Forecasting*, Studies in Income and Wealth, Vol. 17, Princeton University Press for National Bureau of Economic Research, 1955, p. 387.

expression is substituted for u_{1t} in equation 1, the following relationship is obtained:

$$(4) \qquad S_t = S(Y, X_1, \ldots, X_n) + aD(Y, X_1, \ldots, X_n) - aD_t + u_{3t}$$

Quarterly data from 1948-55 support the hypothesis of a negative relation between the propensity to save and the propensity to purchase durable goods. The regression of personal saving, deflated by population (N) and the consumer price index (P), on disposable income and durable goods spending, both similarly deflated, yields:

$$(5) \qquad S/NP = 0.419\,Y/NP - 1.19\,D/NP - 274 \text{ (in 1947-49 dollars)}$$

The coefficient of determination (R^2) is 0.72. The inclusion of durables as a variable leads to a substantial improvement over the usual saving-income relationship. It eliminates 60 per cent of the unexplained variation, and the standard error of estimate (adjusted for degrees of freedom) is lowered from \$23 to \$15.[4] The estimate of the regression coefficient of durables in equation 5 is significantly different from zero but not from minus unity. Thus the results are consistent with the hypothesis that an excess of spending on durables is simply additive to total consumer expenditure. The findings suggest that efforts to predict the propensity to buy durables are potentially capable of contributing substantially to the success of forecasts of economic activity. However, sizable unexplained variation is evident in the other components of consumer spending. Also in the twelve observations provided by annual data for 1929-40 the inclusion of durables fails to aid the explanation of personal saving. Obviously the durables component is not the sole contributor to the variability of consumer behavior. Nevertheless, during the postwar years, any information by which durables expenditures could have been successfully forecast would have materially improved the forecasts of aggregate consumer spending.

EVIDENCE ON BUYING INTENTIONS

Criteria of Predictive Ability. Data on intended purchases of household appliances and of new automobiles are reported in the Survey of Consumer Finances (SCF) and periodic surveys conducted by the Survey Research Center (SRC). These intentions run substantially below realized purchases. Therefore an aggregate "blow-up" of survey buying plans is a hopelessly

[4] The expenditure and income data are taken from the *National Income Supplement, 1954*, and from the July 1956 issue, *Survey of Current Business*, Dept. of Commerce. Years before 1948 were omitted because of the prevalence of excess demand for consumer durables during the immediate postwar period. The saving-income relationship for quarterly data for 1948-55 is:

$$S/NP = 0.248\,Y/NP - 242 \text{ with } r^2 = 0.32$$

The durables–income relationship derived from the same data is:

$$D/NP = 0.143\,Y/NP - 27$$

poor forecaster of total purchases. However, the intentions data can have predictive value so long as they bear some stable relationship to purchases. A one-to-one relationship is not a requirement nor is it necessarily superior to, say, a two-to-one relationship.

In a number of appraisals of the predictive value of intentions data, the direction and magnitude of change in intentions to buy from one year to the next were compared with the change in actual purchases.[5] The technique of comparing pairs of adjacent years has the merit of not requiring a one-to-one relationship, but it has other drawbacks. It ignores potentially useful information from earlier years with the result that, under certain conditions, one unsuccessful survey may produce two poor forecasts. Suppose that intentions decline markedly from one year to the next, and yet purchases rise. If, in the following year, intentions recover at all, the technique of paired comparison implies a further rise in purchases even if plans to buy are still below the level of the initial observation. Usually it would seem preferable to attach some weight to the relative levels of plans and purchases during the first year.[6] Another questionable feature of the technique is the emphasis on direction of change which is frequently associated with paired comparisons. The nature of the survey data creates no presumption that the intentions expressed by households are more likely to distinguish a possible 5 per cent increase in durables spending from a possible 5 per cent decrease than from the alternative possibility of a 15 per cent increase. Nor is it clear in terms of the objectives of general business forecasting that one discrimination is more vital than the other.

The whole body of evidence from time-series data can be utilized efficiently through the technique of regression analysis, the technique adopted here to appraise the predictive value of the data on intentions to buy durable goods.

Car Intentions and Purchases. All of the annual SCF surveys provide data on new car buying plans. However, since the volume of new car purchases was supply-determined well into 1948, 1949 is the first year when buying plans might be expected to have predictive value, and the first year to be considered here. SCF surveys covering 1949-55 yield seven observations on plans to buy. The periodic surveys of June and October 1954 and June and October 1955 provide four more for a total of eleven. The periodic survey of September–October 1953 and the mid-year SCF survey of July 1949 report car purchase intentions without indicating whether the reference is

---

[5] See George Katona and Eva Mueller, *Consumer Expectations, 1953-56,* Survey Research Center, University of Michigan, 1956, pp. 57-60; Irving Schweiger, "The Contribution of Consumer Anticipations in Forecasting Consumer Demand," *Short-Term Economic Forecasting*, pp. 466-470; and see also "Report of Consultant Committee on Consumer Survey Statistics," pp. 302-307.

[6] If, however, there is reason to believe that the relationship between intentions and purchases is changing, it would be wise to rely most on recent observations. Also, if there is evidence of serial correlation in the relative levels of intentions and purchases, use of ratios of observations from succeeding years might eliminate this problem.

to new or used cars. With the latter observations "all car" intentions total thirteen.[7]

Survey respondents are classified into four groups: (1) "definitely will buy," (2) "probably will buy," (3) "may buy, but undecided," and (4) "do not expect to buy." The treatment of the two middle groups presents what has been called the "cutting-point" problem.[8] To what extent should they be included among intended purchasers? All studies to date have bracketed group 2 with group 1. But group 3 has been variously treated. It has been added to the number of prospective purchasers, it has been added with a half weight to this category, and it has been added to the number of prospective nonpurchasers.[9] All three methods were tried by the author. By a trivial margin, the inclusion of "may buy" respondents among the intenders with half weight yielded the best results; so, for lack of a better criterion, it is the method employed here.[10] However the percentage of respondents in the "may buy" category proved sufficiently well-behaved over the sample data to render the cutting-point problem insignificant for present purposes.

The SCF reports percentages of spending units in the various intentions categories while the periodic surveys report in terms of families. However the data on car intentions from the latter source have been rendered comparable with those of the annual surveys by use of a technique suggested by the Survey Research Center.[11] When the percentage of spending units classified as "intenders" (those who definitely or probably will buy, plus half of those who may buy) is multiplied by the number of spending units in the economy, a measure of planned automobile purchases is obtained. Thus the intentions variables are:

M = fraction of spending units intending to buy a new car times number of spending units (in millions)

A = fraction of spending units intending to buy any car, new or used, times number of spending units (in millions).

The intentions series are desired in order to predict the aggregate number of new cars purchased by households over the subsequent year. The best available series for measuring actual purchases is that on new passenger car registrations, even though it includes government and

---

[7] Data on intentions are taken from the various SCF reports as published in the *Federal Reserve Bulletin* and from the tabulations on periodic surveys from Katona and Mueller, pp. 54, 62.

[8] Lansing and Withey, p. 416.

[9] Katona and Mueller, p. 94.

[10] There is evidence from re-interview data that spending units which express a greater degree of certainty in their plans are more likely to fulfill their intentions. See Lansing and Withey, pp. 418, 435-436 (Tables 23, 24, 53, and 55); and Robert Ferber, *Factors Influencing Durable Goods Purchases*, Bureau of Economic Research, University of Illinois, 1955, pp. 44-46.

[11] Katona and Mueller, p. 59 note.

business acquisitions.[12] The monthly series on registrations was cumulated for twelve months commencing with the month of the survey. For the SCF surveys, annual data were used.[13] The dependent variable is:

P = new passenger car registrations for twelve months beginning with the month of the survey.

Following are the results of regression estimates of P on M covering 1949-55 and June and October 1954 and June and October 1955 and of P on A for the same dates and for the same dates plus July 1949 and September–October 1953:

Eleven observations:

(1) $P = 0.79M + 2.72$ (millions of autos); $r^2 = 0.40$

(2) $P = 0.59A + 1.75$; $r^2 = 0.49$

Thirteen observations:

(3) $P = 0.47A + 2.50$; $r^2 = 0.38$

Although these relationships are not statistically significant, they indicate that over this period nearly half of the variation in new car purchases is accounted for by the intentions data.

If the forecaster uses the intentions data to predict the number of new car purchases, he must presumably make a separate and independent projection of the dollar value per auto in order to forecast consumer expenditure on new cars. Alternately, he can rely on the SCF series on the median planned expenditure of those who plan to buy new cars. This series can be used in conjunction with the data on the number of planned purchases (i.e., the variables A and M defined above) to form a measure of intended consumer expenditures on new cars.[14] The intentions variables are then:

B = A times median planned expenditure on new cars
N = M times median planned expenditure on new cars.

The Department of Commerce supplies annual estimates of consumer spending on new cars which are employed below as the measure of the

[12] These are compiled by R. L. Polk Co. and reported monthly in *Survey of Current Business.*

[13] When intentions data are taken from periodic or mid-year surveys as well as from the annual SCF surveys, there is some overlap in the series of realized purchases for the subsequent year. Thus some of the observations of actual purchases are interdependent.

[14] Median planned expenditure is not recorded in the published reports on the periodic surveys. The figure employed here in these cases was the reported median planned expenditure for the annual SCF closest in time to the periodic survey. Revised estimates for median planned expenditure in 1952-55 surveys were published in the March 1957 *Federal Reserve Bulletin.* The revisions have not been incorporated into the calculations. Casual inspection suggests that they would have produced only negligible differences in the results.

actual expenditure series, denoted by Q.[15] Following are the estimated regressions of Q on N and Q on B:

Eleven observations:

(4) $Q = 3.82 + 0.73N$ (billions of dollars); $r^2 = 0.66$

(5) $Q = 3.40 + 0.44B$; $r^2 = 0.67$

Thirteen observations:

(6) $Q = 3.37 + 0.45B$; $r^2 = 0.66$

These results may be compared with those obtained by relating consumer car expenditure to current aggregate disposable income (Y) for corresponding periods of one year, with the intentions data ignored.

Eleven observations:

(7) $Q = 0.062Y - 4.18$ (billions of dollars); $r^2 = 0.66$

Thirteen observations:

(8) $Q = 0.057Y - 2.95$; $r^2 = 0.66$

The intentions data perform just as well as disposable income in explaining consumer expenditures on new cars, yielding almost identical correlation coefficients. While this merely offers the forecaster an alternative as good as one already open to him, there is some appeal in the alternative. Disposable income must itself be predicted and is subject to error, while the intentions data are known once survey results are available.

The most interesting possibility raised by the findings is that the intentions data and disposable income employed jointly may yield better results than either taken alone. Multiple regression estimates, which employ both Y and one of the intentions series (B or N) as independent variables, are as follows:

Eleven observations:

(9) $Q = -3.00 + 0.039Y + 0.45N$ (billions of dollars); $R^2 = 0.82$

Thirteen observations:

(10) $Q = -2.35 + 0.035Y + 0.28B$; $R^2 = 0.81$

[15] Commerce's estimate of consumer expenditure on "new cars and net purchases of used cars" (Table 30, line 61 of the *National Income Supplement, 1954* and the July issue of *Survey of Current Business*) was used for the annual surveys. A quarterly series was constructed from the quarterly data on consumer spending for "automobiles and parts" (Table 51, line 3), using the annual data to eliminate the portion of the Commerce quarterly series covering purchases of car parts and accessories. These quarterly series, cumulated for four quarters beginning with the quarter starting closest to the date of the survey, were used as the estimates of the dependent variable for the periodic surveys. The data employed in equations 1 through 6 may be found in Appendix Tables A-1 and A-2.

The multiple regressions produce a marked improvement over the results of the simple regression equations. The income or intentions data, taken separately, leave unexplained about a third of the variance of car expenditure over the sample period. When the variables are employed together, the unexplained portion is reduced by nearly half, and amounts to less than a fifth of the variance.

Certain theoretical considerations suggest the use of income change, rather than the level of income, as a supplement to the intentions variable in explaining actual purchases. The intentions variable presumably reflects the income expectations of households. When realized income during the forecast period exceeds anticipated income, actual expenditure is likely to be high relative to intentions. Thus, the level of actual spending on cars would be related to (1) intended purchases reported at the start of the period and (2) the difference between realized and expected disposable income. In the absence of a direct measure of expected income, the level of income prevailing at the time of the survey may serve as a proxy, so that unexpected income change is approximated by actual income change. The second independent variable is then:

ΔY = disposable income during year of forecast minus disposable income (seasonally adjusted at annual rates) in quarter preceding year of forecast.

The estimated regression of Q on N and ΔY for the eleven available observations is:

(11) $Q = 3.25 + 0.143 \Delta Y + 0.67N$ (billions of dollars); $R^2 = 0.79$

The income-change variable does supplement the intentions measure in the sample. By a trivial and highly inconclusive margin, however, its performance is not so good as that of income level (equation 9).

Table 1 shows the success of these alternative methods of forecasting car purchases compared with that of naïve models for the calendar years 1950-55. The naïve forecast is that car purchases in the year ahead will equal those of the preceding year, so the percentage error here is simply the percentage change in purchases. For both the number of car registrations and the level of expenditure, the naïve forecasts are distinctly inferior to "predictions" based on the regression equations utilizing SRC buying plans and/or an income variable. The regressions incorporating both an income and intentions variable are most successful. The results are somewhat suspect since the estimates of regression coefficients were derived from a sample which included the observations of plans and purchases for the periods covered in the table. Nonetheless, the results are encouraging. While good fits over a small sample cannot guarantee good forecasts, the evidence suggests that intentions data for car purchases deserve a place of importance in forecasts of consumer spending on this item.

TABLE 1

Comparison of Forecasts of Car Purchases Based on Buying Plans, Income, and
Naïve Models, 1950-1955

(*percentage error*[a])

	REGISTRATIONS		NEW CAR EXPENDITURES			
YEAR	Naïve $(P_t = P_{t-1})$	Regression on M (Eq. 1)	Naïve $(Q_t = Q_{t-1})$	Regression on Y (Eq. 7)	Regression on Y and N (Eq. 9)	Regression on ΔY and N (Eq. 11)
1950	+24	−1	+23	+16	+11	−18
1951	−25	+3	−16	−11	+6	+6
1952	−22	−21	−9	−30	−15	−4
1953	+27	−3	+25	−5	−5	0
1954	−3	+1	−5	−13	−6	+7
1955	+23	+16	+28	+13	+13	+13
Average absolute percentage error (1950-55)	21	8	18	15	9	8

a Computed as [(actual−predicted) ÷ actual].

Plans and Purchases of Major Household Durable Goods. Data on the
percentage of spending units planning to buy major household items are
supplied by the SCF surveys. Comparable data are not available from the
periodic surveys. Widespread excess demand did not persist so long after
the war for household goods as for cars. Hence, the first observation of the
series here considered is drawn from mid-1947. Eleven observations are
provided by the annual surveys of 1948-55 and the mid-year surveys of
1947-49. Intended purchases are again measured by summing the percentages of respondents who respond "definitely will" or "probably will"
buy and half of those who state "may buy." For comparison with actual
flow data, the intentions are converted into dollars by use of data on
median planned expenditure.[16] Thus, the intentions variable is:

H = fraction of spending units intending to buy furniture or major
   household equipment times number of spending units times
   median planned expenditure.

This intentions variable is tested for its ability to predict actual consumer
expenditure on major household durables (W) for a one-year period
beginning with the quarter in which the survey was held.[17] In the

[16] Revised estimates of median planned expenditure for 1952-55 SCF surveys have
not been incorporated. Some calculations suggest that they would lead to a more favorable appraisal of buying intentions. For the mid-year surveys, median planned expenditure was not reported. The figure employed here is the mean of the figures given
for the adjacent pair of annual surveys.

[17] An annual series of consumer expenditure on major durable household goods is
obtained by summing lines 27, 28, and 81 of Table 30 in *National Income Supplement,
1954*, and the July 1956 issue of *Survey of Current Business*. Quarterly data from line 4

regressions below, its performance is compared with that of aggregate disposable income (Y) for the sample of eleven observations:

(1) $W = 0.98H + 4.9$ (billions of dollars); $r^2 = 0.41$

(2) $W = 0.027Y + 2.3$; $r^2 = 0.83$

(3) $W = 0.024Y + 0.19H + 2.5$; $R^2 = 0.84$

In these data, planned expenditure is a fair, though inferior, substitute for the knowledge of disposable income in the year ahead. It does not add to the information obtained from an accurate forecast of income.[18]

Buying Plans and Total Consumer Expenditure on Durable Goods. It is also possible to test the ability of plans to buy household durables and cars, taken together, to aid in the explanation of total consumer expenditure on durable goods. For the seven annual SCF surveys from 1949 to 1955, a combined intentions series can be obtained as a sum of planned expenditure on new cars (N, as defined above) and major household durables (H). Approximately two-thirds of total consumer durables spending is accounted for by the items thus covered.[19] A measure of planned expenditure in relation to income is obtained by dividing the combined buying plans by aggregate disposable income. The resulting variable $[(N+H)/Y]$ is employed in an attempt to explain residuals, for the calendar year following each survey, from an estimated linear regression of durables expenditure on disposable income.[20] The residuals are positively related to $[(N+H)/Y]$ over the sample of seven observations. Of the variance of the residuals, 37 per cent is explained by the ratio of planned spending to income.

This finding, like the results on car intentions, points toward a favorable appraisal of the predictive value of the intentions data. However, the correlation coefficients and standard errors of estimate indicate that a substantial amount of variability in consumer durable spending cannot be foretold by the intentions series alone or in combination with disposable income. Furthermore, the results are not statistically significant. While statistical significance could not reasonably be expected with so few observations, one must concede the possibility that chance alone could have produced the encouraging pattern of relationships observed above. Fortunately, the evidence supplied by cross-section data buttresses the

[18] Juster finds a superior time-series record of prediction for household durables with intentions data taken from Consumers Union mail surveys.

[19] Excluded are such items as jewelry, watches, tableware, lamps, rugs, eyeglasses, books, sporting equipment, and durable toys.

[20] The durables–income regression equation is that described in footnote 4. Annual residuals were taken as the mean of the quarterly residuals for each calendar year.

of Table 51 are used to interpolate the annual series to obtain the figures required in conjunction with the three mid-year surveys. Data on which estimates of H and W are based are available in Tables A-1 and A-3.

time-series findings, thus increasing one's confidence that the observed relationships are not attributable purely to chance.

EVIDENCE FROM CROSS-SECTION DATA

When identical spending units are interviewed twice, the durable goods purchases reported in the second interview can be compared with the intentions expressed in the first interview. In such comparisons, the "objective" characteristics of families should be held constant as they can be through the use of multiple regression techniques. If, for example, upper-income families report more intentions and make more purchases, one must determine whether the intentions data add anything to the information supplied by the income variable. The criterion of predictive value is whether, among households with identical financial and demographic characteristics, there is a larger percentage of buyers among those which had planned to buy than among those which had planned not to buy. By this criterion, intentions data were found to have substantial predictive value in several studies of SCF re-interview samples.

In their tabulations of the 1948-49 re-interview sample, Lansing and Withey showed that, within any economic group, those expressing intentions to buy consistently purchased more frequently than nonplanners. In a multivariate regression analysis of the 1952-53 re-interview sample, Tobin found that planned expenditure on durables was a highly significant supplement to financial and demographic variables in explaining actual expenditure by a household. Using the same data but a different set of explanatory variables, Klein and Lansing reached the same conclusion. In this volume, Eva Mueller reports the results of a panel study conducted from 1954 to 1957. In each of four separate periods, plans to buy augment her other variables significantly.[21]

Skepticism has been expressed on the relevance of findings from cross-section data to an appraisal of the aggregative predictive value of anticipations data.[22] This matter can be clarified by formal analysis. Suppose that, at the beginning of year t, an entire population is interviewed about its plans to purchase some homogeneous durable good, and a fraction (p) of the population reports intentions to buy, while the remaining fraction $(1-p)$ plans not to buy. Re-interviews at the end of the year establish that a fraction (r) of those planning to buy made purchases and that a fraction

[21] James Tobin, "On the Predictive Value of Consumer Intentions and Attitudes," *Review of Economics and Statistics*, 1959; Lansing and Withey, pp. 417-440 (see also Albert G. Hart's comment on the Lansing-Withey paper in the same volume, pp. 496-497); L. R. Klein and J. B. Lansing, "Decisions to Purchase Consumer Durable Goods," *Journal of Marketing*, October 1955, pp. 109-132; and see also Ferber, pp. 42-51.

[22] George Katona, "Federal Reserve Committee Reports on Consumer Expectations and Savings Statistics," *Review of Economics and Statistics*, February 1957, p. 41; see also Schweiger, pp. 459-460.

(s) of the "nonintenders" also bought the item. Then, of the entire population, the fraction making purchases (x) is given by the identity:

(1) $x_t \equiv r_t p_t + s_t (1 - p_t)$ or, alternatively, $x_t \equiv s_t + (r_t - s_t) p_t$

If the census of intentions and realizations is conducted each year, a set of observations on x, r, p, and s will be obtained and r and s can be interpreted as random variables with population means, R and S, respectively. If the intentions data are to have predictive value at the microeconomic level, R must exceed S; that is, the probability of purchase by a planner must exceed that for a nonplanner. If intentions are to have predictive value in the aggregate, x and p must be positively related over time, so that plans and purchases for any year tend to move together.[23]

In the special case where r and s are both independent of p, the condition that intentions data have predictive value on a cross-section basis ($R > S$) is both necessary and sufficient to insure that they have predictive value in the aggregate. In fact an estimate of the linear regression of x on p will yield a slope coefficient which has an expected value of precisely ($R - S$).[24]

More generally, the analysis shows that, when $R = S$, x and p can be positively related only if p is positively related to s and/or r. If the intentions data have no predictive value at the household level, they may still have predictive value in the aggregate if either the probability of fulfillment by intenders or the probability of purchase by nonintenders varies directly with the volume of plans to buy in the whole economy. In such a situation, intentions to buy stimulate purchasing, but they are no more likely to influence those who express the intentions than those who do not. Expectations are somehow symptomatic of the atmosphere but do not supply any evidence about the individuals who express them. Such a mode of behavior,

---

[23] To avoid unnecessary complexity, the discussion abstracts from the other explanatory variables which would be employed in both cross-section and time-series analyses. Also ignored is the mathematical possibility of a perverse relationship between plans and purchases, such that $R < S$ and x is negatively related to p.

[24] The proofs of the above propositions may be outlined in the following way. If a positive relationship between x and p exists, the expected value of M_{xp} will be positive, where M_{xp} is the sample convariance of x and p computed from a random sample of N years. Now,

$$M_{xp} = \frac{1}{N}\left(\sum_{t=1}^{N} x_t p_t\right) - \bar{x}\bar{p}$$

$$= \frac{1}{N}\left(\sum_{t=1}^{N} s_t p_t\right) - \bar{s}\bar{p} + \frac{1}{N}\left(\sum_{t=1}^{N}[(r_t - s_t)p_t(p_t - \bar{p})]\right)$$

$$= (\bar{r} - \bar{s})M_{pp} + \bar{p}M_{rp} + (1 - \bar{p})M_{sp} + M_{rpp} - M_{spp}$$

If r and s are both independent of p, the expected values of M_{rp}, M_{sp}, M_{rpp}, and M_{spp} are all zero; therefore the expected value of M_{xp} is given by: $E(M_{xp}) = (R - S)M_{pp}$, which is positive if, and only if, $R > S$.

In an estimated regression of x on p, the estimated slope coefficient ($\hat{a}$) equals M_{xp}/M_{pp}. Therefore,

$$E(\hat{a}) = E(M_{xp})/M_{pp} = (R - S)$$

though not inconceivable, is highly unlikely where voluntary economic decisions are concerned.[25]

If intentions data have predictive value at the microeconomic level, they can fail to have a predictive value in the aggregate only if p is negatively related to s and/or r. In such a case, the probability of purchase by either intenders or nonintenders would vary inversely with the volume of buying plans so as to nullify the higher probability of purchase by the intenders. Here, an individual unit is discouraged from buying by the purchase plans of other households. Unless there is excess demand, and the volume of actual purchases is exclusively determined by supply, this mode of behavior seems equally implausible. In short, the analysis suggests that re-interview findings have a direct bearing on the aggregative predictive value of expectational data. Therefore the positive results obtained by Lansing–Withey, Klein–Lansing, Mueller, and Tobin strongly reinforce the time-series evidence on the usefulness of intentions data.

OTHER EXPECTATIONAL VARIABLES

The SCF and SRC surveys also provide information on households' expectations for their own incomes and financial welfare, the state of business conditions, and the movement of prices. Available too, are data on attitudes. The latter are not specifically forward-looking; they relate to the respondent's evaluation of his present financial situation relative to the recent past and his evaluation of current market conditions. Nobody has seriously suggested that these expectations are likely to have direct predictive value, but they may provide insight into the future course of consumer spending and saving as indirect predictors. Some of the information supplied by series on the other expectations and attitudes of households will undoubtedly overlap that contained in the intentions data. One would expect the volume of purchase plans reported to be influenced by consumers' appraisals of current and prospective buying conditions and their economic prospects. However, a knowledge of the underlying expectations and attitudes might aid the forecaster in estimating the volume of plans that will be fulfilled and the volume of unplanned purchases.

One plausible view is that plans to buy are predicated upon certain assumptions about personal income prospects and the business outlook. If these assumptions are unduly optimistic, the ratio of actual to planned purchases will be low; if they are unduly pessimistic, the planned purchase

---

[25] Suppose that, in an annual autumnal survey, individuals were asked whether they expected to contract Asian flu in the coming year. Presumably in 1956 almost all would have said no. A year later, however, some would have said yes, either pessimists or people who preferred to say yes even though they really thought the chance was less than fifty-fifty. In comparison with 1956, the 1957 survey would display predictive value in the aggregate; yet it might well have none on a cross-section basis. The population can sense the presence of flu viruses in the atmosphere and still be totally unable to predict who will be stricken.

ratio will be higher and the level of unplanned purchases will be high. At a given level of intended purchases and with a given set of beliefs held by the forecaster about other sectors of the economy, the more bearish consumers are, the more bullish the forecaster should be about the consumer sector. The 1948-49 SCF re-interview sample provides evidence in support of this position. Of all spending units which had in early 1948 reported no plans to buy a car during the year, about one-third received more income than anticipated. This group accounted for nearly two-thirds of the unplanned purchases of new cars. The one-fifth of the nonintenders who received less income than expected during 1948 accounted for only 4 per cent of the unplanned purchases. Similarly, the fulfillment of plans to buy was substantially greater for those spending units which received more income than anticipated than for those which received less.[26]

But a diametrically opposite interpretation can be placed on the attitude and expectation responses of households. Adherents to this view would argue that the prospect implied by these data is, in effect, additive to the level of the intentions data. Optimism about general business, personal financial prospects, and market conditions is treated as reinforcing the expansionary implications of a high level of intentions to buy. As Lansing and Withey argue (page 408), "All the data—consumers' ability to buy, their willingness to buy, and their expected purchases—should form a consistent picture. To the extent that this internal consistency appears in fact, one can have confidence in the conclusions drawn."

It is thus argued that, for any given level of intended purchases, the more optimistic consumers are, the higher will be the level of actual purchases. If it can be established that plans made by optimistic households have a higher probability of fulfillment, the forecaster can weight the plans by the degree of optimism expressed by respondents in other questions, just as he may weight the plans by the degree of certainty attached to the intention by the respondent. Of the households reporting no plans to buy, some may simply have no articulated plans at the time of the survey, others may be particularly negligent or cautious in failing to mention purchases which have a strong likelihood of being made. In that event, one might hope to gain information about the probable level of purchases by nonplanners from responses on the related expectation and attitude queries.

The theoretical arguments are inconclusive. While differing on the proper use, both sides agree that other expectations data can be profitably employed in conjunction with buying intentions. The empirical record, however, does not support this contention. The Consultant Committee on Consumer Survey Statistics appraised the predictive performance of data on expectations and attitudes by comparing the responses obtained in the SCF surveys through 1954 with aggregate time-series data on the ratio of expenditure on durables to disposable income and the ratio of liquid

[26] Lansing and Withey, Table 43, p. 428.

saving to disposable income.[27] No evidence of predictive value was found, and the authors concluded that these queries, "unlike questions on intentions to buy, do not appear . . . to distinguish between the kinds of favorable attitudes that encourage buying of durable goods, other physical assets, and liquid saving."[28]

Recent calculations by the author confirm these results. Using the additional observations available for SCF and periodic SRC surveys conducted in 1955 and 1956, the author made various attempts to relate expectation and attitude responses to the durables spending–disposable income ratio (D/Y) and the personal saving–disposable income ratio (S/Y) for subsequent periods of varying length. None of the expectation series displayed any real explanatory value. Slightly encouraging results were obtained from one of the attitude series, the evaluation of durable goods markets ("good time to buy"). This series was also singled out by the Consultant Committee as a possible exception to the otherwise negative results. Eleven survey observations of this question, covering 1953-56, show a slight positive correlation with D/Y and a negative correlation with S/Y for the quarterly period following the survey. Ten per cent of the variance of D/Y and 24 per cent of variance of S/Y are explained by the responses on "good time to buy." [29]

Katona has argued that, "Instead of testing the predictive value of each attitude separately, the relation of clusters of attitudes should be studied."[30] To study such clusters, he and Miss Mueller constructed an experimental index of consumer attitudes which covers responses to eight questions: two on buying plans for cars and houses, three on external expectations about price movements and business conditions, one on personal financial anticipations, and two attitude series relating to the respondent's current financial situation and his evaluation of current market conditions.[31] The eight series are individually indexed and given equal weight in forming the combined index.

In mimeographed releases and publications on the periodic survey, Katona and Mueller have shown the index in conjunction with quarterly data on the ratio of durables spending to disposable income. Sometimes the charts have been headed, "Do consumer attitudes lead durable goods sales?" Since D/Y was used as the measure of durable goods sales, this implied the reasonable a priori hypothesis that a favorable level of consumer attitudes should be associated with a high rate of durables spending relative to income in the period following the survey.

The question they pose can be investigated by drawing on observations

[27] "Report . . . on Consumer Survey Statistics," pp. 308-316.
[28] *Ibid.*, p. 312.
[29] The independent variable is the percentage of favorable responses minus the percentage of unfavorable responses with noncommittal answers ignored.
[30] Katona, "Federal Reserve Board Committee Reports . . . ," p. 41.
[31] Katona and Mueller, pp. 91-105.

from eleven surveys dating from late 1952 to late 1956.[32] In this sample, the attitude index displays ability to forecast the durables–income ratio for one and two quarters following the survey. However, an index consisting of only the two plans-to-buy components predicts just as well—in fact, a trifle better; while an index of the remaining six components performs less well. Shown below are the proportions of variance (r^2) explained in nine simple regression estimates, employing as dependent variables (1) the durables–income ratio for the quarter following the quarterly period of the survey (D_1/Y_1); (2) the durables–income ratio for the second quarter following the survey quarter, (D_2/Y_2); and (3) the mean of the durables–income ratio for those two quarters, $[0.5(D_1/Y_1 + D_2/Y_2)]$:[33]

Dependent Variable	Attitude Index	Plans to Buy	Attitude Index Excluding Plans to Buy
D_1/Y_1	0.28	0.30	0.20
D_2/Y_2	.13	.23	.05
$0.5(D_1/Y_1 + D_2/Y_2)$	.29	.31	.19

In this sample of data, clusters of attitudes added nothing to the predictive value of intentions to buy.

One might also expect the index of consumer attitudes to suggest the future course of total consumer spending in relation to income, and thereby to offer insight into those variations of the personal saving–disposable income ratio that are not associated with durables spending. In the sample of eleven observations, the attitude index assists in forecasting S/Y for the first quarter following the survey but does not explain any portion of S/Y for the next quarter. In the prediction of S_1/Y_1, it is once again the two plans-to-buy components which account for the success. The inclusion of other attitudes in the total index detracts from the predictive value of plans to buy. The portions of the variance of S_1/Y_1 explained by the alternative expectation variables are:

Attitude index	0.28
Plans to buy	.35
Attitude index, excluding plans to buy	.16

Miss Mueller reports that, for the same eleven surveys, the index constructed of the two plans-to-buy components is inferior to both the total attitude index and the attitude index excluding plans to buy in explaining D/Y for a two-quarter period.[34] The explanation for the divergence of her

[32] Data for surveys from 1952 to 1955 are taken from *ibid.*, p. 100. For the three 1956 periodic surveys, some data were available in mimeographed SRC releases; other required data were supplied to the author by the SRC through the kind cooperation of Ernest Lilienstein.

[33] All estimated slope coefficients are positive, corresponding in sign with a priori beliefs.

[34] See her paper in this volume.

results from those presented above lies in the timing of D/Y. When a survey is taken in the first month of a quarter, Miss Mueller uses D/Y for that same quarter and the next quarter. The D/Y variable used in this paper starts uniformly with the quarter following the quarterly period of the survey. While this leads to differences in dating for a number of surveys, the difference is particularly important in the case of the October 1954 survey. In that survey, plans to buy were very high while other attitude variables were near their mean. In the last quarter of 1954, D/Y was rather low; in the first and second quarters of 1955, it was extremely high. Hence, when the survey data are compared with D/Y for I and II 1955, intentions are excellent predictors while other attitudes are very poor. However, when the relevant period is taken to be IV 1954 and I 1955 as in Miss Mueller's study, intentions overpredict D/Y.

In the final analysis, the divergent results produced by the alternative techniques of dating suggest that eleven times-series observations cannot yield conclusive findings on the relative forecasting value of intentions and other anticipations, particularly since the various expectation measures are themselves closely correlated in aggregative data. However cross-section results are relevant and these point uniformly toward a negative evaluation of consumer anticipations data other than plans to buy. For example, Tobin's study of the 1952-53 re-interview sample of the SCF reveals that, unlike intentions data, the information on other expectations and attitudes —whether taken singly or in combination—fails to supplement the financial and demographic explanatory variables.[35] Tobin's substantive conclusions are equally applicable to the empirical findings in Miss Mueller's analysis of the Center's re-interview panel. In none of the four periods under study did she obtain a statistically significant relationship between durables purchases and an attitude index (excluding plans to buy) when intentions were taken into account. These are powerful tests based on samples of about seven hundred households. When the estimated regression coefficients of an attitude index are uniformly insignificant, grave doubts are cast on the existence of the hypothesized relationship at the level of the household. And a variable which has no predictive value at the microeconomic level is most unlikely to forecast successfully in the aggregate.

Katona is undoubtedly on firm ground in arguing that little has as yet been proved about the predictive value of intentions, and of other expectations and attitudes.[36] Additional empirical research, on both the aggregative and microeconomic levels, would be most welcome. Nevertheless, at

[35] In their study of the same data, Klein and Lansing reach the same general conclusion, although they find some slight value in the evaluations of personal financial situations ("better off"); see pp. 119-120, 128-131. For a bit of negative evidence on "better off" from the 1948-49 re-interview sample, see Table 45 of Lansing and Withey, p. 429. The series on evaluation of market conditions ("good time to buy"), which showed some promise in time-series evidence, had no predictive value in the cross-section studies.

[36] Katona, "Federal Reserve Board Committee Reports . . . ," p. 43.

this point it appears that the burden of proof falls on those who would contend that the predictive value of intentions data can be materially augmented by information on attitudes and other expectations. The empirical record to date obliges the forecaster to weigh heavily the SRC intentions data; on the basis of currently available evidence, he cannot have equal confidence in other measures of consumer expectations and attitudes.

Investment Expenditure

NONFARM RESIDENTIAL CONSTRUCTION

During the past decade, between 20 and 30 per cent of gross private domestic investment has consisted of nonfarm residential construction. Expenditure on new housing has not been a particularly volatile component of capital spending, but it has moved erratically. For example, it rose in 1950 along with other components of investment but fell by 13 per cent in 1951 while plant and equipment spending, GNP, and disposable income continued to rise. In 1954, housing rose by 13 per cent while the rest of private capital formation declined, and in 1956 it fell by 8 per cent despite the boom in plant and equipment spending.

As this record of variation suggests, poor results would have been obtained in recent years from techniques which predict residential construction on the basis of time-series relationships of that component to disposable income, GNP, or other large aggregate flows.[37] Also, because of the frequent turning points, techniques which extrapolate recently observed trends in the housing sector would not have predicted accurately. Instead the forecaster can use "objective" series on family formation; the existing stock of housing; financial variables relating to mortgage markets; and building permits, contract awards, and the number and value of housing starts. He also may consider two expectation series: one, compiled by *Fortune*, records the plans of homebuilders; the other, reported by the SRC, covers the plans of prospective home buyers.

The potential relative contribution of buyers' and builders' plans is a matter of analytical interest. The predictive value of buyers' plans is likely to depend on the rapidity and flexibility with which builders adjust their output to current demand. For built-to-order homes, output is directly determined by demand. Also, builders of large developments may be able to respond rapidly to surprises in demand by adjusting the total number of homes to be included in the project as well as by revising the schedule of

[37] The author has found that expenditures on new housing and on household durables have not moved together as fractions of disposable income in recent years. However, residential building and consumer spending on cars, both expressed as ratios to disposable income, exhibit a surprisingly close relationship in quarterly data for 1948-56, with $r^2 = 0.61$. A variety of theoretical reasons could be advanced to account for this pattern.

construction. In these cases, buyers' plans should be more heavily weighted. However, lags in the adjustment of supply are likely to be widespread. Product differentiation and the lengthy planning period preceding the start of construction make it difficult for builders to recognize and respond to shifts in demand. Therefore, the plans of the builders might be the dominant consideration over the short run.[38]

The survey data on both buyers' and builders' expectations may be readily employed in conjunction with data on the number and value of housing starts. The latter series perform admirably in forecasting nonfarm residential construction for a few months ahead. This is not surprising since the construction of any house is a fairly lengthy operation. In any short period the bulk of construction activity is done on units started in the previous period. The pattern of typical progress in the construction of a house has been determined by field studies and is used by the Departments of Labor and Commerce to estimate the expenditure on residential construction for any month. They apply weights to the value of work started in that month and each of several previous months. The pattern is such that an average of about half of all nonfarm residential construction expenditure in a given quarter is attributable to dwelling units started in the immediately preceding quarter. Another 10 per cent of expenditure is typically associated with starts in earlier quarters. Consequently, only about 40 per cent of expenditure is on units begun in the current quarter.[39] Knowledge of the value of work started in recent months is thus an excellent indicator of residential construction expenditure in the next quarter. Quarterly forecasts made on this basis would have been highly successful from 1950 to 1956.[40] However, the forecaster cannot be satisfied with such a short lead. He may attack the problem of longer range prediction by attempting to forecast the value of work started and, in pursuing this objective, he may turn to the anticipations data supplied by *Fortune* and SRC.

Both of the anticipations series relate to the probable number of new housing starts rather than to their prospective value. Data on the value and

[38] There is no inventory component of unsold new houses in the national product accounts. Thus all production of housing shows up as new residential construction. This contrasts with the treatment of consumer durable goods. For example, excessive optimism in the production decisions of refrigerator manufacturers would be reflected initially in higher inventory investment with no change in the consumer durables component.

[39] See *National Income Supplement, 1954*, p. 125; and *Techniques of Preparing Major BLS Statistical Series*, Dept. of Labor, Bull. 1168, December 1954, pp. 8-15, and 19-21. Quantitative information on the activity patterns has been kindly supplied to the author by Arnold E. Chase, Chief, Division of Construction Statistics, Bureau of Labor Statistics.

[40] In calculations made by the author, data on the value of contract awards for residential construction did not equal the value of starts series in predictive ability. It should, of course, be recognized that the official estimates of actual expenditure are derived from the value of starts series.

number of starts indicate that the value per dwelling unit has risen sub-stantially in recent years, both because construction cost has risen and because people are buying "more house." The upward movement has been fairly steady with value per unit rising by substantially more than con-struction prices. From 1950 to 1956, annual increases in value per unit remained in the narrow range of 5 to 8 per cent, except for a rise of only 1 per cent in 1952. During this period, ability to forecast the number of starts accurately would have insured reasonably successful forecasts of the value of activity, and it seems likely that this condition will prevail in the future.

Data on buying intentions for houses are of the same character as the purchase plans for consumer durables. The annual SCF surveys from 1948 to 1955 and periodic surveys of June and October 1954, and June and October 1955, present twelve observations on the percentages of res-pondents planning to buy houses in the following year. In recent surveys intentions to buy new and old houses have been combined. Intended purchasers are again defined as those respondents reporting they "will" or "probably will" buy and half of those stating they "may buy." The per-centage of intended purchasers is multiplied by the number of spending units (or in the case of the periodic surveys, the number of families) in the economy to form the intentions variable (J). The latter is used in an attempt to explain a dependent variable (S), which is the number of new housing starts in the twelve-month period beginning with the month of the survey.[41] The estimated regression of S on J is:

(1) $S = 641 + 0.15J$ (thousands of dwelling units);   or $r^2 = 0.39$

The standard error of estimate is slightly over 100,000 dwelling units, a sizable margin of error. However, aggregate disposable income for each period, deflated by construction prices, explains only 32 per cent of the variance and is unable to assist the intentions series when both are em-ployed as potential explanatory variables.

Data on the plans of homebuilders are compiled by *Fortune* through interviews with between three and four hundred building firms, stratified by size, in thirty-five or more cities. Each builder is asked what percentage change he expects in his housing starts relative to the previous year. The percentage estimates are combined, weighted, and applied to the level of starts in the previous year in order to obtain a prediction on new housing starts for the calendar year.[42] The survey is conducted early in the year, and results are presented in the "Business Roundup" section of the April 1959 *Fortune*. The results are thus available at approximately the same time as the SCF data on buying intentions, and only slightly after

[41] See Tables A-1 and A-4 for data.
[42] A detailed discussion of the techniques employed in the homebuilding survey may be found in "Report . . . on General Business Expectations," pp. 582-584.

reliable estimates are made available for the fourth quarter of the preceding year.

There are six observations on the predictive value of the survey covering 1951 to 1956. Each time the homebuilders overestimated starts in the year ahead, indicating a possible bias which might be corrected. However, three of the errors amount to only 2 or 3 per cent while three are substantial. In the three bad years (1953, 1955, and 1956), respondents were re-interviewed in late summer.[43] Like homebuilders in the aggregate, the respondents in the sample were not fulfilling their plans. "Tight money" was the primary reason offered. According to the builders, the high cost and lack of availability of mortgage funds affected adversely both the ability of households to acquire homes and the ability of the builders to finance work in progress with construction loans. Restrictive monetary policy might well have surprised builders (as well as other groups in the economy) in 1953 and in 1955. However, in order to accept the "tight money" explanation in 1956, one must assume that, as of the start of the year, the builders anticipated a substantial relaxation in financial markets and reported their housing plans accordingly. It is particularly difficult to form a judgment here. One must wait for more observations to learn whether the homebuilders' survey continues to predict effectively in years of easy money and whether it contains any useful information in years of tight money.

The relation of buyers' plans and sellers' plans to the actual number of housing starts for the years 1951-56 is shown in Table 2. Also included are the results which would have been obtained with two alternative naïve models: one projecting housing starts for the year ahead at the seasonally adjusted annual rate for the last quarter of the preceding year, the other predicting the same level as the whole of the previous year.[44] The percentage error of forecast of the second naïve model is simply the percentage change in housing starts from one year to the next. The hits and misses of the homebuilders' survey stand out in the comparison. It is the best of the four predictions in 1951, 1952, and 1954 but the poorest in 1955 and 1956. The buying plans, as utilized in equation 1 of this section, overpredict badly in two of *Fortune*'s three lean years (1953 and 1956) and underpredict seriously in 1954.[45] The average absolute percentage errors

[43] Re-interview results are presented in "Business Roundup," *Fortune*, October 1953, September 1955, and September 1956.

[44] The first series is based on revised data presented in *Survey of Current Business*, March 1957, p. 20. The seasonally adjusted series omits the small number of publicly financed dwelling units started; the predictor was adjusted upward to allow for the omission.

[45] The performance shown in the table for SRC data in 1956 is actually the percentage error of the October 1955 periodic survey in predicting starts from October 1955 through September 1956. The figure on housing intentions in the 1956 SCF includes all of the "may buy" respondents. If adjusted to the concept of intentions used here, it would also have yielded an excessively high forecast of 1956 housing starts. The six observations of consumer surveys used as predictors here were included in obtaining the estimated regression equation by which the "forecasts" are made.

431

TABLE 2

Comparison of Forecasts of Housing Starts Based on Anticipations
Data and Naïve Models, 1951-1956
(*percentage error*[a])

			NAIVE MODEL	
YEAR	REGRESSION ON SRC BUYING PLANS	"FORTUNE" SURVEY OF HOMEBUILDERS	*Based on Fourth Quarter of Previous Year*	*Based on Whole of Previous Year*
1951	−5	−3[b]	−11	−28
1952	+5	−2[b]	+10	+3
1953	−11	−9	−5	−2[b]
1954	+11	−2[b]	+12	+10
1955	+5[b]	−9	−5[b]	+8
1956	−14	−20	−8	−19
Average absolute percentage error (1951-56)	8.5	7.5	8.5	11.7
Root-mean-square percentage error (1951-56)	9.3	9.9	8.9	14.8

[a] Computed as [(actual-predicted) ÷ actual].

[b] Best (or tied for best) of the four predictions for any given year.

and root-mean-square errors summarize the performance of the four methods. Both measures point to the ability of the anticipations series and of data from the most recent quarter to improve on the full-year naïve model. However, differences in the average error of the three superior predictors are trivial and the rank order is different for the two measures of performance.[46]

Neither the buying plans nor the sellers' expectations display any consistent ability to improve on the information contained in the latest data on housing starts in these six years. The survey data on buying plans were superior to aggregate disposable income in predicting housing starts in the available observations. Since the income variable commands attention in any forecast of housing, data on buying intentions presumably also deserve careful scrutiny. The fact that SRC data on buying intentions have not consistently surpassed the fourth-quarter naïve model means only that buying plans, taken alone and employed in a particular manner, do not contain more information than the most recent data on housing markets. However, there may be more profitable ways to use the buying plans than in the simple regression technique applied above. They might be combined with the recent rate of starts, or used in conjunction with certain demographic or financial variables. Such explorations might be guided by micro-economic evidence on fulfillment of home buying plans but, because

[46] The change in rank order is attributable to the heavier weight given to large deviations by root-mean-square error.

home-buyers change their place of residence, there have been no re-interview studies on this matter to date. The three years of successful prediction by the homebuilders' survey are impressive and this anticipations series might be complemented by other variables. On the basis of the inconclusive evidence from time-series data, survey results on both buying and building intentions deserve inclusion among the various pieces of evidence that must be weighted and combined by the forecaster of GNP when he considers residential construction.

OTHER FIXED INVESTMENT

Valuable information on future expenditure on new plant and equipment is supplied by two surveys of business investment plans, one conducted jointly by the Securities and Exchange Commission and the Department of Commerce and the other by the McGraw–Hill Publishing Company. The surveys project gross fixed investment by nonfarm business for the calendar year. The Commerce–SEC annual survey is conducted between late January and early March; results are presented in the March issue of *Survey of Current Business*. Results of the McGraw–Hill survey appear a few weeks later in *Business Week*. In recent years, McGraw–Hill has also made a preliminary survey of investment intentions in the fourth quarter of the preceding year. In addition to their annual endeavor, SEC and Commerce compile investment plans for each quarter early in the preceding quarter and again at the start of the quarter in question.

The Commerce–SEC intentions data are expressly designed to forecast the series of actual new plant and equipment expenditure by United States business, which is reported on a quarterly basis. The series is not a component of the official national product accounts. It covers the bulk of the sum of two components, "producers' durable equipment" and "other new construction" (i.e., other than residential nonfarm). The items in producers' durable equipment and other new construction excluded from plant and equipment expenditure are farm equipment and construction, construction by private nonprofit institutions, capital outlays charged to current expense, and equipment and construction expenditures by independent professionals. However, even after allowing for these items, the totals are unequal, and no official reconciliation is available. Fortunately the discrepancy is neither large enough nor volatile enough to cause serious trouble. The ratio of plant and equipment spending to the two GNP entries has remained between 72 and 76 per cent since 1951 and the dollar difference between these magnitudes has not changed by more than $1.1 billion in any pair of successive years. Therefore accurate forecasts of plant and equipment spending would provide reasonably accurate predictions of the sum of producers' durables and other construction.

Predictive Performance of Investment Intentions. The predictive record of the Commerce–SEC survey has been outstanding. The survey was initiated in 1947, and the past decade of experience has been carefully analyzed under Commerce–SEC auspices.[47] The post-mortems show that, in every year except 1950, the anticipations data were better predictors than a model projecting expenditures at the level of the previous year or a model projecting expenditures at the level of the fourth quarter.[48] The average absolute error and root-mean-square error over the period are much smaller for planned expenditure than for either naïve model. Table 3 summarizes these findings. Similarly, the intentions series was generally superior in predictive ability to extrapolations of the recent rate of change in plant and equipment outlays and to "causal" explanations such

TABLE 3

Comparison of Forecasts of Plant and Equipment Expenditure based on
Anticipations Data and Naïve Models, 1947-1956 and 1948-1956
(*percentage error*[a])

| | | NAIVE MODEL | |
PERIOD	COMMERCE–SEC ANTICIPATIONS	Based on Whole of Previous Year	Based on Fourth Quarter of Previous Year
1947-56:			
Average absolute percentage error	5	13	n.a.
Root-mean-square percentage error	8	17	n.a.
1948-56:			
Average absolute percentage error	3	11	8
Root-mean-square percentage error	6	14	10

n.a. = not available.
a Computed as [(actual-predicted) ÷ predicted].
Source: Figures are calculated from Murray F. Foss and Vito Natrella, "Ten Years' Experience with Business Investment Anticipations," *Survey of Current Business,* January 1957, p. 17, Table 1; and *Survey of Current Business,* June 1956, pp. 6-7; and June 1957, p. 3. See also Natrella, "Forecasting Plant and Equipment Expenditures from Businessmen's Expectations," *Proceedings of the Business and Economic Statistics Section of the American Statistical Association,* 1955-56, p. 127, Tables 2 and 3.

[47] See Irwin Friend and Jean Bronfenbrenner, "Plant and Equipment Programs and their Realization," *Short-Term Economic Forecasting,* pp. 53-98; and two articles by Murray F. Foss and Vito Natrella, "Ten Years' Experience with Business Investment Anticipations" and "Investment Plans and Realization," in *Survey of Current Business,* January and June 1957, respectively. All cited deviations between actual and anticipated outlays are derived by comparisons of (1) the actual percentage change in outlays from year to year with (2) the anticipated percentage change over the estimated outlays of the previous year as of the time of the survey. This standard technique of evaluation is designed to abstract from the effects of subsequent revisions in the estimates of actual investment for the preceding year.
[48] Since no quarterly data for 1946 are available, the naïve model based on the fourth quarter could not be tested for 1947.

as the linear regression of investment on lagged profits used in the Klein–Goldberger econometric model.

The Commerce–SEC record is marred by the presence of two bad years, 1947 and 1950, when actual expenditures exceeded anticipations by 17 per cent and 15 per cent, respectively. The outbreak of the Korean war in mid-1950 accounts for much of the discrepancy in that year. The deviation in 1947 is not so easily explained, but the survey was new, capital goods prices rose rapidly during the year, and supply shortages may have eased more rapidly than purchasers of capital goods anticipated.[49] In 1953 and 1955, the level of actual expenditures exceeded anticipations by 5 per cent and 6 per cent, respectively. In both cases, the survey predicted very small increases over the outlays of the previous year while actual outlays rose 7 per cent each time. In four of the remaining six years, anticipations came within 1 per cent of realized spending; in the other two, the deviations were 3 per cent.

While the McGraw–Hill anticipations have been valuable, the survey did not equal the Commerce–SEC endeavor in predictive performance during the 1948-56 period. Aggregate capital outlays were underpredicted by 26 per cent and 18 per cent in 1948 and 1950 respectively, and overpredicted by 9 per cent in both 1949 and 1951. During the 1952-56 period, however, the average absolute error was only 4 per cent. The anticipations of the McGraw–Hill sample have predicted excellently the outlays of the participating firms: annual errors have been no larger than 4 per cent except for a 10 per cent understatement in 1950.[50] Since the McGraw–Hill sample consists principally of large firms and is not stratified by size, the fluctuations it records are not perfectly representative of investment behavior in the aggregate.

McGraw–Hill's preliminary surveys are of particular interest, since results are reported in November or December, just when GNP forecasting reaches its seasonal peak of activity and long before annual Commerce–SEC anticipations data become available. Anticipated expenditures in the preliminary survey have usually been lower than those reported in the final survey, but the differences have typically been quite small. 1956 is an exception. The preliminary survey predicted an increase of 13 per cent over 1955, while the final survey envisaged a rise of 30 per cent. Outlays actually rose by 22 per cent. Further experience with the survey may indicate how the apparent tendency to underestimate future outlays can be corrected. On the other hand, because the capital budgeting activities of reporting firms are likely to be concentrated in the last quarter, there may be a sharp discontinuity in the relative predictive abilities of surveys conducted before and after the start of the new year.

[49] Foss and Natrella, "Ten Years' Experience . . . ," p. 17; and Friend and Bronfenbrenner, p. 61.

[50] See Tables 2 and 4 in the paper by Dexter M. Keezer, *et al.*, in this volume.

Commerce–SEC quarterly anticipations data have provided valuable assistance in forecasting plant and equipment outlays over a very short-term period. Two reports are available. One is published just before the quarter in question begins, the other just before the quarter ends. From mid-1952 to mid-1956, the first anticipation as published in adjusted form has predicted outlays with a mean absolute error of 2.6 per cent; the second anticipation has diverged from actual outlays by an average of 2.0 per cent.[51] The quarterly series was especially helpful in signaling the downturn in capital spending of late 1953 and the subsequent upturn of early 1955.

Actual capital outlays of business exhibit a marked seasonal pattern with spending particularly low in the first quarter and high in the fourth quarter. Since the reported anticipations do not accurately reproduce this pattern, outlays in the first quarter are significantly overestimated and those of the fourth quarter are substantially underestimated. Since mid-1952, the Commerce–SEC staff has removed these biases by applying a seasonal correction, with a resulting substantial improvement in predictive success.[52] This is an excellent illustration of the proposition that survey respondents who forecast inaccurately can provide the basis for accurate predictions if the response errors follow a determinable systematic pattern.

The average errors in the adjusted quarterly anticipations are only slightly smaller than those for annual planned outlays, and the former do not improve so much relatively on the performance of naïve models. Presumably plans become more definite as the time horizon contracts, but the shorter period covered by the quarterly data increases the difficulty of estimating the precise time of a prospective expenditure because of uncertainty about equipment deliveries, the progress of construction work, and the scheduling of accounting charges.

Techniques for Improving Predictive Ability. There are wide deviations between the intended and realized capital outlays of individual firms. In samples of McGraw–Hill respondents, actual capital spending was within 20 per cent of anticipated outlays in only 39 per cent of all cases for 1949 and 51 per cent for 1954.[53] For 1949 and again for 1955, only about a fourth of the manufacturing firms in the Commerce–SEC sample fulfilled their plans within a 20 per cent range of error. Since large firms were typically the more accurate forecasters, three-fifths of all outlays in 1955 were made by firms in this category.[54] Clearly, the anticipated outlays do not represent fixed and rigid commitments from which firms are unable to deviate. The anticipated outlays definitely have predictive value at the

[51] Foss and Natrella, "Ten Years' Experience . . . ," p. 19.
[52] *Ibid.*, pp. 18-19; and Friend and Bronfenbrenner, pp. 62-63.
[53] See Table 2 in Robert A. Levine's paper in this volume.
[54] Foss and Natrella, "Ten Years' Experience . . . ," p. 20; and Friend and Bronfenbrenner, p. 65.

microeconomic level, but they leave large unexplained residuals.[55] The intentions have been successful aggregative predictors because these residuals have canceled out in the past. The success of the intentions as aggregative predictors is hardly surprising; all aggregative economic relationships that display any stability over time perform far better than their microeconomic counterparts, profiting from a cancellation of the relatively large individual deviations from the cross-section relationship.

It may be purely fortuitous, however, that anticipations reported early in the year are unbiased (or nearly unbiased) predictors of annual capital outlays. Spending plans have a systematic seasonal bias in quarterly projections and a downward bias in annual projections made before the start of the year. The absence of bias in the annual data must stand simply as an empirical generalization. Systematic errors have been discovered for firms in particular size strata: relatively small firms tend to underpredict while very large firms seem inclined to overpredict slightly.[56] Levine suggests a technique whereby anticipated outlays would be classified by size of the reporting firms and each dollar of planned spending in classes which tend to underpredict would be weighted more heavily. And in 1957, the Commerce–SEC survey began to correct for the typical understatement of small manufacturing firms by adjusting their anticipated outlays upward.[57] There is also apparently a bias associated with the size of the anticipated investment program of the firm. Businesses contemplating programs which are large as a fraction of their existing fixed assets tend to overstate their outlays, although they are relatively good predictors. Firms anticipating small percentage additions to fixed assets tend to underestimate their outlays. Apart from these modest qualifications, research efforts have discovered no systematic bias in the annual anticipations. The forces responsible for deviations between actual and planned outlays by individual firms seem equally capable of operating in either direction.

Some influences are random from firm to firm and can be relied on to cancel out in the aggregate in any period. Other forces, however, may influence the capital spending of many firms in the same direction. Economic developments subsequent to a survey may thus produce deviations of outlays in the aggregate from anticipations. For example, when the business outlook changed suddenly and drastically in 1950, plant and equipment expenditure rose markedly above anticipated levels. The survey data faithfully registered the level of investment demand for the state of economic conditions assumed by respondents, but they cannot supply an unconditionally accurate forecast of investment spending. Fortunately, the

---

[55] See Friend and Bronfenbrenner, *op. cit.*, p. 67; and Robert Eisner, "Expectations, Plans, and Capital Expenditures: A Synthesis of Ex Post and Ex Ante Data," *Expectations, Uncertainty, and Business Behavior*, pp. 170-171.

[56] Friend and Bronfenbrenner, *op. cit.*, pp. 69-70; and the papers by Foss and Natrella, and Levine in this volume.

[57] See the paper by Foss and Natrella in this volume.

factors responsible for deviations from plans can be analyzed *ex ante* as well as *ex post*. This involves treating capital expenditure as a function of intentions expressed at a point in time and of the subsequent course of the nonexpectational variables that influence the realization of intentions.[58] The latter influences must be identified and their paths must be predicted and used in conjunction with anticipations data. The procedure suggested is obviously more complicated than the one-input production process by which the anticipations data are directly converted into forecasts of outlays. The forecaster renders his job more difficult and extends his risks by making his forecast of effective investment demand depend on his beliefs about other variables. However, the level of investment does depend on the course of other economic variables, and the forecaster cannot afford to ignore the interdependence.

The Influence of Other Variables. Two nonexpectational variables which appear to have a significant influence on the realization of spending plans are: (1) the prices and availability of capital goods; and (2) the sales and earnings experience of the prospective investing firms.

PRICES AND AVAILABILITY OF CAPITAL GOODS. It has been suggested that, to a considerable extent, "anticipated outlays . . . reflect a planned physical volume of investment valued at prevailing prices, and hence do not sufficiently take account of price factors."[59] To gather further evidence on this matter, the 1956 Commerce–SEC questionnaire asked respondents to give the assumptions about future capital goods prices which underlay their spending intentions. Only about a third of the firms were allowing for a change (almost unanimously, a rise) in prices. Another third had not considered the possibility of price changes, and the remaining third expected no change.[60]

Because firms tend to project current prices into the future and because the short-run price-elasticity of demand for capital goods is apparently low, higher prices typically raise dollar spending above anticipated levels. Levine finds that, when the McGraw–Hill intentions data are interpreted as forecasts of spending in constant dollars, their predictive accuracy is considerably improved.[61] In the absence of independent evidence, prices reigning at the survey date can serve as a fair approximation to the mean assumed level of prices underlying the intentions data. If the forecaster expects a change in capital goods prices, he should alter his estimate of capital outlays in the same direction.

[58] See Friend, "Critical Evaluation," p. 190; and Franco Modigliani and H. M. Weingartner, "Forecasting Uses of Anticipatory Data on Investment and Sales," *Quarterly Journal of Economics*, February 1958, pp. 36-39.

[59] Friend and Bronfenbrenner, p. 63; see also, O. J. Firestone, "Investment Forecasting in Canada," *Short-Term Economic Forecasting*, pp. 234-235.

[60] Murray F. Foss, "Business Expectations for 1956," *Survey of Current Business*, March 1956, p. 20.

[61] Robert Levine, "Plant and Equipment Expenditures Surveys: Intentions and Fulfillment," unpublished Cowles Foundation Discussion Paper, 1956, p. 121.

Changing prices of capital goods are, however, likely to be associated with variations in the availability of investment goods operating in the opposite direction. Spending intentions for plant and equipment are obviously predicated on certain expectations about how fast construction will progress and when equipment will arrive. When excess demand is present in capital goods markets, intentions can be frustrated by the failure of deliveries. Conversely, potential demand not recorded as planned expenditure can be activated by the evaporation of shortages. For 1949 and 1955 manufacturers were asked in the Commerce–SEC surveys to explain discrepancies between realized and anticipated outlays. Easing of the supply situation was the most frequent explanation offered by those who had spent more than anticipated in 1949, and was cited by 17 per cent of the group. Of those who had spent less than anticipated 10 per cent attributed their deviations principally to supply shortages.[62] In 1955, 38 per cent of firms which had spent less than planned and 7 per cent of those exceeding anticipations pointed to supply conditions as a principal reason. During the 1956 boom in capital spending, supply shortages must have been an even more important source of frustration of intended spending. In both 1949 and 1956, the aggregate predictive performance of anticipations was excellent, presumably because unanticipated changes in capital goods prices and in supply shortages operated in opposite directions to a nearly equal extent.[63] However, one cannot rely on always having so precise a cancellation.

If spending intentions were 30 per cent above the outlays of the preceding year, it would be safe to predict an increase in real investment and a rise in capital goods prices. However, the reported quantitative increase in dollar outlays might require adjustment. The forecaster would then presumably have to consider the productive capacity of capital goods producers and the nature of their pricing policies. If he concluded that capital goods production could expand by only 15 per cent and that prices, being sticky, were unlikely to rise by more than 5 per cent, he would have grounds for marking down the projected 30 per cent increase in outlays. If alternatively he concluded that production could expand by approximately 30 per cent and that prices would nevertheless rise substantially, he should revise the reported anticipations upward.

THE INFLUENCE OF SALES AND EARNINGS. According to either an accelerator or a profitability theory of investment demand, actual capital outlays will deviate from anticipations as a result of unforeseen changes in the demand for the output of firms. The accelerator theory specifies that the rise in physical sales engendered by higher demand will put additional pressure on capacity and induce a more rapid expansion of productive facilities. The profitability approach suggests that higher sales produced

[62] Friend and Bronfenbrenner, p. 87.
[63] Foss and Natrella, "Investment Plans and Realization," pp. 12-13, and 24.

by rising demand increase the prospective return from additional capital goods and thus encourage more investment. Manufacturers' explanations for deviations between realized and intended investment support the theoretical belief that unanticipated changes in sales lead to a revision of investment plans. For the recession year of 1949, nearly half of the firms which invested less than they planned and a sixth of those which invested more offered as their principal reason unanticipated changes in sales or net earnings. The same explanation was offered by about two-fifths of firms exceeding plans and a fourth of those spending less than planned in 1955 when, in general, sales and earnings were more favorable than expected.[64]

Time-series data for manufacturing also confirm this theory. Sales anticipations of firms have been compiled in the annual Commerce–SEC surveys since 1948 in order to show the assumptions about demand underlying the capital spending intentions. It is thus possible to relate percentage deviations between realized and planned investment to percentage errors in sales forecasts. Here, the accelerator view emphasizes changes in the *real* volume of sales as a determinant of investment. The profitability argument suggests that changes in the *dollar* volume of sales, reflecting price movements due to shifts in demand, will also stimulate capital outlays. Most analysts would prefer to test both physical sales and dollar sales (and also capital-goods prices). But with a handful of observations, one must choose between the two.

Modigliani and Weingartner adopted the accelerator model and studied the relationship of relative deviations between actual and anticipated real investment, on the one hand, and deviations between actual and expected real sales, on the other. Since all Commerce–SEC data are registered in current dollars, they had to impute certain naïve price expectations to participating firms and to deflate actual spending by admittedly imperfect price indexes. Despite these difficulties, they found that, with annual observations for all manufacturing for 1948-55, deviations in the forecast of real sales were statistically significant in explaining real investment deviations, accounting for 72 per cent of the variance. The regression estimates indicate that each 1 per cent excess of realized over expected sales is associated with a 1.5 per cent increment of real capital outlays over anticipations. The intercept suggests that, in the event of a zero sales error, real investment would exceed anticipations by a trivial 0.5 per cent.[65]

Alternatively, one might follow the profitability view and test the percentage deviation between actual and expected dollar sales as an indirect predictor of investment. In nine time-series observations on manufacturing as a whole for 1948-56, undeflated percentage deviations in sales display a statistically significant relationship with percentage investment deviations,

---

[64] *Ibid.*, p. 13; and Friend and Bronfenbrenner, p. 87.
[65] Modigliani and Weingartner, pp. 39-47.

likewise undeflated. The sales errors explain 77 per cent of the variance of the investment deviations.[66] The slope coefficient estimated by the author is 1.0, indicating that each 1 per cent addition to dollar sales relative to the expected level is associated with a 1 per cent increment in capital outlays relative to anticipations; the intercept of 1.5 suggests that, when sales expectations are accurate, actual investment tends to exceed slightly the anticipated level.

Both approaches indicate that the major portion of investment deviations by manufacturers can be accounted for by unanticipated changes in sales. The findings are, however, based on a handful of time-series observations. Additional evidence may be sought in microeconomic data. Several attempts have been made to study the relationship between investment deviations and sales deviations, both undeflated and expressed in percentages, on a cross-section basis. Levine reports that no significant relationship could be found in 1954 McGraw–Hill data. Friend and Bronfenbrenner find very low correlations in Commerce–SEC data for 1947–49; and Foss and Natrella report similar results for 1955. They do not, however, report their estimated slope coefficients.[67] Eisner finds a low but significant correlation coefficient of 0.17 for McGraw–Hill data of 1950. His slope coefficient for all firms in his sample is about 0.7, not much below the unity value estimated from the time-series data.[68]

The other sets of data which produced low correlation coefficients might also yield fair-sized slopes. Capital outlays are more volatile and more sensitive to random influences than are sales at the level of the firm. Consequently the variance of percentage investment errors is higher than that of sales errors. In the aggregate, however, the investment errors of firms appear to show more cancellation. Thus, sales errors may explain only a trivial portion of the investment errors at the microeconomic level and yet explain a substantial fraction of aggregative investment errors.

When firms experience declines in sales which they attribute to a worsening of their competitive position, they tend to invest more than anticipated in an attempt to catch up with their rivals by lowering costs or improving their product lines. Such distress investment may account in part for the large residuals and low correlations found in microeconomic studies of investment deviations and sales deviations.[69] Deterioration of general business conditions does not appear to stimulate distress investment.

[66] Foss and Natrella, "Investment Plans and Realization," p. 16.

[67] Friend and Bronfenbrenner, p. 94; Foss and Natrella, "Investment Plans and Realization," pp. 16–17; and Levine, p. 115.

[68] Eisner, Table 4, p. 176. Eisner works with actual and planned investment as fractions of gross fixed assets. His slope estimate of 0.047 per cent of gross fixed assets is equivalent to about 0.7 per cent of investment.

[69] Friend and Bronfenbrenner, pp. 83 and 94.

The assembled body of evidence clearly suggests that unexpected changes in sales affect the realization of investment plans. However, there is an obvious need for further quantitative research on the nature of the relationship. When firms are able and willing to adjust their outlays, investment will be more sensitive to sales surprises. For example, sales disappointments are more likely to reduce planned investment in new projects than outlays on projects already in progress.[70] Thus the fraction of aggregate anticipated outlays which consists of carry-over projects may be an important determinant of the relationship between the fulfillment of investment plans and the course of sales. The flexibility of investment plans may depend on the initial expectations of firms. For example, Eisner finds that firms which were optimistic about sales at the beginning of 1950 expanded capital outlays above anticipations more vigorously when sales experiences proved even more favorable than initially expected.[71]

Existing knowledge about the investment–sales relationship can probably be utilized only crudely. When the forecaster expects a future level of GNP (or corporate profits) which seems inconsistent with the sales expectations of firms, the intentions on capital outlays should be adjusted. In this manner, the forecaster is relying on the anticipations data but endeavoring to improve on their accuracy by considering the induced effects of probable changes in sales.

Expectations of Capital Goods Producers. Expectations of producers of capital goods are compiled in a semiannual survey conducted by *Fortune* and summarized in the "Business Roundup" section of the June and December issues.[72] Respondents are asked to project their sales of capital equipment to private firms in constant dollars for the four quarters following the survey. The industries covered by the survey account for about three-fifths of the production of producers' durable equipment. Because of the absence of a reliable quarterly price-deflator for producers' durables and the difficulty of isolating the behavior of industries not covered by the survey, precise calculations on its predictive record are not feasible. However, it is clear that the survey did well in 1952-54, forecasting the downturn of late 1953 and the upturn of early 1955 and indicating with approximate accuracy the magnitudes of change. In both 1955 surveys and in the June 1956 survey, the producers were insufficiently optimistic about investment demand. They predicted substantial rises in sales but not so large as the increases which eventuated. On the whole, the anticipations data recorded by this survey have supplied forecasters with a valuable complement to the data on purchase intentions for plant and equipment.

[70] Foss and Natrella, in this volume.

[71] Eisner, p. 176.

[72] See details in "Report . . . on General Business Expectations," pp. 590-594. The author is indebted to Sanford Parker and Todd May of *Fortune* for further information on this survey.

Inventory Investment. Inventory investment is a small, highly volatile and exceedingly important component of GNP. Fluctuations in the volume of nonfarm inventory investment accounted for a dominant share of the movement in GNP during the 1948-49 and 1953-54 recessions. Thus far the behavior of inventories has defied successful explanation by non-expectational variables.

Inventory changes are even difficult to measure *ex post*. Small errors in the recorded volume of total inventories may produce large relative errors in the estimate of inventory change. Moreover, the national product accounts record the value of change in the physical volume of inventories, excluding revaluations of an existing stock due to price changes. Data on the book value of inventories as shown in the balance sheets of firms must usually be adjusted to eliminate the effects of price movement. As more detailed information on stocks becomes available the Department of Commerce often revises the estimates of past inventory investment— sometimes extensively. Thus the forecaster of inventory investment does not have reliable benchmarks on recent trends and current levels of stocks on which to base his projections. This is an extremely serious handicap.

As a component of national product, inventory investment is unique. Except for imputed output, all other components record a flow of final goods and services from sellers to buyers. Inventory accumulation is a residual consisting of the portion of total output which is not acquired by a final user and remains in the hands of sellers or processors. To some extent the excess of production over sales will reflect a planned increment desired by sellers to adjust to recent or expected change in sales. However, inventory investment may also reflect divergencies between producers' actual and expected sales volume, and the empirical data obviously do not permit a breakdown of the actual inventory change into planned and unplanned segments.

Inventory expectations of business firms are reported in quarterly surveys conducted by *Fortune* and by Dun and Bradstreet. Inventory anticipations can shed light directly only on planned accumulations of stocks for some assumed course of sales. However, the surveys include information on sales expectations which may be used as indirect predictors of the probable trend of unplanned as well as planned accumulation. They have been employed in this manner in an ingenious empirical exploration conducted by Modigliani and Sauerlender. According to their highly tentative findings, the change in inventories over a quarterly period is positively related to the expected change in sales over that period and is also positively, but less closely, related to the actual change in sales. The latter finding suggests that production plans in the aggregate are adjusted quite rapidly when sales change.[73]

[73] Franco Modigliani and O. H. Sauerlender, "Economic Expectations and Plans of Firms," *Short-Term Economic Forecasting*, pp. 333-350.

The inventory anticipations data of *Fortune* and Dun and Bradstreet are most directly relevant to the prediction of the monthly series on the book value of manufacturing and trade inventories, which covers 90 per cent of all nonfarm inventories. One would expect that when revaluations due to price changes are taken into account, the changes in the book value series over quarterly periods would correspond closely to the nonfarm inventory investment component of GNP, but attempts by the author to effect such a reconciliation yielded disappointing results. A perfect ability to forecast both price changes and the book value of manufacturing and trade inventories would still leave a substantial margin of error in the prediction of the inventory component of GNP.[74]

Nevertheless, it is instructive to consider briefly the performance of the inventory anticipations. Each quarter, *Fortune* obtains projections on inventories in constant prices for six months and one year ahead from a sample of about two hundred manufacturers. These are blown up into an estimate of aggregate inventory change for manufacturers.[75] Because the projections for one year ahead eliminate the serious problem of allowing for unrepresentative seasonal patterns in the sample, these longer-term predictions have received most emphasis recently in "Business Roundup." Also, in recent quarters, emphasis was placed on quantitative reports by respondents regarding any undesired excess (or deficiency) of their current inventories relative to the present level of sales.

The absence of a reliable quarterly price deflator precludes quantitative appraisal of the predictive record of the survey. But since its inception in mid-1953, the survey has apparently surpassed naïve models in forecasting. The expectations were particularly successful in forecasting the magnitude and timing of inventory disinvestment in 1954 and the relative stability of stocks during most of 1955. Actual increases in inventories during 1956 exceeded the rises expected by manufacturers.

Various aspects of the Dun and Bradstreet quarterly surveys have been thoroughly analyzed by Millard Hastay.[76] For inventory expectations, he uses regression techniques employing diffusion indexes which summarize responses on the actual and expected directions of change. The survey variables perform extremely well in forecasts of the Commerce series on the book value of manufacturing and trade inventories for fourteen quarters, 1949-52. The dependent variable is inventory change over a full year, including the two quarters preceding the survey. The inclusion of two quarters already elapsed undoubtedly contributes to the excellent fit of the data. Multiple correlation coefficients obtained are in excess of

---

[74] Cf. "Report of the Consultant Committee on Inventory Statistics," *Reports of Federal Reserve Consultant Committees on Economic Statistics*, pp. 445-447.

[75] See "Report . . . on General Business Expectations," pp. 585-590.

[76] Millard Hastay, "The Dun and Bradstreet Surveys of Businessmen's Expectations," *Proceedings of the Business and Economic Statistics Section of the American Statistical Association*, 1954, pp. 93-123, and his paper in this volume.

0.95 for all manufacturers and traders combined, as well as for durable goods manufacturers and for nondurable goods producers taken separately. The results are less satisfactory when the regression equations are used to predict quarterly inventory change, 1953-55. The general pattern of fluctuation is reproduced, but inventory change is consistently over-estimated.[77]

From survey data presented in *Dun's Review*, one can construct diffusion indexes of inventory expectations for all manufacturers and traders for twenty-six quarters over the period 1949-56. The author employed the series as the independent variable in a rather crude model where the dependent variable was the change in Commerce's book value of stocks in the two quarters following the survey. The diffusion index explained 60 per cent of the change in inventories, surpassing the performance of naïve models. Residuals were strongly autocorrelated, however, being positive in the early years and negative in the later ones. It is particularly hard to judge how changing prices influence the results.

At present, in forecasting inventory investment, the analyst has little on which to rely with confidence. The achievements of the Dun and Bradstreet data and those of the *Fortune* survey, while encouraging, are inconclusive. With existing evidence, one cannot render a verdict on the usefulness of anticipations data in forecasting inventory investment. Further experience and experimentation are required to form a judgment. The success of capital spending intentions as predictors leads one to hope that expectations data on stocks and sales, properly collected and interpreted, can similarly assist in forecasting inventories.

[77] See "Report . . . on General Business Expectations," pp. 539-548.

Appendix A

TABLE A-1

Data on Household Buying Intentions, 1947-1956

SURVEY DATE	MILLIONS OF SPENDING UNITS OR FAMILIES (1)	PERCENTAGE OF SPENDING UNITS PLANNING TO BUY				MEDIAN PLANNED EXPENDITURE	
		New Car (2)	Any Car (3)	Household Durables (4)	All Houses (5)	New Cars (6)	Household Durables (7)
		%	%	%	%	$	$
1947 July	48.0			25.00			220
1948 Jan.–Feb.	49.0			24.60	6.05		240
1948 July	49.9			22.50			245
1949 Jan.–Feb.	50.8	9.55[a]	14.72[a]	27.10	6.00	1,990	250
1949 July	51.6		16.30[a]	24.50			270
1950 Jan.–Feb.	52.5	8.90	14.95	26.40	7.05	1,920	290
1951 Jan.–Feb.	52.2	5.30	9.70	24.55	6.30	1,970	300
1952 Jan.–Feb.	53.0	5.55	10.65	21.35	5.40	2,300	290
1953 Jan.–Feb.	53.9	7.45	12.60	29.15	7.20	2,500	300
1953 Sept.–Oct.	48.3[b]		11.70				
1954 Jan.–Feb.	54.0	6.50	11.85	24.95	5.40	2,500	300
1954 June	48.9[b]	8.60	14.70		7.50		
1954 Oct.	49.1[b]	10.40	18.05		8.45		
1955 Jan.–Feb.	54.2	7.70	13.00	26.10	7.60	2,700	250
1955 June	49.7[b]	8.80	15.50		7.15		
1955 Oct.	50.1[b]	9.10	16.00		7.95		
1956 Jan.–Feb.	55.0	7.00	13.15	26.15	7.50	2,810	290

[a] Adjusted for change in classification of respondents in later periods.
[b] Families.
Source: Reports on the January-February Surveys of Consumer Finances in the *Federal Reserve Bulletin*, Board of Governors of the Federal Reserve System, and George Katona and Eva Mueller, *Consumer Expectations, 1953-1956*, Survey Research Center, University of Michigan, 1956, pp. 54, 62, and 76. March 1956 revisions of estimates of median planned expenditures have not been included. All intentions percentages are sum of "will buy," "will probably buy," and one-half of "may buy."

TABLE A-2

Data on Intended and Realized Car Purchases, 1949-1956

| | INTENDED | | | | REALIZED | | |
| | Spending Units Planning to Buy | | Planned Expenditure | | New Car Registrations | | Actual Expendi- |
SURVEY DATE	New Car (M) (1)	Any Car (A) (2)	New Car (N) (3)	Any Car (B) (4)	Per Month (5)	Per Year (P) (6)	tures on New Cars (Q) (7)
	(thousands)		*(billions)*		*(thousands)*		*(billions)*
1949 Jan.–Feb.	4,851	7,478	$9.65	$14.88	403	4,836	$7.9
1949 July		8,411		16.15	459	5,508	8.7a
1950 Jan.–Feb.	4,673	7,849	8.97	15.07	527	6,324	10.2
1951 Jan.–Feb.	2,767	5,063	5.45	9.97	422	5,064	8.8
1952 Jan.–Feb.	2,942	5,645	6.77	12.98	347	4,164	8.1
1953 Jan.–Feb.	4,016	6,791	10.04	16.98	478	5,736	10.8
1953 Sept.–Oct.		5,851b		14.63	459	5,508	10.2a
1954 Jan.–Feb.	3,510	6,339	8.78	16.00	461	5,532	10.3
1954 June	4,305c	7,388b	10.76d	18.47	552	6,624	12.4a
1954 Oct.	5,206c	9,063b	14.06d	24.47	579	6,948	13.7a
1955 Jan.–Feb.	4,173	7,046	11.27	19.02	597	7,164	14.4
1955 June	4,474c	7,904b	12.08d	21.34	576	6,912	13.5a
1955 Oct.	4,659c	8,216b	13.09d	23.09	527	6,324	12.5a
1956 Jan.–Feb.	3,850	7,230	10.82	20.32	496	5,952	12.0

a Derived by adjusting cumulated quarterly data on consumer spending for "automobiles and parts," *National Income Supplement, 1954*, and the July 1957 issue, *Survey of Current Business*, Dept. of Commerce, Table 51, line 3 in the four quarters starting closest to the survey date. Annual data were used to eliminate the portion covering purchases of car parts and accessories.

b Includes $20,000 for the intentions of secondary spending units.

c Includes $10,000 for the intentions of secondary spending units.

d Median planned expenditure is that of the nearest annual survey (see text).

Source: *Col. 1*—The product of Table A-1, cols. 1 and 2. *Col. 2*—The product of Table A-1, cols. 1 and 3. *Col. 3*—The product of Table A-1, cols. 1, 2, and 6. *Col. 4*—The product of Table A-1, cols. 1, 3, and 6. *Col. 5*—The monthly average of new passenger car registrations for twelve months folllowing the survey, "Monthly Business Statistics," *Survey of Current Business*. *Col. 6*—Present table, col. 5 times twelve. *Col. 7*—Consumer expenditure on "new cars and net purchases of used cars," *National Income Supplement, 1954*, and the July 1957 issue, *Survey of Current Business*, Table 30, line 61.

TABLE A-3

Data on Intended and Realized Purchases of Household Durables, 1947-1956
(*billions of dollars*)

Survey Date	Intended (H)	Realized (W)
1947 July	2.6	7.5
1948 Jan.–Feb.	2.9	7.6
1948 July	2.8	7.2
1949 Jan.–Feb.	3.4	7.3
1949 July	3.4	7.8
1950 Jan.–Feb.	4.0	9.0
1951 Jan.–Feb.	3.8	8.7
1952 Jan.–Feb.	3.3	8.7
1953 Jan.–Feb.	4.7	9.0
1954 Jan.–Feb.	4.0	9.1
1955 Jan.–Feb.	3.5	10.2
1956 Jan.–Feb.	4.2	10.6

Source: *Intended expenditures*—The product of Table A-1, cols. 1, 4, and 7. *Realized expenditures*—Consumer expenditure on major durable household goods. *Annual series* —The sum of lines 27, 28, and 81 of Table 30, *National Income Supplement, 1954,* and the July 1957 issue, *Survey of Current Business.* Mid-year surveys—The cumulated quarterly data on consumer spending on "furniture and household equipment," Table 51, were used to interpolate annual data.

TABLE A-4

Data on Intended and Realized Purchases of Houses, 1948-1956

SURVEY DATE	INTENDED	REALIZED	
	Planned Purchases of Houses (J) (I)	Monthly Starts (2)	Starts in Year Following Survey (S) (3)
	(thousands)		
1948 Jan.–Feb.	2,965	78	936
1949 Jan.–Feb.	3,048	85	1,020
1950 Jan.–Feb.	3,701	116	1,392
1951 Jan.–Feb.	3,289	91	1,092
1952 Jan.–Feb.	2,862	94	1,128
1953 Jan.–Feb.	3,881	92	1,104
1954 Jan.–Feb.	2,916	102	1,224
1954 June	4,058	111	1,332
1954 Oct.	4,572	114	1,368
1955 Jan.–Feb.	4,119	111	1,332
1955 June	3,897	104	1,248
1955 Oct.	4,357	96	1,152
1956 Jan.–Feb.	4,125	93	1,116

Source: *Col. 1*—The product of Table A-1, cols. 1 and 5. *Col. 2*—Average number of monthly new housing starts in the twelve months following the survey from "total number of new dwelling units started," *Monthly Labor Review,* Dept. of Labor, Table F-6 or Table F-5 (before December 1954). *Col. 3*—Present table, col. 2 times twelve.

Appendix B

Further Experience with
Anticipations Series, 1957–58

The years 1957 and 1958 provide further observations on the predictive value of the anticipations data considered in this paper. This appendix is designed to review the information obtained in the period since the body of the paper was written.

Automobiles. Demand for new cars was weak in the period from 1956 to 1958, with registrations falling from over 7 million new cars in 1955 to just below 6 million in both 1956 and 1957 and then to about $4\frac{2}{3}$ million in 1958. Predictions derived from a naïve persistence model are thus too high for both 1956 and 1958. Predictions of registrations derived from SCF new car buying plans (M, as defined in text) do better, but still over-predict 1958 purchases considerably. Disposable income consistently overpredicts expenditure on new cars for 1956–58 when utilized in the regression equation of Q on Y shown in the text. When the dollar volume of SCF new car buying plans (N) is used with income to estimate new car expenditure, forecasts are somewhat more accurate, but still uniformly too high. Only the regression equation utilizing income-change (ΔY) and buying plans (N) performs well; it achieves a high degree of accuracy for 1956–58. These results are shown in Table B-1, which parallels Table 1 of the text.[1]

TABLE B-1

Comparison of Forecasts of Car Purchases Based on Buying Plans, Income, and
Naïve Models, 1956–1958

(*percentage error*[a])

	REGISTRATIONS		NEW CAR EXPENDITURES			
YEAR	*Naïve* ($P_t = P_{t-1}$)	*Regression on M* (*Eq. 1*)	*Naïve* ($Q_t = Q_{t-1}$)	*Regression on Y* (*Eq. 7*)	*Regression on Y and N* (*Eq. 9*)	*Regression on ΔY and N* (*Eq. 11*)
1956	−20	+3	−20	−13	−9	+2
1957	+1	−1	+8	−13	−11	+4
1958	−29	−18	−26	−47	−32	−4

[a] Computed as [(actual-predicted)÷actual].

[1] After the regression estimates of the paper were computed, the Dept. of Commerce revised expenditure data on new cars systematically upwards for years since 1950. Expenditure data for 1956–58 taken from the July 1959 *Survey of Current Business* have been adjusted downwards by the author to accord with the unrevised data for earlier years which were utilized in the regression estimates. These adjustments are necessarily crude and hence the percentage errors shown in the table should be taken as approximate.

Household Durables. Expenditures on major household durables (*W*, as defined in the text) showed little variation from 1956 to 1958 and would thus have been predicted very accurately by naïve forecasts. Spending fell by about 1 per cent or $100 million from 1956 to 1957 and again from 1957 to 1958. The simple regression on income (equation 2 of the relevant section in the text) also is accurate with errors of about 0 and 4 per cent in 1957 and 1958, respectively.[2] On the other hand, the regression on SCF buying plans (equation 1 of the text) underpredicts expenditure on major household durables by about 10 per cent in both 1957 and 1958. Results obtained from the use of both SCF intentions and income (equation 3) are slightly inferior to the use of income alone. These observations are consistent with the indications in the text that SCF buying plans for major household durables have not demonstrated significant predictive value in aggregate time-series data.

Residential Construction. Private housing starts fell by 10 per cent from 1956 to 1957 and rose by 15 per cent from 1957 to 1958. Plans to buy homes reported in the SCF survey of early 1957 incorrectly pointed to strong demand for housing. A forecast of starts for 1957 derived from the regression on plans shown in the text would have been 20 per cent too high. In 1958, however, the forecast of housing starts based on the same estimated regression equation is almost perfectly accurate, coming within 1 per cent of the mark. The *Fortune* homebuilders' survey predicted well in both years, running 4 per cent too high in 1957 and about 5 per cent too low in 1958. Its 1957 performance is equaled by the fourth-quarter naïve model, but a naïve forecast based on 1957 IV misses the sharp upswing of 1958. The 1957 and 1958 results thus provide additional evidence of the predictive value of the *Fortune* survey of builders.

Plant and Equipment Outlays. The Commerce–SEC survey of plant and equipment spending extended its impressive predictive record in 1957–58. The annual survey for 1957 indicated a $6\frac{1}{2}$ per cent increase in outlays over 1956. Realized spending was up by over 5 per cent, thus deviating from plans by merely 1 per cent. In 1958, the annual anticipations pointed to a 13 per cent decline in outlays. Actual expenditure fell by 17 per cent or 4 per cent more than plans.

Investment deviations for manufacturing were positively related to errors in sales forecasts for 1957 and 1958, as in previous years. In 1957, capital spending by manufacturing firms expanded by 7 per cent in comparison with a planned increase of 10 per cent. The negative investment deviation of 3 per cent was associated with a 6 per cent overprediction of sales, as manufacturers expected an 8 per cent increase in sales and experienced a rise of only 2 per cent. In 1958, manufacturers planned a reduction of capital outlays of 17 per cent and actually cut back invest-

---

[2] Again, data for recent years have been adjusted in an attempt to eliminate the effects of systematic Commerce revisions for earlier years.

ment by 28 per cent. Their sales, meanwhile, fell by 8 per cent in contrast with an expected decline of 2 per cent.

First anticipations in the quarterly Commerce–SEC survey predicted well in 1957–58 and called the turning points of 1957 IV and 1958 IV accurately. First anticipations were consistently too high during these eight quarters, however, and their mean deviation of 4 per cent did not match their accuracy in the 1952–56 period. Second anticipations, while generally also too high, had a mean deviation of 2 per cent, equaling their performance for earlier years.

Inventory Investment. The *Fortune* inventory survey had moderate success during 1957–58. Business first reported expected liquidation of stocks in the May 1957 survey, with mild decumulation scheduled over the succeeding four quarters. Similar reports were obtained in the surveys of August and November 1957. Actually, inventory investment turned negative in 1957 IV. At no time did firms predict the massive liquidation of inventories that marked the first three quarters of 1958. In August 1958, they accurately anticipated a cessation of disinvestment in 1958 IV and a return to positive inventory change in 1959 I.

COMMENT

ELMER C. BRATT, Lehigh University

I am in substantial agreement with Okun's paper, and will comment principally on the procedural problem of the use of anticipatory data in a gross national product model. Initial entry of anticipatory data in the form of *ex ante* magnitudes which may be adjusted to obtain estimates of *ex post* values might well be considered an ideal solution. The chief difficulty with this procedure is not the unreliability of forecasts based on anticipations but uncertainty about the weight given the forces over which the decision maker has no control. If anticipations data made clear what related industrial and general business movements were assumed, forecasters could check the assumptions with an analytical model to evaluate their validity. However, we are far from attaining such a model.

Pragmatically, initial entry in the GNP table will involve anticipatory or analytical figures, depending on which are most readily adjusted. Let us consider in this light the various expenditure groups Okun covers.

The use of survey data as the initial entry for consumer durable goods is impractical. Not only does the Federal Reserve figure not become available until March, too late for the model which is usually set up in the fourth quarter of the preceding year, but also expenditures for durable goods are vitally dependent upon disposable income. The relationship to savings should not be expected to be of forecasting value. Generally expenditures for durable goods will be positively related to personal savings because both tend to be positively correlated with disposable income.

Immediately after the war the relationship between disposable income and durable goods sales was vitiated by shortages. One of the most serious mistakes made in postwar forecasts was the assumption that demand would not spill over to nondurable goods; that total expenditures would be held down by unavailability of durable goods. Since then, income changes have proved a good but not infallible guide to the pattern of demand. The acceleration of durable goods sales and disposable income (i.e. second differences) was in the same direction from 1950 until 1956, when disposable income began to accelerate slightly while advance in the sale of durable goods slowed down. Durable goods expenditure and disposable income in current dollars rose together in 1953 and 1955. A slight decline in durable goods was paired with a slight rise in disposable income in 1954, an occurrence readily explained by the recession. The improved position of consumer stocks, especially of automobiles, accounts for divergent movements in 1956.

Under these conditions it seems wise to adopt the recommendation of the Task Force on Consumer Survey Statistics and use consumer durable goods expenditure expected in relation to disposable income as a point of departure. The first adjustment is for the condition of stocks in consumers' hands. This is difficult to estimate, and the Survey Research Center correctly notes that no simple satiation rules apply. Some indication is given by the price of second-hand goods. It is also important to make adjustments, partially qualitative, for changes in replacement demand, models available, dealer margins, and the use of consumer credit. Finally, total adjustments are checked with the indications given by survey data. Okun's conclusion that there is some correlation between the survey indications and the residuals from a regression on disposable income provides some support for this approach.

In the case of residential construction, we must also start with an analytical estimate. It has long been known that disposable income is of little help in forecasting housing starts over the short run. Important assistance is provided by data on household formation. The reference is to total household formation; nonfarm household formation has not been very helpful in recent years because of dynamic factors, such as migration. Contrasting the movement in household formation from March of year one to March of year two with change in starts between the calendar years—in effect assuming starts move with household formation nine months later—we find the direction of movement has been the same each year from 1952 to 1957.

Using a similar lead, total household formation moved with the total deflated dollar value of housing put in place except for a minor variation in 1953. Despite a slight decline in net household formation in 1953 and a leveling of general business activity, a slight increase occurred in housing construction values. The difference may be partly due to the timing of the

452

effect of household formation. In any case, the value per house should be determined separately.

The relationship described must be looked at in terms of family formation because some hope exists for forecasts of various types of families coming into being. Therefore, in dealing with residential construction, the chief explanatory variables are disposable income, number of households, and the changing size of husband-wife families. Apparently the *Fortune* housing survey figure involves a great deal of momentum, that is, the plans of contractors seem to be principally dependent on the amount of construction they have been doing. The use of these figures remains in an experimental stage.

The survey figures on plant and equipment expenditures can be effectively filled in the model initially, especially since preliminary McGraw–Hill figures become available in the fall. It is important, however, to make adjustments based on analytical estimates. Allowance must be made for the expected movement in investment by new companies, an important factor which is reflected poorly if at all in the surveys. Projective analysis of total activity with respect to turning points is also indicated. Unless or until experience proves otherwise it is prudent to assume that the surveys will reflect the influence of general business conditions most poorly at such times. Particular attention should be given to the firmness of current programs, credit availability, and shifts in the formation of new companies. If a recession occurs, it is important to develop some estimates of the extent to which continued investment in construction projects started in better times actually represents unplanned investment.

Inventory investment is difficult to deal with because of the difficulty of separating the planned and unplanned components. The initial figure in the GNP model is most often best obtained by using a lagged relation to sales—inventories can be expected to increase as sales have increased in the recent past. If a turning point is imminent, the method will breakdown because of unplanned inventory accumulation or run-off. Inventory estimates must then be developed from the pattern of market adjustment expected in various areas. The available breakdown on inventories and sales is rather unsatisfactory, but it may help to indicate the extent and character of unplanned inventory change. Near turning points the most important aggregative method of segregation is through the difference in movement of finished-goods and raw-materials inventories; the latter are generally accepted as planned.

As suggested, the most workable model assumes that inventory investment is planned except when turning points, shortages, or other contingencies intervene. Better information on planned inventories may be forthcoming from surveys of inventory anticipations, and the *Fortune* survey certainly should not be ignored. However, such surveys must still be looked on as experimental.

Currently the use of surveys on expectations is founded largely on the record such data have achieved when applied to actual forecasting. Nevertheless, their principal potential value for forecasting is not the extent to which they provide independent forecasts. Careful analysis, along the lines suggested by Hart and Hastay and perhaps cruder formulations, is essential to an understanding of intentions, anticipations, and outlook variables. Even a rough segregation of the part of anticipated changes which is due to intentions from the part dependent upon influences over which the decision maker has no control would represent a major step forward. Also, we need sharper theoretical formulations to explain the relation of intentions to economic change. Economic changes could be employed more effectively in economic analysis if better understood in terms of the measurable aspects of prevailing expansionary and contractionary movements. We would then have a firmer basis for introducing the outlook effect. These problems are of vital importance in practical forecasting work.

GEORGE KATONA, Survey Research Center, University of Michigan

There is apparently some disagreement about the function of survey data on consumer attitudes, expectations, and intentions. Therefore it appears useful to recapitulate the position of the Survey Research Center.[1]

When we ask consumers, in sample interview surveys, whether during the next year they expect to buy a car, expect prices to go up, or expect good or bad times for the country as a whole, we are not interested in their forecasts but in their general "sentiment." We want to find out whether they feel more or less confident, optimistic, or secure than they did six or twelve months earlier when other representative samples were asked the identical questions. We collect this information because we postulate that consumer demand depends on willingness, as well as on ability, to buy.

A conclusion that consumer willingness to buy has increased or decreased is justified if successive surveys disclose consistent and significant changes in several relevant attitudes and expectations. Having observed changes in the state of confidence of the universe (from which the sample was drawn), we expect that concomitant changes in the behavior of the universe are taking place.

Studies of the origin of changes in consumer attitudes indicate that the relative importance of financial factors (ability to buy) and psychological factors (willingness to buy) varies from time to time. Sometimes attitude

---

[1] For a further statement, see George Katona, *Psychological Analysis of Economic Behavior*, McGraw–Hill, 1951; George Katona and Eva Mueller, *Consumer Attitudes and Demand, 1950-52*, Survey Research Center, University of Michigan, 1953; George Katona, "The Predictive Value of Data on Consumer Attitudes," *Consumer Behavior, Volume II*, New York University Press, 1955; and George Katona and Eva Mueller, *Consumer Expectations, 1953-56*, Survey Research Center, University of Michigan, 1956.

changes conform with changes in income and business activity. At other times, however, attitudes change autonomously. For instance, in June and October 1954, following a slight recession and at a time of stable personal incomes, changes in economic attitudes and expectations indicated an improvement in consumer willingness to buy. Divergence between income and attitude trends appeared also in 1949, 1951, and 1957.

The primary reason for collecting data on psychological factors influencing behavior is to improve the diagnosis of the prevailing situation.[2] Psychological data have predictive value only if we assume that nothing "new" will take place during the forecast period. Government and business action may have consequences which will contradict the indications derived from consumer attitudes. In addition, consumer sentiment may undergo changes (though past findings indicate that the attitudes and expectations of broad groups of people, unlike those of individuals, rarely change abruptly except under the impact of major events).

Expectations relating to the respondent's own financial situation or actions, and expectations regarding the economy as a whole, both reflect the respondent's sentiment. (Okun presents a different view in his paper.) There are situations in which personal financial expectations are favorable in spite of a general *malaise*; then general business expectations often provide valuable additional information about what influences behavior. Expressed intentions to buy differ from personal expectations only insofar as there are some people who at the time of a survey have already placed an order for a new car, or who have discussed the question with their families and are firmly resolved to proceed with the purchase within a short time. But the question—"Do you people expect to buy a car during the next twelve months?"—was intentionally formulated to elicit affirmative answers not only from "planners" but also from people who evaluate the prospect of purchase optimistically.

In order to validate data on consumer attitudes or expectations, the behavioral concomitants of changes in attitudes and expectations need to be analyzed separately for each available observation. This procedure, based on a small number of independent observations, has been carried out graphically by the Survey Research Center. It is also possible to experiment with more rigorous tests which consider all available observations jointly by comparing changes in attitudes, expectations, and intentions, with (1) changes in aggregate consumer behavior (especially purchases of durable goods) at the time of the survey (i.e. both shortly before and after) and (2) changes in aggregate consumer behavior after the survey.

Tests comparing expressed attitudes, expectations, and intentions with

[2] George Katona, "Federal Reserve Board Committee Reports on Consumer Expectations and Savings Statistics," *Review of Economics and Statistics*, February 1957, p. 41; and George Katona, Appendix C to *An Appraisal of Data and Research on Businessmen's Expectations*, Board of Governors of the Federal Reserve System, September 1955, pp. 177 ff.

recent past and subsequent behavior "can be carried out at the aggregate as well as at the individual level. Both kinds of tests are needed and are useful."[3] To make individual tests, one must interview the same sample at least twice, and preferably several times. If only two interviews are available, one can test the rate of fulfillment of expressed intentions to buy. In attempting to test differences in subsequent behavior of people who are initially optimistic and pessimistic, however, a timing problem arises. Among the optimists, some may have bought durable goods shortly before the measurement of attitudes and may not buy any for some time thereafter. Expenditures on automobiles may show a negative serial correlation because many more people buy a car every two or every three years than every year. When three consecutive interviews with identical people (panels) are available, it is easier to solve the timing problem, as well as to test the predictive value of changes in attitudes. Extended panel studies, moreover, may enable us to make several individual tests, rather than one, to test hypotheses about differential effects in different circumstances.

Even if panel studies are available, individual tests face difficulties. Aggregative tests may yield statistically significant correlations while individual tests conducted at the same time show only small differences between attitude groups (in the expected direction).[4] Most demographic, inventory, and personality variables vary so little in the aggregate over short periods that they can be considered noise or nuisance variables in short-run prediction. In small sample re-interview studies there may be so much noise from other variables that it becomes difficult to tell whether the important predictive variables do or do not have the expected relation to behavior. (This difficulty is increased by the fact that attitude data collected from individuals are more affected by reporting errors than are group data.)

The Survey Research Center, being greatly interested in the re-interview both for individual tests and for other methodological reasons, has carried out two re-interview surveys in connection with the SCF (in 1948-49 and 1952-53). Both studies were used for investigating the validity of expressed intentions to buy.[5] Neither is suitable for constructing an index of attitudes and for carrying out individual tests with attitudes or expectations other than intentions to buy. First, the SCF (in contrast to the periodic surveys conducted by the Center) includes too few of the crucial expectations

[3] Katona and Mueller, *Consumer Expectations, 1953-56*, p. 2.

[4] Cf. Okun's statement, made in reference to the SEC–Commerce Department surveys, that "All aggregative economic relationships that display any stability over time perform far better than their microeconomic counterparts." See also Eva Mueller, "Effects of Consumer Attitudes on Purchases," *American Economic Review*, December 1957.

[5] J. B. Lansing and S. B. Withey, "Consumer Anticipations: Their Use in Forecasting Behavior," *Short-Term Economic Forecasting*, Studies in Income and Wealth, Vol. 17, Princeton University Press for the National Bureau of Economic Research, 1955; and L. R. Klein and J. B. Lansing, "Decisions to Purchase Consumer Durable Goods," *Journal of Marketing*, October 1955.

questions.[6] Secondly, there is too long an interval—one year—between the two interviews. Finally, people who in the course of the year changed their residence are excluded. Consequently since movers purchase more durable goods on the average than nonmovers, the crucial variable, expenditures on durable goods, is underrepresented.

The Survey Research Center has endeavored for many years to carry out panel studies characterized by (1) several successive interviews with the same representative sample, (2) interviews conducted at six-month intervals, and (3) interviews including as many movers as possible. This was made possible in 1954 through a grant by the Ford Foundation. Data collection for the panel was finished in the spring of 1957. The results of the first attempts at carrying out individual tests using a comprehensive index of consumer attitudes have been presented to this Conference by Eva Mueller. As stated by Miss Mueller, the work on individual tests is far from completed.

Okun refers, with approval, to a statement of mine written a few years ago which said that no definite judgment is as yet possible about the relative predictive value of buying intentions and other attitudes. He goes on, however, to say that on the basis of currently available evidence the forecaster cannot have the same confidence in measures of consumer attitudes as he may have in intentions data. I believe that this is an incorrect conclusion. I submit Miss Mueller's calculations (in this volume) on the relations between attitudes and aggregates sales of durable goods (rather than the sales–income ratio) as one important piece of evidence.

A second piece of evidence became available in 1957. According to the June 1957 periodic survey of the Survey Research Center, data on buying intentions (especially for automobiles) were about as frequent at that time as a year earlier. But data on attitudes and expectations toward personal finances, business conditions, and market conditions showed a substantial and statistically significant decline during the first half of 1957. The Center published these findings in July 1957 under the title "Consumer Optimism

---

[6] For instance, the 1952-53 SCF re-interviews contain only two clearly usable attitude questions—"Are you better or worse off than a year ago?" and "Is this a good or bad time to buy durable goods?" Neither of them refers, however, to expectations. A further question asks about one-year income expectations. This question is insensitive to changes in feelings and attitudes (see Katona and Mueller, *Consumer Attitudes and Demand, 1950-52*, pp. 69ff.) and has therefore been excluded from our attitude surveys. The question used in those surveys—"Do you think that a year from now you people will be better off financially, or worse off, or just about the same as now?"—differs from the income expectation question, even though it is the least sensitive component of our index. It is not possible to construct a comprehensive index of attitudes from the 1952-53 survey questions. It is therefore to be regretted that Okun refers to Tobin's study of the 1952-53 re-interviews to support his notions about the function of "other expectations and attitudes." Since the 1952-53 SCF surveys did not contain sufficient data (except on intentions to buy), Tobin's analysis of "other expectations and attitudes" is entirely inconclusive on this point.

Weakening."[7] Thus changes in consumer attitudes rather than in buying intentions proved early indicators of forthcoming purchase trends. It does not follow, of course, that this will always be the case. Studies of the predictive value of consumer attitudes and intentions will have to continue.

ROBERT EISNER, Northwestern University

It may be useful to analyze further the theoretical basis for Arthur Okun's interesting consideration of observed relationships between deviations of realized from planned investment and deviations of realized from expected sales. Working from the acceleration principle, if we assumed instantaneous adjustment of capital stock to sales, both anticipated and realized, we would write:

(1) $$K_t^e = b(S_t^e)$$

and

(2) $$K_t = b(S_t)$$

where K equals capital stocks, S equals sales, the superscript e indicates that the variable is expectational, and b is the desired capital to sales ratio which, it is presumed, businessmen also realize. The subscript t indicates the end of the time period for the stock variable, K, and the interval over which the volume or rate of flow is measured for flow variables like S (and I, below). Subtracting equation 1 from equation 2 and then dividing by equation 1 gives the following result:

(3) $$\frac{K_t - K_t^e}{K_t^e} = a'\left(\frac{S_t - S_t^e}{S_t^e}\right)$$

where a', of course, equals one.

But the slopes which Okun reported related not to the percentage deviation of capital stocks but to the percentage deviation of actual from anticipated *investment*. If depreciation or capital consumption is unaffected by the deviation between actual and expected capital stocks (as may reasonably be assumed, at least as an approximation), we can substitute $I_t - I_t^e$ for $K_t - K_t^e$, where I denotes gross capital expenditures. Hence, since a' equals one we can, after substituting and multiplying both sides by K_t^e/I_t^e write

(4) $$\frac{I_t - I_t^e}{I_t^e} = \frac{K_t^e}{I_t^e}\left(\frac{S_t - S_t^e}{S_t^e}\right)$$

Thus the long-run slope would equal K_t^e/I_t^e, which is of course far above the values, in a rather wide neighborhood of unity, noted by Okun.

[7] "Consumer Optimism Weakening," mimeographed report issued by the Foundation for Research on Human Behavior and the Survey Research Center, University of Michigan, July 1957.

Offering a rough estimate based on the 1950 investment to 1949 gross fixed asset ratio of 0.088 which Okun culled from my own study, this slope would have an order of magnitude of ten or eleven.

But if we are concerned not with the ultimate adjustment of capital stock to a change in sales but with the adjustment of capital stock within a specified period, equation 4 does not carry us very far. For the crucial question becomes the dynamic one of speed of adjustment and, in large part, the estimate of distributed lags in the investment function or the partial accelerator coefficients of the Hicksian Trade Cycle model.[1] Slope coefficients of the variety noted by Okun which had a value of unity, for example, would then reflect merely the fact that roughly one-eleventh of the total adjustment took place in the time period defined.

My estimates indicate slopes of the regression of $(I_t - I_t^e)/K_{t-1}$ on $(S_t - S_t^e)/S_{t-1}$ of 0.047 for all firms and the interestingly higher 0.093 for firms which had expected an increase in sales.[2] These may be converted to approximately 0.7 and 1.4 in Okun's regression. In the course of further work with more recent McGraw–Hill surveys, I hope to secure a number of more reliable estimates, for different years and different categories of firms, of this important adjustment relationship with which Okun is concerned.

EVA MUELLER, Survey Research Center, University of Michigan

Arthur Okun refers repeatedly to the "divergence" between the results of his aggregative test and mine. In part this divergence is due to differences in what he and I consider the most appropriate forecasting period. Okun relates attitudes and buying plans to purchases in the two quarters following the quarter in which a survey was made, even if the survey was completed at the beginning of a quarter. In the "October 1954" survey, for instance, most of the interviews were completed by the middle of October. Yet Okun relates attitudes as of that time to purchases in the first half of 1955, ignoring the crucial fourth quarter of 1954. In my calculations, where surveys were taken at the beginning of a quarter, purchases in the current and the following quarter were used as the dependent variable.

Yet this timing problem is not the real issue here. Coefficients of determination below 0.40, based on only eleven time-series observations, are far from being statistically significant. And the same holds for small differences between several coefficients of that order of magnitude. Hence where D/Y is used as the dependent variable, no conclusions can be

[1] Cf. L. M. Koyck, *Distributed Lags and Investment Analysis* (North–Holland, Amsterdam, 1954) and my own "Expectations, Plans and Capital Expenditures: A Synthesis of Ex Post and Ex Ante Data," *Expectations, Uncertainty, and Business Behavior*, Mary Jean Bowman, ed., Social Science Research Council, 1958, and "A Distributed Lag Investment Function," *Econometrica*, January 1960.

[2] Eisner, Chap. XII, Table 4.

drawn about the relative forecasting value of attitudes versus buying plans or of Okun's selection of a forecasting period versus mine.

The real point of difference between Okun's tests and those of the Survey Research Center is that in our opinion the relation of attitudes to D or ΔD is a more valid test of the forecasting value of attitudes than the relation of attitudes to D/Y (see the discussion in my paper). When D or ΔD is used as the dependent variable in the aggregate test, consumer attitudes (excluding buying plans) consistently explain a much larger part of the variance than buying plans. Moreover the tests based on D and ΔD yield higher correlation coefficients and also larger differences between the coefficients of determination for consumer attitudes and for buying plans than do any of the tests using D/Y. To be sure, with only eleven observations even relatively large coefficients of determination must be regarded as highly tentative.

Regarding the cross-sectional test, Okun's statement that "cross-section results are relevant and these point uniformly toward a negative evaluation of consumer anticipations data other than plans to buy" is hardly warranted. The data presented in my paper show a weak (and hence statistically not significant) relationship between attitudes and spending for three separate periods of time—consistently in the expected direction. Taking one period at a time, the probability that this relationship could have arisen by chance is too great to permit a conclusion (at conventional confidence levels) that attitudes of individuals influence their spending. However, the repetition of the relationship in three periods considerably reduces the likelihood that this is a chance occurrence. In statistical terminology, in guarding against an error of Type I (mistaken rejection of the null hypothesis), we must not fall into an error of Type II (mistaken acceptance of the null hypothesis). The best available evidence at the microeconomic level suggests that consumer attitudes other than plans to buy do have some influence on subsequent discretionary spending, although further studies are needed to substantiate present findings.

Author Index

Subject Index

Acceleration principle: and fixed investment, 363, 439–440, 458–459; and inventory investment, 96, 139–140, 144–147. *See also* Sales anticipations; Sales changes

Accuracy of aggregate anticipations or forecasts: in Canadian investment surveys, 352–353; in Commerce–SEC investment surveys, 352–353, 388–390, 433–435, 436, 450–451; in Dutch forecasts, 31–36, 43, 45–48, 51–52; in *Fortune* survey of capital goods producers, 442; in Joint Economic Committee projections, 49–50; in labor force anticipations, 188–192, 198; in McGraw–Hill capacity surveys, 375–376; in McGraw–Hill investment surveys, 352–353, 372–374, 435; methods of measuring, 30, 45–48, 50; predictive value in relation to, 4–5; in railroad shippers' forecasts, 188–192, 198, 206–211. *See also* Forecast errors; Predictive value

Accuracy of consumer opinions on economic conditions, 69–72, 74

Accuracy of individual consumer or firm forecasts: in Canadian investment surveys, 352, 354; capital goods supply conditions and, 397, 402–403, 404–405; in Commerce–SEC investment surveys, 352, 354, 390–391, 436; cyclical factors in, 399–402; of direction of change in investment, 400–401; growth rate of firms and, 361–367; industry variation in, 396–397; in McGraw–Hill investment surveys, 352, 354, 360–368, 375, 436; methods of measuring, 354–360; price changes and, 398–399, 438–439; sales expectations and, 360–361, 363–365, 367–368, 401–402, 405, 439–442, 458–459; scale of investment and, 392–396, 397, 399–400, 401, 404; size of firm and, 199, 361–362, 365, 391–396, 397, 402, 404, 437; supply conditions for capital goods and, 388, 395–398, 402–405, 438–439. *See also* Forecast errors; Predictive value

Adjustment of forecasts for effect of forecasts, 46, 47, 50

Assets or debt as influence on consumer purchases, 177

Attitudes, *see* Consumer attitudes

Buying intentions, *see* Consumer buying intentions

Buying-price anticipations, 96, 115–126, 135

Canadian capital expenditure survey, 351, 352, 353, 354

Canadian employment forecast survey, 199–203

Capital appropriations survey: backlog data, 312–314; 318–319; cancellation data, 317–318, 320; comparison with Commerce–SEC data, 304–306, 311–312; comparison with McGraw–Hill data, 312; cycles in new appropriations, 308–312, 313–314; data made available by, 306–308; definitions and coverage, 299–306, 323; diffusion in new appropriations, 314–316; forecasting use of, 48, 318–324; seasonal fluctuations, 308, 323–324

Capital goods shortages, *see* Supply conditions for capital goods

Collinearity due to common price element among variables, 138, 140, 147

Commerce–SEC investment surveys: accuracy of aggregate anticipations in, 352–353, 388–390, 433–435, 436, 450–451; accuracy of individual firm anticipations in, 352, 354, 390–397, 402, 436–437; comparison of coverage with NICB capital appropriation survey, 304–305, 306; comparison of data with NICB capital appropriation survey, 311–312; cyclical patterns in, 399–401; definitions used in, 356–357, 433; direction of change anticipations in, 400–401; industry breakdown of actual and anticipated investment, 388–390, 396–397; plant and equipment data in, 395–396; predictive value of, 433–435, 436, 450–451; sales anticipations errors in, 401–402, 405, 440, 441; scale of investment and accuracy of anticipations in, 392–397, 399–401, 404–405; size of firm and accuracy of forecasts in, 391–396, 397, 402, 437; supply conditions for capital goods and accuracy of, 388, 395–398, 402–403, 404–405, 438–439; understatement by small firms, correction for, 437